CITY *of* EROS

CITY of EROS

New York City, Prostitution, and the Commercialization of Sex, 1790–1920

TIMOTHY J. GILFOYLE

W·W·Norton & Company
New York London

Printed in the United States of America
First Edition

The text of this book is composed
in 11/13 Fairfield Medium
with the display set in
Snell Roundhand Script and Fairfield Medium
Composition and manufacturing by
the Maple-Vail Book Manufacturing Group.
Book design by Margaret M. Wagner

Library of Congress Cataloging-in-Publication Data

Gilfoyle, Timothy J.
City of Eros : New York City, prostitution, and the commercialization of sex, 1790–1920 / by Timothy J. Gilfoyle.
p. cm.
Includes bibliographical references (p.) and index.
1. Prostitution—New York (N.Y.)—History. 2. Sex oriented business—New York (N.Y.)—History. I. Title.
HQ146.N7G55 1992
306.74′09747′1—dc20 91-45024

ISBN 0-393-02800-3

W.W. Norton & Company, Inc.
500 Fifth Avenue, New York, N.Y. 10110
W.W. Norton & Company Ltd.
10 Coptic Street, London WC1A 1PU

1 2 3 4 5 6 7 8 9 0

To my wife,

MARY ROSE ALEXANDER

my mother,

MARY DOROTHY NORTON GILFOYLE

my father,

JOSEPH DANIEL GILFOYLE

my brother,

GERARD PAUL GILFOYLE

and in memory of my brother,

DANIEL MARTIN GILFOYLE

CONTENTS

Appendixes

LIST OF ILLUSTRATIONS

Maps

Tables

FIGURES

There are some questions so painful and perplexing that statesmen, moralists and philanthropists shrink from them by common consent; and of all these questions prostitution is the darkest, the knottiest, and saddest.

—George G. Foster, *New York Naked,* 1850

INTRODUCTION

THE Reverend William Berrian slowly climbed the steps leading to his pulpit. His cautious and deliberate movements reflected the final, hesitating thoughts on his impending sermon. Remaining oblivious to the chilly January winds outside, the minister stepped to the lectern and faced his congregation. Berrian's Trinity Church had long served to protect its members not only from the harsh New York winters but from many of the social realities of nineteenth-century Manhattan. Founded in 1698, Trinity was the oldest parish in the city and probably the wealthiest in the New World. Its plentiful holdings in real estate alone were among the most valuable in the United States. Trinity's parishioners included some of the young republic's most distinguished figures—Alexander Hamilton, Robert Fulton, Albert Gallatin, and Richard Varick. But this Sunday, Trinity's minister planned to deliver no ordinary sermon.

For almost three decades, Berrian had occupied what many considered to be the most prestigious parish post in the United States. Upon succeeding the late Bishop John Hobart as rector of Trinity in 1830, Berrian proved to be an inspirational, farsighted steward. During the horrific cholera epidemic of 1832, instead of fleeing the city, as did many of his parishioners, Berrian gallantly ministered to the needs of the sick and dying. He defended the church from political opponents who sought to alter the Trinity charter during the 1850s. And he directed the physical and financial growth of the parish and its numerous chapels, culminating in the completion of New York's tallest structure in 1846—Richard Upjohn's new Trinity Church. By midcentury, many considered it "the Cathedral of America."[1]

While a model Christian in his virtues, Berrian nevertheless had his vices. And on this Sunday in 1857, he chose to make them public. Gazing over the single richest religious congregation in the land, the pious man matter-of-factly proclaimed, "[D]uring a ministry of more than fifty years I have not been in a house of ill-fame more than ten times!"[2]

The congregants, and other New Yorkers reacted with surprising aplomb. Berrian's frank admission attracted no calls for his resignation. Barely a peep was heard in the city's scandal-conscious media. The patrician vestryman George Templeton Strong, sitting in the audience, even believed that Berrian's sermon "did him credit." So commonplace and central was prostitution to metropolitan life that even the philanderings of a prominent minister hardly shocked New York.

By the midnineteenth century, a wide variety of commercial sexual activity existed in the largest American cities. In addition to prostitution, abortion, masked balls, stripteasing "model artist" shows, and pornography were easily available. Urban sexuality was increasingly expressed and restructured to appeal to a male consumer world of entertainment, goods, newspapers, and advertisements. Prostitution, in particular, became a public activity, conducted in the open and visible to unengaged neighbors and observers. Brothels flourished in all parts of the city. Streetwalkers claimed the most celebrated avenues as their personal turf. Courtesans worked in the foremost theaters, concert halls, and hotels. And many others advertised in guidebooks, in newspapers, and with personal cards. This blatant commercialization transformed activities and behavior with little material "value" into objects with exchange value. For the first time in American life, with the opportunity to resort to prostitutes on a massive scale, sex became an objective consumer commodity.

More significantly, Berrian's single sentence evoked the contradictions and ambiguity surrounding prostitution. For roughly a century, from 1820 to 1920, new sexual subcultures of prostitutes and "sporting men," organized around an "underground" economy, grew and expanded. Numerous bourgeois contemporaries like William Berrian saw these "dangerous classes" and their "underworld" as a threatening, subterranean countersociety. Yet they were active participants in this social universe. In the end, this underworld erected alternative norms that rejected many of the legal restrictions regulating sexual behavior. For this reason, prostitution and other commercialized expressions of sexuality were at the forefront of public debate and social relations in New York City. Not until the era of Progressive reform and World War I did these issues recede from public view and cultural discussion.

Sexual behavior was hardly a private matter. Prostitution ultimately affected police definitions of crime, municipal politicians' maintenance of power, the use of urban real estate, and the status of women. Fears of commercial sex in New York alone generated concern from such diverse citizens as the health reformer Sylvester Graham, the labor leader and communitarian Robert Dale Owen, the physician Elizabeth Blackwell, the poet and editor Walt Whitman, the ministers Charles Parkhurst and Adam Clayton Powell, Sr., the mayors Fernando Wood, W. R. Grace, and Abram Hewitt, the millionaire philanthropist John D. Rockefeller, Jr., and, of course, that naysaying purity reformer Anthony Comstock. At different periods, legalization of prostitution was seriously considered and publicly debated. And by the turn of the century, the famed English sexologist Havelock Ellis, contemplating similar social conditions in London, even considered prostitution to be a necessary product of civilization and urban life.[3]

Prostitution functioned at the nexus of social relations in the nineteenth-century city. Bourgeois Americans sought to create an ideal world of public and private spheres separating vice from virtue, the illicit from the licit, the disreputable from the respectable. But such a divided, binary vision never conformed to reality. Prostitution blurred neat and easy distinctions between good and evil. "Respectable" institutions and individuals directly supported and participated in the "disreputable" underworld of New York. Ultimately, prostitution and the corresponding commercialization of sex exposed the limits and contradictions in the ways nineteenth-century New Yorkers defined "freedom."

Selling oneself for cash for the purpose of sexual intercourse had complex and confused meanings for nineteenth-century Americans. In the extreme, any woman who engaged in premarital intercourse was labeled a prostitute. In this study, I have avoided such stereotyping and employed the term only when money was exchanged. I have also tried to distinguish prostitutes from women who provided sex for other forms of payment: rent, food, clothing, or entertainment. Although there was frequent overlap among such women, "treating" was not the same as prostitution.

Prostitution, of course, was no new phenomenon. As in most eras of history, it was then part of a compendium or range of sexualities. While commercialized forms of sexuality thrived in New York, for example, John Humphrey Noyes promoted his theories of "complex marriage" and "marital continence" in Oneida, New York. Sylvester Graham founded

"Grahamite boarding houses" in order to protect men from "venereal indulgence." And Joseph Smith and Brigham Young instituted polygamy in Mormon communities in the West. What made prostitution different was its integration into an expanding urban network of commercial enterprise and entertainment. In New York, from 1820 to 1920, sexual intercourse became an activity increasingly directed by economic and market forces. Prostitutes, together with abortionists, pornographers, distributors of contraceptive aids, and the organizers of various leisure institutions in which they flourished, turned sexuality into something to be sold, displayed, and utilized to yield income. Sex became a profit-making venture. Subject to the conditions of commerce, sex was no longer restricted to nonpecuniary satisfactions. It was part of the public culture, structured by the market, organized into institutions, ranging from the brothel to the theater, that guaranteed commercial efficiency, ostentation, and publicity. Sexuality thus lost some of the mystical and spiritual functions it enjoyed in earlier eras.[4]

To understand this seamy side of city life is to understand how much of American society functioned. This story moves from the poorest European immigrants to leading families of wealth and power, bearing names like Livingston, Lorillard, and Hearst. Sexuality, transferred to the commercial marketplace, was characterized by increasing promiscuity, bodily objectification, and greater public intimacy (especially in the street, saloon, concert hall, and theater). As a personal, intimate, and nonmarketable commodity, commercialized sex illustrated one significant conquest of the market in nineteenth-century America.[5] And perhaps the ultimate lesson of this story is that whenever a civilization relies upon the market to determine its major priorities, the social by-products are never "free" or without cost.

CITY *of* EROS

1

HOLY GROUNDS

After visiting New York City in the 1760s, John Watt described it as "the worst School for Youth of any of his Majesty's Dominions, Ignorance, Vanity, Dress and Dissipation, being the reigning Characteristics of their insipid Lives." Such moralistic reports of prostitution periodically appeared in the public records of the eighteenth-century city. Residents and travelers occasionally mentioned seeing a few "courtesans" promenading along the Battery at the southernmost tip of the small city. Dr. Alexander Hamilton, for example, noted the Battery's prostitutes in 1744 walking "amidst the iron guns and 32 pounders." For the most part, however, such descriptions were exceptional. Colonial New York was preeminently a seaport with a population of less than twenty thousand in 1760 and under thirty thousand on the eve of the American Revolution. Not surprisingly, prosecutions of colonial prostitutes were rare.[1]

The little prostitution that existed flourished in streets and taverns close to the docks and wharves. The most prominent prostitution district after 1770 and into the early nineteenth century was the famed "Holy Ground." In the two blocks along Church, Vesey, and Barclay streets, the city's most expensive "houses of debauchery" prospered on land owned by the Episcopal church and adjacent to King's College (later Columbia University). On the eve of the Revolution, one observer remarked that over five hundred "ladies of pleasure [kept] lodgings contiguous within the consecrated liberties of St. Paul's [Chapel]." A few blocks north, at the entrance to King's, Robert M'Robert claimed that dozens of prostitutes provided "a temptation to the youth that have occasion to pass so often that way." The often quoted traveler Hector St. John de Crèvecoeur repeated similar concerns when he spied the "dissipations and pleasures" near the college. Lieutenant Isaac Bangs visited the area in 1776, concluding that "nothing could exceed [the prostitutes] for impudence and immodesty." He complained that half his troops frequented the ladies of the district. He especially worried about soldiers contracting "the Fatal Disorder," namely, venereal disease. In the end, Bangs found little with which to empathize in the Holy Ground. "The whole of my aim in visiting the Place at first was out of Curiosity, as was also that of the chief of the Gentlemen that accompanied," he wrote. "[A]nd it seems Strange that any Man can so divest himself of Manhood as to desire an intimate Connection with these worse than brutal Creatures."[2]

Prostitution thrived during the British occupation of Revolutionary New York City. First, large numbers of prostitutes congregated at the foot of Broad Street in the temporary houses replacing those destroyed in the fire of 1776. Nicknamed Canvass-town and Topsail Town after the material used for roofs, the buildings were described by William Duer as "cheap and convenient lodgings for the frail sisterhood, who plied their trade most briskly in the vicinity of the shipping and the barracks." The small district of prostitutes thrived until economic development pushed it elsewhere after 1800.[3]

A more infamous example of colonial prostitution is to be found near the end of the conflict with England. A British agent by the surname of Jackson allegedly imported some three thousand white and black females from England and the West Indies—prostitutes and respectable working girls snatched from their homes in seaport cities. Upon their arrival, Jackson domiciled them in Lispenard Meadows, on the northern edge of town. According to two historians, "harlots flourished brazenly as these dives prospered." Labeled "Jackson whites" and "Jackson blacks" they were quickly driven from the town upon the evacuation of the British. More recently, however, the anthropologist David Cohen has questioned the validity of this story. Finding no historical evidence, Cohen believes the tale to be folklore and legend.[4]

From the close of the Revolution and into the nineteenth century, prostitution remained minimal and concentrated along specific streets (map 1). The Frenchman Moreau de St. Méry noted in 1794, "Whole sections of streets are given over to streetwalkers for the plying of their profession." Women "of every color can be found in the streets, particularly after ten o'clock at night, soliciting men and proudly flaunting their licentiousness in the most shameless manner." Three small areas, in particular, stood out. First, the irreverent Holy Ground, behind St. Paul's Chapel, remained the leading district of deviance. In 1802, more than a score of residents complained to the Common Council (the elected local assembly) about the "idle and disorderly loose women" on Barclay Street who behaved "in such a manner as [was] too indecent to relate." A convenient passage between the East and Hudson rivers, Barclay Street was usually filled with sailors, shipyard workers, and prostitutes "who frequently . . . behave[d] with great incivillity."[5]

A second neighborhood was George Street. Just off the City Common (later City Hall Park), this prostitution district was two short blocks from the Park Theater and close to the East River wharves. After 1800, certain residents and early neighborhood associations deplored the proliferating "houses [of ill fame] in George and Charlotte Streets frequented at unreasonable hours by idle Negroes and other dissolute persons." Farther up the river was a final zone of prostitutes, on East George Street, an area on the outer, northeast fringe of the city in the midst of shipping, dock, and marine industries. Typical was an 1812 Common Council report complaining about the "droves of youth" who journeyed to these outskirts of the city for their "depredations."[6] District attorney records verify that prostitution was concentrated in these neighborhoods during the postwar years. Between 1790 and 1809, for example, two-thirds of the nearly two hundred indictments for prosti-

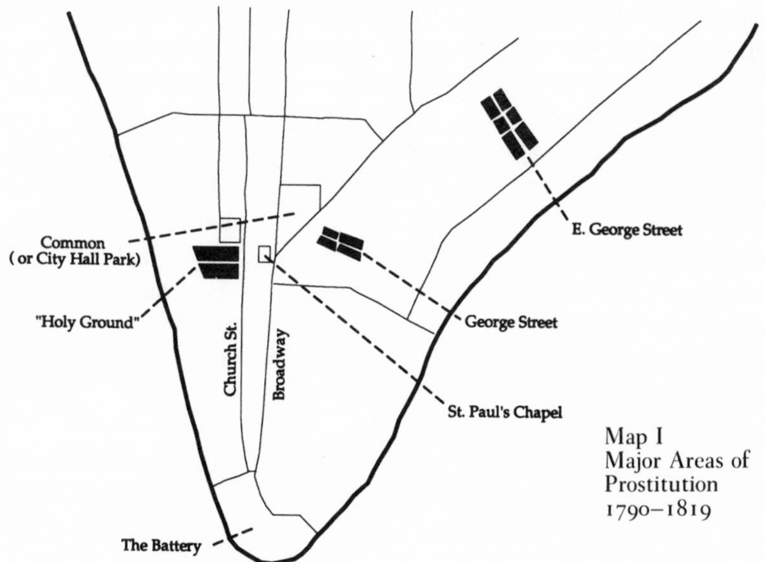

Map I
Major Areas of
Prostitution
1790–1819

tution were for illicit activities near the East River docks, 26 percent on East George and George streets alone.[7]

For several decades after the Revolution, then, prostitution in New York was a comparatively orderly, controlled enterprise, restricted to a few blocks and physically linked to the city's waterfront commerce. Illicit sexuality was isolated and segregated. Little streetwalking occurred outside these clearly defined areas. Solicitation usually happened indoors or on small, remote streets out of the public eye. Compared with European counterparts, early republican New York had little commercial sex. During a visit in 1818, the English labor reformer William Cobbett was struck by the relative absence of crime and visible prostitution. "[M]en go to bed with scarcely locking their doors; and never is seen in those streets what is called in England, a girl of the town."[8]

In general, this was not surprising. Eighteenth-century American society provided few opportunities for spontaneous and imaginative sexual exploration. Crude housing, crowded sleeping arrangements, and the watchful eyes of family and church members were unlikely to foster sexual experimentation. In North America, concupiscence was primarily confined to the family. The clients of prostitutes, for the most part, were visitors, soldiers, and the poorest transients wandering from city to city. As both a social practice and a sexual institution, prostitution functioned on the fringe of urban society before 1820. Although some overly sensitive observers complained of the "debauchery" in Boston, Philadelphia, and New York, there was relatively little commercial sex in the colonies and the early republic. The historian Lawrence Stone has concluded that prostitution was rare in eighteenth- and early-nineteenth-century America, especially when compared with its incidence in England. In one sense, the Puritans and their fellow colonizers successfully established a city of God "upon a hill."[9]

With this limited experience and history, New York proved to be ill prepared for the ensuing century.

Part I

ANTEBELLUM NEW YORK, 1820–1870

2

SEX DISTRICTS

ALTHOUGH the physical act undoubtedly remained the same, New York experienced a kind of sexual revolution after 1820. That year the newspaper, *Niles' Register* proclaimed that the "public show of extravagance, audacity, and licentiousness of the women of the town," demanded "the corrective interposition of the magistrates." For the first time, citizens were so "scandalized and public opinion [so] outraged" that police officers were ordered to report all prostitutes sighted on Broadway and on Gotham's other major arteries. What at first seemed to be a short-term problem turned out to be a century-long phenomenon.

By midcentury, New York had become the carnal showcase of the Western world for native-born Americans and foreign visitors alike. In 1848, the Norwegian traveler Ole Raeder declared, "New York is the Gommorha [*sic*] of the New World, and I am sure it may well be compared with Paris when it comes to opportunities for the destruction of both body and soul." Police Chief George Matsell admitted that prostitution in New York increased during the late 1840s and into the 1850s. "If prostitution continues so," wondered a concerned Walt Whitman in 1857, "and the main classes of young men immerse themselves more and more in it, as they appear to be doing, what will be the result?" The answer was simple, Dr. William Sanger despondently remarked two years later: "Every day makes the system of New York more like that of the most depraved capitals of continental Europe. . . ."[1]

For many, the most telling evidence of this change was spatial. In antebellum New York, certain public areas and urban real estate were increasingly defined by the preponderance of commercial sex. Nothing better symbolized this than the best-known thoroughfare, Broadway. From City Hall Park to Houston Street, the "noctivagous strumpetocracy" was a nightly presence. Whether it was, in Whitman's words, a "notorious courtesan taking a 'respectable' promenade" in the afternoon, or the "tawdry, hateful, foul-tongued, and harsh-voiced harlots" after dusk, Broadway was a mart for prostitutes. *Nymphes de pave* studded with jewelry flashing from their breasts and bare arms collected in groups of five or six along the corners of New York's major avenue. Called "cruisers" by some, many worked in conjunction with the Broadway hotels or nearby brothels. "One is so accustomed to the sight of these gaudily dressed butterflies," reported the *Tribune* in 1855, "that the streets look very strange without them."[2]

Throughout the antebellum era, nighttime pedestrian explorers repeatedly mentioned this carnal display on Gotham's major avenue. "Our magnificent Broadway," lamented John D. Vose, "is almost rendered useless to our virtuous maidens by the courtezans who infest it." In periods when police officers cracked down on the most blatant of exhibitions, the streetwalker simply "dragged her foot" in a conspicuous manner to signal her mission. "Indeed, this renowned street has no great reason to boast over the more notorious, . . . more open, scenes of the 'Point' and 'Hook,' " wrote Harrison Gray Buchanan. Only in its luxury, its "gentility, . . . and its outward semblance of virtue" was it superior. Broadway, he concluded, had "as much profligacy as any other equal section of the city."[3]

One might dismiss many of these pronouncements and others like them as the exaggerated fears of moral reformers. Undoubtedly, most nineteenth-century analyses and descriptions of prostitution were laced with self-righteous assumptions and judgments. But beyond the rhetoric, hyperbole, and prescriptive warnings to real behavior, these impressions still spoke to a dramatic change in sexual activity. Indeed, contemporaries' fixation on only the most blatant manifestation of prostitution ignored numerous other ways it became increasingly entrenched in urban life. Streetwalking was part of a less visible network of institutions and customs that grew more accepted and formalized as the nineteenth century progressed. When it came to prostitution, geography reflected sociology.

Perhaps the most visible evidence of this changing sexual ethos was the rapid rise in the number of brothels and so-called bawdy houses. By the 1820s, conservative estimates claimed New York had at least two hundred brothels. At the end of the Civil War, the number exceeded six hundred in one police report. Sanitary reformers and physicians, during their investigations of health conditions and overcrowding in the city's tenements in the same year, inadvertently counted over five hundred such establishments. Furthermore, a systematic examination of district attorney indictments, police court records, and brothel guidebooks from the era confirms that these estimates were not far off the mark.[4]

The popularity of Broadway with prostitutes and their clients was, in part, a function of this rapid proliferation of houses of prostitution throughout New York. Yet, Broadway was only the most evident and, in some ways, a superficial example. Observers frequently cited the Battery, in lower Manhattan, the famed Bowery, uptown, and Paradise Square, in the heart of Five Points, as worthy competitors for the initial exchanges of prostitutes and their clients. Because antebellum New York had few parks and little public space, these broad thoroughfares and small, open squares functioned like the formal malls and parade grounds in major European cities. Each provided an open, public space for men to meet prostitutes or prospective lovers. In a city of isolated strangers, these areas teemed with voluptuous reminders of sexual encounters

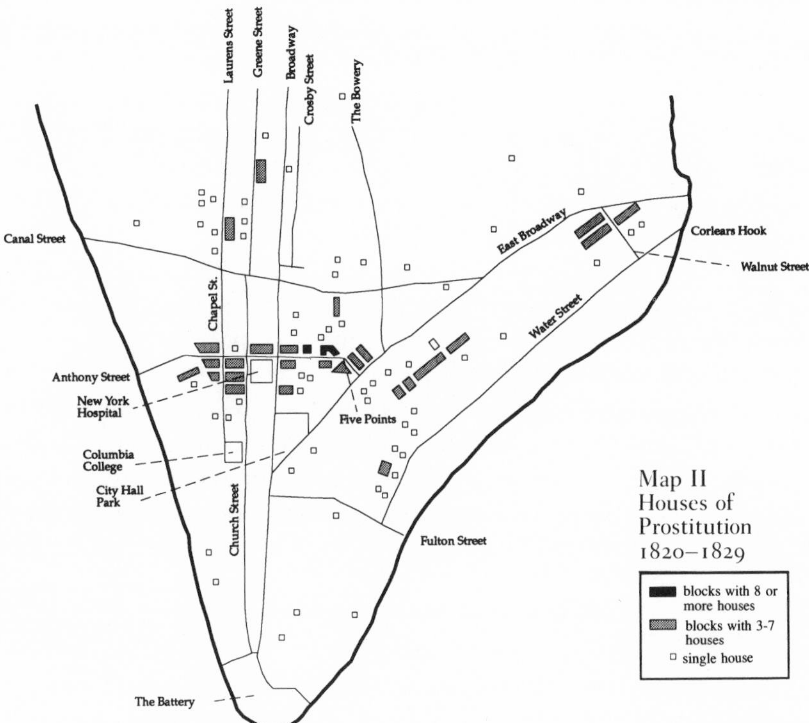

Map II
Houses of Prostitution
1820–1829

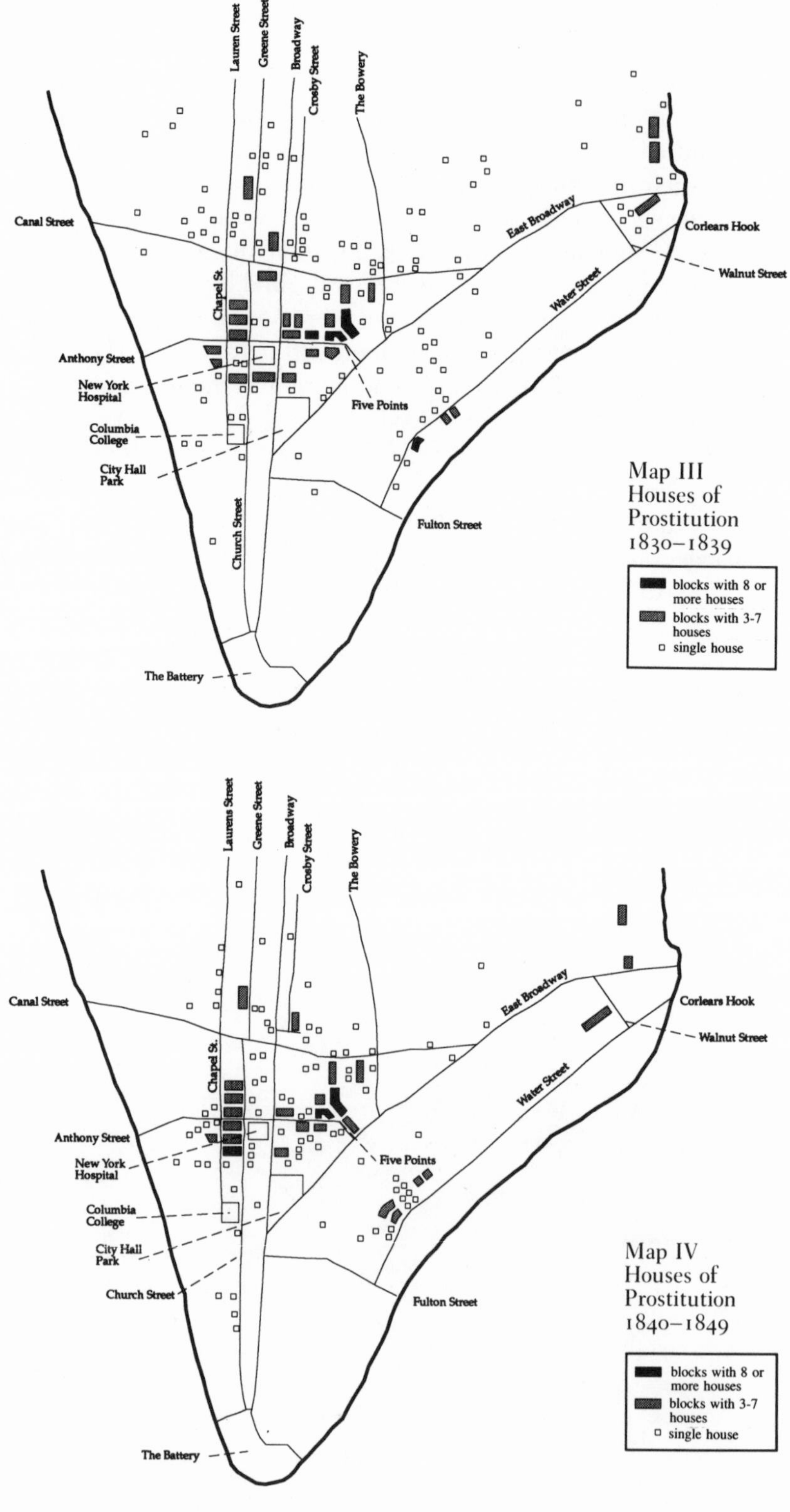

Map III
Houses of
Prostitution
1830–1839

Map IV
Houses of
Prostitution
1840–1849

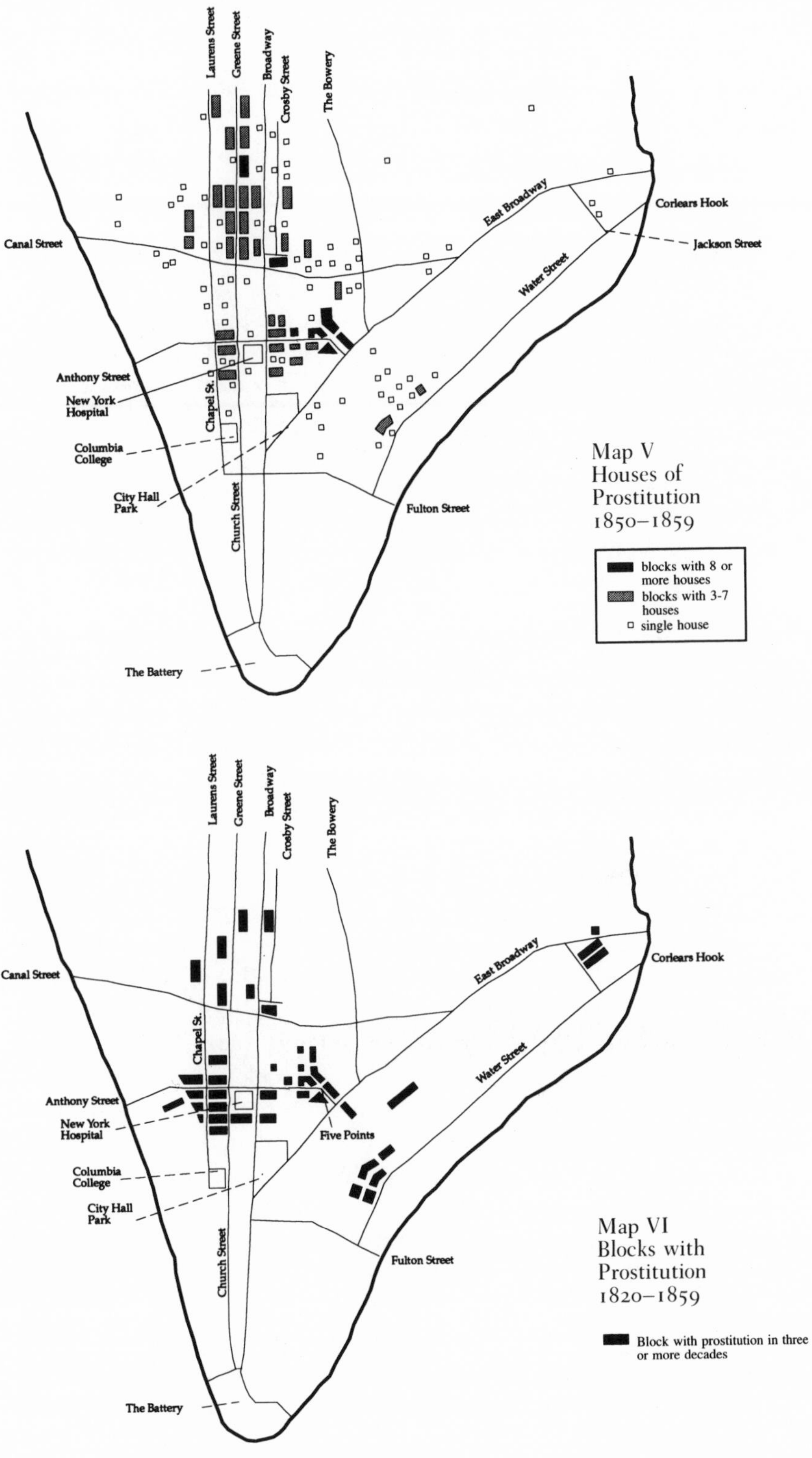

Map V
Houses of
Prostitution
1850–1859

Map VI
Blocks with
Prostitution
1820–1859

offering men a short-term respite from loneliness and an opportunity for physical intimacy.[5]

Even areas associated with wealth and social status were not immune from feeling the effects of this sexual geography. Streetwalkers traversed the Battery, at the southernmost tip of Manhattan, just across the street from the homes of leading merchants. To the north, prostitutes could even be found "above Bleecker Street," generally considered the elite suburb and "the boundary between the business and pleasure quarters of the town." There, prostitutes worked in Greenwich Village (on Thirteenth Street) and in Chelsea (on West Twentieth and Twenty-first streets). Residential working-class areas had blocks that bore designations like Slamm's Row, the Arcade, Rotten Row, and the Female Rialto and were filled with prostitutes. And in poor areas like Five Points, the West Side, and along the East River prostitution thrived. Throughout New York, noted the *Herald,* one found "the strange and disreputable anomaly of theaters, churches, and houses of ill-fame all huddled together in one block."

In fact, no neighborhood dominated trade. These latter three areas, for example, had roughly equal portions of the city's prostitution by the 1820s. Five Points contained the most brothels, but its concentration was unimpressive compared with that of the East River dockfront in the three decades before 1820 or with the Broadway entertainment district after 1850. The only known guidebook from the period, Butt Ender's *Prostitution Exposed,* revealed that Five Points, the West Side, and the Lower East Side respectively contained 31 percent, 25 percent, and 20 percent of the city's best-known and most alluring brothels.[6] No single area enjoyed a monopoly on these habitats of sex (see maps 2 to 7).

A major impetus behind the increasing application of New York's real estate to the sex trade was that it offered windfall profits to the neighborhood landlord. "Let us avoid all ambiguity here," exhorted Walt Whitman. "The tenants so desirable by these landlords are women whose pursuits we best indicate by the avoidance of direct mention." Indeed, as urban planning and development were increasingly "privatized" during the nineteenth century, responsibility for governing and economic development shifted from the public to the private sector. Private individuals assumed the costs of civic improvements—laying roads, building wharves, erecting bridges, dredging harbors. Private property was seen as a means to overturn autocratic privilege in a centralized government. More than any other urban enterprise, real estate investment verified the privatization of the city. And because real estate affected the economic foundation of the city, its disposition constituted incrementalized city planning.[7] The individuals, therefore, who controlled real estate ultimately determined the physical pattern of prostitution in the metropolis.

The new real estate system that emerged in New York after 1800 created attractive conditions for renting to prostitutes. Increasingly, landowners began consolidating their holdings. They often leased real estate for intervals of twenty-one to ninety-nine years, usually to entrepreneurial merchants, brokers, shopkeepers, and speculative builders, who in turn sublet buildings to other tenants. Out of these arrangements, a hierarchy emerged whereby one individual owned the land, a second the building, and a third the lease. "Capitalists, seeking large profits," concluded John Vose, "combine in the manner described." By midcentury, another observer admitted that the "most costly and splendid buildings in New York" stood on leased ground, with the owners paying a ground rent. Major landlords like Trinity Church possessed real estate that encompassed wharves, ferries, dock privileges, depots, stores, hotels, theaters, churches, private mansions, and, later, tenements. Throughout the nineteenth century, urban real estate, structured in this fashion, offered the single most important source of leisured wealth in the nation.[8]

As real estate evolved into a specialized business after 1820, landlords sought new ways to extract greater profits. In an era predating the high-rise office building, real estate interests relied upon residential structures to generate revenue. But after 1830, landlords failed to develop sufficient numbers of housing units, for several reasons. First, the immigrant and working-class populations grew faster than the middle class, thereby creating a market for a new multifamily dwelling form—the tenement. By converting older houses to multiple tenant use or by constructing tenements, landlords quickly increased gross rental income. Second, the panic of 1837–43 stunted housing construction in New York on the eve of massive European immigration. The streams of Irish and German immigrants fleeing famine and revolution created in the city a dearth of available housing units. Finally, at midcentury, commercial development attracted increasing amounts of construction capital, further depleting the city's housing stock. In 1846, one city journal maintained that New York rents were "extravagant beyond all belief." With decent homes annually renting for between $700 and $1,000, skilled workers (earning, on the average, $300 per year) and small-business men complained about the difficult and intolerable situation.[9]

Given a market that generated high rates of rental profit, landlords sought innovative ways to maximize their income. Tenement landlords, in particular, worried that their working-class tenants would not meet high rental payments on time. Prostitution was one salient solution. Furthermore, law enforcement officials did little to discourage landlords from renting to prostitutes. The district attorney, for example, sometimes refused to prosecute well-known prostitutes, because of excessive court costs and frequent acquittals. Successful convictions were frequently undermined by minimal penalties. Even when appellate courts came to the defense of tenants unwittingly forced to live with prostitutes, they did nothing to punish guilty landlords. At midcentury, the Reverend Samuel Prime recognized that city officials virtually licensed some forms of prostitution and ignored others. "If a miserable hole in Orange Street becomes so offensive that the peace of the city requires its purgation," he wrote, "the old hag who keeps it will be snaked to the police office. . . . But hundreds of houses close by the houses of our magistrates spread their allurements before the eyes of our youth, . . . and the shield of the law protects the portal."[10]

Prostitutes, of course, did not spread themselves out uniformly. Certain neighborhoods did emerge as strongholds of commercial sex between 1820 and 1850. A rough hierarchy of prostitution zones appeared with four different forms of concentration in several communities: (1) the fluctuating zones or blocks of streetwalking prostitutes, (2) a large cluster in Five Points, (3) ribbon developments along Church and Chapel streets and extending north into Laurens Street, and (4) small clusters throughout Manhattan, but especially along the East River in Water Street and Corlears Hook (see maps 2–6).[11] While none of these neighborhoods dominated the sex trade, each attracted significant amounts of prostitution. Indeed, the most commercialized parts of the business were found in these poor, working-class areas. Yet, compared with medieval German cities which had sex districts centuries old, or Paris, which had had brothels in the same area since the Middle Ages, or even San Francisco later in the century, with its seventy-five-year-old Tenderloin, antebellum New York shows a geography of prostitution that was fragmentary, dispersed, and short-lived.[12] Several of these neighborhoods, however, deserve closer attention.

Five Points

IF ONE community was equated with crime and the antebellum underworld, it was Five Points (see figures 1 and 2). Located on a landfill atop the former site of the Collect Pond, Five Points was considered by a wide range of observers to be the most notorious slum in the West-

Fig. 1 Five Points
From Valentine's Manual *(1859)*

Fig. 2 Five Points, 1827
Museum of the City of New York

ern Hemisphere. One visitor called it "as miserable a haunt of vice and misery as . . . was ever . . . witnessed in Europe." A grand jury labeled it "a rendezvous for thieves and prostitutes." The journalist George Foster insisted that "nearly every house and cellar [was] a groggery below and a brothel above." A former fireman claimed that numerous citizens feared and "shunned the locality; all walked blocks out of their way rather than pass through it" and submit to violence-prone ruffians, gangs, and other "shoulder-hitters." Another writer advised readers that one "needed not only a 'guidebook,' but a *club*" to visit the neighborhood. The only solution to the problem of Five Points, concluded Ned Buntline in 1848, was for it to be "burned to the ground."[13]

To moralizing contemporaries, Five Points was synonymous with drink, danger, and debauchery, "the spot where black and white promiscuously mingle, and nightly celebrate disgusting orgies." Its reputation induced Europeans to make it a required stop on their visits to New York in order to compare it with similar neighborhoods back home. In one reformer's crude summary Five Points was "the most notorious precinct of moral leprosy in the city" and prostitution its "most open and shameless of vices." On Broadway, wrote another, "vice [was] gilded"; in Five Points, "exposed in naked deformity."[14]

In the four decades before the Civil War, Five Points housed the poorest of New York's laborers and immigrants. Its narrow, crooked streets and filthy, dismal alleys made it seem more medieval than modern. Houses, divided into small, cramped, uncomfortable apartments, appeared "ready to tumble together in a vast rubbish heap." In one dwelling, "every floor [was] without a chair, table, or any other article of furniture save a cooking utensil. . . . Few beds were found in any of these apartments, with inmates sleeping or lying on a heap of filthy rags, straw, and shavings." In an alley house off Baxter Street, something in the form of shelves substituted for beds, "on which lay men and women nestling in the straw, and partially covered with rags." Upstairs three beds accommodated fifteen men, women, and children. In numerous lodging houses, people of both sexes huddled together, "some almost in a state of nudity." In one extreme case, several prostitutes resided in a house where, according to one report, there was not a door and floor, nor roof.[15]

Many of these descriptions of Five Points undoubtedly reflected the moralistic, evangelical biases of the age, and should be read with care and a certain skepticism. Nevertheless, they do reveal something of the city's growing social divide. Five Points, as a neighborhood, differed from other areas because it was the social melting pot of New York's underground economy. Along Broadway and the Bowery, gambling dens openly advertised. In 1827, one newspaper estimated there were 190 illegal lottery offices in New York, mainly along Broadway. Two Bowery entrepreneurs, William McDonald and Nathaniel Weeks, admitted to earning about $500 in weekly profits from their gambling operations. A stranger might suppose, concluded one observer, that "one half of our citizens got their living by affording the opportunity of gambling to the rest." Pawnbrokers, dealers in secondhand goods, and unlicensed junk shops lined the streets.[16] Five Points, indeed, offered a very congenial environment for illegal entrepreneurship.

In Five Points, sex was a readily accessible part of the underground economy. From 1830 to 1839, for example, twenty-seven of the forty-three blocks (63 percent) surrounding Paradise Square housed prostitutes on at least one occasion, inducing the *Sun* to proclaim, "[I]f ever immorality and licentiousness were presented in more disgusting forms, . . . we have never yet beheld them." Prostitutes walked the streets day and night, sharing the same buildings with poor families and other dependent groups like children, the elderly, and the infirm. "I found that the children lived in the brothels," wrote one reporter, "and that as soon as the school was out the children returned to their residence and saw and conversed, and ate, and drank, and slept with the cast off of both sexes."[17]

Five Points prostitution was defined partly by its public display. Along its western edge, the Bowery and Chatham Square were a bourse of sex. The patrician George Templeton Strong claimed that after nightfall, amid the theaters, saloons, dance halls, and cheap lodging houses, the thoroughfare overflowed with "members of the whorearchy in most slatternly *deshabille.*" Once elegant eighteenth-century residences like that of the merchant Edward Mooney at 18 Bowery now served as brothels. West of the Bowery, Paradise Square was the crossroads of Five Points. The Old Brewery, a former liquor manufactory converted into the largest boardinghouse in the neighborhood, was its most notorious building (figure 3). Rooms upstairs accommodated transient visitors, many of them prostitutes. Saloons dotted its vast basement and numerous ground-floor entries. According to one observer, "women, bare-headed, bare-armed, and bare-bosomed, stared in the doorway or on the sidewalk, inviting passers-by, indiscriminately, to enter, or exchanging oaths and obscenities with the inmates of the next house, similarly employed." Adjacent to the Old Brewery was an infamous alleyway dubbed Murderers' Row.[18]

Just around the corner, along Centre and Anthony streets, "were

Fig. 3 Old Brewery, Five Points, 1852
From Valentine's Manual *(1853)*

those exchanges where cyprians sold their shame," Florry Kernan remembered. Saloons like Cow Bay and Cut-Throat Alley attracted hundreds of people. In 1826, some Anthony Street residents lamented that the "number of houses of bad fame and the attraction of vagrants [had] been increasing for several years [making it] . . . intolerable to the inhabitants and dangerous for people to pass through the streets." On the single blockfront bounded by Anthony, Leonard, Orange, and Centre streets, there were at least seventeen domiciles of sex in each of the four decades from 1820 to 1859. And an adjoining block usually contained ten or more similar establishments.[19]

Neighborhood protests, however, were of little avail. Privacy was expensive, housing was overcrowded, and sexuality was simply unconcealed. Prostitutes seeking customers transformed Anthony Street into a promenade of frolicsome sensuality. Keepers of brothels encouraged public carousal and displays, while the wide-open windows permitted passersby to spy upon women "in carnal connection." Vainglorious streetwalkers often pulled up their garments and exposed themselves to potential customers. Even copulation could be public. The watchman Isaac Wessells, for example, remembered arresting John Quin on a hot summer evening in 1838 for fornicating with a black woman in an Anthony Street lot. Similarly, Isaac and Rebecca Davis on another occasion "exposed their nakedness and at four different times, laid down and had or attempted to have carnal connection, which collected a great mob," which cheered them on.[20]

The sometimes interracial character of public sexuality in Five Points attracted periodic attention. Indeed, Five Points offered the most racially integrated milieu in antebellum New York. The Reverend Samuel Prime, during a police-escorted nocturnal tour, was astounded by the "motley multitude of men and women, yellow and white, black and dingy, old and young, . . . a set of male and female Bacchanals dancing to the tambourines and fiddle; giggling and laughing . . . and making 'night hideous' with their lascivious orgies." Prime's racist preconceptions unwittingly unveiled a diverging sexual morality in Five Points. The sharp spatial boundaries typical of black prostitution later in the century were absent in antebellum New York. Rather, the racial divisions characteristic of much of nineteenth-century America vanished in this mixture of promiscuity, poverty, and loneliness.[21]

Indeed, from the end of the Revolution to the 1830s, black New Yorkers enjoyed a wider range of freedom than ever. As Shane White has shown, African-Americans, some recently freed and others fleeing slavery, moved to New York and enjoyed comparative autonomy, opportunity, and success. The vehement racism that appeared after 1830 was less developed or overt. This tolerance probably affected even leisure-time and sexual behavior in the city. For example, as early as 1801, the saloonkeeper Solomon Bell entertained black and white men in his establishment. By midcentury, the best-known dance hall in Five Points, Dickens Place, was operated by Pete Williams, a successful black saloonkeeper.[22]

For much of the antebellum period, in fact, black-run establishments in Five Points were popular and attracted much attention. While the houses of black prostitutes like Catherine Phillips, Ann Johnson, Jane Morgan, and Charlotte Carter did business strictly with African-American customers, numerous Five Points saloons and brothels accommodated black and white prostitutes and a similarly mixed clientele. In the 1820s, the black madam Hannah Lewis employed only white women in her Anthony Street brothel. A single raid by municipal authorities in 1830 concluded in the arrest of 133 individuals, among them "several well-dressed white men, found in the hovels of negroes." Haunts like the Diving Bell, Swimming Bath, and Arcade on Orange Street, as well as the Yankee Kitchen, Cow Bay, and Squeeze Gut Alley nearby, were well known for promoting miscegenational sexual intercourse.[23]

Some African-American proprietors assumed leading roles in the underground economy of Five Points. Many managed, George Foster claimed, "to become house-keepers and landlords, and in one way or another scrape together a good deal of money. They associate upon at least equal terms with the men and women of the parish, and many of them are regarded as desirable companions and lovers by the 'girls.' " Many black proprietors had white wives or mistresses, which frequently caused further consternation. To Foster, "their influence in the community [was] commanding."[24]

These open, commercial displays of interracial prostitution did not pass without some controversy. White residents in Five Points occasionally singled out the rowdy or immoral behavior of their black neighbors. James Bowser, a black saloonkeeper on Broadway and Reed Street, was accused of keeping his business open all night. There was "no street in the city of the lowest, character," asserted the neighbors in 1825, "where a greater nuisance exists than that cellar." Similarly, inhabitants of Anthony Street complained about the "mobs of blacks" that often collected in front of saloons. And when a "party of amorous whites in breeches fell desperately in love" with some black prostitutes just north of Five Points, reported one newspaper, they "routed their sable rivals." Still another observed that residents were upset "at the sight of two fine-looking men, fighting and swearing to see which shall lodge where previously some buck negro swell . . . revelled—in a strapping negress' bed." To some contemporaries, interracial sex, or "amalgamation," was "worse, by far, than sodomy."[25]

That contemporary writers and newspapers repeatedly discussed successful African-American proprietors and prostitutes probably reflected white fears of black sexual supremacy and racial integration. Relegated to the margins of nineteenth-century economic and social life, black women were frequently portrayed as highly sexed and motivated by carnal impulse. Fears of "racial pollution" linked white society's discomfort with issues of sexuality and race relations. By typecasting blacks as sensual, irrational "savages," whites could define themselves as superior.[26]

On occasion, outrageous exhibitions by black prostitutes even stimulated social unrest and political turmoil. With the ascendancy of the antislavery movement after 1830, leading abolitionists and defenders of black civil rights were accused of advocating "racial amalgamation," a contributing factor to riots in the 1830s. Even "respectable" elites, according to the historian Leonard Richards, discussed sexual passion in a vehement, exaggerated manner.[27] Sexuality was thus politicized in antebellum New York. Over time, intercourse between black and white heterosexuals was less a private matter of personal choice and more an issue of public intervention. Anxiety over economic competition from blacks induced some whites to play on fears of interracial sex in order to attack the civil rights goals of the antislavery movement.

Behind these scenes of public carnality stood the landlord. The most prolific entrepreneur of Five Points vice came from one of the leading early American families. John R. Livingston, from the famed clan of Claremont, was the brother of Chancellor Robert R. Livingston, one of the nation's "founding fathers." Born in 1755, John Livingston was a supporter of the American Revolution and a soldier in the Continental army. Seeing the war as an impediment to immediate personal advancement, Livingston resigned shortly after its commencement in order to pursue his own business ventures. One historian of the Livingston family has concluded that John saw the Revolution as a prime opportunity for personal profit. He considered conducting business trips to Great Britain and Holland during the hostilities, only to be dissuaded by his more patriotic brother and Robert Morris. Those bits of advice, however, did not discourage him from privateering, because of "the big money in it." As early as 1776, Livingston embarked on secret trade and illegal commerce with England or its allies. For John Livingston, patriotism and loyalty took a backseat to individual profit. "Poverty," he admitted, "is a curse I can't bear. . . . [W]ith it a man had better not exist."[28]

One secure means of avoiding poverty was investment in the city's real estate market. To the Livingston family's already significant landholdings in Manhattan, John Livingston added more shortly after the war, and in 1788 he gained control of property in what later became Five Points. By 1791, Livingston had purchased and leased property just west of Broadway, an area later filled with houses of prostitution. After 1800, Livingston steadily purchased property, some of it from family members, in the area around the Collect Pond, on Orange and Anthony streets. When Edward Livingston, for example, was forced to sell property in 1811, John paid $400 for his real estate in a city-sponsored auction. As Five Points emerged as an entrepôt of sex, Livingston profited from prostitution, and throughout the 1820s and 1830s he bought and sold land in the heart of the neighborhood.[29] By 1828, Livingston had come to control at least five brothels on Anthony Street near Paradise Square.

Conscious of the increasing value of Manhattan real estate, Livingston did not limit his holdings to Five Points. In 1802, he bought at least twelve lots west of Broadway along Thomas Street, and he continued to purchase and sometimes sell property on Thomas and Anthony streets in the ensuing decades. Shortly after his death in 1851, his heirs sold portions of the Thomas Street property for over $35,000.[30]

Livingston's control of this property, as well as of other habitats of prostitutes, was substantiated in the annual tax assessment records of the municipality. From 1820 to 1850, Livingston was listed as the owner / occupant of more than thirty documented houses of prostitution. Among his tenants were some of the best-known madams in the city—Abby

Mead, Rosina Townsend, Mary Wall, and Elizabeth Brown. Livingston's ownership of so many establishments gave his madams greater flexibility in their operations. If neighbors complained, or the watch harassed, or business declined, prostitutes moved to other Livingston-owned brothels. Abby Mead, for instance, lived at 28 Anthony Street from 1824 to 1826 and then moved to 41 Thomas Street during 1827 and 1828, both Livingston properties. Rosina Townsend followed a similar pattern of movement, working at 28 Anthony Street in 1828 before relocating to the Livingston-owned brothel the City Hotel, at 41 Thomas Street, for six years. It was in this brothel that the murder of the famed courtesan Helen Jewett occurred in 1836.[31]

Livingston was hardly oblivious to his role as New York's leading landlord of vice. Outside of Five Points, his lots and houses were frequently the only brothels on a block, and he usually lived within walking distance of his properties. Neighborhood protests did little to deter Livingston from renting to prostitutes. In 1826, for example, seven Five Points men petitioned the district attorney because "the number of houses of bad fame . . . [had] been increasing for several years . . . to such a degree that they [were] intolerable to the inhabitants and dangerous for people to pass through the streets." Among those blamed for the problem was John R. Livingston, who then owned property at Anthony and Little Water streets. Four years later, George Chapman protested that from his front window, he spotted females across the street "parading . . . in a state of nature, with the front window open to the street." Simply arresting them was fruitless, as any "vacancy in the brothel may be filled in twenty minutes." The problem, he surmised, could be eliminated only "by cleaning out the houses, indicting their keepers and [John R.] Livingston, their agent, who lets these houses with a knowledge of their infamous purposes."[32]

Livingston was not an isolated example of genteel profiteering in the sex trade. For instance, John F. Delaplaine, an importer, commission merchant, and scion of a rich New York family, enhanced his fortune when he married the wealthy daughter of Isaac Clason. By 1845, Delaplaine was worth an estimated $150,000.[33] But some of this wealth was tainted with prostitution. In 1848, for example, he rented a Walker Street brothel to Anson House, who then subleased the dwelling to Rachel Porter. Four years later, he was accused of supporting the establishment of Maria Mitchell on Crosby Street. When the district attorney prosecuted Delaplaine for running a Church Street brothel, the indictment charged that the wealthy merchant was no neophyte in the business and controlled several other establishments in New York.[34]

Livingston and Delaplaine were not aberrations or social misfits among New York's wealthy landlords. An examination of landowning patterns in the heart of Five Points reveals that other well-known families profited from the sex trade. On the block touching Paradise Square and bounded by Anthony, Orange, Leonard, and Collect (later Centre) streets, the landlords included some of the richest individuals and families in the nation. The tobacco entrepreneur George Lorillard, for example, came from a family that by midcentury boasted a total wealth in excess of $3 million. In 1818, he purchased ten lots on this block from the city for $5,400 and retained control until his death.[35] The Fisher family, first Leonard, a wealthy "gentleman," and later his namesake son, a dentist with wealth estimated at $100,000 in 1845, controlled a stretch of brothels along Centre Street during the 1830s. According to an 1836 police court trial, Leonard Fisher's wife personally and actively rented the brothels to known prostitutes and madams. Other members of the family owned similar properties across the street. And in 1839, George Fisher replaced George Lorillard as the owner of two Centre Street houses, an indication that the Fisher family was expanding its brothel holdings in the community.[36] Well-known political figures also owned brothels. Matthew Davis, an early machine politician and the "true founder of Tammany Hall," openly profited from commercial sex in Five Points.[37]

Prostitution was also an avenue of upward mobility for less affluent property holders. James Ridgeway, a house carpenter residing just north of Five Points, began buying property on Anthony and Little Water streets in 1812; between 1821 and 1835, he made at least eleven separate purchases in the heart of Five Points. Over time, Ridgeway invested in more-expensive real estate. His earliest transaction in 1821 cost only $525. But in 1829, his purchases included lots and houses ranging in price from $1,500 to $2,000; by 1834, he had accumulated enough capital to spend $7,750 on a single lot. And in 1850, his estate contained at least eight houses of prostitution. Ridgeway clearly controlled the property he purchased. Every year, he dutifully paid his real estate taxes and was consistently listed as the owner / occupant for some of the leading houses of prostitution in Five Points.[38] While Ridgway's bonanza was partly attributable to a construction boom, a significant portion of his financial estate was derived from the toil of the prostitutes he housed and protected.

The hegemony of landlords, their agents, and prostitutes is well illustrated by the unsuccessful proposals to raze Five Points between 1829 and 1834. Responding to a petition of 2,400 landholders and lessees, the Street Committee of the Common Council in 1829 admitted that the area was in "ruinous Condition" and occupied by the "most degraded and abandoned of the human species." It recommended destruction of the most offensive buildings. Yet, when a coalition of large Five Points landlords, including John R. Livingston and Peter Lorillard, and lessees like the grocers and brothel keepers Patrick Collins and Elijah Valentine, was formed, the proposal failed. The economic interdependency of large landlords and their brothel-sponsoring agents illustrated the limits of nineteenth-century municipal intervention in land use and sexual regulation. What some perceived to be a nuisance in fact increased the value of property.[39]

The West Side

DURING the first half of the nineteenth century, no other neighborhood better epitomized New York's division into two cities, one for the rich and one for the poor, than the West Side below Canal Street (officially the Third and Fifth wards). Important institutions dotted the area. The Astor House, the so-called Granite Pile, was the leading hotel in the city for decades, its construction "intended doubtless to commemorate the wealth and taste of the proprietor, John Jacob Astor." Nearby, New York Hospital physically separated the West Side from Five Points. The city's oldest institution of higher education, Columbia College, with its pastoral, tree-shaded square, occupied a site off Park Place. A block away on Barclay Street was its medical counterpart, the College of Physicians and Surgeons. To the north, John McComb's St. John's Chapel faced the bucolic Hudson Square, "one of the loveliest residential districts," with its railing "as high and as handsome as that of the Tuilleries," in Paris.[40]

Alongside these institutions settled the city's elite. Between 1820 and 1840, three-story row houses and mansions along Broadway, Park Place, and Barclay, Murray, Warren, and Chambers streets contained the stately homes of wealthy families like the Roosevelts, Aspinwalls, Astors, and Grinnells. "Aspinwall's house in College Place was probably the most luxurious and magnificent in the city," concluded one visitor. And in 1845, the wealthy shipbuilder John Cox Stevens built a Greek temple for a residence. Designed by the apostle of American Greek Revival, Alexander Jackson Davis, the mansion combined Greek and Tuscan styles with a colonnaded porch, capped dome, and two floors of large windows. Some considered it the most magnificent edifice in the city. "The Palais Bourbon in Paris, Buckingham Palace in London and Sans-Souci in Berlin, are little grander than this residence of a simple citizen in our republican city," testified the former mayor Philip Hone.[41]

After 1830, however, these wealthy citizens resided in proximity to numerous houses of prostitution. Along Church and Chapel streets, continuing north of Canal Street into Laurens Street (Rotten Row, as it was nicknamed), were many expensive brothels. Church Street, wrote one exaggerating critic, contained "fifteen hundred women of ill-fame," housed in opulent brothels patronized by "venerable" old men. Another described the street as "a foul lazar thoroughfare of prostitution." Well-known Church Street brothels run by Mrs. Lee and Susan Pratt were only a block from Philip Hone's house during the 1830s. A decade later, at least seven houses of prostitution were within three blocks of Hone's former abode, including some on the very same block.[42] Similarly, the Leonard and Church Street brothels of Stacy Pitcher and Elisa Post were within a block of the former mayor Walter Bowne's and the merchant Cornelius Low's residences in 1839. Margaret Duvall's expensive bawdy house on Warren Street faced the respectable homes of the lawyer John Anthon, the auctioneer Simeon Draper, and the merchants Ogden Haggerty and Joseph Hudson. When Henry Clay visited the city in 1849, he stayed with his friend Egbert Benson on the same block. At the intersection of Church Street and Park Place stood the mansions of Assemblyman Thomas McElrath and William Douglas. Their Park Place neighbors a few steps away included the banker Isaac Jones, the merchants Silas Bronson and George Douglas, and the disorderly house of Reuben Parson, Henry Colton, and Henry Collins.[43]

Brothels were attracted to this neighborhood by a new urban development—the hotel. After John Jacob Astor opened the Astor House in 1836, others soon followed. As the initial large hostelries appeared on Broadway, prostitution grew more entrenched one and two blocks west on Church and Chapel streets. During the 1830s, for example, at least thirty-four houses of prostitution in the city (13 percent of the total) were within two and a half blocks of a hotel, and most were in the West Side. By the next decade, the figure nearly tripled, to ninety-six (46 percent). Some, like Mary Benson's Church Street brothel, were reputed to be the favorite resort of patrons from the Astor House and American Hotel. During the 1850s, this locational trend reached its apogee as nearly 80 percent of the houses of prostitution along the West Side remained within two and a half blocks of a major hotel.[44]

Prostitutes also gravitated toward exclusively male institutions in the neighborhood. Columbia College and the neighboring College of Physicians and Surgeons, for instance, had prostitutes for neighbors during most of the antebellum era. One Chapel Street house was even a resort primarily for young men under twenty-one years. And along Church Street, brothels greeted students arriving and departing from Columbia's west side entrance.[45]

The high tax assessments of the West Side's houses of prostitution illustrated their exclusivity. During the 1830s, the median assessment for the known houses of prostitution on Church Street was $4,300. In contrast, Five Points' Anthony Street brothels had a median assessment of only $2,750.[46] This pattern of comparatively high property values in the West Side, especially on Church Street, continued past midcentury; values eventually surpassed $5,500. One observer admitted that Church Street was "justly styled as a 'hard place.' " Yet its houses were "as richly and luxuriously furnished, and . . . exhibit[ed] as much magnificent display as any in Broadway or Bleecker street."[47]

Although distinctions in class and status separated the brothels of the West Side from those of Five Points, they shared a notable amount of interracial sex. Sandwiched between the opulence surrounding Hudson Square in the north and Columbia College in the south was "African Grove." Located on Church Street between Duane and Anthony streets, behind New York Hospital, this was the largest and most significant enclave of blacks in the city by midcentury. As early as 1798, Diane Shessee ran a Warren Street saloon attracting black and white patrons. In 1806, Grace Robinson's Chapel Street brothel catered a racially integrated clientele. Until it was suppressed by the watch, a black male named John Williams ran a cellar saloon on Broadway opposite City Hall Park as late as 1818. Nearby residents complained of observing "white women in bed with black men" and mobs of blacks loitering in front of the popular Anthony Street saloons. Church Street residents maintained in 1833 that the black prostitute Adeline Sales brought men to her apartment who immodestly walked about the building with only their shirttails covering them. Even the brothels near Columbia College were known to include African-American prostitutes among their occupants.[48]

Despite the residential character of parts of the West Side, at times it was impossible to walk along some streets without enduring verbal abuse from prostitutes or their clients. During the 1820s, for example, residents of Anthony and Chapel streets testified that the prostitutes attracted such unruly crowds that "wives and daughters [could not] go out in the evening to the grocery or church without being insulted or crowded off the walk by the frequenters of these abominable houses." In 1841, Andrew Surre complained that his block on Walker Street was "unsafe for respectable females to pass through . . . after nine o'clock at night owing to the constant run of prostitutes and other persons of ill name and fame resorting." Similarly, White Street between Broadway and Church was long "pestered with lewd women cruising up and down the street, frequently collecting five or six together, . . . using the most obscene language, as well as accosting every man." George Templeton Strong remarked that Chapel Street was full of "all sorts of cits [cyprians] and cockneys and pert nurses and perter misses and dirty loafers and Corinthians."[49]

Water and Cherry Streets

IN 1857, Walt Whitman believed that the poorest prostitutes resided along the East River. "The hardest houses of all are those in Cherry, Water, and Walnut streets," he declared. "Here the prostitutes are generally drunkards. . . . You see the women half exposed at the cellar doors as you pass. Their faces are flushed and pimpled. The great doings, in these quarters, are at night." Serving the migratory population of sailors and travelers. Water Street was a center of prostitution longer than any other part of New York. Bustling with the activity of trade, the East River wards (Second, Fourth, and Seventh) contained an unusual mix of vice and wealth. Cherry Street, for instance, was a major avenue of mansions until the 1840s. As late as 1866, a few "first-class citizens" still resided in the central portion along the East River.[50] And the major countinghouses of leading merchants like Abiel A. Low, Moses Grinnell, and Arthur and Lewis Tappan were located along Fulton and South streets.

Residents and visitors alike noted the coarse and bawdy activity on Water and Cherry streets. At midcentury, a police report pronounced this area one "of the most riotous and disorderly localities perhaps in the city." Others declared it *the* worst quarter in New York. Formerly elegant mansions along Pearl, Cherry, and Dover streets crowned with elaborately carved stone trim were converted into tenements and brothels. With the exception of a few storage buildings, Water Street from Peck Slip to Roosevelt Street was full of sex. The "whole of these two blocks," complained one uptown visitor, "is . . . entirely occupied as houses of prostitution of the most degrading and infamous character." The women along Water Street wrote Matthew Hale Smith, "are the lowest and most debased of their class. . . . Crime and vice has done its worst with them. . . . Their dress is flashy, untidy, covered with tinsel, while they are loaded down with brass jewelry. . . . Their dresses short, arms and necks bare, and their appearance as disgusting as can be conceived." Another investigator in 1853 counted thirty-eight houses of prostitution on Water Street, accommodating 138 young girls, and twenty-two similar abodes on Cherry Street. On the latter thoroughfare, prostitutes exposed "their naked persons before the windows to attract . . . the notices of persons passing by." "No one would have believed," lamented the reformer Charles Loring Brace in 1854, "that in less than half a century, a London St. Giles or Spitalfields would have grown up in New York. . . ."[51]

The prostitution in the Water Street area differed from that found in Five Points and the West Side. Whereas the brothel was a major institution of vice in these neighborhoods, saloon and cellar prostitution predominated in Water Street and vicinity. Adjoining the once stately mansions in the neighborhood were two-story houses whose lower floors were commonly used as liquor shops, their basements as dance saloons, and their upper stories "divided among the unfortunate class of women" who worked below. The infamous slum of Gotham Court was located at 36 and 38 Cherry Street. Resorts like the Bay of Biscay, Hong Kong, Canary Bird Hall, and the Band Box dominated neighborhood life. The most common visitors to the areas were sailors, many of them lured there to be robbed by prostitutes' accomplices. And like their counterparts in Five Points and the West Side, black and white prostitutes on Water and Cherry streets shared the same urban turf. A variety of saloons and brothels were said to be resorts where blacks and whites could "amalgamate." "Here," Brace exclaimed, "the wages of the day laborer pass to the harlot."[52]

Although reputed to be poor, Water Street brothels were more valuable than their counterparts in Five Points. In 1835, Water Street houses of prostitution had a medium assessment of $3,800 and those in Cherry Street an assessment of $4,700. At the same time, the median value of Five Points brothels was only $2,750.[53] If housing values are a fair indication, prostitutes in Water and Cherry streets worked in quarters surpassed only by their sisters in the West Side.

Water Street and Corlears Hook prostitutes were also known to work in the various ferries along the East River. Within two decades after Robert Fulton opened the city's first ferry service, connecting Manhattan with Brooklyn at the foot of Fulton Street, there were numerous terminals near the Water Street and Corlears Hook brothels. The high volume of traffic provided an easy cover for males from Brooklyn and elsewhere in search of sex. Any day of the week, as many as twenty-five to thirty prostitutes preparing for a "matrimonial exchange" could be discovered in the Fulton Street ferry house, mingling with less promiscuous women. In fact, by the 1840s, 82 percent of the prostitution along the East River was within two and a half blocks of a ferry station. Pimps and "travelling streetwalkers" were known for recruiting newly arriving girls at steamboat and ferry stations. "In that rush," observed Junius Browne, "all classes are mingled, lawyers and ladies, merchants and beggars, . . . bar-keepers and artists, courtesans and prudes. . . ." At times, prostitutes' activity was so overt that another observer summarily concluded that the ferry house was "the theater."[54]

Action in the street, however, evoked the greatest controversy. In 1846, Ellen Robinson declared that it was becoming increasingly impossible to live in her Water Street tenement because prostitutes were "continually in the habit of sitting half naked on the front stoop." Similarly, a watchman arrested Edward Hogan and Catharine Riley in 1839 for "lying on a stoop in Oliver [Street] . . . in the act of having criminal intercourse with each other." Even when prostitutes and their customers were not exposing themselves, their obscene behavior did little to endear them to their neighbors. In 1841, over 150 residents in the vicinity complained that the "neighborhood is robbed of peace and quietness by the midnight orgies of the miserable and degraded inmates that throng the streets and frequently assault and beat unoffending passers by." It was "unsafe as well as unpleasant and disagreeable for the respectable females residing in that part of the city to venture [out] at any hour either of the day or night." Even when indoors, residents insisted that the howling and the screaming outside were intolerable.[55]

Organized community action had little effect. During the 1860s, Kit Burns's Sportsman's Hall, with its widely known rat and dog pits, attracted the "most depraved and infamous on the entire New York island," charged one critic. By the mid-1870s, the Water Street area was considered by some to be "unrivaled" as "the worst district in the city." Efforts to improve the neighborhood, or even control prostitution, met with little success. The children in the area, reported the Children's Aid Society in the 1870s, were representative of the poorest people in New York. "They have been sent . . . out of the cellars and brothels . . . for which the Fourth Ward has become so notorious."[56]

The Hook

"CIRCUMAMBULATE the city on a dreamy Sabbath afternoon," advised Herman Melville. "Go from Corlears Hook to Coenties Slip. . . . What do you see?—Posted like silent sentinels all around town, stand thousands upon thousands of mortal men fixed in ocean reveries." Amid these labourers and seamen was the final landmark of antebellum

Fig. 4 Cigar Store near Corlears Hook, 1843
From Valentine's Manual *(1857)*

prostitution—Corlears Hook. Located at the easternmost end of Manhattan at Grand Street, the Hook attracted a small cluster of wild saloons and inexpensive brothels, with most of the latter along Walnut (later Jackson) Street. Only seven blocks in length and adjacent to the city's bustling shipyards, coal and granite dumps, mills, and the Allaire Iron Works, Walnut Street probably had the highest concentration of commercial sex in New York. In 1839, one guidebook claimed there were thirty-two houses of assignation and eighty-seven brothels in this part of New York. Even allowing for the exaggerated claims of the guidebook, most of the dwellings in Corlears Hook were devoted to the sale of sex (see figure 4).[57]

Prostitution in the Hook was the most impoverished in the city. The median assessment for all Walnut Street houses, irrespective of use, was half the value of the major brothels in Five Points and considerably less than that of those on Church Street. Compared with the values on Anthony ($2,750) and Church streets ($4,300), prostitutes and residents alike on Walnut Street endured some of the least desirable housing in New York. By the end of the Civil War, a sanitary inspector admitted that brothels were not only numerous in the area but also "of the lowest and vilest kind."[58]

The heavy concentration of poor, working-class women made the Hook the most competitive area of prostitution. Proprietors turned to strong measures to attract customers. At Daniel Lane's dance house, for example, two teenage girls stood in front enticing apprentice boys to enter, "to the great destruction of their morals," in the opinion of one neighbor. Some proprietors even resorted to violence and physical intimidation. When Charles Badeau of Walnut Street complained to the police about the ubiquitous commercial sex on his block, his dwelling was attacked by a mob led by Mary Lawrence, daughter of the brothel keeper Catherine Lawrence. Upon invading his premises, they made a "great noise and turbulence and . . . destroyed his wood furniture."[59]

"*IN SPEAKING* of the locality of the houses of ill-repute in the great city," concluded George Ellington at midcentury, "it would be more difficult to state where they are not, than where they are."[60] The spread of prostitution to seemingly all parts of New York was partly the product of New York's real estate revolution. As the real estate industry grew more specialized and the working-class population multiplied faster than the middle class, landlords relied upon tenancy and residential property to generate revenue. New York's first large tenant districts quickly became its first slums. Areas like Five Points, the West Side, Water Street, and Corlears Hook grew overcrowded and run-down. Prostitution enabled landlords in such areas not only to extract higher rents but also to stabilize their businesses by displacing poorer tenants who frequently failed to pay rent. In this fashion, the first commercialized "sex districts" were linked to the rise of impoverished tenant neighborhoods with a floating, transient population easily exploited by an underground, market economy.

As illicit sex became an increasingly attractive form of capital investment available to a variety of property holders, it benefited a diversity of socioeconomic groups in the city. For descendants of the colonial gentry like John R. Livingston, entrepreneurial artisans like the carpenter James Ridgeway, and the groggery keepers like Patrick Collins, prostitution was an attractive venture in real estate. For the working class, prostitution was simply a means to escape the close threat of poverty. Middle-class artisans used prostitution as a quick vehicle up the ladder of economic success. And for the rich, prostitution offered a secure form of speculation in a boom-and-bust age of economic unpredictability. "The most sanctified sinner, who pays the highest rent in the most fashionable church," charged one critic, thus "acquits his conscience."[61]

The changing geography of prostitution reflected its multiple layers and complexity. In Five Points, the most public and interracial forms of commercial sex thrived. The brothels of the West Side were shaped by their proximity to wealth. And prostitution along the East River was associated with saloons, cellars, and poverty. Needing to walk only ten minutes from their domiciles before confronting a prostitute or house of ill fame, antebellum New Yorkers thus shared their residential space with various entrepreneurs of sex.

3

"THE WHOREARCHY"

MORE than any other phenomenon, female prostitutes challenged the idyllic sexual morality of the growing urban middle class. As increasing numbers of women moved outside the family for financial reasons, female behavior, grounded in the realities of the nineteenth-century urban economy, presented an alternative vision of sexuality and its purposes. Lucy Ann Brady epitomized this subculture of young women. Born in New York City around 1820, Brady grew up in an impoverished household. We know little of her childhood, except that early on she was attracted to the company of her peers. By her teenage years, she regularly attended the theater. Soon thereafter, she began sleeping with its male patrons.

Brady's incorrigible sexual behavior induced her parents to commit her to the House of Refuge, a semipublic institution for juvenile delinquents. After a seventeen-month stay, she was "reformed" and apprenticed as a servant—but to little avail, because she ran away a short time later. For the next year, Brady lived a life of continual transiency. One night, for example, she met a steamboat captain who coaxed her to Mrs. Potter's Greene Street house of assignation. She stayed with him three days and nights before returning home. When another man paid five dollars for her services a few days later, she spent the night with him in an Orange Street brothel. The next day, after visiting a girlfriend in an oyster saloon, she accompanied a male stranger to a Mercer Street brothel. After returning to the saloon, she joined her friend and two other men in still another Orange Street house of prostitution, where they remained for the night.[1]

Brady's sexual experiences were representative of the increasingly visible subculture of prostitutes. A native-born New Yorker, she began prostituting as a young teenager, selling her body on an occasional basis. She was never "seduced" or forced into "white slavery." She worked for a short time as a servant, an occupation frequently associated with prostitution in the minds of many contemporaries. Her part-time prostitution indebted Brady to no one madam or institution. Her visits to the "third tier" in a theater, a house of assignation near Broadway, a brothel in Five Points, and a saloon elsewhere exemplified the institutional variety and fluidity of antebellum prostitution. At some point, her work was interrupted by municipal authorities, who placed her under arrest and kept her off the streets. But her activity was regulated by neither clock nor calendar. In most cases, the decision to prostitute hinged on a short-term need for money and a moment's entertainment. Brady's temporary resort to prostitution was typical of many young prostitutes in New York.

At first, behavior such as Brady's confused and confounded contemporaries. George Templeton Strong, for example, complained that prostitutes were so numerous and visible that New York was infested with a "whorearchy." "No one can walk the length of Broadway without meeting some hideous troop of ragged girls, from twelve-years old down, . . . with thief written in their cunning eyes and whore on their depraved faces," he wrote in 1851. In this world of poverty, a new underclass of female children made their home. "On a rainy day such crews may be seen by dozens," Strong wrote. "They haunt every other crossing and skulk away together, when the sun comes out and the mud is dry again. And such a group is I think the most revolting object that the social diseases of a great city can produce. A gang of blackguard boys is lovely by the side of it."[2]

Many like Strong were unsure where to draw the line between hard-core prostitution and simple promiscuity. But by the 1860s, observers like George Ellington recognized the existence of "treating"—young girls offering sex as a "way of receiving presents from their gentlemen admirers." Different from prostitutes, such females, Ellington admitted, were "in the under-world, but not of it." Convinced that 99 percent of all prostitutes ended up dead shortly thereafter, Ellington nevertheless cited numerous examples to the contrary. A pair of middle-class sisters from Westchester, for example, routinely visited Chatham Street saloons and brothels, "remaining there for a week or two, and then returning home, the parents believing that they had been visiting friends." Upon their arrest, they agreed to stop and reform. To Ellington's surprise, they later married "well and happy. Their parents or friends never heard of their adventures in the 'big city.' "[3]

These inconsistent, anecdotal descriptions of illicit intercourse often revealed more about the boundaries of nineteenth-century sexuality than about who actually was a prostitute. And few statistics were as inexact and divergent as those pertaining to the population of prostitutes. Then as later, the number changed daily, varied widely in the course of any year, and reflected the prejudices of observers.[4] Most nineteenth-century estimates, however, fell into two broad categories. First, clerics, purity reformers, and some proponents of prostitution tended to inflate statistics. In numerous examples, aggregate figures often surpassed 20 percent of the total female population between sixteen and thirty years of age. In 1833, for instance, the *Journal of Public Morals* estimated that 10,000 resided in the city. During the 1840s, different aldermen and newspapers insisted that New York had between 10,000 and 50,000 prostitutes. A guidebook published in 1855 under the nom de plume of Charles DeKock claimed that they numbered 25,000. At the end of the Civil War, Bishop Simpson of the Methodist-Episcopal Church claimed that the population of New York's prostitutes surpassed the total membership of his diocese (for greater detail, see table 1).[5]

These figures gave the false impression that New York was the site of an ongoing orgy. Sympathizers even admitted as much. In 1833, for instance, the *Journal of Public Morals* concurred that the figure of 10,000 prostitutes was surely exaggerated, but it nevertheless continued to employ that figure. Similarly, the minister and reformer Samuel Prime conceded in 1847 that the calculations of 10,000 and 20,000 prostitutes were too high. Since approximately 70,000 women in New York were between sixteen and thirty-six years old, one out of every seven young women would have been a prostitute.[6] Estimates of 50,000 prostitutes, over 70 percent of all females between fifteen and twenty-nine, were easily dismissed as exaggerations.

Police reports contradicted these figures but were, in their own way, equally unreliable. For one thing, they tended to be inconsistent. From October 1845 to January 1846, for example, the police counted 331 brothels with 1,146 prostitutes. In the ensuing three months, however, the figures dropped to 183 and 686, respectively. In fact, the police repeatedly underestimated the number of prostitutes in New York. In 1866, Police Superintendent John Kennedy claimed there were just over 2,500 prostitutes living in 560 brothels. Yet, only eight years earlier Dr. William Sanger, in what was undoubtedly the most systematic exami-

TABLE I
ESTIMATED NUMBER OF PROSTITUTES IN NEW YORK, 1816–1913

Year	*Number*	*Approximate Percentage of Young Females*	*Houses of Prostitution*	*Source Type*
1816	6,000–8,000			minister
1818	1,200			watch
1831	1,388	4%		watch
1833	10,000	27%		purity reform paper
1833	700	2%	220	purity reform paper
	15,000	41%	1,150	purity reform paper
1839	10,691	27%		brothel guide / purity reformer
1845			302	police
1846 (Jan.)	1,146	2%	331	police
1846 (May)	686	1%	183	police
1846	10,000	14%		alderman
	7,000	10%	1,000	police
1847	20,000	28%	400	alderman & minister
1848	18,000	26%	1,000	author
1849	10,000	11%	1,500	author
1849	50,000	71%	700	alderman & newspaper
1852	12,000	10%	1,800	author
1855	25,000	21%		brothel guide book
1858	6,000	5%		Charity Hospital doctor
1864	2,123	2%	599	police
1866	20,000	16%	502	minister & sanitation report
	2,690	2%	615	police
1867	10,000	8%		minister
	12,000	8%	773	magazine
	2,700*	2%	350*	purity reformer
	21,000	13%		reform organization
	2,562	2%	697	police
	25,000	20%		newspaper
	5,000*	4%		reform organization
1869	1,968*	1%	492*	journalist
	20–25,000	16–20%		author
1870			600	newspaper
1872	1,223	1%	464	police
	20,000	12%	601	minister
1880	11,000	6%		newspaper
1908†	10,000	3%		reformer
1910†	30,000	8%		settlement reformer
	6,000	2%		grand jury
1912†	36,000	9%		reform organization
	3,000	1%		reform organization
1913†	26,000	7%		Dept. of Justice
	15,000	4%		Kneeland study

* "Professional" prostitutes or "first-class" brothels only. For sources, see note 4, chapter 3.
† Figures are for Manhattan only.

nation of the century, personally interviewed 2,000 committed to the Charity Hospital. For political reasons, the police continually underestimated the total amount of prostitution in order to stem criticism by the city establishment and religious hierarchy. While police statistics accurately gauged the number of brothels and full-time prostitutes in most commercialized districts, they no doubt ignored the vast amount of part-time prostitution in the city's expanding tenement and working-class neighborhoods.

Despite their wide range of reliability, some tentative conclusions emerge from these and other statistics. Most likely, the total number of full-time and occasional prostitutes exceeded the low figures (under 5 percent) given by the police and never reached the excessive numbers (over 20 percent) of the reformers. Probably 5 to 10 percent of all young nineteenth-century women in New York (between fifteen and thirty years in age) prostituted at some point. Periodic depressions may have pushed the number above 10 percent.[7]

The major factor inducing young women to sell their bodies was the low wages for female labor. The "unjust arrangement of remuneration for services performed," wrote the *Sun* in 1833, "increases the temptation to licentiousness." As teenage women moved to the city in growing numbers after 1800, a large pool of cheap female wage labor appeared.[8] Because sewing and other forms of outwork were seasonal, female employees constantly shifted from one shop to another in an industry plagued with massive underemployment. The *National Laborer* estimated women's pay at no more than 37.5 cents per day in 1836. In 1845, nondomestic labor earned only $2.00 per week, according to the New York *Tribune*. With a cost of living averaging from $1.50 to $1.75 a week, this left little for other expenses. After the Civil War, conditions worsened and New York seamstresses complained of earning only 20 cents a day in a city where the cheapest room available cost about a dollar a week. "[F]emale prostitution," concluded George G. Foster, "is the direct result of the inadequate compensation for female labor."[9]

Abundant evidence confirms the existence of economic incentives for women to become prostitutes. Young girls in the House of Refuge from 1820 to 1860 frequently mentioned the low wages they earned as servants. More than a quarter of the females surveyed by Dr. William Sanger in 1858 (525 of 2,000) offered "destitution" as the primary cause of their prostitution, convincing him that prostitution was mostly a function of low wages and irregular employment. Male employers "drive a woman to starvation by refusing her employment, and then condemn her for maintaining a wretched existence at the price of her virtue," he remarked. Over half the prostitutes Sanger questioned reported earning three dollars or less per week in regular, gainful employment; 27 percent of them made only a single dollar each week. As the Female Moral Reform Society similarly reported, women "can't live by plain sewing in New York," so they resort to "houses of infamy for food and shelter."[10]

Like peddling, scavenging, and ragpicking, prostitution turned something with little value into something with cash value. When work was slow or money slack, milliners, servants, and peddlers alike resorted to prostitution. For example, Mary Weston admitted that she alternated between domestic service and "going on [the] town" as a way to supplement her meager income. Hannah Lewis peddled carpets during the day and brought men to a Benson Street house of assignation once or twice a week to make a few extra dollars.[11] Many prostitutes did not view it as a full-time occupation. Twenty-nine-year-old Ann Wallace, for instance, claimed she "live[d] partly by prostitution." Sharing a room with another woman in Five Points, Patty Penn likewise admitted she was a part-time prostitute, claiming that when she "gets work she does it and when she cannot get it she does without it." Margaret Turner was even more blunt: "I sometimes go out to days work [*sic*] and also live by prostitution."[12]

Others lived off prostitution and nothing else. Fourteen-year-old Harriet Newberry earned four to five dollars per night as a prostitute in a Chapel Street whorehouse and thereby managed to pay even her comparatively high rent of five dollars per week. After her "willing" seduction by a Frenchman in 1834, Sarah Jane Chapman solicited men on Broadway and the Bowery, charging two dollars apiece to the two or three men with whom she slept. Mary Ann Pitt was more direct than most when she stated in 1866 that she simply preferred prostitution to work. One young prostitute put it bluntly: "I know what making money is, sir. I am only fourteen, but I am old enough. I have had to take care of myself ever since I was ten years old, and I have never had a cent given to me. It may be a sin, sir, . . . but God will forgive. . . . The rich do such things and worse, and no one says anything against them."[13]

By the antebellum years, certain types of female employment had in the public mind become linked to prostitution. Those of servants, chambermaids, tailoresses, and milliners were the most common occupations of women who became prostitutes. A report by the Female Moral Reform Society in the 1830s held that servants and chambermaids together accounted for about a quarter of the city's total (see table 2 for a detailed breakdown). In the next several decades, the proportion of prostitutes who worked as servants rose even further. In 1859, Dr. William Sanger found that 47 percent of the prostitutes committed to the Almshouse were former servants. And despite the rise in factory work, the propor-

TABLE II
OCCUPATIONAL BACKGROUNDS OF NEW YORK CITY PROSTITUTES, 1839

Occupation	*Total Number*	*Known Prostitutes*	*Occasional Prostitutes*	*Occupational Percentage**
Milliners	1,920	328 (17%)	520 (27%)	44%
Dressmakers	983	107 (11%)	240 (24%)	35%
Tailoresses	2,450	484 (20%)	923 (38%)	58%
Fur Sewers	810	223 (28%)	318 (39%)	67%
Artificial Florists	507	89 (18%)	103 (20%)	38%
Plain Sewers	708	135 (19%)	192 (27%)	46%
Straw Sewers	706	72 (10%)	163 (23%)	33%
Shoe Binders	980	231 (24%)	318 (32%)	56%
Type Rubbers	370	90 (24%)	167 (45%)	69%
Sock Makers	1,450	206 (14%)	526 (36%)	50%
Chair Gilders	267	44 (16%)	96 (36%)	52%
Umbrella Sewers	1,134	262 (23%)	637 (56%)	79%
Hat Trimmers	839	167 (20%)	246 (29%)	49%
Book Folders	1,210	203 (17%)	260 (21%)	38%
Cloth Cap Makers	821	80 (10%)	394 (48%)	58%
Upholsters	380	61 (16%)	157 (41%)	57%
Chambermaids	983	139 (14%)	480 (49%)	63%
Servants	5,220	847 (16%)	1,183 (23%)	39%
Total	21,738	3,768 (17%)	6,923 (32%)	49%

* "Occupational Percentage" is the total number of known and occasional prostitutes divided by the total number of each occupation.

SOURCE: Based upon a report by the New York Female Moral Reform Society in Butt Ender, *Prostitution Exposed; or, A Moral Reform Directory* (New York, 1839).

tion of dressmakers and tailoresses remained consistent. Whereas 16 percent of all prostitutes were engaged in such work in 1839, on the eve of the Civil War 11 percent were in the leading garment trades.[14]

In the popular imagination, milliners and servants were frequently equated with lax sexual morals, if not prostitution. The *Weekly Rake,* for example, claimed milliners' shops contained "pretty women . . . intrigues, love matches, seductions, and many other things." Semifictional and salacious stories of milliners and servants picking up men and bringing them to nearby brothels were staples of popular lore. Pictures of milliners and servants in the *Whip,* for example, showed them in vulnerable or revealing poses. In "The Chambermaid," the amorous master of the house wrapped his arm around his female employee while she held a broom conspicuously between his legs in graphic phallic symbolism (figure 5). Indeed, some madams employed such businesses as fronts. Mary Gambel, a noted prostitute, kept a dressmaking establishment, and "from the outward respectability of her shop, no lady of character would hesitate to enter," reported one observer.[15]

In demographic terms, native-born and Irish women accounted for

Fig. 5 "The Chambermaid" (Whip, *9 April 1842), Courtesy American Antiquarian Society*

the most significant numbers of prostitutes. The few existing sources from 1840 to 1870 suggest that prostitutes were usually from the northeastern United States or Ireland, under twenty-three years of age, and recent migrants to the metropolis. Interestingly, immigrant prostitutes seem to have gravitated toward streetwalking, whereas native-born women tended to prefer brothels as a work environment.[16] The oldest women involved in the life were madams, whose average age exceeded thirty-three years. Indeed, the pattern that emerged from these sources confirmed many contemporary impressions.[17] Even at the height of Irish immigration in 1848, the *Advocate of Moral Reform* insisted that over half the prostitutes in New York City came not from abroad but from the countryside of the United States.[18]

The most common problem affecting prostitutes was venereal disease. William Sanger discovered that at least 40 percent of the prostitutes he studied confessed that they contracted syphilis or gonorrhea at least once. Most likely, an accurate count would have exceeded that figure. New York Hospital, for example, the city's leading medical facility in the nineteenth century annually reported that syphilis and gonorrhea combined were their most often treated diseases and ailments. Only rheumatism, fevers, and fractures approached venereal diseases in number of aggregate cases. Physicians like Sanger who warned the public about the dangers of contagion belonged to a frequently ignored minority. Not until the end of the century would the public recognize the health risks posed by untreated venereal disease.[19]

More shocking than venereal disease was the youthfulness of many prostitutes. Prior to 1820, an occasional madam recruited teenage girls. For example, after Rosanna McCaleb physically forced thirteen-year-old Betty Whiteman to copulate with "a man named George" by holding her legs, Whiteman worked in McCaleb's brothel. Similarly, when Moll Sanders tried to recruit thirteen-year-old Catherine Woolsey into her Chapel Street house, Woolsey refused, saying she knew "what the said Moll was."[20] But these were exceptional cases; only rarely did the names of very young prostitutes appear in the public record.

By the 1830s, however, child prostitution was a major public concern. Addressing the Society for the Reformation of Juvenile Delinquents, the former mayor and longtime reformer Stephen Allen concluded that the harsh socioeconomic realities of the marketplace were producing more and more teenage prostitutes. Most, he wrote, "have fallen from the combined influence of poverty, neglect, ignorance and bad company, rather than because of individual or voluntary depravity." After 1840, dozens of child prostitutes as young as eleven were found "loafing about City Hall each night, for the basest of purposes." Girls peddling flowers, apples, or matches on the streets were known for their salacious consorts and "loose characters." Around midcentury, police reports claimed that as many as 380 "juvenile harlots" lived in a single police district and that another 10,000 children roamed the city thoroughfares. Similarly, an 1862 Children's Aid Society study found homeless nine- and ten-year-old girls peddling sex late at night near the theaters, leading James McCabe to conclude, "[A]t ten the boys are thieves, at fifteen the girls are all prostitutes."[21]

Numerous brothels actually encouraged youthful carnality. In 1839, city authorities discovered five teenagers, ranging in age from sixteen to eighteen, committing "indecent" acts when they broke up Catharine Badger's disorderly house. Fifteen-year-old girls were known to bring men picked up in the street to Charity Jennison's Five Points establishment in the 1820s and to Louisa Daly's Madison Street house a decade later. During the 1840s, Louisa Acker had more than a score of young girls in her brothel, most ranging from twelve to fifteen years of age, and one as young as nine. Mary Ann Concklin's Anthony Street house had numerous girls under fifteen. Police Officer William Bell expressed little surprise when he learned that a small fifteen-year-old girl working in a Front Street junk shop "was in the habbit of going aboard coal boats in that vicinity and prostituting herself."[22] Teenage girls even worked in tandem. For example, Adaline Pioneer and Susan Baker, each fourteen years old, brought numerous men to Mrs. Webber's house of ill fame on Church Street. One neighbor testified that Pioneer brought at least four men there in ten days. Still other brothels specialized in ten- to fourteen-year-old girls.[23]

Reformers attributed the visible rise of teenage prostitution to the wanton seduction of young innocents by hedonistic philanderers. The penny press, employing sensationalist methods aimed at increasing readership, depicted the city as full of confidence men and sexual leeches eagerly plotting the conquest of young, virginal nymphs. Court cases confirm there was some truth to the charge. For example, Eliza Noe, an apprentice tailor living with Ann Clark, was compelled by her employer to have intercourse or risk a beating. Sixteen-year-old Martha Garrett was found in the bawdy house of Jacob and Louisa Acker in the summer of 1836. Moving to New York in 1833 to learn a trade, she lived with relatives until her seduction and abandonment by a Pearl Street tailor. Parents occasionally brought abduction charges against boyfriends or brothels when their daughters ended up in a house of ill fame. Retribution was not easy, however. When Ann Blaylock rescued her daughter from Catherine Anderson's Orange Street brothel, she was attacked and thrown into the gutter by the women in the house.[24]

Sermonizing reformers aside, young women were not usually prisoners of flesh merchants. Tales of forced sexual exploitation obscured the larger reality of a prostitute's life. Some teenagers used prostitution as a vehicle to escape parental discipline. A seventeen-year-old Connecticut girl ran away from home to work in a brothel because, as she said, "Mother is cross, and home is an old, dull, dead place." Trying to apprehend her seventeen-year-old daughter in a brothel, Matilda Waterbury overheard her daughter say, "Don't let my mother know it for she will kill me." Similarly, after leaving a Water Street brothel, William Ross's niece was "enticed back again to the same house five times in succession." Three moves by her family did little to discourage her predilection for prostitution. Although the parental tensions and social dynamics within these families remain unclear, many young females chose to prostitute. Indeed, fewer than one-fifth of the girls in the House of Refuge contended they were seduced and forced into prostitution. And at midcentury, Dr. William Sanger reported that only 14 percent (282 of 2,000) of the Almshouse prostitutes gave seduction as the primary impetus behind their turning to prostitution.[25]

Young women committed to the House of Refuge reflected the rise of teenage prostitution and its attendant problems. Established in 1825 by the Society for the Reformation of Juvenile Delinquents, the House of Refuge was considered more capable of fighting prostitution than was a Magdalen society (for reformed prostitutes), because of its preventive focus. "Those more advanced in years," argued one annual report, "are unfit subjects for our establishment, and likely to exercise a corrupting influence." Most child and teenage prostitutes committed to the House for Refuge came from broken homes. Well over half had a parent who died or abandoned the family while the girl was still very young (table 3). These young prostitutes tended increasingly to be either foreign-born or the offspring of immigrants. From 1825 to 1829, only 33 percent of the parents had foreign roots and only 16 percent of the girls themselves were born abroad. With the advent of massive Irish and German immigration, this changed dramatically. From 1845 to 1849, some 79 percent of the prostitutes' parents were immigrants, as were 38 percent of the prostitutes themselves. Finally, few of these prostitutes came from families of skilled laborers.[26] Most of the children and teenagers who fell into prostitution and were later committed to the House of Refuge came from those families that suffered the most deleterious effects of industrial capitalism in New York. The majority were orphaned or abandoned girls who lacked authority figures capable of providing for them or controlling their behavior.

The women surveyed by Dr. William Sanger both corroborated and departed from the stories of those in the House of Refuge. For example, over 50 percent of the 2,000 prostitutes he questioned came from fami-

TABLE III
NEW YORK CITY PROSTITUTES IN HOUSE OF REFUGE

Years	*1825–1829*	*1830–1834*	*1845–1849*	*1865–1869*
Number	48	55	47	81
Median Age	15	15	15	16
Lowest Age	8	8	14	12
Foreign-Born Parents	33%	45%	79%	75%
Foreign-Born	16%	18%	38%	21%
Born in NYC	52%	40%	38%	37%
Born in NYS	13%	18%	9%	23%
Born in U.S.	19%	16%	13%	15%
Unknown Birth	0%	8%	0%	4%
Parents Dead or Runaway	65%	65%	62%	51%
Domestics	25%	7%	38%	15%
Father Skilled	13%	2%	2%	5%
Theater Prostitute	4%	13%	2%	0
Brothel Prostitute	48%	20%	49%	63%
Streetwalker	17%	24%	19%	4%

SOURCE: House of Refuge Papers, vols. 1–6, 14–18, 28–31, New York State Archives, Albany.

lies where a parent died before they were twenty. Similarly, most parents suffered from alcoholism. More significant were the parental occupational backgrounds. Unlike the poor girls committed to the House of Refuge, the overwhelming majority in Sanger's sample belonged to families with middle-class or skilled artisanal parents. About 6 percent of the fathers enjoyed high status or wealth. Another 35 percent practiced middling or petty bourgeois professions, including 22 percent who were farmers. Still another 31 percent had fathers who were skilled artisans. Nearly three-quarters (72 percent) of the women, in fact, appear to have enjoyed at least a stable agrarian or artisanal-class upbringing.[27]

When all available sources are considered, the greatest predictor of prostitution was not ethnicity, birthplace, or even class. Rather, the death of a parent, especially the father, with its economic and psychological impact, was the most often shared variable in the personal histories of these women. As prostitutes increasingly came from families of farmers and artisans, the images of downward mobility traditionally associated with the literature of prostitution proved to be more than just exaggerated metaphors.

Some parents made prostitution a family affair. Observing that impoverished artisans sold the sexual favors of their wives and children, the Englishman Francis Place concluded that poverty and chastity were incompatible. The same was true in New York. Ann Donnelly, for instance, encouraged her daughter Sarah to streetwalk and use their Thompson Street apartment for prostitution. Susan Brown's Corlears Hook parlor house usually contained three to five prostitutes, two of whom were her own daughters. While living in a Chapel Street house, Solomon Lincoln tolerated his wife's and daughter's trading sex for cash. Elizabeth Dayton's mother worked as a prostitute and brothel keeper on Orange Street while fifteen-year-old Elizabeth streetwalked outside. When Jane Kane's Irish-born father died, her mother asked the fifteen-year-old to work in an Elm Street brothel. After thirteen-year-old Charlotte Willis's parents separated in 1828, she and her mother became prostitutes. Residents in a Water Street house insisted that the most notorious and disorderly prostitutes in the apartment of William Shaw were his own daughters, who nightly lay seductively in bed with their doors open. Similarly, Bridget Mangin's two daughters worked in her bawdy house on Worth Street in 1855. Cecelia Smith continued her prostitution even after she married; fourteen-year-old Julia Decker joined her married sister as a prostitute. And after arriving from Ireland, fifteen-year-old Mary O'Daniel was forced into the trade by her aunt and boardinghouse keeper Bridget McCarthy.[28] For the widowed mother, the downwardly mobile journeyman, and the poor immigrant, prostitution was not a violation of moral propriety but a necessary part of the household economy.

If family members did not encourage prostitution, female peers sometimes did. By her sixteenth birthday, for example, Fanny Bayles had been a prostitute for four years, usually in the houses of Adeline Miller. Bayles coaxed fourteen-year-old Sarah Cornwell into the business, arguing that she could then give up work and "be able to get many things." When Cornwell agreed to try, Bayles brought her to Miller's Orange Street house and "into a bedroom where a gentleman was sitting and there left her, and the gentleman got up and locked the door after her and then told [her] to undress and go to bed and he then had carnal connection with her which [was] the first time . . . with any man." Losing her virginity earned her two dollars. Likewise, eighteen-year-old Louisa Slowly brought Catharine Blaunelt, four years her junior, to William Murray's Elm Street house of prostitution for her sexual initiation. Fourteen-year-old Mary Hood claimed that Irish-born Bridget Perry initially induced her to have sex "with strange men." But when her parents came to remove her, she moved to another house to escape them. Mary Ann Blakely, a part-time prostitute living on Catharine Street, continually tried to persuade her roommate Maria McMann, a servant girl, to work with her. Sometimes mere persuasion by a madam was sufficient. Catherine Foot was noted for offering young teenagers to her customers at her White Street house of prostitution during the 1820s. In each case, Foot won the confidence of a young girl before arranging a session with a man.[29]

The most visible manifestation of this peer subculture among prostitutes was the "third tier." Like their English counterparts, New York theaters promoted an erotic atmosphere. Leading establishments like the Bowery, Chatham, Olympic, and Park theaters permitted prostitutes in the uppermost tier of seats. "Public prostitution [in the theater] is not noticed by law," admitted one observer. First-time middle-class visitors incredulously conceded that they "had not even dreamed of the improprieties then publicly tolerated in the 'third tier' and galleries." As much as one-fourth of the Broadway Theater, insisted another, was reserved for prostitutes. For over three decades, prostitutes claimed the third tier as their own social space. Numerous citizens complained that the third tier set the tone of the whole establishment. Theaters, wrote one reporter in 1842, "have degenerated into assignation houses—lounges for bawds and their victims—lust palaces." Likewise, women attending the theater were assumed by the prudish to be on "the most convenient and best lighted path to perdition."[30]

By midcentury, these recruiting networks of teenage females produced a certain collective identity among prostitutes. While the transitoriness of prostitution made such identifying bonds short-lived, they were noticed by outside observers. For example, George Wilkes was impressed to find that if a young man was "permanently attached" to a specific prostitute and secretly visited another one, "some of the inmates of the latter place [felt] it to be a matter of conscience to send word to the injured female." "They would expect as much to be done in their own behalf," he wrote. "Such is the common law . . . of this class." Similarly, after observing prostitutes for over a year as a physician in the Charity Hospital, William Sanger commented on the sympathy and kindness they displayed toward each other. When one was released, for example, other prostitutes would "club their scanty resources to supply her needs." If illness plagued one of their number, they provided medical assistance as nurses. In instances of disciplinary action, loyalty to their "prostitute class" induced them to stand together. "Their fidelity to each other," concluded Sanger, "is strongly marked." In limited cases, the bonds of affection lasted beyond their prostitution. In 1869, for example, Junius Browne claimed that one group of "unfortunate women" organized a club, recognizing "prostitution as unavoidable in the present condition of society. They make no effort toward reform, but aim to help with money those who are sick, indigent or aged." Befriending "a great many of their fallen sisters," they had, Brown believed, saved some "from self-destruction."[31]

Within this fluid, female subculture, the phenomenon of child prostitution reflected a transformation in urban sexual behavior and efforts to regulate it. The true extent, then as now, of sex between children and adults, remains an unanswered question. The issue is further complicated by definitions of childhood, adolescence, and adulthood that vary across cultures and time. Philippe Ariès has argued that the "practice of playing with children's privy parts formed part of a widespread tradition" in western Europe before 1600 and remains acceptable in some contemporary cultures. While similar sexual activity probably occurred in colonial and preindustrial America, it was largely hidden from the public eye. But as urban working-class children helped supplement their family incomes by peddling, huckstering, and scavenging, their activities merged with the shadier arts of crime and prostitution.[32]

The sale of one's virginity brought the greatest remuneration. Fourteen-year-old Ann Kerrigan was seduced by the English wine merchant John Ryan while working in a Murray Street porter house. After paying the proprietor $50 for the initial copulation, Ryan paid Kerrigan $20 a week for nearly two years to be his mistress. Another fourteen-year-old, Ruth Hudspeth, ran away from her home in New Jersey when she met a Frenchman who paid $50 to fornicate with her. Thereafter she earned $5 for every act of sexual intercourse with him until she was discovered by her aunt.[33] Even in poor areas like Five Points, intercourse with a virgin cost $10. In a job market offering teenage girls paltry incomes of $35 to $50 per year, the prospect of such income for one's maidenhood could be quite persuasive.

The minimal information on rape in New York partly confirms the inclination of some antebellum males to seduce very young girls. James Stanford, for example, told a fellow Water Street boarder that the young child Eliza Morrison "would make a wicked piece when she got a little bigger." Rather than waiting, he simply raped her. Indeed, about one-third of all the rape and attempted rape cases prosecuted by the district attorney from 1810 to 1876 involved female victims aged twelve or less. Children under twelve were at least twice as likely to be victims of rape or attempted rape as were older children. Although the majority of all rape victims appear to have been single women over nineteen, the large number of young females who were sexually attacked indicates that they were preferred sexual objects of some men in nineteenth-century New York.[34]

In many cases, young girls could even prostitute without risking pregnancy. Social historians have shown that nineteenth-century working-class women usually did not reach sexual maturity and the age of menarche until they were about fifteen. Comparatively less physically developed than twentieth-century girls of the same age, ten- to fifteen-year-olds had fewer fears of unwanted pregnancy than their older sisters in the profession. This "built-in" form of birth control and the diminished likelihood of a young girl's having venereal disease may have encouraged men to seek liaisons with younger women. Furthermore, an erroneous nineteenth-century sexual theory held that intercourse with a virgin would cure venereal disease. When James Campbell, for example, raped seventeen-year-old Eliza McKinsey, his accomplice egged him on, saying, "Get it in; she will clean you out; her blood is fresh, and you will get rid of all disease."[35]

Government did little to discourage such sexual exploitation. The low age of consent in New York (ten years) was hardly a deterrent. Although a few states set the age at twelve, it was not until after 1885 that numerous states bowed to popular pressure and raised the age. By 1889 New York's consent age was sixteen and by 1895 eighteen.[36] Before 1880, if a teenager was willing and her parents consented or were absent or ignorant, no legal obstacle prohibited men from having sexual intercourse with her.

This combination of familial, social, and political factors surely encouraged many young females to resort to prostitution. But probably the most attractive feature was the possibility of economic advancement, best exemplified by the madam. Although most women who prostituted did so for only a short time, some made it a career. Their longevity reflected how prostitution served as an avenue of mobility—a road that, if not paved with gold, provided a modicum of comfort and stability. During the early nineteenth century, some entrepreneurial prostitutes successfully accumulated savings and property. Stereotypical descriptions of a prostitute's life as five years of dissipation followed by death ignored those prostitutes who eventually became madams, acquired real and personal property, and remained in the profession for decades.

The leading prostitute in post-Revolutionary America was Eliza Bowen Jumel. Born in 1775 in Providence, Rhode Island, to a prostitute, she entered her mother's profession at an early age and moved to New York at age nineteen, working as a supernumerary in a theatrical troupe. According to one historian, "everybody who was anybody in New York knew her or knew about her" during the height of her career, from 1794 to 1800. She soon ingratiated herself with the French-born wine merchant Stephen Jumel, who married her in 1804. Because her reputed background created difficulties in socializing with the Knickerbocker elite, Jumel bought the old Roger Morris mansion above Harlem in 1810. When Eliza outlived her husband by forty years, her economic charms quickly surpassed her physical ones. Living in perhaps the most elegant domicile on Manhattan, she was considered the wealthiest woman in America for several decades. By 1833, her fortune was seductive enough to attract Aaron Burr into a short-lived marriage with her.[37]

More significantly, some prostitutes garnered wealth on their own, without the benefit of marriage. For example, during the first quarter of the nineteenth century, Maria Williamson (alias Williams and Willis) ran, according to one contemporary, "one of the greatest Hoar Houses [*sic*] in America." By 1819, she accumulated enough capital to purchase her brothel and real estate for $3,500. Gaining ownership of her establishment, Williamson immediately invested in similar nearby businesses and by 1820 owned five houses of prostitution on Church Street. A year later, she controlled brothels on Duane and Church streets. And the value of her real property was hardly insubstantial, the row of Church Street houses ranging in value from $1,000 to $2,800 each. Their combined assessment was $10,000.[38]

Jumel's and Williamson's success established precedents for other prostitutes shortly thereafter. By the 1840s, the most successful were virtual celebrities. Adeline Miller (alias Furman), "a damsel who has been on the town for twenty years," according to George Templeton

Strong in 1839, was a notable example. Miller acquired considerable wealth in her three-decade career as a prostitute. As early as 1821, she ran a Church Street brothel and owned personal property valued at $500. In the ensuing decades, she leased brothels on Elm, Orange, Duane, and Reade streets at various times. On at least one occasion, she was an "absentee" madam of a Cross Street brothel. By the 1840s, she was the subject of repeated attacks by the *Whip*, being called "the grey-haired hag" and "the most wicked procuress in the city." Her children were allegedly well educated and followed "noble pursuits." One issue even satirized Miller by linking her with the "Millerism" of the Adventist evangelical preacher William Miller. When he predicted that the end of the world would come in 1843 or 1844, the journal was skeptical. "The fellow who is peopling our mad-houses and helping to fill grave-yards and undertakers' pockets, must certainly be Mother Damnable Miller's brother," charged the *Whip*. "Both are working for the devil." By 1855, her possessions in her Church Street house alone were valued at $5,000.[39]

The best-known prostitute in antebellum America was Julia Brown. (see figure 6). The subject of numerous commentaries, Brown began her career by working with Miller in the 1830s. Shortly thereafter, she started running her own Chapel and Church Street brothels. When the National Theater burned down one Saturday morning in 1841, George Templeton Strong remarked that its walls "tumbled on a new and very magnificent temple of Venus, kept . . . by that respectable person Mrs. [Julia] Brown, and demolished one half of it." The damage, however, did little to thwart her prosperity. By 1842, her "two thousand dollar" parlor house on Leonard Street, with its elegant stage chairs from the same National Theater, was the most famous in the metropolis. Brown was even sighted at the magnificent balls and parties given by New York's Bleecker Street elite. Critics accused her of greediness and of gouging her prostitute tenants for more money; her admirers simply called her Princess Julia. So notable was her house that it became the subject of one unproduced play. Rumor had it that Brown even earned a visit from Charles Dickens during his travels through America.[40]

Other prostitutes, such as Elizabeth Forsythe, Charity Jennison, Mary Wall, and Phoebe Doty, displayed an equally impressive upward mobility after 1820. Living at 5 White Street in 1820, Forsythe possessed personal property valued at $300. A year later, residing in Church Street next door to Adeline Miller's house, she owned property assessed at $500. In 1824, she purchased a brothel on Orange Street for $3,400. For the next seven years, she resided at the same house with personal property estimated to be worth $1,000.[41] Likewise, from 1822 to 1826,

Fig. 6 "A Grand Ball with Julia Brown"
(Flash, *1843), Courtesy American Antiquarian Society*

Charity Jennison appeared in the tax assessment records as the owner / occupant of Grand and Orange Street brothels, the latter valued at $1,400. In 1839, she moved to a house twice as expensive, on Cross Street. Similarly, after starting out in Five Points in 1809, Mary Wall was "said to be rich" and living on Mercer Street, according to a tax assessor in 1826.[42] And Phoebe Doty lived in a Five Points brothel from 1821 to 1823, retaining $600 in personal property. During the 1830s, when she lived in a Church Street house, that amount rose to $800. By decade's end, she had acquired $2,000 of personal property for her Leonard Street brothel. During the 1840s, she was one of New York's leading prostitutes, holding extravagant public halls and attracting frequent mention in the nation's "sporting press."[43]

For some, prostitution brought not only wealth but also fame. By the 1840s, numerous madams and prostitutes had achieved celebrity status. After the murder of the prostitute Helen Jewett in 1836, Rosina Townsend and her City Hotel brothel were consistent topics in the penny press from Maine to Charleston. Similarly, the *Libertine* insisted that if Phoebe Doty and Adeline Miller rented the Park Theater to recount their experiences, "the house would be crammed if the *entrance* was five dollars a *head.* The bigger the harlot now-a-days the more money is made." The city's sporting press weekly described the activities of madams like Celest Thebault, Ann Thompson, and Jane Williams. Rebecca ("Lady") Weyman reportedly dressed and traveled as a "fashionable lady" when shopping at A. T. Stewart's Marble Emporium. Sophia ("La Belle") Austin, a frequent compatriot of Weyman's, ran "one of the best" brothels—"orderly and supported by chaps who do such business in the dark."[44]

Other successful prostitutes frequently camouflaged their business by posing as widows running "female boarding houses." Emily Tucker, a longtime madam of "a house of the very worst kind," was usually listed as a widow. Similarly, Maria Adams, proprietor of the famed 55 Leonard Street brothel, appeared as a widow in the 1855 state census. Labeled grass widows by critics, such women often enjoyed the highest personal property assessments on their blocks. In the sixty-six houses and buildings on Elm Street in 1821, for example, Mary Dixon and "Widow" Goodwin, with their $500 and $200 in personal property, were the richest residents on the street. Nearby, Hannah Kinsman and Lydia Waters, with personal property of $500, ranked among the nine wealthiest residents on their Leonard Street block.[45]

By midcentury, a well-developed network of female brothel proprietors thrived in New York. Throughout most of the antebellum period, women increasingly became the operators of brothels, boardinghouses, and houses of assignation. Only in areas where prostitution occurred primarily in saloons and dance halls were men or married couples more likely to have control of the business.[46] During the 1850s, at least thirty-five madams operated brothels for a minimum of four years. Some, like Jane Winslow, Rebecca Weyman, Maggie Lewis, and Kate Rowe, remained at one address for years at a time. Others, like Cinderella Marshall, Maria Stewart, Emma Soule, and Maria Adams, moved among different houses within the same neighborhood. The most successful, among them Julia Brown, Kate Ridgely, and even lesser-known madams like Mrs. Leslie, Mrs. Van Ness, Mrs. Wilson, and Mrs. Palmer, continued in the business for over a decade.[47] Prostitution thus enabled certain women to acquire a degree of autonomy and lead semi-independent economic lives. Because of the changing boundaries of acceptable sexual display, successful prostitutes enjoyed access to previously closed avenues of mobility and wealth. "Whether we choose to see it or not," admitted George Ellington, "the *demi-monde* is, ever before and about us."[48] For these women, prostitution was a good business proposition.

ASTONISHED by the independence of young American females, the Frenchman Alexis de Tocqueville, in his famous 1835 study of American culture, remarked, "[I]n no other country is a girl left so soon or so completely to look after herself."[49] This seemingly newfound autonomy attracted the attention of numerous nineteenth-century observers in the young republic. In various publications, ranging from sober advice books to sensational novels, young women were increasingly central subjects of discussion and debate. Nothing, however, was more controversial than and evoked such fear as their sexuality.

After 1820, the collective social profile of prostitutes in New York was transformed. Although there was never a "typical" prostitute or a "typical" prostitution experience, several important changes can be discerned. The accumulation of personal property and the attention enjoyed by the most entrepreneurial of these women indicated that after 1820 an affluent, but migratory, class of prostitutes flourished in Gotham. In a world of imperfect choices, these women did not view prostitution as deviance or sin; rather, they considered it a better alternative to the factory or domestic servitude. At the end of the 1830s, guidebooks advertised the leading "women of the town," the media highlighted their activities, and residents complained about New York's "whorearchy."[50] Landlords and madams thereby rationalized commercial sex, transforming it into a visible commodity of consumption and thereby creating a pattern of domination, subordination, and hierarchy among different groups of prostitutes.

Increasingly, large numbers of young girls, some only ten to twelve years of age, resorted to prostitution to sustain themselves and their families. Others wanted to break the bonds of familial control and gain a measure of personal independence. Sexual intercourse was not a dark deed for such teenagers. There emerged informal familial and female networks in which adults and prostitutes encouraged female family members, friends, and acquaintances to prostitute themselves. When commodity production moved out of the artisanal shop, it incorporated large numbers of females and thus converted women's wage work from a marginal to critical component of the New York economy.[51] Occasional prostitution gave young females a measure of independence from this economic reality. No boss or pimp controlled their labor, their time, or their leisure. Since some men were willing to pay extravagant sums for sexual relations with children and teenagers, sex posed a powerful financial temptation. As New York gave birth to a new industrial economy, its reverberations not only transformed sexuality into a new commodity but turned prostitution into a distinctive part of the urban female economy.

In one final sense, prostitutes were divided beings. At this critical juncture in their lives, sexuality was an act of commerce, a form of personal finance. Yet, at other points, as the example of Lucy Brady reminds us, sex was something else. It could be personal and romantic, potentially loving. Then as later, most observers viewed sexuality as a unity—it was wholly one kind of activity or wholly another. When the boundaries of a singular act of sexual intercourse overlapped, intersected, or merged, confusion and fear often resulted. In one sense, the estimates of large numbers of prostitutes, by themselves, meant little. The Eliza Jumels and Julia Browns belonged to a minority. Rare were the women who remained prostitutes for a substantial portion of their lives. The significant point is that many women chose or felt compelled at some point to engage in prostitution in numbers unmatched in New York's history, either before or since.

4

BROTHEL RIOTS AND BROADWAY PIMPS

ON A COLD November evening in 1836, Mary Gambel quietly sat in the well-furnished living room of her Crosby Street brothel, awaiting the next customer. Hearing a noise in the parlor entryway, she stood up and casually walked out to investigate. Suddenly and without warning, she was confronted by seven men. Frozen by surprise, she neither moved nor uttered a response. The men immediately "fell upon her with their fists" and began violently beating her. To their surprise, Gambel fought back, tenaciously scratching and gouging her assailants. So formidable was her resistance that one attacker finally "drew a sword cane and stabbed her in the nose . . . and left her face and nose most shockingly cut and injured." By the time help arrived, the belligerents had fled.[1]

Such seemingly spontaneous "mob" violence was nothing new in antebellum America. Historians, in fact, now label the 1830s as New York's "decade of riots." At times, it seemed that anyone could be a victim, irrespective of status and wealth—an affluent merchant, a black worker, an innocent voter on his way to the polls. Whether in antiabolition riots (1834 and 1835), election day riots (1834), or "flour riots" (1837), disgruntled citizens frequently took the law into their own hands. Recent examinations by historians of these and similar violent incidents reveal that riots were hardly unique to New York. Rather, they were emblematic of profound social change taking place throughout the Western world. In most cases, "crowd behavior" was a collective attempt to achieve unfettered social equality and political fairness, a reaction against the arbitrary distribution of justice and a vindication of time-honored traditions. When perceived rights were ignored or violated, especially by agents of the state, rioting to redress grievances was a common resort.[2]

Brothel riots, as they were labeled by city officials, were not peculiar to antebellum New York.[3] Similar attacks on prostitutes periodically occurred in Europe from the fifteenth to the nineteenth century, as well as in other American locales. In New York, soldiers during the Revolution claimed they were mistreated by "ladies of pleasure" and then sacked several whorehouses. Similarly, in 1793, the future mayor Philip Hone witnessed a remarkable attack on a house of prostitution that included the destruction of mahogany tables, windows, and looking glasses and terminated with the dispersal of "Mother Carey's chickens." At the height of the onslaught, another observer, Dr. Alexander Anderson, reported that the "air was filled with feathers, and the street with rags and fragments." The mob's excesses did not cease with "this Mother Damnable." Men "continued their riotous proceedings several successive nights, and many houses of ill-fame in other parts of the city were demolished and their miserable inmates driven naked and houseless into the streets." In 1799, a crowd of nearly one thousand gathered to destroy a Murray Street brothel, only to be thwarted by the timely intervention of the mayor and local magistrates. Two years later, an assemblage of over two hundred Haitians, hoping to liberate twenty slaves, attacked Madame Volunbrun's reputed brothel. Likewise, the disorderly house of William and Catharine Mackline on George Street was besieged by four men in 1807. Five years later, several hundred rioters tried to pull down a brothel on James Street.[4]

These incidents of mob action against prostitutes were sporadic and infrequent. In each instance, mobs sought to close a brothel and put it out of business. Personal assaults or homicides were rare. Most encounters resulted from particular circumstances unrelated to prostitution itself—the castration and murder of a soldier, the seduction of the daughter of a popular ship pilot, the removal of black slaves to the South, or the murder of a fellow seaman in a whorehouse. In most cases, the attacks resembled the spontaneous "extrainstitutional," retributive actions during the Revolutionary era that the historian Pauline Maier has described. They represented a recourse to justice when civil authority failed. To Philip Hone, perched in a tree over Madame Carey's house, they even had the quality of a spectator sport. Violence was inflicted only upon property, not upon individuals. As reactions to specific events, brothel attacks in the colonial and early republican eras were limited, isolated forays against the private property of misbehaving citizens. Heads did not roll in brothel riots, and mobs did not turn to butchery.[5]

After 1820, physical violence against prostitutes increased dramatically. On nearly seventy occasions, brothels, "female boarding houses," or prostitutes themselves were attacked in the years between 1820 and 1860. And over forty such incidents occurred in the 1830s. Many of these riots focused on more than buildings and personal property. Increasingly, individual females were assaulted. Rather than being an isolated victim, Mary Gambel was part of a trend (for a list of riots, see appendix 2).

Some of these vigilante acts against prostitutes continued the colonial tradition of limited, extrainstitutional violence. In these cases, the perpetrators' actions were premeditated and well designed and organized. The participants had clear notions of how to enter the house and specific intentions of what to do inside. Repeated attacks by certain individuals, the circumspect behavior inside the brothel, the "respectable" backgrounds of some offenders, and the accusation by prostitutes that city officials encouraged certain assaults suggest premeditation and calculation. The prostitute's property, not her person, took the beating. The accoutrements of a prostitute's trade—her bed, furniture, glassware, and crockery—were destroyed.

Testimony by prostitutes themselves reflected the vigilantes' well-planned and limited goals. Early one morning in 1842, for example, Jane Williams's house was stoned and then forcibly entered by three men who simply destroyed her furniture. Similarly, Mary Wall admitted five potential customers to her house after they arrived in a hack one evening in 1833. After sitting down, they requested a drink, inquired about her glasses and decanters, and then "grabbed a fire shovel and commenced breaking . . . all most everything on the sideboard." Likewise, the four men who entered Mary Ann Davis's house on Centre Street "behaved in a very noisy and disorderly manner, breaking tumblers, cursing and swearing and when they were going away they took one of her decanters." George Gale and Bentley Curran participated in four brothel attacks during a two-week period in 1831. Forcibly entering Elizabeth Baker's establishment on several different occasions, they broke her windows, destroyed her stoop, and committed "many outrages of an . . . offensive nature." Finally, Isaac Roberts celebrated Christmas in 1851 by leading forty men to Catherine Cauldwell's brothel on Lispenard Street, "to give a benefit," in their words. Once inside, Roberts gave orders to "ribbon everything," and his accomplices put tumblers in their pockets, broke a sofa, and destroyed a piano stool. Before departing, they heaved stones through the front window.[6]

The limited scope of these brothel attacks sometimes reflected neighborhood opposition to prostitution. When Catharine Brown obtained a lease on a King Street house in 1833 and proceeded to conduct an open brothel, neighbors protested. Their opposition and anger, however, went unheeded by public officials. Finally, members of a neighborhood mob seized the moment and took their own vigilante action. They entered the house, destroyed Brown's belongings, and chased her away. Brown never returned.[7]

Other assaults, however, appeared to be random and solitary. Drunken, disorderly, and delirious males often became incensed when a prostitute or madam denied them their heart's desire. John Evans, for example, was arrested for throwing stones at the house of Eliza Vincent after she "refused him admittance." Similarly, James Van Dine broke into Rebecca Weyman's house "by forcing open the windows and shutters . . . there behaved in a most riotous and disorderly manner." One January evening in 1834, William Green traversed Church Street, hopping from groggery to brothel, his drunken enchantment terminating only when he broke a brothel window.[8] Even personal acquaintance afforded little protection for vulnerable prostitutes. For example, Adeline Miller complained that several men she knew repeatedly visited her house, stealing in and then doing as they pleased. Similarly, Hannah Fuller was awakened by William Ford early one summer morning in 1844. After kicking in her door, he removed his boots and pants, carried her to the bed, and attempted "to ravish and . . . carnally know her." Only the last-minute intervention by the watch prevented the rape. Fuller later dropped the charges because Ford was an "old friend."[9]

Women on the street had even less protection from such assaults. Mary Smith, a Leonard Street prostitute, was walking home in 1832 after an evening at the Park Theater when William Nosworthy seized her "in a grossly rude and indecent manner and raised her clothes so as to expose her nakedness to the passers by."[10] The increasing frequency of these attacks during the 1830s reflected, in part, the growing perception that prostitutes were fair game for the aggressions of frustrated males.

The most threatening form of assault was "the spree" or "row." Fueled by male camaraderie and substantial quantities of liquor, gangs of rampaging drunks moved from one saloon or brothel to another, becoming increasingly obnoxious and violent at every stop. This intoxicated conviviality convinced Edgar Allan Poe that the spree was "the mad excess of a counterfeit hilarity—the joint offspring of liberty and of rum."[11]

Sprees were usually arbitrary, unplanned, and unstructured. In 1834, John Lawrence, Henry Flender, and a dozen others attempted to break in to several Chapel Street brothels, but settled instead for spattering the front doors with mud. On another occasion, Samuel Anderson, Charles Dykes, and their chums failed in their effort to break into a brothel on Anthony Street, retreated to the street, and launched stones through the front windows. According to another criminal indictment, a gang of seven young men out on a "frolick . . . proposed to see Mother Brown" and proceeded to smash in the door of her Collect Street house. Finally, William Weed brought eight to ten accomplices "to take possession" of Eliza Swinson's Chapel Street brothel, but they stoned her "castle" only after she locked them out.[12]

Many sprees evolved into scenes of sadistic terror. The three rioters who stoned Amanda Smith's house on Franklin Street also "destroyed her furniture, knocked her down, beat her on the face and head so as to blind her entirely, and after having knocked her down, kicked her." The invaders, charged the district attorney, then beat her crippled son William "in a most shameful and outrageous manner." Witnesses testified that the same men forced their way into two other Orange Street brothels, "making a great noise and disturbance, breaking the furniture." Likewise, John Golding led four other men into Elizabeth Rinnell's Crosby Street house and demanded food, drink, money, and entertainment. After their drunken orgy, Golding assaulted and beat Rinnell. On another occasion, Jane Williams refused to open her brothel door to a dozen men. Two then forced their way through a window, punched Williams in the head, and opened the front door, allowing the remainder to come in and stampede about the house. Similarly, when John Williams entered an Anthony Street brothel, he threw oil of vitriol in Mary Ann Duffy's face, severely scarring her. And when Edward Halliday and friends broke into a Bancker Street house, each one "drew a sword and slashed before them, [and] wounded Sarah Smith, the woman of the house, in the face."[13]

The threat of rape was common in many of these brothel riots. Five men, for example, broke into Eliza Logue's Thomas Street house when she refused them admittance. After breaking the cookery and throwing a lamp at the head of a prostitute, they strangled Logue and "threw her across the foot of a bed and endeavored by force and violence to have connection with her." Only the nearby watch, hearing the commotion, prevented the consummation of the act. In 1840, after beating Mary Lee, Benjamin Waldron and his gang followed her as she tried to escape, striking "her in the face several times and threaten[ing] to commit other outrages." In another instance, more than ten laborers broke into Eliza Ann Potter's Suffolk Street house, violently assaulted her, and "threatened to pickle" and rape her before hastily departing.[14]

What sort of men were these "brothel bullies"? Indictments by the district attorney listed 80 percent as ordinary laborers and the remainder as semiskilled workers (1 percent), skilled artisans (19 percent), and white-collar professionals (under 1 percent). Most rioters lived in the same ward as the prostitute they attacked or in a neighboring one. Less than a quarter resided in more distant areas of the city. While most were working-class laborers, brothel rioters crossed class lines. In 1831, for example, the attorney James Lozier joined a neighbor, the grocer Charles Taylor, and two others in attacking Adeline Miller's Elm Street brothel.[15] The instigators of these assaults, therefore, were not simply disenchanted "rabble," parts of unruly mobs, professional criminals, or clearly defined deviants but "respectable" elements of society as well. Indeed, it appears that their behavior was tolerated and sometimes condoned by neighbors and the municipality.

More important, brothel riots were part of a larger transformation in the patterns of male leisure and social behavior. Simultaneously with the sudden rise in brothel riots, America experienced an increase in communal drinking among men. According to the historian W. J. Rorabaugh, such group intoxication was commonplace after 1820 and endowed the participants with feelings of liberty and independence while inducing a sense of equality. The group drinking binge was an ideological inebriation; to be drunk was to be free. Liquor therefore increased the American male's sense of autonomy.[16]

Brothel sprees were an extension of such drunken displays of egalitarianism. If liquor offered an illusion of freedom, the brothel riot promoted male sexual supremacy. Men lost their inhibitions and individual accountability. Participants unleashed pent-up frustration by attacking a visible independent and sometimes materially successful woman. Whereas a vigilante attack on a house of prostitution was a public protest, a spree was a source of fun. As mock-heroic skirmishes of pride and violation, such attacks were an aggressive form of misogynist, masculine recreation, a means to assert male prerogative and supremacy at the expense of a hapless, vulnerable prostitute. The spree offered an illusion of power to powerless men.[17]

Linked to these intoxicated revelries was the emergence of a particular male, working-class subculture in New York. Numerous observers by midcentury complained of the "schools of vice" that encouraged prostitution, prize-fighting, and drunkenness. According to Elliot Gorn, hard social choices and limited economic opportunity taught many males to value physical prowess and verbal bravado. Fighting was often the primary expression of such a culture.[18] In a world full of potential violence, economic unpredictability, and psychological insecurity, sexual assault on successful prostitutes promised some men a moment of independence, autonomy, and honor.

Prostitutes, however, did not always passively accept these physical assaults. In 1843, for instance, an angry Amelia Norman stabbed one of her clients in the chest on the steps of the Astor House. Only a deflection by his rib prevented the knife from piercing his heart. On another occasion, when John Briggs became uncontrollably drunk and disorderly in Phoebe Doty and Moll Stephens's brothel, one prostitute tried to shoot him with a pistol. Similarly, Mary Gambel, upon being stabbed in the nose, scratched her assailant's face so badly that nearly a month later she was convinced that "he must [still] carry the marks with him."[19]

Most important, antebellum prostitutes used the law to protect themselves. Before the creation of a municipal police force in 1845, criminal prosecution in New York was a private matter. Individual citizens, not public officials, initiated most criminal charges. Shrewdly bringing legal proceedings against their aggressors, prostitutes utilized the machinery of the state to defend their interests and property rights, firmly entrenching their profession in the social fabric of the metropolis. Even streetwalkers sought legal redress when threatened or attacked. For example, when a drunken male approached and kissed a prostitute promenading on Broadway, she objected to his uninvited sexual advances and had him arrested. On another occasion, Jane Williams charged Jim Waters with assaults after he struck her when she abandoned him on the street for another client. Waters unapologetically justified his actions: "I had no notion of letting her off," he insisted. "She wanted to go away with another fellow cause he was dressed a little better than I was."[20] Williams, unsatisfied, fully prosecuted her assailant. Instead of retreating to the domestic hearth, numerous prostitutes asserted themselves by every means at their disposal.

Just as the extreme behavior of men in brothel attacks revealed a transformation in attitudes toward prostitution and the nature of male violence in antebellum society, the use of the legal system by prostitutes to defend themselves was equally important. Private prosecution during the prepolice era gave prostitutes the power to define crime and protect their own property and "commerce." These prostitutes did not see themselves as "fallen women." They publicly defended their personal integrity and private property instead of succumbing to violent intimidation, and they refused to act as fugitives from justice. Such prostitutes rejected a defensive, a reticent posture when subjected to violent terror. By asserting their rights, they forswore surrender.

Forcing the resolution of these conflicts into a public forum, prostitutes turned the municipal government into their agent and protector. For example, they summoned the watch when attacked and prosecuted violators upon arrest. Some rioters consequently considered the watch a protector of the brothel. In 1829, when Marshal Joseph L. Hays tried to arrest three men in the process of destroying Miss Robins's house of ill fame, the culprits temporarily took him hostage, too. Another time, Charles Taylor and Charles Jennings berated the watch who removed them from Adeline Miller's house, "saying it was a damned shame that watchmen should receive pay for protecting whore houses."[21] Outraged by the destruction of their property, prostitutes brought their assailants to court. Rioters were thus compelled to repair the damage even when the judge knew about the illicit carnal activities of the plaintiff. Although the district attorney records provide no clue as to the final decisions in most cases, on at least twelve occasions the courts convicted the riotous defendants. At other times, men eluded conviction only because the prostitute dropped the charge.[22]

In this ironic fashion, the state both defended and protected prostitution. Unlike earlier societies which barred testimony from prostitutes, or later forms of legal intervention which sought to regulate, control, and hinder the independence of prostitutes, antebellum New York saw governmental power invoked for their benefit. When prostitutes exercised their property rights, the municipality was compelled to defend prostitution and prosecute its more violent enemies. Since antebellum government was devoted primarily to protecting the interests of taxpayers and private property, a bewildered municipality faced an unappealing, imperfect choice: suppress sexual deviancy, punish prostitutes and thereby violate their (and ultimately others') property rights, or punish their male aggressors and tolerate the existence of prostitution. In the end, the state chose to defend property, and thus prostitution, at the expense of other laws and the prudish sensibilities of many New Yorkers. In 1842, even the sporting journal the *Whip* concluded that the "brothel bully" had gone out of fashion. "Robberies, and even murders, at brothels were not infrequent" during the 1830s. "Now they are seldom heard of."[23]

Brothel riots represented the nexus where changes in gender relations and the underground economy met. Outside the home, prostitutes were among the most visible women in the industrializing antebellum city. One newspaper lamented that "a new code of ethics" had emerged by 1836, glamorizing the prostitute with her gold watch, splendid earrings, and embroidered stockings, at the expense of "a poor hardworking man, who sticks to one woman, . . . his wife." Indeed, by 1825, madams like Maria Williamson were successful enough to own several brothels and they play an active role in New York's lucrative real estate market. Later on, others like Rosina Townsend, Adeline Miller, and Julia Brown became public figures appearing on the front pages of the penny press, in the diaries of the city's gentry, and in guidebooks sold at corner newsstands. The *Herald* asked when "was there ever found an instance of the open and shameless defence of the character of a public prostitute?" Why, indeed, had leading prostitutes become models "of truth and virtue"?[24] At a time when gender roles were in the initial stage of redefinition and the "cult of domesticity" was gaining ground, the behavior of some prostitutes served as a vivid counterpoise.

These actions by prostitutes probably affected the way many Americans viewed women outside the household. The historians Christine Stansell and Mary Ryan, for example, have shown how antebellum society grew increasingly restless over the public activities and mobility of working women in general. Similarly, contemporaries feared that women in public places risked destructive physical harassment. "There are strange things said of attacks upon females in the streets of New York, . . . if alone," reported *Niles' Register* in 1831. The former mayor Philip Hone proclaimed that some outrage was committed nightly by "young ruffians who prowl the streets insulting females."[25] For women, the message was clear—get off the streets, stay in the home.

At the same time, between 1820 and 1850, women had greater control and influence over prostitution than in any other period. Low wages in the factory and the household made prostitutes the best-paid women workers in the nineteenth-century city. And the willingness of many prostitutes to prosecute their violators in the public arena illustrated their confidence in their own individual rights. Many of the women who were attacked—Jane Williams, Mary Wall, Mary Gambel, Rebecca Weyman, and Adeline Miller—were among the best-known prostitutes and madams in New York City, celebrities in their own right. The rise of violence against prostitutes and brothels, in part, reflected a widening gap between certain groups of men and women in the sex trade. Brothel attacks increased at the very moment when political and other forms of rioting were increasingly suppressed and held in disrepute. Just as some white men terrorized black proprietors of small businesses, oyster shops, churches, and theaters, others found the increased economic and social power of prostitutes threatening.[26]

Furthermore, many of the houses attacked appear to have been "private" brothels—places with high prices, exclusive clients, and admittance by appointment only. In certain respects, private brothels illustrated a widening gender *and* class division between increasingly affluent madams and less successful male artisans and workers. Male rioters, quite likely, sought to make private brothels more public. All prostitutes, irrespective of economic rank or celebrity status, were public women and should be available to all men. Efforts to limit accessibility, in the mind of the brothel bully, violated custom and male prerogative.

While antebellum gender relations were being transformed, so was New York's growing underground economy. A close examination of certain brothel attacks reveals several important political influences that ultimately signaled changes in the organization of prostitution in the city. In 1836, for example, John Chichester and his politically connected gang attacked at least three bordellos. Entering Jane Ann Jackson's Chapel Street brothel with bats, they destroyed windows and shutters and threatened to cut Miss Jackson's throat. Chichester's consorts then broke into Eliza Ludlow's house and forced her to serve brandy; they concluded their guzzling by tossing the glasses in the fire. Then they "abused the inmates of the house," burned a rug, broke a bench by hurling it at a prostitute, and threatened to toss one woman out the window.[27]

Active though it was, Chichester's gang gave pride of place to Thomas Hyer's. From 1836 to 1838, Hyer's group raided at least four brothels. Once, upon breaking into Ellen Holly's house in 1836, they grabbed an inmate and, "by the most forcible and violent means," gang-raped her. Although convicted for the deed, Hyer a year later led the same culprits into Mary Banta's house, destroyed her tableware, and knocked an inmate unconscious. Within the next two decades, his violent habits were rewarded with the American heavyweight boxing championship and important political alliances. Hyer, for example, boxed and defeated James ("Yankee") Sullivan in 1849. But by 1852 the two had reconciled their pugilistic and political differences, "and with a troop of their respective friends paraded Howard and Mercer streets and their respective neighborhood, making the night hideous with their drunken orgies," according to the *Tribune*. Forming alliances with the nativist Bill Poole, the Democrat Mike Walsh, and the Republican William Seward, Hyer gained control of the prostitution, saloons, and gambling dens along Mercer Street in the two decades before the Civil War. The pugilist turned politician cast such a memorable shadow over New York that half a century later the famed ward boss George Washington Plunkitt invoked Hyer's memory during his discussions on Tammany Hall (figure 7).[28]

While motives were less evident in other attacks, participants often enjoyed significant political connections. For example, the rioters who

Fig. 7 Tom Hyer
New-York Historical Society, NYC

destroyed Jane Weston's, Sarah Ferguson's, and Adeline Miller's belongings were white-collar workers and skilled laborers, allegedly acting on orders from Justice John Bloodgood and Street Inspector Daniel McGrath. In 1834, Phoebe Doty accused William H. Tuttle, a clerk for the mayor, and John L. Martin, a tavern keeper, of attacking her bawdy house and commencing "a work of outrageous and disorderly conduct . . . by squirting upon them . . . dirty water." On a separate occasion, Andrew R. Jackman, a City Hall officer and future city assessor and common school trustee, and seven other skilled workers broke into Mary Adams's Thirteenth Ward establishment. While inside, they accosted an inmate, wrapped her up in a straw mat, and rolled her down the stairs.[29]

The political links between these public officials and "public" women were not entirely new. In fact, the association of legal authority with illicit sex was an old one. As early as 1810, for example, John DeLacy complained that disorderly-house keepers used physical threats and municipal protection to evade prosecution. The "wretches," he concluded "are encouraged and counselled by profligate and dishonest brothel marshals with whom their crimes and interests are interwoven." Similarly, in 1806, the watchmen James Skaats, Frederick Storms, and Samuel Dunn were charged with "going to a common dance house and there joining in dancing with the common girls and their associates." And in

1810, a city marshal himself was arrested for running a disorderly house by the East River. Proprietors like Patrick McDermott of East George Street used law enforcement officials to arrest prostitutes for stealing when they left his establishment. In 1815, Ebenezer Burling concluded that city marshals were little more than "brokers among the prostitutes."[30]

In some cases, corruption charges reached as far as the mayor's office. In 1806, George and Amelia Benwood testified in court that "the mayor had given [them] a license to keep a whore house and dance house and a tavern." Similarly, William Lowe "declared that the mayor had given him . . . a license to keep a public whore house and given him privilege to whip or cow hide any of the girls or whores he may have in his house."[31]

But these early examples of municipal duplicity were informal, inconsistent, and subject to the whims of individual officers and political officials. It is doubtful any mayor in the early republic gave a socially marginal saloonkeeper license to operate a brothel. But the rise of competitive party politics brought a new relationship between the municipality and the prostitute. The gangs led by Hyer, Chichester, and others played critical roles in the distribution of power and the early formation of the antebellum political machine. As Amy Bridges has argued, wealthy elites in New York concentrated on federal and state issues, while local concerns and grass-roots organization were left to a new political animal—the career politician. The rich and the well-born thus dominated national party politics, and local career politicians minded the neighborhood political store. To control their fiefdoms, ward-based politicians often employed gangs to keep opponents away from the polls, guard ballot boxes, and enforce political conformity. Hyer, for example, was allied to the nativist "Bowery B'hoys" who, according to Alvin Harlow, were not as vicious as rival Five Points gangs and had a tendency "toward the political rather than the purely savage or criminal."[32]

But if local politicians controlled votes, they lacked money. In order to establish a secure financial base, ward politicians resorted to bribery and extortion of neighborhood proprietors. Saloons, gambling dens, and houses of prostitution paid tribute in return for local officials' ignoring laws regulating such activities. As prostitution became a significant revenue source for the local political boss, gangs were probably used as a means to control and police brothel keepers and their inmates. During the 1840s, for example, one journalist concluded that some brothels were "under the special protection of the bloods of the aristocracy." In addition, the private prosecution of brothel rioters, effective in individual and isolated cases, was inadequate against more public, collective violence. Employing terror, politically motivated gangs restructured the most highly organized forms of prostitution and established a financial foundation for the political machine for the remainder of the century.[33]

The brothel riots of the 1830s thus marked a turning point in the structure of prostitution and sexual politics in New York. Thereafter, it appears that ward bosses enjoyed direct ties with the promoters of prostitution and cooperated with local police in systematically extorting and protecting successful brothels. For example, the U.S. marshal Isaiah Rynders openly derived political support from the proprietors of brothels and saloons with prostitutes. Similarly, Congressman John Clancy ran the prostitute-filled Ivy Green saloon on Elm Street, where Rynders's empire Club frequently met. Even a police court justice and conservative Whig like Robert Taylor, a onetime mayoral nominee, routinely visited brothels without a second thought, searching for evidence in criminal cases. In 1850, when Police Officer John J. McManus arrested most of the saloon and brothel keepers in Five Points, Alderman Patrick Kelly quickly came to their aid. Similarly, Michael Norton, an Irish immigrant who represented the Fifth and Eighth wards as alderman, state senator, assemblyman, Tammany district leader, and district court judge between 1864 and 1889, was known for his alliances with the underworld. In 1865, John Acton, president of the Board of Police, complained that Norton's neighborhood was "a pandemonium of thieves, prostitutes and murderers" and that Norton took "it upon himself to become the champion of these desparate and dangerous classes."[34] By 1840, this combination of political and police control of New York's underground economy had grown more entrenched, and it persisted for the remainder of the century.

This complex mixture of gender relations, violence, and political corruption gave rise to a new participant in commercial sex—the "pimp." As brothels were attacked more frequently during the 1830s, men for the first time were hired to provide protection. Both madams and prostitutes admitted that men lived in their houses to discourage physical attacks or perform services such as buying groceries, repairing the house, or serving the guests. The controversial editor George Wilkes claimed that many of these "gentlemen brothel pensioners" enjoyed significant political connections and met "with considerable toleration from a portion of society." By midcentury, numerous writers were similarly speaking out against the "fancy-men" of prostitutes and the "necessary evil pimps." Many enjoyed ties to local political figures. George Foster insisted that "[n]ine-tenths of these villains" were "red-hot politicians" who served "to keep the City Government for the most part in the wrong hands."[35]

While such pimps did not exert complete control over the tenants in a house of prostitution, they served as a visible reminder of a brothel's need for physical protection and political tolerance. Streetwalkers, on the other hand, required a more dominating type of pimp, especially after 1830. Physical harassment and frequent arrests were common parts of a streetwalker's life. Unless their prostitution was only occasional, streetwalkers employed male partners or "lovers" to assist and protect them. "Scarcely any public women," wrote George Wilkes, "are for any length of time without their pensioners." Similarly, the writer George Thompson claimed in semifictional descriptions of New York's prostitutes, "[It] is well known that almost every gay girl [prostitute] of the pave has a 'bosom friend,' who protects her and is the recipient of her caresses during the absence of *cash* customers."[36]

Pimps were, by the 1840s, "an essential *attaché* to a brothel as . . . a pretty woman to a cigar store," according to one observer. Others ridiculed them for existing "on the money gained by prostitution." Described as "sleek, pale-faced and *moustached,*" they stood in front of Broadway and Park Row cafés and prowled the environs of Five Points and Corlears Hook. By the 1850s, a visible, well-established system of pimps existed in New York. When Mayor Fernando Wood instigated a campaign against streetwalkers in 1855, pimps appeared with them in court. Commonly referred to as "Broadway Statues," they stood in front of the "monster" hotels along New York's best-known avenue (figure 8). These "scamps have the audacity to address [women] without ceremony," complained one reporter, "and if their advances are received with indignation, . . . the wretches apologize and plead mistake." The corner of Broadway and Broome Street was a notorious hangout for pimps waiting for prostitutes to hand over their earnings before resuming their chores. The writer Junius Browne in 1869 remarked that most "cryprians on the town" relied upon these "roughs," "lovers," and "protectors" who "strike her thrice for every kiss."[37] By the midnineteenth century, pimps were a standard feature of New York prostitution. They remain so today.

"IN THIS WORLD," Herman Melville once wrote, "sin that pays its way can travel freely, and without a passport; whereas Virtue, if a pauper, is stopped at all frontiers."[38] But in antebellum New York, the cost to prostitutes who wanted to operate freely was high. And perhaps the greatest price was physical coercion. Brothel riots represented the most evident danger for women involved in the sex trade. But in a larger sense, such violence spoke to a broader issue. Male hatred of and hostility toward women, rather than moving underground or being marginalized, grew more pronounced during these years. In some cases, gender virtually became a sufficient cause for violence. Rioting, rather than

Fig. 8 "Broadway Statues"
From Jonathan Slick, Snares of New York *(1879)*

upholding traditions, redressing legitimate grievances, or reacting against social injustice, served as a vehicle for certain men to control and intimidate certain women.

Indeed, these violent acts may represent the dark side of the otherwise egalitarian subculture of the Bowery. Even those working-class males—the "toughs," "brothel bullies," and "fire laddies"—who operated in the Bowery milieu, men like Tom Hyer, John Chichester, and their cohorts, reveled in their assaults upon women. Some of them may have defended the honor and rights of "Bowery G'hals" on occasion, but given the opportunity, the same men inflicted physical harm on prostitutes and madams elsewhere. Clearly, these males believed they had the right to control, if not physically coerce, prostitutes and other public women. And such attacks quite likely had an impact that went beyond the specific encounter. Just as lynchings in the American South later in the century extended psychological control far beyond their immediate victims, brothel riots probably imposed similar behavioral constraints upon prostitutes.[39]

Violence inflicted upon prostitutes, of course, never embodied the whole essence of antebellum gender relations in New York. Yet, if male assumptions regarding women were expressed within structures of emotion and feeling rather than as a body of explicit ideas, as Christine Stansell and others have argued, antebellum brothel riots were emblematic of a new attitude toward prostitutes and women in public life. The escalation of violence against prostitutes and their residences reflected, in part, changing power relations between antebellum men and women.

The efforts of these men to extend their power over autonomous and sexually independent women were never completely successful. In many cases, their violence was greeted with defiance. Through self-defense, utilization of the legal system, and the adoption of pimps, embattled prostitutes protected themselves. But in the final analysis, the victors in this struggle were not prostitutes or madams. For individual prostitutes, reliance upon pimps, while never total and always in flux, represented a loss of autonomy. Furthermore, the willingness of certain municipal officials to tolerate, if not endorse, violence against prominent prostitutes marked a turning point in New York's underground economy. The ultimate beneficiary of this was the ward politician. As Tammany Hall emerged as the controlling political force of Gotham, violent gangs now allied to neighborhood machine representatives used extortion, force, and outright terror to restructure commercial sex and ensure male hegemony over the profits of prostitution.

In 1836, one extraordinary act of intimate violence carried the meaning of this sexual transformation in New York to the rest of America.

5

SPORTING MEN

It seemed like just another violent event in New York's "decade of riots." The body of twenty-three-year-old Helen Jewett lay lifeless in her room, discovered by her madam, Rosina Townsend, on an April morning in 1836. Within days, however, the incident was a national cause célèbre, and for three months the events surrounding the murder held center stage in the drama of New York. Jewett—erudite, glamorous, seductive, and youthful—was the most celebrated prostitute in New York's most popular brothel. Her murder proved to be the city's most intensely covered story of the decade.[1]

The events surrounding the eve of 9 April 1836 quickly became public. Townsend testified that on the night of the murder, nineteen-year-old Richard P. Robinson visited Jewett with the intention of spending the entire evening (figures 9–10). Robinson was a frequent guest of Jewett's, usually under the alias of Frank Rivers. Quietly arriving at 9:00 P.M., Robinson immediately went to Jewett's room. Townsend remembered serving a bottle of champagne to the couple around 11:00 P.M. The night proceeded uneventfully, and shortly after midnight Townsend and her girls retired to their respective rooms. Suddenly, at 3:00 A.M., the madam awoke. Investigating her parlor, she noticed that a globe lamp was out of place. Townsend knew that only two residents in the house had such a lamp, so she picked it up and climbed the stairs to return it. She went first to

Fig. 9 "The Real Helen Jewett" (1836)
Courtesy American Antiquarian Society

Maria Stevens's room, but found it bolted. The madam then walked to Helen Jewett's room next door and found it unlocked. When Townsend opened the door, smoke unexpectedly billowed out into her face. Momentarily shocked, she quickly recovered and retreated down the hallway, threw open the window, and screamed for the watch. After catching her breath, the madam returned to the room and entered. On the bed lay an unconscious Jewett, her head dripping blood and badly smashed. By now, her body was partly consumed in flames (figure 11). Townsend doused the fire and hastily looked around the house for evidence. Downstairs she noticed that the rear door was ajar. And in the

Fig. 10 "Richard P. Robinson" (1836)
Courtesy American Antiquarian Society

back and adjoining yards lay a hatchet and Robinson's cloak.

The circumstantial but overwhelming evidence led to the quick indictment of Robinson. From the start, the trial attracted national attention. The presiding judge, Ogden Edwards, was a leading Whig politician, as well as a grandson of the theologian Jonathan Edwards and a cousin of Aaron Burr. The public quickly learned that the defendant was a highly valued clerk in Joseph Hoxie's profitable Maiden Lane garment business. Robinson's presence in the house the night of the murder made a guilty verdict seem likely. The crime's violence and sexual origins attracted considerable attention, and nearly everyone had an

Fig. 11 "Ellen Jewett . . . female" (1836)
Courtesy American Antiquarian Society

opinion. "This is the most awful case of depravity, murder, and arson, the fruits of licentiousness and bad passions," wrote the former mayor Philip Hone in his diary. To another, Robinson was simply "the Satanic youngster."[2]

More significant was the reaction by the New York press. Prior to 1835, early American newspapers put advertisements and related commercial information on their front pages. Journalistic etiquette traditionally demanded that tales of sex and scandal be omitted altogether from the city's daily press. But the editor James Gordon Bennett and his recent upstart, the *Herald*, saw opportunity in a slain prostitute. Hoping to expand the paper's market appeal, Bennett devoted three months of unprecedented front-page coverage to the murder and trial. Within weeks, a biography of Robinson with "extracts" from his diary was published to satisfy public demand.[3]

Penny papers like the *Sun* and *Transcript* in New York, as well as others in Philadelphia, Boston, and Albany, quickly joined the fray with their own front-page episodes of delicious carnality and salacious fantasy. Jewett was at once a "goddess," "the Venus of that Paplios of destruction," "the beautiful ruling spirit of that palace of perdition," and one who "gave grace to licentiousness—elegance to its debauchery." One published letter described Jewett as "as sweet a companion now as ever. Oh! lovely creature, what form! what a figure! what a fine bust! Your lineaments, rich lips, full bust. Your mind too, is of the first order." As the *Herald* proclaimed, the Jewett murder agitated "the public mind beyond any event that was ever heard or saw in any city."[4] The trial's national publicity, in effect, initiated the era of the sex scandal in the penny press.

Quickly taking sides, the penny press moralized. Bennett's *Herald* believed Robinson innocent; the *Sun* and *Transcript* found him guilty. Each accused the others of being "advocates of prostitution and wickedness." More important, each made the trial a starting point "to open a full view upon the morals of society." Jewett was a symbol of "the whole frame of society which debauch young women and young men, and root out virtue and morality." It was no secret, one paper proclaimed, that business had a "new code of ethics," and clerks and merchants entertained themselves in such houses, "opening the doors of fashionable profligacy and vice to the innocents from Missouri, Ohio and the west and the south." The Jewett murder was the "natural result" of a society that fostered and protected such commercialized sexuality. "We are all guilty alike," remonstrated the *Herald.*[5]

The intensified coverage, however, did little to render justice. On 8 June 1836, Robinson was acquitted (figure 12). Robinson supporters, it was rumored, had bribed jurors and garnered false testimony on the defendant's behalf. Most considered it a great miscarriage of law. Two years later, for instance, Philip Hone summarily described the verdict as "the foulest blot on the jurisprudence of our country."[6]

Public fascination with the trial was no aberration. The persons of Jewett and Robinson brought out numerous submerged sexual tensions of antebellum America. Jewett, whose real name was Dorcas Doyen, was born to Welsh immigrants in Augusta, Maine. Orphaned at age thirteen, she was adopted by a local judge. As a teenager, however, she was banished from her adopted home because of her sexual liaisons with a sailor and a banker. Living for short periods in nearby Portland and Boston, she eventually made her way to New York, supporting herself by working in several brothels. Attractive, intelligent, and refined, Jewett was a popular regular in the third tier of the Park Theatre. By 1835, she had several suitors competing for her attention, some even willing to marry her. At the time of her murder, she owned clothing and jewelry valued at more than $1,500.

Jewett represented two contradictory fears of many nineteenth-century critics of prostitution. The loss of her virginity through innocent teenage sexuality and its devolution into prostitution embodied middle-class fears of downward mobility. "Step by step had Dorcas Doyen descended the course of a life of common shame," noted one writer a

Fig. 12 "The Trial of R. P. Robinson" (1836)
New-York Historical Society, NYC

decade later. One erotic mishap, and the fall from respectability to social marginality was likely, if not guaranteed. Jewett's case saw the feared and final result—death. On the other hand, Jewett never truly suffered economic want. Rather, prostitution provided her with male paramours, a handsome residence, desirable possessions, and personal autonomy. In sum, she was wealthy, free, and female. Jewett simultaneously represented the dangerous, "inevitable" results of sexual freedom alongside the tangible benefits of a career in commercial sex.[7]

Like Jewett's, Robinson's sexual behavior was laden with symbolism. Born into a highly respectable Connecticut family, he typified the new, young, single male in New York, the "nabob," unencumbered by apprenticeship, employer control, or church stricture. Robinson admitted that his boss was concerned only with his duties at the store, never inquiring how Robinson passed his nights. "I was an unprotected boy, without female friends to introduce me to respectable society, sent into a boarding house, where I could enter at what hour I pleased—subservient to no control after the business of the day was over," remembered Robinson.[8]

To the American public in 1836, Richard Robinson was on trial for more than just the murder of Helen Jewett. As the boardinghouse, peer group, and market economy replaced the craft household, family, and "moral economy," young men frequented brothels and visited women in assignation houses in growing numbers. Robinson himself bragged of the numerous women at his command: "It was first one girl and then another, till like the Grand Turk I had a harem, and only threw the handkerchief to the one I chose." Critics cited Robinson's "intense selfishness" and his tendency to hold "everything secondary to his own advantage." "What else can be expected of . . . youths similarly situated," concluded one writer, who "are brought from the quiet routine of country life, to be plunged into the midst of all the intoxicating pleasures and dazzling temptations of this great Bable of enjoyment."[9]

Robinson's promiscuous adventures aptly illustrated the restructuring of male sexual behavior in New York after 1820. Numerous young men courted prostitutes, "kept" women, paid their rent, and assumed aliases to hide such activities. Sexual desires were now expressed through institutions of public leisure and commercial exchange—the theater, the boardinghouse, and the brothel. More significantly, Robinson's behavior was defensible in the minds of his supporters. Jewett was a social leech out to ruin a rising but poor clerk, a female threat to "Young America." Indeed, "no man ought to forfeit his life for the murder of a whore," concluded some apologists. As the cry for justice in the murder of a prostitute rang out, Robinson's contemporaries saw themselves on trial. Many ran to his defense. There "appears to be a fellow-feeling in the audience," Philip Hone noted during the proceedings; "I was surrounded by young men about his own age, apparently clerks like him, who appeared to be thoroughly initiated into the arcana of such houses." The event so polarized New York that the prostitute's partisans donned "Helen Jewett mourners"—white beaver hats with a black band of crepe halfway up the crown—as badges of opposition to the defenders of her accused murderer. Not to be outdone, Robinson's sympathizers jammed into the City Hall courtroom daily, wearing "Frank Rivers caps" as their symbol of solidarity.[10]

In that tiny, overcrowded municipal chamber, New York and the rest of America confronted a changing sexual ethos. Robinson not only murdered a woman but, more important, also challenged the emerging "respectable," bourgeois, Christian morality. In the years following the Second Great Awakening, the values of self-control, chastity, domesticity, sobriety, and frugality were espoused by Protestant and Catholic clergy, male and female moral reformers, and entrepreneur and small merchant alike. Severe social restrictions increasingly limited intimacy between young men and women as the nineteenth century progressed. Long before the phrase was popularized by a twentieth-century president, these groups admonished young Americans to "just say no."

Robinson's sexual behavior mocked these ideals. For the next decade, it was a national topic of discussion (figures 13–16 reflect the ongoing interest in the case). More than any single person, Robinson put the tension of what constituted "respectable" sexuality on public view. Above all, his popularity among large numbers of urban youths represented the emergence of a "sporting male" culture. Organized around various forms of gaming—horse racing, gambling, cockfighting, pugilism, and other "blood" sports—sporting-male culture defended and promoted male sexual aggressiveness and promiscuity. For young men like Robinson, bachelorhood was the ideal. Prostitution, sexual display, and erotic entertainment brought excitement to a prosaic world. Respectable, reproductive heterosexuality, in contrast, was associated with femininity and female control. Self-indulgence, not self-sacrifice, meant freedom; unregulated sex was the categorical imperative for the sporting male.

The most conspicuous sexual ethic of this subculture was its defense of prostitution. The short-lived sporting press, typified by story papers and journals like the *Rake,* the *Whip,* the *Flash,* and the *Libertine,* were among the most forthright advocates of male sexual freedom. While much of their coverage aped the penny press in its tendency to exaggerate and sensationalize, their appeal rested upon a positive view of male heterosexual indulgence. "Man is endowed by nature with passions that must be gratified," argued the *Sporting Whip,* and no blame can be attached to him, who for that purpose occasionally seeks the woman of pleasure." Another insisted that brothels were "as necessary as bread or water." Similarly, it was "a mistaken idea" to assume that a woman who engaged in "illicit intercourse with one or two men, gradually sinks and sinks deeper into the abyss of shame," claimed the *Weekly Rake.* Even the admired females of classical Greece like Sappho and Phryne were common harlots or kept mistresses. One journal defended prostitutes as "very charitable and feeling," many visiting the almshouse and helping the poor. Others were depicted as artists with "poetic effusions, . . . indicative of a cultivated and reflecting mind." Prostitution, argued yet another journal, should be legalized and regulated. The "cause of morality is not served by the suppression of open brothels; they are as essential to the well-being of society as churches."[11]

Elements of this male subculture, especially with its "rough amusements," existed before 1820, when prostitution was centered in the dock areas of New York. Among mariners and longshoremen, prostitution was viewed as an ordinary part of a jack-tar's life. Along the East River, reported one official, "the denizens of Corinthian haunts in the vicinity

Fig. 13 right. Helen Jewett (1849)

Fig. 14 below. The Murder (1849)
Both from George Wilkes, The Lives of Helen Jewett and Richard Robinson *(1849)*

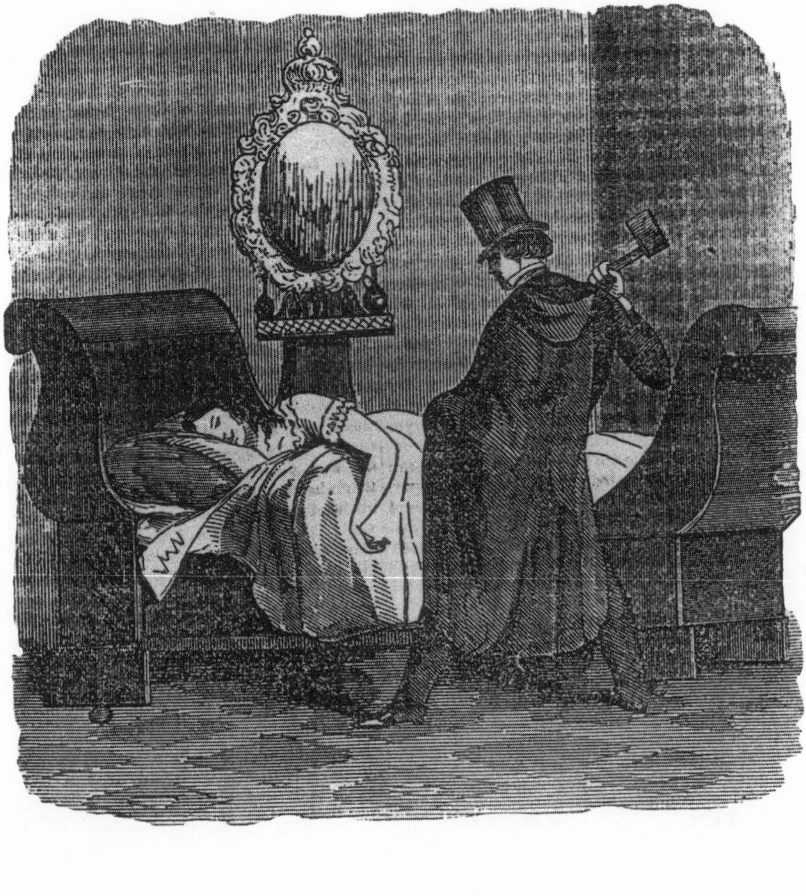

Fig. 15 Helen Jewett (1887)

Fig. 16 Richard Robinson (1887)
Both from George Washington Walling,
Recollections of a New York Police Chief *(1887)*

of the docks" beckoned seafaring visitors to enter the taverns. One mother complained in 1811 that Thomas and Rachel Greer's notorious Walnut Street brothel by the East River was disrupting her family. Her eldest sons "kept a miss" in the house "by the name of Nancy and . . . spen[t] considerable money there to support her." It was only a matter of time, she feared, before their younger siblings would follow.[12]

Some sailors acknowledged that they slept with prostitutes most of their nights on shore. James Jones, for example, arrived in port and immediately went to Daniel Truesdale's Corlears Hook tavern and "fell in with a girl by the name of Polly Miller with whom he slept that night." George Gould and a shipmate admitted that they cohabited with Catharine Butler and Betsey Hill for several nights until Hill's former lover interrupted their visit. Even at midcentury, Walt Whitman noted that the "hardest houses" of prostitution were those in Cherry, Water, and Walnut streets, adding, "Sailors, canal-boatmen, young fellows from the country, etc. go regularly there." Similarly, Florry Kernan recalled that "[i]t was a jubilee, indeed, to the landlords of [Five] Points when the crew of a United States ship-of-war got paid off."[13]

The few surviving arrest records for the early nineteenth century tend to confirm that most clients of prostitutes were less than affluent visitors to New York. For example, of the thirty-seven identifiable males arrested in houses and saloons with prostitutes from 1811 to 1813, only fourteen were listed in city directories. The majority (62 percent) were new residents, visitors, or transients.[14] Before 1820, it appears, prostitutes attracted only a small portion of the male population as clients, and remained a marginal entertainment.

The 1830s witnessed an expansion of this male sexual fraternity, along with several noticeable changes that continued into the twentieth century. Most evident was its youthful character. Increasingly, large numbers of young males—clerks and apprentices, immigrants and native-born, tourists and residents—visited prostitutes. The ever greater transiency of urban life and the changing structure of work disrupted older traditions of courtship for young men. As bachelorhood and the postponement of marriage grew commonplace, sexual activity outside marriage and courtship rituals grew more common. Second, married men frequented prostitutes in increasing numbers, integrating this group of men into the subculture of male promiscuity. Finally, the rise in male sexual activity with prostitutes was never entirely confined to specific economic classes or social groups. Undoubtedly, distinctions of wealth, ethnicity, race, age, and even styles of dress periodically surfaced. But in the broad context of male heterosexual behavior, the institutions and customs that sponsored commercial sex tended to promote male camaraderie. Gender identification more often overwhelmed divisions based upon class, religion, and ethnicity. Sporting-male culture, in effect, displaced older rules and traditions governing sexual behavior for young, married, and "respectable" men. By the age of the Civil War, the writer George Ellington could conclude that many "fashionable bloods and old fogies, known rakes, and presumedly pious people, wealthy bachelors and respectable married men, fast sons and moral husbands" consorted with prostitutes. If this became widely known, Ellington feared, it would "convulse society."[15]

The youthfulness of New York's sexual epicures, as the case of Richard Robinson illustrated, drew attention in a variety of quarters. In 1833, for example, Alexander Polsty lamented that his fifteen-year-old was "a constant frequenter" of the prostitutes in Francis Legg's Anthony Street saloon. "[H]e stays all night," said Polsty, "sleeping with . . . the female inmates. . . ." Others noted that the majority of clients "were half grown boys of the very worst kind." Forming crowds outside some houses of ill repute, the youths committed some of "the grossest indecencies in the neighborhood." Others lamented how such youthful behavior was tolerated even by middle-class women. "It often happens, that young men who are *known* to frequent the *dens* of infamy and vice," wrote one critic, "are freely admitted to the society of ladies." Another clerk who attended fancy balls and visited with New York's elite females openly supported a mistress. "And yet," remonstrated one observer, "no young man in the whole city is more popular with the ladies."[16]

By midcentury, journalists and doctors were convinced that sex with prostitutes was the norm for young male New Yorkers. "Mere boys, of the rising generation, have their fancy women, or favorite prostitutes," noted one newspaper. In 1857, and 1858, Walt Whitman observed that "the majority of nearly grown and just grown lads" in Brooklyn and New York "feel perfectly at home in the most infamous places—and . . . look for their pleasures mostly there."[17] Although "respectable society" ignores the growing practice, he wrote,

> the plain truth is that nineteen out of twenty of the mass of American young men, who live in or visit the great cities, are more or less familiar with houses of prostitution and are customers to them.—A large proportion of the young men become acquainted with all the best known ones in the city.

Large numbers of married men also visited brothels. "The enormous increase of prostitution in New York," concluded the *Whip* in 1842, "has . . . augmented vice in the married station." Numerous articles and stories in the sporting press pointed to the growing frequency with which married men resorted to brothels. For these and other reasons, the police court justice Robert Taylor routinely visited brothels during the 1840s and searched for evidence in divorce cases.[18]

Most significant, neither the benefits of privilege nor the trappings of wealth discouraged visits to the whorehouse. That frequent commentator on New York life, George Templeton Strong, claimed in 1853 that morals and manners, "even among the better class of young men about town," glorified the prostitute. Fearing the larger implications for American society of such a development, Strong wondered, "Was there ever among the boys of any city so much dissipation redeemed by so little culture and so little manliness and audacity even of the watchman-fighting sort?" Among "the best classes of Men" living in New York and Brooklyn, Walt Whitman admitted, "the custom is to go among prostitutes as an ordinary thing. Nothing is thought of it—or rather the wonder is, how can there be an 'fun' without it."[19]

Specific incidents involving noteworthy New Yorkers supported such generalizations. The wealthy merchant Thomas H. Smith, for example, married a young prostitute in 1839. "I did not believe the rumor before," Strong conceded. "[H]is blushing bride is a protégée of that respected female, Mrs. [Adeline] Miller of Duane Street, a damsel who has been on the town for twenty years." Less than a year later, Smith's "amiable bride" left him and fled to Europe with a nineteen-year-old paramour.

Similarly, the former mayor Cornelius Van Wyck Lawrence consorted with prostitutes, until the proprietor and madam of "the Red House" in Harlem, "a noted sporting place," played on Lawrence's fears of public disclosure. "It seems the gentleman and lady have been living on Lawrence ever since he committed this indiscretion and bleeding him freely," concluded Strong. And at midcentury, the sewing machine entrepreneur Isaac Singer and the politico Daniel Sickles similarly drew public attention for their philandering with prostitutes.[20]

Still other observers noted the popularity of prostitutes with segments of wealthy New York. In 1846, their frequency induced the *Tribune* to conclude that three-quarters of the sexual relations in New York were "venal, licentious, and adulterous." In his path-breaking study of New York prostitution in 1859, Dr. William W. Sanger conceded that almost "everyone can specify acts now tolerated in respectable families which, so far as being permitted fifteen years ago, would have . . . warrant[ed] the expulsion of the offender from the domestic circle." Middle-class professionals like Sanger and Strong equated the increasing recourse to prostitutes with a deteriorating sexual morality." Words cannot express the destitution and nakedness, moral and mental, the threadbare and ragged state of intellectual dilapidation into which . . . wealthy, weak minds . . . sooner or later sink," wrote Strong. After the Civil War, George Ellington was convinced that at least two of every three men of wealth and leisure in New York devoted "a certain portion of their time and wealth to some fair one."[21]

Sporting-male sexuality, in effect, consistently challenged and often confused emerging divisions based upon social class, work, and education. As commercial sex became an intrinsic part of urban masculinity and male sexuality, definitions of respectability were undermined. Frequenting prostitutes was not "confined to any particular grade," observed the *Whip* in 1842. "Perhaps such manners exist more amongst the lower classes than others, but all have a touch of them." College "patricians" were as likely "as any town blackguard" to hire women for sex. From lowly clerks to aristocratic merchants, "thousands of boys met constantly in the street in company with prostitutes."[22]

Some distinctions centered on certain character types, which Ned Buntline termed "fancy men for the upper ten-thousand" and "fancy men for the lower million." To an extent, these groups replicated certain class-oriented divisions. But as Elliot Gorn has shown, fancy men were a large, heterogeneous mix of wealthy and poor, educated and ignorant, fashionable and ragged. Leisure activities, not work, defined the fancy. In the boxing ring, gambling den, and saloon, a "rough" egalitarianism reigned. Whereas in Europe sporting males were equated with "gentlemen," in New York older patterns of deference and social behavior broke down. The "mass of sportsmen," George Foster wrote, "are the hundreds of individuals of whom one recognizes figures that no language names, and who gather round certain haunts in the Bowery and elsewhere."[23]

The "fancy man of the lower million" was most often linked to the Bowery. Known for his "bloody bulldog spirit," the "Bowery B'hoy" was young, working class, independent, and rowdy. Writers like George Foster and John Vose portrayed them as revelers in pugilism and prostitution. "The gambling house, the house of prostitution, the groggery," insisted Foster, "are the habitual sphere where he expends his active life." The family, for these men, was "a myth." Few of the refinements of "high" culture made their way into the world of the Bowery. Some sporting males also enjoyed close associations with New York's criminal underworld. The initiators of the numerous brothel attacks during the 1830s and 1840s, for instance, came from this violent group of sporting men. Still others closely associated with the underground economy lived with prostitutes, many as their "chosen lovers" or pimps. This "class of community," noted the *True Flash* in 1841, "start about the town well dressed, supported by the small change and extras of the frail sisterhood."[24]

In contrast, "upper-tendom b'hoys," dandies, and nabobs prized cuff links over fisticuffs. The quintessential dandies were fastidious in dress and detached in manner. They were known for their flashy outfits, finger rings, watch chains, leather boots, and "fashionable" behavior. They aspired to be part of the "upper crust" and "the *bon ton.*" They displayed "polished manners" and "the ways of a gentleman." At the same time, they were described by observers as "knaves" and "rascals." Critics castigated them as part of the "Puppy order" and "conceited fops." Indeed, the dandies moved between the "respectable" world of elite society and the criminal underworld of Gotham. Indulging in wine, women, and pleasure, "the fast boy of Young America" was, according to Charles Astor Bristed, "dressy, vulgar and good-natured."[25]

The dandy combined elitist pretensions with democratic values. "I am a rich man's son," claimed the protagonist in John Vose's semifictional *Leaves from the Diary of a Broadway Dandy,* "yet I prefer to be in full, 'one of the people,' in every sense of the word." Money and brawn were not the primary measures of man, but rather his leisure and sexual pleasures. The dandy inhabited a world of unlimited extramarital sensuality. Full of sexual bravado, he enjoyed kissing at age six; by fifteen, he engaged in "serious flirtations" with teenage heiresses. As a young adult, he visited as many as seventeen ladies daily, evidence that his "love affairs [were] pretty strong." The dandy sponsored elaborate balls filled with prostitutes—"how the Eighth Ward abounds with beautiful girls," he proclaimed. Indeed, such "fancy men" pursued "careers of male prostitution" through the seduction and extortion of married women with "careless and indulgent" husbands. The dandy rejected all rules of sexual propriety. "[I]f a young lady made love to me, . . . it was not my fault but hers!" The "sporting fancy gentry," declared another writer, were "not usually trapped into marriage with much facility."[26] Whether Bowery B'hoy or Broadway dandy, sporting-male culture broadly equated sexual promiscuity and erotic indulgence with individual autonomy and personal freedom.

This bachelor ideology was further elaborated by Donald Mitchell. Although Mitchell has been forgotten in the twentieth century, he was considered one of the great English-language stylists in his own time. His writings appeared in many a schoolchild's *McGuffey's Reader,* and he frequently contributed to *Harper's, Knickerbocker,* and *Atlantic* magazines. Among his most influential works was *Reveries of a Bachelor,* which appeared in 1850 and remained popular and in print into the twentieth century. In *Reveries,* Mitchell articulated the bachelor attack on the "feminized" family and the trappings of domestic life. Matrimony "has a great deal of fire in the beginning, but it is a fire that consumes all that feeds the blaze," he concluded. It only turned men into "captives" of women. A wife "will tear the life out of you," warned Mitchell, "making you pay in righteous retribution of annoyance, grief, vexation, shame, and sickness of heart." Marriage only brought new and irresolvable troubles—in-laws asking for money, nauseating cooking, trite conversation, materialistic demands, fading love, estranged attachments, and dead children. For Mitchell, the wife, in the end, was simply "the prostitute of fashion."[27]

Mitchell celebrated the autonomy and the freedom of the single male life. "Can a man stake his bachelor respectability," he asked, "his independence and comfort, upon the die of absorbing, unchanging, relentless marriage, without trembling at the venture?" No intelligent male, "free to chase his fancies over the wide world," would choose marriage and its claim on his time, his trouble, and his thought. Nothing was more pitiful than a wearied bachelor who conformed and consigned himself to what others called "a nice match." Most important, marriage compromised male sexuality. Mitchell relished the diversity of beautiful young women and the opportunities they offered the bachelor. "My fancy would surely quicken . . . if [a woman] were in attendance," he argued. "Surely imagination would be stronger and purer, if it could have the playful fancies of dawning womanhood to delight in."[28]

The popularity of these literary exposés of sporting-male sexual behavior sheds some light on the way many men perceived their social conditions. Most midnineteenth-century cities had a large, unmarried male population, between 20 and 40 percent of all the men under thirty-five. Sporting life was a growing part of urban culture by the second quarter of the nineteenth century. During the 1820s and 1830s, for example, observers noted the expensive carriages that lined up nightly in front of James Roberts's prostitute-filled dance house in Greenwich Village, Mary Bowne's Elm Street brothel, and numerous Canal Street houses. After surveying the city's voluminous sex trade, reporters for *McDowall's Journal* corroborated similar charges, adding that the clientele was not only wealthy but so plentiful that some brothels had to turn away customers. One busy brothel reportedly served twenty-eight clients in half an hour. "The dress and appearance of these men," reporters concluded, "resembled that of men of wealth and fashion."[29] Brothels, theaters, and groggeries were filled with country merchants, businessmen, and clerks, "the inhabitants of the self-righteous and self-styled virtuous villages and hamlets . . . , men who are thought to be so virtuous at home, [but] go to the brothel . . . when they visit the city."[30]

Such impressionistic accounts might be dismissed as the exaggerated fears of outraged reformers and defenders of a more restrained sexual morality. And indeed hard evidence regarding nineteenth-century male sexuality remains sparse and elusive. The absence of opinion polls and participant-observation studies, combined with the sometimes outlandish judgments of middle-class observers and the closeted nature of much of this activity, makes definitive conclusions almost impossible. Yet the diversity of opinion on this increasingly visible male promiscuity was striking. Patrician figures like Philip Hone and George Templeton Strong, working-class mouthpieces like the *Subterranean,* the women's rights defender Elizabeth Blackwell, the "purity" reformers Anthony Comstock and the editors of the *Advocate of Moral Reform,* and "bohemians" like Walt Whitman and the editors of the sporting press all noted this sort of male behavior. Taken together, such judgments surely amount to more than hypersensitive warnings of moral decay.

Even the supposedly sharp distinction between those who frequented the Bowery and those who went to Broadway, often seen by contemporaries and later historians, as indicative of class divisions, was in fact quite fluid, and the areas were economically integrated. Despite its elite reputation, for example, Broadway was by the 1840s an outpost for the working-class gangs led by John Morrissey and Bill Poole, each of them headquartered a block away along Church and Mercer streets, respectively. Still other gangs centered in the Bowery, such as Tom Hyer's, were allied to counterparts on Broadway. Hyer's compatriots frequented

Broadway establishments as well as their own on the Bowery. At the same time, Broadway was increasingly known for its plethora of prostitutes and pimps, most working out of the many brothels on adjoining and parallel streets. Finally, by the 1850s, this section of Broadway was also the heart of New York's "bohemia," vividly described and popularized by Walt Whitman. While New York's leading boulevard attracted many expensive hotels, theaters, and restaurants, the wealthy were by no means Broadway's primary clientele.[31]

Furthermore, these descriptions of male promiscuity were partially confirmed by a surprising number of men who publicly admitted to sexual intercourse with prostitutes. Arrest records, especially those involving panel house and pickpocket victims—clients of prostitutes robbed during their sexual encounters who hoped to retrieve their stolen articles—provide a window on the hidden world of nineteenth-century male sexuality. For example, Jesse Chatterdon of Queens admitted he lay in bed with Kate Male and "they embraced and fondled with each other." Later he realized he was missing $300. Similarly, on the night he lost $500, John D. Moore had instructed a hackman, "[T]ake me to a house where there are some girls." He ended up in a Tenderloin brothel. After Robert Johnson was robbed by Carrie Smith during an 1865 visit, he admitted that he had followed her to a Crosby Street brothel and "there went to bed" with her. In another case, Mary O'Connor confessed she robbed Darius Eastman of Brooklyn because he treated her badly. "He gave me only ten cents," she cried, "and he had sexual intercourse with me, and I only thought it was a dollar bill he had in his pocket."[32] Over and over again, robbery victims acknowledged in courtroom testimony that they "went to bed" with the women. Increasingly, affluent resident males prosecuted prostitutes in panel house and pickpocket cases. From 1862 to 1870, in 55 percent of the cases brought to trial, the male victims were city residents. For many men, the loss of personal property outweighed any loss in moral standing or public embarrassment such legal action brought.[33]

Certain institutional supports and leisure activities fostered the expansion of sporting-male sexuality in antebellum New York. The theater was the most controversial. By the late eighteenth century, London theaters like Drury Lane and Covent Garden were known for their elegant courtesans and *femmes d'amour,* and Americans were keen to make comparisons. In New York, Washington Irving noted that the theater promoted flirtatious fantasies for all. After attending the Park Theater in 1802, he observed that women in the expensive boxes were "studious to please; their charms were set off to the greatest advantage; each box was a little battery in itself, and they all seemed eager to outdo each other in the havoc they spread around. An arch glance in one box was rivalled by a smile in another."[34]

Stage entertainment was an indisputably popular activity in antebellum New York. By the 1820s, New York allegedly had more theaters than any other city of comparable size in the world. A wide range of attractions—dramas, summer gardens, concerts, lectures, operas, German language plays, and "blood and thunder" melodramas—competed for an ever-growing urban audience. George Templeton Strong noted the immense throngs of all classes, lured to the opera in Castle Garden in the 1850s. "Everyone goes, and nob and snob, Fifth Avenue and Chatham Street, sit side by side fraternally on the hard benches." The *Advocate of Moral Reform* maintained, "[T]he poorer classes are as much addicted to amusement as the rich, and seeking it in its approved forms, they patronize the theatre in larger numbers than those more affluent. . . . They are journeymen, clerks, and agents, . . . or they are porters, apprentices, and nameless classes of vicious boys." Theater patrons were a microcosm of American society. It was, as Lawrence Levine has argued, a kaleidoscopic, democratic institution offering a widely varying bill of fare to all socioeconomic groups and classes.[35]

Despite popular appeal, drama remained a symbol of moral corruption and unrefined culture for many. "The good is mixed up with the bad," admitted the former mayor Philip Hone in 1841. "Shakespeare and Jim Crow come in equally for their share of condemnation, and the stage is indiscriminately voted immoral, irreligious, and what is much worse, *unfashionable.*" Another former mayor and early reformer, Stephen Allen, charged that theaters were "the leading cause of the depravity of youth of both sexes." Charles Loring Brace of the Children's Aid Society complained, "[H]omeless boys and newsboys waste their time going to theaters and gambling away what little money they possess." George Foster argued that the stage emphasized "intrigues with married women, elopements, seductions, bribery, cheating, and fraud of every description—set off with a liberal allowance of *double entendre.*" The prevalence of profanity and "broad indecency" did little more than "excite the animal passions and . . . the lowest and most depraved of human tastes."[36]

The close relationship of sporting-male sexuality and theater was reinforced in the divorce trial of America's famed tragedian Edwin Forrest. Besides being America's most popular actor, Forrest was by mid-century a symbol of sexual individualism and freedom for the sporting male. Mrs. Forrest's eminent lawyer, Charles O'Conor, used the testimony of Caroline Ingersoll, an assignation house keeper, to incriminate the actor. Forrest originally denied any impropriety, but when Ingersoll took the stand, she charged Forrest with consorting with women at various houses of assignation in the city. From 1846 to 1851, Forrest "was the habitual frequenter of a house of prostitution." The evidence "punched the great tragedian much harder than any evidence singled out in the opening," according to George Templeton Strong. His wife's legal victory was greeted with singular outrage by Forrest's admirers. When Mrs. Forrest elected to speak at Brougham's Lyceum a month later, Strong considered it "a most absurd step" and feared a repeat of the Astor Place riot. The "chivalry of the Bowery," he reported, "is said to be in fierce wrath at the verdict against her husband."[37]

What Forrest practiced offstage was promoted by theater owners inside. The secluded, semiprivate balcony labeled the third tier was reserved for sporting men to rendezvous with willing women. Managers defended the practice, arguing that prostitutes were a necessity in order for theaters to attract men and remain profitable. "Ah, Mitchell," proclaimed the *Rake,* refering to the owner of Mitchell's Olympic Theater, "your little band of musicians and large one of pretty legs, voluptuous breasts, and bright eyes bring all the money into your treasury." George Foster satirically concluded in 1850, "[T]he respectable and virtuous public will not visit an assignation, even though it be called a theater."[38]

Even the elite Park Theater, with its reputation for elegant, aesthetic drama, an exclusive clientele, and sponsorship by John Jacob Astor and John Beekman, hardly discouraged prostitution. During Tyrone Power's historic 1838 performance, at least eighty prostitutes roamed the third tier in search of customers. City marshals were sometimes called upon to remove patrons and prostitutes for their "very outrageous, turbulent and noisey" behavior. Francis Grund critically concluded, "[F]ew ladies . . . are ever seen at the theater; and the frequenting of them, even by gentlemen, is not considered a recommendation to their character."[39]

The Bowery Theater was nationally known for its sexual excursions from propriety (figure 17). Its raucous productions and Bowery B'hoy clientele earned it the nickname the Bowery Slaughterhouse. The *Herald* considered it "without exception the worst and wickedest [theater] that ever stood a month in any city under heaven." Prostitutes working in Chapel Street brothels openly attended performances at the Bowery. One prostitute remarked, "[W]e girls always patronize the Bowery—moreover the manager here is a very clever man." A journalist concurred, claiming that sporting-male sexuality in the Bowery Theater outrivaled the unrestrained debauchery depicted in Hogarth's *Rake's and Wanton's Progress.* "[O]aths, shouts, shrieks from the throats of drunken outcast bands, and leprous male prostitutes, saluted the ear, and blasphemous confusion reigned supreme." Walking about, one could observe "males and females in strange and indecent positions in the lobbies, and

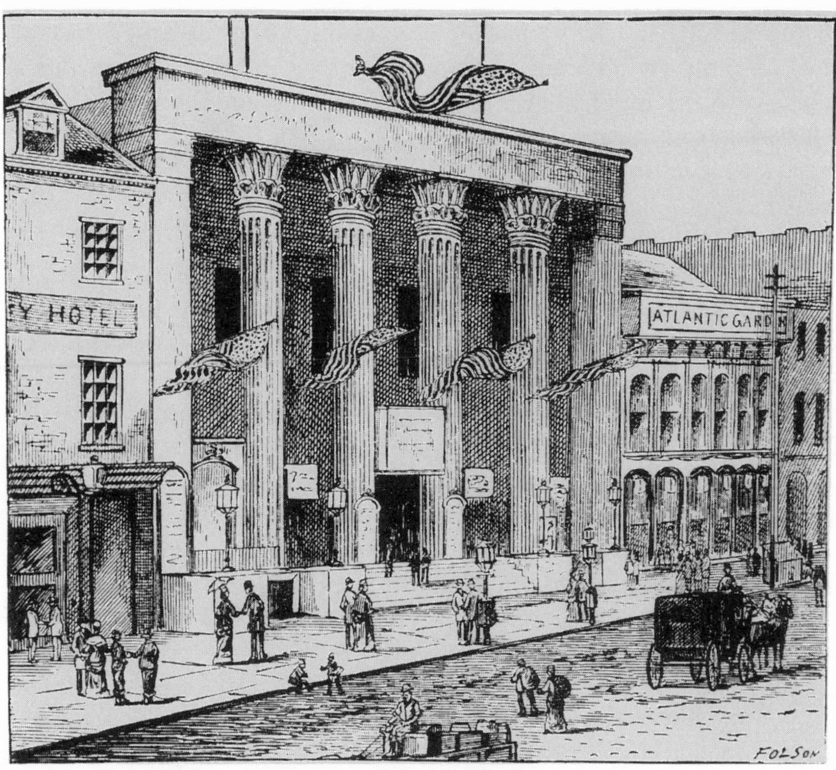

Fig. 17 The Bowery Theater
From George Washington Walling, Recollections of a New York Police Chief *(1887)*

sometimes in the boxes." So blatant was the lubricious activity in the Bowery that it lacked only a few front bedrooms to make it complete. "There is not a dance hall, a free-and-easy, a concert saloon, or a vile drinking place," reported one Englishman in the 1830s, "that presents such a view of the depravity and degradation of New York as the gallery of a Bowery theater."[40]

Theaters promoted sporting-male sexuality not only in the third tier but in the brothel as well. For example, Mary Benson's and Julia Brown's houses on Church Street were favorite resorts for men attending Palmo's Opera House. Mrs. Bowen's establishment on Leonard Street was directly opposite the National Theater. Leonard Street residents in 1839 complained that the prostitutes in Jane Williams's house "frequently go to theatres unattended by gentlemen and as they state visit the third tier." Some houses were even physically connected to a theater. Behind the Park Theater in Theater Alley, for example, was a brothel explicitly for actors. In addition, Rebecca Fraser ran a brothel on the short street in the early 1820s before moving around the corner at Ann Street in 1825. For nearly a decade, from 1831 to 1839, Mrs. Newman ran a house with at least eight girls only a few doors behind the Park.[41]

Brothels and theaters enjoyed close spatial ties. The six major theaters operating from 1820 to 1829, for example, were located within two blocks of a house of prostitution. During the ensuing two decades, theaters like the Bowery, Broadway, Chatham, Lafayette, National, and Park shared their blocks with similar prurient establishments. Until it burned down in 1841, the National Theater was next door to Julia Brown's famous brothel. By the Civil War, six of fourteen Broadway theaters were sharing the same block as a house of prostitution, often in the rear of the theater, along Mercer or Crosby Street. Other theatrical establishments were never more than a block from a brothel.[42]

Yet these well-known theaters actually restrained blatant carnal display when compared with the "sub-theater." After 1830, these small establishments did not even bother restricting public sexuality to the third tier. Stephen Allen, in an 1838 report to the Society for the Reformation of Juvenile Delinquents, wrote that small, minor theaters, short on "respectability," were "more injurious to the morals of the city than the older establishments." Because of the small size of these institutions, prostitutes were not segregated, but ventured freely through the premises. The lure of quick profits from cheap titillation encouraged the unregulated growth of these burlesque palaces for several decades. "At many of the smaller theaters things have been carried to an outrageous pass," wrote George Foster in 1849. The sub-theater, indeed, was "little better than a brothel turned inside out." "The city is utterly dismal," declared George Templeton Strong a decade later. "I'm thinking of course of lager-beer saloons and low theaters."[43]

Toleration of sporting-male sexuality only encouraged dance halls, saloons, and supper clubs to reach out for the same clientele. Saloons, such as those along City Hall Park, frequently divided the rear or upstairs area into small cubicles for prostitutes. Similarly, expensive restaurants sometimes provided boxes, or "private supper rooms," where customers dined and copulated with prostitutes. Although in the early nineteenth century some taverns encouraged dancing, by 1840 there were numerous dance houses where prostitutes mingled in the audience, looking for potential customers. Since many saloons provided a small area for dancing when they hired musicians to entertain their customers and since dance halls served large volumes of liquor, the two types of institutions were frequently indistinguishable.[44]

A number of factors help explain why this sporting-male world became such an integral part of New York culture after 1820. First, the city attracted a large, transient male population. New York, wrote Samuel Halliday in 1861, was "a population of *strangers* in a strange land." The registers of leading New York City hotels as early as 1835 counted nearly 60,000 guests annually. In the same year, approximately 22,000 crewmen aboard ships entered Manhattan. By 1860, the number of visiting seamen had tripled. Furthermore, from 1840 to 1855, 68 percent of the 3.2 million immigrants arriving in the United States landed in New York. And during the decade preceding the depression of 1857, over 2.2 million persons came through the port.[45]

Second, family life endured new pressures as New York industrialized and grew into a modern metropolis. Many young males found it more and more difficult to marry and raise a family. By the 1820s, city apprentices and journeymen were increasingly exploited by their employers as the old artisan system broke down and gave way to one of wage labor. Greater disparities between rich and poor were apparent by the Jacksonian era, and it became harder for unskilled laborers and journeymen workers to support a family.[46] Some complained that only men with sufficient wealth in New York could afford to court, marry, and maintain a family.

Paradoxically, some working-class men felt compelled to marry (while still avoiding a family) for economic reasons. As the "family wage" became the popular standard of paid labor, working-class men required the domestic labor of a wife in order to maintain themselves more easily. For men earning less than $250 annually before 1860, this was almost a necessity. Even men earning this amount enjoyed a clear advantage in marrying because a wife's labor brought in considerably more money than her maintenance cost.[47] Such circumstances probably encouraged men to marry more for economic reasons and less for romance, sex, or love, thereby separating physical intimacy from marriage.

Third, courtship habits and customs in New York City changed considerably after 1820. The transient population, the rising importance of the teenage peer group, and the decline of apprenticeship and church regulation transformed teenage and adult sexual relations. As early as 1819, John Pintard complained about the balls and parties of New York's elite. Among the few forums for young New Yorkers to meet members of the opposite sex. Pintard saw "but little benefit, in the way of matches, resulting from all these public fairs where young ladies are exhibited for market." He took solace, however, in the thought "that not a single marriage, of all the young ladies exposed for sale, at these entertainments has taken place this season." Generally, Pintard considered the young men "too profligate" and the ladies "too extravagant," reflecting a great change in "the conceptions of morals" since his days of courtship.[48]

Pintard astutely identified a new trend in urban courtship. After 1820, even the selection of a spouse was subject to the vagaries of the market. "Personal" ads appeared for the first time in local papers. Many males openly expressed frustration in finding female companions. In the 1840s, for example, young mechanics placed newspaper advertisements seeking the attention of young ladies between fifteen and twenty, reiterating their good moral character and desiring to change their "present solitary lives of celibacy for the more pleasing and social life of conjugal bliss." Admitting that their method was unusual, the young workers expressed the hope that the "irksomeness of introduction, acquaintance and courtship [would] justify [them] in making this public address." By the 1860s, "personals" were a regular feature in New York newspapers.[49]

In rural and small-town America, courtship rituals and customs were less subject to the rules of the market. In New York, though, the difficulty in finding marriage partners for men and women alike was so pronounced that eventually a cottage industry of "marriage brokers" appeared. "They marry as they buy a house or sell a horse, invest in real estate, or go abroad," noted Junius Browne. "The reason they remain unwedded is because they don't find time to look for a wife." James McCabe similarly reported that "matchmakers" regularly advertised in city papers. And even frustrated parents of single young males were induced, according to Elizabeth Blackwell, "to provide a mistress for their sons, in the hope of keeping them from houses of public debauchery."[50]

Finally, discontent over the enhanced power of women within marriage probably induced many men to visit prostitutes. As writers and reformers like Catherine Beecher, Harriet Beecher Stowe, Sarah Hale, Horace Bushnell, and others articulated the ideals of female domesticity, women were increasingly held responsible for family and child-rearing matters. While never universal, and differing across class and ethnic lines, this ideological construct had evolved into a pattern of behavior for most middle-class Americans by the midnineteenth century. The average American woman enjoyed increasing power and autonomy within the family, especially over matters of sexuality and reproduction. In addition, lecturers and writers like Dio Lewis and Henry Wright found that information pertaining to female control of fertility and sexuality was highly popular and well received by women after midcentury. Male licentiousness and "marital excess" were favored topics of interest and complaint among females in the United States. Increasingly, the American middle class idealized male sexual control and self-restraint within the family and depicted women as "passionless."[51] Quite likely resentful of this female power and its "petticoat government" ruling sexuality and family life, men sought sexual pleasure elsewhere.[52]

WHEN the Reverend William Berrian of Trinity Church admitted to occasional brothel visits in New York, George Templeton Strong candidly observed that the admission was hardly startling. Such visits were commonplace. The "significance lies in the fact that he has been so seldom," said Strong, "and in the surprise with which one hears of even one visit every five years on an average."[53] For numerous nineteenth-century American males, whether young men like Richard Robinson or older ones like William Berrian, aspects of masculinity, social status, and self-esteem rested on demonstrating a promiscuous, heterosexual orientation. In a rapidly changing urban environment, sex meant more than physical gratification or reproduction; it frequently determined a portion of one's identity.

Sporting-male sexuality was centered on what might be labeled a promiscuous paradigm. This model of behavior rested on an ethic of sensual pleasure that, on the one hand, distanced men from women's "feminine weakness" and emotional attachments and, on the other, bonded them with other males. This paradigm of sexual behavior and the institutions it fostered embodied more than just a youth culture, for it included older adult males. Sporting men were more than just bachelors, for numerous married men participated in their activities. And they were more than rowdy Bowery B'hoys, because dandies, nabobs, and "fancy men" belonged to the fraternity. Undoubtedly, certain divisions were reflected in the different venues of commercial sex. The rich patronized elegant parlor houses, and members of the working class visited streetwalkers or cheap boardinghouses. Some brothels admitted only men of a particular race or geographic origin. Broadway dandies and Bowery B'hoys hardly joined hands in their nocturnal excursions. But these men shared an infatuation with prostitution and promiscuous sexual behavior. In this sexual context, sporting-male ideas and activity served to promote a certain gender solidarity among nineteenth-century urban males. Through the milieu of commercial sex, urban heterosexual males demarcated part of their subculture.

The glorification of male heterosexual freedom and bachelorhood permeated not only New York but much of America. From frontier communities to eastern cities, sporting-male culture grew ever more prominent during the course of the nineteenth century. Male heroes like Davy Crockett, for example, reveled in the sexual autonomy that came with frontier life. As the historian Carroll Smith-Rosenberg has shown, Crockett's popularity stemmed in part from his misogynist orientation and exhibitionist, nonreproductive sexuality. Crockett's almanacs were filled with veiled references to masturbation and homosexuality, unsupervised courtship, and cathartic violence. The family was for Crockett, as for the sporting male, a female preserve organized to control and restrain his sexual freedom. Even his nickname—"the gentleman from the cane"—inverted the language of respectability and lampooned the emerging sexual norms of middle-class America. Not surprisingly, Crockett's largest audience was found not on the frontier but in the growing urban centers of the eastern seaboard.[54]

As sporting-male culture grew prominent, efforts to define middle-class respectability became more pronounced in New York and elsewhere. Bourgeois thought gradually divorced reproduction from sexual pleasure; one sign of this was the burgeoning literature on sexual abstinence and self-control. Physical intimacy between young men and women brought disdain and opprobrium. Furthermore, commercial leisure institutions promoted commercial sex, and this only widened the social gaps separating young men and women. Sporting-male life in nineteenth-century New York thus offered a kind of liminal social space, even an alternative culture, between the more clearly defined worlds of respectability and criminality. Here men could assume different identities, sometimes multiple identities, that departed from dominant social mores. In search of relationships offering individual expression and sexual promiscuity, men increasingly resorted to commercial venues. Dismissing fears and warnings of disease and degradation, these men chose sexual indulgence over continence.

Part II

HALCYON YEARS

Lust and wickedness are acceptable to me,
I walk with delinquents with passionate love.
I feel I am of them—I belong to those convicts and prostitutes
And henceforth I will not deny them—for how can I deny myself?

—Walt Whitman, *Leaves of Grass*[1]

6

"SHOULDER HITTERS," PORNO KINGS, AND POLITICIANS

THE emergence and growth of two distinct subcultures of prostitutes and sporting men by the midnineteenth century was part of a far-reaching transformation of New York's social structure. Intercourse was only one of many sexual activities increasingly organized around commerce, exchange, and consumption. For the first time, various forms of sexual behavior were available to a mass audience. Abortion, pornography, "model artist" striptease shows on the Bowery and Broadway, the concert saloon, the sporting press, and the appearance of a large, exclusive entertainment and sex district were reminders of changing sexual norms. By 1870, even guidebooks to houses of prostitution admitted that Gotham's previous decade had brought great changes "in the moral tone and character of its inhabitants."[2]

The most striking evidence of the prominence of commercial sex at midcentury was in the use of urban space and real estate. As sex became an increasingly expensive and profitable commodity, New York's first exclusive, large-scale sex district appeared. From 1850 to the early 1870s, the area bounded by the Bowery and by Canal, Laurens, and Houston streets (called SoHo in the late twentieth century) emerged as the center of the sex business. "Not only did the felon and fancy female [prostitute] hold forth in this district," argued the *National Police Gazette*, "but likewise the so-called sporting element, which was then made up of 'shoulder hitters,' dog-fighters, gamblers, actors and politicians."[3]

This district differed in two important ways from previous neighborhoods that saw significant amounts of prostitution. First, it lacked a large impoverished working-class population. The city's earlier zones of prostitution were geographically scattered, physically run-down, and populated by poor immigrants and African-Americans. In contrast, this new district was characterized by recent, well-built housing and few low-income residents. Well-known madams like Eliza Pratt, Jane Winslow, and Kate Rowe operated brothels in the district during these years. One observer remarked, "[T]hese dwellings are generally in a cleanly condition both externally and internally." Thomas Butler Gunn similarly conceded that these houses were "stylishly built" structures, not the "mean-looking tenements" typical of earlier neighborhoods with lots of prostitutes.[4] Commercial sex had become less a function of poverty and unemployment and more the product of entrepreneurs supplying a demand.

Second, this strip of Broadway and the surrounding community formed part of a growing leisure economy and entertainment district. Large department stores, new theaters, expensive restaurants, and gaudy saloons lined the boulevard. Significant amounts of private capital were invested in the neighborhood, epitomized by "monster" hotels like the St. Nicholas, New York's first "million dollar" building. Earlier districts like Five Points and Corlears Hook, in contrast, had never been upscale entertainment or tourist centers, especially for the middle classes. Such areas failed to attract similar forms of capital investment and remained distinctive parts of an alternative, underground economy. Just as certain streets and neighborhoods were by this time devoted to specific functions and economic purposes (as Wall Street was to finance), the area surrounding Broadway above Canal Street became famous for the erotic.

Broadway was the axis of this new entertainment and sex district. After 1850, the eight blocks along Broadway above Canal Street bustled with daytime shoppers in fancy clothing stores, furniture outlets, photographer studios, and artist galleries. Brooks Brothers, Lord and Taylor, Tiffany, and Mathew Brady were among the leading enterprises. And when the sun went down, the boulevard came alive with myriad leisure and entertainment establishments. Walking north, one passed the City Hotel, Fellow's Opera House, the Coliseum, Minerva Rooms, Mechanics Hall, Wallack's Theater, the Carlton House, the St. Nicholas Hotel, the Prescott House, the Collamore Hotel, Wood's Marble Hall, the Metropolitan Hotel (owned by William Marcy Tweed), Niblo's Garden Theater, the Smithsonian Hotel, Olympic Theater, Stuyvesant

Map VII
Broadway
Entertainment
District, 1855–1859

■ House of Prostitution

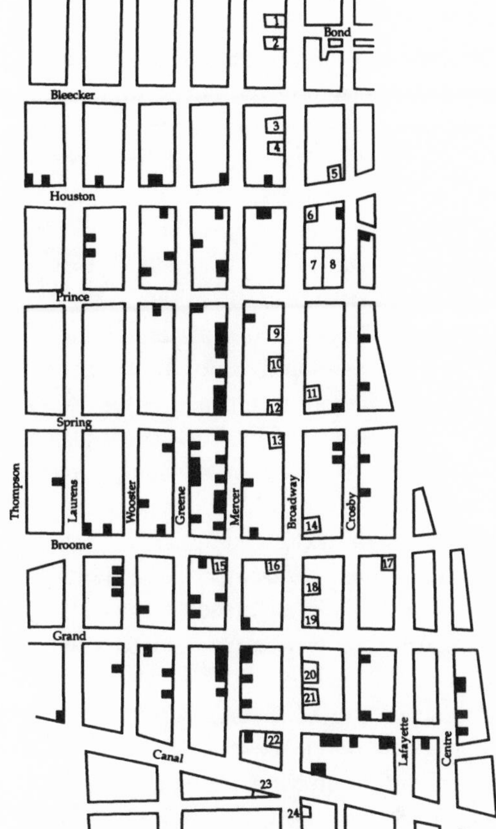

1. Metropolitan Hall/Tripler Hall
   677 Broadway
2. Old Stuyvesant Hall
   Broadway, above Bleeker
3. Pfaff's Cafe (after 1856)
   645 Broadway
4. Laura Keene's Varieties/Olympic Theater
   624 Broadway
5. Hotel de L'Europe
   550 Houston Street
6. Smithsonian Hotel
   604–606 Broadway
7. Metropolitan Hotel
   580 Broadway
8. Niblo's Garden Theater
   Prince & Crosby streets
9. Henry Wood's Marble Hall
   561 Broadway
10. Taylor's Saloon
    555 Broadway
11. Collamore Hotel
    532 Broadway
12. Prescott House
    531 Broadway
13. St. Nicholas Hotel
    519 Broadway
14. Carlton House
    496 Broadway
15. Mercer House
    453 Broome Street
16. Wallack's Theater
    485 Broadway
17. French and Spanish Hotel
    413 Broome Street
18. Mechanics Hall/Bryant's Minstrels
    472 Broadway
19. Minerva Rooms
    460 Broadway
20. Coliseum/City Assembly Rooms
    446 Broadway
21. Fellow's Opera House/Campbell's Minstrels (formerly Mitchell's Olympic Theater)
    444 Broadway
22. City Hotel
    429 Broadway
23. Brandreth House
    415 Broadway
24. New Haven House
    414 Broadway
25. Florence Hotel
    400 Broadway

Hall, and Metropolitan Hall (see map 7). Minstrel shows played nightly at Fellow's Opera, Mechanics Hall, and Wood's Marble Hall. Billiard rooms drew men of all ages and backgrounds. Saloons, liquor shops, and restaurants attracted even larger nighttime crowds.

Throughout the 1850s, a diverse clientele populated Broadway at night. Tourists and the well-to-do rubbed elbows with "bohemians and bummers," in the words of Walt Whitman. Wealthy New Yorkers wined and dined in the leading hotels or restaurants like Delmonico's before rushing off to Niblo's or Wallack's Theater. Numerous Broadway barrooms were located literally underground, below the street. Pfaff's Café (after 1856), Taylor's Saloon, and Platt's Saloon were noted for their cavernous interiors and dimly lit decors. Pfaff's and Taylor's, in particular, enjoyed a reputation as centers for the emerging bohemian and artist subculture in New York. Still other sporting types and working men gathered in Bill Poole's Bank Exchange, Johnny Lyng's Sportsmen's Headquarters, and Stanwix Hall.[5]

Nearly all the hotels along this section of Broadway accommodated prostitutes, some discreetly, some not. "Fallen women of the higher classes," observed the author James D. McCabe, Jr., "abound at the hotels." Another writer claimed that a Broadway hotel was a "potent temptation." Prostitutes, in fact, were "the very best customers" for hotels, according to George Ellington. They attracted more patrons, purchased the hotels' extra services, and were stable sources of income. "The rich miner of mines, the oil speculator, . . . the wealthy European on a tour of inspection, the merchant from the Western city . . . , and the capitalist seeking for an investment,—all these have an overplus of money, and all put up at the very best hotels in the city," noted Ellington. "It is not long before Anonyma finds them out."[6]

Broadway saloons and restaurants also attended to more than just the gastronomic needs of their visitors. The Eureka, Rialto, Evening Star, and Metropolitan Garden saloons, for instance, were all known for their numerous prostitutes. More controversial were restaurants with "private supper rooms." Police Officer Henry Quinn admitted that most restaurants in the vicinity catered in some degree to prostitutes and their clients. James McCabe had these in mind when he wrote that the "principal uptown restaurants [were] largely patronized by disreputable classes." Prostitutes came "to pick up custom, and men to find such companions." Even the "nominally respectable places" were heavily patronized by these groups. Other establishments exhibited "licentious pictures" in their private rooms. Saloons with "upstairs drinking rooms" were similarly described as "primary schools of debauchery," attracting men otherwise unlikely to venture into a brothel.[7]

Broadway, in particular, became Gotham's golden mile of whoredom. "After dark," Walt Whitman admitted in 1857, "any man passing along Broadway, between Houston and Fulton streets, finds the western sidewalk full of prostitutes, jaunting up and down there, by ones, twos, or threes—on the look-out for customers." Most disconcerting to Whitman was that many were "quite handsome" and might under better circumstances have made "respectable and happy women." The Frenchman Ferdinand Longchamp made a similar point a few years later. All large urban centers have their "dens of corruption." But in most cities, prostitution receded from the public gaze and dwelled in remote and isolated streets. New York was different. It "may be doubted whether vice shows itself elsewhere so impudently," he suspected. "[H]ere it displays itself on the most favorite thoroughfare of New York, one which is a sort of Parisian Boulevard for New Yorkers, and at the same time, the pride of commercial men."[8]

By 1870, the erotic nightlife on Broadway had expanded. From Grand Street to Union Square and Fourteenth Street, and then again from Madison Square at Twenty-third Street to Thirtieth Street, Broadway was a magnet for streetwalkers. In the areas near Houston and Greene streets, as many as fifty women would pass by around midnight. The most attractive streetwalkers could be found in the vicinity of Madison Square. "Almost without exception," Edward Crapsey wrote, "they seem in the faint light of the streets to be dressed with elegance and taste, to be handsome in feature and form, and to have left in them something of womanly reserve and modesty."[9]

Directly behind the hotels and theaters on both sides of Broadway, Mercer, Greene, Wooster, and Crosby streets were known for their rich collection of brothels. From 1850 to 1870, in fact, the streets off Broadway contained over 40 percent of the city's prostitution. A typical guidebook described the locale as full of "sumptuous star courtesan[s]" and assignation houses where "love [was] deceived, [and] betrayed." When doctors and sanitary inspectors examined the city's neighborhoods for signs of contagious disease, their reports listed brothels as a separate category, like stores, markets, factories, churches, and tenements. In 1866 alone, they counted 208 brothels and houses of assignation in the neighborhood off Broadway. Teenage girls, "attired in the most gorgeous style of short dresses, low necked and short sleeves, with broad sashes, red garters, and wreaths upon their heads," were common sights in these houses. Such brothels and concert saloons advertised in the daily newspapers. Still others issued their own calling cards to attract customers. Walking the streets of New York, foreign visitors like Edward Dicey were struck by the crowded windows "with wretched half-dressed, or undressed women." New York, he concluded, had "about the most shameless exhibition of public vice [he had] ever come across, even in England or Holland."[10]

The attractive neighborhood and municipal tolerance provided a stable environment for houses of prostitution. Madams in this district remained in business at the same residence for long periods, avoiding the normally frequent moves to escape detection, harassment, and prosecution. According to the leading directories, at least thirty-four brothels operating in 1855 were still thriving in 1859, sixteen under the same owner or occupant listed in tax assessment records. Despite their high visibility, only one of them was ever prosecuted by the district attorney during that time.[11]

Wealthy landlords did little to discourage the salacious use of their real estate. During the 1850s, Walt Whitman noted that landlords raised rents because they knew prostitutes would pay them. "Whole hosts of these [women] have been advancing uptown of later years, and outbidding the workingmen on the question of rent," he remarked. Even the "respectable" were not exempt. Peter Lorillard, of the tobacco family, for example, owned two Howard Street brothels. More common were the likes of William Simers, who recognized a good, quick investment. Labeled a charlatan physician, a "quack advertiser," and a leader in "humbug," Simers obtained a thirty-year lease for three Mercer Street properties in 1821 and immediately built three first-class brothels, leasing one to Mary Wall, one of the richest prostitutes in the city. In 1832, his properties had some of the highest assessments in New York. By the 1840s, he had amassed an estate worth $200,000.[12]

The direct links between real estate, hotels, and prostitution may be seen in the person of Amos R. Eno (figure 18). One of New York's richest men and later owner of the glamorous Fifth Avenue Hotel ("Eno's Folly"), Eno directly controlled some of the leading brothels in the district. Beginning in 1852, he gradually acquired various scattered properties along Mercer and Greene streets. At times working through a third party, Eno rented to publicly known madams like Jane Winslow and Emma Laurian. For several decades, he assiduously monitored these properties, frequently completing physical improvements, ensuring their upkeep, and requiring sureties to compensate him for unpaid rent of tenants.[13]

By midcentury, prostitution was a multimillion-dollar business. William Sanger calculated that the aggregate revenues for those in the trade exceeded $3 million annually. Including additional income from selling liquor and renting houses of assignation, saloons, and the like, the figure doubled. The profits earned in legitimate forms of trade paled in

Fig. 18 Amos Eno

comparison with those from prostitution. In 1855, for example, the individual cash value of manufactured articles like silver wire, oil, soap, and shoes, or in industries like printing, carpentry, shipbuilding, and distilling, was less than $4 million. Only tailor shops in the garment industry, with a cash value of $7.5 million, surpassed that of prostitution. By the end of the Civil War, the gap between profits in customary trade and commerce and that of the underground economy of prostitution was even wider (see table 4).[14]

New York's district attorney confirmed these descriptions of public prostitution. Prior to 1860, the city's chief prosecutor rarely pursued the leading brothels and madams in New York. One 1839 guidebook to brothels directed interested parties to at least 75 specific addresses. Only 5 of them, however, were ever charged by municipal officials during the 1830s and only 10 were indicted in the next decade. By the 1850s, leniency toward prostitution was even more pronounced. Of the 143 different addresses advertised in the city's leading guidebooks, only 7 were charged with any type of disorderly conduct during the entire decade. And by the decade of the Civil War, prostitution was virtually ignored by Gotham's leading law enforcement officers. From 1860 to 1869, a mere eighty-five indictments were issued against the plentiful houses of

TABLE IV
COMPARISON OF THE CASH VALUE OF PROSTITUTION AND MANUFACTURED ARTICLES IN NEW YORK CITY, 1855–1865

	1855	*1865*
Tailor Shops	$7,592,696	—
Prostitution	6,350,760*	—
Silver Wire	3,809,331	—
Steam Engine and Boiler Manufacture	3,292,800	$2,661,000
Shipbuilding	2,593,761	805,000
Gristmills	2,497,719	3,440,867
Chandleries and Soap	2,230,927	1,792,196
Distilleries	2,218,200	1,100,900
Furnaces	2,146,950	2,546,500**
Hot and Cap Manufacture	2,082,502	170,500
Gold and Silver Manufacture	1,966,000	—
Boot and Shoe Manufacture	1,839,100	483,426
Land Oil	1,839,000	—
Butcher Shops	1,763,860	4,350,200
Fish and Whale Oil	1,729,900	364,000
Bakeries	1,727,153	613,310
Gas Manufacture	1,625,500	997,500
Printing	1,545,500	113,500
Breweries	1,377,292	2,320,338
Marble Manufacture	1,154,500	944,300
Sawmills	1,145,000	—

*Total paid to prostitutes and amount spent on liquor, houses of assignation, and saloons with prostitutes.

**Iron foundries and iron rolling.

SOURCES: New York Secretary of State, *Census of New York for 1855* (Albany, 1857), 330–407; *Census of New York for 1865* (Albany, 1867), 420–71, 521; William W. Sanger, *The History of Prostitution* (New York, 1859), 600–606.

prostitution in the city, an average of fewer than nine a year in a city with a minimum of 500 brothels.[15]

An attitude of toleration extended from political leaders to legal magistrates and police officers. The police justice and Whig politico Robert Taylor, as already noted, routinely visited bawdy houses searching for evidence in divorce, criminal, and missing-person cases. Matthew Hale Smith observed that brothel keepers had no motive to hide their business. "The police do not meddle with such, unless they are noisy, disturb the peace, or become a public nuisance," he wrote. "The keepers of such resorts seek custom, and take all possible pains to make their establishments known." As prostitution became more public, better known, and widely advertised, city officials resorted to a policy of "benign neglect" and abandoned any serious effort to eliminate or even suppress it. New York, George Ellington lamented, "will out-Sodom Sodom."[16]

The commercialization of sexuality, of course, was more than just a geographical phenomenon. Its increasing importance was manifest in other leisure institutions. Museums, for example, frequently offered a dash of sex to prospective visitors. In 1850, Dr. Wooster Beach's National Anatomical Museum and Academy of Natural Science, on Broadway, exhibited "figures of men and women naked in lewd, lascivious, wicked, indecent, disquieting and obscene groups, attitudes, and positions." Some exhibits pretended to offer nothing but purely scientific inquiry. Besides diagrams and models of reproductive organs, stages of pregnancy, and dissected breasts, there were examples of "malformations" including a hermaphrodite, a "hottentot female" with an enlarged clitoris, and a model of the physical effects of venereal disease on the human body. The proprietor even displayed a model of "virgin breasts, . . . those rare beauties so peculiar to the female form, without which she would be despoiled of one half her elegance and loveliness." Still other museums permitted soliciting by prostitutes. Even "respectable" museums like P. T. Barnum's famed American Museum conveyed a sense of sexual freedom and were known for "conversations of the other sex." One reporter observed numerous romantic interludes and carnal activities "worthy to be immortalized by the pencil of Caravaggio."[17]

More controversial were theaters that rejected subtlety and sponsored the erotic displays of "model artists." Also called "living statues," "living female paintings," and *"tableaux vivants,"* these were among the most popular entertainments for men after 1840. Onstage, a lone "actress" assumed a stationary pose dressed in tights, transparent clothing, or nothing at all. Themes usually followed a scriptural or classical story, giving the appearance of "high art." "Susannah in the Bath," "Venus Rising from the Sea," and "the Greek Slave" were among the most popular. The female performer, at predetermined points, changed position slightly, thereby permitting the audience a more revealing view. Some theaters even built revolving stages which allowed the performer to expose the more interesting parts of her body to the attentive male audience without moving a muscle. Model artists thus gave New York its first striptease shows.[18]

Palmo's Opera House sponsored a well-advertised performance in 1847, and other theaters followed. In one incident, the performers abandoned their stationary pose and proceeded to dance the polka and minuet while completely nude. "Their gross sights were displayed," reported the *Tribune,* "and men and boys stood at the door distributing prints of naked women to the immense throng of people in Broadway, without the slightest reproof from city authorities." Upon election to office, Mayor Fernando Wood raided these establishments. He still pleased the male throng, however, by parading the seminude performers along Broadway to City

Hall.[19] George Foster remembered police raiding another model-artist exhibition and breaking up

> a squad of naked Olympians . . . wherein Venus was trundled off to the Tombs in a wheelbarrow, minus her chemise, and Bacchus had a narrow escape through the backwindow, leaving his trowsers to the vigilante guardians of the public morals—while the Three Graces—as naked as they were born—made an unsuccessful attempt to scramble, most ungracefully, out at a back basement.

Periodic raids and arrests, however, had little effect. "Instead of ceasing, the exhibitors added to the attractions of their exhibitions," claimed Ned Buntline, "boasting on their show bills of their triumph over law and decency." Model-artist shows were even popular in some upper-class households. Believing that they displayed discipline and self-restraint, genteel couples sometimes permitted such shows during their dinner parties. Visiting New York, Mark Twain remembered (probably with tongue in cheek) the model-artist phenomenon of the 1850s as "that horrid, immoral show . . . [that] everybody growled about." By 1867, however, things had changed. "The model artists play nightly to admiring multitudes," reported Twain. But "now they call that sort of thing a 'Grand Spectacular Drama,' and everybody goes." The titillation led Twain to label it "the wickedest show you can think of." Whereas earlier displays consisted of simply "exhibiting a pack of painted old harlots, swathed in gauze," the new productions included "beautiful clipper-built girls," which laid "a heavier siege to public morals."[20]

Model-artist and striptease shows stimulated the first productions of burlesque in New York. Even elite theaters like Niblo's Garden did little to censor their productions by the 1860s. For example, Alderman Mike Norton remembered seeing about one hundred female dancers in the 1866 production of "The Black Crook" at Niblo's, "most of them wearing the scantiest of attire, the first show of its kind on the American stage to make a feature of the diaphiously *[sic]* draped or semi-nude feminine form." Despite criticism by clerics and moralists, the show ran for 475 performances over sixteen consecutive months, grossing over one million dollars. Similarly, George Templeton Strong heaped praise upon "The White Fawn" two years later, admitting that its popularity and success was attributed to "the well-formed lower extremities of female humanity." Strong concluded that the production was "doubtless the most showy, and the least draped, specimen of what may be called the *Feminine-Femoral* School of Dramatic Art ever produced in New York." The production played before full houses, consisting mostly of enthusiastic men. That same year Lydia Thompson and "her British Blonde Beauty Brigade" made their New York debut. Dressed in tights and exposing arms and breasts, these chorus girls were described by some as "optically edible."[21]

The popularity of sex onstage and the growing tolerance for such theatrical displays contributed to a new entertainment venue—the concert saloon (also called the concert hall). Combining French vaudeville, Italian opera, the German beer garden, and English theater, the concert saloon offered a hybrid brand of entertainment popular among many groups, from native-born, middle-class whites to working-class Irish and German immigrants. Concert saloons were housed in old theaters or three- to four-story buildings. A long bar usually dominated the front room, often decorated with paintings of women in provocative, sensuous poses. To the rear was a stage, which might be little more than a raised platform without any curtain. Concert saloons thus broke the clear spatial division found in theaters, facilitating greater interaction between performer and audience. When vocalists sang, the audience, waiters, and "waiter girls," who were frequently prostitutes, joined in chorus. Performers usually sat in the audience between acts, enabling the women to solicit customers for prostitution in the private rooms and balconies upstairs.[22]

The earliest reference to a concert saloon appeared in 1842. Palmo's and Pinteaux's "musical drinking shops" were the first establishments that sold an entertainment package of music, drink, and sex. Their popularity was almost immediate. "Pinteaux and Palmo are making lots of money," wrote one reporter, "and their success has induced others to follow in their footsteps." Pinteaux's even sponsored balls for Gotham's leading madam, Julia Brown. In 1860, Robert Butler converted the New American Theater, on Broadway, from a dramatic house into a "concert hall" or "music hall." Its immediate popularity rested upon the sale of liquor during performances and the "engagement of handsome and voluptuous waitresses." Calling itself the "Music Hall of the Masses," it ran advertisements promising the "Most Beautiful and Lady-like Waitresses." One observer even claimed (probably erroneously) that in the following year it staged "one of the first nudist exhibitions in America."[23]

By the end of the Civil War, the concert saloon had replaced the theater as the major form of urban entertainment. As "legitimate" theaters, under pressure from purity reformers, redefined the rules of behavior for actor and audience, removing the variety, bawdy, and boisterous material from their performances, popular impulses for cheap but lively entertainment found another outlet. The concert saloon filled the cultural void created by the decline of an egalitarian and democratic theater. By 1866, nearly thirty thousand people nightly attended New York's numerous concert saloons, beer gardens, and music halls. "There are no actors of any . . . note," complained Matthew Hale Smith, "and the pieces put on the stage, except at Wallack's, are a burlesque."[24]

Costume and masquerade balls, displaying similar disdain for sexual modesty, competed with concert saloons. Leading madams sponsored well-publicized and well-attended masked balls throughout the 1840s and 1850s. Julia Brown's was among several Leonard Street brothels known for their "fancy-dress" affairs. Men of wealth and high status regularly attended the prostitute-filled balls of Kate Hastings. On occasion, prostitutes even appeared at elaborate parties sponsored by elite Knickerbockers. In 1841, for instance, George Templeton Strong noticed Julia Brown "with some of her sisterhood" at a magnificent Bleecker Street affair given by Dr. Valentine Mott. At the end of the Civil War, masked balls enjoyed a "reign of prodigality," in the words of one critic. The Ball d'Opera was one of the numerous "French balls" cited as being "masquerades of a low order, [which] degenerated into little better than drunken orgies" where the cancan and other forms of "low entertainment" thrived. Even the balls sponsored by the Cercle Français de l'Harmonie (the sponsor of New York's most popular and well-attended masquerade in the late nineteenth century) were full of prostitutes in various states of undress. Prostitutes became so common at public balls that George Ellington complained in 1869, "[T]his class of women frequent our public assemblages without question, and jostle our wives, mothers and sisters in the throng."[25]

Model artists and brothel balls enjoyed a wider currency thanks, in part, to the spread of pornography after 1840. Improved printing technology and an expanding urban market transformed pornography into a leading growth industry of the urban underground economy. At midcentury, three general forms flourished in New York and other American cities. The first was a direct product of the growth of prostitution—namely, the wide range of guidebooks sold at most corner newsstands and bookstores. These little books, selling for one dollar and small enough to fit into a vest pocket, described for veteran and newcomer alike the most enticing haunts of the sexual underworld. Second, a growing number of salacious literary works with sexual themes, mostly European and often French in subject matter, were sold throughout the city. Finally, a sporting press covered the adventures and institutions of New York's commercial sexual culture, employing the sensationalistic methods of the penny press.

These early ventures into pornography were more literary than visual, containing few illustrations that were explicit, at least by late-twentieth-century standards. When publishers were prosecuted for being "lewd and scandalous," it was written material—brothel addresses, obscene language, sexual gossip—that was the basis of the charge. In many respects, this pornography, with its glorification of "rough" masculinity and sexual promiscuity, helped define New York's sporting-male subculture.

Guidebooks to houses of prostitution were one connecting link between the commercialized world of public sexuality and the fantasies and fears of the nineteenth-century male. Guidebooks did more than serve as directories of the leading courtesans and whorehouses in New York. Their libidinal descriptions and provocative characterizations provided a chimera of sexual extravagance and fantasy for American males. Although such guidebooks appeared in European cities as early as the eighteenth century, the first New York guidebook on record is *Prostitution Exposed* (figure 19), published in 1839 with the fantastic nom de plume Butt Ender. As forms of erotic literature, English guidebooks

Fig. 19 Prostitution Exposed *(1839)*
Collection of Leo Hershkowitz

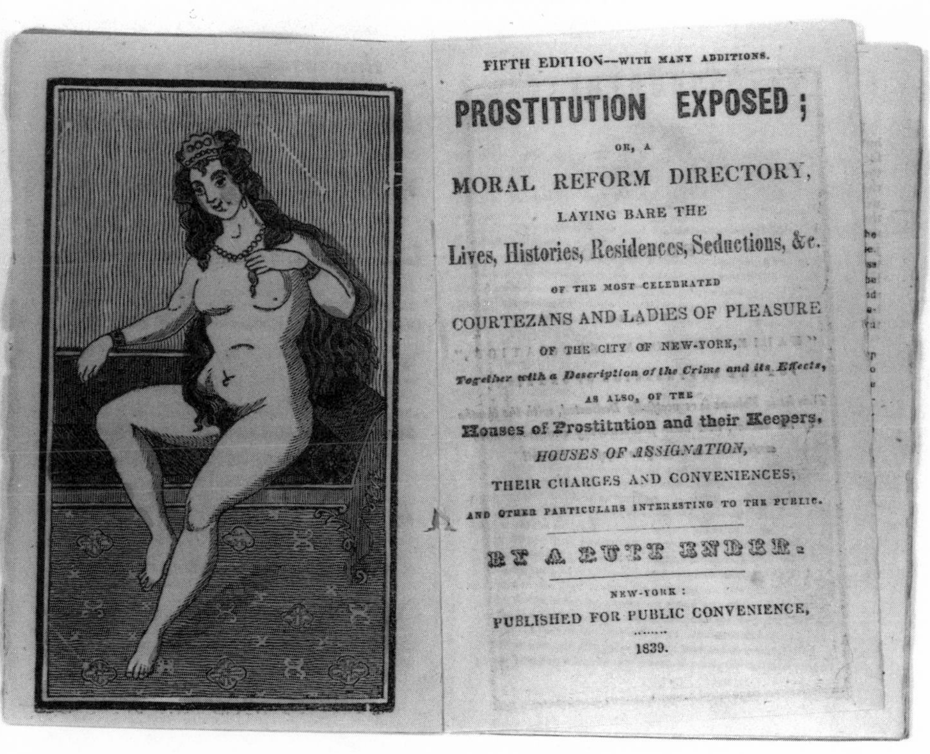

FIFTH EDITION—WITH MANY ADDITIONS.

PROSTITUTION EXPOSED;

OR, A

MORAL REFORM DIRECTORY,

LAYING BARE THE

Lives, Histories, Residences, Seductions, &c.

OF THE MOST CELEBRATED

COURTEZANS AND LADIES OF PLEASURE

OF THE CITY OF NEW-YORK,

Together with a Description of the Crime and its Effects,

AS ALSO, OF THE

Houses of Prostitution and their Keepers,

HOUSES OF ASSIGNATION,

THEIR CHARGES AND CONVENIENCES,

AND OTHER PARTICULARS INTERESTING TO THE PUBLIC.

BY A BUTT ENDER.

NEW-YORK:

PUBLISHED FOR PUBLIC CONVENIENCE,

1839.

tended to be overblown or Rabelaisian in content. Their New York counterparts, in contrast, were priggishly American—pragmatic, straightforward, empirical, and objective. Butt Ender's publication, for example, reproduced occupational and demographic statistics gathered by the New-York Female Moral Reform Society. Others included biographical and family information on leading madams, frequently citing their age, the number of women available, their period of residence at a particular house, and the length of their career in the business. The variety of clientele served was described—southerners, Germans, Frenchmen, sailors, actors at the Park Theater, or visitors at the Astor House, to name a few. Predictably, they justified prostitution as a way to protect virtuous women. "[T]hese 'houses' by affording that gratification," argued one 1855 publication, "are the best safeguards to the virtue of maidens, wives, and widows, who would otherwise be exposed to violence and outrage."[26]

Since these directories to the combat zones of sex were written to entertain as well as to inform, satire was never entirely absent. Butt Ender's *Prostitution Exposed* poked fun at the futile tactics of the Female Moral Reform Society and was whimsically dedicated to these militant female reformers. Furthermore, Butt Ender played on nativist prejudices. Numerous anti-Catholic novels appeared during the 1830s, the most controversial being Maria Monk's *Awful Disclosures of the Hotel Dieu Nunnery of Montreal* (1836), a fabricated, highly erotic account of lurid sexual behavior, priestly cunning, and illegitimate babies behind convent walls. Its sales exceeded 300,000 copies. Depicting convent life as an institutionalized orgy, *Awful Disclosures* has been aptly labeled the "Uncle Tom's Cabin of Know-Nothingism." *Prostitution Exposed* satirized this earthy tale, even referring to brothels as "nunneries."[27] By depicting prostitutes as amorous nuns and brothels as convents full of sexual heretics, guidebooks turned the insecurity of the growing city into forbidden, yet accessible, fantasy.

Traditional pornography likewise grew in popularity. In England, this literature enjoyed a period of popularity during the eighteenth century, but suffered a decline after 1800. Little of it existed by midcentury except for the occasional guidebook on prostitutes. Quite the opposite occurred in New York. Publishers, bookstore owners, and even small newspaper vendors attempted to exploit the popular demand for tempestuous tales of moral turpitude. As early as the 1820s, New York's district attorney prosecuted printers for selling obscene prints and books like *Fanny Hill.*[28] By midcentury, street vendors and bookshops throughout the city sold blatant forms of pornography. According to one newspaper in 1843, nearly every sidewalk stand was substantially "furnished with those things, together with libidinous books with most revolting and disgusting contents." One police raid turned up several thousand prints and books in Henry R. Robinson's Cortlandt Street store. Common and popular titles included *The Cabinet of Venus, The Lustful Turk,* and *The Confessions of a Voluptuous Young Lady of High Rank.* In 1873, Rector Morgan Dix of Trinity Church spoke out against "the nasty illustrated flash weeklies that are sold at every newsstand" in the city.[29]

Endeavors to eliminate sexually explicit material from New York proved futile, and more titles appeared in the bookstores selling illicit sexual materials. *Fanny Hill, The Secret Habits of the Female Sex,* and *The Intrigues and Secret Amours of Napoleon* were typical publications found in many stores. By 1870, America's most famous purity reformer, Anthony Comstock, claimed that pornography was so easily obtained in New York that fines did little to stop its sale, many vendors remaining in the business for years.[30]

The penny press was likewise influenced by the rising demand for sex. If nothing else, coverage of the Jewett-Robinson episode in 1836 and thereafter proved that sex sold. The daily examination of the Robinson trial increased the *Herald*'s circulation in one week to 15,000 per day. Titillating tales with shocking sensuality became a magnet with which to attract a wide readership. The *Tribune,* for example, attacked its competition for publishing "monstrosities of all kinds," including "seductions, rapes, [and] trials of [the abortionist Madame] Costello, with all the disgusting details of her profession." These and other events were "paraded before the whole community, old and young, male and female, so that the public must have become quite well acquainted with the secrets of Licentiousness." Similarly, Charles Dickens derided New York journalism for its "pimping and pandering for all degrees of vicious taste" and characterized reporters as "the vilest vermin and worst birds of prey." An embarrassed Philip Hone condemned "the depravity of the times" reflected by such popular publications. "Everybody wonders how people can buy and read those receptacles of scandal, the penny papers, and yet everybody does encourage them. . . ."[31] More than any other single institution, the penny press transformed the prostitute and abortionist into national celebrities.

The sporting press that thrived after 1840, however, made the penny press look tame. Thaddeus W. Meighan's *Rake,* George Wooldridge's *Whip,* Charles G. Scott, John Vandewater, and William Snelling's *Flash* were published from 1841 to 1843. Similar but less successful publications like the *Libertine* and *Life in New York* appear to have lasted for only a single issue. But the most successful, the *National Police Gazette,* flourished from 1845 to 1933. These weekly journals covered the urban underworld and other forms of "sport." One dedicated itself to "ladies, gossip, gaity and gumption, the stage, turf, fun and frolic." Similarly, the *Libertine* claimed an audience of "epicures" in New York, Philadelphia, Boston, and other American cities. "[T]ales of love, of error, of frailty and of wit" were its subject matter. Sexual titillation was the goal, describing the "[m]emoirs of celebrated females, illustrated, with an exposé of . . . libertines . . . , seductions, and all the failings of the fair sex."[32]

Like the penny press, sensationalistic journalists, and certain moral reformers, the sporting press defended its unprecedented coverage of salacious subjects by feigning objectivity. "We are not the apologists of libertinism. We loathe, detest, abhor, condemn, abjure licentiousness in every form and shape," claimed the *Rake*. "Our part is to hold the mirror up to nature, to show vice in its own image." The *Whip* insisted its primary purpose was to "take a birds' eye view of that wickedness" in the city, to "put in every honest hand a whip." Its editor, George B. Wooldridge, sardonically claimed that his publication was "devoted to the Sports of the Ring, the turf, and city life—such as sprees, larks, criminal conspiracy, seductions, rapes, . . . not forgetting to keep a watchful eye on all brothels and their frail inmates." Similarly, the *New York Sporting Whip* claimed it supported "the suppression of Fornication, Adultery and Seduction" and expressed outrage upon finding madams enticing girls nine to thirteen years old into prostitution. It then listed all their names and addresses.[33] By attacking commercial sex in sensational fashion, the sporting press, like the penny press, glamorized it more.

The appeal of the sporting press rested upon the popularity of commercial sex. Each paper covered a wide range of male sexual pursuits. Advertisements for cures of veneral disease, for example, appeared weekly. The *New York Sporting Whip* had columns entitled "Balls," "Canine" (dog fights), "Fair Sex," "Firemen," "The Turf," "Trotting," "Theatricals," "The Ring," "Walk about Town," and "Vice and Immorality." The *Weekly Rake* frequently included "Tales from the Decameron" on its front page. Another column, "From Our Office Window," described New York's streetwalkers, their origins, and their more attractive qualities. Sexual gossip about sporting men and women was covered in "The Rake Wants to Know" and "Advice Gratis—The Rake Advises." Numerous articles focused on local color. "W.J.," for example, one of the "Bloods of East Broadway," followed "a nymph for miles when he thought it would gratify his lustful desires." Another, "Alfred R——," was a "Blood of Broadway Pave" and "a weak puny youth, . . . [whose] evenings are spent in low bawdy house rum mills; it is a mystery where he obtains the money to support his beastialities." Sometimes it even featured celebrities: "What was it that [the editor] Horace Greeley . . . was talking about to Madame Restelle [the abortionist] in the stairway beside the *Tribune* office?"[34]

Another controversial example of commercialized sex was abortion. As the historian James C. Mohr has shown, doctors and midwives who performed abortions developed specialized practices by the 1840s. The most famous, Madame Costello, Madame Bird, and Ann Lohman, better known as Madame Restelle, advertised "for ladies who have been unfortunate" and "diseases peculiar to females" in the New York daily newspapers. Articles frequently appeared describing and sometimes condemning their activity in the sporting press. By 1840, Restelle herself had offices in New York, Philadelphia, and Newark. During her 1847 abortion trial, she was affluent enough to afford legal counsel from the former district attorney and Tammany Hall leader James T. Brady. Restelle's reputation was so widespread that she was even a subject for popular novelists of the time. By 1870, she resided in a large Fifth Avenue mansion.[35]

Like prostitutes, the city's abortionists enjoyed their greatest period of prosperity from 1840 to 1871. The activities were often linked in the minds of contemporaries. Drs. Thomas ("Lookup") Evans, Jacob Rosenzweig, and Michael A. A. Wolff, as well as female practitioners like Restelle, Julia Grindle, and Ann Burns, were so successful that they could afford large oceanfront homes and substantial estates in New York City by the 1860s. "From 'palatial mansions' in Fifth-Avenue," commented the *Times,* "down to the wretched chambers in the slums of Chatham Street," abortionists accommodated the needs of women from "every rank and condition in life."[36] Ignored for the most part by law enforcement officials, New York's abortionists were left comparatively undisturbed for three decades and were popular "among women of the upper middle strata." Not until the Tweed scandal, the rise of Anthony Comstock, and the creation of the preventive society were abortionists forced to run for cover and adopt more clandestine methods.[37]

The sexual toleration that prevailed in these years sometimes extended to homosexuality. Cultural historians have noted the celebration of male love frequently found in Walt Whitman's poetry, and his references to "sleeping" with various men in his journal, as possible evidence of a nascent male homosexual subculture. And indeed, during the 1840s a small but noticeable one appeared. Reportedly, these men were distinguished by their youth and "feminine appearance and manners." The sporting press insisted that their numbers were growing and that they congregated in the vicinity of City Hall Park and farther south, on Cedar

Street. Many were associated with the theater. Like those of prostitution, cases of sodomy, or "buggery," were seldom prosecuted by public officials during these years. One German visitor claimed that attitudes regarding homosexuality were considerably more lenient in America than in his native land. The historian Michael Lynch, after examining most of the nineteenth-century court records on sodomy charges, has concluded that homosexuality was never perceived as a threat to the family, a psychic disorder, or an ideological danger. There was even greater toleration of homosexuality than of prostitution. Rarely considered a sexual issue, homosexuality was not a scapegoat for social problems.[38]

When criticism of homosexual activity was aired, it focused on effeminate behavior and the foreign origins of the participants. The sporting press was perhaps the most homophobic. The *Whip,* for example, consistently referred to homosexuals as "brutal sodomites," "abominable sinners," and "beasts who follow that unhallowed practice." They were stereotyped as extortionists of "men of respectability." Others were described as foreign threats to American masculinity, being of either French, English, or Jewish heritage. In another issue, the *Whip* attacked stage actors, warning the theater owner Ferdinand Palmo that he had "one of these monsters among [his] performers." Throughout New York, the paper insisted, "sodomites" performed "terrible enormities now winked at."[39]

In his fictional account of the underworld, *City Crimes; or, Life in New York and Boston* (1849), George Thompson evinced similar prejudices. Homosexuals were "beasts in human shape." They had "perverted appetites." They were guilty of "a crime against nature." At a masked ball, the Spanish ambassador "made a diabolical proposal to Josephine Franklin, whom he supposed to be a boy." Most homosexuals, Thompson proclaimed, were part of "the tribe of genteel foreign vagabonds who infest the city."[40]

In some cases, this fictional homosexual world overlapped with the real-life one of the prostitute. In 1836, for example, Peter Sewally, a black thirty-three-year-old lifetime resident of New York, was convicted of grand larceny. It was not his crime or race, however, that attracted attention, but rather the feminine attire he was wearing when arrested (figure 20). Sewally, in some measure, illustrated the ambiguous sexuality found in the subculture of commercial sex. Adopting the alias Mary Jones, Sewally admitted that he lived in a Greene Street brothel, performing cooking and domestic tasks and often greeting male patrons at the door. He frequently dressed in female clothes, he claimed, because he "looked so much better in them." Furthermore, Sewally testified that cross-dressing like this was hardly unique. While living in New York

Fig. 20 "The Man Monster"—Peter Sewally, alias Mary Jones (1836) New-York Historical Society, NYC

and visiting in New Orleans, Sewally insisted that he had "always attended parties among the people of [his] own color dressed in this way."[41]

Quite likely, Sewally's employment in a popular brothel involved more than just cooking and cleaning. It reveals that certain forms of homosexuality, even male prostitution, were probably tolerated and linked to the brothel subculture during these years. Passing references sometimes implied the presence of male homosexuals in certain houses of prostitution. Descriptions of midcentury brothels in the sporting press, for example, occasionally mentioned the presence of "male prostitutes" inside. In addition, several New York district attorneys prosecuted brothels for "harboring" young boys (in contrast to "abducting"), possibly for the purpose of letting them prostitute with male clients. Since the sharp distinctions between homosexual and heterosexual behavior did not appear until the late nineteenth century (the term "homosexual" did not enter English usage until the 1880s), antebellum observers were quite likely describing sexual activity that was later labeled "homosexual."[42]

Most critiques of such effeminate males—"queens" or "fairies," as they were called—focused on their gender behavior, not just on their sexual activity. George Thompson's homosexuals were condemned, for example, because they were "boys who *prostitute* themselves." For similar reasons, homosexuals in brothels were labeled "male prostitutes." Instead of behaving like "normal" heterosexual men, these males assumed the gender roles of women. More important, the historian George Chauncey, Jr., has shown that by the end of nineteenth century many believed that virile or "normal" males accepted sexual advances by homosexual men because they were so highly sexed that even women were unable to satisfy them. Homosexual males were suspected not simply of inverting sexual behavior but rather of adopting "weak" and "passive" female roles.[43] If "men of respectability" were subjected to extortion, and "sodomites" were growing in visibility, as the sporting press charged, then portions of Chauncey's hypothesis might well apply during the antebellum years. What twentieth-century observers would define as "homosexual" was seen merely as homosocial.

In this environment, sexuality was frequently politicized. In 1844, for example, Alderman Caleb S. Woodhull recommended the elimination of the third tier in all city theaters "by exclusion of *frailty* from places of public amusement." Acknowledging the suggestions of "jurists and legislators of esteemed reputation," he rejected the regulation or legalization of prostitution as a solution. Woodhull's report nevertheless instigated a debate, which continued for three decades, concerning the relationship between the state and the prostitute. In 1846, the Common Council required the newly created police force to report all bawdy houses to their captains, a policy that ultimately led to de facto regulation and greater corruption. The state legislature even debated rigid regulation of sexuality. A variety of proposals included incarceration and heavy fines for brothel keepers ($100 to $300), clients of prostitutes ($1,000 to $5,000), adulterers ($500 to $1,000), and the impregnators of young, unmarried females ($1,000 to $5,000).[44] None passed.

Generally, sexual-purification campaigns were infrequent and of little avail. Police Captain John McManus's 1850 raid in Five Points and Mayor Fernando Wood's ill-fated and politically expedient program in 1857 of harassing and arresting the city's streetwalkers were the most prominent political attempts to eliminate prostitution until the moral reconstruction efforts of Anthony Comstock after 1871. By 1860, some reformers were acknowledging the futility of publicly suppressing sexuality. "New evils are to come up, requiring new remedies," admitted the Children's Aid Society. "The crowding of young girls in large factories and shops will generally prevent prostitution, yet it also at times gives occasion for it." Young women, "with the passion for amusement, or the impulse of vanity, . . . are often easily led away." Purity reformers called for a new strategy to counteract New York's emerging libertine culture.[45]

In lieu of moral sanctification, however, still others called for greater sexual toleration. In 1835, Assistant Alderman John J. Boyd of the First Ward offered an alternative to suppression—the legalization of prostitution. Although never formally adopted in New York, proposals like Boyd's were repeatedly debated thereafter. In 1849, for example, Charles P. Daly, chief judge of the Court of General Sessions and the presiding judge in the Astor Place riot trial, recommended the same (figure 21). Withstanding journalistic outrage, Daly considered prostitution a "necessary evil" in a growing metropolis. Ned Buntline, a later critic of Daly's stance, immediately agreed. "[I]f the city government is too weak and sickly to sustain its rights, why not license the gamblers and courtesans, and make the ills which they cannot prevent a source of city revenue." Others concurred, arguing that the municipality prohibited the sale of poisons, invoked quarantine regulations during epidemics, and even prohibited citizens from entering disease-ridden districts. "The gaudy prostitute, however, who teems with death, whose touch is as deadly as the kissings of the asp, and who sows fevers and consumptions in every foul embrace, goes uncorrected in her accursed vocation," maintained one editor. As a sanitary measure, municipal regulation of prostitution would protect whole families and future generations "from the reproductive penalties of the curse."[46]

Other prominent New Yorkers echoed Daly's recommendation. "There are certain propensities and passions inherent in our nature which will have vent in one shape or another, despite all the combined legislative wisdom of communities," argued Walt Whitman. "It has always been so, it is now so, and until some radical change takes place in frail human nature, it will always be so." Harsh laws were futile, a dead letter. Regulating prostitutes would provide "a safety valve for the . . . excesses which would otherwise prey upon the vitals of the community with a far more destructive effect." Blind prejudice, Whitman believed, should never "stand in the way of a tangible benefit."[47]

After a sociological study of the prostitutes incarcerated in the City Hospital, the resident physician William Sanger admitted in 1859 that it was "a mere absurdity to assert that prostitution can ever be eradicated." Antiprostitution laws in New York were worthless and impractical. Remnants of Anglo-Saxon prudery, they contributed to greater evils rather than abating them. In conjunction with compulsory schooling, sex education, and enforcement of marriage laws (which he believed would end many of the causes of prostitution), Sanger supported munic-

Fig. 21 Charles P. Daly

ipal regulation. "Government should be patriarchal in its character, and exercise an effective but parental supervision over all its subjects."[48]

After the Civil War, others echoed Sanger's plea. In 1867, acting on a request by the state assembly, the recently created Metropolitan Board of Health urged regulation. "To acknowledge a vice is not to applaud it," it concluded. The board member and physician Willard Park called for the registration of all city prostitutes. Similarly, Inspector William F. Thomas insisted that since statutes were ineffective in eliminating prostitution, "laws should be enacted to control, by imposing a fine, when disease is found among" the city's prostitutes. The Greenwich Village sanitary inspector Dr. F. A. Burrell concurred. Legalization and medical regulation, he said, are the most efficacious methods "for preserving society from the ravages of a pernicious and inveterate disease, . . . while practically giving it less encouragement than it at present enjoys." After visiting the Seventh Ward, along the East River, a third inspector reluctantly admitted that "something should be recommended to mitigate or stay the ravages of syphilis." For nearly a decade, legalization efforts continued. Something drastic was necessary, the *Nation* insisted in 1867, as prostitution was "becoming more virulent and deadly."[49]

That same year, Judge Charles J. Folger drew up a bill regulating prostitution in New York, but it was never introduced, because of opposition from Susan B. Anthony and other enemies of legalization. And in 1876, a grand jury recommended regulation, concluding, "[L]egislation to suppress prostitution is and must be ineffective. . . . [I]t is an evil impossible to suppress." Its expansion, the jury continued, made property "in many portions of the city . . . almost worthless for occupancy by respectable persons, either for business or for residence." Proponents of legal commercial sex were pragmatic. "The truth . . . must be plainly told, and no prudish delicacy must be allowed to prevent the adoption," wrote Edward Crapsey. While not eliminating prostitution, legalized prostitution would "do more to mitigate it than anything else."[50]

MORE than most of his contemporaries, Walt Whitman was aware of the sexual paradoxes of midnineteenth-century New York. "You prostitutes flaunting over the trottoirs or obscene in your rooms," he wrote in *Leaves of Grass,* "who am I that I should call you more obscene than myself."[51] Even Whitman's poetry recognized a transformation in sexual behavior in antebellum New York. If the years from 1820 to 1920 made up the century of prostitution in New York, the decades between 1836 and 1871 were the halcyon years of commercialized sex. From the Jewett-Robinson affair to the rise of Anthony Comstock and the preventive-society movement in the 1870s, prostitution was a spectacular reminder of a new sexual culture. Seen together, the rise and toleration of prostitution, pornography, model-artist shows, the concert saloon, the sex district, and even the beginnings of a distinct homosexual subculture marked the rejection of an older, preindustrial, patriarchal sexuality. More than ever before, ideas regarding sexual etiquette were shaped and affected primarily by public life in the city, not by the private enclave of the church or the family. Commerce preceded Christianity in determining real sexual behavior. This was a remarkable departure from the community-regulated, noncommercialized structure of preindustrial sexuality.

The new sexual culture gave men unprecedented sexual freedom. It reflected an increasing emphasis on individualism and personal choice in erotic matters. At its foundation, however, this reorganized sexuality was male centered, if not misogynist. More than ever before, women were perceived as objects and images to purchase, judged by their sexual talents, and measured in terms of monetary exchange and value. Perhaps it was no accident that these years also saw increasing abuse of women in the street, violent attacks on brothels, rising levels of assault and battery, and more instances of homelessness, vagrancy, and child abandonment. While women may have benefited from increased accessibility to abortion, in the attempt to move in and out of this commercialized sexual underworld, they faced far more severe constraints than did their male counterparts. Even abortion itself was a procedure fraught with danger and potential loss of life. The historical record tells little about how the average woman perceived and reacted to these changes, but it is unlikely that many applauded.

7 A "GAY" LITERATURE

PROSTITUTES like Julia Brown, Caroline Hastings, and Jane Williams were not just criminal defendants appearing in police indictments or penny press articles. By the midnineteenth century, popular writers and reporters incorporated courtesans into their subterranean portraits of the nocturnal mysteries of the metropolis. Dime novelists, too, treated readers to the same salacious images in their fictional accounts of New York. In publications ranging from newspapers to novels, seductive female characters possessed "voluptuous busts," "exquisitely rounded limbs," "heavenly charms," and "beautiful globes . . . so round and firm."[1] Commercial sex, growing more open and public, contributed to a new commercialized and popular city culture. For antebellum readers, prostitutes were the stuff of literature.

Numerous antebellum novelists introduced living, contemporary prostitutes in their writings on the New York underworld. George Thompson, for example, described an international ring of women labeled *Les Filles de Venus* (Daughters of Venus) in his semipornographic novel *The Countess; or, Memoirs of Women of Leisure* (1849). This "Ladies Free and Easy Club" hatched plots, he wrote, "to catch the thoughtless with the tempting bait" of commercial sex. Thompson filled the organization with characters like the abortionist Madame Restelle, mistress Amelia Norman, and prostitutes Kate

Winslow and Caroline Hastings. Together, they described their perverse and erotic adventures as part of an exaggerated conspiracy of female wealth and evil.

It is significant that these characters were not just products of Thompson's vivid imagination. Rather, all of these women were prominent midcentury figures. Restelle, called "the wickedest women in the city" by abortion critics, was the most prolific practitioner of the trade in America by the 1840s. The "charming" Caroline (or Catherine) Hastings and Kate ("Fanny") Winslow were leading prostitutes in the city, winning frequent acclaim in the sporting press. Whenever Winslow appeared on Broadway or in the Battery, for example, her expensive, horse-drawn carriage drew "the attention of all," according to one reporter. Hastings attracted considerable notice when she physically attacked the editor and writer Ned Buntline for slandering her in his newspaper. And Amelia Norman, a noted prostitute and "kept women," dramatically stabbed her former lover Henry Ballard on the steps of the Astor House in 1843. She was later acquitted of attempted murder.[2]

Thompson was not alone in employing this technique. In his novel *Celio; or, New York Above-Ground and Under-Ground* (1850), George G. Foster "fictionalized" portions of his alleged interviews with two brothel prostitutes previously published in his exposé *New York by Gas-Light* (1850). Harrison Gray Buchanan's *Asmodeus* (1848) described the well-known prostitute Jane P. Williams and her Duane Street house, considered "the most dangerous and detested brothel" by the *Whip*. Buchanan also wrote at great length on Fanny Okille and Julia Brown's brothel at 55 Leonard Street, as well as the noted establishment of Annie Clark at 43 Wooster Street. And the writer John D. Vose mentioned seeing Mrs. Livingston, "an eighth ward heiress," in his fictitious explorations of New York street life in *Fresh Leaves from the Diary of a Broadway Dandy* (1852). One guidebook three years later listed Livingston as a prominent madam in an Eighth Ward brothel.[3]

By merging fiction and nonfiction, antebellum authors created an illusion of authenticity in their dramatic narratives. Again and again, writers stressed the accuracy and realism of their sensational stories. Thompson, for example, bluntly proclaimed that his novels *The Countess* and *City Crimes; or, Life in New York and Boston* (1849) were "not fiction, but . . . fact." The wild and unbelievable tales "may seem impossible," he acknowledged, "but it is all true." Similarly, Ned Buntline (or Edward Zane Carroll Judson) in his best-selling *The Mysteries and Miseries of New York* (1848) insisted that "strange as all may be," the stories were "drawn from *life.*" and George Foster repeated the same at the start of *Celio,* claiming that the book was "drawn from real life."

In these melodramatic accounts, no key was necessary to introduce readers to certain individual characters. The names and images were recognized by most New Yorkers and spoke directly to their experiences. "There are some of them [underworld characters] who cannot fail of being known everywhere," wrote the anonymous author of *Revelations of Asmodeus* (1849), "the originals being of world-wide celebrity."[4]

This transformation of the prostitute into an urban celebrity emerged from a larger literary preoccupation with the "wronged woman" after 1830. As increasing numbers of young urban females entered the labor market, moralists and novelists alike treated seamstresses, factory girls, and female migrants as major subjects. The fallen woman was an integral part of this new antebellum canon. As David Reynolds has shown, several types of moral reform genres evolved out of evangelical Protestantism and the Second Great Awakening. At first, conventional moral reform literature focused on hopeful themes and characters. The blissful home in the pastoral village with nurturing parents and angelic children advertised the deserved results of a life-style of self-improvement and hard work. Rational in tone and restrained in message, such works avoided sensationalism. Ministers like Joseph Tuckerman and William Ellery Channing, reformers like Horace Mann, and novelists like Catharine M. Sedgwick epitomized this style and thought.[5]

As commercial sex became increasingly visible and prevalent in antebellum cities, however, numerous antiprostitution reformers grew dissatisfied with such idyllic imagery and simplistic interpretations of prostitution. Ultimately, they responded with more unconventional styles to advertise their outrage. Beginning with the Presbyterian minister John McDowall in 1833, "immoral" moral reformers openly discussed previously forbidden themes of prostitution and other forms of extramarital sexuality. They defended the airing of soiled social linen as a necessary first step to cleansing society. "Ignorance of vice is no security for virtue," concluded one such author in 1835. But when a grand jury ruled that *McDowall's Journal* was "calculated to promote lewdness," publication ceased. Nevertheless, the subject of sexuality was injected into public debate and popular literature. The ensuing decades witnessed a widespread fascination with prostitution and other forms of illicit sexuality by a multitude of writers, artists, and observers.[6]

Sporting-male descriptions of prostitutes initially countered those of evangelical outrage. Upon the murder of the famed courtesan Helen Jewett in 1836, graphic artists and newspaper reporters portrayed the victim in an alluring, seductive manner. The most notable was Henry R. Robinson, a well-known political cartoonist and supporter of the Whig party. Robinson (no relation to Richard) published several images of the victim and defendant, including one with the murdered Jewett topless in bed (figures 9 and 11). The prints proved to be so popular that Henry Robinson embarked on a short-lived career as a pornographer. When city officials finally closed his printshop in 1842, they discovered several thousand obscene prints and books in his possession.[7]

Fascination with Jewett led to similar prints and illustrations in ensuing years (figures 13–15). By the late 1830s, in fact, guidebooks to brothels began appearing. These publications similarly emphasized the beauty and sex appeal of their subjects. Although little remembered and confined to individual archives and personal collections today, these physically small and socially satirical works probably reached the widest audience of any of the descriptions of prostitutes. Sold in bookstores and corner newstands, Butt Ender's *Prostitution Exposed* (1839) (Figure 19), Charles DeKock's *Guide to the Harems* (1855), and the anonymously published *Gentleman's Companion* (1870) and *Gentleman's Directory* (1870) presented arrays of women willing to satisfy a variety of sexual needs.[8] Even visual images like "Hooking a Victim" depicted streetwalkers, usually considered the lowest prostitutes, as attractive young women in elegant gowns and bonnets, surrounded by gentlemen of substance (figure 22). By these accounts, prostitutes not only enjoyed financial independence but were celebrities of national repute. Far from being a threat to society, these women epitomized the sexual freedoms of urban life for the sporting male.

Most popular authors, however, presented prostitutes in much more deprecating or sentimentalized ways. Ned Buntline, George Foster, and George Thompson, in particular, exploited the public's fascination with commercial sexual culture, but in a style that reinforced the values of middle-class domesticity in their conclusions. Several of Buntline's dime novels—*The Mysteries and Miseries of New York,* and its sequels *Three Years After* (1849), *The B'hoys of New York* (1850), and *The G'hals of New York: A Novel* (1850)—specifically centered their stories on the sporting-male and prostitute subcultures of antebellum New York.[9] The prostitute Isabella Meadows, for example, is depicted as a soiled dove. Coming from a protected childhood and affluent family, Isabella falls in love with the rake Henry Whitmore. But Whitmore's repeated verbal assurances of love leave Isabella unconvinced, especially when she discovers his plans for a "mock marriage." Frustrated, Whitmore finally drugs and seduces her. But Isabella forgives his treachery and remains faithful to Whitmore until he abandons her to a life of prostitution in the well-known brothel at 100 Church Street.

Buntline's New York is a city of extremes, a battleground where the forces of civilization meet those of savagery, represented by innocent

Fig. 22 "Hooking a Victim" (1851)
Museum of the City of New York

virginity and sexual promiscuity, respectively. Dire consequences await the Isabellas, whether they are forced or seduced into the life of the underworld. Sexuality serves as a vehicle transporting any occupant down into the depths of barbarism. Not surprisingly, Isabella is joined by her brother Charles, who follows a similar route to moral degradation by way of gambling. Together, they function as metaphors of warning. Parents should protect their offspring, writes Buntline, "before the arrows in the hands of the unwhipped villains reach your *own* hearts!" Sporting men, like those leading Isabella and Charles astray, look at women "*only* as slaves—things to bend to the pleasure of man."

Women, in particular, face only misery. "Who is there of her unhappy class in this city who do not feel it? Not one! They smile and laugh—they try hard to be gay, but oh what sad and aching hearts beat beneath their bosoms; what agonizing thoughts darken their gayest moments." So deep are the tragedies of prostitutes that they "are praying for death." Isabella, losing all sense of balance and goodness, conspires against Whitmore for the remainder of the novel and its sequels. Her thirst for vengeance culminates in insanity. "Go tell the raving maniac not to be mad," she screams. "[T]ell the serpent not to bite—tell the lion not to play with the lamb—tell the childless widow not to weep, but do not tell me not to be wretched." The novel, however, ends without resolution. In a final confrontation, Charles tries to defend his sister's lost honor but succeeds only in stabbing Whitmore in the shoulder. Charles and Isabella finally leave New York, while Whitmore and his accomplices go free.[10]

Despite the harsh imagery that permeates *Mysteries* and *Three Years After,* Buntline sometimes acknowledges that prostitutes are motivated by economic necessity or financial gain. Some of his "G'hals" are frustrated working girls who "threw up their situations in disgust, and became—*you can easily guess what!*" When the sisters Mary and Susan discuss the need to prostitute in order to pay their rent, virtue is called "an angel's maxim" and the brothel a "woman's last refuge." Indirectly, Buntline defends a woman's choice to prostitute, admitting that "the harlot is better paid for one night's act of shame, than poor honest virtue often gets for a *month's* unceasing labor." In *Mysteries,* he even criticizes the double standard at one point, saying that it is "a poor rule which will forever blast a woman's fame, if she yields to the persuasions of a seductive man; and, at the same time, let the man pass scot-free from censure."[11]

Nevertheless, the most common image of the prostitute was that of the innocent virgin like Isabella, tricked and seduced into commercial sex. In numerous other fictional accounts, young, American-born women are frail, weak, and easily manipulated. Seduction quickly evolves into prostitution, leading down a road with no return. In Marie Louise Hankins's *Women of New York* (1861), for example, Clara Collins, who is seduced by a married man, abandoned, and disowned by her family, ends up a lonely prostitute. After Mary Montgomery is seduced by and married to a bigamist in Eleanor Maria Ames's *Up Broadway* (1870), she suffers sudden descent into prostitution. Even writers critical of the double standard see this condition as final. "[A] woman who once loses her virtue," writes George Thompson in *The Gay Girls of New-York; or, Life on Broadway* (1854), "can never recover her position in society—while the man who sins a thousand times, is a thousand times applauded." Described as "deceived, down-trodden, wounded and cast out," the prostitute finds few sympathizers, according to John D. Vose. Fallen women have "every generous sentiment . . . smothered, every noble effort crushed, every fond hope blasted—all scattered."[12]

Buntline and others frequently invoke the theme of insanity. In *The B'hoys of New York,* for example, Agnes Morton is seduced and forced to become a prostitute. She is "lost—and more, she is a *maniac,*" writes Buntline. "Reason has fled from its throne. . . ." Likewise, George Foster, in *Celio,* initially argues that prostitution is unnatural and "a species of insanity." Henry Williams, in *Gay Life in New-York* (1866), even depicts brothel prostitutes as irrational nymphomaniacs. "I thought I should go mad," exclaims a prostitute describing her own seduction. His kisses "fired me with mad, tempestuous fury." Society associates reason and self-control with goodness and truth, quickly equating evil and sexual promiscuity with the absence of reason. Prostitution is powerful sexuality, and it marks the starting point for all forms of perversity, for criminality, and, ultimately, for insanity.[13]

Themes of seduction, perversity, and insanity also appear in the sensationalist writings of George Foster. Best known for his reportage in the *Tribune* and for his popular exposés *New York by Gas-Light, New York in Slices* (1849), and *New York Naked* (1850), Foster made little distinction between his fictional and nonfictional representations of prostitutes. In *Celio,* for example, he provides personal and anecdotal testimony of two prostitutes, Miss Virginia and Miss Margaret. During Virginia's narration, Foster makes explicit the erotic danger she presents, noting that "her well-formed bosom, partially exposed by the dress she wore . . . heaved tumultuously, and her symmetrical and well-knit frame shivered with passion." Virginia proceeds to describe herself as the daughter of an upstate New York farmer. At age fifteen, she is seduced by a visiting cousin and then by the local minister. Her parents are so distraught upon discovering her sexual activity that her mother dies and her father turns to alcohol and loses his farm. Virginia then walks to New York City to work as a prostitute, quickly becoming a leading figure in the city's brothels.[14]

Virginia, however, is no fallen angel. Indeed, she moves to New York explicitly "to seek and execute revenge upon mankind." Prostitution is a choice on her part, and she admits to having "perverted and unnatural appetites." Her willingness to prostitute is explained as a type of opportunistic witchcraft. "I am a demon—a she-devil," explains Virginia, "as are all women who have lost their virtue; and I mean to make the most of it." Indeed, Foster often employed this image of the prostitute as a kind of urban witch, even in nonfictional accounts. In *New York Naked,* for example, he writes that, once she turns to prostitution, the "woman becomes a demon in her turn, and preys remorselessly upon her insensate victims." Similarly, in *New York by Gas-Light,* Foster claims that the Five Points prostitute is a woman "transformed to a devil and there is no hope for her."[15]

In contrast, Miss Margaret enjoys none of the benefits of a secure upbringing. She grows up amid poverty in a Five Points cellar with drunken parents. As a child, she works as a street sweeper. The temptations of the *pave* prove too great, and by the age of ten, she is running a brothel. Margaret openly defends her life-style. "I don't feel that I have done wrong," she argues. "I live freely and generously, dress like a princess, drink, eat and sleep like a king's mistress, and care for nobody on earth." Foster even strengthens this image by including a footnote quoting a *Sunday Courier* story in 1849 describing a ten-year-old girl recently sent to the House of Refuge for running a house of prostitution.[16]

For the women in these books, prostitution is not simply seduction, fall, and death. Foster overlays his characters with bourgeois themes of domesticity and true womanhood, suggesting that prostitutes react with horror to their lives. But when prostitutes speak, they exhibit an ironic degree of personal agency in their predicament. In a world that forever condemns them for one accident, few alternatives exist. More specifically, sex gives them a certain power that "virtuous" women or honest working girls never enjoy. Prostitutes may have bouts of insanity or depression, but they do not starve or live in abject poverty.

Of course, when prostitutes exhibit such control, the specter of evil is never far behind. For both Buntline and Foster, prostitutes are also nineteenth-century Eves, temptresses on a mission to lure innocent youths down paths of perdition. In *New York by Gas-Light* and *New York in Slices,* Foster describes Broadway prostitutes as "fishers of men," "painted demons," "beldames and she-devils," always in search of "victims." Theater prostitutes, in particular, initiate bargains that corrupt the body and deform the soul "to the likeness of hell." Similarly, prostitutes like Big Lize and Kate Buckley in Buntline's *Mysteries and Miseries* (1848) run panel houses and are professional tricksters, always looking for ways to tempt and fool men. "Having herself been made a victim," Buntline summarizes, the streetwalker looks "for someone to victimise." In Buntline's most extreme depiction, the millionairess Magdalena Van Linden is seduced, married, and abandoned by a confidence man. She then opens a panel house, leads a life of crime, captures her runaway husband, imprisons him in a basement, and starves him to death.[17]

Other novelists repeated this theme of sexual revenge. In Osgood Bradbury's *Female Depravity* (1857), Clara Hopkins induces wealthy Charles Henderson to accompany her to a house of ill fame, hoping to trick him into "seducing" her and thereby force a marriage. Bradbury describes Henderson as "caught in a silken net" and warns about "the attentions and caresses of beautiful, accomplished, yet meretricious women who throng all our large cities." The dangers of the seduced innocent turned prostitute are more sharply illustrated in Bradbury's *Ellen Grant* (185?). After her seduction by a Methodist preacher in her hometown, Ellen moved to New York, "where she became a wanton." When her seducer settles in the city disguised as a doctor, she successfully plots revenge, posing as a mulatto and finally killing him. In still another Bradbury novel, the protagonist remarks, "[T]he truth compels me to say that my own sex are often engaged in the same unholy work, and are quite if not more dangerous than the male anglers; for they know better the weak points, which are first to be attacked."[18]

The prostitute as a source of male ruin knows no bounds in some accounts. In *Revelations of Asmodeus* (1849), the prostitute is "the false slave . . . [whose] pretences of love are only to wheedle him out of more money to gratify her extravagant humors in part, but still more, to lavish on a worthless fellow, whom she really loves with a fond affection." Even when murdered, the prostitute is the culprit. In a fictionalized account of Helen Jewett's life, Joseph Holt Ingraham claims, "*She* was the seducer, *not* he. . . . Her beauty was her power, and she triumphed in it. She felt a sort of revenge against the other sex, and used every art to tempt and seduce and ruin young men."[19] Ultimately, these stark examples of female conspiracy enabled authors to conflate unregulated female sexuality and criminality.

Themes of virginity turned into vengeful insanity reached their height with George Thompson. More than any other writer, Thompson made prostitutes primary protagonists in this literature of sexual pathology. In *The Countess,* for example, the major character, Louisa, acts as a metaphor for the betrayal of republican virtue. Born in New England, granddaughter of a signer of the Declaration of Independence, she is well educated, precocious, and mischievous. "Charm succeeded charm," and by the age of twelve she is a model of beauty, possessing "a form of the most exquisite mold."

Louisa's beauty quickly attracts men and makes women jealous. She manipulates her physical charms to her advantage. While being courted by the son of a wealthy Philadelphia doctor (implied to be Benjamin Rush, the Revolutionary patriot), she wears a loose, low-necked dress expressly to display, in her words, as "much of [her] voluptuous bust as possible." Her methods produce the desired result: "his passions had assumed the realm of reason . . . [and] his hands were soon in close communication with my breasts. . . . His passions rose by degrees, and I saw the proud aristocrat changed to a slave." But when his hand touched her knee and "then still higher," she "broke from his embrace," chastising him for assuming such liberties. Just as dramatically, he proposes marriage. She refuses, whereupon he pulls a knife, promising to kill her and then commit suicide. But failing to act, he quickly apologizes and leaves.[20]

Louisa's parents then move to Boston, where she finds the restrictions placed on her behavior onerous. She rebels in order to experience, as she says, "the pleasures of the world." Louisa proceeds to meet a series of suitors and sporting men, many of whom are so overcome by her that they propose marriage upon a single encounter. But suddenly her father dies, and Louisa is pushed into poverty. Her solution is to move to New York, where she begins a series of complicated intrigues with numerous "gentlemen" of the city. In time, she grows disenchanted with the sexual and moral duplicity surrounding her. After visiting church one day, she resolves to remove her "gay attire" and leaves New York forever.[21]

Louisa's story is a tale of inverted domesticity. Beneath the images of sexual promiscuity and Thompson's semipornographic style is a defense of female purity, piety, and submissiveness. Louisa hopes other girls will "learn a . . . lesson that may be the means of saving their honor and virtue." Elsewhere she proclaims that whenever a woman "stoops to enjoy the passions of the flesh, she falls forever from the high pinnacle on which nature and heaven ordained her to stand." Noble intentions aside, Louisa embodies negative stereotypes of prostitutes. She is full of falsehood and dishonesty. "She knows how to be many women in one," Thompson writes. Like many a "coquette," she spends much of her time scheming to seduce men in order to get their money. Louisa tricks men and women alike into following her, seeking "companions in her pleasure and . . . spread[ing] wide her net . . . with the tempting bait of her charms." And she derives strength from this activity. She relishes how males wilt before her physical allure, seeing respectable men enslaved to her disreputable offerings.[22]

In his later novel *The Gay Girls of New-York,* Thompson resorts to perhaps his most pornographic depiction of a prostitute. The protagonist Hannah Sherwood is the star courtesan of Estelle Bishop's brothel. Sherwood dresses in high fashion, reads novels, drinks champagne, and engages in numerous "amorous delights." In an illustration, she coyly avoids the attentions of her paramour, her limbs and cleavage provocatively exposed, amid the accoutrements of luxury (figure 23). Readers are warned that any client soon becomes a victim, like "a lamb to the slaughter."

But Sherwood is not totally evil. One evening, for example, she prevents Arthur Wallingford, a wealthy alderman, from seducing a virtuous sewing girl in the brothel. Even when Wallingford offers Hannah $300 to go away, she refuses; "courtesan as she was, [she] possessed a good heart," writes Thompson. Sherwood even goes on to humiliate the

Fig. 23 Hannah Sherwood
From George Thompson, The Gay Girls of New York *(1854)*

alderman, forcing him to kneel and apologize. She screams at Wallingford, calling him a coward because he "tremble[s] before a woman."[23]

Sherwood's intervention, however, draws the ire of the brothel's madam. After chastising Sherwood, Estelle Bishop provokes a fight, during which they rip off each other's clothes. When Sherwood gets the better of Bishop, the latter responds by expelling her opponent from the brothel. Sherwood departs, undismayed and self-righteous, with her lover and pimp, Frank Rattleton. Walking along Broadway, they come upon one of her former clients, a prosperous country merchant, lying drunk and unconscious on the sidewalk. Sherwood and Rattleton drag him into an alley and there remove his clothes. Sherwood then strips herself naked and exchanges outfits with the intoxicated hayseed.

Now dressed in male garb, Sherwood and Rattleton go "slumming" in Five Points. There they see "villainous-looking Jews," "half-naked children," and the "hideous population of prostitutes." The two of them spend the evening going from saloon to saloon, "treating" male patrons in each establishment. In one low dive, they meet the fortune-teller

Granny Grizzle, who predicts that Sherwood will become a "victim of the vilest vagabonds of the Points." Sherwood and Rattleton only laugh at her.

Days later, not surprisingly, Sherwood's misfortunes begin. Estelle Bishop, still smarting from her humiliation, approaches Sherwood in a Broadway saloon and throws vitriol in her face. Sherwood is left severely disfigured and blind. At first, Rattleton helps Sherwood adjust to her accident, visiting her in the hospital, finding her a room in a boardinghouse, and professing his faithfulness to her. But not long afterward, he abandons her, running off with the young daughter of the boardinghouse keeper. Sherwood, now absent any means of support, is summarily evicted from her boardinghouse and rendered homeless. In desperation, she agrees to support herself by appearing in a Five Points freak show. When Granny Grizzle appears, Sherwood realizes that the prophecy has been fulfilled: "that I should *meet* her again, but never again see her." Sherwood dies shortly thereafter, broken and alone, buried in a pauper's grave.

Sherwood's tale, of course, fits the standard image of the fallen woman—that the fruits of prostitution are death. And this is reinforced by similar results of other "gay girls" in the novel. Estelle Bishop, for example, upon her arrest for assaulting Sherwood, commits suicide in the Tombs. Mary Sourby, the daughter of the boardinghouse keeper, is seduced by Rattleton and ends up streetwalking on Broadway and dying of venereal disease. And Alice Vernon, seduced in an assignation house, becomes a fashionable prostitute but dies in a low brothel. While Thompson claims some women "are ruined because of their love of dress and finery," and others "are driven . . . by hunger, by want, by privation of every kind," all the women described are victims of male profligacy and seduction.[24]

But Sherwood's character is threatening for several other reasons. Throughout the novel, the reader sympathizes with Sherwood and is repelled only when Thompson injects moral condemnations. She has a "good heart." Forces Sherwood cannot control simply overwhelm her. At points, Thompson himself acknowledges the inequity of her predicament.[25] Most important, Sherwood transgresses not only sexual mores. By defending a female virgin, aggressively humiliating a wealthy political leader, donning male attire, and treating men in Five Points, she inverts nineteenth-century gender roles. "Corrupt" sexual intercourse becomes the origin for any challenge to the division of power between men and women.

This dire imagery departs from popular depictions of European prostitutes, especially those in Eugène Sue's *The Mysteries of Paris* (1843).

Peter Brooks has shown that Sue implies that working-class girls who prostitute can become honest wives. Bourgeois women who descend into prostitution, in contrast, can never be reclaimed and made "respectable." Class for them is an impenetrable barrier to sincere reform. Sue's evolving socialist leanings thus influence the cloak of class distinction that he drapes over his fictional prostitutes.[26] In contrast, sexual intercourse has a leveling effect on the young American female for Buntline, Foster, and Thompson. Whether the daughter of prosperous merchants, hardworking farmers, or impoverished drunkards, the whore is irredeemable. Social origin and previous status count for nothing. The final result for the prostitute is, if not death, surely unhappiness.

These descriptions of New York also lack a prostitute heroine like Sue's own Fleur-de-Marie. Sherwood and even Buntline's Big Liz have admirable qualities, but they prove to be tragic figures. They never evolve into objects of emulation or hero worship. Fiction and nonfiction writers alike emphasize the process by which a woman becomes a prostitute. All assume that once a woman "falls," it is forever. The rigid boundaries of proper sexual behavior make it impossible for any sexually experienced female, not only promiscuous prostitutes, to regain respectability or virtue. Even those courtesans who serve as narrators give voice more to middle-class domestic fears than to female working-class experiences. Morality and domestic culture merge, now defined in physical and biological ways. No matter how innocent, kind, or intelligent, the prostitute is under a life sentence. A woman's status is thus determined by her first sexual intercourse.

The popularity of these fictional and nonfictional accounts did not rest upon their pornographic imagery alone. Authors also embedded their characters in the geography and institutions of commercial sex. Broadway streetwalkers, Five Points prostitutes, opulent Church Street brothels, and model-artist exhibitions appear. Even specific locales like the Bowery Theater, Pete Williams's dance hall, and Julia Brown's parlor house document the intimate details of this less than intimate world. These were the images of New York's antebellum nightlife, scenes residents and visitors witnessed daily. The inclusion of such a readily recognized geography gave these stories a sharp sense of realism, a resonance of authenticity, so often absent from earlier accounts of the metropolis.

Furthermore, the authors explained these "mysteries" and "corruptions" as the product of *very* organized crime. David Reynolds and Michael Denning have shown in other contexts how these works shared a narrative and rhetoric of exposure, of republican virtue threatened by the luxury and decadence of its seducers and leaders. Authors combined artisanal and yeoman suspicion of unproductive commercial capitalism with republican disdain for privilege and aristocracy. But these sexual transgressions are also presented as an organized onslaught against the very moral foundations of the nation. In Buntline's *Mysteries,* for instance, foreign-born criminals meet regularly and report to each other in assembly rooms where they have "formed themselves into a regular confederacy." In *Celio,* Foster posits the existence of an "under-ground universe" with "a regularly organized community of thieves, who have their laws and regulations," which are more rigidly enforced and more faithfully followed than legitimate society.[27] Criminality becomes a way of life. Prostitutes are the female components of this growing, hidden conspiracy. Commercial sex, with its organized, criminal underground, represents an internal threat to domestic and republican tranquillity.

This literature of deviancy influenced later nonfictional accounts of the same. Journalists, for example, routinely assumed that prostitutes who began in luxurious establishments ended up in Five Points hovels. At midcentury, published reports of leading Protestant reform organizations like the Children's Aid Society and the Five Points House of Industry repeated such stories, warning citizens of the dangers of extramarital sex. On the eve of the Civil War, Dr. William Sanger, in his empirically based study of New York's prostitutes, argued that four years was the maximum career span of a prostitute. It is "a totally well established fact that one fourth of the total number of abandoned women in this city die every year," Sanger wrote. A decade later, in *The Secrets of the Great City* (1868), James D. McCabe, Jr., similarly warned women not to deceive themselves. " 'The wages of sin is death.' . . . Once entered upon a life of shame, however glittering it may be in the outset, her fate is certain—unless she anticipates her final doom by suicide. She cannot reform if she would." Likewise, in *The Women of New York; or, The Under-World of the Great City* (1869), George Ellington concluded that the careers of ninety-nine of every hundred prostitutes followed a steady descent to death. They "all end up the same, and, as a general thing add one more mound to the many unhallowed graves." After all, Junius Browne cynically asked in *The Great Metropolis: A Mirror of New York* (1869), "Who ever saw an aged courtesan?"[28]

These nonfictional accounts, however, exhibited a certain moral ambiguity toward the prostitute. Prostitution emerged as a confusing array of images, often within the same text. McCabe, for instance, repeated the standard moral reform refrain that prostitution was forced and drug induced. "Let no one suppose that these women entered upon such wretched lives voluntarily." Yet elsewhere he acknowledged a variety of causes. McCabe even cited stories in which teenage girls deliberately chose prostitution for a variety of material benefits and went on to relatively happy lives. Similarly, George Ellington condemned madams as "female fiends of the worst kind, who seem to have lost all the better qualities of human nature"; at the same time, he recognized that they had "*entrée* to the good society of the metropolis" with "the friends and chosen companions of some of the wealthiest and most intellectual men of the city." Many madams and prostitutes were well educated, surrounded by luxury, and able to enjoy an elegant life-style. "This sisterhood purchase the most expensive dresses, the rarest bonnets, the neatest boots," Ellington inconsistently concluded.[29]

Ellington even provided visual images of the respectable but tempting prostitute. In "A Belle of the Under-World," "The Queen of the Underworld," "Fast Women," and "Women of Pleasure on the Promenade," prostitutes sport the finest fashion and expensive jewelry. They possess thin waists and pretty faces. They parade and ride in carriages in elite settings like Central Park and Broadway. Even the double chinned woman of "The Madam" wears a formal, low-cut dress (figures 24–28). Dressed as respectable ladies with simple necklines and low, tight bodices, the prostitute visually warns readers against the sentimentalist belief that outward fashion is an index to inner character.[30]

BY THE midnineteenth century, commercial sex with its underground economy and subcultures of prostitutes and sporting men was not only a fact of everyday urban life but also a fixture of popular culture. Whether in dime novels by Ned Buntline or in the poetry of Walt Whitman, prostitutes assumed central roles. A distinct literary argot even emerged that categorized and shaped public discussion of the phenomenon. In empirical examinations like William Sanger's, fictional narratives by George Thompson, or popular exposés by James McCabe, one finds energetic descriptions of the "gay world of the great metropolis." The illicit activities of the underworld were "the gayeties of life." Sexually aggressive women were "gay seducers." Prostitutes were "a gay sight," "gay nymphs," "gay sisters," and "gay *figurantés*." The brothel was simply "a house of resort for the gay of both sexes." Seduced women who descended the degrading hierarchy of prostitution only "became gayer than ever." To many, this subculture of "gay girls" represented the immediate dangers of urbanization, "the very vortex of dissipation and frivolity of New York." Although observers like George Ellington noted its irony, "for there is not gayety but on the outside," their preoccupation with the subject highlighted the prominent place of prostitution in urban life.[31]

Commercial sex had achieved an unprecedented level of public dis-

Fig. 24 opposite, above left. "A Belle of the Under-World"

Fig. 25 opposite, above right. "The Queen of the Under-World"

Fig. 26 opposite below. "Fast Women—The Drive in Central Park"

Fig. 27 above. "Women of Pleasure on the Promenade"

Fig. 28 left. "The Madam"
All from George Ellington, The Women of New York *(1869)*

play. Through the popular novel and the urban exposé, the penny press and the story paper for sporting men, the courtesan entered the urban antebellum imagination. This prostitute subculture was such a fixture of New York social life—the madams, the brothels, the streetwalkers, the contrast of great luxury and utter poverty—that by midcentury popular writers transformed it into a "gay" literature. But this genre, like most forms of popular culture, conveyed contradictory images and disguises. Prostitutes could be soiled doves, insane devils, or sources of ruin. As oversimplified symbols, they became vehicles by which to comprehend the incomprehensible underworld of the new metropolis. The erotic was a part of expanding commerce. But like any symbol, the prostitute both highlighted and obscured the reality of the subcultures of commercial sex. For contemporaries, it became impossible to determine the boundaries between hard reality and urban mythology.

8

"BAWDY HOUSES"

ANTHONY COMSTOCK was the most famous purity reformer in American history. Reared in a rural Connecticut family of Puritan descent, Comstock made his way to New York City at the conclusion of the Civil War. He floundered for a short time as a clerk in one of the city's numerous dry goods houses. After 1871, however, he found his calling when he successfully lobbied for a federal antiobscenity law (the famed Comstock Law), organized the New York Society for the Suppression of Vice, and was named special agent by the postmaster general. In the latter role, Comstock was charged with enforcing the statute that bore his name. For four decades, Comstock tracked down what he considered to be smut, lewdness, and filth. By the twentieth century, he could brag that he had destroyed over 160 tons of pornography.[1] More than any other single individual, Anthony Comstock came to define sexual respectability in postbellum America (see figure 29).

Although Comstock concentrated on visual forms of "sexual depravity," on several occasions his moral forays extended to sexual behavior itself. On one June evening in 1878, Comstock calmly entered a well-known Greene Street brothel. Posing as an ordinary customer, he inquired about the house's "Busy Fleas" performances. Convinced he was in the right place, Comstock paid five dollars and sat down to relish the evening's entertainment. Three women thereupon entered the room, danc-

Fig. 29 Anthony Comstock

ing to the house's piano music. According to Comstock, he attentively watched the three women slowly disrobe and seductively expose themselves to several patrons. Then, to his amazement, they placed "their faces and mouths between one another's legs, and lick[ed] or pretend[ed] to lick or suck on another's private parts." Expressing disgust, he arrested the three performers.[2]

Comstock's clandestine crusade, however, was not over. He covertly ventured into yet another brothel, using the same disguise. This time he observed women putting their heads, in his words, "between the legs of one another and their mouths upon the sexual organs or vagina, drinking beer poured upon the vagina of one girl by the other, placing a cigar in the rectum of one of the girls who [had] thrown her limbs and feet above head. . . . Others feigned intercourse with each other and sucked each other breasts." Comstock incarcerated everyone in the house.[3]

Probably no other institution of commercial sex so violated Comstock's conception of proper, reproductive, and private sexuality as the brothel. But his attention to titillating detail was full of irony. Only on rare occasions did Comstock confront this most commercialized example of nineteenth-century sexuality. Throughout his career, he conceded he could do little to remove prostitution in its most obvious form from the city. Comstock's intervention came not in the overt sale of sexual intercourse but rather in the brothel's increasingly popular striptease shows that went beyond simple burlesque. Performances like those Comstock witnessed and a variety of live erotica attracted audiences to brothels for purposes other than copulation. Men sought more than genital gratification. They wanted entertainment. Much to his chagrin, Comstock realized that the brothel was no longer simply a place to purchase sex but, indeed, a popular house of leisure and relaxation.

The brothel was the best-known and most controversial site of sexual intercourse. By the midnineteenth century, it was a highly specialized vehicle of business with its own hierarchy and systems of operation. At different periods, madams like Eliza Jumel, Maria Williamson, Julia Brown, and Rosie Hertz achieved celebrity status and were prominently mentioned in the penny press, visitor memoirs, guidebooks, and even diaries of elite New Yorkers.[4] In time, political reform, changing land use patterns, and the rise of large-scale forms of commercial sex eventually doomed the brothel. By World War I, it was nearly extinct. But for nearly a century, the brothel remained the ubiquitious symbol of commercialized sex in America's leading metropolis.

More specifically, the brothel occupied a liminal position in nineteenth-century New York. Widely attacked in many quarters, it nevertheless remained a leading institution of popular male recreation and female entrepreneurship. In sheer numbers—over six hundred by the age of the Civil War—only saloons outdid them. Critics like the *Tribune* characterized the brothel as one of the "false Institutions and Arrangements in the present system of Society which produce the dreadful social evils." And some like Comstock tried fruitlessly to suppress it. But to many others, the brothel represented a new source of leisure and excitement, the embodiment of an emerging cosmopolitan society rejecting the cultural fig leaves of rural and small-town America. Freedom meant male promiscuity and the easy availability of sex without the responsibilities imposed by family and community. Increasingly left to the dictates of the sexual marketplace, the brothel saw its popularity evidenced by its profitability. "A well-regulated bed-house," conceded Matthew Hale Smith in 1867, "is the most lucrative house in New York."[5]

In the early years of the republic, however, the brothel was a marginal institution found primarily in dockfront areas and associated with taverns. Over half the "disorderly houses" harboring prostitutes from 1790 to 1820, for example, were taverns, inns, or saloons along the East River. Liquor establishments known as grog shops, slop shops, and tippling houses were popular with seamen and transient laborers. To satisfy their customers' lust and to supplement their income, numerous urban taverns were fitted with six to eight beds, usually in a rear room or upstairs. John Fitzpatrick's East George Street tavern was typical. Fitzpatrick sublet all his rooms to "common prostitutes," charging four shillings for every customer they entertained. Staying open all night, Fitzpatrick's tavern catered to every vice. If all the beds were being used, prostitutes simply resorted to Francis Legee's house in the rear alley, where, for a shilling less, they could have a "man lay with them." Part of the seductive arcana of city sex, the tavern was the principal rendezvous for the early American prostitute.[6]

After 1820, though, prostitution tended to move from the tavern to the row house, and brothels drew more and more attention. In the spring of 1833, for example, one of America's earliest purity reformers, the Reverend John McDowall, upon surveying the character of prostitution in New York, discovered that the tavern was no longer the prostitute's major haunt. Rather, McDowall counted at least 172 boardinghouses that accommodated prostitutes and 48 houses of assignation. He estimated that seven hundred or more women worked out of these establishments, usually three or four per domicile. Several months later, a more moralistic observer, whose outrage was surpassed only by his hyperbole, argued that houses of assignation alone numbered over a thousand. And Butt Ender's salacious 1839 guidebook claimed that the city had 266 brothels and 75 houses of assignation. The brothel's prominence, in fact, motivated some militant women to organize the Female Moral Reform Society specifically to expunge it from the city.[7] While these critics ignored the institutional variety of antebellum prostitution (prostitutes were readily found in saloons, theaters, dance halls, tenements, and even restaurants), they rightly noted the new importance of the brothel.

By the late 1830s, two broad categories of brothels had emerged in New York. On one hand, "parlor" or "private houses" offered the most exclusive form of commercial sex. Such establishments protected the secrecy and anonymity of their clients. Indeed, the very label "parlor house" reflected an emphasis on replicating the atmosphere, privacy, and physical environment of the middle-class home. Prostitutes in such elite brothels charged as much as five dollars per customer, a staggering sum to the average male journeyman or worker, who earned between six and fifteen dollars weekly. The high prices enabled these women to restrict their service to a few clients while enjoying the most luxurious work environment. As a rule, only regular visitors were admitted, and new patrons had to obtain invitations, letters of recommendation, or appointments before entering. Furthermore, the affluent clientele allowed private brothels to function with only a small number of women. Houses with more than six inmates were in the minority before 1840. By midcentury, some were identified by the geographical origins of their patrons. On Laurens Street, for example, Mrs. Everett's house fostered a distinctive southern ambience. Two blocks away on Mercer Street, Clara Gordon's brothel indulged only southern "gentlemen." A few houses north, Louisa Kanth entertained and titillated German merchants. And Mrs. Rush's Howard Street bagnio was "the resort of Philadelphia sporting men."[8]

In contrast, "public houses" were open to anyone willing to pay. Secrecy, if any, was minimal. The most popular public brothels, or "bawdy houses," attracted lines of boisterous male patrons outside their doors, eagerly awaiting their turn. Through guidebooks, business cards, and even newspapers, public brothels appealed to male sexual fantasies and advertised their specialized carnal offerings. Sometimes the raucous atmosphere inside and out resembled that of a saloon more closely than that of a parlor house. The time male clients spent with prostitutes was frequently so short that such establishments offered little more than genital gratification. For these patrons, coitus was a public performance and a source of male camaraderie.[9]

By the 1850s, some public brothels had large resident populations, with as many as twenty women offering a diversity of sexual services. These new specialities reflected not only the changing clientele but also how brothels were increasingly defined by their clientele. For example, Sarah Sweet's and A. E. Basteen's Church Street houses provided men with southern "creole" women. During the 1830s and 1840s, Rebecca Weyman's Mott Street house was equipped with "ropes and braces." For the most adventurous, the delights of "French love" were discovered at Miss Mitchell's on Sullivan Street or Miss French's on West Twenty-seventh Street. Still others resorted to drama to attract patrons. Matilda Pinteaux's Duane Street house of prostitution, for example, sponsored model-artist shows—displays of stationary, but naked, women imitating classical sculptures and other well-known female forms found in visual art. Anthony Comstock was by no means the first to witness a brothel striptease. In this "enlightened age," remarked one observer in 1848, such entertainments found at the Odeon or at Madame Pinteaux's were "enough to condemn its character, if it had one previously."[10]

This increasingly specialized brothel prostitution also reflected the changing structure of city land use and domestic housing arrangements. With the decline of apprenticeship and slavery, and the rise of immigration, antebellum households took in boarders for cash payments rather than in exchange for labor. Soon "taking boarders" evolved into a trade. "Few are aware of the extent of boarding house life in New York," lamented Walt Whitman at midcentury. "Thousands of young or 'moderately well off' people, absolutely unable to find the right residence for them, hire a house quite too large, and eke out the rent by sub-letting one, two, three, or more rooms . . . to such lodgers as they can find." Rising rents, considered the highest in the Western world, gave New Yorkers few housing options. In addition, the low wages and transiency of women's wage labor made females undesirable tenants. "Any and every boarding house-keeper is prejudiced against women," insisted Junius Browne in 1868. Most proprietors preferred male tenants and did their "best to avoid taking" women. The wide variety of boardinghouses elicited satires like Thomas Butler Gunn's *Physiology of New York Boarding Houses,* which described a melange of types, ranging from the fashionable and the dirty to the theatrical and the vegetarian, even the Bostonian and the Chinese.[11]

At the same time, other New York landlords increasingly hired leaseholders and agents to collect rents from tenants, including those living in the building and saloonkeepers and grocers whose businesses were downstairs. Responsible for rent collection in a building with sometimes unreliable low-income tenants, these "sublandlords" simply rented to individual prostitutes. When convenient, they converted the building into a brothel. Numerous landlords included clauses prohibiting any "immoral use" of the property, but these were usually a form of landlord protection and routinely ignored by lessees.[12] As cash replaced work in the relationship between tenant and landlord, profit became the latter's goal. And prostitution afforded an easy means to accumulate earnings.

The brothel ultimately integrated prostitution into the city's tax and property structures. Like peddlers, streetwalkers were unaffected by urban real estate policy, and they thereby retained nearly all their earnings. Brothels, on the other hand, gave landlords and lessees hefty profits and the municipal tax collector additional revenue. One reform journal put it bluntly: "in the rent of houses, in the supply of furniture, and in various ways, there is a vast *capital* employed in the traffic of degraded females. . . ."[13] Over time, the brothel helped cement the links among Gotham's growing underground economy, the real estate industry, and the municipal government.

While two- to four-story row houses and boardinghouses proliferated, a sometimes confusing array of bawdy houses appeared. In fact, the distinctions between public brothels, parlor houses, houses of assignation, furnished-room houses, and panel houses were often unclear. A house filled exclusively with prostitutes was outwardly indistinguishable from a female-run boardinghouse with a few tenants. Madams of the leading brothels occasionally camouflaged their establishments as simple boardinghouses. Moreover, numerous keepers of boardinghouses and houses of assignation, hoping to increase their income, permitted prostitutes to reside. And if a prostitute from an assignation house solicited on the street, the establishment differed little from a boardinghouse or even a second- or third-class public brothel. In 1855, at least twenty-eight boardinghouses in the city directory were also clandestine houses of ill fame. City census takers in the 1850s listed obvious brothels as "prostitute boarding houses." By 1870, some brothels were listed simply as "boarding houses." Whether parlor house, bawdy house, or boardinghouse, each served as the house and workplace of the prostitute, thus institutionalizing antebellum prostitution in some type of residential structure.[14]

Similarly, numerous grocers and saloonkeepers rented their upper floors to prostitutes and then supplied them with liquor. Throughout the antebellum period, disorderly houses were sometimes saloons downstairs and brothels upstairs. "Intemperance and prostitution," argued *McDowall's Journal,* "are inseparably connected."[15] Elijah Valentine, for example, was a Mulberry Street grocer who in 1826 controlled five houses of prostitution on nearby Cross Street. Similarly, Dennis Gillespie, also a grocer, changed his residence at least three times during the 1820s, moving between property owned by James Ridgeway and by John R. Livingston. In 1830, he severed his dependence upon these larger landlords when he purchased an Orange Street house for $2,300 at a Merchant's Exchange auction. By 1833, Gillespie was the sole owner or occupant of at least three brothel saloons on Anthony Street.[16]

Successful neighborhood saloonkeepers even developed reputations that extended beyond their neighborhood. The *National Police Gazette* claimed that Wallace Parker was a leading brothel keeper on Water Street, controlling three or four such establishments. Robert B. Gordon's prostitute-filled groggery on Anthony and Little Water streets long remained open despite numerous attempts to arrest him and close down his business. And Edward Swartz avoided conviction despite several arrests for accommodating prostitutes in his Old Bath House, on Pearl Street.[17] In numerous cases, neighborhood storekeepers accumulated savings, purchased leases or real estate, and entered the sex trade.

The fluid structure of prostitution even enabled working-class couples to enter and leave the trade periodically. For example, Anton and Maria Wellerdick operated a boot and shoe store in Greenwich Village after marrying in 1857. Several years later, they left the trade and opened two saloons. By 1869, they were renting a Greene Street brothel, which was primarily run by Maria, a woman described by friends as "industrious," who "tried to save money and pay debts." Although their business ended abruptly when Anton abandoned Maria and New York, it illustrates how skilled artisans, saloonkeepers, and their families slipped in and out of the underground economy. Commercial sex was a means to a supplementary income and a quick profit.[18]

The integration of prostitutes with normal boardinghouse tenants had significant social and economic ramifications. As housing increasingly defined one's status and class, some New Yorkers concluded that all boardinghouses were little more than "respectable purgatories." One newspaper insisted that the boardinghouse was a representative example of the everyday mixing of virtue and vice in New York. "If you have a desire to study man in all his varieties, throw away Shakespeare and put down stakes in a boarding house. More life—real genuine scenes—may be witnessed at one of these places during a period of twenty-four hours than at a tavern or other place of promiscuous resort."[19]

At root, the brothel was a business. The most conspicuous lessee was the madam, often working under an annual lease and suffering the greatest burden of risk. On the eve of the Civil War, Dr. William Sanger discovered that annual brothel rents ranged from $560 to $9,100, with the median hovering around $1,000. Other examples confirmed Sanger's conclusion. Jane Williams, a leading madam, leased her brothel for $900 to $1,000 annually during the 1830s. In 1843, Mary Williams kept a small bawdy house on Grand Street for $500. In some cases, landlords like James Ridgeway supplied their madams with furniture; in others, furniture store owners leased items directly to madams. During the 1840s, for example, a Mrs. Wilson and a Mrs. Curly reportedly made their living simply by leasing furniture to brothels. In addition, for their own protection, landlords levied weekly fees and bonds. Less organized houses were rented by the week. Susan Shannon, for instance, rented John Taylor's Thomas Street house, furniture included, for $25 per week. Some madams, without owning their brothel, bought and insured their furniture and even sublet additional pieces to other brothel keepers. In 1842, the *Whip* proclaimed that many were "amassing large fortunes, by the letting of furniture and houses to the frail sisterhood."[20]

The high turnover of residents in parlor houses and boardinghouses forced proprietors to levy a weekly rent and "bed money"—a portion of their earned fee from each client—on their promiscuous tenants. Throughout the antebellum period, $2 to $5 was the standard weekly charge for prostitutes, the most successful keepers earning monthly rents in excess of $20 from prostitutes. A few brothels imposed higher fees. For example, Eleanor Timple demanded an outlandish $8 per week for room and board in 1808, and John Ward charged $5 per week in his furnished-room house as early as 1817. Prostitutes paid Salona Blanchard $8 per week for residing in her Chapel Street house a decade later. In the 1840s, Adeline Miller reputedly earned $14 per week from each of her brothel residents. During the 1860s, the prostitutes in Elizabeth Fairchild's (alias Stanley) Fifteenth Street brothel paid $8 to $10 a week in rent.[21]

Some leaseholders rented a few units to prostitutes for short periods. For example, Jack Strong rented part of a Leonard Street domicile to prostitutes until other tenants complained about the havoc they wreaked. When James Malone obtained a lease on the building beside his Bayard Street residence, he promptly leased it to prostitutes for eighteen months, until his arrest. Elizabeth Whitehead, a widow with four children, supported her family by taking on as boarders two young women who were occasional prostitutes. In order to support his five children when he lost his job, Thomas Jones rented a room on Walnut Street and allowed the prostitute Hannah Romoun to board there. When thirty-one-year-old Anastasia Bodell's husband was absent for two months, she rented rooms to prostitutes for short intervals. Living in such houses, prostitutes more easily assumed, according to one observer, "the guise of respectable people by day and follow[ed] their vocation at night."[22]

The exorbitant rents did not keep some women from making significant profits. Even smaller operations could meet rents of $500 to $1,000 per annum. Mary Williams, for example, with four prostitutes in residence, whom she charged $5 per week in board, easily made annual profits in excess of $500. "Bed money" surely doubled that figure. Jane Williams also charged her six prostitutes a $5 weekly rent, bringing in gross receipts of at least $1,560 annually. Naturally, with more inmates, the house became more lucrative. On the eve of the Civil War, when male workers and tradesmen earned between $250 and $600, the most successful brothels reportedly earned annual incomes in excess of $26,000.[23]

The more inmates, the more rigid control madams exerted over their work force. Resident prostitutes were prohibited from streetwalking except during slow periods. In 1855, leading houses like the Leonard Street establishments of Cinderella Marshall and Marie Adams employed as many as sixteen and fourteen prostitutes, respectively. On the same block, Ellen Hamilton and Charlotte Brown had a minimum of seven women working for them. During busy periods, madams allowed nonresident prostitutes to "sit in company" with their brothel counterparts, sometimes doubling their work force, to twenty or twenty-five women. After midcentury, leading madams even required their prostitutes to submit to weekly physical examinations.[24]

As the number of brothels and houses of assignation expanded after 1820, competition between different proprietors intensified. William

Thompson complained in 1840 that even with four prostitutes in his Broome Street boardinghouse, he could not meet his expenses. Only with more girls could he make it pay, so Thompson and his madam accomplice, Nancy Flinn, opened an employment office or "intelligence office" to screen and refer potential prospects for their brothel. By the Civil War, some brothel owners were finding it hard to compete with streetwalkers. Living on their own, streetwalkers enjoyed "comparative liberty and independence," thereby avoiding the brothel. Streetwalkers, Walt Whitman declared, "have their own rooms, and 'keep house' by themselves." Other proprietors cooperated among themselves. As early as 1825, a formal network for supplying certain houses of prostitution with young girls existed in New York. Susan Baker for example, obtained girls from Philadelphia to work in her brothel, most of them ranging from fifteen to sixteen years in age. In 1847, Samuel Prime claimed that the city's "sinks of iniquity" were "supplied by importations from the country."[25]

The most successful brothels employed a number of techniques to enhance their reputations and attract customers. Some, when complaints were few, posted pictures of the female residents in the window as a type of advertising (figure 30). Others required resident prostitutes to expose themselves in doorways and windows, beckoning to passersby to enter. The most prominent device, however, was the ball. The leading madams in New York sponsored elegant monthly, and sometimes weekly, balls during the winter season, although critics dismissed them as "low brothel dances." While the public activity centered on dining and dancing, early arrivals were allowed to "amuse themselves with the ladies in the upper rooms." After supper, "the gay *figurantés,*" wearing dresses of silk and satin and tiaras of diamonds, mingled with the guests. When the madam Susan Shannon sponsored her "Cotillion Party and Supper" for visiting country merchants in 1842, "the pretty hostess was dressed in a most magnificent tunic of black velvet," reported one witness. Julia Brown, Rebecca Weyman, Eliza Davenport, and Mary Williams sponsored such events, often with each other's participation. Commenting upon their popularity and success, the *Whip* satirically opposed "the low brothel dance houses" but supported "those of a more respectable nature."[26]

More than the brothel, the house of assignation integrated promiscuous sexuality into nineteenth-century New York's residential life. First appearing early in the century, the house of assignation was by the 1830s a convenient retreat not only for prostitutes but for premarital and adulterous lovers. It resembled a boardinghouse with furnished quarters, but functioned much like a hotel. In his travels, the Frenchman Moreau

Fig. 30 "The Genius of Advertising"
From National Police Gazette

de St. Méry learned that the proprietors of houses of assignation (or "duennas," as he called them) secretly arranged for sexual liaisons between men and young girls. "If the patron wants a different woman," he found, "the duenna provides her with equal complaisance." Houses of assignation thus generated more controversy than brothels in some quarters because of the secretive, unregulated sexual activity they promoted. Their "effect has been to intrude prostitution into circles and places where its presence is never suspected," charged one critic. "To these private places," complained *McDowall's Journal,* "genteel in their outward appearance, resort by day and by night, men and boys, girls and women, of all ages and colours, married and single to commit fornication." Seldom housing more than one or two permanent residents, assignation houses advertised in local papers with "rooms to let to quiet persons" or "rooms . . . where boarders are not annoyed with impertinent questions." The assignation house offorded a secluded rendezvous for secretive couples.[27]

The best-known assignation houses were dubbed the "upper ten." Proprietors like Catherine Jennison cared little about who rented their rooms. For two decades, she took "bed money" from couples who came for only part of the evening. When prosecuted in 1822, Jennison proclaimed "she would never let her beds be idle as long as she could get a dollar for them." In 1839, she was still in the business. Reporters for *McDowall's Journal* corroborated Jennison's defiance. Observing a single house during a five-month period in 1833, the paper concluded that with a voluminous traffic of ten to twenty couples per night, it made a profit of $1,450 annually. Still others, Mary Fowler among them, went to nearby brothels where conditions were ripe and recruited girls to sit "in company" at her place for the evening. By the decade of the Civil War, assignation houses had multiplied. "Women of high position and culture, no less than the unlettered shop girls, resort to the houses of assignation, which are of every grade, from the palaces in the aristocratic quarter of the city to the frowsy rooms in the slums," wrote Edward Crapsey.[28] For young couples, adulterous mates, or streetwalking prostitutes, the house of assignation offered a place for intimacy unavailable in their home.

The competitiveness of the underground economy was reinforced by changing housing patterns by the 1860s. Increasingly, boardinghouses gave way to a new form of lodging—the furnished-room house. Boarding, popular before the Civil War with its personalized, family-oriented structure, allowed for daily monitoring of all female tenants. Lodging, in contrast, changed the relationship between tenant and landlord to one that was strictly commercial and based on rent. Operating without registers, clerks, or nosy landladies, furnished-room houses enabled solitary prostitutes to rent suites, affording them greater independence than the brothel.[29] And like antebellum houses of assignation, furnished-room houses offered discreet accommodations for sexually curious couples.

Generally, furnished-room houses replaced and, to a degree, imitated houses of assignation. Proprietors of furnished-room houses accommodated prostitutes in two ways. First, they respected individual privacy and permitted anyone to rent a room. Since most renting couples were not prostitutes, it was especially difficult for critics to isolate the "disreputable" from the "virtuous." Not surprisingly, some such places were so populated with prostitutes that neighbors mistook them for bordellos. Second, some proprietors of furnished-room houses embraced prostitution so enthusiastically that they admitted only women associated with particular saloons and concert halls. In Union Square, for example, the constant traffic between saloons, concert halls, and furnished-room houses, wrote one businessman, "proves that the latter depends largely on the former for its patrons."[30]

A final offshoot of the brothel, the assignation house, and the furnished-room house was the panel house. From 1820 to about 1900, the dangers of the panel house were frequently mentioned by press, police, and victim. In a typical scenario, astute prostitutes, derogatorily referred to as badgers, worked in groups of three or four, dressed "in the best style," and brought clients to an abode of "respectable appearance." Upon entering a bedroom, the gentleman paid for the sex and proceeded to undress. Then one of two things occurred. An unknown man outside the room might knock upon the door. Immediately, the visibly terrified prostitute insisted he was her husband, hastily dressed the client, and rushed him out a rear exit absent his money. On other occasions, the client undressed, laid his clothing and possessions on a chair by the wall, and jumped into bed with the woman. In the midst of the fornicating, an accomplice, hidden behind a moving panel along the wall, sneaked out and pilfered the money from the victim's clothes. "It makes no difference to this class," wrote one reporter, "whether the man whom they entice into their den is a poor laborer who has got together a few hard earned dollars . . . or . . . a rich gentleman with a plethoric purse."[31]

Panel houses were frequently run by a male landlord or tenant. James Fowler operated a profitable house in Corlears Hook, while William Stein, a thirty-five-year-old German immigrant, controlled a panel game on Laurens Street. The most successful panel house operator of all was Charles Quin. From 1840 to 1851, Quin ran panel houses simultaneously on Staple, Elizabeth, Reade, and Murray streets. An African-American who resided in Five Points, Quin was so well known in the New York underworld that he was a topic of gossip in the city's penny press. Finally, one guidebook noted that parasitical panel house operators were to New York's "public streets what sharks are on the ocean."[32]

After the Civil War, panelhouses attracted increasing fire from critics and victims. For example, when a visitor from Pittsburgh entered a Mercer Street address with two prostitutes in 1879, "they stripped naked and while one of them entertained him in a chair, the other abstracted $100 from his pocket-book." Another visitor near the St. Nicholas Hotel, on Broadway, described how two young prostitutes stopped him and "began to feel around [his body] in the most *vulgar* manner." When he went with them to a nearby house, he returned $100 poorer. Other victims charged that the police tolerated, even protected, panel houses. After James Wilson was robbed in Mrs. M. F. Muller's house, he wrote, "[T]hey do not make any bones of robing [*sic*] you and then kicking you out. . . . [T]hey will get your money from you and if you wish any satisfaction for it, they tell you to get out and if you demand your money back they say 'I'll call a police and have you arrested.' " And in 1876, the president of the Board of Police remonstrated with his captains, saying, "[I]f there is any one crime that carries with it a lower depth of degradation than another, it is the crime of panel thieving."[33]

Threats of reprisal, however, did little to stop the practice. In 1888, one landlord wrote that in some Hester Street houses the "women are there for the purpose of bringing in men as they call them sharks and then when they get them up the stairs they drug and rob him." By the turn of the century, Charles Lomax testified that he had seen at least a hundred men robbed in panel houses on his own block. "If a man was robbed in 116 [West Twenty-sixth Street] by a woman, the woman who committed the robbery, as soon as that man went out, would go over to 133," he reported. "The natural consequence was, when the man went back with a officer to identify the woman who committed the robbery, the woman wasn't in the house. . . ." In their extensive investigations of prostitution, early-twentieth-century vice commissions discovered numerous houses permitting the "bilking" of customers, and even significant numbers of men willing to prosecute prostitutes for their larcenous activity.[34]

The specialized sexual offerings found in antebellum brothels expanded during the Gilded Age. Glamorous first-class houses (sometimes called five- and ten-dollar houses) with full furnishings sometimes paid rents of $1,000 per month or more. Kate Woods's Tenderloin brothel on West Twenty-fifth Street, nicknamed the Hotel de Wood, was reputed to be furnished at a cost of $70,000 in 1870. Generally, "[n]o hotel is more elegantly furnished," wrote Matthew Hale Smith. "Quiet, order, and taste abound. The lady boarders in these houses never walk the streets nor solicit company." James McCabe remarked that the women were "handsome, well-dressed, generally refined in manner, and conduct themselves with outward propriety." Leading parlor houses guaranteed privacy and admitted only discreet gentlemen, providing them piano music as they waited for their sexual entertainment.[35]

Many houses continued to resort to rather ingenious methods to procure business. For example, first-class brothels were equipped with telegraph systems, or "call boxes," which connected them with messenger agencies employing boys to run errands and recruit customers. Even more common were those that placed ads in newspapers like the *Morning Journal, Herald,* and *Tenderloin*. Increasingly, brothels relied on more blatant forms of public erotica as the century passed. For instance, advertising cards, calling attention to specific brothels, were "peddled on the street by boys and young lads."

Leading brothels, nicknamed ladies clubs, were renowned for well-known prostitutes, generally referred to as stars. Among the most famous by the 1880s was Kate Woods's House of All Nations, on West Twenty-seventh Street, with its assortment of beautiful foreign-born women. For the right price, Irish, French, German, English, even Asian, African, and South American females were available. Here, wrote one reporter, "the male rounder could enjoy feminine society from all parts of the universe." After a visit, more than a few young sports bragged "that they may not have travelled extensively, [but] they . . . managed to see a lot of the world in one night."[36]

Even brothels in poor, immigrant neighborhoods of the Gilded Age city exhibited elegance. In the Lower East Side, for instance, one Stanton Street brothel was in

> a neat-looking three-story red brick house, with a new stuped awning at the front door, hanging low, so as to shield the head and shoulders of anyone who might be seen entering or coming out of the house. The windows have shutters, but they are open, while on the interior of the parlor floor windows had heavy flowered curtains, covering the lower sash only.

Inside, the richly carpeted parlor contained about a score of small cherry tables and chairs, "showing that business must be thriving at night."[37]

Besides prostitutes, the best-organized houses of ill fame employed an impressive arrary of pimps, cabmen, and maids. Pimps (or cadets, as they were sometimes called), young men usually eighteen to twenty-five in age, were responsible for securing a steady supply of women for the brothel. Summarily, "[h]is occupation is professional seduction," concluded the Committee of Fifteen, an antiprostitution reform group. For a streetwalker or a "ruined girl," cadets earned five dollars; for a virgin or a "greenhorn," ten to fifty dollars. According to one report, "many of these houses could not flourish unless they had these men to keep up the supply, for it does not drift in fast enough, but must be secured through systematic work." Still other "independent" prostitutes who "sat in company" on weekends supported pimps in return for their protection. "These men work for all houses where they can place girls and make big money." When not seducing or recruiting young, immigrant females, pimps functioned as "runners," "lookouts," and "watchboys," provided protection, ran errands, and passed out advertisements on the street.[38]

Intense competition among proprietors induced them to hire cabmen to bring visitors and interested parties to their houses. As early as the 1850s, Walt Whitman described cabmen as "monsters who first throng around the hapless visitants and seek to devour them, . . . and then after depositing them at destinations proper and improper, demand . . .

excessive fares." By 1888, this was the norm. Describing an expensive Wooster Street brothel, one city resident observed

> that their modus operandi is to stand in with certain hack drivers stationed at the different ferries and that for every "customer" that is brought to them they received ten dollars spot cash regardless of appearances or anything else, and also should he prove to be a good one as the saying is the hackman will undoubtedly receive from fifteen to fifty dollars extra.

"Half the cabbies in the Tenderloin," remembered Cornelius Willemse, "were drawing regular commissions for steering strangers to the houses."[39]

In a city where workers still labored ten to twelve hours per day, six days a week, Sunday was never a day of rest for the brothel keeper. Critics agreed that Sunday was the busiest day for sexual activity in the city. "Between Saturday night and Monday morning," reproved *McDowall's Journal* as early as 1833, "there is more iniquity committed in those dens than in any other two, or perhaps four days of the week." Keepers of brothels and saloons admitted they could ill afford to close, because of the vast demand by working males on their "day of rest." Well into the final decade of the century, young males habitually gathered in front of their favorite brothels, awaiting their turn for an amorous encounter, while indulging in drink and discussion with their conspicuous pals.[40]

Gilded Age brothels frequently promoted sexual practices rarely found elsewhere. More often than not, these specialized exercises were simply excused as "French" imports. "Paris at its worst has been the model for these forms of shame and horror as our own," complained Helen Campbell. In 1878, for example, Belle Rochelle advertised that she gave the "French treatment" in her Chrystie Street house, while other establishments were known as French houses because of their willingness to do "unnatural practices." When Arthur Wilson entered a rear room in a Third Avenue music house, a prostitute-actress whispered into his ear, offering him "French love." The "unnatural acts" and "indecent dances and dinners" considered standard fare in many brothels simply meant oral sex. "There has grown up a great trade in what is known as French houses," concluded Frances Kellor in 1907. "These women will stoop to practices that the ordinary American girl could not be induced to do."[41]

Descriptions of exotic titillation and striptease increasingly found their way into the public record, especially in the city's courts. For example, after paying five dollars in a Tenderloin brothel, a voyeuristic police officer testified to watching six prostitutes strip to their stockings. Then one "placed a portion of a lighted segar in the private parts of another . . . who was lying on her back with her feet elevated to her head." Simultaneously, the other four pretended "they were having sexual intercourse with each other and one . . . took a rubber implement shaped in the form of a Penis, commonly called a dildo," and inserted it. In another undercover investigation, police observed prostitutes "exhibiting the act of sexual connection with an artifical male organ in presence of a lustful gaze of men." Decades later, the Reverend Charles Parkhurst repeated Anthony Comstock's nocturnal adventure and observed the salacious "dance of nature" in a Tenderloin brothel. For fifteen dollars, the female residents dressed up in fashionable Mother Hubbard gowns and proceeded to perform the cancan and "leap frog" in various degrees of undress.[42]

The prominent position of the brothel in the city's underground economy and entertainment culture did not last forever. Beginning in the 1880s, a number of new developments steadily pushed the brothel out of New York's sexual limelight. Most significant was the increasing tendency of prostitutes to work out of furnished rooms, tenements, and hotels. Whereas under 25 percent of Gotham's prostitutes worked in such places during the 1870s, over 85 percent did by the second decade of the twentieth century.[43] The larger scale of these enterprises and their links to concert saloons and cabarets offered a more efficient and effective way to organize commercial sex in the final decades of the nineteenth century.

Women themselves grew less satisfied with the brothel as a place to work. The strict control by the madams and the strenuous physical demands upon a prostitute's body made residence in brothels short. "A girl stays not much more than a month," said one, "unless she brings in good trade." The exorbitant living expenses in parlor houses made them less lucrative for the more ambitious courtesan. By the twentieth century, most prostitutes appeared actively to avoid brothels. Streetwalkers even disparaged brothel prostitutes as "girls . . . afraid to hustle on the street."[44]

Finally, the increasing repression of brothels also contributed to their decline. As preventive societies grew more influential after 1875, Mayors William R. Grace and Abram S. Hewitt closed down many such establishments. Manicure and massage parlors soon replaced brothels in large numbers. "Whenever the police begin to clean up a precinct and drive the well-known places out of business," remarked one police commissioner, "massage parlors at once begin to flourish." The numerous ads in the daily newspapers confirmed the popularity of such establishments. And the continual attack on the brothel after 1890 by Charles Parkhurst and other reformers pushed many more prostitutes into tenements and apartments.[45]

THE fluid institutional structure of prostitution mirrored the transformation of New York's residential housing market after 1820. Profit-hungry proprietors moved easily from one form to another, according to the dictates of circumstance. Like gambling houses and illegal saloons, brothels integrated New York's expanding underground economy into other parts of this unusual service industry. Linked economically to the real estate business, culturally to the theater, concert saloon, and tavern, and politically to the neighborhood tax collector and ward boss, brothels were prominent leisure institutions in nineteenth-century Gotham.

Thanks to their variety, brothels could offer different kinds of commercial sex. The most visible—public or bawdy houses—reflected the growing demand for sexual services by the ever-transient male population passing through New York. In contrast, private parlor houses kept patronage of prostitutes a secret. By protecting male privacy, these brothels offered both physical space and personal isolation for sexual indulgences little tolerated by the nineteenth-century middle class. Away from the watchful eyes of the family and censorious clerics, parlor houses offered an environment for private promiscuity and sexual excitement. Little wonder that to their defenders, they were "temples of love."[46]

To critics, all brothels were little more than intolerable retail marts for commercial sex. Ultimately, the critics prevailed. In 1906, the former police chief William McAdoo admitted that "the breaking up of vice in quarters where it [was] congested . . . resulted in its invasion of tenement and apartment houses." Undercover investigators found that the most notorious of brothel owners had departed from New York to more tolerant environs elsewhere. In lieu of the brothel, prostitutes moved in with pimps to more secretive residences in furnished-room houses, tenements, apartments, and hotels. Thus, the reformer Raymond Fosdick happily proclaimed in 1916 that New York no longer had "a disorderly house of the old type in operation."[47] Gotham's era of the brothel was over.

Part III

Comstock's New York, 1871–1920

9

SEXUAL POLITICS

IF *SPORTING MEN* saw prostitutes and brothels as expressions of freedom, liberation, and the breakdown of earlier constraints upon sexual behavior, moral reformers, on the other hand, equated them with sewers and sin. Besides violating every bourgeois rule of appropriate conduct, the prostitute reminded all citizens of their precarious position in New York's market economy. The whore was a metaphor; her persona embodied fears of "ruin," downward mobility, loss of status, and social marginality. Paradoxically, the prostitute attracted men's homage and society's opprobrium.

Middle-class outrage over prostitution, sporting-male culture, and tolerance of commercial sex was most frequently expressed in antiprostitution reform movements. Prior to 1870, such efforts proved to be sporadic and short-lived. Beginning with Anthony Comstock, however, so-called vice campaigns actively sought to redefine the public limits of sexual behavior. Antiprostitution reformers, for the first time in New York's history, established long-lasting institutions. Their interventionist policies soon raised critical questions about late-nineteenth-century urban society. What, for example, was the function of municipal government regarding sexuality? What was the purpose of an urban police force? And how should cities control the underground economy?

Sexual Politics before 1870

"PURITY REFORM" was not born full grown in postbellum New York. In seventeenth-century Boston, Cotton Mather founded the first known antivice organization in North America, the Society for the Suppression of Disorder. Its goal of shutting down Boston's brothels, however, proved unattainable. The first similar organization in New York, the Society for the Suppression of Vice, appeared in the early nineteenth century. Concerned not only with prostitution but also with Sunday drinking, saloons, and gambling, this short-lived organization conceded that to "attempt to extirpate at once all the vices which they desire to suppress would be to undertake an Herculean task and would excite an opposition formidable both in numbers and activity." Human institutions, laws, and punishments did little to renew the heart. "All that can be done," the report continued, "is to hinder the formation of vicious habits and to prevent those who are already corrupt from corrupting others."[1]

Most early New York efforts to combat social ills took this lesson to heart, circumscribing their ambitions and their reach. After 1815, the Lying-In Hospital admitted only "honest women," while the Asylum for Lying-In Women accepted only those with marriage certificates. Only "repenting victims of seduction" were received by the Magdalen Society, and "syphilitic men" were unwelcome at New York Hospital. Individual reformers echoed these limited goals. In 1827, a former resident physician of New York Hospital and a Magdalen Society founder considered reclamation efforts foolhardy and a "direct encouragement to prostitution." Such women were irretrievable. "Little was to be gained," he concluded, "where the moral sense was so totally depraved as in most of such cases—returning like the dog to his vomit."[2]

In 1831, a new moral reform period began, sparked by the evangelical fires of the Second Great Awakening. With the financial support of Arthur and Lewis Tappan, A. G. Phelps, and William Colgate, the Reverend John R. McDowall founded the New York Magdalen Society and opened a "house of refuge" as a stopping place for penitent prostitutes. An evangelical Presbyterian, McDowall wanted to eliminate, not just control, prostitution. By 1835, a variety of antiprostitution organizations had appeared in New York, including the American Society for Promoting Observance of the Seventh Commandment, the New York Female Benevolent Society, the New-York Society of Public Morals, and the New-York Female Moral Reform Society (NYFMRS). Radically interpreting the cult of domestic womanhood, these reform bodies were angered by prostitution and seduction outside of wedlock. The female-led NYFMRS, in particular, blamed lustful men for the social subordination and sexual victimization of young women.[3]

Religious efforts to quell prostitution continued during the ensuing decades. In 1843, Roman Catholics established the Sisters of Mercy to dissuade Irish girls from falling into prostitution and the Sisters of the Good Shepherd to redeem those who had. Similarly, the American Female Guardian Society was established in 1846 and within two years operated a home for "friendless" women. The city mission movement also expanded and achieved its greatest success with the founding of the Five Points Mission in 1850 and the House of Industry four years later. Even the municipality expressed concern about the growing problem of prostitution. In 1847, the Board of Education established a system of evening schools to provide an alternative to theaters, saloons, and idle activities for men and women. "These poor girls, living in the street, are exposed to great dangers. They become bold, ungoverned, careless," concluded one annual report, "without any pure or kind influences to hold them back."[4]

During the first half of the nineteenth century, most efforts to control or eliminate prostitution originated in private moral reform organizations. In the 1850s, however, the state intervened for the first time on a significant scale. In September and October of 1850, with the support of two police court justices, the district attorney, and the future head of the Five Points Mission, police raided Five Points. During a five-week period, Captain John J. McManus brought indictments against over forty brothels and their proprietors. The massive sweeps provided an environment conducive to evangelical reform and were partly responsible for the establishment of the Five Points House of Industry in 1854. Within two years, the Reverend Louis Pease embarked upon similar efforts to eradicate what he considered to be the sexual jaundice in the nation's foremost slum.[5]

During his initial term as mayor, from 1855 to 1858, Fernando Wood became New York's first chief executive to seek elimination of gambling and prostitution from certain parts of the metropolis. "Chief among the civic notabilia is the Mayor's foray or razzia among the unhappy fallen women who perambulate Broadway," recounted George Templeton Strong, who questioned the legality, if not the motives, of Wood's actions. "What the Mayor seeks to abolish or abate is not the terrible evil of prostitution, but simply the scandal and offence of the *peripatetic* whorearchy." In other words, the mayor moved only against poor streetwalkers, not the chic brothels of Leonard, Church, and Mercer streets. Wood was "popular for his courage in taking the responsibility of action unsupported by precedent and statute," continued Strong. "So rise dictators in degenerate commonwealths."[6]

Although short-lived, the McManus and Wood antiprostitution campaigns marked the initial attempts of the municipality to shape private sexual behavior in nineteenth-century New York. But like their evangelical predecessors, city officials fell far short of their goals to eliminate commercial sex. As Walt Whitman commented on the eve of the Civil War, reform programs achieved little in the way of transforming the behavior of most prostitutes. When arrested and sent to the Tombs or Blackwell's Island, prostitutes became "more promiscuous in their associations thereafter," said Whitman, adding, "They do not resort to their old quarters for fear of arrest, but spread themselves, and the vice and disease ever marching in their train, over the previously uncontaminated parts of the metropolis and its suburbs."[7]

Even the morally optimistic Five Points House of Industry's *Monthly Record* conceded that such "sinful skepticism of the public mind" was based on the "wrong-headed efforts" of New York's moral reform societies. Although founded "for the laudable purpose of recovering the wretched daughters of vice, . . . [they] carried on with so much more . . . zeal than knowledge . . . that they could hardly have any other effect than to draw new victims into the same terrible abyss." Inmate population statistics tended to confirm the limited impact of moral reformers. At midcentury, in a city of half a million people and approximately six thousand prostitutes, the American Female Guardian Society's Home of the Friendless had only 89 inmates, all fifteen years of age or younger. The Institution of Mercy in the Fourteenth Ward had a few more with 103 females. And the famed Magdalen Asylum in the Twelfth Ward housed a mere 11 inmates, ranging from fourteen to twenty years in age.[8]

By 1870, antiprostitution reform had come full circle. Like their early predecessors, midcentury reformers abandoned moral reclamation efforts to salvage the reputations and souls of prostitutes. Houses of refuge for homeless and young women now consciously avoided becoming Magdalen homes (institutions to reform penitent prostitutes).[9] Most antebellum campaigns to eliminate or minimize the impact of prostitution were thus sporadic and short-lived and, except for Fernando Wood's brief excursion into the realm of moral propriety, had little impact upon municipal politics.

The Preventive Society

AFTER the Civil War, the antiprostitution appeal assumed a new dimension. Reacting to pervasive municipal corruption and the increasing visibility of gambling dens, brothels, panel houses, and unlicensed saloons, many New Yorkers became convinced that sexual evil could be eliminated by effective and vigorous action. A variety of purity groups appeared that actively fought proposals by members of the American Medical Association and the New York Society for the Prevention of Contagious Diseases to regulate prostitution. Led by the former abolitionists Aaron Macy Powell and Abby Hopper Gibbons, the New York Committee for the Prevention of State Regulation (1876) successfully defeated several proposals to legalize prostitution during the 1870s. During the 1890s, the organization became the American Purity Alliance. Still others, such as Charles Crittendon, established missions for reformed prostitutes and other "fallen" women.[10]

These antiregulatory groups, however, were preoccupied primarily with the politics of vice in Albany. More influential were those purity advocates who confronted the problem directly in the streets, particularly Anthony Comstock and, later, Charles Parkhurst. Probably the best-known antivice reformers in American history, Comstock and Parkhurst led a five-decade battle to mold manners and morals. "Comstockery," as a captious George Bernard Shaw put it, quickly became synonymous with the American predilection for sexual suppression and moral regulation. These moral reformers created and sustained a new institution, the preventive society, in hopes of reducing erotic temptation in the city.[11]

Preventive societies marked, in part, a reaction against increasing corruption in New York's police force. In 1852, for instance, one observer characterized the police as "partly awed by the blackguards of the brothel and groggery, partly intimate with them." Similarly, in 1875, Mayor William H. Wickham charged that the men in blue were not only inefficient but "demoralized [and] beyond recovery." By the century's end, critics on the state senate's Lexow committee investigating municipal corruption viewed the police "as disturbers and breakers of the peace, . . . a danger not only to the liberty but to the safety of the citizens." Charles Parkhurst asserted, "The guilt of the proprietors [of vice] is not nearly so great as the guilt of a police system that tolerates and fosters guilty proprietorship. It is our police system that is the supreme culprit. . . ."[12]

Equally evil to many reformers were the police courts. One observer pointed out that the majority of magistrates were not even lawyers, while another called them "marvels of stupidity and corruption." Charging that "the police courts of New York are unequalled," Edward Crapsey conceded that even honest judges found little opportunity to fight disorder. Brothels, gambling dens, and saloons openly bribed police to stay in business. After obtaining a warrant, police raided these establishments and forced them to pay for "protection" in exchange for a discharged case or a light sentence. This system of justice, Crapsey argued, discouraged many judges from issuing warrants at all. Another put it simply in 1870: "Municipal law is a failure in New York."[13]

According to purity-minded New Yorkers, municipal tolerance of public commercial sex stimulated licentiousness and government malfeasance. Some even encouraged extralegal, private action. Before the Civil War, George Templeton Strong, for example, predicted that New Yorkers would someday resort to vigilantism. An "organized amateur society of supporters of law would be wholesome," he argued, and it "should employ agents to prosecute violence and corruption rigorously." Strong went onto speculate that such a group might not succeed "unless it went farther and took the law into its own hands," in the manner of the 1850s vigilance committees of San Francisco. Private, vigilante bodies would thus replace the debilitated public instruments of law enforcement.[14]

Strong proved to be an accurate soothsayer, for in 1866 Henry Bergh organized the first such preventive group, the American Society for the Prevention of Cruelty to Animals (ASPCA). Modeled after an English association of the same name, the ASPCA saw its star rise quickly, and by 1876 there were similar organizations in thirteen New York cities, thirty states, Canada, and Italy. When a serious case of child abuse was brought to the ASPCA in 1872, the society's counsel, Elbridge Gerry, subsequently created the Society for the Prevention of Cruelty to Children (SPCC). Like the ASPCA, the SPCC quickly expanded its influence. Within five years, there were over four hundred affiliated organizations in New York, sixteen in other states, and two in France and Italy, each copying the initial society in New York City. At approximately the same time, Anthony Comstock established the Society for the Suppression of Vice (SSV), which he led well into the twentieth century. Finally, the Presbyterian minister Howard Crosby founded the Society for the Prevention of Crime (SPC) in 1878. In the 1890s, Charles Parkhurst assumed control of the SPC, which became the parent organization to the City Vigilance League (CVL) in 1892.[15]

The membership and administrators of preventive societies included the most prominent citizens and reflected a new political consensus emerging in the post-Tweed era. Notables like Peter Cooper, Henry Bergh, Elbridge Gerry, Benjamin D. Hicks, Thomas Acton, and William H. Webb participated in the founding and early administration of several preventive societies. Although most were Protestant and Republican, the Democrats August Belmont and Moses Taylor, the Tammany Hall allies John T. Hoffman, A. Oakey Hall, and James T. Brady, and the liberals William Cullen Bryant and Parke Godwin were also active supporters. In order to avoid rigid evangelical approaches or associations with any specific religious denomination, preventive societies actively sought support from Rabbi Gustave Gottheil and the outspoken Roman Catholic pastor Edward McGlynn. The movement was "from the start purely unsectarian and non-partisan," Charles Parkhurst later asserted.[16]

Although the four preventive societies differed in specific origins, membership, and incorporated charters, they nevertheless showed many similarities. Each concentrated on a specific social vice, envisioned itself as an enforcer of the law, and believed that the spread of social deviancy justified extralegal action. Relations among the preventive societies were characterized by cooperation and only rare displays of sectarian rivalry.

Most important, the preventive society differed from other nineteenth-century antivice and moral reform organizations in method and strategy. The founders of preventive societies believed that most laws were adequate and that lax law enforcement bred moral degeneration. Consequently, the societies adopted their own private, unregulated methods to secure their goals. Second, preventive societies, wholly private in organization and control, won vague law enforcement responsibilities from the state, thereby acquiring a quasi-governmental power other reform groups never enjoyed. Ideologically, supporters of preventive societies argued that crime was institutionalized, that urban depravity originated in well-planned and organized groups. The absence of female participants also distinguished preventive societies from their reform contemporaries. Finally, several key leaders—Howard Crosby and Parkhurst, most notably—opposed the temperance and prohibition goals of many other reformers.[17]

In regard to powers, the SSV's 1873 charter characteristically claimed responsibility for "the enforcement of laws for the suppression of the trade in, and circulation of obscene literature and illustrations, advertisements, and articles of indecent or immoral use." When the U.S. Post Office made Comstock a special agent that same year, the SSV's local powers of prosecution were magnified and its influence thereafter was felt nationwide.[18] Initially empowered to bring complaints on the basis of any law affecting children, the SPCC widened its responsibility in 1876 when Charles Fairchild, the state attorney general, and Benjamin Phelps, the city district attorney, designated it the city's and state's representative in all child abuse cases. And in 1888, the state continued the trend of privatizing law enforcement at the expense of the official police force by permitting SPCC agents to arrest anyone violating child protection laws.[19]

Instead of cooperating with municipal agencies, as had originally been intended, preventive societies competed with them. Torn between loyalty to the law and the fervent hope of eliminating vice, preventive societies developed an ideology that justified extralegal, nonviolent vigilantism and a disregard for legally created local government institutions. Like vigilantes, preventive reformers seized control of public authority in order to suppress and punish crime when they thought due process was inadequate.[20] But unlike typical vigilante bodies, preventive societies were formal, incorporated groups with a legal existence.

In their rhetoric, preventive reformers viewed the city as the frontier. Preventive societies, for example, were initially designed to be an auxiliary to the police force, a type of urban posse. Henry Bergh considered himself a policeman, "although not on the pay roll." Corrupt police officers, lenient courts, and the subversive, underground nature of crime justified extralegal action. "In some degree," editorialized the New York *Times*, "our voluntary associations for the prevention of various evils resemble vigilance committees, regulators, or lynch policemen." Lynchings, claimed another paper, were necessary means of redressing offenses, especially where a trial would only confer "dignity upon a crime which would be derogatory to the security of a community." Any form of obscenity warranted adoption of the lynch law, according to the SSV. By 1901, the City Vigilance League, the Committee of Fifteen, and the Episcopal bishop Henry Codman Potter were actively organizing "vigilante" committees. In the mind of Charles Parkhurst, the preventive society was the city "protecting itself against ravage by volunteer action" because other methods "had proven to be inadequate."[21]

Preventive societies fancied themselves above the law. Comstock, Bergh, and Gerry raided dance halls, brothels, gambling dens, and even rat pits in their efforts to suppress "immoral" behavior. They convinced O. B. Frothingham that "the position assumed by these champions is that of belligerency. The rules they adopt are the rules of war. . . . Their efforts, consequently, are partial, to say nothing of their roughness and violence." In one SSV report, Comstock charged, "You must hunt these men as you hunt rats, without mercy." Similarly, Bergh asserted that vice and cruelty corroded the moral structure of society, thereby requiring "zealous daring" and a disregard of the formal requirements of law. "In times of peace as well as war the element of enthusiasm is material to success; and while the letter of the law should be always paramount, its spirit ought also to be taken into account." Ineffective police raids and municipal action especially vexed reformers. Parkhurst derided such raids as "a form of official playfulness."[22] For preventive reformers, self-defined humanitarian concern overrode the technicality of statutes, justifying a more pragmatic, even if illegal, course of action.

These efforts did not escape condemnation by the police. "I think it is an outrage that [the SPC] should be allowed to make fools of the police and endanger the interests of justice by [its] clumsiness," charged one police inspector. If they have warrants, he argued, "why don't they come to us and intrust us with them?"[23] Years later, Parkhurst and the SPC informed the police that their failure to close disorderly places after presenting a list forced the SPC to adopt its "own scheme of action" in efforts to close the brothels. When the police commissioner refused warrants to private vice societies in 1901, they resorted to their own, violent, destructive raids, in which William T. Jerome and Frank Moss literally swung hammers and sledges in illicit cafés and gambling dens. Finally, in 1909, the tenement house commissioner refused to secure legal evidence against tenement house prostitutes and landlords, and that led members of the SPC to procure the evidence themselves.[24]

The undercover tactics employed by the preventive societies illustrated their disregard for proper legal procedure. In entrapping and arresting a factory owner for attempting to seduce a teenage girl, for example, the SPC asserted that it "voluntarily undertook work which naturally might have been passed over to the Police Department." At other times, preventive societies tried to determine the punishment levied against an offender. When a father admitted that his six-year-old daughter appeared at Harry Hill's concert saloon, the SPCC indefinitely adjourned the case after he promised to stop her performances. Similarly, Sophia Meyers was arrested for operating a brothel on Greene Street, but received a suspended sentence after promising the SPCC that a twelve-year-old prostitute would be put in its custody, that she would close her business, and that thereafter her "home and children would be liable to inspection by the Society's officers." The SPCC frequently persuaded judges to suspend sentences on madams of other brothels if they promised to break up their businesses (for a cartoon critical of these methods, see figure 31).[25]

Comstock, Gerry, and Crosby believed that concert saloons and dime museums were major causes of vice. Most disconcerting were the prostitutes employed as "waiter girls" in such establishments. Attired in

Fig. 31 Robert Minor, "Your Honor, this woman gave birth to a naked child!" From The Masses, *1915, Courtesy Tamiment Institute Library, New York University*

revealing costumes, they moved from table to table, even lap to lap, soliciting customers. In the rear or above the dance floor, single rooms were available where sex could readily be purchased. The most popular concert saloon, Harry Hill's, even developed a national reputation. Dime museums, those "sinks of iniquity," earned Gerry's wrath by admitting children to see their exhibits. Gerry singled out the Tivoli Theater because its "chief attractions were blood and thunder dramas, full of powder, smoke and western bravadoes," which encouraged youths to beg or steal to get admission money.[26] Such attitudes reflected middle-class fears of the emergence of an independent, popular culture, cut off from and uncontrolled by those religious and educational institutions previously responsible for disseminating "culture." In the ensuing decade, the SPC and SPCC forced the closing of Sandy Spencer's Palace Music Hall, the Bowery Garden, the Bowery Varieties Theater, Owney Geoghegan's concert saloon, the Windsor Museum, the Globe Dime Museum, the New American Museum, the New York Museum, and the Deutsches Casino.[27]

Gerry specifically believed that the theater was a direct cause of prostitution and homelessness. Theater companies frequently employed young girls and boys, whose parents were eager to secure additional family income. Gerry charged, however, that the children were often released later during a tour and forced to "seek employment in a lower grade of entertainment." He cited cases where child performers appeared at prominent New York theaters like Wallack's, the Metropolitan Opera House, and the Academy of Music, only to be discovered a year or two later in run-down dives, singing to "an audience composed in a greater part of prostitutes, and where both men and women were drinking and smoking."[28]

Preventive reformers especially feared the increasing commercialization of leisure and the impact of market forces on the family. It was "a foreign theory," believed Gerry, "that children are merely property of the parents, and to be utilized as they see fit for their pecuniary profit and benefit." Preventive reformers defined the proper conduct of responsible parents and children. If a youth was attracted to a morally unfit environment, Gerry considered it his duty to act "to extricate children from dens wherein they have been decoyed with the sure sequence of irreparable injury, disease, and death." Child abuse and police corruption justified the abandonment of public law enforcement "in order to protect those who are unable to protect themselves, especially in dealing with offenders who are wealthy, influential and powerful." Family entertainment groups from home and abroad were thus repeatedly throughout the 1870s and 1880s denied permission to perform in the entertainment center of nation.[29]

Such tactics of surveillance and law enforcement eventually aroused controversy. By the 1890s, the SSV refused to publish details of its work, admitting that its activities were sometimes inconsistent with the law. One state senator maintained that the SPC was "a society . . . at war with the police force . . . and animated by methods of revenge against them." The SPC was even accused of committing "acts of shamelessness" in endeavoring to procure evidence on disorderly houses. John Goff complained that the courts had little control over children "secreted away" from their parents by the SPCC. Although the intent was altruistic, Goff questioned "the wisdom of vesting so much power in any society that has no responsibility to the people." The judge and future mayor William J. Gaynor warned that "societies and private enthusiasts for the 'suppression of vice' should . . . learn the supreme danger of trying to do all at once . . . what can be done . . . only very gradually."[30]

The Vice Campaigns

PREVENTIVE societies were not alone in their alarmist campaigns. After 1880, vice and prostitution were continual themes in municipal life and politics. The tactics and policies adopted by the varied and usually short-lived purity movements were heavily influenced by preventive societies, despite their political or independent origins. The crusades of Mayors William R. Grace and Abram S. Hewitt from 1885 to 1888, the exposés of Charles Parkhurst from 1892 to 1894, the Lexow and Mazet investigations of 1894 and 1899, the Committee of Fifteen from 1900 to 1902, and the Committee of Fourteen from 1905 to 1932 illustrated other prominent attempts by reformers to change the sexual politics of New York.

In 1885, William R. Grace could lay claim to being America's most successful Irish immigrant. Upon leaving his family's prosperous County Cork estate, he worked as a clerk for a shipping company in Peru. Eventually becoming partner in the firm, Grace made it a leading commercial house in South America. During the Civil War, when Peruvian and English interests refused to credit vessels of the U.S. Navy, Grace single-handedly put the resources of his business at the disposal of the Navy. In 1868, the firm expanded and Grace moved to New York, where he led American relief efforts to arrest the Irish famine of 1879 and became the first Irish Catholic mayor in 1880. After losing renomination because of a confrontation with the Tammany leader Honest John Kelly, he made a political comeback in 1884 and was reelected on an anti-Tammany reform ticket.[31]

For nearly two decades following the Civil War, municipal and state officials tolerated prostitution in concert saloons. Although city law prohibited the sale of liquor in theaters and concert halls, those opposed to such activity had a difficult time stopping it. For example, concert saloon proprietors, if rejected for a liquor license by the state excise board, routinely circumvented the law by applying for a theater license from the city. Needless to say, the process could also work in reverse. Furthermore, excise officials often ignored the illegal theatrical productions in saloons and city officials the illegal liquor in concert halls and theaters. Graft was the common inducement. John Koster, proprietor of the popular Koster and Bial's, admitted that were the law enforced, he saw "no other way of doing [business] than to shut up at once."[32]

Grace wanted to end this corrupt relationship. Upon his political resurrection and with the advice of Howard Crosby of the SPC, Grace ordered the police and excise commissioners to eliminate prostitution

Fig. 32 William R. Grace

and gambling in concert saloons. When ignored, Grace charged the excise commissioners with granting illegal liquor licenses to prostitute-filled concert halls and saloons. The commissioners claimed Grace was at fault for granting such places theater licenses, which made the excise licenses void. After a special investigative committee exonerated the commissioners, Grace moved to appoint a new board. From May to July 1886, the members of the former excise board refused to relinquish their offices to Grace's appointees. In what might be labeled a battle for control of the underground economy, the two boards simultaneously issued excise licenses to saloons and concert halls. Finally, in October 1886, Grace authorized police raids and suppressed the leading concert saloons, including Harry Hill's, the Brighton, Sans Souci, the American Mabille, the Cremorne, and the Alhambra. By the year's end, Grace had revoked nine hundred licenses.[33]

Grace's commitment to eliminating prostitution, however, was suspect. Prior to his second term, Grace displayed little interest in purity reform. He disdained partisanship, declaring he would "take no active participation in politics so long as [he was] the Chief Magistrate of the city." He even appointed as city marshal the saloonkeeper Robert Hill, whose MacDougal Street saloon was a well-known spot for prostitutes. When Grace eventually moved against the city's proprietors of vice, the

Brooklyn *Eagle* wondered why "something of this sort was not done long ago."[34]

The motives behind Grace's political transformation appear to have been threefold. First, by 1884 he was a confidant and friend of Howard Crosby of the SPC, and Grace sought Crosby's advice throughout the antivice campaign. Second, Grace's strongest antivice efforts occurred at the height of the Henry George–Abram Hewitt mayoral race, a campaign that at times equated concert hall, saloon, and working-class interests with moral licentiousness. Finally, Grace was personally involved in a political scandal. In September 1885, the press reported that Grace was associated with the Grant and Ward investment scheme that publicly embarrassed the former president Ulysses S. Grant. Grace lost $1 million of city revenues by depositing them in the underfinanced Marine Bank, an institution Grace knew had only $400,000 in capital.[35]

As mayor, Grace devoted scant attention to vice and prostitution during his initial year in office. Only after embarrassing public revelations did Grace begin his moral crusade. Even the state investigative committee Grace supported was widely ridiculed, since the governor himself, as one cynic charged, was "a product of the groggery school of politics" and was expected to do little to hurt the political strength of the saloons. And the committee eventually concluded that Grace, not the excise board, had regulatory control over concert halls. Concentrating on prostitution and the concert hall, Grace deflected critical opposition and earned the support of reformers like Crosby, Felix Adler, Heber Newton, E. L. Godkin, and Theodore Roosevelt. The multiple controversies took their toll on Grace, however, and at the end of his term he wrote, "I am heartily sick of the office and have neither the time nor the disposition to give to it."[36]

The attack on commercial sex did not end with Grace's removal from office. Indeed, his successor, Abram S. Hewitt, was a national figure who expanded Grace's efforts. Coming from an artisan family, Hewitt graduated first in his class at Columbia College and proceeded to make a fortune in iron making, first managing Peter Cooper's Trenton Ironworks and later forming a partnership with his brother-in-law and the future mayor Edward Cooper. As Allan Nevins has noted, Hewitt "might have rivalled Andrew Carnegie had he not turned away from iron and steel when he had won a fortune." Leaving industry for politics, Hewitt was elected to Congress and later managed Samuel Tilden's unsuccessful presidential campaign in 1876. The future U.S. secretary of state Elihu Root called Hewitt "New York's first citizen."[37]

Tammany supporters hoped Hewitt's administration would be more tolerant of sporting-male leisure. But to their disappointment, he quickly

Fig. 33 Abram S. Hewitt

closed down numerous concert saloons, including the Haymarket, Harry Hill's, and Tom Gould's. Interestingly, Hewitt's campaign against the concert hall and public displays of sexuality coincided with a period of great labor unrest in New York City. Henry George's nearly successful mayoral campaign, four violent strikes by streetcar employees in 1886, and Johann Most's exuberant leadership of the anarchist movement reflected increasingly aggressive drives for political and economic power by New York's laborers. While breaking strikes and crushing socialist organizing efforts, city officials cooperated with preventive societies in suppressing the concert hall.

Like Grace's before him, however, Hewitt's moral reform activity smacked of political sophistry. He did little to eliminate the brothel or prostitution in other parts of the metropolis. Forced out of institutions like the saloon and concert hall, where it had thrived for a quarter century, prostitution rapidly spread to the tenement and new areas of the city. And when concerned citizens, ranging from wealthy elites to poor immigrants, complained about prostitutes in their neighborhood, Hewitt did little. Usually, he forwarded formal or written complaints to the police, who merely denied the accusation and continued to tolerate the illegal prostitution.[38] Hewitt's hypocrisy ultimately set the stage for

Charles Parkhurst and New York's most famous antiprostitution crusade, at the end of the century.

DESPITE their sometimes coercive methods of fighting illicit sexuality and crime, preventive reformers and their mayoral supporters proved to be precursors of Progressive reforms like child labor laws, food and drug regulation, public hygiene, and better health care for immigrants as early as the 1870s. Court decisions arguing that "the custody of the child by the parent [was] within legislative regulation" were the product of aggressive action by preventive societies.[39] Acceptance of state intervention in theatrical performances set precedents for similar rulings in later child labor cases. Like many Progressives after 1900, preventive reformers refused to attribute vice and poverty to defective character. Instead, they blamed urban amusements and institutions that fostered unbridled sex and shaped the environment of the immigrant and working-class neighborhood. If a building housed a concert saloon or brothel, new management brought little change. Only outright prohibition did.

Preventive societies privatized "moral" law enforcement. As commercial sex grew more prominent and profitable, private reform organizations intervened in the name of the general, law-abiding public. These societies though little of invading different spheres of private life in behalf of the public interest. Rather than adopting government regulation, they assumed governmental functions. Preventive societies thus acted as a kind of "private" state, vigilantly preserving their own sexual and moral code. In so doing, they occasionally usurped police power and employed extralegal measures in regulating private and leisure-time behavior, giving them an enduring impact upon public police power. Preventive reformers thereby planted and cultivated a consensus on sexual morality in late-nineteenth-century New York that would be harvested in the era of Progressive reform.

10

SEX DISTRICTS REVISITED

THE vice campaigns of Anthony Comstock, W. R. Grace, and Abram Hewitt, while affecting the institutional structure of prostitution in New York, had little impact on its geography. By the end of the nineteenth century, in fact, prostitution seemed to be everywhere. The experience of one anonymous male illustrates the omnipresence of commercial sex in the metropolis. On a warm September night in 1888, he took a leisurely walk downtown. Beginning near Herald Square on Sixth Avenue, in the physical heart of Manhattan, he saw prostitutes whose brightly colored garb spoke, in his words, "a tale of untold misery, . . . like a ship cut loose from her moorings." As he wandered down a cross street, a voice beckoned him. "I turned quickly," he recalled, "and beheld a woman . . . using her best endeavors to persuade me to enter into her abode or in other words to come upstairs and have a good time." He declined the sexual invitation, continuing his pedestrian adventure southward into Greenwich Village. "Passing down there," he wrote, the prostitutes "seemed to get more brazened as I was jostled by several of the women or unfortunates as I passed."

Manhattan became metaphor, as he evoked images of Dante's *Inferno*. The "further down I got, [the] more stepped [*sic*] in sin did these unfortunates appear." Moving through Washington Square, he ventured down Wooster Street and into Grand Street. "I passed along till I got as far as Elizabeth Street, a street that is well known all over New York for its impurity and vice. . . . I hardly reached Hester Street when I was crowded off the sidewalk by a lot of depraved young girls between 14 and 20 years old." On Canal Street, he found the same as he approached the terminus of the Bowery, Chatham Square: "only the girls were more under the influence of liquor and more depraved." He walked along Chrystie Street, in the immigrant district of the Lower East Side. "[I]t was quiet to all outside appearances, but still vice rules its way as the objects at the windows plainly told and the red lights indicated the business that was going on within the walls." When one reaches Bleecker Street, "the same thing occur [*sic*]. Women parading up and down, women in the windows trying to attract attention."[1]

Such descriptions of New York's sexual terrain remained commonplace in the half century following the Civil War. Vigilante methods and moral panegyrics notwithstanding, preventive societies and their allies were unsuccessful in hindering the physical spread of prostitution. "In all the great cities of the United States, . . . the walking of the streets after nightfall by prostitutes has becoming an alarming evil," wrote Edward Crapsey in 1872, adding, "New York is entitled, I am afraid, to preeminence in this respect." Four years later, a grand jury reported that numerous areas of Manhattan were "almost worthless for occupancy" because of the vast array of brothels. At the turn of the century, the Committee of Fifteen complained that the "social evil" prevailed in "alarming dimensions" and threatened New York with its "complete satiation." "As everyone knows," concurred the former police chief William McAdoo in 1906, "the city is being rebuilt, and vice moves ahead of business."[2]

Between 1870 and 1915, a new geography of sex districts emerged in New York. So pervasive was prostitution in New York's leisure and working-class subcultures that observant pedestrians like the foregoing spotted it in most neighborhoods. Entertainment districts with names like the Tenderloin and the Rialto were centerpieces of national folklore and famous for the easy availability of sex. Indeed, such areas contained the most lucrative and commercialized forms of prostitution. Still, blatant sexuality did not fully define such neighborhoods. Prostitutes worked alongside the city's leading theaters, hotels, and restaurants. And while some brothels dominated certain blocks, such establishments usually shared their space with ordinary commercial enterprises and working-class residents.

Less well-known and less commercialized were the growing immigrant and working-class areas on the Lower East Side, on the East Side near Gramercy Park, and in Greenwich Village, just south of Washington Square Park. Even smaller clusters remained below Canal Street, where impoverished, mainly immigrant prostitutes worked in Greenwich and Water streets, Chinatown, and Little Italy. Finally, with the expansion of elevated railroads after 1870 and the opening of the subway in 1904, prostitutes were soon found on the Upper East and West sides, in Harlem, and in some outer boroughs (see maps 8–13).[3] Truly segregated red-light districts never appeared.

Changes in land use patterns and physical development in New York exerted a profound influence upon the geography of prostitution. First, the industrialization of garment manufacturing forced prostitution uptown, along with entertainment, residential, and other less profitable land uses. After 1865, for instance, the industrial and cast-iron edifices of the architects Griffith Thomas, James Duckworth, and Henry Fern-

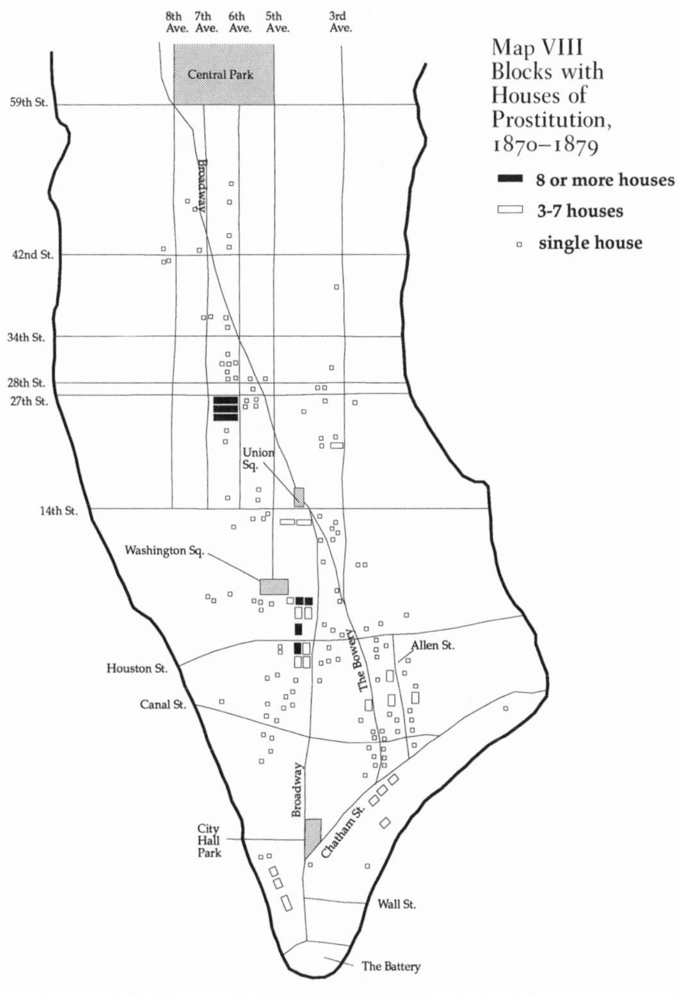

Map VIII
Blocks with Houses of Prostitution, 1870–1879

bach rapidly replaced the brothels along Mercer, Wooster, Greene, and Crosby streets. Real estate in this old sex district around Broadway doubled and tripled in value between 1850 and 1880, hastening the conversion from residential to industrial use. A sanitary inspector making his rounds in the neighborhood after the Civil War concluded that the "large number of houses of prostitution . . . for which this district was . . . so notorious . . . [were] rapidly disappearing from this section of the city, . . . being soon crowded out by the encroachments of mercantile business." Similarly, George Ellington admitted in 1869 that Mercer Street property was so expensive that "warehouses of immense proportions [were] taking the places of the houses where scenes of revelry were once enacted."[4]

A second factor rearranging the geography of sex was a citywide building

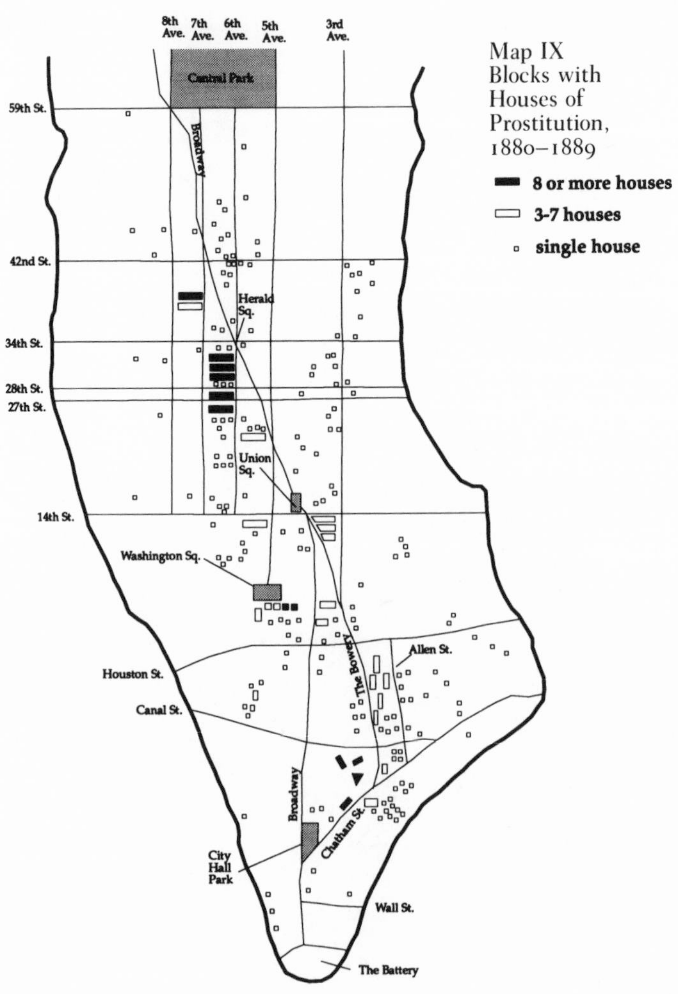

Map IX
Blocks with Houses of Prostitution, 1880–1889

boom. New York, like numerous other American cities, more than doubled its total supply of dwellings between 1870 and 1900. Nowhere was this change more evident than in the construction of tenement houses. In the period 1864–93, the number of tenements in Gotham rose from 15,511 to 39,138. Inhabited almost immediately upon erection, tenements attracted working-class and immigrant populations and dramatically transformed the neighborhood structure of New York. As the tenement replaced the row house as the primary residential type, it contributed to the decline of the brothel as the major form of prostitution. By the end of the century, prostitution in tenements was a major concern of housing reformers.[5]

New York's leading entertainment institutions reacted to these forces and abandoned their older downtown surroundings. Beginning with the

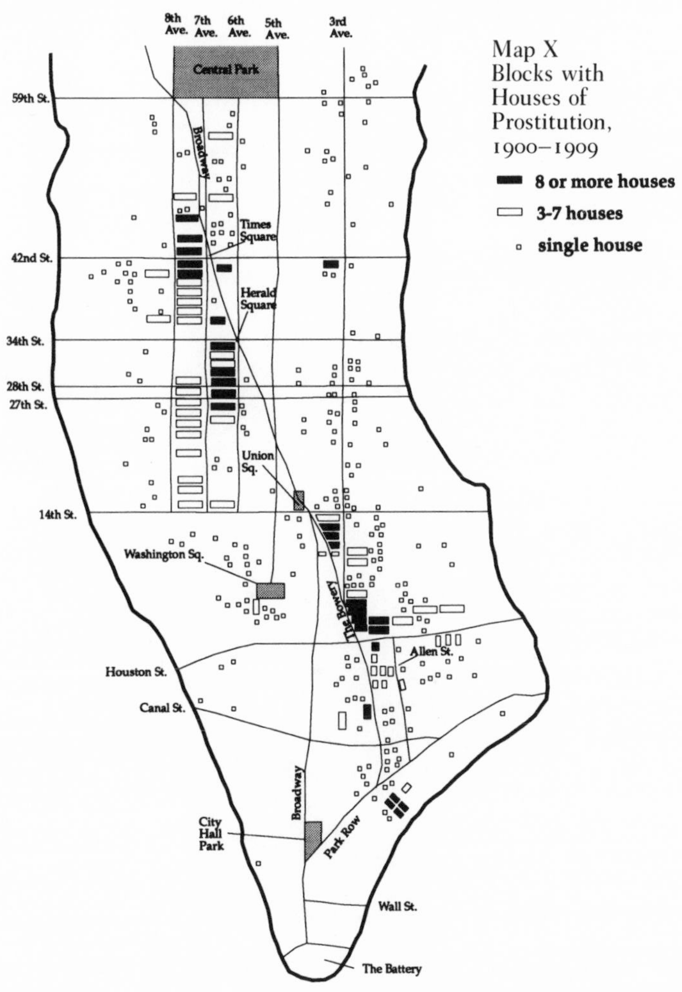

Map X
Blocks with Houses of Prostitution, 1900–1909

Academy of Music's opening on Union Square (Fourteenth Street) in 1854, leading theaters migrated north along Broadway. Many moved into the once elite row house neighborhoods of Chelsea and Madison Square. By 1880, Twenty-third Street was the major theater district. By 1905, Times Square and Forty-second Street made that claim. The most commercialized forms of prostitution quickly followed this uptown movement of entertainment. More than purity reformers, industrial capitalism and urban redevelopment displaced commercial sex.

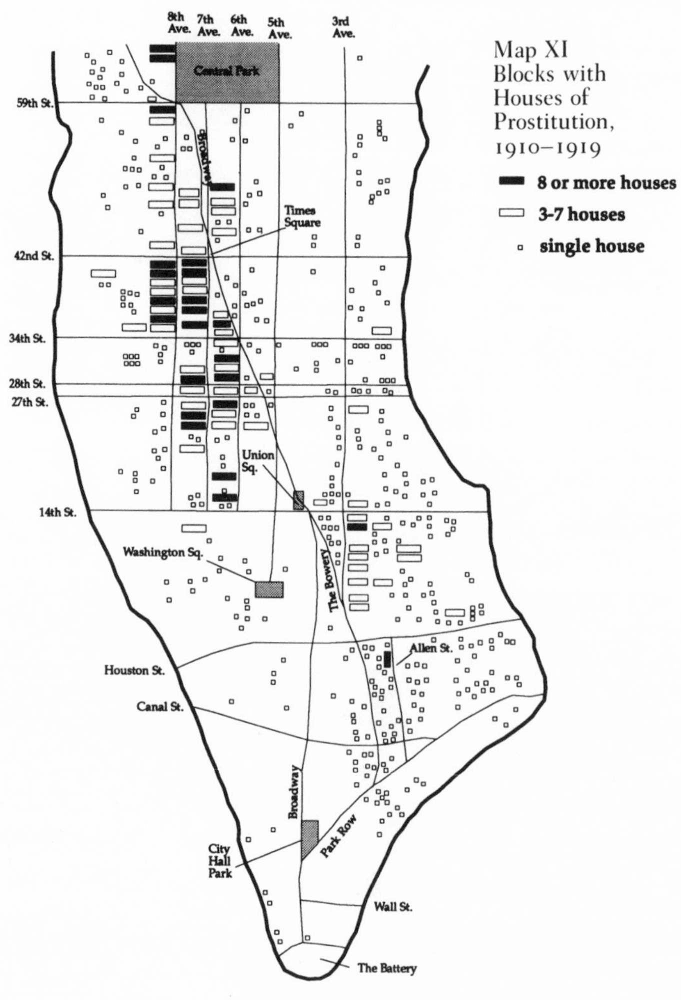

Map XI
Blocks with Houses of Prostitution, 1910–1919

The Tenderloin

THE Tenderloin was the most famous sex district in New York City history. Sandwiched between wealthy Gramercy Park and Murray Hill on the east and working-class Hell's Kitchen on the west, the Tenderloin stretched north from Twenty-third Street between Fifth and Eighth avenues. Its major axis was Sixth Avenue. Throughout the final decades of the nineteenth century, the boundaries of the Tenderloin fluctuated. It progressed up the middle of Manhattan, reaching Thirty-fourth Street during the 1870s, Forty-second Street in the 1880s, and Fifty-seventh Street by the 1890s. According to legend, the Tenderloin's name originated when a corrupt police captain, Alexander S. Williams, upon his transfer to the Twenty-ninth Precinct in 1876, merrily proclaimed, "I've been having chuck steak ever since I've been on the force, and now I'm going to have a bit of tenderloin."[6] The appellation stuck.

The Tenderloin's early history gave few hints of its rise as New York's premier sex district. Led by Clement Clarke Moore and William B. Astor, real estate entrepreneurs between 1830 and 1860 developed the area north of Fourteenth Street into an elite suburban community. By 1860, magnificent brownstones lined its streets. The neighborhood between Fifth and Eighth avenues was even described as having "a superior class of residents than those on the East Side of town."[7]

After the Civil War, the quiet surroundings of this elite community were shattered by the forces of commerce and entertainment. Beginning with Daly's, at Broadway and Twenty-ninth Street, in 1867, several new theaters opened. Within three years, the Grand Opera House (1869), Booth's Theater (1869), and Koster and Bial's (1870) had opened on West Twenty-third Street. By one account, Booth's was "the handsomest theater in the city." And only one block east stood Madison Square Garden (1870).[8]

Hotels also followed, sparked by the opening of the sumptuous, eight-story Gilsey House (1869), with its elaborate Second Empire façade, adjacent to Daly's Theater. The ensuing decade saw the construction of Coleman House, Stuyvesant House, Clifford House, and the Grand Hotel along Broadway. The physical isolation of the neighborhood ended with the opening of New York's first elevated railroad, along Ninth Avenue, in 1871. Finally, department stores, seeking more space and lower rents, invaded the area, beginning with Lord and Taylor and Arnold Constable (both in 1869) along Broadway between Nineteenth and Twenty-first streets. By 1876, Hugh O'Neill and B. Altman had opened similar palaces of consumption a block west on Sixth Avenue. "Ladies Mile" had moved uptown. For two decades after 1870, West Twenty-third Street, from Madison Square to Eighth Avenue, was a dominant thoroughfare in the Tenderloin, filled with hotels, express offices, theaters, saloons, restaurants, and department stores.[9]

The movement of premier theaters into this area continued for over a decade. By 1885, Herald Square was at the center of the Tenderloin. Bisecting it was Broadway, alight in a blazing sea of illumination. The New Park Theater (1873), Daly's Fifth Avenue Theater (1877), San Francisco Music Hall (1878), Wallack's Theater (1882), Brighton Theater (1883), Herald Square Theater (1883), Casino Theater (1882), the Metropolitan Opera House (1883), and Broadway Theater (1880) lined the chic boulevard from Twenty-third to Forty-first Street. "Crowds throng the sidewalks," wrote James D. McCabe, Jr. The "lights of the omnibuses and carriages dart to and fro along the roadway like myriads of fire-flies; the great hotels, the theatres and restaurants, send out their blaze of gas-lamps, and are alive with visitors. . . . All sorts of people are out, and the scene is enlivening beyond description." One police officer remembered that "the Tenderloin drew to its streets most of the visitors and the best people in the city."[10]

This surfeit of entertainment and commerce made the neighborhood undesirable to wealthy New Yorkers, who then abandoned their well-built brownstones for new ones uptown. Landlords unable to attract middle-class residents had two choices: subdivide the houses into multiple-family dwellings for working-class tenants or lease to agents who in turn rented to prostitutes who could afford high rents. The numerous neighborhood theaters made the latter option the more profitable. Thus, the former domiciles of middle-class respectability were transformed into brothels. "[H]ouses of prostitution," remembered one Tenderloin police officer, "lined up in an unbroken row of brownstone fronts." Tenderloin brothels, in fact, occupied some of the most lucrative property in the city. Houses just off Broadway, and others adjacent to such enterprises as Daly's Theater, the Metropolitan Opera House, Wallack's Theater, Carnegie Hall, and the Waldorf-Astoria, were the most valuable bordellos in New York City.[11]

Nearly every street that intersected Broadway and Sixth Avenue above Twenty-third Street housed some prostitutes. Specific blocks, however, developed reputations for their erotic activity. In the 1870s, for example, the Seven Sisters brothels, on West Twenty-fifth Street (between Sixth and Seventh avenues), were preeminent. With well-bred, musically-inclined, "cultured and pleasing companions," these brothels advertised in newspapers and accepted only a formally dressed clientele. As late as

1913, over ten brothels were located on the same street. Another block was known for the enterprising brothels that attracted patrons by putting "pictures of the charming inmates in their windows." Similarly, West Twenty-seventh Street (Sixth to Seventh avenues) had at least twenty-six brothels during the 1870s and fifteen during the 1880s. One neighborhood resident complained that the plentiful number of prostitutes on the street alone made it "almost impossible to go through . . . , especially in late evening unless you are satisfied to turn into the middle of the street."[12]

The plethora of brothels transformed street life. By 1879, Sixth Avenue in particular was "the sidewalk of the *lorettes,* the stomping ground of the well-dressed unfortunates," according to one observer. Another, familiar with London's red-light district, dubbed it "the Haymarket of New York." Observers repeatedly noted how prostitutes rarely conducted themselves "with the outward propriety" they did on Broadway. "[B]y some indescribable wearing of the sealskin saque [*sic*] or the jaunty hat," wrote one critic, the prostitutes "gave the impression that they were of the half-world where dwell most of the heroines of your modern French dramatists and romances." Apart from brothels, prostitutes worked in the many concert saloons that lined Sixth Avenue north of Twenty-third Street. For decades, entertainment entrepreneurs strove for a European cachet and called their places of pleasure the Haymarket, the Strand, the Cremorne, the Cairo, the Star and Garter, and Buckingham Palace. Full of prostitutes, these remained leading institutions of New York's nightlife.[13]

No single block was preeminent in Tenderloin sex. West Thirty-first and West Thirty-second streets, for example, were populated with at least nineteen brothels apiece in the 1880s and had a minimum of ten each during the following decade. Farther north, a string of a dozen or so brothels lined West Thirty-ninth and Fortieth streets (Seventh to Eighth Avenue). Beginning in 1883 with the opening of the Metropolitan Opera House, then the world's largest auditorium, these brothels thrived (figure 34). Operagoers complained about the streetwalkers soliciting men entering and exiting the opera. West Thirty-ninth Street, in particular, drew attention for its French-run bordellos. Dubbed Soubrette Row by the 1890s, these houses "were known all over the country," according to one observer. "The French girls in these houses," wrote another investigator, "resort to unnatural practices and as a result the other girls will not associate or eat with them."[14]

Prostitution was not the only activity found on blocks with large numbers of brothels. During the day, department stores, dry goods establishments, and theater-related services attracted consumers from

Fig. 34 Metropolitan Opera House
Museum of the City of New York

all walks of life. Some brothels shared their block with various industries. The ones on West Twenty-fifth, Twenty-sixth, and Twenty-seventh streets, for example, were close to furniture and refrigerator factories, carpenter shops, mineral water distributors, coal sheds, lumberyards, and small warehouses. Immediate neighbors in other houses included artists, clerks, dressmakers, teamsters, plumbers, and small merchants (see figure 35 for a later example). Ordinary residents complained that even outwardly quiet, residential blocks in the Tenderloin district were in fact "infested by several houses of ill fame." The Reverend Cornelius Praetori of St. Francis Roman Catholic Church, on West Thirty-first Street, lamented that his parish was located practically in the middle of the Tenderloin by the 1880s. "[T]here is no church in the city of New York," declared the pastor, "so near [the] whore houses." Another Tenderloin resident, George Stone, reported in 1887 that "two men came into my house and sat down in the parlor, imagining that they were in one of these resorts, and refused to leave when ordered to do so, calling my wife and daughter all sorts of vile names, and using the most profane language."[15]

Fig. 35 Tenderloin brothels, West 54th Street
From Committee of Fourteen, Annual Report for 1914 *(1915)*

The movement of hotels and theaters up Broadway continued through the 1890s and into the twentieth century. The Knickerbocker and Empire theaters opened in 1893 at Thirty-eighth and Fortieth streets, respectively. In 1895, Oscar Hammerstein opened his stunning, 6,000-seat Olympia Theater, on Broadway and Forty-fourth Street. And from 1903 to 1907, no fewer than nine theaters were constructed in the vicinity, many along Forty-second Street. When the new subway line opened in 1904, the New York *Times* moved to Longacre Square and persuaded the city to rename it Times Square.

This new nightlife attracted prostitutes. By 1901, Committee of Fifteen investigators identified 132 different addresses housing some form of prostitution in the immediate thirty-three blocks of the Longacre Square neighborhood (see map 12). At least 63 brothels, 61 tenements, 8 apartments, and 10 hotels were used by prostitutes. On Saturday and Sunday nights, lines of eager young men formed outside the most popular bordellos. Tammany Hall's Archibald Hadden ran the popular and prostitute-filled German Village and Denver Hotel, on West Fortieth Street. West Forty-second Street from Sixth to Ninth Avenue was thick with streetwalkers. The Reverend Adam Clayton Powell, Sr., contended that his West Fortieth Street church was in "the most notorious red-light district in New York City." There "harlots would stand across the street on Sunday evenings in unbuttoned Mother Hubbards [dresses] solicit-

Map XII
Houses of Prostitution in Longacre Square, 1901

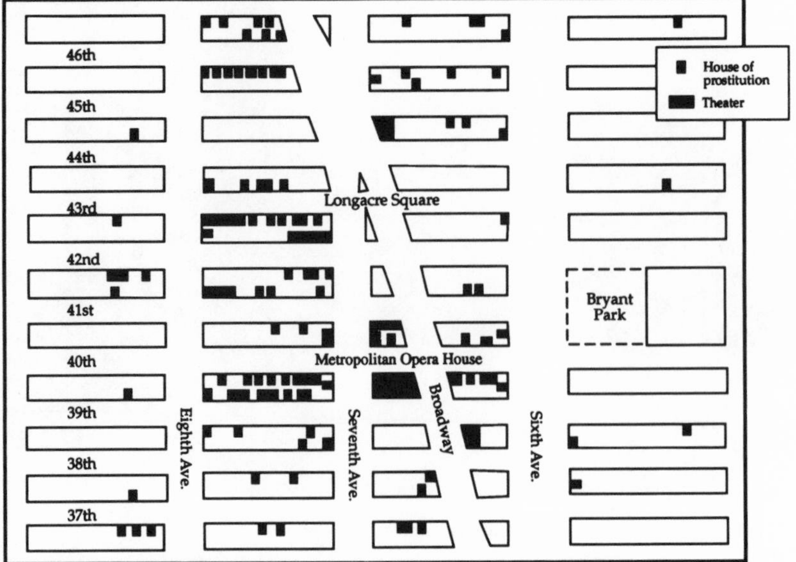

ing men as they left our service." By 1901, the sobriquet Soubrette Row was applied to West Forty-third Street, a block where almost every house was a brothel and directly across from the future site of the *Times*. Observers insisted that Broadway from West Twenty-seventh to Sixty-eighth Street was a two-mile parade of prurient commerce, "ten to twenty prostitutes . . . seen nightly on every block." Such pedestrian activity convinced even the *Times* that "the glittering splendor of 'the Great White Way' does not symbolize the best spirit of the people of New York."[16]

In the half century after 1870, the Tenderloin truly had no center. The use of city streets and real property by prostitutes and their clients moved about not only from year to year but even within different parts of the day. In morning and afternoon, the Ladies Mile, along Broadway, filled with shoppers visiting the department stores and retail outlets. At night along the same strip, prostitutes joined the clientele of restaurants, hotels, theaters, and saloons. A block west, concert saloons and bars dominated a more salacious Sixth Avenue. Blocks of West Twenty-ninth, Thirty-second, Thirty-ninth, Fortieth, and Forty-third streets, off Sixth Avenue or Broadway, consistently housed a minimum of a dozen brothels. When business was booming, as many as twenty such establishments could be counted on each block. For roughly a quarter century, sex pervaded the geographical heart of nighttime Manhattan.

The African Tenderloin

SEX in the Tenderloin was also a racial affair. Black prostitution was relegated to the edge of the sex district along Seventh Avenue from Twenty-third to Fortieth Street, better known as African Broadway. By the 1880s, West Twenty-fifth and Twenty-seventh streets between Sixth and Seventh avenues were frequently noted for the large numbers of African-American prostitutes strolling along the street day and night. Similarly, Father Praetori complained that black prostitutes on West Thirty-second Street made noise, sang obnoxious songs, and "climbed up the windows of the school and called in bad, vile names and spoke . . . bad language to the children."[17]

Like their white counterparts, African-American prostitutes soon moved uptown. By the early 1900s, West Thirty-sixth to Forty-first Street between Eighth and Ninth avenues was filled with black women "soliciting in the streets at any hour of the day or night," according to one account. West Thirty-seventh Street residents remarked that female neighbors stood in front of their houses from early evening to as late as four in the morning with little clothing, "speak[ing] to all men who pass (especially white men) and then tak[ing] them up to their flats." Another complained that on Fortieth Street numerous "colored women walk up and down the street, blocking the passage of white men and boys, and in some cases force them into the gutter, in order for them to get clear of them." On the same street, Adam Clayton Powell, Sr., observed prostitutes snatching the hats off men, forcing men to run into hallways after them.[18]

Most black-run establishments operated with little fanfare or opposition, except for the interracial "black and tans." By ignoring many of the conventions of racial segregation, these establishments drew criticism from many who normally tolerated commercial sex. Charles Gardner, for example, described Nigger Johnson's dance house (a former "aristocratic house") on West Twenty-seventh Street, where "the colored and white races nightly congregated," and fifteen- and sixteen-year-old white females danced with black men. One judge even claimed that such dives, by promoting interracial sex, "put decent places in disrepute."[19]

Judges notwithstanding, racially integrated nightspots like Digg's Hotel, Edmund's (or the Douglas) Theatrical Club, and Percy Brown's Café attracted a racially mixed clientele, especially after 1900. Undercover investigators found that in Walter Herbert's Criterion Club Café there were "a good many white men looking for colored girls, . . . so [there was] always a crowd of streetwalkers on hand." Similarly, Marshall's Hotel, on West Fifty-third Street, was a "high class restaurant for colored people," and despite the "questionable orgies and revels . . . held there nightly" was "perhaps [the] most popular place in town." Its Thirty-fifth Street rival, Baron Wilkins's Place, was "the swellest club in town," with its "high class of sporting people." While attractive brown-skinned women sang popular and suggestive songs, Wilkins discreetly provided private rooms to regular customers and prostitutes. One investigator learned of "a special room where white women and colored men can meet and be protected."[20]

The Rialto

SECOND only to the Tenderloin as New York's amusement center was the Rialto. Geographically centered on Fourteenth Street from Third Avenue to Broadway and Union Square, the Rialto began as an elite residential area. During the 1830s, Samuel Ruggles developed Gramercy Park and its surrounding row house mansions a few blocks north. By midcentury, the Union Square neighborhood was an exclusive community that counted Vanderbilts, Whitneys, and Roosevelts among its residents. The opening of the Academy of Music, on Fourteenth Street, in 1854, however, soon attracted numerous hotels and theaters. By 1870, Irving Hall, Delmonico's Restaurant, Steinway Hall, Theater Français (or Fourteenth Street Theater), Tammany Hall, and the Union Square Hotel and Theater lined Fourteenth Street. Nearby, Wallack's Theater and Robinson Hall offered more nighttime entertainment. Chickering Music Hall (1875), Tony Pastor's Theater in Tammany Hall (1881), Huber's Prospect Garden (1882), and Luchow's restaurant (1886) later added to the wide range of entertainment. Pastor's, in fact, sponsored some of the leading performers of the era, including Lillian Russell, Hart and Harrigan, and Sophie Tucker. Fifth Avenue, within earshot to the west and "the fashionable street, *par excellence,* of New York," continued to be the most prestigious residential thoroughfare in the nation. It was, as the novelist Henry James wrote, an "august precinct . . . marked for high destinies." On the other side of Union Square, the Gramercy Park neighborhood was home to some of New York's leading figures, including Samuel Tilden, Theodore Roosevelt, James Harper, Cyrus Field, and Abram Hewitt. For nearly three decades, Union Square was, as one observer noted, "the show of the high life of New York—the aristocracy—the 'upper ten.' "[21]

The invasion of leisure and commercial enterprises transformed Union Square into a "tale of two cities," according to one sanitary reformer in 1866. Adjoining areas of wealth along Fifth Avenue and Gramercy Park now stood "theatres, museums for men only, drinking palaces, gambling joints, and worse." "It is a district," the reformer noted, "of strong contrasts where rich and poor, healthy and sick, meet together, . . . where the greatest refinement and most stolid indifference are found respectively in the mansion and the cellar." An 1869 Children's Aid Society report on the Union Square neighborhood described "a wild, ragged, dirty, untamable set of children living in cellars, dark holes and miserable shanties." And public officials admitted that the Union Square area was also rich in expensive, neatly kept brothels. Like the Tenderloin, the former brownstone abodes of upper-class New York were adapted to more erotic purposes. Throughout the half century after the Civil War, from "early afternoon to early morning," claimed one nearby resident, "the streets of this section were patrolled by hundreds of women."[22]

Even Fifth Avenue changed at nightfall. During the 1880s, one resident insisted that after dark the avenue from Washington Square to Fourteenth Street was "not fit for any lady to pass, being a perfect rendezvous for fast women and tramps. And the women solicit men in a most disgusting open manner." After years in the neighborhood, he confessed, "[M]y wife is constantly asking me to move out as she (and I cannot blame her) calls it the disreputable neighborhood." Still others recounted the "multitude of bed houses" on Thirteenth and Tenth streets, where prostitutes chanted, "Come up? Got a dollar and a half? O how sweet. Want to come by and have a good time?" Another neighborhood resident recounted that on his way home one evening he passed through Thirteenth Street from Fifth to Sixth Avenue, "and no less than thirteen girls stopped [him] and asked [him] to go inside with them."[23]

After 1890, the Fourteenth Street Rialto underwent another transformation. Wealthy patrons abandoned the district for newer, uptown leisure establishments. The Academy of Music declined and became a combination playhouse. Steinway and Chickering halls were torn down. In 1893, B. F. Keith and Edward Albee introduced vaudeville at the Union Square Theater, quickly attracting imitators and turning Union Square into the leading working-class entertainment district. As Union Square became an extension of the Bowery, sexual behavior grew more blatant. In Stuyvesant and Union squares, streetwalkers joined homosexual males, according to one observer, in search of a "scraping acquaintance with a strange Hercules or Adonis." Reformers and residents described the two squares as places where "tramps male and female haggle and dispute over their price." Third Avenue "has taken on many of the characteristics of the Bowery," concluded Helen Campbell. "I know of no place in the city not even the tenderloin," wrote Charles Sommer, "with the brazen women about twenty to thirty of them who solicit all day long as well as into the night." And by 1900, concert saloons like Theiss's, Wulfer's, and Sharkey's (figure 36) were, in the words of one critic, "three of the largest markets for women which the city ever had."[24]

East Side

THE Tenderloin and Rialto did not have a monopoly on the most expensive houses of prostitution in Gilded Age New York. Half a mile north of Union Square, the genteel East Side and Murray Hill were home to a surprising amount of prostitution after the Civil War. On East Twenty-second Street (between Third and Fourth avenues) imme-

Fig. 36 Tom Sharkey's and the Rialto
From Committee of Fourteen, Annual Report for 1914 *(1915)*

diately above Gramercy Park were at least seven high-priced brothels, attracted in part by the nearby Gramercy Park House, Continental Hotel, and Park Theater. George Ellington similarly reported that much "fashionable prostitution" existed along Fifth and Madison avenues above Twenty-third Street. In the 1880s, houses of prostitution on East Thirtieth Street, only a block from the residence of the merchant and two-time mayor William R. Grace, operated "with no pretense of secrecy." And past President Chester A. Arthur's brownstone, Lexington Avenue from Twentieth to Thirty-fourth Street was a reputed "parade ground for prostitutes" for several decades.[25]

Into the twentieth century, residents claimed that prostitutes and their cohorts operated in an environment of relative impunity. Since the East Side neighborhood south of Fifty-ninth Street was not a major tenement center, most prostitution occurred in brothels, hotels, and boardinghouses. On the eve of World War I, Laura Clapp of the Kips Bay Neighborhood Association insisted that very little prostitution took place in tenements. Instead, she estimated that probably half the furnished rooms between Twenty-eighth and Fifty-ninth streets were used by prostitutes.[26]

Bleecker Street and Washington Square

AS PROSTITUTES from the Rialto traversed Fifth Avenue north of Washington Square, another pocket of Greenwich Village prostitution flourished just south of it. Bleecker Street, once an antebellum seat of fashion and wealth, became the bohemian quarter of Gotham after 1870. Former mansions were converted to stores, restaurants, and saloons, and the area filled with struggling artists, musicians, actresses, ballerinas, seamstresses, and prostitutes. New York University (NYU), just north of Bleecker Street, attracted an amalgam of writers and middle-class families. Between 1880 and World War I, Mayor Edward Cooper, the novelists Edith Wharton, William Dean Howells, Henry James, and Theodore Dreiser, the playwright Eugene O'Neill, the radical journalist John Reed, and the painters William Glackens and Edward Hopper lived near Washington Square. At the same time, residents expressed concern about the increasing visibility of prostitutes. The locality, wrote the real estate agent Frank Houghton in 1887, "is occupied by some very respectable residences and apartment houses, but I fear they will be driven away if the evil . . . is not soon suppressed."[27]

Prostitution near Bleecker Street and Washington Square was not a new development. "This has been going on uninterruptedly for many years past and is well known to everybody," claimed a resident in 1887. The conglomeration of French brothels beside NYU, for example, was dubbed Frenchtown. Their carnal activity frequently spread into the park, making it undesirable to cross, even during daylight. "You can go there any time of the day or night," remarked a local businessman, "and get plenty of invitations to come inside and to go upstairs." From open windows, he complained, "painted creatures . . . call[ed] to the men who pass[ed]—turning the buoyant thoughts of youth into evil courses and encouraging old timers in their evil ways."[28]

Just south of Frenchtown were the rundown brothels of Greene and Wooster streets. Among a largely Italian and black population, half-naked prostitutes sat in the windows "from early in the morning until midnight, soliciting every man as he [went] along." Still others welcomed visitors at the private entrances of corner saloons. Police Captain James Brogan admitted that the numerous domiciles of intercourse thrived because they "conduct their business in a very cautious manner, and . . . admit only those with whom they are acquainted." Julius Lederer declared the law "nothing but a farce" because it "forbids prostitution . . . in New York, but certainly any one passing [below Washington Square] would deny that such is the law."[29]

Prostitutes mixed with other tenants in the community. At night, "girls are in rows walking up and down . . . the block from half past eight until one and two o'clock in the morning," complained one Wooster Street resident. "Sometimes in the summer when it is nice and warm in the evening we leave our door open to get some air. They [the prostitutes] come in and . . . sit in our rooms and we can not get them out unless we say we will go for an officer." One sixteen-year-old recounted that while walking through West Third Street, he had "been stoped [*sic*] some nights by between seven to ten different women, belonging to as many houses." Counting over one hundred brothels in the area, an anonymous resident insisted that "the street walkers [were] harmless compared with the brothels," where five-dollar striptease shows like the "Busy Fleas" included "three girls stripping themselves naked, . . . going through most disgusting exhibitions," and then fornicating with patrons.[30]

South of Bleecker Street was the so-called Coontown, or Negro Alley. Edward Crapsey considered it the worst slum in New York, "the moral cesspool of the metropolis."[31] During the 1880s, its impoverished residents spread north. Thereafter, Thompson Street (between Houston and Third streets) was notorious for interracial sex. One resident insisted, "[It] swarms with negro prostitutes and after nightfall it is absolutely dangerous to pass this locality. In the daytime it is very little better."

Another wrote that "profane language" was "constantly carried on by the colored prostitutes [on Thompson Street] in open day light." Even men could not pass through "without being pulled and halled [*sic*] in a most shameful manner." Still others offered to perform "unnatural acts."[32]

Adjoining streets elicited similar charges. In the vicinity of Sixth Avenue and Third Street, half-naked women sat in the windows as piano music played inside. "[N]ot one man can pass," said a visitor from Hoboken, who "is not called and insulted." A Grand Street brothel was noted for miscegenational prostitution. "Nothing but white women are in the house and no others but negroes are permitted to visit it," charged J. W. Brinkman. Another resident complained that prostitutes congregated on the corner of Grand and Thompson streets "like a flock of sheep throughout the day." Finally, in "the Minettas"—the short, block-long streets of Minetta Lane, Minetta Place, and Minetta Street—poor African-American prostitutes predominated during the last decades of the nineteenth century.[33]

Lower East Side

THE BOWERY and its environs on the Lower East Side were the working-class center of commercial sex.[34] "The Bowery [was] never dead, never even asleep," according to the *Times* (figure 37). Filled with saloons, missions, gin mills, beer gardens, concert halls, dime museums, cigar stores, lodging houses, gambling dens, and theaters, the Bowery offered a smorgasbord of working-class leisure. "It is chiefly the single man with money," wrote F. H. McLean in 1899, "whom the Bowery amusement places endeavor to attract." Gaudily dressed prostitutes of all ages walked the Bowery, soliciting men to join them in the cheap hotels, lodging houses, and tenements in the dark streets off the boulevard. From Houston to Fourteenth Street, the *Herald* reported in 1895, one "can see that vice is not dead in New York . . . . [H]ouses of assignation are to be found all over the district, while raids are most infrequent, and only against the lowest resorts. . . ." The settlement house reformer Mary Simkhovitch remembered that the Bowery in 1898 was "in its full flower and flavor of stage-villainy."[35]

Most prostitution on the Lower East Side occurred in tenements. In the half century following the Civil War, neighborhoods on both sides of the Bowery filled with immigrants. East European Jews were located largely below First Street. Italians settled between the Bowery and Broadway south of Bleecker Street. To the east, Germans lived from First Street to St. Mark's Place. And the Irish were sprinkled through-

Fig. 37 The Bowery, 1895
Museum of the City of New York

out the area. The massive infusion of poor, working residents spurred real estate developers to build large numbers of dumbbell-shaped tenements. By the turn of the century, the Lower East Side was the most densely populated neighborhood in America.

Prostitution was a pervasive part of immigrant life on the Lower East Side. Along with the Bowery, Allen Street, four blocks east, was the most notorious thoroughfare of commercial sex. During the 1890s, for example, Theo Goetze complained, "[In] broad day light you can see them [prostitutes] at their windows and calling to passers by at night. They are so vulgar in front of their houses that any respectable person cannot pass without being insulted by them."[36] Another resident expressed agitation because women could not pass through most streets after dusk "without becoming a victim to the abuse of the paramours who hang around the corners awaiting the proceeds of their concubines." A businessman argued that the "dissipation and indecent exposure indulged in nightly [were] simply shocking to even the hardened eye," with some houses having ten to twenty teenage prostitutes. "It is useless to appeal to the police," said another, "as the very men who are sent out in citizen clothes stand and talk with them and go in saloons and drink with them." One police captain defended such toleration, arguing, "[I]f I get them out of the private houses, they will go into the tenements, which would be worse."[37]

West of the Bowery, in Little Italy, prostitutes were already in tenements. On the street, numerous other ones congregated along Mulberry, Mott, and Elizabeth streets. Nudity and "exposures are of constant occurrence," complained the residents, "the inmates . . . go[ing] about the street ill-clad or carelessly clad or not clad at all." The Italian dives along Mulberry Street housed "tramps and vagrants of the lowest character," reported Police Captain John McCullagh.[38]

Just north of these Jewish and Italian quarters, cafés along St. Mark's Place employed attractive young German women, attired in low-necked gowns. Second Avenue, once considered the Fifth Avenue of the East Side, became "so overrun with the denizens of the pavements and the outcasts from the Tenderloin," according to one observer, "that after dusk no respectable woman" walked the street alone. After 1890, Second Avenue from Houston to Tenth Street was christened Pimp Row. A Committee of Fifteen agent characterized the area as "a tramping ground" crowded with prostitutes. "They are very bold in soliciting men," he continued. "They come up to you, ask you out loud: 'Don't you want to go and have a good time?' " Some of the more aggressive ones actually grabbed potential customers in their efforts to lure them. "They walk in pairs; sometimes you will meet them three abreast. They will back against you and say, 'Come on have a good time.' " According to the Society for the Prevention of Cruelty to Children, no part of the area was immune; brothels located on blocks with new brownstones, respectable groceries, and good tenants.[39]

More than outside observers or vigilante reformers, individual residents corroborated such charges. In 1887, an East Second Street resident concluded that the area was "going from worse to worse," adding, "Evenings when I sit with my family in front of my residence I must be ashamed by the remarks made by the disreputable women." Similarly, Charles Libby complained that the seven furnished-room houses on his East Second Street block were filled with "the most degraded class of Bowery prostitutes." Every night, he continued, "the windows are opened and . . . inmates stand at the windows with only a single garment upon them." After 1880, Bleecker Street from the Bowery to Broadway was full of "numerous dives and other vile resorts in full blast." Describing East Fourth Street between Broadway and the Bowery, one irate resident said, "[G]ood citizens cannot return from the theatre late at night without having things snatched from their persons and being insulted by brazen faced *street walkers!* . . . [T]his street is a den of *brazen women* and pickpockets." One house in particular was notorious, and passing it evoked images of life on the frontier. "Inmates even call to respectable women when passing on the street. They yell like a set of wild indians for young girls to come in." Well into the twentieth century, residents complained about the many hotel and furnished-room house prostitutes who traversed Second and Third avenues.[40]

Below Canal Street

AS LOWER Manhattan emerged as the industrial and commercial heart of the city, prostitutes gradually abandoned their antebellum areas of work. Whereas one-fifth of Gotham's prostitution was south of Canal Street from 1870 to 1879, only 2 percent was there after 1910. Nevertheless, small, isolated pockets of prostitution persisted. For example, adjacent to the Wall Street business district, prostitutes worked in saloons along Greenwich Street, taking men upstairs for intercourse. In addition, immediately south of Wall Street was the Battery Tenderloin, on Whitehall Street, with its "wide open" sex.[41]

The Water Street area, however, remained the most significant and poorest waterfront zone of prostitution, generating comparisons with the poverty-ridden Whitechapel section of London. Amid the rookeries, rat pits, and dance halls, prostitutes "exposed in each window to the public view" plied their trade. In 1893, Helen Campbell described women "hideously painted and bedizened." And another defied "any man to pass there after dark without being shoved about by the women with whom the sidewalk is allways crowded." The most colorful was the ex-prostitute Gallus Mag. A heavy drinker and a saloonkeeper, the so-called Queen of Cherry Street held her skirts with suspenders and was expert at biting off the ears of roughhousing patrons. Over time, she garnered a collection of such trophies, preserved in a bottle of alcohol over the bar.[42]

Just above Water and Cherry streets, hordes of streetwalkers plied their trade in the hotels and lodging houses stretching from the Brooklyn Bridge to Chatham Square at the foot of the Bowery, and along Chambers Street behind City Hall Park.[43] A few blocks north, in the former Five Points area, Chinatown formed a final pocket of prostitution off the lower Bowery. Mott Street from Chatham Square to Hester Street became a virtual marketplace for sex, many of the prostitutes visiting Chinese laundries and soliciting customers among Chinese men. "When arrested and brought into the police courts," said Helen Campbell, "they claim to be the wives of Chinese, and either produce marriage certificates or bring their alleged husbands to swear to the matrimonial relation."[44] Unlike those in Chinatowns in other U.S. cities that imported girls for sexual purposes, prostitutes in New York's

Chinatown were usually white. The interracial flavor elicited the prejudices of law enforcement authorities like Police Commissioner William McAdoo, who considered Chinatown prostitutes "the most wretched, degraded, and utterly vile lot of white women and girls that could be found anywhere."[45]

Above Fifty-ninth Street

WITH the movement of theaters above Columbus Circle and the opening of the subway in 1904, increasing amounts of prostitution appeared north of Fifty-ninth Street. By 1910, commercial sex was found throughout the Upper West Side (see map 13). For example, in apartments across the street from the Century Opera House, on West Sixty-fourth Street, and the Central Opera House, on West Sixty-seventh Street, worked numerous prostitutes. One madam, Louisa Brown, even ran a prostitution ring from four apartments on West Sixty-fifth Street. Residents complained in 1912 that Broadway and Columbus Avenue were filled with streetwalkers from Columbus Circle (Sixtieth Street) to Sixty-sixth Street. On Amsterdam Avenue, resorts entertained patrons with streetwalkers dancing "bare naked." Other enterprising prostitutes even solicited customers on the platforms of the recently opened underground subway stations. By 1914, uniformed patrolmen were responsible for chasing these local peddlers of sex away from the stops between Seventy-second and Ninety-sixth streets.[46]

North of Ninety-sixth Street, prostitution also thrived. "There are many places generally termed Bachelor Quarters," wrote one resident, "which are being utilized by the occupants for immoral purposes." While Columbus Avenue and Central Park West were full of streetwalkers, most prostitutes were attracted to Little Coney Island, a strip of Raines Law hotels, saloons, and dance halls beneath the elevated tracks on 110th Street just south of Columbia University. The best-known establishment, Waldron's Dance Hall, usually had over one hundred prostitutes by midnight on weekends. Numerous prostitutes lived in apartments and tenements in the immediate vicinity from 108th to 111th Street. And for the first time, scores of reports found prostitutes in New York's most famous park. "The benches in certain sections of Central Park," claimed George Kneeland, "presented a most demoralizing spectacle to . . . every one who walked through the park during . . . July and August."[47]

The uptown movement of prostitution after 1900 produced a new district that eventually supplanted the Tenderloin. Harlem, a former village and suburb, was physically integrated into the metropolis with the opening of the subway in 1904. Within a few years, prostitution flourished throughout the neighborhood. In 1908, for instance, A. V. Morgenstern observed that the music and dance halls north of Central Park were "meeting places of the professional prostitutes," who took clients to the numerous "transient hotels" nearby. Along Eighth Avenue, saloons like Chester's, Lynch's, and Pete's were filled with prostitutes, the latter including even " 'men' who talk and act like women." On 125th Street near St. Nicholas Avenue, Café St. Nick, Tony's, the Alhambra Theater Café, and the West End Casino drew comparisons with the old Haymarket. And in the College Inn, a 125th Street rathskeller, college men mingled with show girls and "high class prostitutes."[48]

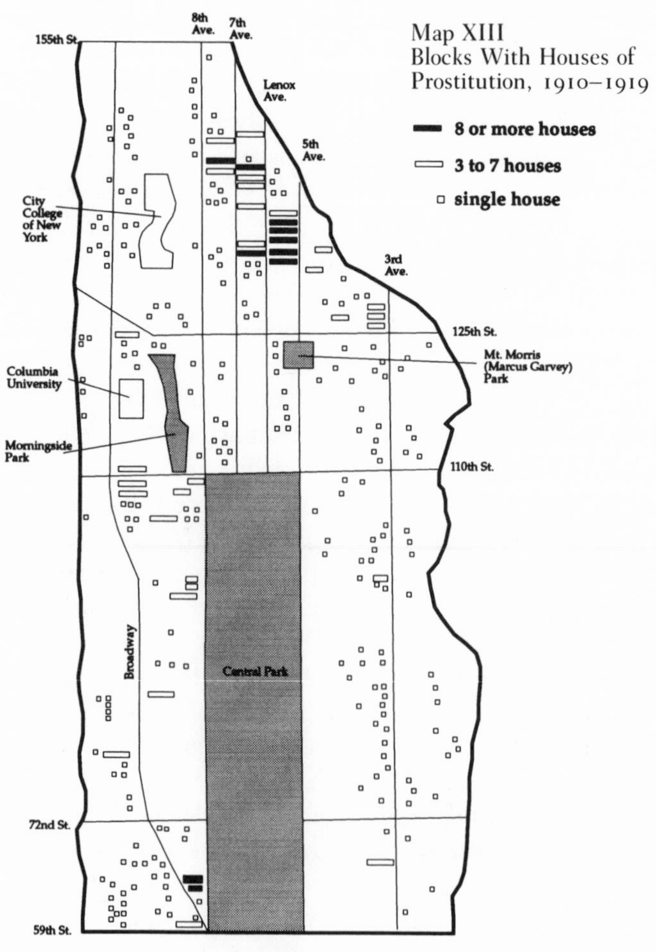

Eugene K. Jones of the National League on Urban Conditions among Negroes admitted that prostitution was a serious problem, causing the "indiscriminate mixing" of prostitutes and regular tenants in apartment houses in Harlem. Indeed, from 1910 to 1919, prostitutes were found on at least 128 of Harlem's 283 blocks. Few questioned one investigator's conclusion as early as 1911 that "conditions in Harlem [were] as bad as in the Tenderloin."[49]

The greater concentration of prostitution, however, was in central Harlem, beside the luxurious apartment houses along Seventh and Lenox avenues north of 130th Street, once dubbed "the best of Harlem." By 1915, some believed it had surpassed the Tenderloin as the city's major vice quarter. On the West Side, at least six blocks from 132d to 137th Street between Fifth and Seventh avenues housed over fifteen domiciles of prostitution apiece. Streetwalkers lined 137th Street from Fifth to Lenox Avenue.[50] Along 135th Street, numerous saloons, cabarets, and rathskellers accommodated prostitutes. "There are so many prostitutes," wrote one Committee of Fourteen investigator, "that they go from one cafe to another looking for business." Connor's, for example, is a "fine place and [the] bar is Al," observed an investigator, who "saw any number of *swell colored* prostitutes go in and out and not for billiards either. It is the swiftest joint uptown." When Baron Wilkins moved from the Tenderloin to Harlem, he attracted white prostitutes working out of the furnished-room houses nearby. According to Duke Ellington, Wilkins's cabaret was Harlem's "*top* spot, . . . where they catered to big spenders, gamblers, sportmen, and women, at all peaks of their various careers." With the construction of the Lincoln, Lafayette, and Apollo theaters after 1912, prostitutes quickly found the neighborhood even more attractive. By the 1920s, it had become the jazz and commercial sex center of New York.[51]

Outer Boroughs

PRIOR to 1910, little commercial sex existed in the boroughs of Brooklyn, Queens, and the Bronx. "The Brooklyn problem is not the professional prostitute, but the casual," wrote Frederick Whitin, "the woman who goes out Saturday nights, the woman who wants to add to her weekly income." One police officer made no distinction between sex for pay and sex for pleasure, arguing that the "professional prostitute cannot live in Brooklyn, [because] the amateur gives her no chance to live."[52]

After 1915, however, prostitution was found outside of Manhattan with rising frequency. John C. Gebhart of the Brooklyn Bureau of Charities admitted that the rigorous enforcement of tenement laws and the Committee of Fourteen's antiprostitution campaign in Manhattan drove the "offenders" to other boroughs, where the prosecution was "less stringent and effective." Eva Roses, for instance, a famous New York madam since 1890, ran a Fulton Street hotel with her husband and a dozen prostitutes in 1911.[53] The vicinity of the Brooklyn Navy Yard, especially Adams Street, was called the Brooklyn Tenderloin. The two-story houses along Sands and Lorimer streets were synonymous with commercial sex. One police inspector attributed the problem to race: "It is true that the neighborhood, like nearly all colonies of negroes, does not possess the quality of morality that would be expected from white people."[54] Along Hamilton Avenue, cigar stores provided ill-disguised fronts for disorderly houses. Union Street was dominated by Italian prostitutes. Finally, Coney Island was known for its "alleged condition of lawlessness and flagrant" prostitution. In the Glass Pavilion, along the Bowery, prostitutes performed onstage and solicited in the audience, offering to bring men to the gallery, where they would "deliver the goods" or perform "an immodest and indecent dance known as the Zulu."[55]

In the Bronx and Queens, islands of commercial sex also existed. For example, one resident found that along Fox Street in the Bronx, prostitutes carried "on flirtations through the window in the daytime in the presence of all who [might] be on the street." And in both boroughs, the popularity of the automobile fostered the spread of prostitution. "Road houses" in Far Rockaway and Rockaway Beach were charged with facilitating the sex trade, although there was probably much more premarital than commercial sex, since many of the houses were visited by ordinary couples.[56]

THIS descriptive catalog of the physical geography of commercial sex reveals why contemporary observers so often understood prostitution in spatial terms. From the Battery Tenderloin in southern Manhattan to Harlem in the north, various types of prostitutes were integrated into the everyday geography of New York. Most often, prostitutes lived and worked in the same neighborhood, making them a noticeable part of the urban milieu. Even in entertainment districts like the Tenderloin, the Rialto, and the Bowery, where the most organized forms thrived, prostitutes shared the community with shoppers and tourists during the day and with theater and restaurant patrons at night. Residents and visitors alike confronted the demimonde while walking along stylish Broadway or the "rough" Bowery. Whether entering the Metropolitan Opera House or Sharkey's Concert Saloon, patrons met prostitutes at the door. On nearby blocks, with their dozens of brothels, working- and lower-middle-class tenants resided and varieties of commercial enterprises flourished.

Ironically, middle-class residents and visitors, instead of understanding the social forces that produced this complex and multilayered sexual geography, most often resorted to explanations that divided the city into reputable and disreputable neighborhoods. They envisioned a city with regions of virtue and vice, of safety and danger, of sunshine and shadow. Surely, they perceived their social environment in that way. But such bifurcated, polarized descriptions reflected a cultural construction, a bourgeois ideal of city life, hardly the physical reality of prostitution. These seemingly antagonistic worlds, in fact, overlapped and intersected in the cultural and leisure spaces of the city. Never segregated to isolated areas, commercial sex permeated all parts of the metropolis.

11

CONCERT HALLS AND FRENCH BALLS

THE geography of prostitution after 1870 illustrated only one of the new dimensions of leisure space in New York. The physical movement of commercial sex reflected the spread of prostitution through New York culture and in different social and class groupings. "We may justly speak of licentiousness as an institution," insisted the female physician, Elizabeth Blackwell, in 1881. "It is considered by a large portion of society as an essential part of itself." So integrated into New York's entertainment world was prostitution that few contested George Kneeland's conclusion in 1913 that wherever "groups of people meet for innocent pleasure or for business, there the prostitute lingers to ply her trade."[1]

Most emblematic of this changing geography of leisure was the concert saloon (or "concert hall"). Between 1870 and 1895, concert saloons and masked balls gradually supplanted theaters and brothels as the most public, commercialized venues for prostitutes. Whereas over half of the antebellum places accommodating prostitutes were brothels, panel houses, assignation houses, and furnished-room houses, less than 10 percent of New York's prostitution took place there after the turn of the twentieth century.[2] Most important, the concert saloon was the precursor of modern urban nightlife—the model for vaudeville and the cabaret. Concert saloons were New York's first nightclubs. For half a century, remembered Cornelius Willemse, "[t]hey were the centers of 'high life' and people flocked to see them from all parts of the world."[3]

Concert saloons generated controversy because of their toleration, if not outright promotion, of prostitution. In most, "abandoned women congregate to try their charms on easily tempted men," wrote one police commissioner. Upon their appearance in antebellum New York, municipal officials tried to regulate and limit the number of concert saloons. But even laws passed in 1862 and 1872 did little to hinder their increase. One newspaper noted, "[T]he excise commissioners say it is not their fault, the police say it is not theirs, and the police courts say it is not theirs." Concert saloons allowed female performers and waitresses to double as prostitutes, soliciting customers as they worked. Some had darkened balconies and private rooms where interested parties could go for intercourse. At others, like Volk's Garden, actresses leaned out of the balconies between performances, exposing their breasts and urging men to come up and "have some fun."[4]

This mixture of intoxication, stage shows, and sexual pleasure introduced a new, more eroticized form of prostitution to New York. Before, men went to brothels or accompanied prostitutes to rooming houses or hotels specifically for sexual intercourse. The whole activity, from their entry into the establishment to their final exit, was more or less a private one between prostitute and customer. While some brothels offered additional services like striptease performances, these were exceptional and, as a rule, carefully monitored by the madam. The best brothels staked their reputation on their discretion. Elite parlor houses even modeled themselves on the domesticated, middle-class household. The typical visit to a brothel was therefore, usually short, quiet, and veiled in secrecy. Concert saloons marked a sharp departure from this. Solicitation was open and public. Privacy was typically confined to the specific act of intercourse upstairs or around the corner in a nearby brothel, tenement, or lodging house. And men went to concert saloons for more than just coitus. Food and drink, song and dance, made concert saloons centers for simple relaxation and ordinary entertainment.

Concert saloons thus established a new organizational model for prostitution. The sex of the brothel was available, but so were the intoxication and camaraderie of the saloon and the entertainment of the theater. By merging these previously segregated leisure activities, proprietors at once gained greater control over the workplace of the prostitute and created a more profitable form of commercial sex. Intercourse was only one item available for purchase from the menu of pleasures. Mixing sex with nonerotic entertainments, the concert saloon effectively pushed the boundaries of prostitution into new areas of leisure.

The best example of this smorgasbord of entertainment was Harry

Fig. 38 Harry Hill's
From James D. McCabe, Jr., New York by Sunlight and Gaslight *(1882)*

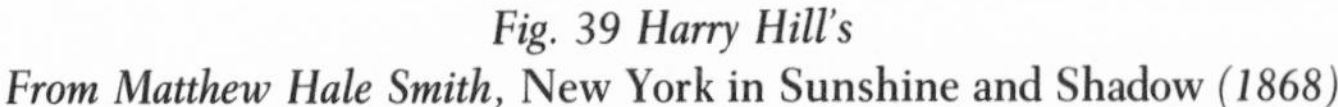

Fig. 39 Harry Hill's
From Matthew Hale Smith, New York in Sunshine and Shadow *(1868)*

Hill's concert saloon (figures 38 and 39). One newspaper insisted that the establishment was so popular that there wasn't "a better known man in the United States than Mr. Hill." "New York without Harry," argued another, "would be almost like 'Uncle Tom's Cabin' without Uncle Tom." An English immigrant and former boxer who won a medal of valor for helping the police in the draft riots of 1863, Hill operated his concert saloon on the corner of Houston and Crosby streets from 1854 to 1886. He offered everything from pugilism to variety shows. Here John L. Sullivan, the world heavyweight boxing champion, made his New York debut. Hill's was one of the first public establishments with electric lights, personally installed by Thomas Edison. And Hill's landlord was none other than P. T. Barnum. Popular with southern planters, congressmen, and judges, Hill simultaneously attracted rugged types from the Bowery and the docks.[5]

If Hill's clientele was mixed, its behavior surely was not. Hill demanded a veneer of respectability. Patrons were required to refrain from obscene language, bad behavior, and poor dress. The demimonde and women of "doubtful character" observed proper conduct. Pleasure-seeking, sporting men, in turn, were expected to treat them like "ladies" and with respect. One journal remarked that although "the shinypated gentlemen who occupy the front row of seats at Niblo's [a "respectable" theater] would pale in horror if found at Harry Hill's, . . . the dancers [at Hill's] come out clad to dance, and do it in regulation style." This standard of decorum and discretion separated Hill's from his wilder, less ordered competitors. By dressing the commercial sex in a veil of respectability, Hill successfully operated his establishment for several decades.[6]

Hill's counterpart in the Tenderloin was the Haymarket, dubbed the Moulin Rouge of New York (figure 40). Despite occasional raids and closings, the Haymarket thrived from the 1870s to the 1910s. A drab, repulsive building by day, it shone at night "with the brilliancy of a Broadway theatre," symbolizing "the licentious life of the avenue," wrote one observer. Its polished dance floor attracted the likes of Diamond Jim Brady, as well as dozens of women, all of whom were admitted free (men were charged twenty-five cents). One observer estimated that the women ranged from seventeen to thirty-five years of age, with a mix of the "extremely young and pretty" and the "fat and homely and awkward." Some were "dressed with taste, . . . others [were] brazen in their conduct." The Haymarket's proprietors, first William McMahon, a onetime professional baseball player, and later Edward Corey, were also "stickler[s] on behavior and demanded outward decency from every patron." Couples who were too erotic in their dancing were expelled. " 'Cheek to cheek' or jazz steps," wrote one, "would have horrified him."[7]

Fig. 40 The Haymarket, at West 29th Street and Sixth Avenue
From Committee of Fourteen, Annual Report for 1914 *(1915)*

Sexual intercourse was readily obtained in concert saloons. In Gunther's Fourteenth Street Palm Garden, for example, the proprietor's wife ran a "hotel" for prostitutes. In another, a reporter remembered being "surrounded by a bevy of nymphs," who smilingly escorted him to a seat, where he was quietly and "lovingly" informed by one that she was ready to obey his commands. "The hint," he understated, "could not be misunderstood by the veriest clown in creation." In one Bowery establishment, a woman exposed a blue satin bodice under her dress to an investigator, promising to "strip off" if he joined her upstairs. At the Liverpool Varieties, another prostitute displayed some creativity when offering herself to a patron by showing him a poem she had written, "so arranged that the initial letter of each word of each successive line spelled an obscene sentence."[8]

In the 1880s, among the most controversial concert saloons were Armory Hall and American Mabille. The latter, also called Bal Mabille and Jardin Mabille, was owned by a leading sporting-world figure, Theodore ("The") Allen. Known for its blatant sexuality, American

Mabille housed "all classes of the *demi-monde,*" according to one reporter, "from the sin-bleared Cyprian of the Bowery . . . to the diamond-bedecked mistress of some wealthy sporting man." Another charged Allen with causing "the ruin of more young girls than all the dive keepers in New York." Allen's counterpart at Armory Hall was Billy McGlory (figure 41). Located amid the rundown tenements and cheap saloons of Hester Street, Armory Hall was a dimly lit auditorium full of plain furniture and a balcony on the sides partitioned into "secret" compartments. Besides the many prostitutes and "waiter girls," significant numbers of young males were present—"painted" like women, dressed in feminine attire and speaking in high, falsetto voices. McGlory's was the best-known nineteenth-century concert saloon that encouraged homosexual activity among its patrons.[9]

Fig. 41 Billy McGlory
From National Police Gazette

Since concert saloons mixed live entertainment, alcohol, and sex, they were frequently confused with theaters, especially in the city's working-class districts. At the Columbia Opera House, on Greeenwich Street, for example, the wine bar was filled with dancing girls and performers dressed in tights and costumes, soliciting patrons. Beside the bar, "French boxes" overlooking the stage offered the privacy necessary for intercourse of all kinds to those willing to pay. Onstage, actresses reportedly performed "almost entirely nude, in diverse lewd, lascivious, indecent and obscene postures and positions." Similarly, in the wine rooms of the Tivoli and Bowery Varieties theaters, "women of the town were in the habit of congregating." At the Eighth Street Theater, one newspaper wrote, "slatternly, reckless young girls" predominated in the audience and the production "became a drunken orgie, the culmination of which was the introduction of two can-can girls, from whom their companions snatched garment after garment until at length they literally danced in nothing except hats, shoes, and stockings." And in 1897, the Society for the Suppression of Vice complained of "atrocious displays in theatres and low play houses," adding, "Matters which were formerly relegated to disorderly houses . . . received the patronage of so-called decent society."[10]

Although some establishments called themselves theaters, they functioned like concert saloons. The Metropolitan on Broadway, for example, sponsored "various impudent, lascivious, lewd, . . . and obscene groupings, dancings, . . . and songs," wrote one observer. One dancer "exposes her person, legs encased in tights, shows her frontpiece and her arse and winds up by falling into the arms of . . . her partner; he catches her and thrusting his hand into her crotch, holds her legs up to open view." The cancan was a feature of each show, and when the performance ended, tables were cleared and women joined in "a general dance and flinging up of skirts and legs and fanning each others' crotches with handkerchiefs." So-called theaters along the Bowery continued admitting prostitutes, and Miner's sold obscene pictures in the aisles, had exhibitions that, critics claimed, "beggar[ed] description for lewdness," and were filled with "gaudily painted and scantily dressed" women.[11]

Dime museums also imitated concert saloons. Elbridge Gerry of the SPCC generalized that most dime museums, especially along the Bowery, were "sinks of iniquity," their audiences consisting almost entirely of prostitutes and "low characters." According to another SPCC officer, the Windsor Museum, on the Bowery, was filled with thirteen- to fifteen-year-old girls, "the majority of [whom] were prostitutes." Nearby, in the New York Museum, "disgusting curiosities [were] exhibited as attractions, [and] performances consist[ed] of vulgar songs and dances, with a number of young prostitutes in the audience." The New American Museum, near Chatham Square, was "the vilest and most disreputable den in the whole of Chatham Square," because the prostitutes were "continually on the go in and out of the museum, and from one seat to another during the performance, accosting the men."[12] Whether called dime museums, theaters, or concert saloons, most of these establishments differed only in label. Each of them served liquor. Stage performances attracted patrons. Performers intermingled with spectators. And prostitutes solicited potential clients in the audience.

Concert saloons and their imitators, however, were not just populated with prostitutes and sporting men. And not all patrons were looking for sex. Gunther's Palm Garden, for example, had families with small girls and boys among its audience. Similarly, Theiss's Alhambra, on Fourteenth Street, was advertised as a family resort that attracted married couples from the neighborhood. "I go there [Globe Dime Museum] with my wife and children," wrote a newspaper agent. "The audience consists of working men and respectable people so far as I can see."[13] Even critics remarked on the mixed clientele of concert saloons. Matthew Hale Smith reported, "Girls of great promise and education; girls accomplished and fitted to adorn any station; girls from country homes and from the city; missing maidens; wives who have run away from their husbands; girls who have eloped with lovers; girls from shops and factories; . . . the wife of an eminent lawyer, showy, flashy and elegantly dressed, and women of a lower degree, all mingle." Edward Crapsey similarly admitted that concert saloons were popular with "respectable" residents of the city.[14]

Certain concert saloons were identified with specific immigrant groups. For example, despite complaints of prostitution, Clarendon Hall, on East Thirteenth Street, was used by groups as diverse as the "98" Club for the Preservation of the Irish Language, the German Carpenters Association, and the Central Labor Union. When McGlory's Armory Hall was threatened with closing in 1889, ten of the twelve testifying in its defense had Irish surnames. The three Chrystie Street concert saloons run by Charles Krumm, Bertrand Meyer, and Ernest Friede were known for their German audiences, "women in short dresses . . . immodestly exposed," and "Tyrolese dances." The Oriental staged operatic performances attended largely by Jews. And the Harlem Circle Casino catered strictly to Swedes and Finns.[15]

Other concert saloons appealed to different races. "Black and tans" allowed not only white and black Americans to interact but sometimes also Asians and Native Americans. In one Bleecker Street establishment frequented by nonwhite males, all the women were white, making it "all the more revolting" to one police commissioner. In one off the Bowery, "women [were] of all shades from ebony black to the lightest of tan colors. Most of the latter were flashilly dressed, but the coal-black ones were generally in plain attire." By the turn of the century, these "mixed-race resorts" were gaining in popularity.[16]

The French Ball

THE demand for new forms of public erotica culminated in the most sexually charged Victorian institution—the "French Ball." Sponsored by the Cercle Français de l'Harmonie, this was an annual erotically charged masquerade held in a leading public auditorium. For over two decades, the Academy of Music (1866–87) housed the proceedings; it was succeeded by the Metropolitan Opera House (1888–90, 1892) and by Madison Square Garden (1891, 1893–1901). The French Ball was probably the most significant public forum for testing the boundaries of urban sexual behavior. According to a frequent participant, one could find everyone from Wall Street businessmen to prostitutes and gay drag queens at masquerades. The annual event included a one-hundred-piece orchestra and was usually sold out, attracting over four thousand participants in 1876 and seven thousand by 1882 (figures 42 and 43).

Masquerades were not unique to late-nineteenth-century New York. In eighteenth-century London, the Haymarket Theatre was renowned for the gorgeous prostitutes attending such events. Similarly, antebellum brothels, taverns, and inns held weekly "balls" to attract customers. Even private households sponsored masked balls, inducing the short-lived Society for the Suppression of Vice to call for their prohibition. In 1829 and 1848, the city reacted by passing laws to restrict such masked affairs. While the former mayor Philip Hone conceded that some masquerades were "conducted with decorum and propriety," he feared their abuse, enabling "licentiousness to go abroad in public places with its face concealed."[17]

Despite vocal opposition and legislative prohibition, masked balls continued to flourish at midcentury. Municipal statutes tended to go unenforced, and during the 1850s the French Association (nicknamed the Friends of Gayety) staged "fancy dress balls" at Tammany Hall. Local ward leaders like Jim Turner also sponsored masked balls, which by one account were "attended by hard characters and a sprinkling of politicians, at which dresses and manners were decidedly free and easy." By the Tweed era, New York's Democratic party organization promoted numerous masquerades as part of its fund-raising efforts. "Young men

Fig. 42 left. French Ball
From National Police Gazette

Fig. 43 below. French Ball
From George Washington Walling, Recollections of a New York Police Chief *(1887)*

were lured by the fascinations spread for them at these monster but usually vulgar entertainments," claimed the *Times*.[18]

The popularity of the masquerade reached its height after the Civil War, and the most conspicuous of these erotic assemblies was the French Ball. Despite the overt sexuality, sponsors of the event aimed at a cross section of New York society and even invited public officials. One observer concluded that male patrons ranged from "maskers plebeian [to] maskers of Knickerbocker descent." A wide variety of females, too, participated. One reporter insisted that there "were modest and well-behaved women, and there were women not burdened with modesty." While most ladies in attendance were usually "of the highest respectability," others came "whose presence would be tolerated only at a masquerade."[19]

For middle-class New Yorkers, the French Ball represented an excursion from propriety to concupiscence. The *Times* described it as "the 'naughtiest' of the respectable masked balls." The annual event offered a liminal social space where participants could probe the limits of public sexual behavior. Through fantasies of dress, New Yorkers temporarily dropped their standard conceptions of proper, "respectable" behavior. "The costumes were daring," wrote one observer; "in many instances they were more than daring." Police Chief George Washington Walling wrote that "women in black tights, women in red tights, women in blue tights, men and women in every picturesque garb imaginable," from that of Cleopatra to that of Oscar Wilde, moved about at the ball. "Husbands and wives often go," Walling observed, but "generally with somebody else's wives and husbands." The ball climaxed in "a bacchanalian orgie—a hot and crazy revel, a whirl of passion."[20]

The public salaciousness of the French Ball called forth controversy and castigation across the political spectrum. The suffragist Victoria Woodhull, for example, characterized the ball as "three thousand of the *best* men and four thousand of the worst women in our city." Some boxes, she stated, are used by men "for the purpose of debauching debauched women; and the trustees of the Academy [of Music] know this." To illustrate, Woodhull described the sexual philanderings of several wealthy males, including one whose name was "one of the oldest and best in the annals of New York society." Both gentlemen came to the ball with fifteen-year-old girls, whom they later seduced in a brothel. To "prove that he had seduced a maiden," wrote an angry Woodhull, one of them triumphantly "carried for days on his finger . . . the red trophy of her virginity."[21]

Conservatives like the purity crusader Anthony Comstock likewise considered the ball nothing more than a big orgy. In 1888, he observed behavior that he described as "the most disgusting and revolting." Comstock further complained to Mayor Abram C. Hewitt that the entire event was marked by "the most offensive exhibitions and indecent exposures of persons, male and female . . . upon the floor and in the private boxes." Similarly, Lecence K. Durand ridiculed the *Herald* for believing that the costumes were Parisian in origin. More accurately, he wrote, they came "from the brothels of Greene and Wooster Streets." In 1895, the antivice fighter John Goff described the French Ball as simply "a standing disgrace to New York for years."[22]

In such a public forum of overt sexuality, "modest man and sensitive women' willingly disregarded "the dictum[s] of fashion." In 1888, a reporter wrote,

> [W]omen who remained closely masked proved that many a respectable female was seeing life in safe disguise. . . . There could not have been less than two hundred pairs of female legs disclosed to points varying between calf and hip. Page custumes, outlining the entire form, were quite common; and many of those who wore long skirts compensated themselves by bareness at the other end. . . . About the most striking fancy costume had a tunic of green leaves, and all the rest was flesh-colored tights. The effect was that of an almost naked woman, with her body showing through the interstices of the leafy garment. Her arms and bosom were wholly bare, and the silken covering of her legs looked exactly like skin. Is it any wonder that she was followed and surrounded by a crowd, and that finally, being caught in a corner by some hilarious Wall Street fellows, she was plucked of the leaves in a jiffy? She was willing to dance in her corset, but the floor managers retired her.

During the 1901 event, police interfered with only one woman, who "with more substance than covering danced out into the centre of the hall and proceeded to do a high kicking whirl." After the police stopped her, she reappeared, "wrapped in a long cloak, . . . enjoying the ball to the limit of enjoyment."[23]

Not surprisingly, prostitutes played an important role in such an atmosphere. John Lemon recognized many of the women from brothels. During the 1894 ball at Madison Square Garden, he witnessed courtesans being thrown from the dance floor into the lower boxes and wine galleries above. There, the prostitutes were dressed "in short skirts and low necks, and some in tights." "[T]heir breasts were exposed very much," Lemon said, "and on several occasions, I saw the men take and loosen the straps, or throw down the straps . . . that held their waists up, and their breasts would fall right out and be exposed to everybody that wished to look at them." This commonplace activity occurred between laughter, kissing, and drinking. One woman even "showed her person right there to a man sitting with her," testified Lemon. As Walling simply put it, the ball was "an assemblage of the higher class demi-monde and the club men of New York City, a congress of the more particular disreputable women and of business and professional men."[24]

Leading madams most often stole the spotlight at the French Ball. At one, a Miss Western, "a woman of much notoriety," inhabited the private box normally taken by the Astor family. Unmasked, she sat tall and proud, wearing an array of diamonds, black satin, a square corsage, and elbow-length gloves. More than two hundred men passed by during the affair to pay her homage. Walling recognized the paradox: "It seemed very odd that the gleaming and glittering creature should be sitting there, enthroned and complacent, in the chair which Mrs. Astor usually occupies. . . ."[25]

In the twentieth century, other organizations sponsored similar masquerades with prostitutes. In 1912, at the Terrace Garden, on the East Side, French students staged several balls with women in "costumes devoid of more than a few inches of skirt" dancing in "the most audacious" manner to "the seductiveness of ragtime music." Many prostitutes covertly worked in tandem with waiters who acted as liaisons with potential customers. On another occasion, the Bronx Boys, a large social club, sponsored a masked ball at the Harlem River Casino, where "complete license reigned between the two sexes." With many prostitutes in attendance, "girls sat on men's laps, [and] men had their arms around the girls, feeling them openly." Similarly, during the Hotel Workers Union ball in 1919 at the New Amsterdam Opera House, "almost every professional prostitute . . . came straggling in" after two in the morning. Investigators spied upon couples in the boxes, in balconies, and on the main floor hugging and kissing. The men acted with virtually unrestrained sexual abandon, according to one report, feeling the "legs and behinds" of countless women, even "putting their hands under women's clothes [and] . . . squeezing their busts."[26]

Real Men

THE popularity of concert saloons and masquerades in the final third of the nineteenth century reflected a subtle but persistent expansion of the sporting-male subculture. Then, as in the antebellum era, sporting men came from all walks of life. Their culture's rising popularity among males of educated and middle-class status, however, generated considerable concern. In 1879, for example, Howard Crosby of the Society for the Prevention of Crime complained that such concert saloons were not only located near the best neighborhoods and finest residences but were also frequented by "sons of our best-esteemed citizens—merchants' and bankers' clerks, book-keepers, and tellers of banks, employees of insurance offices, city, county, and State office-holders." Another observed that outside the prostitute-filled concert saloons along Bleecker Street were "handsome carriages or automobiles in waiting for the aristocratic patrons of [the] den[s] of Moral Perverts." During the 1880s, one visitor reported that The Allen's American Mabille was frequented by "reverend judges and juvenile delinquents, pious and devout hypocrites, bankers, merchants, and libertines." Tenderloin brothels along West Twenty-ninth Street "were frequented by all classes, 'silk hat' roisterers, college boys visiting the city for 'a time,' business men out for a night of gayety, clerks, and working men." In 1882, James McCabe testified that leading brothel madams claimed that most of their customers were not single youths but wealthy married men. The popularity of the sporting-male life-style convinced Elizabeth Blackwell that "all the young women of the middle and upper classes of society . . . [were] brought by these customs of society, into direct competition with prostitutes!"[27]

Less affluent women also publicly complained about their spouses' infidelities. "Please help a mother of five little children to get their father home," one wife implored Mayor Abram Hewitt. "I am a hard working married woman, . . . but [my husband] spends my and his money every week in a disorderly house with common bad woman [*sic*], and does not support me." Mrs. W. Blackburn similarly complained, "My husband is in the habit of spending his money with the women kept in [a brothel], neglecting myself and four children." A Mrs. Wagner lamented that her husband of four years constantly visited an East Thirty-third Street house of prostitution, leaving her "penniless with . . . two little babies." When Mary Meacher's husband began visiting Jennie Wells's house on West Fifty-first Street, his health and morals were destroyed. "He does not care for his children or his home anymore," she cried. "He is like a different man. I have prayed to the good Lord to save him, but its no use."[28]

By some standards, this pattern of male sexual license was even more pronounced at the turn of the century. When questioned about widespread prostitution, for instance, Mayor Robert A. Van Wyck simply responded, "I think those boys do now what I did when I was a boy." Similarly, one Committee of Fourteen investigator learned from J. P. Morgan's chauffeur that his employer routinely employed prostitutes, "conveying his kept women to an apartment he maintained in Westchester County." A study of the brothels outside the Metropolitan Opera

House found that over 550 males visited the block on a weekend night, one house accommodating over 100 in less than three hours. And in her muckraking study of urban poverty, Helen Campbell maintained that if the roll of the clients of prostitutes were called, "it would be found that it includes stockbrokers from Wall Street, great importers, merchants, and representatives from every wealthy class in the city."[29]

Male residents of New York were more willing than ever to admit their sexual activities. Rather than hiding visits to local prostitutes, numerous men openly acknowledged having had such encounters. For example, during the Mazet committee investigations of municipal corruption in 1899, testimony revealed that nearly two hundred men complained to the police of having been robbed by prostitutes during a sexual rendezvous. Nearly two-thirds of the clients (64 percent) lived in the city, more than a quarter (28 percent) in the same ward as the prostitute. For these men, public embarrassment ranked second to the recovery of their personal property. Philandering, in effect, seemed so ordinary that many men felt no compulsion to conceal their behavior. Such actions led police officers like Cornelius Willemse to conclude that prostitution "was an accepted fact in city life and there seemed little that could be done to check it."[30]

Entertainment and residential areas known for their profusion of prostitutes were usually not far from the growing concentrations of bachelor and transient males. By the late nineteenth century and into the twentieth, between one-third and one-half the men over fifteen in Manhattan were unmarried. As early as 1882, James McCabe estimated that over seventy thousand "strangers from distant parts of the country temporarily sojourn[ed] to New York in all periods of the year." For some groups, the gender imbalance was especially severe. From 1880 to 1910, for instance, 80 percent of the Italians arriving in New York City were male. The situation was even more extreme for the Chinese segregated in Chinatown, with a ratio of about thirty men for every woman.[31]

Housing reformers, worried about the overcrowded living conditions such men endured, promoted the construction of lodging houses for transient, homeless males. By 1905, over 60 percent of Manhattan's male lodging houses were in the vicinity of the Bowery. Institutions like Mills House No. 1, on Bleecker Street, and Mills House No. 2, on Rivington Street, accommodated 1,500 and 600 men, respectively. These and other nearby lodging houses provided a ready and steady patronage for prostitutes. In 1917, George Kneeland estimated that the daily clientele for New York's prostitute exceeded 150,000.[32]

> There are thousands of these men in New York. No home ties restrain them; no home associations fill their time or thought. Their rooms are fit only to sleep in; close friends they have are few or none. You can watch them on the streets any evening. Hour after hour they gaze at the passing throng; at length they fling themselves into the current—no longer silent or alone.

During the half century following the Civil War, a combination of social patterns—uneven gender ratios, the postponement of marriage, even marital dissatisfaction—fed the growth of this sporting-male world. In the absence of more detailed studies, one can speculate that the high levels of transiency alone presented difficult obstacles for males and females hoping to establish long-term heterosexual relationships. For men without roots to New York, prostitutes offered an easy and readily available sexual outlet. And significant numbers of men, finding the sexually anesthetized Victorian marriage unsatisfactory in meeting their erotic needs, appear to have indulged in these sporting-male rituals. The male search for sexual pleasure could even be justified as something natural, perhaps most succinctly by the organized-labor leader Samuel Gompers. Upon learning of the War Department policy to promote chastity during World War I, Gompers mocked the effort. "When have fighting men been preached to on the benefits of continence? The millennium has not arrived and until it does your pronouncements of yesterday will not be accepted," he chided. "Real men will be real men."[33]

Residential Sex

ALTHOUGH concert halls and masked balls were the most public institutions propagating prostitution after the Civil War, they were not the only ones. Nothing better illustrates the dynamic quality of prostitution than its emergence in residential and neighborhood life after 1870. Furnished-room houses, tenements, apartments, and local commercial establishments attracted increasing numbers of prostitutes. As early as 1866, one sanitary inspector concluded that "much of the vice, immorality, and crime of our city [was] due to the construction, overcrowding, and mismanagement of tenant-houses." Thirteen years later, another reformer concluded that prostitution and "shocking immorality [were] incident to tenement house life in our city." As tenement construction flourished after 1880, ordinary residents increasingly shared their crowded living spaces with prostitutes. On the Lower East Side, tenement prostitution was a frequently discussed problem. Occupants frequently complained of "half naked" and "unashamed" prostitutes walking in the hallways and using the water closets. In 1901, one Committee of Fifteen investigation discovered prostitutes in every one of the 125 tenements it examined. On another occasion, the committee secured evidence of prostitution in over 300 units in tenement buildings.[34]

Moralistic reformers frequently complained that tenements encouraged all kinds of promiscuity. Robert DeForest of the Tenement House Committee, for example, blamed "dark halls, with all their moral and sanitary evils," for stimulating sexual behavior. Clerics like the vicar at St. Augustine's Church, on the Lower East Side, echoed similar fears that dark staircases gave "constant opportunities and . . . excuses for personal familiarities of the worst kind between the sexes." Others insisted that children in tenements were "tempted, and [became] addicted to habits of immorality." In fact, prostitutes were not alone in their public displays of promiscuity. The limited opportunities for private courtship and socialization between the sexes in tenements only encouraged such behavior. Most youths were simply forced to carry on their personal and intimate relations in the hallways and on stoops of tenements.[35]

The rise of tenement prostitution, especially after 1895, was attributable to several factors. First, landlords saw considerable profit in it. The housing reformer Lawrence Veiller charged that tenement owners rented to prostitutes because they paid higher rents for "an illegitimate use of [the] property." "There is too much money in it," observed one tenement housekeeper in 1903. "[T]he landlord cares only for money . . . ; it's all money, money." As multiple-family dwellings replaced single-family structures after 1870, real estate agents gladly accepted such tenants who paid two to four times the normal rent. Second, the suppression of the brothel, especially after 1885, pushed more and more prostitution into tenements. "I do believe," wrote the former police officer William Murphy in 1914, "that the continual raiding of the 'parlor house' type of disorderly house is practically responsible for the increased number of disorderly [tenement and apartment] flats." As it became difficult to run a brothel without paying substantial bribes, many prostitutes worked out of their own tenement or apartment. Some tenement buildings, generally five to six stories, with twenty to twenty-four units, housed as many as sixteen prostitutes. As the brothel declined, tenement prostitution adopted many of its features. Prices were similar, medical examinations were required by proprietors, advertising was common, and liquor was sold.[36]

Even the antiprostitution campaigns after 1900 barely hindered the spread of tenement prostitution. In 1911, for example, the Bureau of

Social Hygiene found 1,172 "vice resorts" in 575 Manhattan tenements. Two years later, the Tenement House Commission argued that 30 percent of New York's prostitution was in tenements. Veiller conceded the "prostitution in the tenements was a very great evil and the whole city was terribly aroused." Madge Headley of the Charity Organization Society believed in 1914 that tenement prostitution was as rampant then as it had been in "the terrible Red Light days of 1900."[37]

In neighborhoods with few tenements, like the Tenderloin, prostitutes moved into apartments (or French flats, as they were called). "There is no doubt [that prostitutes] have taken principally to flat houses," concluded William Murphy in 1914. "The method of procedure . . . is to get all the apartments [on a floor] occupied by women of their own kind . . . [since] there is little or no chance of complaint." For the most part, tenement and apartment prostitution was the least organized and most casual variety of commercial sex. Arrest records of prostitutes in tenements and apartments showed very low levels of recidivism. Of the 1,881 charged in 1915, for instance, 1,100 were first-time offenders. And law enforcement officials usually found that under 20 percent of the women charged with tenement prostitution were repeat offenders.[38]

In areas with significant levels of tenement and apartment prostitution, commercial enterprises frequently gave entrepreneurship a new meaning. After 1880, prostitutes could be found in cigar stores, lunchrooms, bakeries, delicatessens, and soda water stores. For many local merchants and businessmen, prostitution was a way to attract customers. "It is surely no exaggeration to maintain," George Kneeland admitted, "that prostitution in New York City is widely and openly exploited as a business enterprise."[39]

The most obvious commercial enterprises that acted as fronts for illegitimate sexual activity were manicure, hairdressing, and massage parlors. Euphemisms like the "magnetic water treatment" indicated that more than just a bath could be purchased. During the 1870s and 1880s, daily newspapers like the *World, Morning Journal,* and *Herald* routinely ran advertisements for these camouflaged houses of prostitution. One observer wrote, "[I]t is generally conceded that notices of this nature are but a cloak for another business." After 1900, massage parlors multiplied in the region from West Twenty-third to West Eightieth Street; former brothel madams used them as fronts. The lower volume of business produced higher prices. Massage parlors usually charged more than most brothels, from two to ten dollars per customer.[40]

Ordinary commercial establishments with a male clientele were also used to disguise prostitution. For example, one citizen complained that a Reade Street barbershop routinely sent men two doors away to rendezvous with women "for the purpose of *fucking*." More common, however, was the cigar store. Its clientele was almost entirely male, it functioned in physically limited and narrow spaces, it could legally be open on Sundays, and it required little overhead. Cigar stores frequently served as the meeting places for private male social clubs. These circumstances not only facilitated sex for hire; they also helped men hide their actions from their wives and families.[41]

The Lower East Side, in particular, was filled with such cigar stores. One German immigrant remembered buying a cigar when the storekeeper routinely stated that if he "wanted to be alone with a nice girl, it would cost only one dollar." Similarly, when a prospective customer entered a West Third Street cigar store, the front portion of the store was divided from the back by a curtain, "from behind which emerge[d] half *naked* women whenever a customer enter[ed]."[42] Some cigar manufacturers even encouraged prostitution. When one hopeful tobacconist opened a cigar store on Rivington Street, her supplier David Goldstein advised her "to take in some women." For twenty-five dollars down and fifteen dollars per month, Goldstein bribed the police and "protected" her business. When tenants of a Second Avenue tenement complained about the prostitutes in a ground-floor cigar store, the agent and owner ignored them, saying they "dont care because they [the prostitutes] pay big rent," and advised the tenants to leave. In a Delancey Street store, said another, "they wear short dresses above their knees and on the first floor they sit at the windows with their breasts fully exposed to any one passing by." Louis Goldsticker's cigar store and coffee saloon on Hester Street was so blatant that one neighbor insisted, "[A]n honest man cannot pass by on the block without being insulted by the inmates."[43]

In Jewish and Italian neighborhoods, cafés, soda water restaurants, and "cider stubes" were popular haunts for prostitutes in the daytime and pimps in the evening. As in cigar stores, an open room in the front provided the legitimate area of business while the rear or upstairs portion was set aside for carnal activity. At the Café Tortoni, on Lexington Avenue and Thirtieth Street, for example, the proprietor, Louisa Chandi, allowed women to meet men in the private wine rooms, some of which had beds. Residents complained that "the most shameful and outrageous orgies [were] committed to the disgrace of the street."[44]

Most soda water stores and cider stubes were in the ground floor or the basement of tenements. The wife or lover of the proprietor was usually in charge and an attractive girl sitting inside. "When a man purchases a drink and is charged twenty-five or fifty cents and makes no protest," wrote one investigator, "the way is open for conversation and inducements are made to him, and he disappears in the house."

Soda water restaurants like Cohen's, on Second Avenue, Wallstein's, on First Street, and Bernstein's, on Third Street, were among the better-known Lower East Side establishments, charging as much as two dollars for water and a prostitute. Cider stubes employed prostitutes as waitresses and advertised in ethnic newspapers. Even lunchrooms, bakeries, pastry shops, and delicatessens were used. Open all night, the "sexually decent" mingled with their more flagrant counterparts. Bakeries like Korn's and Elfenbein's, delis such as Litzky's, Steckles', and Ringschules', and the lunchrooms of Schwartsberg, Kerner, and Frisch were leading resorts of prostitutes, their protectors, and clients.[45]

Many of these culinary institutions were in fact operated by former prostitutes and pimps. On the Lower East Side, Isidor Ringschules and Max Schwartsberg were involved in commercial sex before opening their restaurants. Others, like the proprietor of Litzky's and Nathan Steckles, encouraged patronage by prostitutes and their allies by providing bail whenever they were arrested. On one occasion, Steckles interfered with police officers arresting a prostitute in his restaurant and addressed them, according to one of the policeman, in "vile language . . . and threatening to have them dismissed." Little wonder that one investigator remarked, "[Steckles] acts as a friend and the girls feel it is a place where they can make themselves at home."[46]

The Raines Law Hotel

IN 1896, State Senator John Raines introduced and saw passed what he envisioned to be the most far-reaching piece of antivice legislation in nineteenth-century New York. Raines hoped to achieve several goals with the statute: increase state revenues, weaken Democratic party control over the saloon business, protect the Sabbath, and curtail prostitution. The law imposed new and severe restrictions on saloons, raised excise fees to an exorbitant $1,200, required an $1,800 bond on all saloons, to be forfeited upon any violation of the law, and placed Albany in control of all licenses. Hoping to keep working-class saloons closed on Sunday, the Raines Law allowed only hotels with ten or more beds to serve alcohol to patrons. Ironically, the statute produced results entirely contrary to its supporters' intentions.

For much of the nineteenth century, saloons had inconsistently promoted prostitution as a means to bolster their highly competitive liquor enterprise. But by the end of the century, prostitution was becoming more prevalent. Most saloons were controlled by local breweries, which held ironclad mortgages over most saloonkeepers. Increasingly, the difference between bankruptcy and solvency was the prostitute. Although some all-male bastions like McSorley's Ale House refused admittance to any women and discouraged flashy customers who disturbed the conservative workingmen's atmosphere, others were considerably more permissive. Of course, not all the women in saloons were prostitutes, but since some working women engaged in prostitution during periods of unemployment, the line of division could be vague. One policeman concluded that this was common in Fourth Ward establishments by the East River, which were "frequented from time to time by respectable women and by women of questionable character."[47]

Sexually tolerant saloons provoked the wrath of their competitors. A saloonkeeper on East Fourth Street, for example, charged that Jacob Hertz's establishment was a nuisance. "I am a man who runs a salon too in the same block and dont like ta interfere with anybody else, but I dont understand how this Hertz can sell beer and wine and do business here the place is nothing but a dive." More important, local liquor dealers complained that boardinghouses offered prostitutes and liquor without excise licenses, usually at the expense of legitimate saloonkeepers nearby. In areas known for their brothels, like Allen Street on the Lower East Side, saloons almost had to have prostitutes in order to stay in business, and some even permitted them to board. By the Progressive Era, the link between liquor and sex was strong enough that many blamed the spread of prostitution on the saloon.[48]

Before 1896, saloons accommodated prostitutes in several ways. Those lining Chatham Street across from City Hall Park, for example, partitioned the rear space into five or six bedrooms. For a dollar, one could "indulge in the orgies so common there," wrote one critic. Others, such as Albert Rook's Thirteenth Street lager beer saloon, maintained rooms upstairs.[49] Some saloons rented clubrooms to local male groups that in turn brought their own prostitutes. Still others, such as the Oriental House saloon, on Grand and Ludlow streets, had prostitutes from a nearby Eldridge Street brothel come around when customers were interested. At other times, it was "not unusual to see one or two coupels [*sic*] standing at the entrance waiting for others to vacate that they may enter." Finally, some saloons simply let prostitutes solicit their customers and go elsewhere for sexual intercourse. Owney Geoghegan's saloon, "the Bastille of the Bowery," was known for its boxing, its gaudy decorations, and, according to one reporter, the "carnival of debauchery that would make a Black Hills miner in his native hurdy-gurdy go crazy with delight." None of the prostitutes and female boxers who populated Geoghegan's used it for sex.[50]

The Raines Law of 1896 transformed the institutional structure of prostitution and produced a new relationship between the saloon and the hotel. Since the law required hotels to have only ten beds, saloons simply subdivided their rear or upper floor space into small bedrooms. In a matter of weeks, over one thousand saloons became "hotels" by adding beds and taking out hotel licenses. Few people could sleep in a loud saloon, so most establishments just let prostitutes use the rooms with patrons. Some officials did little to enforce the law, best illustrated when one city magistrate defined a meal (to distinguish a hotel from a saloon) as seventeen beers and a pretzel.

Prostitution in hotels was nothing new. Since midcentury, hotels had enjoyed some tenuous links with profitable sex. By the 1880s, the hotel was almost synonymous with it in some quarters. One hotelkeeper lamented that "even the largest and best known [were] mere recruiting stations for the vilest sort of vice." Another admitted that proprietors "had no compunction about the matter as long as [they] got the rent." Brewers and surety companies were willing to issue hotel mortgages because profits, often from prostitution, were high.[51] In 1888, a neighborhood resident wrote that the Compton House, the Bull's Head Hotel, and the Glenham House, on the corner of Twenty-fourth Street and Third Avenue, reaped rich harvests on Saturday nights: "I have . . . within the space of one hour counted as many as twenty couples enter the Compton house." Similarly, along Broadway's Ladies Mile, the Florence Hotel, just north of Madison Square, was full of "lewd women" who called men from the street and nearby hotels. And at the King Edward Hotel, on West Forty-fourth Street, male visitors were routinely asked if they wanted a woman.[52]

The Raines Law effectively eliminated older institutional boundaries that separated various forms of commercial sex. Prostitutes now easily moved among hotels, saloons, concert halls, tenements, and lodging houses in search of prospective clients. Even well-known restaurants and "respectable" saloons converted portions of their establishments into "hotels" after 1896. "Persons who would hesitate to enter a brothel or notorious rendezvous," lamented the Committee of Fifteen, "are easily 'victimized' in the Raines Law hotel with summer garden or roof garden or other facilities for public entertainment." Restaurants like Maurice Sickel's Maryland Kitchen, on Thirty-fourth Street, popular for its southern-style cuisine, soon accommodated prostitutes in private rooms upstairs.[53]

The best example of the increasingly blurred boundaries of prostitution was Luchow's restaurant. Patronized by the likes of Dvořák and Caruso, the establishment was opened in 1882 by the German immigrant August G. Luchow. By 1900, the famed German eatery occupied three buildings facing Union Square and four more on Thirteenth Street. Full of actors, singers, artists, and politicians, Luchow's was mentioned in the same breath as its neighbors—the Academy of Music, Steinway Hall, Tony Pastor's, and Tammany Hall. But by the early twentieth century, police reports classified it as a Raines Law hotel. Investigators claimed that "questionable" women were found in growing numbers inside, including some local streetwalkers.[54]

Raines Law hotels also introduced crude economies of scale to commercial sex. In fact, the most profitable of them were little more than large-scale brothels. Some prostitutes lived in the hotel, as did pimps who recruited and protected them. In the Tenderloin, for example, the Regent, on Twenty-eighth Street, had one hundred prostitutes associated with it. In the Aulic Hotel, on Thirty-fifth Street, were twelve pimps and sixty-five prostitutes. Roach's Hotel housed between thirty and forty women. Others, including Buchwald's, the Bellwood, Nelson's, and McGirr's, operated with fifteen to twenty-five prostitutes, while hotels like the Bergin and Clinton Place accommodated primarily streetwalkers. On the East Side, the Hotel Van Twiller, on Lexington Avenue, had 250 rooms, a dozen regular prostitutes, and four pimps. More-modest hotels like the Delevan, the German Hotel, and the St. Blaise were subdivided row houses that resembled parlor houses from the outside. They had between 15 and 50 rooms that were used by prostitutes who frequented the hotels or nearby saloons. In 1904, the reformer John Peters concluded that 1,205 of the 1,405 registered hotels in Manhattan and the Bronx sponsored prostitution. Even the best hotels often tolerated illicit sex. "It is not an uncommon thing for the more prosperous and well-dressed prostitutes to solicit trade in the lobbies," wrote George Kneeland in 1913.[55]

Proprietors admitted that they were "disorderly" because that was "the only way to make the hotel proposition pay." The bartender in the sixteen-room National Hotel, on Irving Place, for example, reported that 240 couples registered daily, an average of 10 per hour. Annual profits exceeded $200,000. At the Metropolitan Hotel and Winter Garden, a three-story row house with a beer garden and twenty prostitutes, "couples who are well known," noted one investigator, "do not even take the trouble to register for rooms." In the upstairs brothel at the Friendly Inn or Flagelle's, on Mott Street, a dozen teenage girls waited for customers. "Very few of these girls," claimed one investigator, "were spoken to, you simply nod your head or beckon." Most girls performed their service in less than ten or fifteen minutes, one telling a client, "[H]urry up, . . . there is others that want to be fucked as well as you." The popularity of Raines Law hotels prompted brothel madams to refer to them antagonistically as "charity places."[56]

The most successful Raines Law hotels worked in close connection with concert saloons and dance halls. For example, Max Hochstim's Sans Souci concert saloon, on Third Avenue, allowed only women from the nearby Alhambra Hotel to solicit. "Girls assigned there by the hotel came with their credentials and are assigned to a table," wrote one investigator. Similarly, prostitutes from the National Hotel solicited in Wulfer's and Sharkey's concert saloons (figure 36). The National's manager enjoyed "an agreement [with] the concert hall for this privilege for his girls," stated another investigator. So profitable and safe from police harassment were such arrangements that there were "waiting lists" of prostitutes who wanted to work in them.[57]

By the twentieth century, the Raines Law hotel was the leading institution of prostitution in Gotham. "As a consequence, all difficulties that normally lie in the way of soliciting in other notorious parts of the city are removed," concluded the Committee of Fifteen in 1902. "The streetwalker may make any place she chooses the scene of her operations. As a result, solicitation is probably more general in New York than in any other American city." The larger establishments gave prostitutes rebates for every customer, provided bail and legal assistance, allowed prostitutes to "bilk" customers, and even formed their own organization—the Greater New York Hotel Men's Association—to defend their interests. As the famed anarchist and early feminist Emma Goldman put it, the Raines Law hotel "relieved the keeper of responsibility towards the inmates and increased their revenue from prostitution."[58]

The Raines Law hotel also helped transform the concert saloon into the cabaret. As concert saloons let prostitutes leave their premises for hotels, many of the older objections against concert saloons vanished. In many respects, cabarets differed little from concert saloons. The similarities between them, especially in the years 1890–1910, were striking. The first cabarets, for example, appeared in the Tenderloin. Some, like Maxim's, were even operated by former concert saloon proprietors. Performances in both kinds of establishments featured chorus girls and other scantily clad females. Each encouraged spontaneity and interaction between patrons and performers by transferring the performance from the stage to the floor. And prostitutes could be found in both. So strong were the similarities that some critics equated cabarets with Raines Law hotels. The new "white-light district" around Times Square after 1905 was, according to one, "nothing less than a re-incarnation of the old time dive and dance halls, only that they appear in a new dress, richly furnished with dazzling lights inside and outside." While they advertise that no unaccompanied women are allowed, the critic claimed, "everyone knows this is a rule made not to be enforced."[59]

What set cabarets apart from their predecessors was the removal of overt and blatant prostitution from the premises. Men wanting to purchase sex now went to a hotel for the actual intercourse. This enabled cabarets to cultivate an atmosphere of subtle sensuality, allowing middle- and upper-class women to join in the fun. Prostitutes still came to cabarets as they had to the concert saloon, but open soliciting was not tolerated. In place of the system in which individual prostitutes aggressively made their own acquaintances, a whole new series of signals and behaviors was adopted. For example, in Maxim's, on West Thirty-eighth Street, waiters solicited regular or trustworthy guests. At Pekin's, on Broadway, a waiter assured an undercover investigator he "could pick someone up" if he returned later. In Hotel Reisenweber's cabaret (figure 44), where Sophie Tucker reigned, prostitutes arrived with escorts and never solicited. At Child's restaurant, on Columbus Circle, prostitutes in the upstairs chop suey parlor indulged "in the various forms of lovemaking . . . in the semi-privacy of the booths." And the Green Turtle and Bustanoby's were considered "swell houses" because they were "frequented by fast women and streetwalkers of the better type."[60]

This veneer of respectability, however thin, allowed many ordinary females to attended cabarets. At the College Inn, in Harlem, for example, "the audience was about equally divided between the kept-women class, and the absolutely respectable kind that go out for a Saturday evening diversion with a little spice in it," wrote one investigator. He even noticed a family group that included a grandmother. Likewise, Maxim's was "patronized by professional prostitutes, questionable women and also respectable looking women." At Healy's restaurant, on Columbus Avenue, half the women were prostitutes and half "respectable," all escorted. Pekin's was filled with "some evident prostitutes," wrote another, "but the majority of guests seemed to be just plain suckers who thought they were seeing LIFE."[61]

"*STARTLING* as is the assertion," remarked Police Captain Thomas Byrnes in 1886, "it is nevertheless true, that the traffic in female virtue is as much a regular business, systematically carried on for gain, in the city of New York, as is the trade in boots and shoes, dry goods and groceries." Indeed, from genteel restaurants like Luchow's on Union Square to immigrant cigar stores on the Lower East Side, prostitutes adopted a variety of institutional forms after 1870. Brothels, concert

Fig. 44 Reisenweber's Columbus Circle, 1915
Curt Teich Postcard Archives

saloons, cabarets, neighborhood restaurants and stores, and masked balls structured urban sexual behavior, promoting a new sexuality consistently organized around rules of exchange. "Shrewdness, large capital, business enterprise, are all enlisted in the lawless stimulation of this mighty instinct of sex," aptly concluded Elizabeth Blackwell in 1881.[62]

The social boundaries of sexuality in the city were most noticeably altered by these popular leisure institutions. Nightlife establishments were often heterogeneous, interethnic, and sexually integrated. At Harry Hill's, the businessman rubbed shoulders with the Bowery B'hoy. At the French Ball, the prostitute danced arm in arm with the young society matron. And at Maxim's, lines demarcating sexual propriety were invisible. In each, the sexually modest consorted with the sexually vain. Instead of promoting particular values of appropriate behavior, the masked ball, the concert saloon, and after 1900, the cabaret broke them down. And prostitutes occupied subtle yet significant positions in each. Behind visors of disguise and on crowded dance floors thrived New York's imperfect form of sexual democracy.

12

SYNDICATES AND UNDERWORLDS

IN 1894, after the most extensive examination of law enforcement in nineteenth-century New York, State Senator Clarence Lexow concluded that prostitution had been and probably still was "fostered and protected by the police of the city." The police, Lexow insisted, maintained "a partnership . . . in the traffic" of prostitutes, "absorbing the largest part of the resulting profit." Two decades later, another observer concluded that prostitution was still "controlled solely by the Police Department."[1] Whether obtaining evidence, procuring warrants, arresting suspects, or extorting brothel keepers, "New York's finest" helped organize the most commercialized forms of nineteenth- and early-twentieth-century sexuality. The result was an underground, dual economy. Although prostitution was never legal, New York's police and political machine developed an elaborate system of maintenance and control over the most prominent institutions of prostitution. In effect, public sexuality was shaped and protected by a system of de facto regulation during New York's century of prostitution.

Politics contributed to municipal connivance with forces in New York's underground economy in the half century after 1870. First, a decentralized police system gave ward politicians and police captains a remarkable degree of independence. In fact, local district leaders and police captains usually determined police appointments and promotions, much to the chagrin of other municipal officials. Even high-level police authorities complained of their inability to control rank-and-file behavior. In 1879, for example, Police Commissioner Joel B. Erhardt admitted that numerous police captains and officers received "contributions" from gambling halls and houses of prostitution. In 1896, Police Commissioner Theodore Roosevelt similarly conceded that New York's police system was simply a "business of blackmail and protection." Commissioner Theodore Bingham concluded in 1907 that police commissioners and mayors served such short terms that police officer looked to local politicians for support. In turn, politicians "use[d] the platoons of the Police Department to further their own disreputable affairs." Proprietors of commercial sex, wrote a former police commissioner, William McAdoo, "have the votes to give and money to swell the campaign fund, and open pocket-books for those who can protect them from the law."[2]

Second, New York law enforcement was based on informal authority with loose internal discipline. Living in the ward they patrolled, officers enjoyed personal relationships with different elements of the community. Police regularly acted outside standard legal procedures, and individual officers had great discretionary power. Reminiscing in 1931, the former officer Cornelius Willemse said that the nineteenth-century "policeman was respected and feared . . . much more than . . . today. . . . They were powerful, fearless men, [who] dispensed the law with night-stick, seldom bothering to make arrests." Such uncontrolled individualism induced William McAdoo to recommend that policemen be recruited like soldiers, housed in segregated barracks, and rigidly supervised. If they worked in groups and were "divested of all political power," as McAdoo argued, "the subject of dealing with them would be much simplified."[3]

Internal police procedures further discouraged strict enforcement. For failing to close a disorderly house, for example, an officer could be docked five days' pay, roughly twenty to thirty dollars. But in districts with scores of brothels and disorderly saloons, clever policemen earned that much in an evening by shaking down proprietors, hardly an incentive for compliance with regulations. Furthermore, promotion depended on favorable relations with local politicians, who often supported prostitution.[4]

Finally, most police officers took a fatalistic view of prostitution, seeing it as necessary and inevitable. So "long as houses were not located in any neighborhood where they disturbed the peace," said one captain in 1856, "I think it would be better for them to remain there than to be removed to a place where they would disturb the public." In 1887, when the Reverend Cornelius Praetori complained about the row of brothels in front of his church, Captain Alexander Williams said they had been there for over two decades. "What shall I do?" countered Williams. "If I expell them, they will go into tenement houses to infest them." Williams cynically added, "[S]uppose you succeed in expelling them, then all these houses will be empty, for more than twelve years no honest people will occupy them but negroes." Police officers generally maintained that suppression accomplished little. After Abram Hewitt's antiprostitution campaign, for example, a police spokesman charged that "the bad female element [was] being distributed all amongst the respectable parts of the city." In 1901, the police commissioner aptly concluded that houses of prostitution "can't be governed absolutely." He went on, "I can't govern them. I don't see who could. If anybody'll tell me how, I'll do it. We've kept 'em under the surface, out of the public eye, and I think that's all the people want us to do."[5]

Although the police did not control every prostitute and madam in New York, the most lucrative operations were subject to local police approval. After the Civil War, for example, houses of prostitution paid regular "protection fees," the amount depending upon the size and location of the brothel. Those just south of Washington Square paid from $35 to $40; on Bleecker Street, the monthly fees were $20 to $40; on Cherry Street, near the East River, $50; on the Lower East Side, $100 per month. In the Tenderloin, Captain Alexander Williams "fixed the business *[sic]* with the managers of bad houses and gambling houses," according to one resident, requiring from $30 to $100 per month. Profitable concert saloons like the Haymarket, Gould's, and the Cremorne paid monthly fees of $100. To cut down on competition, new madams were charged higher amounts. Those enjoying cozy relationships with local authorities were taxed at lower rates. As one observer glumly mused, "woe unto her who does not have the money ready when the collector makes his appearance. Upon her failure [to pay], . . . she could not remain in the precinct one day."[6]

After the antiprostitution campaigns of Mayors Hewitt and Grace in the late 1880s, police captains imposed even higher "initiation fees." For example, Charles Prime kept a brothel on Bayard Street in the 1880s, regularly paying from $25 to $50 per month to the police, as well as the expected "gift" of $75 to $100 at Christmas. He was raided anyway, and Captain Edward Devery demanded a $500 initiation fee before letting him reopen. Likewise, in 1893, Henry Hoffman paid Wardman Edward Glennon a $500 initiation fee and a monthly $40 protection charge thereafter to run an Allen Street brothel. When the police captain received complaints about the house, Glennon raised the levy to $50. Similarly,

Lena Schwartz paid a $500 initiation fee and $50 per month to operate a Houston Street brothel. Ironically, purity crusades only jacked up prices. In the wake of the Parkhurst campaign, for example, brothels in the Tenderloin and on the Lower East Side required an exorbitant $1,000 initiation fee and a $100 per month payment. And by 1899, some Tenderloin captains were demanding as much as $150 per week.[7]

Such transactions convinced some observers that the police organized all of Gotham's commercial sex. The antiprostitution crusader Frank Moss, for example, argued that the police department was "the most perfect machine ever invented" when it came to illicit sex:

> It knows every prostitute, it knows every house, and no prostitute, no gambler, can live for a moment in any place in the city without being known, and his haunt being known. I find that the police are just as competent to put their hands upon disorderly people in a flat as they are in a whore-house, and my investigations have shown that the people in flats have paid as liberally for protection as the people in whore-houses.

Moss saw the police as an inseparable part of New York's underground economy.[8]

Much of this collusion, however, was not the centralized form of corruption that Moss and his supporters envisioned. Initiation and protection fees, for example, varied not only from one precinct to the next but even within neighborhoods. In one instance, a coffeehouse with a brothel upstairs paid an initiation fee of $350, while poorer Chinatown operations paid only $12 to $20 per month for individual prostitutes and up to $40 for brothels. Even streetwalkers paid $1 to $2 per week to avoid arrest. And all of these payoffs fluctuated according to the whims of individual police officers. When Wardman George Bissert, for instance, learned that Augusta Thurow allowed her female tenants to "entertain" men, he inquired whether she could afford to pay protection money. "I said I could not afford to pay much," Thurow testified, "as many of the rooms were empty, and I gave him $10." A reasonable, albeit corrupt, man, Bissert simply charged her $20 per month.[9]

The linchpins in this network of politicians, policemen, and prostitutes were the individual wardmen and precinct captains. Called a fly cop by some, a wardman was the appointed assistant of the captain, and he knew most of the madams and regular prostitutes in the precinct. Many wardmen and captains were more than euphemistically intimate with the women they were extorting. After observing several brothels on West Tenth and Thirteenth streets, for example, an anonymous resident insisted that it was "a well-known fact . . . that many of the women who frequent[ed] these houses [were] *living with police officers.*" "It is useless to complain to Captain Brogan," wrote another Greenwich Village resident in 1888, regarding the Green Street brothels, "as he is himself a visitor to one of these houses." Similarly, Wardman Frank Hahn was during the 1880s the reputed lover and adviser of the Eldridge Street madam Elizabeth Hartel, at times even living in her brothel. In the Tenderloin, after accidentally being caught in a raid, Captain James Gannon admitted he regularly visited Lizzie Mack's Fifteenth Street bagnio. Even the wife of a police officer, John J. Miller, was accused of running a brothel in the Tenderloin.[10]

Not surprisingly, some brothels operated literally in the shadow of police precinct houses. For example, four Greene Street brothels were immediately behind the Fifteenth Precinct headquarters. "These infamous dens are kept within a stone's throw of the Mercer Street station," complained one neighbor. In the Eighth Precinct, a Prince Street brothel operated for two decades only two doors away from the police station.[11]

By the 1870s, authorities had come to recognize de facto regulation as a well-known fact of life. Mayor William H. Wickham deemed the police "inexcusable and inefficient." Repeated complaints by residents about "the deteriorating influence of such flaunting abodes and resorts of vicious and depraved people" went unheeded, claimed the mayor. "The woman who keeps [the brothel on West Twenty-ninth Street]," wrote H. Cole in 1887, "has the protection of the police and is backed by a well-known politician." After asserting that Ryan's prostitute-filled Canal Street saloon had never "been closed one hour in two years," another citizen claimed, "Mr. Ryan boasts of his pull with the police and says he is paying for protection and intends to get the benefit of his money or raise a row." A sailor in a Lower East Side boardinghouse said that he did "not care for the Police" in cases involving poor, youthful offenders. "The Police can catch them anytime," he declared. On Fifth Avenue, prostitutes filled the street after nightfall, leaving one resident to complain, "[The] police allow it all to go on as if it were quite right and never attempt to interfere with either the women or the tramps." In the Tenderloin, the future mayor John Purroy Mitchel found that police "walked up and down [the street] in the ostensible performance of their duties, [while] solicitation from doors and windows continued within their sight and hearing, and certain of the houses were entered by numerous men while the officer on post stood by indifferent to what was patent to any person upon the street." And after spying upon Bleecker Street prostitutes working unmolested, one observer concluded, "[The police] whose duty it is to prevent crime, are the very ones who countenance it and commit it."[12]

Ironically, citizen opposition to this coercive method of sexual regulation only strengthened police control over New York's underground economy. For example, complaints and negative press coverage induced captains to station an officer in front of more-offensive establishments. Police Commissioner William McAdoo later conceded that this "was something worse than useless." For five or ten dollars, a madam turned her enemy into "a protector or guardian of the place [who] was looked upon with a more than friendly eye." Furthermore, police captains investigated for corruption threatened to run local madams out of business if they testified against them. Little wonder that the *Times* referred to such investigations as "the broadest of broad farces." Captains Allaire and Williams even organized neighborhood petition campaigns with local businesses and allies to prove "what nice and dutyful" captains they were.[13]

Even raids were public relations ploys. Police frequently arrested innocent boardinghouse keepers and ignored their more offensive neighbors. Charles Parkhurst accused police of putting "a spasmodic and temporary end to disorderly conduct in one house here and another there, and leav[ing] midway between two or three of the sort untouched." In 1895, Frank Moss of the Society for the Prevention of Crime concluded that raids were a means to increase payoffs to precinct sergeants, judges, bondsmen, and lawyers. Madams routinely paid desk sergeants $5 and lawyers $10 to $20 to get prostitutes out on bail. For $15, judges gave reduced sentences. By the twentieth century, reformers had come to consider raids worthless. "[T]he promoter expects to be raided and is constantly prepared," George Kneeland explained. For the madam, he continued, "this is part of her job." One woman simply admitted that "it was safer to turn up a dollar or so . . . than go before a magistrate and be locked up.[14]

Like that of the police, Tammany Hall's relationship with the underground economy rested upon the actions of individual members. No directives came from the general committee of the hall. Police Commissioner Theodore Bingham recognized this when he concluded that a great many "minor Tammany workers [were] engaged in running [the] markets of prostitution." Bruns Bocks, for example, an interpreter in the First District Court, operated "a resort for the lowest kind of girls" on Broadway. Robert Hill, keeper of a Macdougal Street saloon with prostitutes, was a city marshal. Individual Tammany Hall clubs regularly required houses of prostitution to contribute to election campaigns. Although she conveniently could not remember its name, the madam Rhoda Sanford paid a "young political organization" $200 and, when necessary, purchased $5 and $10 tickets for local events sponsored by political clubs. Henry and Emma Jones's Bayard Street brothels even had election polls in their basement. And other houses of prostitution served a dual function when Tammany groups like the Owasco Club, the Flyder Association, and the Republican Hackett's Association used them as clubhouses.[15]

Relations between Tammany and the prostitution business were informal and fluid, varying according to the neighborhood and the individual leader. Some local members were directly involved. For example, Tammany's Charles Krammer spent $8,000 renovating a James Street brothel during the 1890s, while politicians like Jim Kelly and Hugo Langerfeld encouraged soliciting in their saloons and hotels near the popular concert halls on Fourteenth Street.[16] In the Tenderloin, the Tammany district leader Sam Paul supported several disorderly houses, while Archibald Hadden was the proprietor of the German Village café, one of the "most notorious and open markets for prostitutes in the city." Similarly, Augusta Thurow's husband, Ernest, belonged to the same Tammany club as State Senator George Roesch. When they had trouble keeping the place open because of neighbors' complaints, he paid the senator a $100 bribe. And Alderman Frederick F. Fleck was the proprietor of the Manhattan Music Hall, on the Bowery, until it was closed in 1901 after a raid by District Attorney Leonard Jerome.[17]

The corruption of local Tammany leaders did not pass unnoticed. In 1907, Pastor James Curry of St. James Roman Catholic Church, on the Lower East Side, the home parish of the future Tammany Hall leader, New York governor, and Democratic presidential nominee Alfred E. Smith, lamented that opposing prostitution was like fighting "an octopus, not with eight or ten heads, but with as many heads as there are ward politicians, and they are not of one party or of the other entirely, but a witch's foul mixture of all parties." No politician could win without such "tainted money." Ultimately, they were the critical agents in the growth of commercial sex. "The fight," Curry concluded, "is not against the policeman, not against the captain, but against the low ward politician."[18]

This irregular mixing of sex and politics did not end with little-remembered district leaders; it occasionally reached the highest echelon of city politics. Some members of Tammany Hall's general committee, its most important deliberative body, operated well-known concert saloons, among them Charles Appell and Tony Gartner. Similarly, Larry Hart, election captain in the Third Assembly District, ran Wulfer's, on Fourteenth Street. Even Big Tim Sullivan, one of the most influential bosses in American history, traveled with prostitutes "almost all of the time" and kept a mistress in an Upper West Side apartment, according to one investigator.[19] Other concert saloon proprietors who allowed prostitutes to roam their establishments were frequently supported by local politicians when they applied for licenses. William McMahon of the Haymarket, for example, was in 1886 described by the ex-alderman Tony Hartmann as "upright." And Congressman William Bennet of Harlem, a member of the Committee of Fourteen, defended a questionable 125th Street cabaret as an "orderly place."[20]

The close relationship between the underground economy and politics provided prominent madams and proprietors access to the best legal talent in Gotham. For example, when Sarah Meyers was tried for running a Wooster Street parlor house, she was defended by a former Tweed Ring mayor, A. Oakey Hall. Likewise, in her 1875 trial, Matilda Street was defended by an ex-judge. As state senator and Tammany district leader, George F. Roesch endorsed the application of numerous Bowery concert saloons and defended a variety of disorderly houses in court. Henry J. Goldsmith, law partner with Little Tim Sullivan, owned a notorious Third Avenue hotel. The special session judge Frederick Kernochan owned a four-story furnished-room house on Fourteenth Street. George H. Engel, special counsel to Thomas Foley, Second District Tammany leader and county sheriff, represented Wulfer's, on Fourteenth Street, and Archie Hadden's German Village, in the Tenderloin. City Magistrate Dan Finn and State Senator William Caffrey defended Hubert Fugazy's Bleecker Street saloon when necessary. New York's leading madam, Rosie Hertz, hired as her counsel Louis H. Reynolds, later a Brooklyn Magistrate's Court judge. And when the corrupt police captain Alexander Williams was tried in 1887, the future U.S. secretary of state Elihu Root was his successful attorney.[21]

Legal intervention in this underground economy reached its apogee in the early twentieth century. Clause 79 of the Inferior Courts Act of 1910 (or the Page Act) provided for a compulsory physical examination of prostitutes. Upon conviction, prostitutes were to be examined for venereal disease by a Board of Health physician and held twenty-four hours while awaiting the results. The Women's Prison Association concluded that the law transformed the medical examiner into "a public procuress" who decided which women were "safe for uses of prostitution" and which were to be subjected to further treatment. New York's court system became, in essence, a "clearing house" for prostitutes, marking those who were "safe for public use." The settlement house reformer Lillian Wald labeled it "a partial form of state regulated vice." The legislation limited public prostitution, as "there were fewer women to be seen on Broadway and those who did resort there conducted themselves in a most careful manner." Although the Court of Appeals ruled the provision unconstitutional in 1911, Magistrate's Court judges nevertheless enjoyed the right to refuse bail to accused prostitutes until they underwent a physical examination for venereal disease. Personal civil liberties mattered little to judges like Jonah J. Goldstein. "Common sense told me that prostitution would lead to venereal disease," argued Goldstein.[22]

The Rise of the Syndicates

BY THE END of the nineteenth century, this elaborate yet informal system of de facto regulation was coordinated by an organized network of "syndicates."[23] Although antiprostitution reformers brought these groups to public attention with their "white slavery" campaigns in the early twentieth century, organized recruitment of prostitutes was hardly new. As early as 1793, Moreau de St. Méry discovered young girls "sold" to Philadelphia brothels for thirty dollars. Throughout the nineteenth century, procurers routinely visited rural towns searching for prospective inmates under the guise of recruiting for factory or domestic work. For example, during the 1830s, Joe Farryall made three or four trips per year to New England and other country towns to recruit or seduce girls for his New York City brothel. Similarly, pimps and husbands of madams frequently went to small eastern cities like Troy, Schenectady, Utica, Reading, and Allentown to procure girls.[24]

Poverty even forced some families to "sell" their children. Annie Wilson of Philadelphia, for instance, sold her teenage daughter to a New York procuress for fifty dollars. A police officer testified he knew of at least half a dozen cases in which Italian fathers "made a regular business of hiring out their children for the purposes of prostitution." By the 1860s, Italian padrones had established a system of bringing young children to the United States, allegedly to work as organ grinders. And some successful madams developed personal connections with compatriots in other cities, shipping young girls to and from New York whenever necessary.[25]

Some entrepreneurs of prostitution resorted to coercion. Although this issue was ignored until the white-slavery campaigns at the turn of the century, earlier examples are occasionally found. The notorious Jacques Monaise, for example, frequently enticed teenage girls into his Church Street house, where he removed their clothes and "exhibited" them to men for five dollars. After giving the girls a small portion of his profit, he released them and instructed them to tell their parents that they were working. Margaret Lyons, a fourteen-year-old seamstress, contemplated suicide after one such experience and stayed away from home, fearing reprisal for her sexual transgressions. When Monaise was finally tried, the members of the jury convicted him without leaving their seats. Such examples of force, however, were infrequent and unconnected to the larger organizational networks that emerged in the final decades of the century.[26]

A far more common recruitment device was the "intelligence office." Early versions of a job referral service, these agencies were often used by young women interested in locating wagework. Although little is precisely known about their methods, most appear to have been comparatively small, informal networks. Some offices inadvertently sent prospective servants to brothels because they were ignorant of the household's clandestine business. For example, one Rivington Street madam's "specialty [was] to get green german girls," by hiring them as servants. As soon as "they [were] in the house she compell[ed] them to go with men," according to one neighbor. If they refused, she beat them. Other Lower East Side residents claimed that madams "established quite a trade in that line."[27] Some recruiters gave jobs to women only upon sleeping with them; other offices readily recruited girls whenever a brothel requested them. In the 1870s, the Society for the Prevention of Crime declared that established agencies recruited young girls in numerous eastern towns and villages through deceptive advertisements. "Traffickers in human flesh and blood," stated the society, "they are unscrupulous and blush at nothing to accomplish their purpose." By the twentieth century, some employment agencies were sending agents to Europe for the purpose of "collecting girls." Not until 1906 did New York State prohibit employment agencies from referring applicants to houses of prostitution.[28]

In most cases, recruiting methods tended to be haphazard and to differ from one individual to the next. For example, Louis Schwartz, a local boss and gang leader on the Lower East Side, personally seduced young women, spent money on them, paid their rent, and, when they became pregnant, encouraged them to work in brothels. A few ethnic gangs profited from recruiting young girls, using dance halls, lunchrooms, cigar stores, and the like to find potential prostitutes. By the twentieth century, gangs led by Paul Kelly, Monk Eastman, and Kid Twist on the Lower East Side were among the better-known examples. Some brothels even operated in concert with one another. For example, in four West Fifteenth Street brothels, girls were obtained from Belle Channing's house at 234 West Seventeenth Street, which was even recorded in Dun and Bradstreet's as a "fast house." Similarly, Libby

Dixon, alias Pollie Dix, supplied prostitutes from her West Fifty-first Street house to other brothels as well as to clients in hotels.[29]

The rise, after 1890, of large-scale leisure institutions with commercial sex and the toleration of prostitution by police, politicians, and real estate interests facilitated the formation of organized networks of proprietors called syndicates. The most successful was the Independent Benevolent Association (IBA). Centered on the Lower East Side, the IBA was initially an informal consortium of local ward politicians, real estate agents, concert saloon owners, and brothel proprietors. The group functioned as part of the Max Hochstim Association, named after a successful Lower East Side concert saloon proprietor with close ties to Tammany leaders and other political figures. By 1896, Hochstim's organization was centralized and incorporated as a fraternal body providing insurance, death benefits, and burial plots to its members. Its membership numbered between two and six hundred.[30]

After Hochstim, the IBA's most notable leader was Martin Engel. A butcher who operated a highly profitable poultry business on the Lower East Side, Engel rose to become an assemblyman and district leader by the 1890s. A stolid, squat, and physically unattractive figure, he lacked the dashing qualities that made bosses like Big Tim Sullivan and George Washington Plunkitt men of mark. Nevertheless, he secured more administrative offices than any other district leader and organized much of the prostitution on the Lower East Side, principally along Allen Street. In the early 1890s, Engel and his brother bought several Allen Street houses for a total of $47,000. When commercial sex was booming, he regularly scheduled physicians to examine prostitutes for venereal disease. After 1900, Engel controlled houses of prostitution in other parts of the city. One of his furnished-room houses on East Sixth Street served as both a local Democratic clubhouse and a brothel. Near Union Square, he was a chief proprietor of the concert saloon Sans Souci and one of three partners in control of the Hotel DuNord.[31]

With Hochstim and Engel as leaders, the IBA dominated much of the prostitution on the Lower East Side. The IBA was a kind of "enterprise" syndicate that was structured around an illegal activity. Its membership adopted an entrepreneurial approach to commercial sex and rarely resorted to violence or coercion to enforce order. Rather, the IBA paid the protection fees, bonds, and legal costs of its members and acted as an abritration board settling disputes and conflicts among those in the business. One pimp admitted that members turned over a certain percentage of their profits to the association. Whenever he needed savvy legal advice, Hochstim hired Charles H. Hyde, a future city chamberlain and law partner of Mayor William J. Gaynor, or Harold Spielberg, a former assemblyman. The IBA included notable Jewish brothel keepers like Jacob and Rosie Hertz, brothel physicians like Joseph Adler, politicians like Assemblymen Philip Wissig and Charles ("Silver Dollar") Smith, as well as lawyers, property owners, and police officers (for an example of a prostitute's health certificate, see figure 45).[32]

IBA members naturally did business with one another. Hochstim, for example, was president of the Third Avenue Amusement Company and owner of the Sans Souci concert saloon and the German Hotel, near Union Square (figure 46). In 1908, he leased the Princess Hotel, in the Tenderloin, controlled since the 1890s by Jacob Oestricher's realty company and long known for its prostitutes. Hochstim's lease, in fact, came from Harris Mandelbaum and Fisher Lewine, two prominent Lower East Side landlords. Hochstim later transferred the lease for a dollar to Charles Fromberg and Beatrice Hirsch, who were also partners in Hochstim's scheme to control the Windsor Hotel, in Harlem. By 1915, Hochstim and his associates were principal owners of the Hotel Lincoln, the Princess Hotel, the Crown Café, and Alt Heidelberg, all in the Tenderloin, as well as the Windsor Hotel.[33]

With their immigrant backgrounds, syndicate members developed business connections with similar figures in Europe, South America, South Africa, and other American cities. By 1906, the IBA reportedly held investments in houses of prostitution not only in New York's Tenderloin and on its Lower East Side but also in Newark, Philadelphia,

Fig. 45 Health Certificate Issued to a Prostitute
Committee of Fifteen Records, Rare Books and Manuscript Division, New York Public Library, Astor, Lenox, and Tilden Foundations

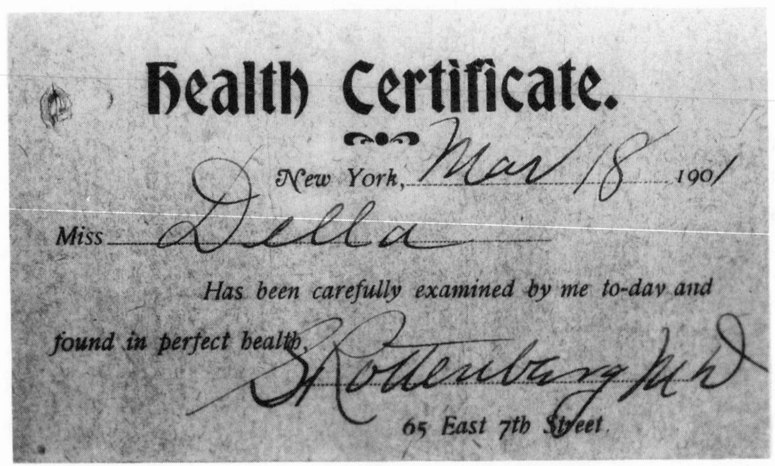

Health Certificate.

New York, Mar 18 1901

Miss Della

Has been carefully examined by me to-day and found in perfect health, S. Rottenberg M.D.

65 East 7th Street.

Fig. 46 Program for Max Hochstim's Sans Souci Concert Saloon (1900) Committee of Fifteen Records, Rare Books and Manuscript Division, New York Public Library, Astor, Lenox, and Tilden Foundations

Chicago, Los Angeles, and San Francisco. Even in New York, IBA members relied on pimps to provide them with women they could employ in their establishments. By 1911, many observers concluded that Jewish immigrants controlled a significant portion of New York's commercialized sex. For example, of the sixty-six establishments that required a cash bond to procure a hotel or excise license (meaning no reputable surety company would back them), thirty were operated by Jewish immigrants.[34]

Syndicate-controlled prostitution enjoyed strong ties to the immigrant community. "Almost without exception these men are foreigners," reported the antivice crusader Hattie Ross in 1909, "and some of them are interested in as many as six or eight places." Similarly, in their 1910 and 1912 examinations of the Tenderloin, the Committee of Fourteen found over fifty French-operated houses and resorts. More than the IBA, the French syndicate actively recruited French prostitutes abroad, many of whom entered as wives, relatives, or maids of their pimp or recruiter.[35] The French syndicate included numerous proprietors of French restaurants like Maurice Chevallier and was headquartered in the Tenderloin. The reformer and investigator Frances Kellor concluded that the French syndicate received less attention because of its experience in more-tolerant French cities, allowing its members to run "their business as nearly compatible with the rules laid down by the police department." Their compliance with local politicians and police convinced the Woman's Municipal League and the City Club that such activity "could not exist without the connivance or acquiescence of the party in power," and they blamed Tammany Hall.[36]

Although this underworld network was developed to an unprecedented degree, the syndicates never took on the impersonal character of the modern corporation, as exemplified by the industrial trusts and vertical monopolies of the era. Business methods remained informal and based on face-to-face meetings. Contemporaries, trying to generate public outrage, often employed the hyperbolic language of muckrakers. Even the term "syndicate" implied that the IBA was the Standard Oil of the underworld. When pressed, critics of white slavery and the "vice trust" could offer little proof. In 1902, for example, District Attorney William T. Jerome admitted that the Committee of Fifteen looked for an international ring "but found no trace of one." The Jewish Kehillah also discovered no such organized "trust" among Jewish immigrants. Even the muckraking journalist George Kibbe Turner, testifying before John D. Rockefeller, Jr.'s grand jury investigating white slavery, admitted that he had exaggerated his charges. The Rockefeller investigation concluded that while the IBA's membership consisted entirely of participants involved in commercial sex, it had never directly recruited women. Rather, "such traffic [was] . . . carried on by various members as individuals."[37]

Landlords and the Underworld

IN HIS 1879 classic, *Progress and Poverty,* the single-tax reformer Henry George blamed the private ownership of real estate for "plant[ing] the brothel behind the church." Although many Americans considered this radical in the 1880s, reformers of the Progressive Era echoed George's proclamation linking property and prostitution. In 1900, for example, District Attorney Asa Bird Gardiner insisted that "the landlord [was] the person to keep his property from becoming a neighborhood nuisance through tenants' violations of the law." Similarly, George Kneeland later held that efforts "to combat prostitution must study the uses of property, especially real property, in such commerce," and lamented that "so many respectable owners of property seem to have no conception of their legal and moral responsibilities." The Committee of Fourteen maintained, "There can be no prostitution without the use of property for that purpose, and property cannot systematically be so used without the consent or collusion of owners and agents."[38]

Most landlords were aware of illicit uses of their property. During the 1880s, police officials reported many brothels and gambling houses to the district attorney, who in turn told property owners to dispossess tenants. Similarly, residents living adjacent to prostitutes usually upbraided building managers, but most complaints were ignored because the prostitution was lucrative. Many tenants feared eviction if they incriminated their landlord. By the twentieth century, landlords were frankly admitting that the removal of prostitutes would result in "financial loss."[39]

Furthermore, multiple subleases made it extremely difficult to trace responsibility. Sometimes the lines of ownership led to the wealthiest families in America. For example, Hamilton Fish, Jr., son of the former New York governor, U.S. senator, and secretary of state, leased a Third Avenue property to William L. Dickel in May 1907. Half a year later, Dickel leased it to John Brennan of Westchester County. Early in 1908, Brennan did likewise with Charles Wundling for the monthly rent of $190. And in March 1908, Wundling assigned the lease for $1.00 to Jacob Hertz, whose wife, Rosie, was the best-known madam in New York City. Similarly, William Randolph Hearst, newspaper editor, aspirant to political office, and millionaire, officially purchased several notorious houses of prostitution in 1913 as part of his scheme to transform the Columbus Circle area into his personal real estate empire. Interestingly, his political opponent Mayor William J. Gaynor claimed that Hearst had bought the properties as early as 1909, keeping the conveyances off the public record, a charge the real estate agent Martin Huberth supported under oath.[40] Thus, the leading elements of American society, at times wittingly abetted New York's underworld of illicit business.

Most leaseholds, however, did not have such complicated arrangements. Leading agents and madams like Jacob and Rosie Hertz usually leased property "to be occupied as a furnished room or boarding or dwelling house" directly from a landlord for four to five years at an annual rent of $1,500 to $1,800. Successful entrepreneurs like the Hertzes might even sublease the property later on, sometimes doubling the rent. They might also, like William H. Falconer, acquire leases for most dwellings on a single block and then rent them strictly to prostitutes.[41]

Agents enabled landlords to feign ignorance. For example, when residents complained to the owners of brothels, the latter often removed the prostitutes in return for no prosecution. Later, the landlord would hire an agent, who then rented to the same prostitutes under different names. George Kneeland noted, "In order to cover up their partnership with vice promoters, certain owners place their property in the hands of respectable agents, who in turn transfer its management to unscrupulous agents." Furthermore, landlords of first-class brothels frequently demanded from the proprietor a bond, which was usually paid by a surety company. Similarly, when Natalie Sonnischsen asked an Upper West Side agent if she could have "visiting privileges" in her furnished-room unit, the agent replied, "[Y]ou can do what you like, . . . so long as you keep quiet and to yourself." He then approvingly patted her shoulder. At another house, the agent was even more frank: "Have all the men you want, but don't let the other tenants know too much about you. Thousands of women receive men callers in New York—it's up to you."[42]

Not surprisingly, landlords courted local politicians, who in turn protected them from prosecution. Bob Nelson, a Tammany member and Tenderloin saloonkeeper, constantly provided bail for prostitutes, using his real estate as security. "I don't know half the people I bail out. I know someone connected with them, and somebody comes to me [with] interest in them, and through them I go their bonds [*sic*]." In one seven-month period, Nelson gave bail over five hundred times, using his real estate to guarantee the bonds.[43]

The most obvious attraction of prostitution for all involved remained its profitability. From the midnineteenth century to World War I, a well-run brothel earned at least $15,000 annually. In 1879, one landlord bought a brothel for $52,000 and within six months brought in a $16,000 profit. During the 1880s, Bleecker Street assignation houses earned $40 to $60 per day, roughly $14,000 to $21,000 annually. Even in the heart of poverty-ridden Little Italy, the proprietor of Flagelle's Friendly Inn, a Raines Law hotel, claimed $400 profits on a busy weekend, or over $20,000 annually. Cheap, run-down units renting monthly for $9 to $10 to regular tenants were leased to prostitutes for $50 to $60. And in the 1890s, the most prosperous concert saloons and brothels paid annual rents of nearly $8,000, usually in long-term (up to ten years) leases.[44]

Even after 1900, when the brothel was in decline, profits remained substantial. George Kneeland's 1913 survey of thirty cheap, one-dollar brothels in the Tenderloin found that the average monthly profit was $2,069, almost $25,000 a year. Eight five-dollar houses averaged $1,415, or nearly $17,000 annually. Profits from brothels alone, Kneeland concluded, were about $2 million per year. Frances Kellor's 1907 study discovered even higher profits; it reckoned that landlords of Tenderloin brothels enjoyed profits of as much as $800 per week, a rate that brought their annual income to $41,600. Citywide, prostitution generated annual profits ranging from $15 million to $20 million in the two decades prior to World War I.[45]

Few occupations at the turn of the century could match such compensation. Upper-level white-collar incomes occasionally passed the $2,000 mark, and some municipal officers earned that amount. Most middle-level white-collar positions, such as those of bookkeeper and clerk, paid about $1,000 annually. The lower echelons of white-collar labor rarely earned more than $700 per year. Industrial workers were paid even less. Only a minority ever received over $500, and most earned between $300 and $500. Department store saleswomen, for example, made approximately $300 yearly.[46] The possibility of earning as much as ten or twenty times more by investing or participating in the underground economy was undoubtedly attractive to many.

The sex lords of New York did accumulate substantial private wealth. While few records exist that allow any systematic analysis of these illicitly obtained riches, contemporaries occasionally spoke about their success. For example, Jacob and Rosie Hertz owned their own horses, coaches, and a home in Brooklyn, and their bank account was reputed to be worth $250,000. Joseph O'Donnell was worth $60,000 in 1887, most of it derived from his Tenderloin dive. And John H. McGurk, proprietor of the notorious Suicide Hall, on the Bowery, was worth $200,000 by 1900.[47]

Police and public officials shared in the profits. The Reverend Dewitt Talmage claimed that some police captains made over $10,000 annually from the proceeds of illicit sex. After serving only two years, one corrupt Greenwich Village police detective bought a $10,000 house, inducing one acquaintance to remark that he educated his son "to be a Roman Catholic priest from the fruits of prostitution and blackmail." The detective's superior, Captain James Brogan, reportedly made over $700 per week from the more than one hundred brothels, gambling dens, and saloons in his precinct. Madame Matilda Hermann testified in 1895 that she had paid approximately $30,000 in protection fees to police officers during her career. On the Lower East Side, minor Tammany officials and members of the IBA reaped annual profits of $20,000 to $30,000, leading the Committee of Fourteen to conclude that twentieth-century New York was "the most profitable field of operations for the prostitute in the United States." As Rudolph Holde cynically wrote Mayor William Gaynor, "Behold how one becomes rich in America."[48]

IN CONTRAST to San Francisco, New Orleans, St. Louis, or Cincinnati, New York City never formally legalized or regulated prostitution. The absence of legal prostitution further prevented the appearance of the kind of formal structures that controlled and organized prostitution in France and Great Britain during the second half of the nineteenth century. Yet, the informal, de facto regulation adopted by Gotham's police and political machine served much the same function. Rarely extending beyond the ward or the precinct, this payoff system was secretive, always fluctuating, and individually controlled. In the most commercialized sex districts, police knew madams, numerous prostitutes, their pimps, and their addresses. The most successful regulated the street life and sexual commerce of the neighborhood. And by the turn of the twentieth century, networks of sex entrepreneurs labeled syndicates had finally emerged.[49]

The de facto regulation of prostitution reflected one inherent contradiction in New York's market economy. Private groups like the Society for the Suppression of Vice, the Society for the Prevention of Crime, and the Society for the Prevention of Cruelty to Children adopted traditional public functions in their efforts to prosecute criminal offenders ignored by the police and others. In contrast, public officials—police and politicians—organized, regulated, and profited from the underground economy, ultimately resorting to private, sometimes illegal, methods of business. Significantly, these police activities frequently extended beyond prostitution. Police officers were also "hired" to protect saloons and gambling dens, even to serve as strikebreakers on behalf of employers.[50] Paradoxically, public officials resorted to entrepreneurial methods in their work, while private organizations assumed law enforcement responsibilities.

13

WHITE SLAVES AND KEPT WOMEN

IN *FIN DE SIÈCLE* New York, the "fallen woman" became a "white slave." This image and stereotype of female victimization reached its apogee in Stephen Crane's *Maggie: A Girl of the Streets* (1893). Praised for its critical realism, Crane's work attracted the interest of contemporaries like William Dean Howells for its graphic depiction of a cruel world indifferent to human action. Futility marked all human endeavor, especially in a work like *Maggie*. But while Crane may have been revolutionary in his urban realism, he came to some rather unrevolutionary conclusions in his treatment of prostitution.

Maggie begins with a depressing image of working-class life in New York. Maggie Johnson, a young, innocent teenager, lives in a rough tenement district near the Bowery. Her family environment is filled with physical violence and material poverty. Her mother is a drunk, her father is abusive, and her brother Jimmie has fallen in with a gang of tough street urchins. Her virtue notwithstanding, the prospects do not appear good for young Maggie.

Despite the despair around her, Maggie is beautiful. In Crane's words, she has "blossomed in a mud puddle." She is more than willing to help her family and begins working in a nearby garment factory. In time, she meets Pete, a local bartender, whom she admires and idolizes. Pete quickly takes advantage of Maggie, introducing her to the twin evils of alcohol and sex. When her parents discover her "fall," they immediately reject her. Even Peter, wary of abuse from his peers, dumps her as his girl. Suddenly, Maggie is forced into the streets. And when she makes a last-ditch plea for help to a gentleman stranger, she is rebuffed. Within months, Maggie becomes a deplorable streetwalker, routinely rejected by prospective clients along the Bowery. The novella reaches its melodramatic conclusion when Maggie jumps into the river and ends her life.[1]

Crane's plot has much in common with earlier portrayals of prostitution by George Thompson, Ned Buntline, and George Foster. Like them, Crane embedded *Maggie* in the geography of vice, a terrain familiar to much of America by the 1890s. His treatment of the Bowery varies little from that of the literary "slumming" missions found in the earlier "mysteries and miseries" of New York. In the end, Maggie is powerless to control the conditions around her. She is destroyed not only by her environment but by her lax morals and willingness to follow a glamorous but false social code. Crane claimed that in *Maggie* he wanted "to show that environment is a tremendous thing in the world and frequently shapes lives regardless." But for Maggie, prostitution is inescapable.[2] Not even a poor working-class female can escape prostitution, marry, and be accepted into working-class life.

Crane was by no means alone in stereotyping prostitutes. Numerous writers after 1870 continued to treat the popular antebellum theme that prostitutes are suicidal figures and fallen women. Commercial sex remained a primary symbol of moral and urban decay. For example, the reformer Charles Loring Brace, in *The Dangerous Classes of New York* (1872), maintained that female sexual intercourse was "the most debasing of all sins." Womanly instincts were naturally inclined "toward the preservation of purity," and any departure produced drastic results. Brace doubted whether society "would ever cure this fatal disease." Indeed, his illustration "The Street-Girl's End" (figure 47) was a prelude to the suicidal results later popularized in Crane's *Maggie.* For similarly horrified writers, such as Edward Crapsey, New York's young prostitutes were "the *enfants terribles* of civilization." James D. McCabe, Jr., in *New York by Sunlight and Gaslight* (1882), describes the Broadway streetwalker as someone whom the "men of the city shun." He adds, "Woe to the man who follows after one of these creatures." McCabe's warnings are even more pronounced regarding the Bowery, where "[v]ice offers every inducement to its votaries, and the devil's work is done nightly upon a grand scale." For the "lost sisterhood," no matter how successful, life ends with "horrible death and a pauper's grave."[3]

Visual images like those found in McCabe associated prostitutes with

Fig. 47 "A Street-Girl's End"
From Charles Loring Brace, The Dangerous Classes of New York *(1872)*

sporting-male life. The women in "Allen's Dance House," for example, are passive subjects in a male environment (figure 48). One young female flies through the air, tossed by her dance partner. To the left, another women is dressed in a see-through skirt, thus being exposed even when clothed. Both women lack control and serve ultimately as playthings for the men. In contrast, "A Fancy Ball at the Buckingham Palace" depicts the glamorous world of the demimonde (figure 49). Sitting among classical statuary, expensive top hats, and bright chandeliers, prostitutes are draped in elegant fashion. Many on the dance floor don masks, symbols of the highly charged sexual setting. Together, the images remind viewers that prostitutes, and thus danger, can be found in most leisure institutions.

Women novelists frequently attacked the double standard and blamed prostitution on social conventions. In *We and Our Neighbors* (1873), for

Fig. 48 "Allen's Dance House"
From James D. McCabe, Jr., New York by Sunlight and Gaslight *(1882)*

Fig. 49 "A Fancy Ball at Buckingham Palace"
From James D. McCabe, Jr., New York by Sunlight and Gaslight *(1882)*

example, Harriet Beecher Stowe criticizes the hypocrisy of middle-class New York. "[T]hings are so arranged in this world that if man, woman or child does wrong," argues one of her characters, "all society is armed to the teeth to prevent their ever doing right again." In the end, Maggie, Stowe's protagonist and fallen woman, asks point-blank, "Why was it such a sin for *her,* and no sin for him?" Similarly, Nixy, the unmarried teenage mother in Elizabeth Stuart Phelps's *Hedged In* (1870), is abandoned and suicidal until rescued by a respectable middle-class family: "Society had hedged her in on every side."[4] Despite their sympathy for the outcast subject, these writers continued to depict female sexuality as sinful, degrading, and dangerous. Young women were pure and passive orphans threatened with sexual danger and coaxed by forces they did not comprehend. Victims of inconsistent social conventions, sexual women were in the end saved only by Christian charity.

This pattern was repeated in popular romance novels. The historian Joanne Meyerowitz has shown that such works commonly pictured the city as a perilous place for women. Heroines were young, white, native-born innocents "adrift." T. W. Hanshew's "Alone in New York: A Thrilling Portrayal of the Dangers and Pitfalls of the Metropolis" (1887) typified this genre. Veteran prostitutes were ugly, haggard, evil women who threatened the innocence of the female newcomer. Whether victim or cause of evil, all prostitutes imperiled virginal purity.[5]

At the century's end, even the new field of criminology supported these stereotypes. Most notably, Caesar Lombroso and William Ferrero's *The Female Offender* employed science to justify a conservative sexual morality. In this book, originally published in Italy and translated into English in 1895, Lombroso and Ferrero argued that prostitution was the product of heredity. Prostitutes shared similar physical characteristics—namely, smaller heads and "cranial capacity," darker hair, smaller feet, longer hands, and obese bodies. The "born prostitute" was more likely to have moles, a hairy body, a low forehead, and a large jaw. After examining the physical characteristics of prostitutes and other female criminals, the authors concluded that "criminality increases among women with the march of civilization."[6]

By the turn of the century, this image of the fallen woman had been replaced by that of the "white slave." With European immigration on the rise, Americans grew more concerned with growing problems of prostitution in American cities. White slavery was so controversial that it was the subject of repeated international conferences. New York was no exception, and several campaigns to eradicate the problem were launched. Its most sensationalist tracts, like William T. Stead's *Satan's Invisible World Displayed* (1898) and the journalist George Kibbe Turner's articles in *McClure's* (1909), stuck to the traditional, moralistic judgments. Purity reformers saw prostitutes as helpless victims, powerless to make rational choices. Vice commissions like the Committee of Fifteen concluded that numerous females entered prostitution "before they were old enough to be responsible for their acts." These crusaders never believed that the decision to engage in prostitution could be a voluntary choice. Even antinativist and humanitarian reformers like Lillian Wald thought that women needed some form of protection. All of them considered sex dangerous and ultimately a threat to the status of individual women.[7]

The white-slave image was so compelling that even the newest entertainment medium, the movies, consistently employed it. The earliest ventures in cinema frequently embraced the views of purity campaigns. As Leslie Fishbein has shown, *Tenderloin at Night* (1899), *The Musketeers of Pig Alley* (1912), and *Traffic in Souls* (1913) echoed vice commission charges that prostitution involved the corruption of innocent virgins by evil men. From 1912 to 1920, white-slavery movies were one of the initial forms of the "exploitation film." Not until after World War I did filmmakers reject this Manichaean image of the prostitute and substitute a more complex and realistic one.[8]

Even sympathizers on the political left considered prostitutes to be white slaves. The socialist George Kauffman, for example, in his best-selling novel *The House of Bondage* (1910), featured a prostitute, Mary Denbigh. Recruited from her Pennsylvania hometown by a Jewish cadet with a promise of marriage, Mary arrives in New York, only to be drugged and sent to a brothel. She resists her degradation but inevitably succumbs and descends the hierarchy of prostitution. In many respects, Kauffman repeats many of the simplistic antebellum republican attacks on commercial sex found in the novels of George Thompson, George Foster, and Ned Buntline. Prostitution serves as a shocking metaphor of American urban life and industrial capitalism: "[W]herever walked the great god Poverty, that great god led Prostitution by the hand." New York is depicted as "an inimical monster" and "an invisible enemy." Capitalism proves to be "a house of bondage" offering young women few opportunities for viable employment. "The social system was too mighty," Kauffman writes. "She could not prevail against it. She must do its bidding."[9]

His radical critique to the contrary, Kauffman retains many of the outworn myths of commercial sex. He believes that most prostitution culminates in death, usually within five years. He sees female sexuality as embarrassing, at the least, if not degenerative. Mary's "captivity had taught her much of bestiality," he writes. The main character, in fact, "was debased and must never . . . permit her degradation to attach to her family." In the novel's conclusion, Mary becomes a syphilitic streetwalker rejected even by her former madam.[10]

The most controversial and far-reaching reinterpretation of the prostitute in literature came with David Graham Phillips's *Susan Lenox* (1917). Written between 1904 and 1911 and published posthumously, the work depicts the sometime prostitute Susan Lenox as a strong, heroic woman continually battling seemingly insurmountable odds. After fleeing a forced marriage in her small midwestern town, Susan ends up in New York City. She eventually engages in nearly every variety of prostitution, working in the Tenderloin, the Bowery, and the Lower East Side. Increasingly, Susan recognizes the impossibility of a single working woman's surviving independently or without male support. "If it was wiser to be good," she asks, "why were most people imprisoned in a life from which they could escape only by being bad?" The novel ends not with Susan's death or final fall but rather with her success as a highly acclaimed stage actress in New York.[11]

Susan Lenox is the first New York prostitute in fiction who is treated as a symbol of female power and independence. Susan ultimately concludes that bourgeois conceptions of virtue and goodness are luxuries for the protected female. For the working woman, these are unattainable standards. Susan recognizes she has few options: "the outcast without friends or family, the woman alone, with no one to lean upon or to give her anything except in exchange for what she had to offer that was marketable." Phillips describes family life in the tenement districts of the Lower East Side as a heartbreaking struggle in which mothers strive to save their daughters not from immorality or living with men outside marriage but from the dangers of poverty and hunger. "In the opinion of these people," Phillips argues, "the life of prostitution was not so bad."[12] Throughout the novel, Susan wrestles with her constant ambivalence toward female sexual behavior. In her ongoing battle, she repeatedly breaks the social boundaries separating the criminal and the respectable worlds. More significant, she continually moves back and forth between these different female subcultures. Acting, marriage, and prostitution are intimately related. For Phillips, the boundaries between prostitutes and other women are not fixed or rigid but rather permeable, malleable, and always in flux.

This unprecedented degree of ambiguity in the character of Susan Lenox reflected, in part, the growing impact of social science. In the new and expanding fields of sociology and psychology, women social scientists challenged the hereditary theories of prostitution. Frances Kellor, Katharine Bement Davis, and Mary Ruth Fernald, for example, were among the first to apply "objective" methods of social science to the problem of prostitutes. In 1900, Kellor published a series of articles in the *Arena* and the *American Journal of Sociology* attacking Caesar Lombroso's theories of biological determinism. Kellor repeated Lombroso's experiments on prostitutes and other female criminals and systematically exposed the weaknesses of his popular thesis. In contrast to Lombroso, Kellor argued that the environment, not heredity, explained the attraction of prostitution for working-class women.[13]

Similarly, Davis, as superintendent of the New York Reformatory for Women at Bedford Hills, wrote some of the first studies of female sexual behavior in the early twentieth century. Davis expanded upon Kellor's environmental interpretation, arguing that prostitutes most often came from low-income or broken families. The ordinary prostitute was pushed into commercial sex on an occasional basis by the absence of adequate wage employment. Although Davis depicted prostitutes as "feebleminded" and mentally handicapped, she, like Kellor, rejected behavioral models that assumed the existence of a criminal female personality. Mary Ruth Fernald, Mary Hayes, and Almena Dawley later reached similar conclusions in *A Study of Women Delinquents in New York State* (1920). They, too, attributed prostitution to poverty, broken homes, and low wages. Compared with domestic service and factory work, prostitution simply offered a better living.[14]

The path-breaking examinations of Sigmund Freud and Havelock Ellis in Europe also made sex a subject of inquiry for Americans. John D. Rockefeller's Bureau of Social Hygiene, for example, commissioned the most influential studies of prostitution: George Kneeland's *Commercialized Prostitution in New York City* (1913) and Abraham Flexner's *Prostitution in Europe* (1914). Both works quickly redefined the public debate on the subject in Progressive Era New York. Later, independent studies like Howard Woolston's *Prostitution in the United States* (1921), George E. Worthington and Ruth Topping's *Specialized Courts Dealing with Sex Delinquency* (1921), and William I. Thomas's *The Unadjusted Girl* (1923) expanded upon environmental themes. While these social scientists saw prostitution as a deviant activity and a reflection of community or family breakdown, all of them recognized the variety and degrees of female sexual behavior. Each attempted, in Thomas's words, to "neither condemn nor ridicule but try to understand" the subject. Thomas was particularly critical of the interpretation of women as "completely good and . . . completely bad." The "line between the professional and the amateur prostitute," he concluded, "has become vague."[15] By 1920, many psychologists and social scientists had come to reject the notion of the prostitute as a social type or born criminal. Environmentalism increasingly replaced heredity and moral damnation as causal explanations for prostitution.

Interestingly, American artists, especially the "Ashcan" school of painters, were among the first to apply environmentalism in their treatment of the prostitute. Between 1895 and 1905, Robert Henri, John Sloan, George Luks, George Bellows, William Glackens, and Everett Shinn moved to New York. Sharing left-wing political sympathies, these artists rejected conventional ideas on beauty, taste, and art. Nineteenth-century American artists, for the most part, had remained tied to European and Renaissance traditions. Popular aesthetics emphasized composition, the human figure, nature, and classical models of the past. Leading artists in the United States painted landscapes, portraits, interiors, and literary themes, not images of urban reality or social criticism.[16]

In contrast, Ashcan painters examined working-class and immigrant life in Greenwich Village and on the Lower East Side. Their efforts to achieve visual realism reflected their interest in city life, especially its ugly and embarrassing moments. Asserting a vulgarity of subject matter and a vigorous style, they chose the prostitute as one of their motifs. These painters departed not only from earlier American artists but also from their modernist and cubist counterparts in Europe—above all, from the elegant and posed female images of Charles Dana Gibson and Montgomery Flagg in the United States. "If historians of the future wish to know what [the] America of city streets was like at the turn of the century," wrote Shinn, "they have only to look at those drawings of the Ashcan painters."[17]

These American painters were most likely influenced by their French counterparts who made the prostitute a major subject during the final third of the nineteenth century. Edouard Manet's *Olympia* (1865) and *Masked Ball at the Opera* (1873) reflected the golden age of the courtesan in Second Empire France, portraying erotic, sexually active, and confident women in a positive way for the first time. Similarly, Edgar Degas's images of female ballet dancers, milliners, laundresses, and bathers introduced in the years 1876–84 a new element of sexual ambiguity. As Eunice Lipton has shown, such women were considered to be "tarts," often forced to rely upon male associates for entertainment, clothing, housing, and supports. Sexual favors were part of the exchange, sometimes amounting to prostitution.[18]

Henri de Toulouse-Lautrec expanded upon this new image of prostitutes. He showed them in everyday life—during their leisure time, at the toilette and at breakfast, and waiting for customers. Absent was any provocative eroticism or voyeurism; instead, prostitutes appeared bored and ordinary. The utilitarian images revealed the prostitutes' aversion to emotional involvement and their tendency to define themselves apart from men. For Toulouse-Lautrec, the brothel was less a center for commercial sex and more a place of female companionship. Men were present, but only on the fringe. Prostitutes may have been humiliated or crippled women, but they retained a sense of dignity, freedom, and even heroism.[19]

In New York, John Sloan was the first artist to address such themes and sympathetically examine the prostitute's subculture. Like Walt Whitman half a century earlier, Sloan roamed the streets of Manhattan in search of appropriate subjects. Admirers hailed Sloan for his critical realism and "relentless truthfulness . . . in showing the trend of some phases of . . . civilization," in the words of one contemporary critic.[20] *The Haymarket* (1907) (figure 50) was the first painting by a serious artist to focus on a well-known habitat of prostitution. Rather than making a moral judgment about the subjects, Sloan portrays the women, most likely prostitutes in their feathered hats, entering the establishment as well dressed and attractive. The Haymarket entrance, with its

Fig. 50 John Sloan, The Haymarket
From the Brooklyn Museum

illumination and flashy entertainment, beckons the subjects as well as the viewer. Images of the concert saloon as a symbol of corruption and darkness are absent. A hint of social disapproval appears only to the left side, where a worried mother pulls her inquisitive young daughter away.

Moving only a block north, Sloan produced a lithograph a year later, *Sixth Avenue and Thirtieth Street* (1908), which depicts a well-dressed woman in the heart of the Tenderloin (figure 51). Contemporaries familiar with the neighborhood would most likely have assumed that she was a

Fig. 51 John Sloan, Sixth Avenue and Thirtieth Street
From the National Gallery of Art, Washington, D.C.

madam or a successful prostitute. But unlike women in nineteenth-century images, this one is neither victim nor temptress. Rather, she is independent and powerful, attracting the attention of the neighbors. She walks upright, pulling on her expensive gloves, her foot pointing forward, and her head turned in a confident manner. Sloan chose such images deliberately. "I have never liked to show human beings when they are not themselves. I think it is an insult to their human dignity. . . . One of the things I so dislike about most socially conscious pictures, is that the artist is looking down on people."[21]

Sloan was also the first artist who exposed the systematic entrapment of prostitutes by the police. In *Before Her Maker and Her Judge* (1913), published as part of Frank T. Shay's essay "The Machine" for the socialist monthly the *Masses,* Sloan depicts a solitary prostitute in court surrounded by unscrupulous legal and police authorities ready to sentence her (figure 52). Compared with her merciless prosecutors, the prostitute stands out as a romantic heroine. Sloan felt strongly about the mistreatment and exploitation of prostitutes in New York. "I spent New Year's eve at the 'night court' in Jefferson Market," he wrote, "the women's court where women are on the basis of their being separate cattle treated 'special.' "[22]

Sloan's images broke new ground by minimizing and undercutting the immorality of prostitutes, making them less marginal and more acceptable. These women were simultaneously accessible and aloof. Their

Fig. 52 *John Sloan,* Before Her Maker and Her Judge
From The Masses, *Whitney Museum of Art*

sexuality was in a state of flux, a subject of debate and redefinition by themselves and twentieth-century society. Instead of depicting the prostitute in a brothel or as an offering for the supporting male, Sloan presented her as she experienced herself and her neighborhood. The prostitute was, in essence, an ordinary working woman. Sloan, in effect, erased the line separating "loose" women from "good" women.

George Bellows, best remembered for his stunning portrayals of tenement life, followed Sloan's lead in treating the confusing sexual boundaries of New York. Characteristically, Bellows's lithograph *The Street* (1917) shows the street peddlers, lunchrooms, rooming houses, and barefoot children along the Lower East Side thoroughfare (figure 53). This lithograph was a reworking of the earlier work *I Was Punchin' His Face* (1914), published in *Harper's,* depicting several young boys being apprehended by the police after an altercation.[23] Whereas the women

Fig. 53 George Bellows, The Street
From the Library of Congress

and their ambiguous sexuality form a minor theme in the earlier rendering, they become the dominant figures in *The Street*. While most of the figures are darkened by the shadow of the elevated rail tracks, the two women are bathed in light. The ladies walk arm in arm, attracting knowing and critical glances from their neighbors. Dressed in fashionable garb, the women display no discomfort with the chaos around them. In fact, they are an integral part of it. The women are not morally depraved, fallen, or erotically tempting. They are ordinary, everyday parts of the urban streetscape. The ambiguity of the scene forced viewers to wonder whether these women, dressed like prostitutes, really were prostitutes.

A Bellows cartoon in 1914 mocked the white-slavery campaigns of the era (figure 54). A white middle-class female and a well-dressed black woman seeking a servant position are engaged in conversation:

> "But if you have never cooked or done housework—what have you done?"
> "Well, Mam, Ah—Ah's been a sort of p'fessional."
> "A professional what?"
> "Well, Mam—Ah takes yo' fo' a broad-minded lady—Ah don't mind tellin' you Ah been one of them white slaves."

The cartoon reminded viewers that purity reformers too often ignored the racial dimension of prostitution. In addition, the distinctive dress of the black female symbolized the rewards of commercial sex. While Bellows did not deal with questions of sexual and economic exploitation, the cartoon turned traditional images of prostitution upside down.[24]

These novel examinations of prostitution in New York at times glamorized prostitution. Sloan and Bellows, in particular, were guilty of sentimentality and naïveté in some of their depictions of the "happy" prostitute. Pain, brutality, and conflict were often absent. Nevertheless, they joined leading social scientists in departing from their predecessors in important ways. For the first time, American intellectuals and artists treated prostitutes as more than simple symbols of immorality or hereditary criminals. By examining the details of the prostitute's existence, social scientists and artists rejected the damning, one-sided moralisms of the nineteenth-century and the white-slavery campaigns of the twentieth. In their place, they created a new image of urban life.

Real Lives

THESE new images, substituting female agency for male coercion, corresponded with how female prostitutes tended to view their activi-

Fig. 54 George Bellows, White Slavery
From The Masses *(1914), Archives of American Art, Smithsonian Institution*

ties. Many saw commercial sex as a routine part of city life and did not regard themselves as fallen women or white slaves. As a teenager growing up on the Lower East Side, for example, Emma Hartig discovered an informal social network in which numerous young prostitutes shared. Moving among brothels and assignation houses during the 1890s, Hartig noted that most inmates were thirteen- to seventeen-year-olds like herself. Her peers provided all kinds of information about prostitution and advice on where to locate such work. "I found out these different places through . . . a great many young girls circulating through all those places on the East Side," she remembered. And when Hartig answered an advertisement for a waitress and discovered that the place was really an "immoral house," she stayed. "They kept me quite nice there," she admitted. "I did not like the place where I was." Similarly, when a former madam was queried about where and how she obtained girls, she curtly responded, "My dear gentlemen, you will find lots of girls yet, the girls know where the houses are."[25]

Evidence of this independent subculture of prostitutes existed before 1900, of course, but was ignored by contemporaries. During the 1870s, for example, the Society for the Prevention of Cruelty to Children concluded that "flower girls" were responsible for introducing many young girls to prostitution. "The business of peddling flowers at night is constantly resorted to as a pretense. . . . They are in the streets at all hours of the day and night, frequenting saloons and houses of ill-repute." Some girls, "rather handsome in features and modest in demeanor," even organized small gangs and practiced "the domestic lay"—blackmailing guilty and innocent merchants "for alleged improper liberties taken with them." All too often, noted one journalist, "the peddler of posies" became "a lady of the camellias."[26]

The success of teenage prostitutes was not lost on their colleagues. Older prostitutes, hoping to appease male fantasies for young sex partners, often disguised themselves to look like children (figure 55). For example, one man, solicited by what he thought was a schoolgirl on Sixth Avenue, quickly realized "that out of the juvenile attire of the bearer of the satchel there peeped a face young and fresh enough, yet by no means that of a child." Prostitutes posing as schoolgirls most often appeared around schooltime, earning the epithet "buzzards in doves' plumes."[27]

Teenage prostitutes were common in many New York brothels. For example, Mary Henry's five-dollar parlor house in the Tenderloin had ten girls ranging in age from fifteen to eighteen, and a Harlem brothel with an allegedly elderly clientele provided partners twelve to eighteen years old. One neighbor complained that "the children talk of it" while they played in the street. Similarly, the Tenderloin madam Sophia "furnished young girls for seduction purposes, usually afternoons for $20 to $25." She even offered her niece from England to her customers, whereupon "she was torn so that they had to employ a doctor," according to one investigator.[28]

The prostitutes' peer group occasionally overwhelmed family strictures. The famed Seven Sisters brothels in the Tenderloin were said to have begun when one young woman, after running a brothel for a time, persuaded six of her sisters to move from their New England hometown to New York and do the same. Other madams, too, recruited girls from their hometowns. More common were cases like that of fifteen-year-old Katie Byrne, who worked in a Tenderloin brothel until

Fig. 55 "A Buzzard in Dove's Plumes"
From National Police Gazette

her mother discovered her secret. "My daughter has been going to this home every day for the past four months," cried her mother, "telling me she was going to work and bringing home her wages every Saturday night . . . and I thought her an innocent girl."[29]

Teenage females in seemingly stable families were not immune to the attractions of prostitution. For example, the fifteen- to seventeen-year-olds in Mrs. George Miller's West Fortieth Street brothel "were Jewish girls of very respectable people." Similarly, thirteen- and fourteen-year-old girls visiting Rosa Langbein's Eldridge Street assignation house "had respectable homes, and their parents were under the impression that they were employed in a factory."[30]

Many teenage prostitutes acknowledged that commercial sex offered tangible rewards and that they considered it easy employment. In fact, prostitutes frequently claimed that they did not even consider that the selling of sex was work. Delia Minsey, seeing "how easy it was to make money," said she wanted "to be a kept woman." Another woman insisted that she became a prostitute after observing girls in her tenement wearing "nice things without working." She went on to say that she "never did any honest work but followed what they did." Similarly, French Viola, a Tenderloin brothel prostitute who averaged twenty-five dollars per week in wages and accommodated as many as 180 clients, incongruously admitted that she "drifted into the business because of the easy time." One woman bluntly told the reformer Felix Adler that prostitution was simply the best alternative. "Good food, fine clothes and the easy life make it attractive," she declared.[31]

As women entered the world of wage labor in larger numbers after 1870, prostitution was attractive to some. Most female occupations paid very low and inadequate wages. In the garment industry, for example, women averaged between six and twelve dollars per week in wages. Schoolteachers and clerks rarely made more than ten. In contrast, prostitutes admitted to earning thirty dollars per night in concert saloons and fifty dollars a week streetwalking along Broadway.[32] This willingness on the part of some women to choose prostitution over other forms of labor reflected an alternative attitude regarding their bodies. Their view of the meaning of coitus was very different from that of middle-class Americans. For the prostitute, commercial sex offered a better and more appealing form of employment and life-style.

For many of these teenage prostitutes, assignation houses, hotels, and concert saloons provided greater freedom than did brothels. In the row of assignation houses on East Thirteenth Street, near Union Square, a neighbor complained that it was "not an uncommon thing for very young and seemingly innocent girls to be seen going in there heavily veiled." Girls as young as twelve and thirteen, for example, brought men to Mary Lester's house on the block. Elsewhere in Greenwich Village, Minnie Brooks offered twelve- and fourteen-year-old girls in her house. Despite their "outside respectability," the three hotels at Twenty-fourth Street and Third Avenue attracted large numbers of fourteen- and fifteen-year-old females "of the shop girl class." In Richard Hill's Harlem concert saloon, young girls allegedly "entice[d] men into [the] wine rooms where the orgies [were] carried untill daylight." And ten- to fifteen-year-old girls solicited men in the Globe, Windsor, and New American dime museums on the Bowery, bringing men to nearby assignation houses.[33]

The same was repeated in cigar stores. Annie Bushein, for example, provided girls of fifteen years and under to customers. In similar businesses on the Lower East Side, large numbers of German girls under sixteen waited on customers and asked if they wanted "to go up stairs or back." One reporter concluded, "[T]he girls in them do not look as common as those in the lower east side houses or on the Bowery. Some of them are rather bashful and look as if they have not been in the business very long."[34]

For other young women, however, the decision to prostitute was not easy. Emma Goldman said of her decision to streetwalk on Fourteenth Street to raise money for her lover, the anarchist Alexander Berkman, "I felt no nervousness at first, but when I looked at the passing men and saw their vulgar glances and their manner of approaching the women, my heart sank. . . . I wanted to take flight, to run back to my room, tear of my cheap finery, and scrub myself clean." When her first customer realized she was a novice, he simply gave her ten dollars and instructed her to go home. She never tried prostitution again.[35]

Goldman's confused and contradictory feelings about prostitution illustrate the fluidity and constantly tested social terrain of this subculture. As Kathy Peiss, Joanne Meyerowitz, and others have argued, many young girls at the turn of the century bartered their bodies on an occasional and irregular basis, blurring the line between sex for hire and sex in courtship. Men "treated" women to drinks, theater tickets, and other incidentals in exchange for various sexual favors, ranging from flirtatious companionship to sexual intercourse. Young women offered themselves to men not just for money but for company, presents, and amusement. While they were not truly promiscuous, neither were they models of decorum; they moved in and out of the trade quite easily.[36]

Even vice investigators by the early twentieth century recognized the diversity of prostitution and female sexual behavior. Charles Briggs, working undercover on behalf of the Committee of Fourteen, admitted that a wide range of female sexual activity occurred in cabarets and concert saloons. So varied was this behavior that Briggs constructed his own, four-tier hierarchy in describing and evaluating it. First, skilled working women like store clerks, telephone operators, and stenographers frequently displayed "loose" morals and enjoyed a high level of "sexual intimacy with their male companions." Most of them, however, never engaged in prostitution. Briggs talked with one department store clerk who admitted that she made special arrangements to stay out so that her family would not catch on. She expressed interest in going out "all night if . . . she received a little present for doing so." Other women, whom Briggs defined as "near whores" or "whores in the making," were "sporty in appearance" and commonly called "wise ones" for their "experience in obtaining money through sexual intercourse." A third group he considered to be occasional prostitutes, who sold themselves only "if the circumstances [were] right." Finally, "kept women" and the professional prostitutes made little secret of what they did.[37] Whereas mid-nineteenth-century reformers and writers often saw female sexual activity in simplistic, black-and-white terms, investigators like Briggs implicitly recognized that prostitution was a constructed category. Levels and degrees of prostitution were often determined simply by how people defined it.

Briggs was not alone in his observations. Other investigators independently came to similar conclusions. One, for example, found "that only a portion of the girls [in a cabaret] 'were out for the money'; some of them were 'straight,' [meaning] that the girls had sexual relations only with one man at a time." At Klyberg and Freeney's saloon, on Fourteenth Street and Sixth Avenue, another investigator found women he described as "decent and some who follow[ed] the business of prostitution." And J. B. Beers, investigating Raines Law hotels in Harlem, saw prostitutes and ordinary working-class women socializing in the same institutions.[38]

The wide range of female sexual behavior reflected the variety of personal economies and financial circumstances that encouraged women to prostitute. Working-class married women, in particular, engaged in occasional prostitution in times of economic hardship. For instance, John H. Sheidhauer's wife was arrested several times for soliciting while he was a patient at the Charity Hospital. Likewise, when Emma Dale's sailor husband was away, she resorted to prostitution for financial sustenance. Louisa Baker prostituted herself because her husband made only two dollars a day and she was "destitute." Mary Mass claimed that her husband died while she was pregnant and left her with no means of support. When the husband of C. A. Lawrence eloped with another woman, she started streetwalking "to provide for her child and herself." Nellie Brown simply said "she had no other way of making a living."[39]

Prostitution, for some, was part of the "family wage." Instances abound in which husbands encouraged their wives or parents their children to prostitute in order to contribute to the household income. From 1888 to 1892, for example, Rachel Marks peddled her children to various houses of prostitution on the Lower East Side. When she was arrested and her children sent to the House of Mercy, she moved to Brooklyn to run a house on Fulton Street. Yet in 1895, after rejoining her English husband and moving to the Williamsburgh neighborhood in Brooklyn, she requested that her children be returned. In another case, a Mr. Del-Paul ordered his wife to entertain other men, even though their four children were sometimes forced, according to investigators, "to witness the nightly orgies enacted at home." In 1888, the owner of a Forsythe

Street cigar store offered his fifteen-year-old daughter to the keeper of a boardinghouse, "where in a short time she would have a young man for a lover; and could earn $20 a week and no hard work." A seventeen-year-old Jewish girl worked in a Tenderloin brothel avowedly to support her parents. Lizzie Dannenberg, a thirty-four-year-old German immigrant and janitoress, encouraged her fifteen-year-old daughter to engage in prostitution. These common practices led the physician and women's rights activist Elizabeth Blackwell to assert, "The great mass of poor women are often regarded as the subjects to be used for the benefit of the upper classes."[40]

Most often, however, it was living alone and earning low wages that induced many young females to choose prostitution. In an economy still structured around a family wage, the absence of traditional familial support resulted in economic hardship. As early as 1879, one newspaper estimated that sixty thousand young females in New York depended solely upon themselves for support. Similarly, by 1900 nearly 20 percent of the adult working women in New York City were living in lodging houses or boardinghouses by themselves. Prostitutes testified to the resulting dire economic circumstances. One told an investigator that she simply could not survive on her weekly six-dollar salary at the Siegel and Cooper department store. But for nine dollars more, she promised to lead a "honest" life. After permanently injuring her back, the chorus girl Estell Lavett decided she simply made more money in a brothel. Even the Committee of Fifteen, for all its charges of white slavery, admitted that many women in "a time of distress" resorted to prostitution as "their readiest means of support." Finally, Katharine Bement Davis's 1912 survey of 671 prostitutes recognized that family and "personal" problems were the greatest inducement to prostitution.[41]

The occupational background of Gotham's prostitutes after 1900 reflected the low-paying jobs most women were forced to accept. Of nearly five hundred prostitutes who related personal histories in a 1912 Night Court survey, department- and small-store clerks made up 30 percent. Servants, houseworkers, and chambermaids together totaled another 24 percent. Interestingly, new occupations also appeared in significant numbers. As a single skilled occupational group, office workers, stenographers, telephone operators, and teachers accounted for 15 percent of New York's prostitutes, as did actresses and factory operatives.[42] Although some careful observers like Maude Miner of the New York Probation and Protective Association believed that slightly more women in domestic service (including waitresses in hotels and restaurants, laundry workers, and so on) were prostitutes than factory workers, the declining percentage of servants who became prostitutes was attributable to the steady national decline in the number of domestics from 1870 to 1900. Not surprisingly, the low remuneration servants received partly explained their tendency to resort to prostitution as well to various other forms of crime.[43]

Selling sexual favors, however, rarely afforded a woman complete independence. Whether their tie was to a pimp, a parent, a policeman, a proprietor, or a madam, prostitutes were never fully self-sufficient workers. Women in brothels were indebted to their brothel keeper; streetwalkers, to their pimp. In saloons, soda water and cider stubes, cigar stores, and lunchrooms, occasional prostitutes worked at the sufferance of the owner. Women in furnished-room houses, concert saloons, and hotels divided their proceeds with proprietors and pimps, who often provided protection, bail, and even customers.[44]

While some young women considered prostitution to be "easy" work, conditions could be rather onerous. Some prostitutes worked at an astonishing pace. According to account books in one fifty-cent brothel, one prostitute copulated with 273 men in two weeks, an average of 19 per day (her high was 28 in a day), earning $136.50 for the house. Two other prostitutes in the same house saw an average of 120 and 185 men each week, respectively, one seeing as many as 49 in one day. The surprisingly high volume was contingent upon each woman's willingness to spend sixteen hours daily at the task. Many often worked in intense, short spurts. For example, one girl in a Delancey Street house had intercourse with 58 different men in a single three-hour period. Madge Williams made $58 one evening in 1909, meaning that she had intercourse with at least 29 men. One French-born prostitute in the Tenderloin claimed she accommodated about 180 clients weekly. And streetwalkers, working out of the National Hotel, near Union Square, returned with different clients every ten to twenty minutes.[45]

The most lucrative forms of prostitution were also quite competitive, and this probably put a heavy physical burden on prostitutes. Police and court surveys of brothel inmates, for example, revealed the most were in the house several months or less. In John and Josephine Fisher's Greene Street brothel, the four residents were there two months, six weeks, and eleven and three days, respectively. As one woman told an investigator, "a girl stays not much more than a month unless she brings good trade," and soon exchanges places in other houses. Working in a parlor house, twenty-eight-year-old Blanche Coleman complained that she earned so little money that she opted for streetwalking. On West Third Street, Police Captain James Brogan observed that prostitutes and tenants alike were "continually moving from one location to another and in many instances, [did] not occupy the same apartments for more than a week or month."[46]

Evidence of the short careers of most prostitutes is even found in arrest records. Court statistics show that of 5,175 different females convicted of prostitution from 1900 to 1913, 55 percent appeared only once and only 10 percent were convicted five or more times. Recidivism declined further between 1916 and 1922, when under 4 percent of over 6,000 women had more than one conviction. Even so-called "professional prostitutes" moved in and out of the trade. For example, Hattie Ledyne was arrested over one hundred times in a two-and-one-half-year period. Yet, whenever a nearby saloonkeeper needed a servant, she would quit prostituting to work for him.[47]

Popular stereotypes pinned the blame for prostitution on immigrants. However, the most reliable information from the turn of the century shows that most New York prostitutes were American-born. The U.S. Senate's Immigrant Commission, for example, found that of over 2,000 prostitutes arrested in four months of 1908 and 1909, almost three-quarters were American-born.[48] In a 1912 survey of over 1,000 streetwalkers in New York, 69 percent were native-born. A later study of 647 prostitutes by Katharine Bement Davis showed that 63 percent were American-born whites, 13 percent American-born blacks, and 24 percent foreign-born. Finally, a sampling of women who passed through Women's Court from 1914 to 1917 confirmed these findings. Significantly, as the percentage of immigrant prostitutes declined during World War I, greater numbers of African-American prostitutes appeared in the courts.[49]

Immigrant prostitution attracted so much attention, in part, because it appeared in the most visible and commercialized institutions in the Tenderloin. For example, of the 464 women found in Tenderloin hotels in one Committee of Fourteen survey, 30 percent were French, 20 percent Jewish, and 6 percent German. Of those remaining, at least 38 percent were American-born, including 18 percent Irish-American and 7 percent African-American. Similarly, the 187 women whom investigators counted in 32 boardinghouses and brothels in the Tenderloin included only 13 percent who were American-born. Over half (51 percent) were Jewish and more than a third (36 percent) French.[50] Finally, on the basis of their religious affiliation, it seems likely that many native-born prostitutes came from second-generation immigrant families. In 1912, for example, 44 percent of the more than 10,000 prostitutes who went through the city's courts were Catholic, 35 percent Protestant, and 18 percent Jewish. In general, Catholic, Protestant, and Jewish women resorted to prostitution in numbers roughly equal to their proportion in the city's population.[51]

A final noteworthy change by the twentieth century was the apparent aging of New York's prostitutes. According to George Kneeland, the average entry age by the second decade of the century was seventeen. When professionals, such as teachers, resorted to prostitution, they were usually over the age of twenty. Furthermore, in a Committee of Fourteen study between 1905 and 1910, only 11 percent of the women sentenced in Women's Court were nineteen years old or younger, the greatest number (33 percent) twenty-four to twenty-five. By World War I, prostitutes appeared to be getting even older. A Committee of Fourteen investigator patrolling Broadway in 1918 remarked, "[M]ost noticeable is the large number of older women on the streets around the ages of 30 to 40 or more, well dressed and full of rings, etc. It has been the rule to find the young ones in the past but business is better and these older ones can even make it go." In a sampling of prostitutes in the Women's Court a year later, a surprising 56 percent were over twenty-six years old. Similarly, the average age of over a thousand prostitutes surveyed, dispersed in saloons, concert halls, hotels, and the street, was twenty-five.[52] The weight of evidence implies that by the second decade of the twentieth century, fewer teenagers and more young adult women relied upon prostitution to remedy economic or personal distress.

Not surprisingly, those who worked in the parlor of brothels enjoyed longer careers than those who toiled in the bedroom. The spotty records that describe madams during these years show that some stayed in the business for decades. Kate Woods, for example, did so for nearly half a century. After running the Hotel du Wood during the 1870s, she managed the famed House of All Nations in the ensuing decade. By 1909, her West Forty-first Street house was a "clearing house" for numerous Upper West Side establishments. Similarly, Kitty Mack survived thirty-nine years as a madam, Annie Grey thirty, Virginia Dallafind twenty-four, Elizabeth Hartel twenty, and Lucy A. Rogers thirty-six, the latter reportedly at the *same* address. Male proprietors also remained in the business for decades.[53]

Like ordinary prostitutes, madams frequently changed their residences. For example, in 1870, Josephine Fisher and her husband ran a West Twenty-seventh Street brothel. Six years later, they operated a Greene Street house south of Greenwich Village. By 1886, Fisher controlled three Tenderloin establishments, and by the early twentieth century, she was back in a different pair of brothels on West Twenty-seventh Street. Similarly, Minnie Wiener changed houses almost every year. In 1888, for example, she was at 74 Forsythe Street; in 1898, at

199 Forsythe Street; a year later, at 201 Allen Street; in 1900, at 199 Allen Street; and in 1901, at 203 Eldridge Street. Likewise, during the 1870s, Nellie De Camp worked in the Tenderloin and then in several East Side houses, before moving to West Fifty-second Street, residing in several on that street. Eva Roses moved to Brooklyn in 1911, after twenty-two years in the business and in at least five different Lower East side brothels.[54]

One reason that madams moved so much was that the most successful often controlled more than one establishment. Emma DeForrest, whom Anthony Comstock arrested after watching a "Busy Fleas" performance in her brothel, ran two houses by the time she was thirty-nine. Tenderloin madams, in particular, were the most likely to run several brothels. In 1888, for example, May Brown ran two adjoining houses on West Thirty-first Street. And after 1900, Ada Shaw, who owned her own horses, carriage, and brownstone after ten years in the business, controlled two West Twenty-eighth Street brothels, while May Livingston and Annie Grey ran three brothels apiece in the heart of the Tenderloin.[55]

One of the most successful was Matilda Hermann. Shortly after immigrating from France in 1882, Hermann opened a brothel along West Third Street. Operating under a lease, she appears to have had some previous experience in Europe in the trade, and she quickly recruited her sister to assist her in the business. Within a few years, they jointly ran six brothels along West Third Street. Their monthly rents were quite high. At a time when the average three-room unit on the Lower East Side rented for $13.50 per month, the Hermanns paid monthly rents ranging from $75 to $110. When one of their houses was later sublet as a private home, its monthly rent was only $40. Their high overhead, however, did not inhibit their financial success. By 1891, they had accumulated enough capital to purchase two of the houses on the block, one for $12,500. Conflicts with the law, though, eventually forced Matilda out of the business, but not before corrupt police officials paid her $1,700 to abandon the houses.[56]

The most famous madam in turn-of-the-century New York was Rosie Hertz. Saving enough from her own prostitution, she and her husband, Jacob, opened several brothels on the Lower East Side during the 1880s. Within a decade, they were successful enough to purchase other pieces of Manhattan property. By 1901, the Hertzes controlled at least five brothels and Raines Law hotels along East First Street, including the Hertz Sample room, the Maine Saloon, and the Hertz Hotel. Like many native-born Americans, once they had accumulated enough savings, they moved to the suburbs, in this case to affluent Borough Park, in Brooklyn. The epitome of the "white slaver," Hertz was called by one judge the "godmother for prostitutes." Another critic considered her "as much a public feature of the lower East Side . . . as the Brooklyn Bridge."[57]

Hertz's success, however, was short-lived. As antiprostitution campaigns grew stronger after 1905, Hertz was forced to pay higher protection fees to police officers. In the process, she reportedly squandered a fortune estimated at $250,000 before her conviction in 1913. After nearly three decades in the business, Hertz was tried for graft and sentenced to a year in jail, an event that one observer claimed was "the most severe blow which [had] befallen the old ring of disorderly housekeepers in many a year."[58]

Rich madams like Matilda Hermann and Rosie Hertz, however, were the exception. Most others were much less entrepreneurial and were motivated by survival needs rather than by opportunities for wealth. One part-time madam, for example, insisted that she and others entered the business "from pure necessity." When Annie Smith's policeman husband died, she opened a brothel on West Twenty-seventh Street as a way to support her four children. Similarly, Rhoda Sanford, after working as a housekeeper in several brothels and in dire need of support for her children in Brooklyn, entered the business in 1892 after a madam and former employer provided her with an initial $3,000 mortgage. On one occasion, after being raided, she sent the girls away and ran the place as a furnished-room house. Five months later, she brought them back and ran it "on the quiet." Another houseworker, twenty-seven-year-old Lena Schwartz, ran a Houston Street brothel until she experienced difficulty making money.[59] Generally, the substantial protection fees and frequent raids reduced madams' net income to about 15 percent of their gross receipts. One claimed that "when trade got dull," she did not earn enough even to pay the protection fees. "As I could not pay it," she said, "I sold my furniture and am now destitute."[60]

Female boardinghouse keepers often permitted prostitutes to "lodge" with them as a means to supplement their own rent. Before she was evicted, for example, sixty-year-old Hannah Harris derived support "from a few dissolute women, . . . to whom she furnished lodgings." Indeed, the practice of housekeepers' renting to prostitutes was an ordinary part of city life. The German widow, mother, and café proprietor Flora Walters testified, "I did not think it was so bad."[61]

The position of madams seems to have worsened during the final decade of the nineteenth century. As in the antebellum era, in the years 1870–1900, the majority of identifiable proprietors were females. As long as the brothel remained a signal institution of commercial sex, madams and boardinghouse keepers enjoyed considerable influence in

Fig. 56 Lucy Rogers's brothel
From Committee of Fourteen, Annual Report for 1915–16 *(1917)*

the city's vice economy. Prostitutes simply relied upon the brothel as their place of work. But with passage of the Raines Law in 1896, a major shift occurred. Individual prostitutes increasingly worked out of concert saloons and Raines Law hotels, thereby gaining a measure of independence from brothels.[62] Ironically, in the very years when the white-slave controversy focused attention on the brothel and the coercive practices of some proprietors, female prostitutes probably felt less institutional coercion in their work. It was simply easier for them to bring clients to a tenement, apartment, or hotel for sexual intercourse.

As a consequence, the ensuing two decades saw the number of brothel madams decline considerably. In 1916, when authorities arrested the madam Lucy A. Rogers and closed down her Tenderloin brothel (figure 56), some claimed it marked the end of an era. Her business on West Fifteenth Street had noticeably fallen off during her thirty-six years in the business. Only one prostitute was found working for her, and that woman did not even live there. The establishment had become little more than a boardinghouse.[63] The termination of Lucy Rogers's career as a madam reflected the changing social structure of prostitution in New York. New real estate investment patterns, alternative institutions with commercial sex, and greater municipal repression undermined the importance of the brothel. By the eve of America's entry into World War I, the brothel madam had lost her prominent role in the business.

14

UNDERMINING THE UNDERWORLD

On 13 *March* 1892, from his pulpit in the Madison Square Presbyterian Church, the Reverend Charles Parkhurst launched the most famous antiprostitution campaign in New York history. Only a week earlier, the minister, accompanied by the private detective Charles W. Gardner, had traversed the city, hoping to ignite a political inquiry into vice and sexual crime. In church, Parkhurst described the sexual plague he had observed on this tour of the metropolis (figure 57).

On Water Street, Parkhurst charged, the women solicited "with the same air that a Grand Central Station hackman asks you to 'have a cab.' " Once he was inside a saloon, women taunted the disguised minister with "Hey whiskers, going to ball me off?" In Bowery concert halls, young girls sat on men's laps, encouraging any advance, "no matter how vile it was." Fifty women accosted Parkhurst and Gardner as they passed along Bleecker Street, in Greenwich Village, only a stone's throw from police headquarters. In a nearby brothel, he witnessed an exhibition of the "French circus" and, in the Tenderloin, a similar burlesque entitled the "dance of nations." The curious cleric even ventured into the Gold Rule Pleasure Club, with its small rooms and homosexual boys with painted faces, falsetto voices, and the airs of young girls.[1]

Parkhurst's campaign was hardly the first of its kind. During the 1830s, Protestant evangelical reformers led

Fig. 57 Charles Parkhurst

by the Reverend John McDowall and the Female Moral Reform Society called for the eradication of the brothel. Two decades later, evangelical Methodists founded the Five Points Mission with similar goals. Anthony Comstock's periodic raids of popular brothels stirred up controversy after 1870. Mayors William Grace and Abram Hewitt instigated similar campaigns during the 1880s. Parkhurst's crusade, however, departed from these earlier forays of moral outrage. Whereas previous attacks had been short-lived and quickly forgotten, Parkhurst's ushered in a new era of antiprostitution reform lasting over a quarter century. In one sense, the period of Progressive reform in New York City began with Parkhurst's assaults on sexual turpitude. Prostitution became a sustained, central concern for groups determined to solve the most salient urban problems: investigators of municipal corruption, antivice commissions, settlement house leaders, women's organizations, social hygienists, purity reformers, and wealthy businessmen. All, in their own ways, were determined to undermine the underworld.

Parkhurst's concern was not simply with prostitution but also with politics, specifically Tammany Hall. In dramatic fashion, Parkhurst put the political machine on the defensive. The minister was among the first to charge the police and the machine with being pillars of organized crime. Tammany, Parkhurst insisted, was not a political party but "a commercial corporation organized in the interest of making the most possible out of official opportunities." The police represented "organized municipal criminality," the machine, "the organization of crime." Parkhurst saw little advantage in preaching the Gospel to young men on Sunday if they were only "going to be sitting on the edge of a Tammany-maintained hell the rest of the week."[2]

Not all contemporaries reacted favorably to Parkhurst. Some, like the author Robert Walsh, faulted the minister for his coercive tactics and predicted failure. Fearing that prostitution would be forced into hotels and homes, Walsh wrote that a "judicious toleration of necessary evil [was] perhaps the surest way to prevent its indiscriminate spread." The Reverend William O'Brien Pardow, whose St. Francis Xavier Roman Catholic Church was in the middle of the Tenderloin, charged Parkhurst with "inducing evil [rather] than restraining it." Another minister concurred that Parkhurst's actions would only push prostitution into previously untouched neighborhoods. The Congregationalist minister and Social Gospel advocate Washington Gladden warned Parkhurst about mixing politics with religious duty, arguing that a linking of theological agendas with party politics would only create confusion. Even Parkhurst's detective companion believed that the minister "was only a man trying to justify a position into which he had foolishly placed himself." Yet others, such as the Reverend J. O. Peck, lauded Parkhurst and his fellow purity reformer Anthony Comstock as the two greatest men "in moral heroism and Christian courage."[3]

Publicly, Parkhurst envisioned an ecumenical, nonpartisan reform movement in which a variety of religious and secular organizations united in an effort to establish honest government. Parkhurst's ministerial vocation, his evangelicism, and his occasional attacks on the Roman Catholic church for its support of Tammany Hall convinced many that he was just another nativist. But Parkhurst argued that his organization attracted Protestants, Catholics, and Jews who "mingle[d] harmoniously in its councils, and co-operate[d] in its work." Theologically, Parkhurst tended to turn his back on his conservative coreligionists. He believed in evolution and a liberal interpretation of Christianity. "[B]elieving the Bible," he asserted, "is not quite the same as believing everything there is in it." Disdaining denominationalism and a fire-and-brimstone Protestantism, he urged ecumenical solutions to social and sexual problems.[4]

In order to fight prostitution and corruption, Parkhurst even offered an alternative vision of city government. Founding the City Vigilance League in 1892, he established offices in the city's thirty assembly districts and endeavored to create a metropolitan, grass-roots organization. Instead of resorting to Albany and state legislation, he wanted a massive, internal, neighborhood-based social activism. Parkhurst intended each district's group to familiarize itself with every building, every owner, and every occupant. They would monitor the quality of sanitation and cleanliness of the streets and gather information on tenement, lodging house, and excise violations in the district. In effect, the central office of the Vigilance League would act as a "shadow government," which even had corresponding departments modeled after those in City Hall.[5]

Parkhurst's movement enjoyed some short-term success. In 1894, after Governor Roswell P. Flower vetoed a state appropriation for a special legislative committee to investigate Parkhurst's charges, the Chamber of Commerce financed a formal investigation. Chaired by State Senator Clarence Lexow, a Republican from Nyack, and directed by the reformers John W. Goff, William Travers Jerome, and Frank Moss, the "Lexow committee" compiled five volumes of evidence documenting municipal abuse, police corruption, and sexual exploitation. Moss, counsel for the Society for the Prevention of Crime (SPC) and the Owners and Business Men's Association of West Twenty-seventh Street, was known for devising private methods to fight police corruption and prostitution.[6] These efforts provoked public outrage and contributed to the successful mayoral campaign of the millionaire and reform candidate William L. Strong in 1894.

While Parkhurst's long-term goal of revamping the structure of municipal government was unrealized (Tammany Hall regained the mayoralty in 1896), his battle against prostitution generated more support. In 1899, the Republican party leader Thomas Platt ordered another state investigation (called the Mazet committee, after its chairman) into city corruption, producing another five volumes describing municipal malfeasance. A year later, the Episcopalian bishop Henry Codman Potter and his fellow minister Robert Paddock repeated the tactics of Parkhurst, launching the first antiprostitution campaign of the twentieth century. Comparing New York City to Caesar's Rome, Potter assailed the "rapacious licentiousness" throughout the city and called for the formation of a 25,000-member vigilance committee comparable to San Francisco's in the 1850s. Potter's call persuaded the Chamber of Commerce to act, and at the year's end it organized the Committee of Fifteen.[7]

The committee was one of the initial "vice commissions" of the Progressive Era. Like Parkhurst, the wealthy businessmen, academics, and reformers on the committee sought to overthrow Tammany by exposing its direct ties to prostitution. Allied with the SPC, the City Vigilance League, the Citizens Union, and the City Club, the Committee of Fifteen linked diverse political groups in New York, including Republicans, fusionists, reform Democrats, and anti-Croker Tammany men. Comstock's Society for the Suppression of Vice (SSV), the Public Education Association, the Hebrew Educational Alliance, the Settlements Association, the Church Association for the Advancement of Labor, and the Central Federation of Churches and Christian Workers aided the committee in varying capacities. Initially, the committee was concerned with gambling; by early 1901, though, leaders of various women's organizations, including Elizabeth Grannis, Elizabeth Cady Stanton, Carrie Chapman Cott, and Mary White Ovington, urged the committee to examine prostitution.[8] The members considered vice to be a glaring example of municipal inefficiency affecting future economic development. "New York is now the most expensive place in the world in which to do business," claimed Charles Stewart Smith, "and business will seek a more favorable atmosphere unless we purge the city." Committee members readily conceded they did not expect to eliminate prostitution, but hoped to end its links to municipal government.[9]

What attracted attention to the committee, however, was its support of the vigilant, antivice tactics of Judge William Travers Jerome. An ally and sometimes an accomplice of Frank Moss of the SPC and the City Vigilance League, Jerome instigated a series of spectacular raids early in 1901. From January to October, relying upon the Committee of Fifteen's investigative evidence, Jerome physically invaded and closed forty-five brothels and sixty-nine gambling dens. Wielding an ax during these moral crusades, Jerome proclaimed, "This is the law. The police won't enforce it. It is for the citizen to act." Although his draconian methods drew critical fire from some members of the committee, the judge attracted support in some neighborhoods for his attack on unpopular pimps, police, and Tammany politicians. By the end of the year, he had been elected district attorney in a campaign that swept the reformer Seth Low into the mayor's office.[10]

The committee's greatest impact came in the attention it focused on tenement house prostitution. By 1901, numerous newspapers publicized the committee's support for the new tenement law recommended by the Tenement House Commission. For the first time, city reformers attacked property owners. Felix Adler, a Committee of Fifteen member and longtime housing reformer, recommended that landlords be held responsible for prostitution. "The tenement, with its vast population," wrote Adler, "is becoming a kind of public institution, which cannot properly be dealt with from the point of view regarding it as a private house." By imposing $1,000 penalties upon owners of tenements and apartments who tolerated prostitutes, the Tenement House Law of 1901 placed a new burden of responsibility upon landlords. The legislation was also unsympathetic toward individual prostitutes. Any woman convicted of tenement prostitution was considered a vagrant and confined to prison for a maximum of six months. Lawrence Veiller admitted that the penalty was "much more severe" for tenement prostitution in order "to make it attractive for the prostitutes to leave the tenement houses and go into regular houses of prostitution."[11]

While the Committee of Fifteen successfully inaugurated a temporary policy of repression and a new tenement law, it had only a marginal effect on the city's prostitution. Within two years of the committee's disbandment, the problem was worse than before. The $1,000 penalty was rarely, if ever, collected. More important, the Raines Law of 1896, originally intended to suppress prostitution and regulate liquor sales, had done the reverse. The new legislation prohibited Sunday liquor sales everywhere except in hotels with ten or more beds. Instead of reducing the number of saloons, the law simply increased the number of brothels, and saloons subdivided rear and upper parts of their buildings into cheap "hotel rooms" for illegitimate use.

The proliferation of Raines Law hotels led to the founding of the Committee of Fourteen. A spin-off of the Anti-Saloon League comprising settlement house workers, temperance advocates, clerics, housing reformers, and businessmen, the committee described itself as "a permanent commission with a powerful backing representative of every class." Its membership included well-known reformers like Lawrence Veiller, Frances Kellor, and Mary Simkhovitch and was funded by wealthy New Yorkers like Andrew Carnegie, Edward Harkness, Jacob Schiff, and Felix Warburg. When the committee reorganized itself in 1911, John D. Rockefeller, Jr., became its most important fund-raiser; he himself often contributed as much as $2,500 annually. The committee proved to be a durable organization, lasting twenty-seven years before disbanding in 1932.[12]

The committee both borrowed and departed from earlier antiprostitution groups. Much of its support originated from its predecessor Committee of Fifteen, whose records the new body inherited. In addition, both organizations adopted the vigilant method of nineteenth-century preventive societies. For example, one SPC official working on behalf of the Committee of Fifteen admitted that when the police failed to perform their duty, the committee was "going to do it." Likewise, the Committee of Fourteen declared that if the district attorney did not enforce injunction laws, it would "act independently."[13]

Unlike previous antiprostitution reformers, however, the Committee of Fourteen accepted commercial sex as an unavoidable part of city life. "Certain things must be recognized," declared the committee's chairman, Frederick H. Whitin. Prostitution is "an accompaniment of civilization; that the crowding in the cities, an increase of luxuries and the postponement of . . . marriage, all tend to increase it." Echoing earlier arguments calling for the legalization of prostitution, Whitin surmised that if prostitution was eliminated "unquestionably, a terrible increase in the crimes of rape and seduction and abortions and illegitimate births" would result. "It is so deeply bedded in the constitution of society," agreed Raymond Fosdick, "that only direct surgical processes, involving violent alterations, can really hope to remedy it."[14] He doubted that such extreme measures were worth it.

Nonetheless, the committee did embody Progressive reform ideals. "It is my belief and hope," stated Whitin in 1913, "that while we as human [*sic*] have come from the animal, we are moving onwards and upwards towards the ideal which we hold of divinity." Prostitution would never be eradicated, yet New York in 1910 was "a great improvement" over what had existed one and two decades earlier. Whitin did not "think it a wild guess" that with woman's suffrage, the "doctrine of masculine sex necessity" would be in "limbo with many other seemingly impossible things to change."[15]

The Committee of Fourteen was the most successful antiprostitution organization in New York City history, achieving an impressive array of reforms. Within a year of its founding, for instance, the committee formulated and successfully lobbied for the Prentice Law, which cut the number of Raines Law hotels by more than half and persuaded Buildings Bureau officials to revoke liquor licenses in unsafe buildings.[16] Later accomplishments included the establishment of Night Court in 1907, a special jurisdiction where all prostitutes were arraigned by the same presiding justices in order to ensure uniformity of disposition.[17] The disorganized Magistrate's Court was coordinated and unified, and the Court of Special Sessions was enlarged. The committee cooperated with local improvement associations fighting prostitution in the Gramercy, Chelsea, and Hell's Kitchen neighborhoods, as well as with the Kehillah (Welfare Committee of the Jewish Community). It even succeeded in enlisting brewers and surety companies in its campaign, forcing them to sever connections with saloons permitting prostitution. In Albany, the committee lobbied for stricter enforcement of liquor laws, regulation of disorderly houses, and stiffer penalties for landlords of tenements with prostitutes. With the support of State Senators Robert Wagner and Walter Herrick, an injunction and abatement law was passed in 1914 penalizing property owners who tolerated prostitutes.[18]

The Committee of Fourteen owed its popularity and longevity to an unprecedented coalition of support. After 1900, a wide range of groups and individuals cooperated in efforts to eliminate the most public forms of prostitution. Settlement house leaders like Lillian Wald, Mary Simkhovitch, and Frances Kellor supported legislation to protect female immigrants from being coerced into prostitution. Settlement house volunteers like Rose Livingston, dubbed the Angel of Chinatown, went on "rescue missions" to help immigrants she believed had been forced into prostitution. Purity groups ranging from Anthony Comstock's SSV, the Anti-Saloon League, the National Vigilance Committee (1907), and the American Purity Alliance (1909) made white slavery a national issue. Spokesmen in the medical community like Dr. Prince Morrow, founder of the American Society of Sanitary and Moral Prophylaxis (1905), Dr. O. Edward Janney, and Abraham Flexner rejected the nineteenth-century medical arguments in support of regulation. Instead, they urged suppression. And muckraking journalists like George Kibbe Turner, Lincoln Steffens, and William Stead depicted prostitution as the ultimate manifestation of municipal corruption in their attacks on Tammany Hall.

Much of this movement, including the Committees of Fifteen and Fourteen, was funded by wealthy industrialists. The Chamber of Commerce, for example, sponsored the Lexow investigation in 1894, and its leaders were active in both committees. Similarly, John D. Rockefeller, Jr., not only was the major financial contributor to the Committee of Fourteen but also headed a grand-jury investigation of white slavery. Rockefeller wealth, in fact, provided considerable financial support for the New York Social Hygiene Society, the Bureau of Social Hygiene (1911), and the American Social Hygiene Association (1913). The bureau, in turn, funded the influential studies on prostitution by George Kneeland and Abraham Flexner.[19]

The Committee of Fourteen reflected the diversity of groups involved in Progressive reform. Nearly all parts of the purity and antiprostitution movements supported the committee: purity reformers wanting to suppress any discussion of sexuality, social hygienists fighting prudery and venereal disease, settlement house workers seeking protection of immigrant women, muckrakers attacking municipal politics, tenement house reformers linking prostitution to inadequate housing, and social scientists treating prostitution as a serious subject of academic inquiry. By

1910, at least twenty-six organizations existed to discourage or prevent women from engaging in prostitution. Thirty more independent clubs provided "opportunities for friendship, recreation and training" for young females. An additional fourteen groups were devoted primarily to reform work. And three state agencies assumed correctional responsibilities.[20]

What began as a clerical attack on vice and political corruption by Charles Parkhurst evolved into the scientific and "objective" study of deviant sexuality. This coalition of Progressive Era reformers ultimately forced a restructuring of prostitution and the underground economy. Upon eliminating the majority of Raines Law hotels, the committee hoped to eliminate other forms of commercial sex and sporting-male behavior. And elements of this coalition, led by the Anti-Saloon League, began a campaign to prohibit the sale of alcohol nationally. In this sense, the antiprostitution movement mirrored the changing nature of urban reform.[21]

The End of the Century of Prostitution

ON THE EVE of America's entry into World War I, antiprostitution reformers believed they had accomplished the impossible. "I am speaking without exaggeration when I say that for a city of its size," opined Raymond Fosdick, New York "is the cleanest city in the world." Although prostitution still existed, Fosdick charged that it was declining "under frontal attack" and changing its form. Another reformer noted that "with the closing of the town the disorderly women [had] largely resorted to flats and cheaper apartment houses to continue their business." Similarly, the Committee of Fourteen concluded that the "old-fashioned resort, where prostitutes sat around waiting . . . practically [had] been eliminated in New York City." Even the Bowery had lost most of its "disorderly resorts." Repression combined with the twin inventions of the skyscraper and the telephone to make the brothel and streetwalker obsolete. In her private apartment, the "call girl" rarely strayed into the public eye.[22]

After decades of visibility in theaters, concert saloons, masked balls, cabarets, and streets, prostitution waned in the early twentieth century. It became a clandestine, underground activity. Brothels did not advertise their existence. Prostitutes no longer openly plied their trade in concert halls, cabarets, and nightclubs. And streetwalkers disappeared from the major avenues and boulevards. In the words of the Committee of Fourteen, 1920 was "the low water mark in prostitution."[23] Gotham's century of prostitution was over.

Ironically, during the "Roaring Twenties," when New York was, in one description, "naked, profane, blasphemous and salacious," commercial sex grew less public and increasingly covert. For example, the Committee of Fourteen insisted, "New York has less open vice than any other of the world's largest cities." Prostitution was "almost entirely clandestine," street solicitation "exceptional," and "no public disorderly resorts of the open type [existed], nor of the semi-private type known as parlor houses." Organized houses with a dozen or more women disappeared.[24]

Even white slavery declined. Investigators noticed that clubs and speakeasies with prostitutes in the 1920s bore "very little resemblance to the old-time white slave traffic." "Instead of a white slave traffic," concluded one report, "the traffic is what might be termed a traffic in hostesses." A League of Nations report in 1927 similarly noted that although the traffic flourished in other countries, the United States was "hard to enter, and still harder to use as a base of operations." When Charles ("Lucky") Luciano was convicted of running New York's largest prostitution syndicate in 1935, there was no suggestion that he employed or imported immigrant females. Rather, the prostitutes came from the nearby factory towns of New York, Pennsylvania, and Ohio. The "white slaves of former times," concluded the Committee of Fourteen, were "a thing of the past."[25]

The trend continued throughout the Great Depression. Myles A. Paige told Mayor Fiorello LaGuardia in 1936 that only two forms of prostitution existed in Harlem—secluded call girls in apartments and occasional streetwalkers. Neither was a major problem, however, since a police crackdown removed most street soliciters and since call girl and apartment prostitution was "not such a great menace to the community because of its secrecy and seclusion." By 1938, the settlement house reformer and Committee of Fourteen member Mary Simkhovitch remarked that although sexual immorality still abounded, "the old red-light days [had] gone."[26]

Those involved in commercial sex admitted that procuring a prostitute required diligent effort. In 1919, a saloonkeeper said, "[I]f anybody comes in a place the first time and nobody knows him, he has a hardship to pick up a woman." Only after visiting an establishment several times was it possible "to pick up a girl in New York." Likewise, a bellboy in the Martinique Hotel, on Herald Square, complained that the police were "very strict around here now even on the streets." Even taxi drivers admitted to riders that they were ignorant of the location of "regular Cat Houses." Streetwalkers were so severely suppressed that most were reluctant to approach unfamiliar men because of the strict law enforcement. In one example, a newsboy employed in the subway station near the Bloomingdale's department store served as a "go-between" for prostitutes working out of a nearby cafeteria. As brothel and hotel prostitution declined, many prostitutes operated the "team way," relying upon pimps, hotel bellboys, theater ushers, restaurant waiters, and taxi drivers to procure customers.[27]

Antiprostitution reformers relished the manifest decline of prostitution, often taking most of the credit for it. But factors other than Progressive reformist zeal explain the change. Whereas unprecedented demographic growth, residential transiency, deplorably low female wages, new real estate patterns, and a sporting-male ideology and subculture undermined older patterns of sexual behavior after 1820, alterations in these same social forces by the early twentieth century stimulated new and reorganized forms of prostitution. No single development accounts for this; rather, it was the by-product of a constellation of critical events. Just as public prostitution characterized urban life from the War of 1812 to World War I, so its decline marked a significant transformation in metropolitan life.

Even the most visible changes, such as the decline of the Tenderloin as a prostitution center, were the result of forces other than Progressive reform. New uses of real estate, for instance, were considerably more influential. Between 1880 and 1920, the three- to six-story structures were in many areas of New York gradually replaced by skyscrapers and high-rise apartments. Among other things, apartments allowed greater amounts of privacy and secrecy than tenements or specialized brothels. More important, twentieth-century office buildings replaced many of the nineteenth-century dens of prostitution. In the Tenderloin neighborhood, for example, office space rose from less than 10 percent of the total real estate in 1900 to 43 percent by 1935. The erection of Pennsylvania Station from 1900 to 1910, in particular, spurred considerable redevelopment, especially in hotel construction. And south of Forty-second Street, large lofts and garment factories replaced the rows of brothels and boardinghouses after 1920. Ultimately, these changing land uses in the Tenderloin pushed out prostitution as a primary source of profit for midtown real estate interests.[28]

Government intervention also played a role in the decline of public prostitution. For the first time in American history, federal and municipal governments actively suppressed commercial sex in New York. The passage of the Mann Act in 1910, for example, made the transportation of women across state lines for such purposes illegal. While its importance was more symbolic than real in drastically curtailing prostitution, it nevertheless hurt organized syndicates. In 1915, all forms of prostitution were rendered illegal by the state legislature, removing the earlier encumbrances that inhibited prosecution. More important, within two weeks after the United States entered World War I, Secretary of War Newton Baker created the Commission on Training Camp Activities, chaired by Raymond Fosdick, specifically to protect soldiers from prostitutes and venereal disease. For two years, the commission treated illicit sex as a subversive, national security threat and led the most aggressive attack on prostitution in the nation's history.[29]

After the war, the federal Immigration Acts of 1921, 1924, and 1929 significantly cut the number of transient men and women in New York City. Annual immigration to the United States, most of which passed through New York, averaged approximately 820,000 between 1900 and 1909, topping the 1.2 million mark in 1907. But that figure dropped considerably beginning with World War I. During the 1920s, the annual influx of foreigners was halved, and by the 1930s the number had fallen to under 70,000 per year, including a low of 23,068 in 1933.[30] With considerably fewer transient males moving through New York, the demand for prostitutes diminished.

Prohibition also transformed prostitution. Passage of the Volstead Act in 1919 outlawed many of the venues of the prostitute—namely, saloons, concert halls, and cabarets. As illegal and more secretive alternatives appeared—most notably, the speakeasy—prostitutes were quickly attracted. Speakeasies encouraged prostitutes to abandon the street and brought them into less public environments. By its very nature, the speakeasy operated in a furtive manner, unable to advertise its existence and thereby making prostitution less noticeable. Like the drinking of alcohol, the consumption of sex became more of an underground activity.

Even municipal government treated prostitution differently. Until the Progressive Era in the early twentieth century, there was no statutory definition of prostitution. No law expressly prohibited soliciting in a saloon, dance hall, or furnished-room house. Instead, prostitution was a condition of vagrancy and being female. And even when prosecuted, prostitutes were usually treated like disorderly persons, charged with simple misdemeanors and never with felonies. Men patronizing prostitutes were rarely arrested. More important, common law never implicated the owners of a house of prostitution or considered them as accessories; it thereby encouraged, charged critics, "the use of property for immoral purposes on account of its higher revenue." Defense attorneys of prostitutes even claimed that as long as a woman lived alone and did not disturb her neighbors, it made "no difference how many men visit[ed] her and [had] sexual intercourse with her." With the passage of the Herrick Injunction and Abatement Law in 1914, most of these legal loopholes vanished.[31]

Such dramatic changes in government policy forced New York's political machine to adopt a new attitude toward commercial sex. As the historian Daniel Czitrom has discovered, Tammany Hall began cutting its support of ward leaders connected with New York's underground economy. With the election of Charles Murphy as grand sachem in 1902, Tammany officials distanced themselves from prostitution. The efforts by the Committee of Fourteen to expose saloons and surety companies that fostered such activities further encouraged Tammany to look elsewhere for revenue. And by 1910, numerous police officials working with elements of the underground economy had started replacing prostitution with gambling as a source of income.[32]

As sex entrepreneurs were compelled to operate much more secretly, a new organizational structure for prostitution appeared. Male "bookies," as they were called, controlled large numbers of prostitutes and madams, placing (or "booking") such women in different houses and apartments and moving them around from week to week. Reminiscent of the "Orpheum circuit," whereby popular films moved among movie palaces on a weekly basis, booking replaced bonding as a way to extort payments from prostitutes and madams. By 1930, this flexible and highly secretive method was the prevailing form of syndicate prostitution.[33]

Changes in government policy also affected longtime critics of commercial sex. During the 1920s, municipal reform and feminist agendas moved in new directions. Specifically, the antiprostitution appeal declined among reformers, and the elimination of prostitution was no longer a priority. In 1935, the Women's City Club of New York, the League of Women Voters of New York City, and the Women's Prison Association of New York recommended that prostitution be treated strictly as a medical, psychiatric, and social problem, not a criminal act. And when prostitutes were hauled into court during the 1930s, even Helen P. McCormick, counsel of the Brooklyn Women's Court Alliance, and Samuel Markus of the Society for the Prevention of Crime supported medical examinations for venereal disease, dismissing earlier generations' fears of abuse and informal regulation by the municipal court system.[34]

The medicalization of prostitution was not unique to New York. Public efforts promoting greater education and consciousness regarding venereal disease increasingly blamed prostitution as a major source of disease and public danger. Beginning with World War I and continuing during the 1930s with Thomas Parran's campaign, the American public was made increasingly aware of the health risks of indiscriminate sex.[35] As intercourse became an acceptable topic of public discussion, the potential dangers of promiscuity drew increased attention. Naturally, some blamed the prostitute, making her a serious health risk in the minds of many men.

A third factor—better wages and working conditions for women—rendered prostitution less necessary for many women. From 1910 to 1920, for example, the national proportion of female workers in non-manual jobs rose from 17 percent to 30 percent. Women made real gains in certain service-sector occupations. Those of telephone and telegraph operator, clerk, bookkeeper, saleswoman, buyer, designer, decorator, and copywriter were among the new, well-paying white-collar jobs for women. As Alice Kessler-Harris has shown, by the 1920s a larger percentage of employed women were laboring in these jobs (25.6 percent) than in manufacturing (23.8 percent), domestic service (18.2 percent), or agriculture (12.9 percent). Most important, in the office and department store, work and pay were steady and secure.[36]

Finally, American heterosexual behavior underwent significant changes after 1900. An increase in premarital sex, for instance, made prostitution less necessary or attractive for male and female alike. Furthermore, the homosocial patterns of nineteenth-century leisure, including the sporting-male subculture, were increasingly replaced by more heterosexual forms of entertainment. As historians like Kathy Peiss and Lewis Erenberg have shown, large dance halls and cabarets after 1910 attracted a wide range of women, many of whom attended unescorted. "Charity girls," or women offering themselves to strangers, not just for money but for presents, attention, or simple pleasure, made the need for prostitutes less imperative. As "treating" grew more common, it undermined commercial sex.[37]

Sexuality within marriage also changed. After 1920, intercourse was seen less as a commodity and part of an exchange relationship because of changing expectations attached to it within marriage. The rise of "affectionate" marriage, the "companionate wife," "masculine domesticity," and the "sexualization" of women in the initial decades of the twentieth century fostered what Paula Fass has termed the "democratization of family relations." The ideals of emotional warmth, amicability, and affection replaced rigid Victorian authority and responsibility as the defining qualities of the American family. Equally significant, sex was increasingly seen as a legitimate physical function, a crucial part of married life, and a basic expression of love within marriage. The increasing acceptance and availability of artificial birth control contributed to this change. Heterosexuality was transformed, but within older, monogamous traditions restricting sex to marriage. Sexual intercourse was a positive good, the acme of love, and, most important, the hallmark of equality in marriage.[38]

Earlier marriage also cut the large supply of rootless, single men and women. Whereas over 82 percent of the males and over 53 percent of the females twenty to twenty-four years in age were single in 1890, those figures had declined to 72.6 percent and 47.5 percent, respectively, by 1920. Additionally, whereas only 55 percent of the American population was married in 1890, some 60 percent was in 1920.[39] The rising incidence of youthful marriage significantly lowered the number of bachelor males exposed to the sporting-male subculture, as well as single females who needed to work as prostitutes to support themselves. Since American males no longer postponed marriage as in the past, prostitutes were less necessary for many of them.

The greater tolerance of premarital sex, the growing role of intercourse within marriage, the easier access to contraceptives, and a changing demography combined to weaken the importance of prostitution in New York. This trend was confirmed decades later by the sexologist Alfred Kinsey. In his path-breaking study of American sexual behavior, Kinsey found that the frequency of sexual intercourse with prostitutes by American males declined by one-half to two-thirds from 1926 to 1948.[40] During the first half of the twentieth century, it appears, American men increasingly rejected the prostitute as a sexual outlet.

The combination of these forces resulted in a new conception of male heterosexuality. In growing numbers, middle-class men rejected the double standard and sporting-male sexuality, especially within marriage. For too long, Dr. Prince Morrow noted, society has separated women "into two classes," demanding chastity from one and sexual gratification from the other. "It thus proclaims the doctrine, immoral as it is unhygienic, that debauchery is a necessity for its men." As the historian David Kennedy has pointed out, the attack on the double standard and the union of science with romance created a new attitude toward marital sexuality that made birth control, monogamy, and, ultimately, sexual pleasure more acceptable to many American males.[41] Whereas much sex and romance had occurred outside the home, and frequently in the brothel, during the nineteenth century, by the early twentieth century they were key ingredients in American courtship and marriage.

The decline of prostitution reflected other important changes in American sexuality after World War I. While the 1920s frequently evoked images of the seductive flapper and the secluded speakeasy, sexual conservatism underlay much American behavior. As states passed laws making prostitution illegal, for instance, commercial sex increasingly came under the control of centralized state authority and more rigid governmental scrutiny. Furthermore, the repression of prophylaxis, the "conspiracy of silence" in treating venereal disease, active public censorship of birth control, the criminalization of abortion, public fears of sexual psychopaths, increased homophobia, and fears of new dances displayed the sexual apprehensions of many Americans. Even seemingly revolutionary new activities like unchaperoned dating, "petting," premarital sex, and artificial birth control were marriage oriented in goal and focus. While morality no longer meant silence or chastity, promiscuity was hardly condoned.[42]

From the vantage point of this long history, prostitution and sexual intercourse in New York City experienced a three-part evolution from 1790 to 1920, changing from a "sacred" to a secular phenomenon and returning once again to the sacred. In 1800, prostitution, the institutions accommodating it, and the places where it flourished were geographically marginalized and socially isolated. Commercial sex had but little impact on the surrounding urban society. After 1820, however, sexuality was increasingly organized around and by market forces. It was treated more and more like a secular commodity, invested with exchange value, for the benefit of heterosexual males. Prostitution moved from the fringe to the core of city social life. Promiscuous sexuality now defined leading institutions of the nineteenth-century city—concert saloons, theaters, masked balls, brothels, and cabarets. Subcultures of prostitutes and sporting men, linked to an alternative society frequently labeled the underworld, became important elements in the social structure and public life of the metropolis. Commercial expressions of sexuality played an integral role in neighborhood, leisure, and female life, infusing private, intimate relations with economic value and epitomizing the secularization of sexuality. For the right price, sex was an advertised commodity in the commercial marketplace.

The steady decline of prostitution and the ensuing romance of marriage after 1910 evidence the "resacralization" of sexuality. Indeed, midway through the Progressive Era and particularly following World War I, American sexuality grew more exclusive, monogamous, and constricted. For men, the promiscuous paradigm that defined sporting-male sexuality waned as a defining characteristic of urban social life. Compared with the heavily sexualized entertainment districts, blatant prostitution, French brothels, and masked balls of nineteenth-century New York, and especially the halcyon years 1840–71, sexuality in Gotham was now more physically confined and less publicly provocative. Even advertisers who employed sexual themes after 1920 did so subliminally and usually with an orientation toward the family, monogamy, and reproduction. Tolerance for sporting-male behavior and commercialized forms of sexuality declined. Early in the twentieth century, just as Americans invested children with sentimental and religious meaning, they did the same to sex.[43]

Perhaps nothing symbolized these changes better than the Haymarket. For decades, this Tenderloin concert saloon had long remained a center of prostitution and sporting-male nightlife. Its popularity drew the ire of many a purity reformer, even leading to temporary closings by Mayors W. R. Grace and Abram Hewitt during the 1880s. The Haymarket was also a subject of interest for the artist John Sloan (figures 40 and 50). But during the second decade of the new century, the Jewish immigrant and onetime garment cutter William Fox turned it into a movie house. Rather than fighting reform, Fox joined it, transforming Gotham's most sexually promiscuous concert saloon into a brightly colored, Grecian-style movie palace. Soon a leading Hollywood magnate, Fox pushed out the prostitute and introduced a "proper" atmosphere to popular entertainment.[44] Here an institution and space once devoted to commercial sex succumbed to new market demands and new forms of leisure.

This is not to say that prostitution vanished from the face of the metropolis. Then as now, sexual behavior was dynamic, beset with tensions and contradictions. Trends and countertrends appeared simultaneously, sometimes side by side, making widespread generalizations about these sexual manners problematic. Prostitution—a symbol of social degeneration for some and a public and popular activity for many others—was characterized, in part, by its ambiguity. Indeed, prostitution was more than just sex for hire; it was contested cultural terrain. Commercial sex surely remained a part of the city's nightlife and social structure after 1920. But the public decline of prostitution, with its increasing marginalization, reflected the rise of new institutions of leisure, changing heterosexual relations, and new boundaries of acceptable social behavior. New York's century of prostitution had ended.

PROSTITUTION represented a fundamental paradox in the nineteenth- and early-twentieth-century city.[45] For women, nothing better symbolized blatant, unfettered exploitation; yet few other kinds of labor offered such large financial rewards. Voracious, hedonistic males quite likely saw this era as one of liberation and easy sexual exploration, a time of unbounded personal freedom. But close up, that freedom was ultimately limited by the pocketbook and what it could or could not buy.

The milieu of the underground economy offered a variety of alternative subcultures, some of which countered the dominant, sexually prescriptive mores of the age. But discriminations rooted in gender, class, race, and other types of difference ensured that the benefits of these subcultures were never equally shared.

Few echoes remain of New York's century of prostitution. In place of the plentiful Five Points brothels described by Dickens on Anthony (now Worth) Street stand the middle-income housing project Chatham Towers, the Jacob Javits Federal Building, the New York County Courthouse, and Thomas Paine and Columbus parks. Along First Street, once the turf of Rosie and Jacob Hertz, sit abandoned buildings and empty lots. The lucrative Tenderloin brothels adjacent to the old Metropolitan Opera House have vanished, replaced by garment factories and large warehouses. And on West Forty-third Street, the site once occupied by the French houses of Soubrette Row, sits the headquarters of the New York *Times*. The disappearance of these physical reminders of an earlier sexuality is appropriately symbolic. Prostitution at the end of the twentieth century is "invisible," no longer widespread in its physical and social presence. More prurient than controversial in public interest, prostitution occupies a comparatively marginal and obscure position in New York life. Just as the skyscraper epitomizes the new metropolis, the dearth of physical structures from a past New York exemplify a former sexuality now gone.

Appendix 1

A SELECTION OF BROTHEL OWNERS IN NEW YORK CITY, 1820–1859

Below is a selection of specific houses of prostitution located on real estate owned by John R. Livingston, John F. Delaplaine, and James Ridgeway. Along with the addresses are the years of ownership, the assessed valuation of the real property, the leaseholders and tenants and their years in the house (if known), and the assessed valuation of their personal property (if known). Sources for the lists include Record of Assessment (by ward), 1800–60; New York City District Attorney Indictment Papers, Court of General Sessions, 1790–1860; Police Court Papers, 1800–60, all in New York City Municipal Archives and Records Center; New York City Land Title Registrations, Pre-1917 Conveyance Records, Office of the City Register; Butt Ender, *Prostitution Exposed; or, A Moral Reform Directory* (New York, 1839); Charles DeKock, *Guide to the Harems* (New York, 1855); Free Loveyer, *Directory to the Seraglios* (New York, 1859). For those interested in a more detailed breakdown by selected streets, see Timothy J. Gilfoyle, "City of Eros: New York City, Prostitution, and the Commercialization of Sex, 1790–1920" (Ph.D. diss., Columbia Univ., 1987), appendix 2.

BROTHELS OF JOHN R. LIVINGSTON

Address and Tenants	*Years*	*Real Property Value*	*Personal Property Value*
39 Thomas Street			
John Edwards	1820	$3,000	$100
John Mortan	1820		$100

BROTHELS OF JOHN R. LIVINGSTON (*Continued*)

Address and Tenants	*Years*	*Real Property Value*	*Personal Property Value*
John Peter	1820		$100
4 men	1821		
Elisa Smith	1825		$1,000
Caroline Anders or Andrews	1826–29		$1,000
Mary Wall	1830		$1,000
Susan Scott	1831–37		$500–$1,000
Mrs. Kelly	1859	$5,500	
39½ THOMAS STREET			
C. Sammis	1825	$3,000	$200
? Telfair	1825		$100
Mary Ann Jones	1826		$500
Mary Wall	1827		$1,000
Ann Perkins	1828–30		$300–500
Miss Ross	1831		$1,200
Hannah Baker	1832	$4,300	$500
40 THOMAS STREET			
C. Sammis	1825	$3,000	$200
? Telfair	1825		$100
40½ THOMAS STREET	1850–59		
41 THOMAS STREET			
Abby Mead	1827–28	$1,200	$500
Rosina Townsend, alias Thompson	1829–35		$500
48 THOMAS STREET			
Catharine Sands	1825	$2,000	$1,000
70 CHAPEL STREET			
Ann Mills	1820	$2,400	
72 CHAPEL STREET			
William Marsh	1820	$2,400	
74 CHAPEL STREET			
Susan Fields	1829		
76 CHAPEL STREET	1829–50		
106 CHAPEL STREET	1838–50		
19 ANTHONY STREET			
Catherine Sands	1820	$2,400	$300
24 ANTHONY STREET			
Betsy and David Howland	1820	$2,000	$100
J. C. Shute	1825		
Sarah Jennings	1826		
Elizabeth Brown	1827–31		$500
Catherine Near	1832		
26 ANTHONY STREET			
Catherine Fitch	1824–26	$2,000	$600
Catherine Skilman	1827–28		
Sophia Peterson	1829		
Mary Francis	1831–32		$300

Address and Tenants	*Years*	*Real Property Value*	*Personal Property Value*
28 ANTHONY STREET			
Abby Mead	1824–26	$2,000	$1,000
Almira Sterns	1827		
Rosina Townsend, alias Thompson	1828		
Ann Boyd	1829		
Mrs. Thomas	1830		$200
Mrs. Shott	1831		
30 ANTHONY STREET			
J. Hannable	1824–26		$200
Rossana Cisco	1824–26		$300
John Sickles	1827		
John Sickles	1828		
Fanny Nelson	1828		
John P. Signer	1829		
William H. Butler	1831		$600
A. Lark	1833		$300
140 ANTHONY STREET			
Robert B. Gordon	1826	$3,600	$300
141 ANTHONY STREET			
John McGinnis	1826	$2,000	$100
142 ANTHONY STREET			
Mary Jenkins	1826	$2,000	$500
145 ANTHONY STREET	1826	$2,000	
152 ANTHONY STREET	1830		(R. R. Livingston estate)
153 ANTHONY STREET	1828–30	$2,200	(R. R. Livingston estate)
154 ANTHONY STREET			(R. R. Livingston estate)
Robert Gordon	1828	$3,000	$500
155 ANTHONY STREET	1828–30	$2,200	(R. R. Livingston estate)
157 ANTHONY STREET	1828–30		(R. R. Livingston estate)
William Wright	1828		$300
38 ORANGE STREET	1833–37	$3,000	(R. R. Livingston estate)
40 ORANGE STREET	1833–37	$3,000	
42 ORANGE STREET	1830		
141 ORANGE STREET			
John McGinnis	1826	$2,000	$100
143 ORANGE STREET			
John Baris	1826	$2,000	$100
145 ORANGE STREET			
William Vandewater	1826	$2,000	$100
147 ORANGE STREET			
Joseph Rushlow	1826	$2,000	$100
149 ORANGE STREET			
Sarah Tuttle	1826	$2,000	$800
60 CROSS STREET (corner Little Water St.)			
Bernard Fagan	1826	$1,800	$100

Address and Tenants	*Years*	*Real Property Value*	*Personal Property Value*
BROTHELS OF JOHN R. LIVINGSTON (*Continued*)			
62 Cross Street	1832		
64 Cross Street	1832		
66 Cross Street	1832		
68 Cross Street	1832		
BROTHELS OF JOHN F. DELAPLAINE			
98 Lombardy Street			
Robert C. Folger	1825	$2,200	$500
Widow Ann Horton	1825	$2,200	$1,000
567 Broadway	1829		
(Prince St., and 3 adjoining empty lots)			
67 Anthony Street			
Mary Springer	1831–35	$3,500–$4,000	$1,000
34 Walker Street			
Rachel Porter	1848–59		
37 Crosby Street			
Maria Mitchell	1852		
213 Church Street			
Margaret Murphy	1848		
Fanny Howard	1849		
BROTHELS OF JAMES RIDGEWAY			
14 Catherine Lane	1826–28	$1,800	
136 Anthony Street	1826	$2,400	
138 Anthony Street	1826	$3,500	
142 Anthony Street	1830–50	$3,000–$4,500	(1832–36)
144 Anthony Street	1830–50	$3,000–$4,500	(1832–36)
146 Anthony Street	1850		
147 Anthony Street	1821	$2,000	
148 Anthony Street	1828–50	$1,600–$5,250	
(corner Little Water St.)			
150 Anthony Street			
(corner Little Water St.)			
Dennis Gillespie	1826	$3,500	$500
56 Cross Street	1850		
(corner Little Water St.)			
148 Leonard Street	1836	$6,000	
(George Lorillard estate)			
154 Leonard Street	1832		
(George Lorillard estate)			
156 Leonard Street	1832–36	$1,950	
158 Leonard Street	1832–36	$2,250	

Appendix 2

RECORDED ATTACKS ON HOUSES OF PROSTITUTION, 1820–1860

MOST antebellum attacks (or riots) on houses of prostitution are found in the New York City District Attorney Indictment Papers, Court of General Sessions; and the Police Court Papers, both in the New York City Municipal Archives and Records Center; and the New York *Sun* (22 Jan. 1833; 3 Sept. 1833; 4, 11, 12 Feb. 1834; 11 March 1834; 5, 17 May 1834; 27 June 1846). Some occupations and addresses of rioters are listed in city directories. See *Longworth's City Directory*, 1825–55; *New York As It Is* (New York, 1833). For the convenience of interested scholars, individual indictments listed below are arranged according to the date of their indictment, not the day of the attack. Some indictments did not specifically mention prostitution, but the address or participants involved were cited in other sources. These attacks are marked by an asterisk (*). Repeat offenders are designated by the letter *r*. Nearly every indictment listed the occupation of rioters as "laborer," even when they were skilled craftsmen or white-collar workers. Occupations and addresses below are from the city directories.

Date of Case	*Victim and and Address (Ward)*	*Rioter, Occupation and Address (Ward)*
11 March 1820	Sarah Smith, 185 Bancker St. (7)	Edward Halliday, mariner, 29 Hester St. (13) Thomas McDile David Conklin
	*	

Date of Case	*Victim and and Address (Ward)*	*Rioter, Occupation and Address (Ward)*
9 Jan. 1821	Daniel and Susan Dey, 99 Rivington St. (10)	David Johnson tailor, 98 Mott St. (6) John Fogel baker, 188 Spring St. (14) William Hopkins butcher, 46 Broome St. (14) Cornelius Schuyler butcher, 287 Bowery (14)
Sept. 1821	Mary Brown	Edward Daugherty Orange St. (6) Charles Daugherty 20 Catherine St. (7) John Carroll apprentice, 219 Church St. (5) Michael McGuire 48 Vesey St. (5) James Bucken 110 Mulberry St. (6) Walter Roberts James McLaughlin milkman, 118 Bancker St. (7)
15 Dec. 1824	Harriet Lyons, 165 Church St. (5)	John Lee 109 Mulberry St. (6) John Snell leather dresser, 145 Orange St. (6) William Hatfield turner, 55 Harman St. 20 Others
14 July 1825	Mary Gambel, 25 Crosby St. (14)	Alexander Fink, tavern, 149 Bowery, home, 148 Forsyth St. (10) Others Unknown
10 April 1826	Susan Inyard, Chapel and Anthony Sts. (5)	William Bates Oliver William Simpson Oliver
14 April 1826	* Charlotte McDonald, 35 Leonard St. (5)	John Rapelye, clerk Others Unknown
17 Nov. 1827	Ann Gregory	r John Harrison, ship carpenter, 109 Lombardy St. (9) John Van Houter, carpenter, 213 Washington St. (3) Jacob Hampshire r Daniel Spinnage, pilot, 80 Roosevelt St. (7) Edward Faulkner George Gordon, watchmaker, 156 William St. (1)
6 June 1828	Eliza Thompson and Catherine Goff, Ann St. and Theater Alley (4)	Daniel C. Mygatt 10–12 Others

Date of Case	*Victim and and Address (Ward)*	*Rioter, Occupation and Address (Ward)*
12 Jan. 1829	Miss Robins, 441 Broadway (8)	John S. Anderson George Clinch, butcher, 196 Mulberry St. (14) Owen Geary, tailor, 179 Varick St. (8) Others Unknown
16 Jan. 1829	Rachel Pruyne, 21 Laurens St. (8)	Isaac Horshea William Small T. Jacocks Mary Ann Carr, dressmaker, 52 Mott St. (6)
10 Oct. 1829	Mary Ann Davis, 20 Centre St. (6)	r Alexander Fanning John Mathews Samuel Beaty, cartman, Orange St. (6) Thomas Kelso, deputy pilot, Port of N.Y. 6 Roosevelt St. (4)
12 Nov. 1829	* Rebecca Hilton, 97 Pitt St. (11)	James Wardlean George Remsen Samuel McGraw Robert Moore, paver, 22 Gay St. (9)
7 Jan. 1831	Rebecca Weyman, 37 Elm St. (6)	James Van Dine
7 Jan. 1831	* John Rollison, 157 Anthony St. (6)	William Cozine Phillip Boyle Henry Gay Robert Campbell, smith, 109 Leonard St. (6) r Alexander Fanning
7 Jan. 1831	* Elizabeth Miley, 2 Mercer St. (8)	Edward White, painter, 73 Charlton St. (15)
10 Jan. 1831	Margaret McDonald, Little Water and Anthony Sts. (6)	r Alexander Fanning John McGowan Others Unknown
15 Feb. 1831	* Eliza Sayre (wife of Baxter, shoemaker) 45 Orange St. (6)	John Furnell Others Unknown (about 100)
23 April 1831	Elizabeth Baker, 97 Chapel St. (5)	r George Gale r Bentley Curran
25 April 1831	Elizabeth Baker, 97 Chapel St. (5)	r George Gale r Bentley Curran
1 May 1831	Elizabeth Baker, 97 Chapel St. (5)	r George Gale r Bentley Curran

Date of Case	Victim and and Address (Ward)	Rioter, Occupation and Address (Ward)
2 May 1831	Phoebe Doty, 167 Church St. (5)	r George Gale Enoch Carter
12 May 1831	Adeline Furman, 39 Elm St. (6)	r John Harrison Denton Furman Martin Bownosan
10 June 1831	Susan Patterson, 26 Centre St. (6)	Alexander Jackson, 106 Liberty St. (1) Others Unknown
14 June 1831	Adeline Furman, alias Miller, Elm St. (6)	James Lozier, attorney, 89 Beekman St. home, 65 Division St. (10) Jeremiah Dodge, ship carver, 75 Columbia St. home, 264 Rivington St. (13) Charles Taylor, grocer, 64–66 Division St. (10) Charles B. Jennings
12 March 1832	Mary Bowen, 112 Leonard St. (6)	r William Nosworthy, Others Unknown
6 Dec. 1832	Ann Pullis, 89 Cross St. (6)	r Townsend Pearsall, seaman (6) Others Unknown
12 Dec. 1832	Rebecca Weyman, 37 Elm St. (6)	John B. Damon Samuel Jones, alias William Kendall
18 Dec. 1832	Mary Bowen, 112 Leonard St. (6)	Hiram Aclus r John Boyd John McCary Josephus Cushman Thomas Millicane John McCormick William David Charles Gardner Jeremiah Harris Samuel Jones Henry Reese James Martin William Wade Richard Whitney Richard Schuyler
2 Jan. 1833	Unknown Prostitute 12 Anthony St. (5)	Samuel Anderson Charles Dykes
11 March 1833	Mary Wall, 472 Broome St. (8)	r Charles B. Valentine Other 4 Unknown
13 March 1833	Unknown Prostitute Park Theater (2)	r Charles B. Valentine Charles Pearsall, cabinetmaker, 262 Grand St. (10) r Daniel Spinnage, pilot, 97 Madison St. (7)

Date of Case	*Victim and and Address (Ward)*	*Rioter, Occupation and Address (Ward)*
		James M. Thompson Edward Davis carpenter, 7 Jersey St. (1) Others Unknown
3 Sept. 1833	Eliza Vincent	John Evans
23 Sept. 1833	Unknown Church St. (5)	William Green, Broadway and Wall St. (1)
15 Jan. 1834	Phoebe Doty, 9 Desbrosses St. (5)	William H. Tuttle, mayors' clerk John L. Martin, tavern keeper William Nichols Jeremiah O'Mera, tavern keeper, 65 Leonard St. (5) Others Unknown
3 Feb. 1834	Unknown Chapel St. (5)	John Lawrence Henry Flender, baker, 79 Clinton St. (13) Other 12 Unknown
11 Feb. 1834	Margaret A. Roberts, 24 Anthony St. (5)	John Phillips, Vesey St. (3)
10 March 1834	Eliza Swinson, 123 Chapel St. (5)	William Weed, merchant or shoemaker, 100 Fulton St. (2) Other 8–10 Unknown
14 March 1834	* Mary Ann Grosvenor 26 Anthony St. (5)	r Townsend Pearsall, mariner
9 April 1834	Julia Brown, 64 Chapel St. (3)	
16 Nov. 1834	Mary Adams, Clinton and Delancey Sts. (13)	Charles Kemp John K. Reyerson, tailor, 28 Ludlow St. (10) Joseph B. Smith, butcher, 51 Fulton St. (2) home, 64 North St. (11) Samuel Hill, butcher, 15 Clinton St. (13) home, 51 First St. (11) Henry Avis James Johnson, butcher, 1 Fulton St. (3) home, 86 Delancey St. (13) Andrew Jackman, City Hall officer home, 101 Elizabeth St. (14) Jacob Vogle, butcher, 27 Clinton St. (13) home, 50 First St. (11) Others Unknown

Date of Case	*Victim and and Address (Ward)*	*Rioter, Occupation and Address (Ward)*
8 April 1836	Eliza Ann Potter, 150 Suffolk St. (11)	Francis Hanratty William Fargo Henry Steers John Rhodes Samuel Allen James Fowler Aaron Fowler Thomas Whiting
8 April 1836	Eliza Ludlow, 75 Greene St. (8)	r John Chichester, Bowery (6) Coon Gaines, stable keeper (6)
7 May 1836	Elizabeth Jeffries 95 Chapel St. (5)	r John Chichester, Bowery (6) r John Boyd r Alexander Hamilton, mason, 82 Elizabeth St. (6) or 714 Broadway
11 May 1836	Jane Ann Jackson, 99 Chapel St. (5)	r John Chichester Bowery (6) r John Boyd Benjamin S. Penniman
20 Nov. 1836	Mary Gambel, 28 Crosby St. (14)	Garret Dikeman, laborer (6) James Morton, laborer (6) George Wilkes, laborer (6) Thomas Thorne, laborer (6) William Story, laborer (6) Benjamin Story, oyster house, 64 Barclay St. (6) Lewis Blanch, laborer (6)
13 Dec. 1836	Jane Weston, Duane St. (5)	r James Graham, clerk, 53 Lumber St. (1) r William C. Rider, bartender, 505 Pearl St. (6) r Henry Bertholf, mason, 76 Amos St. (15) r James Cole, engineer, 38 Hubert St. (5) r George Mayne, printer, 29 Madison St. (4)
13 Dec. 1836	Sarah Ferguson, 44 Orange St. (6)	r James Graham, clerk, 53 Lumber St. (1) r William C. Rider, bartender, 505 Pearl St. (6)

Date of Case	*Victim and and Address (Ward)*	*Rioter, Occupation and Address (Ward)*
		r Henry Bertholf, mason, 76 Amos St. (15) r James Cole, engineer, 38 Hubert St. (5) r George Mayne, printer, 29 Madison St. (4)
13 Dec. 1836	Adeline Miller, alias Furman, 44 Orange St. (6) and 133 Reade St. (5)	r James Graham, clerk, 53 Lumber St. (1) r William C. Rider, bartender, 505 Pearl St. (6) r Henry Bertholf, mason, 76 Amos St. (15) r James Cole, engineer, 38 Hubert St. (5) r George Mayne, printer, 29 Madison St. (4)
13 Dec. 1836	Ellen Holly, 20 Centre St. (6)	r Thomas Hyer, porterhouse keeper (6) r Franklin Fisher r James Darby r Abraham Vanderzee, alias Van Walkingburgh, binder, 74 Thompson St. (8) James Harrington
13 Dec. 1836	* George and Susan Needham, 153 Anthony St. (6)	r Thomas Hyer, porterhouse keeper (6) r Franklin Fisher r James Darby r Abraham Vanderzee, alias Van Walkingburgh, binder, 74 Thompson St. (8)
13 Dec. 1836	* Henry H. Marshall, 155 Anthony St. (6)	r Thomas Hyer, porterhouse keeper (6) r Franklin Fisher r James Darby r Abraham Vanderzee, alias Van Walkingburgh, binder, 74 Thompson St. (8)
20 Feb. 1837	Amanda Smith, 3 Franklin St. (5)	Daniel Samis Joseph Westervelt Samuel Conover, mason, 81 Barrow St. (15)
10 Jan. 1838	Mary Banta and Elizabeth Raymond, 105 W. Broadway (8)	Michael Roberts, laborer (3) Richard Burns, laborer (3) r Abraham Vanderzee, binder, 74 Thompson St. (8)

Date of Case	*Victim and and Address (Ward)*	*Rioter, Occupation and Address (Ward)*
		Alexander Hogg, 72 Broad St. (1) r Alexander Hamilton, mason, 82 Elizabeth St. (6) or 714 Broadway r Thomas Hyer, porterhouse keeper (6) Stephen Gordon, laborer (3) Henry Chase, laborer (3) Lewis Walsh, laborer (3)
25 Dec. 1839	Mary Ann Misener, 24 Anthony St. (5)	William Hubbard Charles Brewster Robert McKibbin John Buckman John Smith Others Unknown
3 Jan. 1840	Susan Shannon, 74 Chapel St. (5)	John Cherry William Ward bootmaker, 78 Canal St. (6) James Ward Alexander Ketcham Charles Hamblin
9 Jan. 1840	* Francis Biddle, Church and Leonard Sts. (5)	Charles Wilson Henry Drayton James Brown James Kerr
7 March 1840	* Mary Lee, 249 Houston St. (11)	Benjamin Waldron Bill Warrington
13 Feb. 1841	Frances S. Perry, 70 Grand St. (8)	Stewart Thorp George Dalton, laborer, Christopher and Bleecker Sts. (9) William Knowlton George Warner Barry Brighton William Stevens John Conclin James C. Denny "Painter Jack" painter, 4th and Grove sts. (9)
11 Feb. 1842	Elizabeth N. Rinnell, 19 Crosby St. (14)	John Golding, City Hall Officer, 160 Rivington St. (10) Other 4 Unknown

Date of Case	*Victim and and Address (Ward)*	*Rioter, Occupation and Address (Ward)*
10 April 1842	Eliza Logue, 19 Thomas St. (5)	John Timpson, grocer, 101 Fulton St. (2) Thomas Brown, Other 3 Unknown
28 Aug. 1842	Jane B. Williams, 22 Manhattan Pl. (6)	r William Ford, boot crimper, 22 Watts St. (5) John McCloster George Remus
20 Oct. 1842	Jane B. Williams, 133 Reade St. (6)	Stephen Mott, caulker, 151 Goerck St. (13) or surveyor, 113 Prince St. (8) Other 11 Unknown
10 Aug. 1844	Hannah Fuller, 117 Walker St. (6)	r William Ford, boot crimper, 22 Watts St. (5)
27 June 1846	Mary Ann Duffy, 52 Anthony St. (5)	John Williams
25 Dec. 1851	Catherine Cauldwell, 60 Lispenard St. (8)	Robert Isaacs, laborer (1) Other 40–50 Unknown
15 Jan. 1852	* Ferdinand Palmo, Broadway and White St. (5)	Michael Moody John Buckley John Rogers Other 100 Unknown
22 Sept. 1857	Thomas and Mary Phipps, 78 Oliver St. (4)	Patrick Flynn, boardinghouse, 104 Oliver St. (7) John Moore, boardinghouse, 75 Oliver St. (7)
23 Feb. 1860	William and Mary Grover, 277 Water St. (7) saloon	Joseph Stevens, grocery clerk, 217 Water St. (7) Daniel Simpson, bartender, Water St. (7) George Collinger, hackman, Water St. (7)

NOTES

Commonly Used Abbreviations

AAS	American Antiquarian Society Collections, Worcester, Massachusetts
AHR	*American Historical Review*
AJ	*Amerasia Journal*
AQ	*American Quarterly*
ASR	*American Sociological Review*
ASPCA	American Society for the Prevention of Cruelty to Animals
CAS	Children's Aid Society, New York City
CSS Papers	Community Service Society Papers, Columbia University
C14P	Committee of Fourteen Papers, New York Public Library
C15P	Committee of Fifteen Papers, New York Public Library
Daly Papers	Charles P. Daly Papers, New York Public Library
DAP	District Attorney Indictment Papers, Court of General Sessions, New York City Municipal Archives and Records Center
FHQ	*Florida Historical Quarterly*
FS	*Feminist Studies*
HLP	Harriet Laidlaw Papers, Schlesinger Library, Harvard University
IRSH	*International Review of Social History*
JAH	*Journal of American History*
JIH	*Journal of Interdisciplinary History*
JHG	*Journal of Historical Geography*
JSH	*Journal of Social History*
JUH	*Journal of Urban History*
Lexow Committee	New York State Senate, *Investigation of the Police Department of New York City* (Albany, 1895)
LWP	Lillian Wald Papers, Columbia University
MARC	New York City Municipal Archives and Records Center
Mazet Committee	New York State Assembly, *Special Committee Appointed to Investigate Public Officers and Departments in the City of New York* (Albany, 1900)
MCC	*Minutes of the Common Council of the City of New York* (New York, 1917)
MP	Mayors' Papers, New York City Municipal Archives and Records Center
NDQ	*North Dakota Quarterly*
NPG	*National Police Gazette*
NYH	*New York History*

NYHS	New-York Historical Society Collections
NYPL	New York Public Library Collections
PCP	Police Court Papers, New York City Municipal Archives and Records Center
PHR	*Pacific Historical Review*
RAH	*Reviews in American History*
RHR	*Radical History Review*
SPC	Society for the Prevention of Crime
SPCC	Society for the Prevention of Cruelty to Children
SSV	Society for the Suppression of Vice
VQR	*Virginia Quarterly Review*
WMQ	*William and Mary Quarterly*

Introduction

1. Matthew Hale Smith, *Sunshine and Shadow in New York* (Hartford, 1868), 279 ("Cathedral"). Berrian lived from 1787 to 1862 and served as rector from 1830 until his death. He was baptized in Trinity, confirmed in St. George's, ordained deacon in St. John's, and ministered in St. Paul's, all chapels of Trinity. For more on Berrian, see Morgan Dix, ed., *A History of the Parish of Trinity Church in the City of New York* (New York, 1906), 4:121–57, 467–78; *Trinity Church Bicentennial Celebration* (New York, 1897); *Narrative of Events Connected with the Bicentennial Celebration of Trinity Church, New York* (New York, 1898), 9–10. Among Berrian's important works are *Facts against Fancy, or, A True and Just View of Trinity Church* (New York, 1855) and *An Historical Sketch of Trinity Church* (New York, 1847).
2. Allan Nevins and Milton Halsey Thomas, eds., *The Diary of George Templeton Strong* (New York, 1952), 1:318. For similar charges, see Calvin Stowe's complaints about Methodist ministers' frequenting New York City brothels at midcentury. See Edmund Wilson, *Patriotic Gore* (New York, 1962), 20–21.
3. Havelock Ellis, *Studies in the Psychology of Sex* (New York, 1906 and 1936), 4:288–89, 304.
4. Among the ancient Egyptians and Greeks, copulation was sometimes regarded as an act of worship. See Fernando Henriques, *Prostitution and Society: A Survey—Primitive, Classical and Oriental* (New York, 1962), 1:20–85. To Romans, sex and its imagery had a mystical, not lustful, function. See Walter Kendrick, *The Secret Museum: Pornography in Modern Culture* (New York, 1987), 10. For other, noncommercial social views of prostitution, see Ellis, *Studies,* 4:242–49; on the European Middle Ages, see Jacques Rossiaud, "Prostitution, Youth, and Society in the Towns of Southeastern France in the Fifteenth Century," in *Deviants and the Abandoned in French Society: Selections from the "Annales,"* ed. Robert Forster and Orest Ranum (Baltimore, 1978), 1–31. For other examples of nineteenth-century sexuality, see Louis J. Kern, *An Ordered Love: Sex Roles and Sexuality in Victorian Utopias—The Shakers, the Mormons, and the Oneida Community* (Chapel Hill, N.C., 1981); John D'Emilio and Estelle B. Freedman, *Intimate Matters: A History of Sexuality in America* (New York, 1988); Michel Foucault, *The History of Sexuality: An Introduction,* trans. Robert Hurley (New York, 1978); Stephen Nissenbaum, *Sex, Diet, and Debility in Jacksonian America: Sylvester Graham and Health Reform* (Westport, Conn., 1980). On the importance of a "public" culture, see Thomas Bender, *New York Intellect: A History of Intellectual Life in New York City, from 1750 to the Beginnings of Our Own Time* (New York, 1987). My thinking on the development of social boundaries is influenced by Emile Durkheim. See his *Rules of Sociological Method,* trans. Sarah A. Solovay and John H. Mueller, ed. George E. G. Catlin (New York, 1966), 47–75. On commercialization in America, see Jean-Christophe Agnew, "The Consuming Vision of Henry James," in *The Culture of Consumption: Critical Essays in American History, 1880–1980,* ed. Richard Wightman Fox and T. J. Jackson Lears (New York, 1983), 67–84.
5. For another example of this process, see Viviana A. Zelizer, *Pricing the Priceless Child: The Changing Social Value of Children* (New York, 1985), 20.

Chapter 1 Holy Grounds

1. I. N. Phelps Stokes, *The Iconography of Manhattan Island, 1498–1910* (New York, 1912), 4:581; Floyd M. Shumway, *Seaport City: New York in 1775* (New York, 1975), 1–30. For the Watt quotation, see Carl Bridenbaugh, *Cities in Revolt: Urban Life in America, 1743–1776* (New York, 1955), 318.
2. Stokes, *Iconography,* 4:862; Edward Bangs, ed., *Journal of Lt. Isaac Bangs, 1776* (Cambridge, Mass., 1890), 29–30, 59–60. For the de Crèvecoeur quotation, see *Magazine of American History* 2 (1878): 749.
3. Stokes, *Iconography* 5:1194, 1204, 1343; William A. Duer, *Reminiscences of an Old New Yorker* (New York, 1867), 10.
4. Roi Ottley and William J. Weatherby, eds., *The Negro in New York: An Informal Social History, 1626–1940* (New York, 1967), 40–41; David Steven Cohen, *The Ramapo Mountain People* (New Brunswick, N.J., 1974), 3–24.
5. Kenneth Roberts and Anna M. Roberts, trans. and eds., *Moreau de St. Méry's American Journey, 1793–98* (Garden City, N.Y., 1947), 156; Stokes, *Iconography,* 862; Petition of 23 Residents to Common Council, 21 Sept. 1802, Common Council Papers, Box 20, MARC; *MCC,* 5:603 (10 July 1809).
6. *MCC,* 7:72 ("droves"); *Moreau de St. Méry,* 156, 173. For petitions, see *MCC,* 3:393 (21 Nov. 1803); 5:192 (11 July 1808); 5:266 (19 Sept. 1808). George Street, later renamed Spruce Street, was the dividing line between the Second and Fourth wards. East George Street was in the Seventh Ward and later renamed Market Street. Charlotte Street was a block east and renamed Pike Street. Another 15 percent of the indictments were in the Seventh Ward, many of which were probably on or in the vicinity of East George Street. By 1808, the physical development along Broadway had reached as far north as Anthony Street and the vicinity of the Collect Pond. To the east, the city spread as far as Grand Street on the Bowery and Montgomery Street in the Seventh Ward. In fact, only small parts of the Fifth, Sixth, and Seventh wards remained undeveloped. Nothing except the filling of swampland and the Collect slowed their conversion to completely developed real estate. The best description of New York's physical development can be found in Department of the Interior, Census Office, *Tenth Census of the United States, 1880: Report on the Social Statistics of Cities* (Washington, D.C., 1886), vol. 18, map facing p. 555; James Grant Wilson, *Memorial History of New York City* (New York, 1893) 3:208.
7. DAP, for the years 1790–1819.
8. Quoted in Ned Buntline, *The Mysteries and Miseries of New York* (New York, 1848), 5:87.
9. For an example of a prosecution, see New York City Miscellaneous Manuscripts, Box 35, 3 Feb. 1752, NYHS. On the eighteenth century, see Mary P. Ryan, *The Cradle of the Middle Class: The Family in Oneida County, New York, 1790–1865* (New York, 1981), 36–37; Lawrence Stone, *The Family, Sex, and Marriage in England, 1500–1800* (New York, 1977), 527, 616–20. Citing various complaints of vice in colonial cities, Carl Bridenbaugh admitted that most had only a few cases of prostitution annually and that many complaints concerned adultery, premarital intercourse, drunkenness, and gambling. See his *Cities in the Wilderness: Urban Life in America, 1625–1742* (New York, 1938), 72–73, 226–27, 388–89, and *Cities in Revolt,* 121–22, 316–19.

Chapter 2 Sex Districts

1. *Niles' Register,* 14 Oct. 1820; Ole M. Raeder, *America in the Forties,* trans. and ed. Gunnar J. Malmin (Minneapolis, 1929), 230; Walt Whitman, *New York Dissected,* ed. Emory Holloway and Ralph Adimari, (New York, 1936), 7; *Weekly Journal of Commerce,* 14 June 1849, quoted in Edward K. Spann, *The New Metropolis: New York City, 1840–1857* (New York, 1981), 572. The Matsell remark was in the *Times,* 23 Jan. 1852. For similar fears, see Samuel B. Halliday, *The Little Street Sweeper; or, Life among the Poor* (New York, 1861), 332; *Advocate of Moral*

Reform, 1 Feb. 1850, 15 Nov. 1838; *Fireman's Own,* 6 Oct. 1849, in Daly Papers, Scrapbook 21, p. 62; *NPG,* 22 June 1867.

2. Whitman, *New York Dissected,* 119–21; Allan Nevins and Milton Halsey Thomas, eds., *The Diary of George Templeton Strong* (New York, 1952), 1:217–18; *Tribune,* 30 March 1855. Also see Edward Crapsey, *The Nether Side of New York* (New York, 1872), 53, 65; James D. McCabe, Jr., *The Secrets of the Great City* (Philadelphia, 1868), 46–47, 110, 303–5; Matthew Hale Smith, *Sunshine and Shadow in New York* (Hartford, 1868), 427; *Advocate of Moral Reform,* 15 Jan. 1849. The terms "Nymphes de pave" and "cruisers" are in *The Gentleman's Directory* (New York, 1870), 10, copy in NYHS. On the importance of Broadway as a cultural symbol, see Peter Bacon Hales, *Silver Cities: The Photography of American Urbanization, 1839–1915* (Philadelphia, 1984), 58–61.
3. Harrison Gray Buchanan, *Asmodeus; or, Legends of New York* (New York, 1848), 10, 58; John D. Vose, *Seven Nights in Gotham* (New York, 1852), 121. Prurient accounts of Broadway were described in fictional and nonfictional literature. See George G. Foster, *New York by Gas-Light, with Here and There a Streak of Sunshine* (New York, 1850), 5–11; idem, *New York in Slices, by an Experienced Carver* (New York, 1849), 7–13, 98–100; Ned Buntline, *The Mysteries and Miseries of New York* (New York, 1848), 1:9–10; John D. Vose, *Fresh Leaves from the Diary of a Broadway Dandy* (New York, 1852), 70; McCabe, *Secrets,* 46–47, 110.
4. *McDowall's Journal,* May 1833, listed 59 streets with houses of prostitution, 19 of which never appeared in any other records for that decade. Municipal reports in *Documents of the Board of Aldermen* (New York, 1846), 12:384 (doc. 21), 542 (doc. 33) listed over 300 houses. Butt Ender, *Prostitution Exposed; or, A Moral Reform Directory* (New York, 1839), claimed that there were 266 brothels and 75 houses of assignation (341 total), although it provided addresses for only 78 places. In Citizens' Association of New York, *Sanitary Condition of the City: Report of the Council of Hygiene and Public Health* (New York, 1866), 26, 37, 59, 67, 81, 96, 137, different sanitary inspectors counted a total of 502 brothels. For more on district attorney and court records, see note 6 below.
5. Nevins, *Diary of Strong,* 1:259–60; *Times,* 28 March 1880. On streetwalkers in European malls and parades, see Mark Girouard, *Cities and People: A Social and Architectural History* (New Haven, 1986), 186, 192; Ronald Pearsall, *The Worm in the Bud: The World of Victorian Sexuality* (Harmondsworth, Eng., 1969), 14, 65. On prostitutes in the Battery, see Prudden v. Murray, 5 Aug. 1838, Box 7451, PCP; *Rake,* 9 July 1842, copy in People v. Meighan, 8 Aug. 1842, DAP. On the Bowery, see note 18 below.
6. *Herald,* 1 June 1841; Charles Astor Bristed, *The Upper Ten Thousand: Sketches of American Society* (New York, 1852), 41 ("above Bleecker"). On Bleecker Street, see Junius Henri Browne, *The Great Metropolis: A Mirror of New York* (New York, 1869), 372–73. On the Battery, see PCP, Box 7451, Prudden v. Murray, 5 Aug. 1838; *Rake,* 9 July 1842, copy in DAP, People v. Meighan, 8 Aug. 1842. Slamm's Row was on Delancey Street between Norfolk and Essex streets. The Arcade was in an alley on Elizabeth Street between Hester and Walker streets. The Female Rialto was at the foot of Rivington Street. See Butt Ender, *Prostitution Exposed.* Rotten Row comprised the three poorly maintained blocks of Laurens Street just above Canal Street and was filled with cheap brothels. Plagued by riots in 1834, Assistant Alderman Tallmadge called for the city to purchase the land or close the street to make it safe and orderly. See *Niles' Register,* 28 June 1834; Butt Ender, *Prostitution Exposed.* Laurens Street (later West Broadway) was not fully improved until 1870. See Nevins, *Diary of Strong,* 4:322. For more on Rotten Row, see the daily journal of Charles Loring Brace, 11 April 1853, p. 21, CAS Records, New York City. I am indebted to Tara Fitzpatrick for this source.

   To measure the amount of prostitution over time and trace its spatial movement, I plotted over 1,500 specific addresses from 1790 to 1869 that I located. The majority of addresses were found in DAP and PCP. Other sources included Stephen Allen Papers, Court Minutes, 1819, and Tavern Complaints, 1822; William Bell Diary, 1850–51, both in NYHS; Butt Ender, *Prostitution Exposed;* Free Loveyer, *Directory to the Seraglios in New York, Philadelphia, Boston, and All the Principal Cities in the Union* (New York, 1859); Charles DeKock, *Guide to the Harems; or, Directory to the Ladies of Fashion in New York and Various other Cities* (New York,

1855); *Sun; Herald; Times; National Police Gazette.* To avoid exaggerating or inflating the amount of prostitution, I included only places and individuals accused of the specific disorderly conduct charge of prostitution (frequently written as "whorring" in indictments). I disregarded other disorderly charges. While some of these establishments were involved with housing prostitutes, the lack of absolute certainty led me to reject their inclusion. Addresses in the district attorney indictments were from cases that usually originated from a citizen's complaint. If unresolved in police court, the case was presented to a grand jury, which led to the indictment. These tended to be the most offensive cases and probably represent only a small portion of the hundreds of complaints that never made it past the police court magistrates. Finally, many houses of prostitution, especially those in brothel guidebooks, never appeared in the police and court records. The maps and figures that follow, therefore, are a conservative measurement and may even underestimate the levels of prostitution in New York. For examples of reports with greater numbers, see note 4 above.

To measure the physical movement of prostitution over time and space, I divided the city into neighborhoods consistent with their ward numbers and physical separation by major thoroughfares. Since neighborhoods and their perceived boundaries were vague and imprecise, this was an admittedly imperfect method. Nevertheless, it was the best means of breaking the physical city down into smaller constituent parts in order to measure geographical change over time. The neighborhoods and their boundaries were the following: Wall Street area—south of Fulton Street (First Ward and parts of Second and Fourth wards); West Side—north of Fulton Street, west of Broadway to Hudson River, south of Canal Street (most of the Third and all of the Fifth wards); East River dock area—north of Fulton Street, east of Chatham Street, Park Row, and East Broadway to East River, south of Canal and Grand streets (most of the Fourth and Seventh wards); Five Points—area bounded by Broadway, Canal Street, Centre Street, Hester Street, Bowery, Chatham Street, Park Row (all of the Sixth and part of the Fourteenth wards); Lower East Side—Bowery, Houston Street, East River, Grand Street, and East Broadway (all of the Tenth and Thirteenth and part of the Eleventh wards).

The neighborhood distribution of houses in Butt Ender's *Prostitution Exposed* was consistent with cases prosecuted by the district attorney and police court magistrates. Five Points, the West Side, Wall Street, and SoHo differed by only 6 percent or less. Butt Ender found a higher percentage in the Lower East Side (20 percent to 7 percent) and a lower amount in the East Dock (7 percent to 20 percent). Of the 75 addresses cited, the breakdown by neighborhood was as follows: Five Points—31 percent (23); West Side—25 percent (19); Lower East Side—20 percent (15); SoHo—16 percent (12); East Dock—7 percent (5); Wall Street—1 percent (1). A compilation of all available sources yielded the following percentage distribution of New York's houses of prostitution by neighborhood:

Years	*Number of Addresses*	*East Dock*	*Five Points*	*West Side*	*Wall Street*	*SoHo*	*Other*
1790–1809	182	65	6	21	7	0	.5
1810–19	245	55	15	22	5	0	4
1820–29	253	30	30	26	2	8	4
1830–39	271	17	35	20	0	16	11
1840–49	207	19	36	28	4	11	3
1850–59	336	8	32	12	2	41	7
1860–69	99	10	12	8	5	45	19

Addresses were based on whether a single location was cited one or more times for prostitution violations by any source. If the same address was cited more than once in a decade, it was counted only one time.

7. Sam Bass Warner, Jr., *The Urban Wilderness: A History of the American City* (New York, 1972); idem, *The Private City: Philadelphia in Three Periods of Growth* (Philadelphia, 1968), 3–11, 108–17, 202–3; Joyce Appleby, "Defining the Public Realm," *RAH* 12 (1984): 200.

8. Elizabeth Blackmar, "Re-walking the 'Walking City': Housing and Property Relations in New York City, 1780–1840," *RHR* 21 (1979):137–38; idem, *Manhattan for Rent, 1785–1850* (Ithaca, N.Y., 1989), 28–95, 243–45; Kenneth T. Jackson, *Crabgrass Frontier: The Suburbanization of the United States* (New York, 1985), 134; Smith, *Sunshine and Shadow,* 278 ("splendid buildings"); Vose, *Seven Nights,* 116 ("capitalists").
9. *NPG,* 19 Dec. 1846; Sean Wilentz, *Chants Democratic: New York City and the Rise of the American Working Class, 1788–1850* (New York, 1984), 117. On real estate specialization, see Blackmar, *Manhattan for Rent,* chaps. 6, 7.
10. Samuel Prime, *Life in New York* (New York, 1847), 169. On excessive prosecution costs, see DAP, People v. Brown, 25 May 1842, 17 Oct. 1842. For examples of acquittals, see DAP, People v. Brown, 12 May 1826; People v. Brown, 10 Jan. 1827; People v. Powell, 28 Sept. 1842; People v. Davis, 7 July 1843; People v. Switzler, 12 Feb. 1855. Examples of district attorneys and judges refusing to prosecute prostitutes or their proprietors, despite favorable evidence, are in DAP, People v. Johnson, 9 June 1834; People v. Feeks, 5 Nov. 1841; People v. Bloomfield, 8 Nov. 1841; People v. Brown, 11 April 1842; People v. Rooney, 23 May 1851, 20 Sept. 1853. For examples of low fines and short jail sentences, see *NPG,* 23 May 1846; DAP, People v. Yates, 28 Sept. 1842; People v. Tucker, 13 July 1842, 8 Feb. 1843, 10 July 1843; People v. Clover and Gauger, 14 July 1843. The New York Court of Errors ruled that if a tenant was prevented from "beneficial enjoyment" of the property because a prostitute shared the same dwelling, the tenant was excused from payment of rent. But this decision only allowed the tenant to leave; it did not force the landlord to eliminate the prostitution. See *Pendleton v. Dyett,* 4 Cowen 581 (Aug. 1825); *Dyett v. Pendleton,* 8 Cowan 727. I am indebted to Elizabeth Blackmar for this citation. Prior to 1915, prostitutes who did not solicit in streets or tenements were not guilty of any offense in New York City. See Committee of Fourteen, *Annual Report* (New York, 1921), 26; idem, *Annual Report* (New York, 1915), 3; *McDowall's Journal,* June 1833; Richard Symanski, *The Immoral Landscape: Female Prostitution in Western Societies* (Toronto, 1981), 83–88. For a comparative view on statutes, see Mary P. Ryan, *Women in Public: Between Banners and Ballots, 1825–1880* (Baltimore, 1990), 97–103.
11. For other small clusters, see note 6 above. This model departs from that of Richard Symanski, who argues that, geometrically, locales of prostitution tend to be strongly linear, extending along a main thoroughfare, with minor soliciting on side streets. See his *Immoral Landscape,* 37. In order to measure the degree of concentration of houses of prostitution over time, I compared blocks with documented prostitution to the total number of occupied or developed city blocks. A high ratio indicates a greater physical concentration of prostitute activity. As is seen below, the ratio of addresses to blocks declined from 2.28:1 in the 1820s to 1.95:1 in the 1830s. Although the ratios had increased to 2.20:1 by midcentury, they still remained below those of the 1820s. Because of the absence of specific addresses, it was impossible to compute similar ratios for the years 1790–1819. The high percentage in the East River dock area and especially on George and East George streets would seem to indicate, however, that the concentration ratios for this period were higher. Significantly, in the 1850s, the concentration jumped to 2.48:1, statistical evidence that the most exclusive prostitution was gravitating to the Broadway entertainment district north of Canal Street. The physical concentration ratios over the course of the century were as follows:

Years	*No. of Plotted Addresses*	*No. of Blocks*	*Ratio*
1820–29	210	92	2.28:1
1830–39	253	130	1.95:1
1840–49	198	90	2.20:1
1850–59	323	130	2.48:1
1870–79	434	163	2.66:1
1880–89	619	254	2.44:1

Years	No. of Plotted Addresses	No. of Blocks	Ratio
East Dock	59	17	3.47:1
Lower East Side	93	35	2.66:1
Tenderloin	174	61	2.85:1
1890–99	426	161	2.65:1
East Dock	18	5	3.6:1
Lower East Side	114	31	3.68:1
Tenderloin	151	64	2.36:1
1900–09	1,196	359	3.33:1
East Dock	50	15	3.33:1
Lower East Side	149	39	3.82:1
Tenderloin	499	117	4.26:1
1910–19	2,196	749	2.93:1
East Dock	17	15	1.13:1
Tenderloin	696	163	4.27:1
West Harlem	331	95	3.48:1

For sources and a more precise breakdown by individual neighborhood, see note 6 above; Timothy J. Gilfoyle, "City of Eros: New York City, Prostitution, and the Commercialization of Sex, 1790–1920" (Ph.D. diss., Columbia Univ., 1987), 356–57.

12. Symanski, *Immoral Landscape,* 38. In San Francisco from 1880 to 1934, prostitution was always in the area between the commercial and residential districts. See Neil Larry Shumsky and Larry M. Springer, "San Francisco's Zone of Prostitution, 1880–1934," *JHG* 7 (1981):74.
13. Charles Dickens, *On America and the Americans,* ed. Michael Slater (Austin, Tex. 1978), 123; Foster, *New York in Slices,* 22–25; Buntline, *Mysteries and Miseries,* 1:74; Edward Dicey, *Six Months in the Federal States* (London, 1863), 16–17 ("miserable a haunt"); J. Frank ("Florry") Kernan, *Reminiscences of the Old Fire Laddies* (New York, 1885), 39–41. Five Points's name was derived from the five streets that met in Paradise Square: Anthony (later Worth), Orange (later Baxter), Cross (later Park), Mulberry, and Little Water (gone).
14. Joel H. Ross, *What I Saw in New York* (Auburn, N.Y., 1851), 101–2; *Ned Buntline's Own,* 6 Oct. 1849, in Daly Papers, Scrapbook 21, p. 68; Five Points House of Industry, *Monthly Record* (June 1858), 25; ibid. (May 1860), 17; Citizens' Association, *Sanitary Condition,* 81; Buchanan, *Asmodeus,* 45 ("naked deformity").
15. DAP, People v. Mayor ("unwholesome smells"), 30 May 1862; *McDowall's Journal,* Nov. 1834; McCabe, *Secrets,* 190–91; *Advocate of Moral Reform,* 1 Sept. 1848; Smith, *Sunshine and Shadow,* 204; Five Points House of Industry, *Monthly Record* (June 1858), 42–43 ("state of nudity"); Halliday, *Little Street Sweeper;* 208–15 ("not a door"); Nevins, *Diary of Strong,* 1:259–60; Citizens' Association, *Sanitary Condition,* 77.
16. DAP, People v. McDonald, 12 March 1828; *Niles' Register,* 13 Jan. 1827. McDonald and Weeks were at 36 and 38 Bowery, respectively. In 1850, the policeman William Bell made over thirty-five arrests of unlicensed junk dealers in a small, five-block stretch along Orange Street. See William H. Bell Diary, 1850–51, pp. 5–7, 22, 26, 34, NYHS. On the working-class street economy, see Blackmar, *Manhattan for Rent,* 170–82.
17. *Sun,* 29 May 1834; *McDowall's Journal,* 1 Sept. 1848, Jan. 1833; Butt Ender, *Prostitution Exposed.*
18. Foster, *New York by Gas-Light,* 54 ("bare-bosomed"); *NPG,* 13 Dec. 1845, 13 May 1848; Nevins, *Diary of Strong,* 1:259–60. For other descriptions, including fictionalized versions, see Buntline, *Mysteries and Miseries,* 1:82–85; 2:92–95; 3:6; Vose, *Seven Nights,* 36, 18–19; George Thompson, *The House Breaker; or, The Mysteries of Crime* (New York, 1848), 3–4. On the Bowery, see *Fireman's Own,* 6 Oct. 1849, in Daly Papers, Scrapbook 21, p. 69; *Tribune,* 14 March 1855; Whitman, *New York Dissected,* 5–6; *NPG,* 3 Nov. 1866; Butt Ender, *Prostitution*

Exposed. Constructed by a wholesale meat merchant in 1789, 18 Bowery, is considered the oldest row house standing in Manhattan. See John Tauranac, *Essential New York* (New York, 1979), 4–5. For a record of its prostitution, see PCP, Box 7446, 26 April 1834. On streetwalkers, see *NPG,* 13 Dec. 1845; Nevins, *Diary of Strong,* 1:259–60; Spann, *New Metropolis,* 344.

19. DAP, People v. Tuttle ("number of houses"), 11 Oct. 1826; Kernan, *Reminiscences,* 40–41. Full of thieves, beggars, and prostitutes of all ages and races, the "Alley" averaged two murders a year at midcentury. See Five Points House of Industry, *Monthly Record* (April 1861), 465–68. In conveyance and tax assessment records and fire insurance maps, this is block no. 166. Specific addresses for houses of prostitution are in DAP. 1820–59; PCP, 1820–60; Butt Ender, *Prostitution Exposed;* DeKock, *Guide to the Harems.*
20. PCP, Box 7439, Wark v. Wheeler, 2 Aug. 1827; Ackerman v. Morgan, 8 June 1826; Box 7436, Johnson v. Robinson, 12 April 1820; Box 7451, Wessells v. Quin, 30 Aug. 1838; DAP, People v. Davis, 14 Oct. 1824. For later examples of sexual intercourse in the streets, see DAP, People v. McCall, 20 Sept. 1850; People v. Maier and Day, 4 March 1868.
21. Prime, *Life in New York,* 175–76. On the segregation of black prostitution in Harlem after 1900, see chapter 10. New Orleans's Storyville in the early twentieth century segregated blacks in the worst locations—those farthest from the major entry points and principal saloons and became "a ghetto within a black ghetto." See Symanski, *Immoral Landscape,* 138–42.
22. Shane White, *Somewhat More Independent: The End of Slavery in New York City, 1770–1810* (Athens, Ga., 1991); idem, "A Question of Style: Blacks in and around New York City in the Late Eighteenth Century," *Journal of American Folklore* 102 (1989): 24–44; Foster, *New York by Gas-Light,* 72–76; People v. Bell, 10 Oct. 1801, DAP; Buntline, *Mysteries and Miseries,* 1:90–91; 2:79–85; Vose, *Seven Nights,* 77–87.
23. PCP, Box 7437, Walton v. Lewis, 8 May 1822; *Niles' Register,* 19 June 1830. On black brothels, see DAP, People v. Stackhouse, 12 Oct. 1824. Phillips and Johnson lived at 23 Collect Street, Morgan at 79 Mulberry Street, and Carter at 146 Orange Street. See DAP, People v. Phillips, 11 Nov. 1825; People v. Carter, 18 Feb. 1842; PCP, Box 7439, Handy v. Morgan, 9 Jan. 1826. For more examples of interracial prostitution, see DAP, People v. Acker et al., 14 Oct. 1806; People v. Scott, 13 Dec. 1815; People v. Lolly, 16 May 1827; People v. McGinnis, 11 July 1828; People v. Andrews, 17 May 1832; People v. Reed, 20 Jan. 1847; People v. Franklin, 20 Sept. 1850; PCP, Box 7445, Thomas v. Mulligan, 26 Sept. 1833; *NPG,* 17 July 1847; Hackett Books, 5 Oct. 1866, vol. 1, NYPL.
24. Foster, *New York by Gas-Light,* 56.
25. *New York Sporting Whip,* 28 Jan. 1843 ("sable"); *Whip,* 12 March 1842 ("sodomy"); DAP, People v. Bowser, 11 June 1825.
26. Clarence Walker, "How Many Negroes Did Karl Marx Know? Peculiarities of the Americans" (Paper delivered at Barnard College, New York City, 7 April 1989); Winthrop Jordan, *White over Black: American Attitudes toward the Negro, 1550–1812* (Chapel Hill, N.C., 1968), 158–62.
27. Leonard L. Richards, *"Gentlemen of Property and Standing": Antiabolition Mobs in Jacksonian America* (New York, 1970), 40–46, 114–15.
28. George Dangerfield, *Chancellor Robert R. Livingston* (New York, 1960), 97, 112; John R. Livingston to Robert R. Livingston, 11 Oct. 1776, 2 Feb. 1777, 11 Feb. 1780, 127 July 1782, Robert R. Livingston Papers, NYHS. A picture of Livingston's house on Broadway in 1798 is in John A. Kouwenhoven, *The Columbia Historical Portrait of New York* (New York, 1972), 102. For more on the Livingston family, see Edwin Brockholst Livingston, *The Livingstons of Livingston Manor* (New York, 1910).
29. Livingston gained control of lots on block 166 in 1788 through an indenture from Margaret Livingston. See Pre-1917 Conveyance Liber 59, p. 265, 6 Nov. 1800. On later purchases, see Lease from Elliston Perot to John R. Livingston, 14, 15 Sept. 1791; Conveyance from Collin Van Gelder to Livingston, 22 Sept. 1791, both in New York City—Deeds, Box 10, NYHS. On the Edward Livingston transaction, see Pre-1917 Conveyance Liber 91, p. 395, 29 March 1811; Liber 79, p. 190, 23 Jan. 1808. For examples of Livingston's activity on block 166

(Anthony, Leonard, Orange, and Centre streets), see the following Pre-1917 Conveyances: Liber 142, p. 270, 27 March 1820; Liber 174, pp. 338, 341, 8 April 1824; Liber 179, p. 363, 1 Sept. 1824; Liber 181, p. 47, 1 Sept. 1824; Liber 213, p. 494, 14 Feb. 1827; Liber 221, p. 220, 17 May 1827; Liber 290, p. 191, 3 Dec. 1832. Most information on real estate holdings in this study is derived from New York City Land Title Registrations, Pre-1917 Conveyance Records, Office of the City Register, and Record of Assessments (by wards), 1800–60, MARC. Several difficulties emerged in tracing ownership patterns through conveyances: (1) not all deeds and transactions were recorded, and some were kept private; (2) lot numbers changed as land was subdivided and developed, making it difficult to trace ownership patterns precisely; and (3) lot location in a deed was frequently described in measurements from the corner of the block and other points, further complicating the process by requiring a surveyor. Tax assessment records offered a more consistent record because they followed each address year by year and listed who paid the tax and thus controlled the property. Because the vast amount of prostitution during this period ruled out a comprehensive survey of ownership patterns, I examined those addresses on streets with five or more houses of prostitution in decades from 1820–29, 1830–39, and 1850–59. For a more detailed listing of the landholding patterns in the most commercialized areas of prostitution, see the appendixes and Gilfoyle, "City of Eros," appendix 2.

30. On the profitability of real estate, see John R. Livingston to Robert R. Livingston, 23 Feb. 1804, Robert R. Livingston Papers. Livingston purchased the Thomas Street property from Effingham and Mary Embree for a total of 4,126 pounds. See the following Pre-1917 Conveyances: Liber 63, pp. 37–42, 19–21 Oct. 1802. For other transactions involving Livingston, see the following Pre-1917 Conveyances: Liber 69, p. 422, 3 May 1803; Liber 115, p. 599, 26 June 1816; Liber 204, p. 77, 4 April 1826; Liber 634, p. 230, 7 May 1853; Liber 642, p. 163, 16 May 1853; Liber 647, p. 128, 2 June 1853.

31. DAP, People v. Robinson, 19 April 1836; Record of Assessments, Fifth Ward, 1824–28. On brothel owners in London, see Pearsall, *Worm in the Bud,* 350.

32. Livingston addresses in the city directory were 67 Broadway, 1796–1815; 2 Greenwich Street, 1820–22; 204 Duane Street, 1824–31; and 164 Duane Street, 1835–39. Although he did not die until 1851, Livingston's name disappears from the city directories in 1840. See *Longworth's Directory* for the respective years. The petitions are in DAP, People v. Tuttle, 11 Oct. 1826; People v. Wall, 13 July 1830. Since only one tenant or lessee is listed with Livingston in the tax assessment records, it is unlikely he was ignorant of the background of that tenant to whom he was entrusting his real property.

33. Moses Yale Beach, *Wealth and Biography of the Wealthy Citizens of New York City* (New York, 1845), 10.

34. The specific addresses were 34 Walker Street, 37 Crosby Street, and 213 Church Street. See DAP, People v. Porter, 17 May 1848; People v. Mitchell, 14 May 1852; People v. Delaplaine, 19 Oct. 1849. In 1825, Delaplaine also controlled 98 Lombardy Street, which never appears in any other records as a house of prostitution. However, the large amount of personal property ($1,000) of the female occupant, Widow Ann Horton, casts suspicion upon the establishment. See Record of Assessments, Seventh Ward, 1825. In 1860, Isaac C. Delaplaine was elected to Congress as a fusionist Democrat. See Nevins, *Diary of Strong,* 3:90.

35. Pre-1917 Conveyance Liber 126, pp. 290–94, 25 March 1818; Beach, *Wealthy Citizens.* Evidence of the continuous Lorillard family control of the portions of this block are in Liber 407, p. 27, 5 May 1840; Liber 410, p. 487, 13 Dec. 1843. Also see Gilfoyle, "City of Eros," appendix 2.

36. Pre-1917 Conveyance Liber 139, p. 398, 21 Sept. 1819; Liber 350, p. 29, 2 Feb. 1836. In 1830, Leonard Fisher controlled every house from 14 to 24 Centre Street; nos. 16 to 20 were known brothels. By 1838, the same properties were listed under the names of other members of the Fisher family. See Record of Assessments, Sixth Ward, 1830, 1838, 1839. On Mrs. Fisher's active involvement, see PCP, Box 7449, Wooldridge v. Smith, 20 July 1836.

37. In 1829, however, Davis was forced to sell much of his property to pay off his indebtedness. See Pre-1917 Conveyance Liber 256, p. 405, 9 Dec. 1829; Liber 274, p. 398, 10 June 1831.

On Davis, see Jerome Mushkat, *Tammany: The Evolution of a Political Machine, 1789–1865* (Syracuse, 1971), 36. Walter Bowne, mayor of New York from 1829 to 1833, bought land on this block early in the century. See Pre-1917 Conveyance Liber 68, p. 483, 7 April 1803.

38. Pre-1917 Conveyance Liber 152, p. 1, 5 March 1821; Liber 256, p. 390, 1 Dec. 1829; Liber 256, p. 405, 9 Dec. 1829; Liber 313, p. 590, 1 Aug. 1834. Other purchases by Ridgeway can be found in the following Pre-1917 Conveyances: Liber 167, p. 402, 16 July 1823; Liber 274, p. 398, 10 June 1831; Liber 291, p. 632, 12 Feb. 1833; Liber 329, p. 165, 1 April 1835; Liber 338, p. 231, 26 June 1835; Liber 336, p. 348, 27 June 1835; Liber 343, p. 294, 10 Nov. 1835; Liber 352, p. 117, 8 March 1836; Liber 401, p. 345, 6 Nov. 1839; Liber 407, p. 27, 5 May 1840; Record of Assessments, Sixth Ward, 1832–36. During the same time, Ridgeway was also listed as the owner of 148, 154, 156 (a known brothel), and 158 Leonard Street. Ridgeway lived in a multiple-family dwelling on Grand and Elm streets with his wife and three children. See DAP, People v. Ridgeway, 11 July 1815.

39. *MCC,* 17:587 (26 June 1829); 18:11–12, 19–20 (20 April 1829). The best analysis of this controversy is Blackmar, *Manhattan for Rent,* 169–82. On Collins, Valentine, and other lessees, see Gilfoyle, "City of Eros," appendix 2.

40. On the Astor House, see Duer, *Reminiscences,* 40; Charles Lockwood, *Manhattan Moves Uptown* (Boston, 1976), 41–42. For descriptions of the area, see William A. Mercein, *City Directory* (New York, 1820), 94; Nathan Silver, *Lost New York* (New York, 1967), 151–52; Kouwenhoven, *Columbia Historical Portrait,* 140; Daniel Curry, *New York: A Historic Sketch of the Rise and Progress of the Metropolitan City of America* (New York, 1853), 218; Mrs. (Frances) Trollope, *Domestic Manners of the Americans* (London, 1832), 160; Ezekiel Porter Belden, *New York: Past, Present, and Future* (New York, 1849), 33; Nevins, *Diary of Strong,* 1:17.

41. Enhancing the prestige of the neighborhood, Columbia College and surrounding property owners persuaded the Common Council in 1831 to rename part of Chapel Street "College Place." See *MCC,* 19:706 (9 May 1831). Cox's home was on Columbia's property at the southeast corner of Murray Street and College Place. See Allan Nevins, ed., *The Diary of Philip Hone, 1828–1851* (New York, 1927), 861; *Columbia Alumni News* 35 (July 1944): 3–5; Silver, *Lost New York,* 115; Lockwood, *Manhattan,* 91–92, 144; Nevins, *Diary of Strong,* 1:x, 272. By 1845, over fifty of the richest New York households lived in the West Side. A compendium of New York's elite, Beach, *Wealthy Citizens,* included at least fifty-seven families who lived in the Third Ward. The names were checked with *Longworth's City Directory* (New York, 1845). On Chambers Street between Broadway and Chapel Street being filled with wealthy merchant houses from 1810 to 1840, see Blackmar, *Manhattan for Rent,* chap. 3.

42. Buntline, *Mysteries and Miseries,* 5:100 (1,500 women); *Three Years After: A Sequel to the Mysteries and Miseries of New York* (New York, 1849), 23–25; Vose, *Seven Nights,* 43, 127 ("lazar"). The addresses were 35 Warren Street, 55 West Broadway, 11 or 13 Church Street, *NPG,* 22 May 1847, 4 July 1846, 16 May 1846; 35 West Broadway, DAP, 7 Sept. 1842; 36 West Broadway, DAP, 17 April 1846; 14 Church St., DAP, 19 Nov., 2 Dec. 1844; 19 Park Place, DAP, 16 Feb. 1846, *NPG,* 18 April 1846. For more on Rotten Row, see note 6 above.

43. Pitcher lived at 50 and 55 Leonard Street and 154 Church Street. Post lived at 58 Leonard Street. Bowne and Low (with $100,000 in personal property) resided at 41 and 71 Leonard Street, respectively. On Duvall, see *NPG,* 22 May 1847. The respective Warren Street addresses were 36 for Anthon, 10 for Draper, 35 for Duvall, 8 for Haggerty, and 18 for Hudson. All of the men were listed in Beach, *Wealthy Citizens.* On Clay's visit, see Nevins, *Diary of Hone,* 877. On the brothels, see DAP, People v. Parsons, 16 Feb. 1846; People v. Collins, 18 April 1846. Bronson, Jones, and George Douglas lived at 4, 19, and 17 Park Place, respectively. Interestingly, the address cited for the disorderly house is the same as that of Douglas, whose wealth of $700,000 made him one of the richest men in the United States. For William Douglas, see Nevins, *Diary of Hone,* 480.

44. Benson lived at 100 Church Street. See Butt Ender, *Prostitution Exposed.* A decade-by-decade breakdown of antebellum houses of prostitution within 2.5 blocks of a hotel revealed the following:

Years	*Number*	*Percentage of All Houses*
1830–39	34	13
1840–49	96	46
1850–59	170	51

45. On Columbia College students going to Church Street brothels, see Buchanan, *Asmodeus.* On antebellum campus life, see Columbia University, *A History* (New York, 1904), 121. For Chapel Street, see PCP, Box 7444, Marshal v. King, 26 July 1832. Block 86 was directly south of the Columbia campus. The following were cited for prostitution: 28 Church Street (1834), 11 or 13 Church Street (1846), and 14 Church Street (1844). See PCP, Box 7446, 24 May 1834; *NPG,* 16 May 1846; DAP, Cases for 19 Nov. 1844 and 2 Dec. 1844. In 1857, Columbia moved uptown to a location on Madison Avenue.
46. Record of Assessments, Fifth and Sixth Wards, 1830–39, MARC. The Church Street houses and assessments were $1,800 for 99; $10,000 for 100; $5,500 for 102; $4,800 for 104; $4,300 for 110; $4,000 for 118; $2,400 for 167. For Anthony Street, they were $3,000 for 130; $2,500 for 141; $2,500 for 151; $4,000 for corner of Little Water Street. Assessed tax values of land were only a fraction of their market value and varied according to government policies and the political influence of property owners. These and the following figures thus offer only a rough, comparative measurement for land values.
47. Buchanan, *Asmodeus,* 88. The Church Street assessments were $17,000 for 92; $10,000 for 100; $5,500 for 102; $5,500 for 104; $5,500 for 130; $6,500 for 136; $4,000 for 142. For Anthony Street, they were $6,000 for 133; $4,000 for 139; $2,500 for 140; $3,000 for 142; $3,000 for 143; $3,000 for 144; $2,700 for 145; $3,000 for 146; $2,700 for 147; $2,800 for 148; $5,300 for 150; $3,000 for 151; $3,900 for 153; $3,200 for 157; $1,800 for 159; $2,000 for 161; $1,500 for 163. See Record of Assessments, Fifth and Sixth wards, 1850–59, MARC.
48. New York State, Secretary of State, *Census of 1855* (Albany, 1857), 8; DAP, People v. Shessee, 5 April 1798; People v. Williams, 13 Aug. 1818; People v. Meyers, 16 Aug 1815; People v. Stackhouse, 12 Oct. 1824; PCP, Box 7444, Riker v. Sales, 1 June 1833. Black prostitutes were to be found at 71 and 72 Chapel Street. See PCP, Box 7439, Snow v. Gerand, 18 Dec. 1826; DAP, People v. Johnson, 11 June 1821. For similar charges of racially mixed activity, see DAP, People v. Jackson, 12 Aug. 1822; People v. Scales, 22 Feb. 1842; People v. Berry, 11 June 1846.
49. On the 1820s, see DAP, People v. Campbell et al., 11 Jan. 1820; People v. Blanch, 16 June 1826. On the five-block stretch of Chapel Street between Murray and Thomas streets stood at least fourteen houses of prostitution. On Surre, see DAP, People v. Murthe, 12 Oct. 1841. On White Street, see *Tribune,* 14 March 1855; Nevins, *Diary of Strong,* 1:72. "Corinthian" was synonymous with whoremonger and "cyprian" with prostitute. See Pearsall, *Worm in the Bud,* 502.
50. Whitman, *New York Dissected,* 6; Citizens' Association, *Sanitary Condition,* 100; Lockwood, *Manhattan,* 118. On Henry Rutgers developing the Seventh Ward as an elite residential area, see Blackmar, *Manhattan for Rent,* 101–2. At midcentury, 6 of the 200 richest men in New York lived in the area. William Crosby lived in the Rutgers mansion, occupying the complete block bordering Cherry, Jefferson, Monroe, and Clinton streets. The others lived on Madison, Rivington, and East Broadway.
51. State of New York, Assembly, *Report of the Commissioners of the Metropolitan Police* (Albany, 1858), 15. On Water and Cherry streets, see William Ross to McYoungs, 5 Sept. 1851, in DAP, People v. Gayand, 19 Nov. 1851; Smith, *Sunshine and Shadow,* 232–34; DAP, People v. Dawson, 15 April 1857; CAS, *First Annual Report* (New York, 1854), 3–4; idem *Sixth Annual Report* (New York, 1859), 33–34; Handwritten Report of E. G. Gerry, Statistics on Immorality and Crime in the Fourth Ward, Aug. 1853, CAS Records. For a semifictionalized account, see Buntline, *Mysteries and Miseries,* 1:33–40; 2:12–15. By 1855, the Fourth Ward was a poor neighborhood inhabited by laborers and sailors. See Mary Christine Stansell, "Women of the

Laboring Poor in New York City, 1820–1860" (Ph.D. diss., Yale Univ., 1979), 88. For a description of tenement life in the area, see Crapsey, *Nether Side,* 110, 117.

52. CAS, *Sixth Annual Report,* 33–34; Foster, *New York by Gas-Light,* 76–80. On Gotham Court, see Robert W. DeForest and Lawrence Veiller, eds., *The Tenement House Problem* (New York, 1903), 1:78–80. In the 1820s, Bancker Street (later Madison) was the major thoroughfare with prostitutes, many of them African-Americans. See DAP, People v. White, 6 April 1822; People v. Fagan, 15 July 1823; People v. Clark, 12 March 1823; Anonymous, *Mysteries of New York* (Boston, 1845), 31. But by the 1840s, Water, Cherry, Roosevelt, and Front streets were filled with similar activities. On robbing sailors, see J. S. Buckingham, *America: Historical, Statistic, and Descriptive* (London, 1841), 1:25–26; *NPG,* 20 Feb. 1847; DAP, 9 July 1841. On Bancker Street brothels and saloons, see DAP, People v. Akins, 14 July 1819; People v. McLaughlin, 15 Sept. 1818. On the interracial character of Water and Cherry streets, see DAP, People v. Hardenbrook, 4 June 1828; People v. Johnston, 9 Aug. 1847; PCP, Box 7445, Coghlin v. McGown, 20 May 1833.

53. Two decades later, while assessments of domiciles in Five Points increased by only several hundred dollars, the Water Street houses enjoyed a median assessment of $3,500 to $4,000 from 1853 to 1857. See Record of Assessments, Fourth and Seventh wards, 1833–37, 1853–57. The Water Street assessments for 1835 were $3,000 for 267; $2,000 for 278; $1,700 for 331; $3,800 for 366; $4,000 for 370. The Cherry Street assessments were $5,000 for 35; $4,500 for 81; $4,700 for 87; $3,300 for 97; $3,300 for 110; $7,000 for 112; $5,700 for 206. By 1853, the Water Street assessments had risen as follows: $3,500 for 274; $2,300 for 306; $4,300 for 310; $5,200 for 314; $3,200 for 317; $3,600 for 382; $11,000 for 396. In 1857, they were $3,600 for 274; $2,200 for 306; $4,300 for 310; $6,000 for 314; $3,100 for 317; $4,000 for 382; $11,000 for 396.

54. *Advocate of Moral Reform,* 2 Oct. 1848; *NPG,* 24 Aug. 1867; Browne, *Great Metropolis,* 103. For ferry and steamboat stops, see W. Hooker, *Plan of the City of New York* (New York, 1817), Columbia Univ. Map Collection, no. 362; D. H. Burr, *Map of the City of New York* (New York, 1837), Columbia Map Collection, no. 359. A decade-by-decade breakdown of the houses of prostitution within 2.5 blocks of a ferry revealed the following:

Years	*Total Number and Percentage*		*East River Docks*	
1820–29	15	6%	15	20%
1830–39	20	7%	17	37%
1840–49	32	15%	32	82%
1850–49	13	4%	13	52%
1870–79	12	3%	11	28%
1880–89	25	4%	24	41%
1900–09	38	3%	31	62%
1910–19	19	.8%	1	6%

For sources, see note 6 in this chapter and note 3 in chapter 10.

55. DAP, People v. Scott ("midnight orgies"), 9 July 1841; People v. George ("half naked"), 21 Nov. 1846; People v. Rochford, 20 Sept. 1850; PCP, Box 7452, Oakley v. Hogan, 15 Oct. 1839. For other examples, see People v. Gibbons, 21 Sept. 1841; PCP, Box 7450, Seaman v. Sandford, 30 Sept. 1837; Box 7438, Ayman v. Williams, 21 June 1824; *NPG,* 29 Dec. 1866.

56. CAS, *Twentieth Annual Report* (New York, 1872), 12; idem, *Twenty-second Annual Report* (New York, 1874), 61; J. F. Richmond, *The Institutions of New York* (New York, 1871), 471–74 ("unrivaled").

57. Herman Melville, *Moby-Dick; or, The Whale,* ed. Harold Beaver (New York, 1972), 93–94. For a description of the area on Madison and Monroe streets, see Thomas Butler Gunn, *The Physiology of New York Boarding Houses* (New York, 1857), 226, 278–80. I found only one documented case of black proprietors in the records I examined. Morris and Betsy Sands ran a bawdy house on Walnut Street in 1830. See DAP, People v. Sands, 13 May 1830. On the number of brothels, see Butt Ender, *Prostitution Exposed.* For a physical description of area,

see John W. Harrison, *Map of the City of the New York Extending Northward to 50th Street* (New York, 1851), Library of Congress. There were thirty-nine and forty-one houses on Walnut Street in 1822 and 1828, respectively. See Record of Assessments, Seventh Ward, 1822, 1828.

58. Citizens' Association, *Sanitary Condition,* 106. Walnut Street was poorly recorded in the tax assessment records. House numbers were often unlisted, making it impossible to trace specific addresses of brothels over times. In determining the median values, I therefore included all houses. The number of houses assessed ranged between twenty-three and forty-one. Their median and average assessments for a range of years were $1,000 and $1,100 in 1822; $1,400 and $1,268 in 1828; $1,000 and $1,197 in 1833; $2,400 and $2,488 in 1839, $2,200 and $2,435 in 1853; $2,200 and $2,509 in 1857.
59. PCP, Box 7436, Parker v. Hacket and Thurston, 25 Sept. 1820; DAP, People v. Lane, 12 Dec. 1822; People v. Lawrence, 12 Dec. 1831.
60. George Ellington, *The Women of New York: or, The Under-World of the Great City* (Burlington, Iowa, 1869), 196.
61. Vose, *Seven Nights,* 115.

Chapter 3: "The Whorearchy"

1. Brady v. Porter, 16 Nov. 1835, Box 7448, PCP. For similar examples, see the following in the House of Refuge Papers, New York State Archives, Albany, vol. 28, Cases of Rossanna Cavenaugh, Lena Metzger, and Margaret McGuirk; vol. 29, Case of Louisa Hyams; vol. 30, Cases of Anna M. Poole, Mary A. Anderson, and Josephine Williams; vol. 31, Cases of Rosa Herschfield and Kate Schaffer. Unfortunately, the records give a very incomplete picture of the length of time the girl had been or continued to be a prostitute. For other examples, see People v. Wood, 7 Aug. 1818, People v. Bryson, 25 Sept. 1840; People v. Bodell, 8 March 1847, all in DAP.
2. Allan Nevins and Milton Halsey Thomas, eds., *The Diary of George Templeton Strong* (New York, 1952), 2:57; 1:217–18, 262, 294. Also see Charles Loring Brace, *Our Pauper and Vagrant Children* (New York, 1859); Edward Crapsey, *The Nether Side of New York* (New York, 1872), 142.
3. George Ellington, *Women of New York; or, The Under-World of the Great City* (Burlington, Iowa, 1869), 179–83, 193, 200. For similar examples, see pp. 211, 216–17, 237–39.
4. Estimates of the population of prostitutes can be found in the following: *Working Men's Advocate,* 20 Aug. 1831; *McDowall's Journal,* Jan., May, Oct. 1833; *Journal of Public Morals,* 7 March, 8 July 1833; Butt Ender, *Prostitution Exposed; or, A Moral Reform Directory* (New York, 1839); *Tribune,* 21 March 1846, supplement; *Evening Post,* 18 Nov. 1846; Samuel Prime, *Life in New York* (New York, 1847), 164–66; Ned Buntline, *The Mysteries and Miseries of New York* (New York, 1848), 5:100; *Documents of the Board of Aldermen,* 12:384, 539, 542, 778–82 (docs. 21, 33, 47); George G. Foster, *New York in Slices, by an Experienced Carver* (New York, 1849), 4, 30; *Globe,* 27 Jan. 1849; *Fireman's Own,* 6 Oct. 1849, in Daly Papers, Scrapbook 21, pp. 67–69; John D. Vose, *Seven Nights in Gotham* (New York, 1852), 43, 113; Charles DeKock, *Guide to the Harems; or, Directory to the Ladies of Fashion in New York and Various Other Cities* (New York, 1855); William W. Sanger, *The History of Prostitution: Its Extent, Causes, and Effects throughout the World* (New York, 1859); Citizens' Association of New York, *Sanitary Condition of the City: Report of the Council of Hygiene and Public Health* (New York, 1866), 26, 37, 59, 67, 81, 96, 137; *Nation,* 21 Feb. 1867; *NPG,* 16, 23 Feb. 1857, 28 Dec. 1857; 9 Oct. 1880; Matthew Hale Smith, *Sunshine and Shadow in New York* (New York, 1868), 371–72; James D. McCabe, Jr., *The Secrets of the Great City* (Philadelphia, 1868), 283–85; idem, *New York by Sunlight and Gaslight* (Philadelphia, 1882), 474; Ellington, *Women of New York,* 173; Junius Henri Browne, *The Great Metropolis: A Mirror of New York* (Hartford, 1869), 538; Crapsey, *Nether Side,* 24, 146; Rosenstern to Whitin, 10 Sept. 1913; Whitin to Bierhoff, 21 Jan. 1913, both in Box 2, C14P; George Kneeland, *Commercialized Prostitution in New York City* (New York, 1913), 100; Christine Stansell, *City of Women: Sex and Class in New York,*

1789–1860 (New York, 1986), 172–73, 276; Richard Symanski, *The Immoral Landscape: Female Prostitution in Western Societies* (Toronto, 1981), 20; James F. Richardson, *The New York Police: From Colonial Times to 1901* (New York, 1970), 27; Edward J. Bristow, *Prostitution and Prejudice: The Jewish Fight against White Slavery* (Oxford, Eng., 1982), 160. The percentages of young females given in table 1 are based on approximations of census data for females aged fifteen to twenty-nine: 37,000 in 1830; 117,673 in 1855; 122,235 in 1865; 172,777 in 1875; 386,026 (Manhattan only) and 726,320 (all boroughs) in 1910; and for those aged sixteen to thirty-six for the 1840s (70,000). See New York (State), Secretary of State, *Census of 1855* (Albany, 1877), 119; *Tribune,* 14 Nov. 1845; U.S. Bureau of the Census, *Thirteenth Census of the United States, 1910: Statistics for New York* (Washington, D.C., 1913), 602.

5. *Journal of Public Morals,* 7 March, 8 July 1833; Butt Ender, *Prostitution Exposed;* Daly Papers, Scrapbook 21, pp. 67–69; DeKock, *Guide to the Harems;* Smith, *Sunshine and Shadow,* 372; McCabe, *Secrets,* 283–85.
6. *Journal of Public Morals,* 7 March, 8 July 1833; Prime, *Life in New York,* 164.
7. Several other pieces of evidence support this tentative conclusion. First, Sanger claimed that he interviewed approximately one-third of the city's prostitutes. His cohort, however, ignored healthy streetwalkers, first-class prostitutes in the city's leading brothels, and occasional prostitutes in tenements. His estimate of 6,000 prostitutes—5 percent of all young females—was probably too low. Second, a health study on the impact of overpopulation and tenement life conducted by the Citizens' Association of New York in 1866 unintentionally discovered at least 502 houses of prostitution. And some physicians performing the ward-by-ward survey ignored numerous brothels in districts where they thrived. Finally, prostitution was found in most residential areas of the city (see chapter 2), a fact few contemporaries acknowledged. The approximate decade-by-decade prostitute population of antebellum New York was as follows:

1830–39	1,850 to 3,700
1840–49	3,500 to 7,000
1850–59	6,100 to 12,000
1860–69	6,500 to 13,000

Also see *Documents of Board of Aldermen* (New York, 1846), 12:542, 782; Crapsey, *Nether Side,* 146; *NPG,* 23 Feb. 1867; McCabe, *Secrets,* 285. Sanger claimed that prostitution increased 20 percent with the panic of 1857. See his *History of Prostitution,* 475. The high figures found in Butt Ender, *Prostitution Exposed,* were collected during the panic of 1837.

8. *Sun,* 14 March 1833; James A. Henretta, *The Evolution of American Society, 1700–1815: An Interdisciplinary Analysis* (Lexington, Mass., 1973), chap. 2; Allan Stanley Horlick, *Country Boys and Merchant Princes, The Social Control of Young Men in New York* (Lewisburg, Penn., 1975), 11; Joseph F. Kett, "Growing Up in Rural New England, 1800–1850," in *Anonymous Americans: Explorations in Nineteenth Century Social History,* ed. Tamara K. Hareven (Englewood Cliffs, N.J., 1971), 1–16.
9. George G. Foster, *New York Naked* (New York, 1850), 151; Stansell, *City of Women,* 109, 226; idem, "The Origins of the Sweatshop: Women and Early Industrialization in New York City," in *Working-Class America: Essays on Labor, Community, and American Society,* ed. Michael H. Frisch and Daniel J. Walkowitz (Urbana, Ill., 1983), 78–103; Alice Kessler-Harris, *Out to Work: A History of Wage-Earning Women in the United States* (New York, 1982), 59–60, 78; *Advocate of Moral Reform,* 1 Sept. 1852; Amy Gilman Srebnick, "True Womanhood and Hard Times: Women and Early New York City Industrialization, 1840–1860" (Ph.D. diss., SUNY, Stony Brook, 1979). On the seasonal shift of nineteenth-century English workers, see Gareth Stedman Jones, *Outcast London: A Study in the Relationship between Classes in Victorian Society* (Harmondsworth, Eng., 1971), 40. The *Herald,* 25 Oct. 1857, reported that prior to the panic of 1857 wages had improved, as shirt sewers working at home earned four to five dollars per week and those in the factory five to six dollars per week.
10. *Advocate of Moral Reform,* 15 April 1848. Of the 2,000 prostitutes Sanger studied, 27 percent (534) earned $1, 17 percent (336) earned $2, 12 percent (230) earned $3, and 6 percent (127) earned $4. Since a third (663) gave no income, these figures are conservative estimates. More

than a quarter (513) of Sanger's interviewees claimed they were prostitutes by "inclination." See his *History of Prostitution,* 488, 526–30. For individual examples, see House of Refuge Papers, vol. 3, Cases of Ann Kerrigan and Mary Baldwin; vol. 6, Case of Sarah Jane Chapman; vol. 18, Case of Catharine Hughs. By 1819, even skilled artisans had difficulty meeting their living expenses. The basic expenses for a family of five averaged between $6.50 and $7.00 per week. Tailors and journeymen with irregular employment averaged only $6 per week. See Sean Wilentz, *Chants Democratic: New York City and the Origins of the American Working Class, 1788–1850* (New York, 1984), 50.

11. House of Refuge Papers, vol. 3, Cases of Mary Weston and Harriet Newberry; vol. 6, Case of Sarah Jane Chapman; vol. 17, Case of Hannah Lewis; vol. 29, Case of Mary Ann Pitt. The House of Refuge kept few records on what motivated young girls to become prostitutes. Some cases do reveal a willingness on the part of most to enter the life. Nearly half (seven of fifteen) of the young prostitutes in 1867 were runaways, and the following two years saw even higher percentages of young girls who left home to become prostitutes of their own accord. See House of Refuge Papers, vols. 30, 31. In 1868, seven to eleven were runaways, and in 1869, six of six. Unfortunately, the earlier records were not as detailed about the backgrounds of prostitutes. The carnal enthusiasms of female children and teenagers in the House of Refuge were even noticed by Stephen Allen. In 1840, he admitted that the female division "presented many more difficulties than the boys' department." "Derelictions from virtue in females, are looked upon . . . with an uncompromising disapprobation and severity," he continued. "As far as possible, we have endeavored to place them far away from cities and from their acquaintances. . . ." See Managers for the Society for the Reformation of Juvenile Delinquents, *Fifteenth Annual Report* (New York, 1840), 14.
12. People v. Butler, 11 July 1814; People v. Turner et al., 15 Feb. 1840, both in DAP.
13. House of Refuge Papers, vol. 3, Case of Harriet Newberry; vol. 6, Case of Sarah Jane Chapman; vol. 29, Case of Mary Ann Pitt; CAS, *First Annual Report* (New York, 1854), 26 ("the rich"). On women freely choosing prostitution, see *Tribune,* 21 March 1846, supplement.
14. Sanger, *History of Prostitution,* 524; Butt Ender, *Prostitution Exposed.* As significant as these numbers are, some other occupations showed an even larger proportion of prostitutes (percentages in parentheses): umbrella sewers (79), type rubbers (69), fur sewers (67), tailoresses (58), cloth cap makers (58), upholsters (57), shoe binders (56), chair gilders (52), and sock makers (50). And only three occupations—those of artificial-flower makers (38), dressmakers (35), and straw sewers (33)—had under 40 percent of their numbers working as prostitutes. In London, sewing and prostitution were the only two eighteenth-century occupations open to uneducated females from poor families, and irregular employment tended to mix the two up. See Lawrence Stone, *The Family, Sex, and Marriage in England, 1500–1800* (New York, 1977), 617. Because no precise labor force data are available before 1850, the accuracy of this survey is problematic. In 1845, the *Tribune* estimated that 50,000 women were employed in manufacturing, a statistic the historian Carl Degler has dismissed as exaggerated. The figures in *Prostitution Exposed* are more believable. For example, excluding servants and chambermaids, the 1839 report recorded 15,535 women in manufacturing. This is compatible with the manuscript schedules of the New York State Products of Industry Census examined by Amy Gilman Srebnick listing 30,304 in 1850 and 23,167 in 1860. Degler gives the 1860 female manufacturing population as 24,721. The occupational breakdown, however, raises questions of the 1839 data. In those industries with 25 percent or more female workers, the differences with Degler's figures are as follows:

	1839	*1860*
Milliners	1,920	1,043
Fur Sewers	810	500
Artificial Florists	507	390
Umbrella Sewers	1,134	706
Hat Trimmers	839	205
Cloth Cap Makers	821	134
Straw Sewers	706	3,000

On the basis of these comparisons, the 1839 figures appear inflated. One possible explanation is that different occupational categorization schemes were employed in 1839 and 1860. For data on the 1860 female manufacturing population, see Carl N. Degler, "Labor in the Economy and Politics of New York City, 1850–1860" (Ph.D. diss., Columbia Univ., 1952), 96–127; Srebnick, "True Womanhood," 53–55. The New York Magdalen Society charged in 1831 that hundreds of servants clandestinely worked as prostitutes after hours. See Faye E. Dudden, *Serving Women: Household Service in Nineteenth-Century America* (Middletown, Conn., 1983), 213–19.

15. *Weekly Rake,* 9 July 1842 ("intrigues"); *New York Sporting Whip,* 4 Feb. 1843. "The Chambermaid" is in *Whip,* 9 April 1842; "The Milliner Apprentices," in *Whip,* 22 Jan. 1842; "The Milliner's Shop," in *Weekly Rake,* 9 July 1842. On Gambel and others, see *Whip,* 8 and 22 Jan. 1842; People v. Fink et al., 14 July 1825; People v. Dikeman et al., 14 Dec. 1836, both in DAP. In 1859, Sanger found the number of milliners and dressmakers working as prostitutes to be declining. Of the 2,000 he studied, only 6 percent (121) were dressmakers, 5 percent (105) tailoresses, and 2 percent (41) milliners. See his *History of Prostitution,* 524.
16. The sources include Mayor Fernando Wood's crackdown on streetwalkers in 1855; "panel house" arrests; Sanger, *History of Prostitution;* and the state censuses of 1855 and 1870. Of the 39 arrested in the Wood raid, 25 were Irish and 7 native-born. See *Times,* 24 May 1855. The district attorney prosecuted at least 68 women for running panel houses in the period 1840–69; 39 percent were from Ireland, 23 percent from other European countries, 9 percent from New York City, 9 percent from New York State, 8 percent from Middle Atlantic states, 5 percent from New England, 3 percent from Canada, and 3 percent from the rest of the United States. See DAP, 1840–59, 1862–69. Sanger found that 62 percent (1,238 of 2,000) of the women he studied were foreign-born, the largest proportion being Irish (35 percent of total). See Sanger, *History of Prostitution,* 455–61, 536. That figure corresponded with the 1860 census, which found 65 percent (44 of 68) of the prostitutes in the Blackwell's Island Workhouse from Ireland (28 percent were native-born). See Federal Census of 1860, Population Schedules for New York City, Blackwell's Island, ZI-108, reel 24, pp. 103–21. Of the women in brothels, 73 percent claimed the United States as their birthplace in 1855 and 78 percent in 1870. Of the foreign-born prostitutes, the largest number came from Ireland, but they accounted for only 16 percent of the total in 1855 and 11 percent in 1870, and that was considerably less than the proportion of Irish in the city's overall populace. New England and New York State combined were the birthplace of 42 percent of the city's prostitutes in 1855, a considerably greater percentage than the 14 percent born in the city. By 1870, a reversal in this pattern had emerged, as 36 percent listed the city as their birthplace and only 31 percent New England and New York State. These data are based upon a comparison of addresses found in DeKock, *Guide to the Harems,* and the anonymous *Gentleman's Companion* (New York, 1870) with New York State Census of 1855 and Census of 1870, Manuscript Schedules, New York County, Hall of Records. Unfortunately, the censuses did not record the address of each household, and I had to search for the names of madams as household heads by ward and election district. Although I failed to find all the houses in each guidebook, I did find enough houses to compile a limited social profile of their inmates. Of the 188 prostitutes found in the 1855 census, 89 gave an occupation. The majority (78 percent) were listed as "prostitute." The breakdown was as follows: prostitutes, 69; dressmakers, 6; tailoresses, 6; housekeepers, 2; and teacher, corset maker, embroiderer, and fur sewer, 1 each.
17. Census data indicate that brothel prostitutes tended to be older than streetwalkers. In 1855, their average age was 23; by 1870, it had fallen to 21.6. Madams showed an even greater range in ages. Although some were under 20 (one in 1855, two in 1870), as well as over 50 (three each in 1855 and 1870), most surpassed 30 years of age. In 1855, the average madam was 36; in 1870, 33. The migratory tendency of New York's prostitutes was further confirmed by their length of residence in the city. In 1855, the average length of time a prostitute had lived in the city was six years. Excluding the city-born lowers the average to four years. Madams, as expected, had been in the city longer—an average of fifteen years. The 1870 census, unfortunately, did not provide similar information. Sanger's data also indicated that parlor house pros-

titutes were mostly native-born. See his *History of Prostitution,* 549–58. A similar trend was found for Philadelphia in the 1880 census. See Carlisle, "Prostitutes and Their Reformers," 94–96.

18. *Advocate of Moral Reform,* 1 Nov. 1848. The overall data on the nativity of prostitutes were so mixed that it was impossible to draw a firm, final conclusion. For example, Samuel B. Halliday believed that by 1860, most prostitutes were immigrants. See his *Little Street Sweeper; or, Life among the Poor* (New York, 1861), 235–36. Hsia Diner has concluded that Irish women rarely indulged in sexual immorality. While the Irish surely had strict gender and sexual boundaries, many still resorted to prostitution, although they probably never matched the native-born percentage. See Diner, *Erin's Daughters in America* (Baltimore, 1983), 106–7, 114. For another example of Irish prostitution, see Dennis Clark, *The Irish in Philadelphia* (Philadelphia, 1973), 102–3.

19. The records on venereal disease in New York are poor. While New York Hospital issued annual reports that provided statistics on all diseases treated there, most of the patients in the figures below were probably men. The annual breakdown was as follows:

	Syphilis	*Gonorrhea*	*Rank with Other Diseases*
1800	65	14	1
1810	292	—	1
1820	216	—	2
1830	158	—	3
1840	183	47	1
1850	289	—	2
1860	272	54	1
1870	10	4	—
1880	19	—	1

See State of the New York Hospital and Bloomingdale Asylum, *Annual Reports* (New York, 1801–81); Sanger, *History of Prostitution,* 487–88; John S. Haller and Robin M. Haller, *The Physician and Sexuality in Victorian America* (Urbana, Ill., 1974), 252–70; Allan M. Brandt, *No Magic Bullet: A Social History of Venereal Disease in the United States since 1880* (New York, 1985), 9–13.

20. DAP, People v. McCaleb, 11 March 1813, People v. Saunders, 5 Feb. 1819. I found few cases of very young prostitutes in the DAP, 1790–1820.

21. Managers of the Society for the Reformation of Juvenile Delinquents, *Thirteenth Annual Report* (New York, 1838), 19–20 (Allen); *NPG,* Library of Congress Microfilm, 2:26, 28, 203; *Advocate of Moral Reform,* 11 Feb. 1850; Metropolitan Police, *Annual Report* (New York, 1865), 9–10; CAS, *First Annual Report* (New York, 1854), 3–4; idem, *Ninth Annual Report* (New York, 1862), 20–21, 33; DAP, People v. Nickeney, 16 Sept. 1868; McCabe, *Secrets,* 46–47, 110; Halliday, *Little Street Sweeper,* 142–43. Flower selling was a common way for girls to flirt and meet young men in other U.S. cities. See Suzanne Lebsock, *The Free Women of Petersburg: Status and Culture in a Southern Town, 1784–1860* (New York, 1984), 219–20.

22. PCP, Box 7453, Kieman v. Badger, 1 March 1839; Box 7437, White v. Jamison *(sic),* 4 Sept. 1822; Box 7447, Dugan v. Daly, 15 Dec. 1834; William H. Bell Diary, 10 June 1851, NYHS. Interestingly, when Bell was informed of the child's prostitution, he chastised the junk dealer, not the guilty youth. On Acker and Concklin, see *New York Sporting Whip,* 18, 25 Feb. 1843.

23. PCP, Box 7448, Hunt v. Baker, 8 Oct. 1835. Ann Pioneer, mother of Adaline, was a servant and said her daughter was "ungovernable." For other examples of prostitutes under sixteen years old, see *New York Sporting Whip,* 4 Feb. 1843; *Tribune,* 2, 10 April 1846; *Sun,* 3 April, 12, 14 May 1834; *NPG,* 21 Nov. 1846, 2 Jan., 10 April, 15, 22 May 1847, 28 Oct. 1848; DAP, People v. Bartlett, 13 Aug. 1821; People v. Furman (Miller), 13 Dec. 1821; People v. Sterling, 14 June 1847; PCP, Box 7438, Forbes v. Jackson, 17 April 1824; Box 7439, Hammond v. Lawrence, 2 June 1826; Box 7444, Blaylock v. Anderson, 9 Aug. 1832; Box 7445, Bogert v. Brun, 10 Aug. 1833; Box 7449, Sparks v. Acher, 29 July 1836. On brothels special-

izing in ten- to fourteen-year-old girls, see DAP, People v. Appell, 18 Dec. 1854; *NPG,* 15 May 1847. For similar complaints of promiscuous eight- to fourteen-year-old females in Philadelphia, see Kenneth Roberts and Anna M. Roberts, eds., *Moreau de St. Méry's American Journey, 1793–1798* (Garden City, N.Y., 1947), 311–13.

24. DAP, People v. Clark, 18 Dec. 1829; PCP, Box 7449, Sparks v. Acker, 29 July 1836; Box 7444, Blaylock v. Anderson, 9 Aug. 1832. For other examples, see PCP, Box 7446, Murphy v. Daw, 20 Feb. 1834; Walsh v. Clark, 24 May 1834; Box 7935, Baker v. Stewart, 23 Aug. 1843; Box 7449, Hines v. Blanchard, 19 Sept. 1836; DAP, People v. Bourne, 11 May 1829; People v. James, 15 Sept. 1840; People v. Switzler, 12 Feb. 1855; People v. Boomstadt, 22 Sept. 1855; People v. Henry, 22 Sept. 1855; People v. Sexton, 15 Sept. 1858; *Advocate of Moral Reform,* 1 Sept. 1838; Ellington, *Women of New York,* 177. On "intelligence" or employment offices being used to seduce and recruit young girls for brothels, see *MCC,* 12:133, 266, 295, 464.

25. McCabe, *Secrets,* 296; Ross to McYoungs, Cases for 19 Nov. 1851; People v. Abraham, 12 May 1814, both in DAP. Waterbury's daughter admitted she frequently visited brothels. For a similar case, see DAP, People v. Fluries, 16 July 1817. Sanger, *History of Prostitution,* 488; House of Refuge Papers, vols. 14–18. Percentages for other years examined were 2 percent (1) for 1825–29; 18 percent (10) for 1830–34; 15 percent (7) for 1845–49; and 1 percent (1) for 1865–69.

26. Managers of the Society for the Reformation of Juvenile Delinquents, *Thirteenth Annual Report,* 21; idem, *Twenty-eighth Annual Report* (New York, 1853), 13; House of Refuge Papers, vols. 1–6, 14–18, 28–31. Surprisingly, only a small percentage of those in the House of Refuge had intemperate parents. Compared with Sanger's and other nineteenth-century reformers' preoccupation with this problem, these figures are probably very accurate. The breakdown was 2 percent in 1825–29, 5 percent in 1830–34, 4 percent in 1845–49, and 9 percent in 1865–69. The skilled occupations of fathers included those of blacksmith, carpenter, fruit shop proprietor, ship carpenter, stevedore, and tobacconist in the period 1825–29; a Connecticut landlord in 1830–34; ship carpenter in 1845–49; and boardinghouse keeper, cabinetmaker, machinist, and policeman in 1865–69. Although the number of foreign-born prostitutes declined in the period immediately following the Civil War, three-quarters of their parents were immigrants.

27. Sanger, *History of Prostitution,* 535–36, 539, 544. I classified the 77 occupations Sanger found according to the model in Michael B. Katz, *The People of Hamilton, Canada West: Family and Class in a Mid-Nineteenth-Century City* (Cambridge, Mass., 1975), appendix 2. The numerical breakdown by occupational categories was: I (High) – 111 (6%); II – 703 (35%); III – 615 (31%); IV – 184 (9%); V (Low) – 259 (13%); VI (Unidentifiable) – 131 (7%). Historians are divided on the Sanger study. Marcia Carlisle faults Sanger for disbelieving any statistic that suggested prostitution was not a killer disease. For example, Sanger concluded that the rates of abortion, venereal disease, and alcoholic parents were underreported. See Carlisle, "Prostitutes," 92. Amy Gilman Srebnick criticizes the survey for seeing uncontrolled female sexuality lurking in every poor New York City ward and assuming that working women were morally lax. See her "True Womanhood." I tend to agree with Christine Stansell, who recognizes that Sanger avoided the blanket moral condemnations of antebellum reformers and adopted a more dispassionate and environmentalist interpretation. If anything, he was sympathetic to their plight, seeing them as victims of poverty, low wages, male lust, and hard luck. See Stansell, *City of Women,* 177–78.

28. Mary Thale, ed., *The Autobiography of Francis Place, 1771–1854* (Cambridge, Eng., 1972), xxv, 87–88; PCP, Box 7438, Lewis v. Donnelly, 26 Aug. 1824; Box 7446, Popham v. Lincoln, 21 Dec. 1833; Box 7447, Driscoll v. Shaw, 7 Aug. 1835; Box 7953, Pease v. Mangin, 1 Aug. 1855; DAP, People v. Brown, 17 Dec. 1850; People v. McCarthy, 20 Jan. 1852; House of Refuge Papers, vol. 2, Case of Elizabeth Dayton; vol. 4, Cases of Charlotte August Willis; vol. 5, Cases of Cecelia Smith and Julia Decker; vol. 17, Case of Jane Kane; *NPG,* 28 Oct. 1848. For other examples of family prostitution, see PCP, Box 7438, Prince v. Ward, 27 July 1824; DAP, People v. Stoutenburgh, 11 April 1812; People v. Fraser, 21 July 1840; People v. Bodell,

8 March 1847; Five Points House of Industry, *Monthly Report* (Aug. 1858), 74–75. Marcia Carlisle found a significant number of children living in brothels with their prostitute mothers, as well as husbands tolerating prostitution by their wives. See her "Prostitutes," 105–11. For examples of married prostitutes continuing in the business without the approval of their husbands, see the following bigamy cases in DAP: People v. Johnston, 13 June 1825; People v. Givens, 9 April 1830; People v. Browne, 21 Oct. 1839; People v. Grovier, 15 March 1861. For other examples of married prostitutes, see Sanger, *History of Prostitution,* 474–78, 512–13, 516. For a semifictional account of mothers encouraging daughters to prostitute, see Harrison Gray Buchanan, *Asmodeus; or, Legends of New York* (New York, 1848), 84–86.

29. DAP, People v. Furman (Miller), 13 Dec. 1821; People v. Murray, 9 Jan. 1849; People v. Perry, 11 June 1849; People v. Blakely, 12 Dec. 1828; People v. Foot, 11 Nov. 1822.

30. *New York Sporting Whip,* 18 Feb. 1843 ("lust palaces"); *NPG,* 13 Dec. 1845 ("perdition"); Foster, *Slices,* 90 ("the law"); *Rake,* 24 Sept. 1842, 1 Oct. 1842; *Times,* 28 Sept. 1861. For an overview, see Claudia D. Johnson, "That Guilty Third Tier: Prostitution in Nineteenth Century American Theaters," in *Victorian America,* ed. Daniel Walker Howe (Philadelphia, 1976), 111–20.

31. George Wilkes, *The Lives of Helen Jewett and Richard Robinson* (New York, 1849), 78; Sanger, *History of Prostitution,* 548; Browne, *Great Metropolis,* 453. See also Samuel Prime, *Life in New York* (New York, 1847), 178. For an attack on the subculture of prostitutes and "kept women," see *Weekly Rake,* 9 July 1842. For a closer examination of the subculture of brothel prostitution, see Patricia Cline Cohen's forthcoming book on the Jewett / Robinson affair.

32. Philippe Ariès, *Centuries of Childhood: A Social History of Family Life,* trans. Robert Baldick (New York, 1962), 100–119; Christine Stansell, "Women, Children, and the Uses of the Streets: Class and Gender Conflict in New York City, 1850–1860," *FS* 8 (1982): 308–35; idem, *City of Women,* chap. 10; Ronald Pearsall, *The Worm in the Bud: The World of Victorian Sexuality* (Harmondsworth, Eng., 1969), 359–68, 430.

33. House of Refuge Papers, vol. 3, Case of Ann Kerrigan; vol. 4, Case of Ruth Hudspeth. Kerrigan was dismissed when she started seeing other men. DAP, People v. McCarthy, 20 Jan. 1852. The price of virginal sex appears to have risen during the first half of the nineteenth century. In 1805, Eleanor Timple charged only five dollars to sleep with thirteen-year-old Rhody Duff in Timple's brothel. See DAP, People v. Timple, 8 April 1805. According to Steven Marcus, popular pieces of English pornography like *My Secret Life* (1888) discussed urgent male desires to deflower virgins. See Marcus, *The Other Victorians: A Study of Sexuality and Pornography in Mid-Nineteenth-Century England* (New York, 1964 and 1974), 156–57. For a fictional account of a man paying fifty dollars to seduce a virgin, see Osgood Bradbury, *The Belle of the Bowery* (Boston, 1846), 60.

34. DAP, People v. Stanford, 7 Nov. 1823. The ages of victims of rape and attempted rape in cases prosecuted by the New York City District Attorney break down as follows:

	1790–1799	*1800–1809*	*1810–1819*	*1820–1829*	*1830–1839*	*1840–1849*	*1850–1859*	*1860–1869*	*1870–1876*
Total Cases	5	11	27	16	32	51	71	105	128
Age									
1–9	1 (20%)	1 (9%)	5 (19%)	6 (38%)	2 (6%)	8 (16%)	11 (15%)	28 (27%)	26 (20%)
10–12	1 (20%)	1 (9%)	3 (11%)	4 (25%)	8 (25%)	7 (14%)	6 (8%)	10 (9%)	13 (10%)
13–15	0	0	1 (4%)	2 (13%)	3 (9%)	4 (8%)	4 (6%)	7 (7%)	9 (7%)
16–18	0	0	1 (4%)	0	1 (3%)	2 (4%)	7 (10%)	3 (3%)	7 (5%)

	1790–1799	1800–1809	1810–1819	1820–1829	1830–1839	1840–1849	1850–1859	1860–1869	1870–1876
19 or more	0	0	1 (4%)	0	1 (3%)	4 (8%)	6 (8%)	6 (6%)	13 (10%)
Age Unknown	3 (60%)	9 (82%)	16 (59%)	4 (25%)	17 (53%)	26 (51%)	37 (52%)	51 (49%)	60 (47%)
Married	0	5 (60%)	7 (30%)	2 (13%)	7 (22%)	6 (12%)	4 (6%)	9 (9%)	9 (7%)
Widow	0	0	1 (5%)	0	0	2 (4%)	0	1 (1%)	1 (1%)

Source: DAP, 1790–1877, MARC.

Most prosecution records did not give the age or marital status of the victim except when she was under eighteen years of age or married. For the most part, the women listed under "age unknown" above were probably single adults. My tabulation of cases differs slightly from Christine Stansell's because these rapidly deteriorating records are organized by indictment date and it is difficult to find all relevant cases when paging through the manuscripts. See Stansell, *City of Women,* 257, 278. Unfortunately, these court records fail to provide an answer to the question why men sought out such young girls as sexual companions.

35. Peter Laslett, *The World We Have Lost: England before the Industrial Age* (New York, 1965 and 1984), 84; People v. Campbell, 11 April 1870, DAP.

36. David J. Pivar, *Purity Crusade: Sexual Morality and Social Control, 1868–1900* (Westport, Conn., 1973), 141–43. For a recent examination of consent legislation, see Mary E. Odem, " 'The Girl Problem': Sexual Regulation of Female Minors, 1880–1930" (Ph.D. diss., Univ. of California, Berkeley, 1989).

37. William Cary Duncan, *The Amazing Madame Jumel* (New York, 1935), quotation on p. 62; Milton Lomask, *Aaron Burr: The Conspiracy and Years of Exile, 1805–1836* (New York, 1985), 395–401; Nathan Schachner, *Aaron Burr: A Biography* (New York, 1937), 511–14.

38. The quotation is from Anonymous to Mayor Cadwallader Colden, 8 Sept. 1820, in DAP, People v. Williams, 12 Sept. 1820. Williamson was reputed to have abandoned and disgraced daughters of well-to-do merchants in her houses. Williamson purchased 104 Church Street from Isaac Minard in 1819. See New York City Land Title Registrations, Pre-1917 Conveyance Records, Office of the City Register, Liber 137, p. 25 (block 148, lot 20). From 1820 to 1824, Mary Williams is listed as owner of 98 ($1,000), 102 ($1,800), 104 ($2,800), 106 ($2,000), and 110 ($2,400) Church Street. From 1815 to 1819, no such addresses appear in the assessments, and there is no record of her name under any other property on the street. It seems that the houses were newly built in 1820. After 1824, the title changes to the "estate of Mary Williams." Williams was also associated with 158 Duane Street and 150 Church Street. See Record of Assessments, Fifth Ward, 1815–25.

39. Nevins, *Diary of Strong,* 1:114; *New York Sporting Whip,* 4 March 1843 ("devil"); 18 Feb. 1843 ("hag" and "procuress"). Miller lived at 167 Church Street in 1821; 32 Orange Street in 1822–26; Elm Street in 1831; 44 Orange Street in 1831; 133 Reade Street in 1836–42; 134 Duane Street in 1839, 1842; Church Street in 1843; 130 Church Street in 1855. In 1826, she was involved with the prostitution at 85 Cross Street. See Record of Assessments, Fifth Ward, 1821, 1855; Sixth Ward, 1822; Butt Ender, *Prostitution Exposed;* DAP, People v. Miller, 11 Oct. 1826; People v. Concklin, 10 Aug. 1843; People v. Harrison et al., 12 May 1831; People v. Lozier et al., 14 June 1831; People v. Graham, 14 Dec. 1836; *Whip,* 25 Dec. 1841; 1, 8, 22 Jan. 1842; 5, 12, 26 Feb. 1842; 22 April 1842.

40. Nevins, *Diary of Strong,* 1:162 ("Venus"); 1:170 ("Bleecker Street"); *Whip,* 22 Jan. 1842 (play); 16 April 1842 (chairs), 4 June 1842; *Weekly Rake,* 5 Nov. 1842 ($2,000); 12 Nov. 1842 (Dickens). Brown lived or worked at the following: 133 Reade Street (1834), 64 Chapel Street

(1834), 100 Church Street (1839–42), 55 Leonard Street (1842–48), and 53 Wooster Street (1855–59). See People v. Brown, 11 April 1842, 25 May 1842, Sept. 1846, all DAP; Case of 23 May 1842, Box 7934; Velasquez v. Brown, 9 April 1834, Box 7446, both in PCP; Record of Assessment, Fifth Ward, 1846, MARC; *NPG,* 15 Aug. 1848; Butt Ender, *Prostitution Exposed;* DeKock, *Guide to the Harems;* Free Loveyer, *Directory to the Seraglios in New York, Philadelphia, Boston, and All the Principal Cities in the Union* (New York, 1859); *Libertine,* 15 June 1842; *Weekly Rake,* 5, 12, 26 Nov. 1842; most of the issues of *Whip* and *New York Sporting Whip* from 1841 to 1843.

41. Miller and Forsythe respectively leased 167 and 169 Church Street from Stephen Baxter in 1821. See DAP, People v. Tuttle, 11 Oct. 1826; Record of Assessments, Sixth Ward, 1820–31. Forsythe bought 42 Orange Street from Charles and Elizabeth Weeks and John and Mary Trigleth in 1824. See Pre-1917 Conveyance Liber 178, p. 312. Record of Assessments, Sixth Ward, 1831, listed her address as 44 Orange Street.

42. Record of Assessments, Sixth Ward, 1822–26 (95 Orange Street), 1839 (94 Cross Street); DAP, People v. Lane, 18 Feb. 1826 (Grand Street); Butt Ender, *Prostitution Exposed.* Jennison sometimes appeared as "Jamison" and "Gennison." From her grandmother's will, one can infer that Jennison came from an affluent family. When Grandmother Charity Jennison died in 1827, she divided her trinkets, clothing, and apparel to her daughter Elizabeth and granddaughter Charity and her real estate among her five children. See Record of Wills, Liber 61, p. 475, 27 Nov. 1827, County Clerks Office, Hall of Records. Wall lived at 40 Cross Street (1809), the Fifth Ward (1840), 39 Thomas Street (1826–32), 472 Broome Street (1833). See People v. Wall, 13 Feb. 1809, 11 Aug. 1810; People v. Valentine, 11 March 1833, all in DAP; Record of Assessments, Eighth Ward, 1826; Fifth Ward, 1830–32.

43. Doty lived at 123 or 125 Anthony Street in 1820, at 129 Anthony Street in 1821–23, at 167 Church Street in 1830, and at 29 Leonard Street in 1839. See Record of Assessments, Sixth Ward, 1821–23; Fifth Ward, 1839; Butt Ender, *Prostitution Exposed; Whip,* 5 Feb. and 12 March 1842.

44. *Libertine,* 15 June 1842; *New York Sporting Whip,* 28 Jan. 1843, 25 Feb. 1843; *Rake,* most issues in 1842. On Thebault, see *New York Sporting Whip,* 28 Jan. 1843; *Weekly Rake,* 26 Nov. 1842; *Rake,* 1 Oct. 1842. Numerous "widows" appeared in tax records in Five Points during these years. See Record of Assessments, Sixth Ward, 1825–45, especially for Mott, Orange, and Mulberry streets.

45. Dixon and Goodwin lived at 37 and 39 Elm Street. See Record of Assessments, Sixth Ward, 1821. For examples of brothel keepers as "grass widows," see *Rake,* 1842 (no. 11), AAS; Harry L. Williams, *Gay Life in New-York! or, Fast Women and Grass Widows* (New York, 1866). On Tucker, see *Weekly Rake,* 22 Oct. 1842, 26 Nov. 1842; the numerous cases in DAP, 13 July 1842, 28 Sept. 1842; 8 Feb. 1843; 10 July 1843; 9 April 1846; 11 June 1849. On Adams, see DeKock, *Guide to the Harems;* Free Loveyer, *Seraglios; NPG,* 7 Aug. 1847; 1855 New York State Manuscript Census for New York City, Ward 5, Election District 1, no. 108. On 55 Leonard Street, see Buchanan, *Asmodeus,* 11.

46. On the network of madams and their profits, see Ellington, *Women of New York,* 166–71, 244–59; Sanger, *History of Prostitution,* 554, 549–52; McCabe, *Secrets,* 286–89. A male grogshop proprietor in Five Points reportedly left a fortune of $50,000 when he died. See Five Points House of Industry, *Monthly Record* (April 1861), 465–68. The proprietors of houses of prostitution that could be identified according to gender and neighborhood broke down as follows:

	Wall Street	*East River Dock*	*Five Points*	*West Side*	*Lower East Side*	*SoHo*	*Greenwich Village*	*Tenderloin*	*Total (%)*
					1820–1829				
Males	3	35	14	6	1	1	1	0	61 (22%)
Females	2	27	65	62	8	21	1	0	186 (68%)
Couples	0	14	6	3	0	2	0	0	25 (9%)

	Wall Street	*East River Dock*	*Five Points*	*West Side*	*Lower East Side*	*SoHo*	*Greenwich Village*	*Tenderloin*	*Total (%)*
					1830–1839				
Males	0	16	29	3	4	2	0		54 (20%)
Females	2	23	59	63	16	35	1	1	200 (73%)
Couples	0	7	4	2	2	4	0		19 (7%)
					1840–1849				
Males	3	39	35	13	0	6	0	1	97 (43%)
Females	3	11	39	46	4	17	0	1	121 (54%)
Couples	0	2	2	0	0	1	1	0	6 (3%)
					1850–1859				
Males	7	19	71	9	4	19	2	4	125 (35%)
Females	2	5	45	30	4	124	2	6	218 (61%)
Couples	0	3	6	0	0	3	0	2	14 (4%)

For sources, see DAP, 1790–1860, MARC.

Disorderly-house charges against women usually involved prostitution. Prosecution of men included a wider range of charges: gambling, drunkenness, quarreling, and running unlicensed saloons. For more on these charges, see Timothy J. Gilfoyle, "City of Eros: New York City, Prostitution, and the Commercialization of Sex, 1790–1920" (Ph.D. diss., Columbia Univ., 1987), 148–49, 200.

47. On Winslow, see DeKock, *Guide to the Harems;* Free Loveyer, *Seraglios.* Maggie Lewis lived at 6 Thomas Street at least in the years 1850–52 and at 6 Thompson Street in 1855–59. See *Guide to the Harems; Seraglios;* and *Herald, Report of the Forrest Divorce Case* (New York, 1852), 13. Kate Rowe lived at 21 Greene Street from 1855 to 1859. See *Guide to the Harems* and *Seraglios.* Marshall was at 54 Leonard Street and 105 Mercer Street in 1855 and at 406 Canal Street in 1862. See *Guide to the Harems;* 1860 Federal Manuscript Census Schedules for New York, Ward 2, Election District ?, no. 34, and Ward 11, Election District 8, no. 53; People v. Marshall, 12 Nov. 1862, DAP. Adams lived at 3 Franklin Street in 1847, 55 Leonard Street in 1855, and 3 Clark Street in 1859. See *Guide to the Harems; Seraglios;* and 1855 New York State Census Manuscript Schedules for New York City, Ward 5, Election District 1, no. 108. Mrs. Palmer lived at 71 Elm Street in 1855, 80 Reade Street from 1855 to 1859, and 112 Spring Street in 1870. See *Guide to the Harems; Seraglios;* and *Gentleman's Companion.* Rebecca Weyman (alias Willis) lived at and probably owned 62 Mott Street from 1836 to 1850. See Record of Assessment, Sixth Ward, 1836–50, MARC. Mrs. Wilson lived at 61 Canal Street in 1851, 19 Crosby Street in 1859, and 123 Crosby and 156 East 22d streets in 1870. See Bell Diary, 27 March 1851, p. 84; *Seraglios; Gentleman's Companion.* Mrs. Van Ness lived at 149 Mercer Street from 1855 to 1859 and 102 East 22d Street in 1870. See *Guide to the Harems; Seraglios; Gentleman's Companion.* Mrs. Leslie lived at 44 Greene Street from 1855 to 1859 and 30 West 12th Street in 1870. See *Guide to the Harems; Seraglios; Gentleman's Companion.* At midcentury, one courtesan living in an expensive hotel reportedly earned $25,000 annually. See Ellington, *Women of New York,* 210.
48. Ellington, *Women of New York,* 163.
49. Alexis de Tocqueville, *Democracy in America,* ed. J. P. Mayer, trans. George Lawrence (New York, 1969), 2:590.
50. Nevins, *Diary of Strong,* 1:262, 294.
51. Stansell, *City of Women,* 105–29, 155–68; Wilentz, *Chants Democratic,* 24–48.

Chapter 4 Brothel Riots and Broadway Pimps

1. DAP, People v. Dikeman et al., 14 Dec. 1836.
2. Paul Gilje, *The Road to Mobocracy: Popular Disorder in New York City, 1763–1834* (Chapel

Hill, N.C., 1987). The literature on eighteenth- and nineteenth-century crowd behavior is voluminous. For a short historiography of American crowds from 1750 to 1840, see Timothy J. Gilfoyle, "Strumpets and Misogynists: Brothel 'Riots' and the Transformation of Prostitution in Antebellum New York City," *NYH* 68 (1987): 46–48.

3. Records of brothel attacks are in the New York City District Attorney Indictment Papers, Court of General Sessions, MARC, and the New York *Sun*. In the former, the defendant was usually charged with "rioting" and not simply assault and battery. The indictment did not always describe the dwelling under attack as a house of prostitution, but in most cases, the individual proprietor appeared in other indictments for operating a disorderly house. Furthermore, the physical description of the attack, the interior arrangement of the house, and the behavior of the men and women involved frequently indicated that it was a house of prostitution. For examples of attacks on prostitutes, see Lawrence Stone, *The Family, Sex, and Marriage in England, 1500–1800* (New York, 1977), 616; Nancy Tomes, " 'A Torrent of Abuse': Crimes of Violence between Working-Class Men and Women in London, 1840–1875," *JSH* 11 (1978): 337; John C. Schneider, *Detroit and the Problem of Order* (Lincoln, Neb., 1980), 20–31, 121; Jacques Rossiaud, "Prostitution, Youth, and Society in the Towns of Southeastern France in the Fifteenth Century," in *Deviants and the Abandoned in French Society: Selections from the "Annales,"* ed. Robert Forster and Orest Ranum (Baltimore, 1978), 1–31. On the absence of attacks on prostitutes, see Marcia Carlisle, "Prostitutes and Their Reformers in Nineteenth Century Philadelphia" (Ph.D. diss., Rutgers Univ., 1982), 31.

4. On Madame Carey, see Allan Nevins, ed., *The Diary of Philip Hone* (New York, 1927), 339; Dr. Alexander Anderson Diary, Oct. 14, 15, 1793, Columbia Univ.; Kenneth Roberts and Anna M. Roberts, eds., *Moreau de St. Méry's American Journey, 1793–1798* (Garden City, N.Y., 1947), 312. Other attacks are mentioned in Edward Countryman, *A People in Revolution: The American Revolution and Political Society in New York, 1760–1790* (Baltimore, 1981), 41; Edward Bangs, ed., *Journal of Lt. Isaac Bangs, 1776* (Cambridge, Mass., 1890), 29–30; I. N. Phelps Stokes, *The Iconography of Manhattan Island, 1498–1910* (New York, 1912), 5:1301, 1370, 1550; DAP, People v. Marcelle et al., 9 Oct. 1801 (Volunbrun); People v. Perry, 10 Oct. 1807. On the racial implications of the Volunbrun attack, see Shane White, " 'We Dwell in Safety and Pursue Our Honest Callings': Free Blacks in New York City, 1783–1810," *JAH* 75 (1988):450–51. For other attacks, see People v. Varian et al., 11 April 1812; People v. Rioters, 9 July 1814, all in DAP.

5. Pauline Maier, *From Resistance to Revolution: Colonial Radicals and the Development of American Opposition to Britain* (New York, 1972), chap. 1. Maier mentions similar attacks on brothels during the colonial period. For other examples of antiprostitution violence in the antebellum period, see John C. Schneider, "Public Order and the Geography of the City: Crime, Violence, and the Police in Detroit, 1845–1875," *JUH* 4 (1978): 193. The final sentence paraphrases Bernard Bailyn, ed., *Pamphlets of the American Revolution, 1750–1776* (Cambridge, Mass., 1965), 1:581–84.

6. DAP, People v. Ford, 28 Sept. 1842 (Williams); People v. Valentine, 11 March 1833 (Wall); People v. Kelso et al., 10 Sept. 1829 (Davis); People v. Rapelye, 14 April 1826; People v. Gale, June 14, 1831; People v. Isaacs, 19 March 1852. A year later, Cauldwell still resided at the same address. See People v. Roberts, 15 Sept. 1853. For similar examples, see DAP, People v. Oliver et al., 10 April 1826; People v. Harrison et al., 17 Nov. 1827; People v. Ramsen et al., 12 Nov. 1829; People v. White, 7 Jan. 1831; People v. Cozine, 7 Jan. 1831; People v. Jackson, 10 June 1831.

7. DAP, People v. Brown, 6 Dec. 1833. For examples showing the difficulty residents had in removing prostitutes through official channels, see DAP, People v. Clark, 17 Oct. 1834; PCP, Box 7953, Davis v. Mills, 6 Dec. 1855.

8. *Sun*, 3 Sept. 1833, 22 Jan., 11 Feb. 1834; DAP, People v. Van Dine, 7 Jan. 1831. Roberts was probably a prostitute because in other breaking-and-entering cases, the newspaper coverage describes the victim as living in a "respectable" house or family. See *Sun*, 12 Feb. 1834. This part of Anthony Street was also a major zone of prostitution from 1820 to 1850.

9. On Furman, see DAP, People v. Harrison et al., 12 May 1831. On Fuller, see DAP, People

v. Ford, 10 Aug. 1844. Ford, however, was convicted of assaults on three police officers who arrested him. For other cases of violence involving Ford, see DAP, People v. Ford, 10 Oct. 1842, 11 July 1844.

10. DAP, People v. Nosworthy, 12 March 1832. Nosworthy was a leader in an unrelated attack on Mary Bowen's Leonard Street brothel. See appendix 2.

11. Edgar Allan Poe, "The Mystery of Marie Roget," in *The Complete Tales and Poems of Edgar Allan Poe* (New York, 1938), 197. On sprees, see Allan Nevins and Milton Halsey Thomas, eds., *The Diary of George Templeton Strong* (New York, 1952), 1:22–24, 62, 84.

12. *Sun,* Feb. 4, March 11, 1834; DAP, People v. Buckan et al., Sept. 1821; PCP, Box 7445, Stewart v. Anderson and Dykes, Jan. 2, 1833. For similar examples, see DAP, People v. Mygatt, 6 June 1828; People v. Valentine et al., 13 March 1833.

13. Most of these cases are in the DAP. See People v. Samis, 20 Feb. 1837; People v. Golding, 11 Feb. 1842; People v. Mott, 20 Oct. 1842; People v. Small, 16 Jan. 1829; People v. Halliday et al., 11 March 1820. For similar cases of physical violence on madams and prostitutes, see DAP, People v. Johnson et al., 9 Jan. 1821; People v. Lee et al., 15 Dec. 1824; People v. Anderson et al., 12 Jan. 1829; People v. Dikeman et al., 14 Dec. 1836; People v. Wilson, 9 Jan. 1840.

14. DAP, People v. Timpson, 11 April 1842; People v. Henrietta, 8 April 1836; People v. Waldron et al., 17 March 1840; *Herald,* 9 Jan. 1836. Waldron was later indicted in another unrelated attack. See DAP, People v. Waldron, 11 Feb. 1840. The charge was later dropped when he joined the Methodist church.

15. DAP, People v. Lozier et al., 14 June 1831. On their occupations and addresses, see Gilfoyle, "Strumpets and Misogynists," 57. The wards and addresses of the rioters were based, first, on city directories and, second, on the ward given in the standard indictment, if it differed from the address attacked. The term "brothel bullies" was used by George Templeton Strong. See Nevins, *Diary of Strong,* 4:113. Since writing "Strumpets and Misogynists," I have discovered more examples, which revise my earlier figures. In sixty-nine known or suspected attacks on disorderly houses from 1820 to 1860, 184 individuals were indicted (many more were arrested, but not recorded). At least 19 of the defendants were repeat offenders involved in two or more attacks. In identifying rioters, I used the city directory. The ward numbers and occupations recorded on the standard indictment form tended to be inconsistent and unreliable. In most cases, the ward listed was *where* the crime occurred and contradicted other information in the indictment and city directories. Even when skilled occupations were given in the defendant's testimony, the indictment frequently listed him as "laborer." See DAP, People v. Tuttle, 15 Jan. 1834; People v. Chichester, 8 April, 11 May 1836; People v. Graham et al., 13, 14 Dec. 1836. The 17 semiskilled workers included 8 grocers and saloon keepers, 2 boardinghouse keepers, 1 apprentice, 1 cartman, 1 female dressmaker, 1 mariner, 1 milkman, 1 stable keeper, and 1 turner; the 35 skilled workers included 7 butchers, 2 river pilots, 1 ship carver, 2 bakers, 3 tailors, 3 masons, 1 printer, 1 binder, 1 bootmaker, 1 boot crimper, 1 cabinetmaker, 3 carpenters, 1 caulker, 1 leather dresser, 1 painter, 1 paver, 1 smith, and 1 watchmaker. (Three others had several listed for the same name, but all were either skilled or professional occupations); and the 8 white-collar or professional workers included 3 clerks, 1 engineer, 1 attorney, and 3 City Hall or mayor's officials. For a convenient classification scheme on preindustrial riots, see George Rudé, *Paris and London in the Eighteenth Century: Studies in Popular Protest* (New York, 1970), 18–23. These brothel riots departed in several ways from the earlier forms of preindustrial collective violence described by Rudé and others. First, much violence was inflicted on the persons, not simply on the property. While some assaults were planned and had political motives, many were virtually spontaneous forms of terror and personal assault. Second, unlike those who attacked agents of the state such as soldiers, tax collectors, or government officials, who often fought back with greater ferocity than the mob, brothel bullies encountered minimal physical opposition. Finally, since prostitution always existed in New York, its preservation as an institution was an unlikely motive behind their behavior.

16. W. J. Rorabaugh, *The Alcoholic Republic: An American Tradition* (New York, 1979), 150–52, 161.

17. David Grimsted has similarly argued that Jacksonian rioters attacked groups less powerful and influential than they were. Their victims tended to be "the oppressed, the unpopular, and the unprotected." See "Rioting in Its Jacksonian Setting," *AHR* 77 (1972): 388–410.
18. Elliot J. Gorn, " 'Good-Bye Boys, I Die a True American': Homicide, Nativism, and Working-Class Culture in Antebellum New York City," *JAH* 74 (1987): 388–410.
19. *NPG,* 2 Jan. 1847; DAP, People v. Dikeman et al., 14 Dec. 1836; DAP, People v. Norman, 23 Nov. 1843. Most interestingly, the prostitute in the Astor House stabbing, Lydia Brown, alias Amelia Norman, was acquitted of her crime. See *Subterranean,* 27 Jan. 1844, copy in DAP, People v. Walsh, 8 Feb. 1844. For a case of Julia Brown stabbing an assailant, see DAP, People v. Brown, 21 Nov. 1842. On rising levels of female violence, see *Niles' Register,* 19 July 1828.
20. *Sun,* 5, 17 May 1834. For another discussion of Jane Williams, see Harrison Gray Buchanan, *Asmodeus: or, Legends of New York* (New York, 1848), 92–94. For an example of prostitutes attacking a customer for leaving with a blanket, see DAP, People v. Brown, 13 Aug. 1822. On the importance of private prosecution of crime, see Allen R. Steinberg, *Prosecution, Politics and Popular Life in Philadelphia, 1800–1880* (Chapel Hill, N.C., 1989).
21. DAP, People v. Anderson et al., 12 Jan. 1829; People v. Lozier et al., 14 June 1831. For corruption as early as 1815, see Ebenezer Burling to Humane Society (ca. 1815), Society for the Suppression of Vice and Immorality Manuscripts, reel 3, John Jay Papers, NYHS.
22. For examples of prostitutes winning, see DAP, People v. Small et al., 16 Jan. 1829; People v. Gale, 14 June 1831; People v. Nosworthy, 12 March 1832; People v. Tuttle, 15 Jan. 1834; People v. Graham and Cole, 14 Dec. 1836; People v. Hyer et al., 17, 19 Dec. 1836. On convictions, see *Sun,* 11 March 1834; DAP, People v. Halliday et al., 11 March 1820; People v. Small, 16 Jan. 1829; People v. Chichester, 11 May 1836; People v. Hyer, 13 Dec. 1836; People v. Thorp et al., 13 Feb. 1841; People v. Golding, 11 Feb. 1842; People v. Timpson, 11 April 1842; People v. Isaacs, 25 Dec. 1851; People v. Moody et al., 15 Jan. 1852. On prostitutes dropping charges, see DAP, People v. Samis, 20 Feb. 1837; People v. Pearsall, 6 Dec. 1832; People v. Ford, 10 Aug. 1844. Marcia Carlisle and John C. Schneider found that antebellum Philadelphia and Detroit prostitutes also turned to the legal system to defend their rights and property. See Carlisle, "Prostitutes," 36–40; Schneider, *Detroit and the Problem of Order,* 20–21.
23. *Whip,* 8 Jan. 1842. For an example of prohibition of testimony by prostitutes, see Leah Lydia Otis, *Prostitution in Medieval Society: The History of an Urban Institution in Languedoc* (Chicago, 1985), 65–68. On American and English efforts to regulate prostitution, see David J. Pivar, *Purity Crusade: Sexual Morality and Social Control, 1868–1900* (Westport, Conn., 1973), 51–71; Judith R. Walkowitz, *Prostitution and Victorian Society: Women, Class, and the State* (Cambridge, Eng., 1980).
24. *Herald,* 23, 26 June 1836. For front-page stories, see *Herald* and *Sun,* 13–30 April 1836, 7–20 June 1836, and *Whip,* 9 July 1842, copy in DAP, People v. Wooldridge, 14 July 1842. Maria Williamson appears in New York City Land Title Registrations, Pre-1917 Conveyance Records, Office of City Register, Liber 137, p. 25, 15 May 1819; Record of Assessments, Fifth Ward 1820–25, MARC. On the popular attention given to prostitutes, see Nevins, *Diary of Strong,* 1:114, 133, 170; 2:270; Robert Taylor Diary, 14 Feb. 1846; 4, 17 April 1846; 17, 18, 20, 21, 22, 23 Nov. 1846; 5, 6, 17 Dec. 1846; 6 Jan. 1847, NYPL; George Wilkes, *The Lives of Helen Jewett and Richard Robinson* (New York, 1849), 73, 124–26. The literature on the "cult of domesticity" is voluminous. I have been most influenced by Nancy Cott, *The Bonds of Womanhood: "Woman's Sphere" in New England, 1780–1835* (New Haven, 1977); Barbara Welter, "The Cult of True Womanhood, 1820–1860," *AQ* 18 (1966):151–75; Suzanne Lebsock, *The Free Women of Petersburg: Status and Culture in a Southern Town, 1784–1860* (New York, 1984); Carroll Smith-Rosenberg, *Disorderly Conduct: Visions of Gender in Victorian America* (New York, 1985).
25. Stansell, "Women, Children, and the Uses of the Streets: Class and Gender Conflict in New York City, 1850–1860," *FS* 8 (1982): 309–35; Mary P. Ryan, *Women in Public: Between Banners and Ballots, 1825–1880* (Baltimore, 1990); Amy Gilman Srebnick, "The Murder of Mary

Rogers: Identity, Sex and Class in Mid-Nineteenth Century New York City" (Paper delivered at the Annual Meeting of the American Historical Association, New York City, Dec. 29, 1985); *Niles' Register,* Jan. 8, 1831; Nevins, *Diary of Hone,* 435, 451. For examples of attacks on women, see *Tribune,* March 13, 1844, March 27, May 1, 1846.

26. See the following DAP cases for attacks on leading prostitutes: People v. Ford, 28 Sept. 1842; People v. Mott, 20 Oct. 1842 (Jane Williams); People v. Valentine, 11 March 1842 (Mary Wall); People v. Dikeman et al., 14 Dec. 1836; People v. Fink et al., 14 July 1825 (Gambel); People v. Lozier, 14 June 1831; People v. Cole et al., 16 Dec. 1836; People v. Harrison et al., 12 May 1833 (Miller); People v. Van Dine et al., 7 Jan. 1831; and PCP, Box 7445, Weyman v. Danon and Jones, 12 Dec. 1832 (Rebecca Weyman). On the transformation of antebellum rioting in New York, see Gilje, *Mobocracy.* On the distinction between "public" and "private" brothels, see chapter 8.

27. People v. Chichester, 8, 11 May 1836. One of Chichester's accomplices, John Boyd, only four years earlier had broken into Mary Bowen's Leonard Street domicile with a gang of fourteen males and destroyed her furniture. See PCP, Box 7445, People v. Boyd et al., 18 Dec. 1832. The Chichester gang is mentioned in Samuel Prime, *Life in New York* (New York, 1847), 180; *Herald,* 15, 25 April 1836; Herbert Asbury, *The Gangs of New York* (New York, 1927), 29; Paul O. Weinbaum, *Mobs and Demagogues: The New York Response to Collective Violence in the Early Nineteenth Century* (Ann Arbor, 1979), 151, 155. Their headquarters was at 44 Bowery.

28. DAP, People v. Hyer, 17 Dec. 1836; People v. Roberts et al., 10 Jan. 1838; *Tribune,* 10, 12 March 1855; William L. Riordon, *Plunkitt of Tammany Hall,* ed. Arthur Mann (1905; reprint, New York, 1962), 86. Among Hyer's accomplices was Abraham Vanderzee, who earned a position on the police force when it was created in 1844. See D. T. Valentine, *Manual of the Corporation of the City of New York* (New York, 1846), 59. Hyer's gang operated out of saloons at 42 and 50 Bowery, Poole's on Mercer Street, and John Morrissey's on Church Street (the "downtown gang"). Hyer was a pallbearer at Poole's funeral. See Asbury, *Gangs,* 87–100; Frank Moss, *The American Metropolis* (New York, 1897), 2:397. On Hyer's alliances with Walsh and Seward (whom he supported at the 1860 Republican convention), see Sean Wilentz, *Chants Democratic: New York City and the Rise of the American Working Class, 1788–1850* (New York, 1984), 328; Alvin F. Harlow, *Old Bowery Days: The Chronicles of a Famous Street* (New York, 1931), 301, 306. The best and most recent work on Hyer is Elliot J. Gorn, *The Manly Art: Bare-Knuckle Prize Fighting in America* (Ithaca, N.Y., 1986), 38–39, 81–97, 113, 123–24, 134.

29. DAP, People v. Graham, 13, 14 Dec. 1836; People v. Tuttle, 15 Jan. 1834; People v. Ryerson et al., 10 Dec. 1834. On the addresses and backgrounds of the accused, see Gilfoyle, "Strumpets and Misogynists," 62.

30. DeLacy to Police Justices in DAP, People v. Miller (Furman), 13 Oct. 1810; Oblinis to Fairlie, 18 March 1806, Watch Folder, Box 28, Common Council Papers, New York City Municipal Archives and Records Center; DAP, People v. Smith (McDermott), 18 Oct. 1810; Report of Ebenezer Burling to Humane Society, 1815, reel 3, John Jay Papers, NYHS. Captain Thomas Darling of the Third Watch District was even fined ten dollars for assaulting a Church Street prostitute in 1809. See *MCC,* 5:603. City Marshal John DuBarre was accused of operating a similar enterprise on the other side of town near the Hudson River a year later. And with his wife, Maria, he was subject to frequent prosecution by the district attorney. See DAP, People v. DuBarre and Peltie, 9 April 1810 (DuBarre was arrested with Marie Peltie); People v. DuBarre and Wood, 10 Oct. 1811 (DuBarre was arrested with Sarah Wood in their Thomas Street brothel); People v. John and Maria DuBarre, 13 Oct. 1810 (Seventh Ward), 11 April 1811 (Water Street). The DuBarres sometimes brought complaints against proprietors of competing houses. See DAP, People v. Willacy, 9 Dec. 1811. In another instance, John DuBarre personally arrested thirteen inn and tavern keepers on East George Street in the Seventh Ward for "whorring." See DAP, People v. Marshal et al., 13 August 1810.

31. DAP, People v. Benwoods, 4 June 1806; People v. Lowe, 15 Jan. 1806. The Benwoods lived in the Sixth Ward and Lowe in the Seventh. By 1809, the Benwoods moved to East George Street. See DAP, People v. Benwood, People v. Lund, 2 March 1809. On the association of

the watch and prostitution, see *Flash,* 24 July 1842, copy in DAP, People v. Scott, 10 Aug. 1842; People v. Anderson et al., 12 Jan. 1829; People v. Lozier et al., 14 June 1831. In 1833, vagrancy was defined to include prostitution, giving constables greater authority to arrest lewd women. See *McDowall's Journal,* June 1833. Vagrancy also included begging, drunkenness, and contracting a venereal infection. After 1845, the police force was supposed "to prevent all disorderly and suspicious persons from mingling in bodies brought together for unlawful purposes, or in places of public resort," to report "all bawdy houses," and to caution strangers and others from going into such places. See *Documents of the Board of Aldermen* (New York, 1845), no. 57, 6 March 1844 (see art. 1, sec. 8; and art. 4, sec. 4).

32. Amy Bridges, *A City in the Republic: Antebellum New York and the Origins of Machine Politics* (Cambridge, Eng., 1984), 73–77, 126–36, 152–53; Harlow, *Old Bowery Days,* 188, 205, 296–301. Prostitutes were sometimes the cause of political skirmishes. In the 1840s, for example, the former boxer and politician Tom McCann allegedly fought the heavyweight champion and future congressman John Morrissey to "win" Kate Ridgely, madam of a Duane Street brothel. Ridgely soon thereafter became McCann's mistress. See *NPG,* 11 Sept. 1880.

33. *New York Sporting Whip,* 28 Jan. 1843 ("bloods"). Some attributed Mayor Fernando Wood's election to the organizational support from "the dens of debauchery, vice and crime." See *Tribune,* 3 Sept. 1856. By the 1850s, New York had an unofficial system of financial payoffs that required local officeholders to pay sums ranging from $5,000 to $20,000 in order to secure a nomination. See *Herald,* 1 Nov. 1858, quoted in William Mills Ivins, *Machine Politics and Money in Elections in New York City* (New York, 1887), 130–31. On the inadequacy of private prosecution against public, collective violence, see Steinberg, *Prosecution.*

34. Taylor was usually accompanied by other judges or police captains on his visits. See Robert Taylor Diary, 17, 18, 20, 21 Nov., 6, 17, Dec. 1846, 6 Jan. 1847, NYPL. On extortion and protection, see *Tribune,* 16, 22 March 1855; *Herald,* 10 March 1855; DAP, People v. Werner, 21 Nov. 1859. Rynders, a Jacksonian Democrat, founded the Empire Club in 1844 and was appointed marshal in 1857. Blamed for fomenting the Astor Place riot in 1849, he remained a topic of discussion even after his death in 1885. See William H. Bell Diary, 26 April 1851, NYHS; *NPG,* 24 Jan. 1845, 7 Feb. 1885; J. Frank ("Florry") Kernan, *Reminiscences of the Old Fire Laddies* (New York, 1885), 52–54; Invitation to William R. Grace, 1 Feb. 1882, MP 84-GWR-12; George Washington Walling, *Recollections of a New York Police Chief* (New York, 1887), 47; Moss, *American Metropolis,* 2:377–78. On Clancy, see *NPG,* 11 Sept. 1880. On McManus and Kelly, see letters of Patrick Kelly to John McKeon, District Attorney, Nov. 1850, in DAP, People v. Waley et al., 26 Oct. 1850; People v. McGowan, 16 May 1851. The toleration and extortion of prostitutes was not uniform; some like Alderman Hart and Captain John J. McManus openly fought and opposed their district's underworld, but they were exceptional. See *NPG,* 3 Jan. 1846. On Norton, see Edwin P. Kilroe, comp., "Skeleton Outline of the Activities of Michael Norton, 1839–1889," manuscript, 1 April 1938, NYHS; *Herald,* 24 Aug. 1865.

35. Wilkes, *Lives,* 45–46 ("toleration"); George G. Foster, *New York in Slices, by an Experienced Carver* (New York, 1849), 48. *McDowall's Journal* reported that boardinghouses acting as fronts for parlor houses usually employed one man for such purposes. See *McDowall's Journal,* May 1833; PCP, Box 7448, Bennett v. Pearce, 9 Nov. 1835; DAP, People v. Shannon, 19 April 1836; People v. Smith, 25 July 1840. For other examples of pimps, see Ned Buntline, *The G'hals of New York: A Novel* (New York, 1850), 37, 62; idem, *Three Years After: A Sequel to the Mystery and Miseries of New York* (New York, 1849), 40, 44, 47; John D. Vose, *Fresh Leaves from the Diary of a Broadway Dandy* (New York, 1852), 73; Henry L. Williams, *Gay Life in New-York! or, Fast Men and Grass Widows* (New York, 1866), 64, 88.

36. Wilkes, *Lives,* 45–46; George Thompson, *The Brazen Star; or, The Adventures of a New-York M.P.* (New York, 1853), 37; idem, *The Gay Girls of New York; or, Life on Broadway* (New York, 1854), 23. For another example of "fancy men" as pimps, see Anonymous, *Revelations of Asmodeus* (New York, 1849), 17–20.

37. William W. Sanger, *The History of Prostitution: Its Extent, Causes, and Effects throughout the World* (New York, 1859), 486, 556; George Ellington, *The Women of New York; or, The Under-*

World of the Great City (Burlington, Iowa, 1869), 303–5; Junius Henri Browne, *The Great Metropolis: A Mirror of New York* (Hartford, 1869), 70–71, 440–41; *NPG,* 8 Dec. 1866, 8 June 1867; *Tribune,* 28, 29 March 1855; James D. McCabe, Jr., *The Secrets of the Great City* (Philadelphia, 1868), 290; *Whip,* 8 Jan. 1842 ("attaché" and "moustached"); *New York Sporting Whip,* 4 March 1843 ("money gained"). Mike Walsh referred to certain political opponents like Jack Magnus and George B. Wooldridge as "pimps." See *Subterranean,* 29 July 1843, 7 June 1845, copies in DAP, People v. Walsh, 29 July 1843, 18 June 1845. Some men who recruited customers for gambling houses were called pimps. See Buchanan, *Asmodeus,* 45. This evidence contradicts more recent arguments that attribute the first appearance of pimps and male dominance of commercialized prostitution to greater police harassment after 1890. See Ruth Rosen, *The Lost Sisterhood: Prostitution in the Progressive Era, 1900–1918* (Baltimore, 1982), 33, 40; Stansell, *City of Women: Sex and Class in New York, 1789–1860* (New York, 1986), 171; John D'Emilio and Estelle B. Freedman, *Intimate Matters: A History of Sexuality in America* (New York, 1988), 136. Jacques Rossiaud found prostitutes with pimps in fifteenth-century France. See his "Prostitution, Youth, and Society," 18.

38. Herman Melville, *Moby-Dick; or, The Whale,* ed. Harold Beaver (Harmondworth, Eng., 1972), 138.
39. Jacquelyn Dowd Hall, " 'The Mind That Burns in Each Body': Women, Rape and Racial Violence," in *Powers of Desire: The Politics of Sexuality,* ed. Ann Snitow et al. (New York, 1983), 328–49. For an interpretation that emphasizes class ties over gender solidarity in the Bowery subculture, and sees sexual hostilities going underground or becoming marginalized during these years, see Stansell, *City of Women,* 23, 96–99. On prostitution as the quintessential symbol of male sexual coercion, see Ellen Carol DuBois and Linda Gordon, "Seeking Ecstasy on the Battlefield: Danger and Pleasure in Nineteenth-Century Feminist Sexual Thought," *FS* 9 (1983): 7–25.

Chapter 5 Sporting Men

1. The most recent work on the Jewett murder is Patricia Cline Cohen, "The Helen Jewett Murder: Violence, Gender, and Sexual Licentiousness in Antebellum America," *National Women's Studies Association Journal* 2 (1990): 374–89; John D. Stevens, *Sensationalism and the New York Press* (New York, 1991), 34–53. I am indebted to Professors Cohen and Stevens for sharing this work with me while it was still in manuscript. Reminiscences of Jewett are in George Washington Walling, *Recollections of a New York Police Chief* (New York, 1887), 25; *NPG,* 26 Aug. 1882; Allan Nevins and Milton Halsey Thomas, eds., *The Diary of George Templeton Strong* (New York, 1952), 1:15, 23–24; Nevins, ed., *The Diary of Philip Hone* (New York, 1927), 206–7, 214, 372. The events were extensively covered from 12 April to 30 June 1836 in New York's *Herald, Sun,* and *Transcript.* A manuscript record of the trial proceedings is in People v. Robinson, 19 April 1836, DAP. Printed copies of the trial include Richard P. Robinson, *The Thomas Street Tragedy* (New York, 1836); idem, *Trial of Richard P. Robinson before the Court of Oyer and Terminer, on the Second of June, 1836, for the Murder of Ellen Jewett* (n.p., n.d.). Robinson's case was put forth in his *A Letter from Richard P. Robinson . . . to His Friend, Thomas Armstrong* (New York, 1837); idem, *A Sketch of the Life of R. P. Robinson, the Alleged Murderer of Ellen Jewett* (New York, 1836). Also see George Wilkes, *The Lives of Helen Jewett and Richard Robinson* (New York, 1849). There were inconsistencies in Jewett's first name. Townsend and her prostitutes referred to the victim as Helen. Robinson and other observers called her Ellen. After locating a copy of her signature, Patricia Cline Cohen has concluded that she was Helen. See Cohen, "Helen Jewett Murder," 375; Cohen to Gilfoyle, 28 Aug. 1989 (letter in my possession).
2. Nevins, *Diary of Hone,* 206–7, 372. I have lost the newspaper citation for "Satanic youngster."
3. Historians of American journalism attribute nationwide changes in journalistic practice to the coverage of the Jewett-Robinson case. Some even credit Bennett with the first journalistic interview (of Rosina Townsend). See Stevens, *Sensationalism;* Dan Schiller, *Objectivity and the*

News: The Public and the Rise of Commercial Journalism (Philadelphia, 1981), 57–65; Niles G. Nilsson, "The Origins of the Interview," *Journalism Quarterly* 48 (1971):101–13.

4. *Herald,* 13 April 1836.
5. *Herald,* 13, 14, 15, 30 April 1836, 9, 10, 21, 23 June 1836. Also see *Niles' Register,* 16 April 1836.
6. Nevins, *Diary of Hone,* 206–7, 372. Hoxie was in 1833 listed in the city directory as a tailor at 83 William Street. By 1835, he had moved to 101 Maiden Lane. He lived at 132 Madison Street. See *Longworth's Almanac* (New York, 1833–41). Sean Wilentz has described Hoxie as an evangelical master artisan, craft entrepreneur, temperance reformer, and abolitionist. He was a member of the General Society of Mechanics and Tradesmen, as well as of the American Institute. See Wilentz, *Chants Democratic: New York City and the Rise of the American Working Class, 1788–1850* (New York, 1984), 202, 207, 263, 281. In the week of Robinson's acquittal, Edwards imposed heavy fines on journeymen tailors convicted of labor conspiracy, a decision with important ramifications for the city's budding trade union movement, for it provoked one of the largest labor demonstrations in antebellum America a few days later. The timing of the two events is provocative, but it is unclear whether the emerging class divisions between downwardly mobile journeymen tailors and upwardly mobile nabob clerks (like Robinson) were overcome by gender solidarity in the Jewett-Robinson case. No detailed descriptions of Robinson's supporters at the trial exist. Wilentz argues that, in the mid-1830s, New York journeymen included all trades and occupations in their movement but restricted membership to "wage earners." See Wilentz, *Chants Democratic,* 253, 289–93. For examples of the longtime interest in the case, see Anonymous, *The Truly Remarkable Life of the Beautiful Helen Jewett* (New York, 1880); Walling, *Recollections.*
7. Wilkes, *Lives,* 7, 30, 54. On money's negative impact on perceptions of Jewett's character, see Robinson, *Letter,* 8.
8. Robinson, *Letter,* 5–7; Wilkes, *Lives,* 58–60, 65–68. After examining all of the literature on the Jewett-Robinson affair, Patricia Cline Cohen now doubts that Robinson wrote *A Letter.* See Cohen to Gilfoyle, March 1991 (letter in my possession). Nevertheless, the passage quoted here illustrates contemporary fears regarding the temptations of urban life.
9. Ibid.
10. Wilkes, *Lives,* 125; Nevins, *Diary of Hone,* 210–11; Cohen, "Helen Jewett Murder," 375–77. On fears of youthful, unregulated sexuality and linkages to prostitution during the 1830s, see Mary P. Ryan, *Cradle of the Middle Class: The Family in Oneida County, New York, 1790–1865* (New York, 1981), 116–30. For more on the emergence of middle-class standards of morality and restraint, see Carroll Smith-Rosenberg, *Disorderly Conduct: Visions of Gender in Victorian America* (New York, 1985), 79–89, 109–64; Ronald G. Walters, ed., *Primers for Prudery: Sexual Advice to Victorian America* (Englewood Cliffs, N.J., 1974). For an insightful analysis of the larger evolution of "sport," "the fancy," and their relationship to working-class culture, see Elliott J. Gorn, *The Manly Art: Bare-Knuckle Prize Fighting in America* (Ithaca, N.Y., 1986). On the early beginnings and organization of middle-class etiquette and definitions of proper behavior, see Karen Halttunen, *Confidence Men and Painted Women: A Study of Middle-Class Culture in America, 1830–1870* (New Haven, 1982). For arguments that the latter half of the eighteenth century was the most sexually tolerant period in American history, see David H. Flaherty, "Law and the Enforcement of Morals in Early America," *Perspectives in American History* 5 (1971): 207–53; Stephen Nissenbaum, *Sex, Diet, and Debility in Jacksonian America: Sylvester Graham and Health Reform* (Westport, Conn., 1980), 26–33; Daniel Scott Smith and Michael S. Hindus, "Premarital Pregnancy in America, 1640–1971: An Overview and Interpretation," *JIH* 5 (1975): 537–70; Ortho T. Beall, Jr., "*Aristotle's Master Piece* in America: A Landmark in the Folklore of Medicine," *WMQ,* 3d ser., 20 (1962): 207–22; Carl Bridenbaugh, *Cities in Revolt: Urban Life in America, 1743–1776* (New York, 1955), 121; Ellen K. Rothman, *Hands and Hearts: A History of Courtship in America* (New York, 1984), 46–49.
11. *Sporting Whip,* 28 Jan. 1843; *Rake,* 9 July 1842 ("necessary"); *Weekly Rake,* 30 July 1842; *Whip,* 8 Jan. 1842, 5, 26 March 1842. For a semifictional defense of prostitution, see Anonymous, *Reflections of Asmodeus; or, Mysteries of Upper-Tendom* (New York, 1849), 56–57. On the

importance of story papers during these years, see Michael Denning, *Mechanic Accents: Dime Novels and Working-Class Culture in America* (London, 1987), 10–11.

12. DAP, People v. Flyn et al., 11 Aug. 1798; People v. Jackson, 8 June 1803; People v. Greer, 8 May 1811.
13. People v. Truesdale, 7 Sept. 1816; People v. Battis, 15 Oct. 1818; Walt Whitman, "On Vice," in *The Uncollected Poetry and Prose of Walt Whitman,* ed. Emory Holloway (Garden City, N.Y., 1921), 1:6; J. Frank ("Florry") Kernan, *Reminiscences of the Old Fire Laddies* (New York, 1885), 42. For a short, fictional description of the role of prostitution in seamen's lives, see Herman Melville, *Redburn* (New York, 1963), 175, 245–46. For other examples, see DAP, People v. Pearsall, 11 Dec. 1840; Citizens' Association of New York, *Sanitary Condition of the City: Report of the Council of Hygiene and Public Health* (New York, 1866), 100; Minutes of 8 Oct. 1912, Box 13, SPC Papers.
14. The names of the clients are in DAP, Cases for 7 Sept., 5 Nov. 1811, 14 Sept. 1812, 13 Sept. 1813. The names were traced in *Elliot and Crissy's New-York Directory* (New York, 1811); *Longworth's American Almanac, New-York Register and City Directory* (New York, 1811 and 1813); William Elliot, *Elliot's Improved New-York Double Directory* (New York, 1812). Similarly, in panel house robberies between 1822 and 1859, 41 percent of the victims were city residents. While only 36 percent were identified as living outside New York, the remaining anonymous victims were unlikely to have been New Yorkers. The victims numbered twenty-two; the addresses of five of them were unknown. The names of panel house victims were found in DAP, Cases for 25 Sept., 11 Dec. 1840, 10 Aug. 1843, 4 Jan., 20 June 1844, 11 Sept., 17 Oct. 1845, 9 April, 3 June 1846, 6 Oct., 14 Nov. 1848, 16 Feb., 12 April 1849, 8 July 1850, 14 June 1858, 18 Jan., 16 May 1859; PCP, Box 7437, Cases for 30 Oct. 1822, 25 Aug. 1823; Box 7448, 9 Nov. 1835; *NPG,* 16 May 1846, 19 June 1847. Sometimes newspapers mentioned the names and addresses of clients of prostitutes, but not in significant numbers. Five men so named in 1834 and one in 1847 were city residents, although none appeared in any city directory. See *Sun,* 23 March, 9, 16, 17 May 1834; *NPG,* 2 Jan. 1847.
15. George Ellington, *The Women of New York; or, The Under-World of the Great City* (Burlington, Iowa, 1869), 220–21.
16. *Herald,* 10 June 1836; *Advocate of Moral Reform,* 15 July 1836 ("dens"); 15 Jan. 1837 ("popular"). Specific cases are in DAP, People v. Greer, 8 May 1811; People v. Legg, 10 July 1833.
17. *Whip,* 1, 8 Jan. 1842 ("boys"); Whitman, "On Vice," 2:6; idem, "New York Dissected," in *New York Dissected,* ed. Emory Holloway and Ralph Adimari (New York, 1936), 217–18. For a similar complaint, also see DAP, People v. Burns, 22 Feb. 1842. For similar stories later in the century, see "A Heartbroken Mother" to Hewitt, 15 July 1887, MP 87-HAS-29; Forrester to Gaynor, 16 Aug. 1912, MP GWJ-55; Hardy to Hewitt, July 1887, MP 87-HAS-28; Walsh to Police Commissioner, 13 Oct. 1910, MP GWJ-17.
18. *Whip,* 1, 8 Jan. 1842; Robert Taylor Diary, 14 Feb., 17, 18, 20 Nov., 5, 6 Dec. 1846, NYPL. For examples of married men with prostitutes, see DAP, People v. Knapp, 9 Nov. 1811; People v. Nicholls, 6 Jan. 1815; People v. Powell, 11 July 1826; People v. Ehman, 17 April 1846.
19. Nevins, *Diary of Strong,* 2:117; Whitman, "On Vice," 1:6.
20. On Singer, see Walling, *Recollections,* 327–29. The Lawrence scandal is in Nevins, *Diary of Strong,* 1:114, 133; 2:270. Lawrence was mayor of New York from 1834 to 1837. For a recent examination of Lawrence, see Eric H. Monkkonen, *America Becomes Urban: The Development of United States Cities and Towns, 1780–1980* (Berkeley, Calif., 1988), 117–20. Sickles brought a prostitute with him to Great Britain when he served as secretary to the U.S. ambassador James Buchanan. See W. A. Swanberg, *Sickles the Incredible* (New York, 1956), 83–84, 91–94, 310, 339.
21. *Tribune,* 21 March 1846, supplement; William W. Sanger, *The History of Prostitution: Its Extent, Causes, and Effects throughout the World* (New York, 1859), 572; Nevins, *Diary of Strong,* 3:222; Ellington, *Women of New York,* 166.
22. *Whip,* 1, 8 Jan. 1842. For another image of wealthy young and married men in brothels, see Harrison Gray Buchanan, *Asmodeus; or, Legends of New York* (New York, 1848), 27–30.
23. Ned Buntline, *The Mysteries and Miseries of New York* (New York, 1848), 1:19–20; 2:28–33;

George G. Foster, *New York Naked* (New York, 1850), 127. The best overall analysis of this subculture is Gorn, *Manly Art.*

24. Foster, *New York Naked,* 128–29; John D. Vose, *Seven Nights in Gotham* (New York, 1852), 34–35; Anonymous, *Revelations of Asmodeus,* 17–18; Henry L. Williams, *Gay Life in New-York! or, Fast Men and Grass Widows* (New York, 1866), 66; *True Flash,* 4 Dec. 1841; *Whip,* 19 March 1842; Ellington, *Women of New York,* 185, 203, 235–36. For more on the Bowery and working-class life in New York, see Alvin F. Harlow, *Old Bowery Days: The Chronicles of a Famous Street* (New York, 1931); Wilentz, *Chants Democratic.* For other descriptions of the Bowery B'hoy, see Charles H. Haswell, *Reminiscences of New York by an Octogenarian* (New York, 1898), 270–71; Abram C. Dayton, *Last Days of Knickerbocker Life in New York* (New York, 1882), 164–65; Benedict F. Giamo, "On the Bowery: Symbolic Action in American Culture and Subculture" (Ph.D. diss., Emory Univ., 1987). For a different interpretation of Bowery sexuality and gender relations, see Christine Stansell, *City of Women: Sex and Class in New York, 1789–1860* (New York, 1986).
25. Buntline, *Mysteries and Miseries,* 1:19–20; 2:28–33; idem, *The B'hoys of New York* (New York, 1850), 7–8; Anonymous, *Revelations of Asmodeus,* 18–20; *Weekly Rake,* 1 Oct. 1842 ("fops"); John D. Vose, *Fresh Leaves from the Diary of a Broadway Dandy* (New York, 1852), 30, 85; Charles Astor Bristed, *The Upper Ten Thousand: Sketches of American Society* (New York, 1852), 6, 10. On the broader cultural meaning of nabobs, see Peter G. Buckley, "Culture, Class and Place in Antebellum New York," in *Power, Culture, and Place: Essays on New York City,* ed. John H. Mollenkopf (New York, 1988), 25–52.
26. Vose, *Leaves,* 12, 17–18, 24, 52–53 ("fault"); Anonymous, *Revelations of Asmodeus,* 12 ("facility"), 18–20, 47–49 ("male prostitution"); *Whip,* 8 Jan. 1842. On the image of unlimited sensuality, see George Thompson, *The Gay Girls of New-York; or, Life on Broadway* (New York, 1854), 63. For a leading fictional account of the "man of pleasure," see Warren Baer, *Champagne Charlie; or, The Sports of New York* (New York, 1868), and the character of Gus Lorrimer in George Lippard, *The Quaker City* (Philadelphia, 1845), 87–89.
27. Donald G. Mitchell, *Reveries of a Bachelor; or, A Book of the Heart* (New York, 1850), 10–16, 28–37, 65 ("fashion"), 90 ("fire"). *Reveries* first appeared in *Southern Literary Messenger* in 1849. Its popularity led to its reissue in 1863, 1883, and 1907. On Mitchell's background, see Waldo H. Dunn, *The Life of Donald G. Mitchell* (New York, 1922), vii, 225, 237, 399.
28. Mitchell, *Reveries,* 7 ("die"), 19–20 ("dawning womanhood"), 127 ("match"). Similarly, George Templeton Strong considered marriage to be "voluntary slavery" and said he was "becoming more and more of a misogynist every day." See Nevins, *Diary of Strong,* 1:162.
29. DAP, People v. Bowne, 14 Oct. 1829; People v. Collins, 14 Sept. 1831; *McDowall's Journal,* Jan. 1833. The house of ill fame was Mrs. Collins's at 123 Canal Street. James Roberts's dance house was at Broadway and 13th Street. See DAP, People v. Roberts, 16 Aug. 1826. Charity Jennison's Orange Street brothel was usually filled on Sunday nights. See DAP, People v. Lane, 18 Feb. 1826. Elliot Gorn estimates that 40 percent of men twenty-five to thirty-five years old were unmarried in the midnineteenth-century city. See his *Manly Art,* 141–42.
30. *Journal of Public Morals,* 7 March 1833; *Advocate of Moral Reform,* 16 Oct. 1848. On the Irish bachelor subculture and its relationship to sporting life, see Benjamin G. Rader, *American Sports* (Englewood Cliffs, N.J., 1983), 97–100. For observations that clients of prostitutes were primarily visitors to New York, see Francis J. Grund, *The Americans in Their Moral, Social, and Political Relations* (Boston, 1837), 39. On visitors in the Tenderloin after 1870, see *Times,* 28 March 1880; Cornelius W. Willemse, *Behind the Green Lights* (New York, 1931), 12–13.
31. On the Hyer-Poole alliance, see *Tribune,* 10, 12 March 1855. Hyer's gang was headquartered in saloons at 42 and 50 Bowery, Poole's on Mercer Street, and Morrissey's on Church Street. Hyer was allied to Poole by 1852. See Herbert Asbury, *The Gangs of New York* (New York, 1927), 87–100; Frank Moss, *The American Metropolis* (New York, 1897), 2:397; Harlow, *Old Bowery Days,* 301–6. On the diverse mix of people on Broadway by the 1850s, see chapter 6; Elliot J. Gorn, " 'Good-Bye Boys, I Die a True American': Homicide, Nativism, and Working-Class Culture in Antebellum New York City," *JAH* 74 (1987): 388–410. On prostitutes and

pimps along Broadway, see chapters 2 and 4. On bohemians, see Elizabeth Kray, *A Walk through the SoHo District with Walt Whitman* (New York, 1981); chapter 6.

32. DAP, People v. Male, 13 Dec. 1866; People v. Haggerty, 13 June 1865; People v. Smith, 15 Dec. 1865; People v. Mason, 13 Sept. 1866. Robbery was not the only occurrence that made clients willing publicly to reveal their illegal sexual behavior. Males sometimes urged public officials to close a brothel where they had contracted venereal disease. See MP 87-HAS-28; Davis to Edson, 10 May 1884, MP 85-EF-10.

33. Of the forty-four men, twenty-four (55 percent) were from New York City, nine (21 percent) visitors, six (14 percent) from Brooklyn, Queens, or New Jersey, and five (11 percent) unknown. The twenty-six who gave monetary amounts stolen averaged $149. Some carried substantial sums of cash—$500 in one case, over $250 in four other cases—and five others had expensive watches purloined. The names were found in DAP, Cases for 13 June 1862, 4 March 1863, 7 June, 18, 25 Nov. 1864, 5, 14 Jan., 5 April, 5 May, 13, 20 June, 7 July, 8 Aug., 6, 17, 18, 25 Oct., 16 Nov., 15 Dec. 1865, 13, 20, 24 Sept., 13 Dec. 1866, 20 Feb., 17 June, 11, 20 Nov. 1867, 22 Jan., 7, 11, 20 May, 4 June 1868, 21, 22 Jan., 10, 15, 18, 24 Feb., 22 March, 24 June, 15, 29 July 1869, 15 Nov. 1870; *NPG,* 3 Nov. 1866. For a brothel raid where a majority of clients (seven of twelve arrested) were listed in the city directory, see *NPG,* 27 April 1867, and *Trow's New York City Directory* (New York, 1867).

34. William C. Young, ed., *Documents of American Theater History* (Chicago, 1973), 1:51–52; *McDowall's Journal,* Sept. 1834. On comparisons of English and American theaters, see James Hardie, *Descriptions of New York* (New York, 1827), 339.

35. Nevins, *Diary of Strong,* 2:59, 455–56; *Advocate of Moral Reform,* 1 July 1849; Lawrence Levine, "William Shakespeare and the American People," *AHR* 89 (1984): 40–42. For similar remarks, see J. S. Buckingham, *America: Historical, Statistic, and Descriptive* (London, 1841), 1:47–48; Charles Lockwood, *Manhattan Moves Uptown* (Boston, 1976), 121; Mary Henderson, *The City and the Theater: New York Playhouses from Bowling Green to Times Square* (Clifton, N.J., 1973), 87; Young, *Documents,* 1:54–55. For other insightful analyses of the antebellum theater, see Peter C. Buckley, "To the Opera House: Culture and Society in New York City, 1820–1860" (Ph.D. diss., SUNY, Stony Brook, 1984); David Grimsted, *Melodrama Unveiled: American Theater and Culture, 1800–50* (Chicago, 1968).

36. Nevins *Diary of Hone,* 572; George G. Foster, *New York in Slices, by an Experienced Carver* (New York, 1849), 101; *Advocate of Moral Reform,* 15 Jan. 1852; CAS, *First Annual Report* (New York, 1854), 11; Stephen Allen to John Dix, 3 March 1842; Allen to Walter Bowne, 17 March 1824; Allen to John Morse, 1 April 1824, all in Stephen Allen Papers, NYHS. On efforts to regulate theaters, see Timothy J. Gilfoyle, "City of Eros: New York City, Prostitution, and the Commericalization of Sex, 1790–1920" (Ph.D. diss., Columbia Univ., 1987), 100–101, 145–46. On theater bifurcation, see Buckley, "Opera House," 139–61.

37. Caroline Forrest won alimony of $3,000 annually and was permitted to remarry; Edwin was not. See *Herald, Report of the Forrest Divorce Case* (New York, 1852), 6, 13, 87–88, 161, 187; Franklin Walker and G. Ezra Pane, eds., *Twain's Travels with Mr. Brown* (New York, 1940), 245–46; Alexander K. McClure, *Old Time Notes on Pennsylvania* (Philadelphia, 1905), 1:256–57; Nevins, *Diary of Strong,* 2:81–85; Wilentz, *Chants Democratic,* 258. On other divorce trials (Peter Strong's and Egbert Viele's) that jammed courtrooms and drew great public attention, see Nevins, *Diary of Strong,* 4:53–54, 314, 365.

38. *Rake,* 24 Sept. 1842, 1 Oct. 1842; Foster, *New York in Slices,* 90 ("the law"); idem, *New York by Gas-Light, with Here and There a Streak of Sunshine* (New York, 1850), 86–87 ("virtuous"); *NPG,* 13 Dec. 1845; Claudia D. Johnson, "That Guilty Third Tier: Prostitution in Nineteenth-Century American Theaters," in *Victorian America,* ed. Daniel Walker Howe (Philadelphia, 1976), 111–20. On the third tier in the 1850s, see Sanger, *History of Prostitution,* 557–58.

39. DAP, People v. Valentine, 13 March 1833; *Advocate of Moral Reform,* 20 Oct. 1848; Grund, *American,* 77; *Rake,* 1 Oct. 1842. On Power, see *Advocate of Moral Reform,* 15 Nov. 1838; 2 Oct. 1849; 1 Jan. 1838. Foster later contradicted himself and said the Broadway Theater was respectable. See his *New York Naked* (New York, 1850), 146. On the Chatham Theater, see

Rake, 1 Oct. 1842; *New York Sporting Whip,* 18 Feb. 1843. On theater riots, see DAP, People v. Elliot, 8 Feb. 1794; People v. Mitchel et al., 12 Dec. 1828. The Park Theater burned in 1820; it reopened a year later under the proprietorship of Astor and Beekman. Walt Whitman believed that the Park was the exception to the problem of prostitution in the theater. See Whitman, "Miserable State of the Stage," in *American Theater as Seen by Its Critics, 1752–1934,* ed. Montrose J. Moses and John Mason Brown (New York, 1934), 70–71.

40. Frances Trollope, *Domestic Manners of the Americans* (London, 1839), 2:162–63 ("elegantly decorated"); *Herald,* 29 Aug. 1836, quoted in Young, *Documents,* 92; *Sun,* 2 April 1834 ("we girls"); *New York Sporting Whip,* 4, 11 Feb. 1843 ("blasphemous confusion"); John M. Murtaugh and Sarah Harris, *Cast the First Stone* (New York, 1957), 205 ("depravity and degradation").

41. Butt Ender, *Prostitution Exposed; or, A Moral Reform Directory* (New York, 1839); DAP, People v. Ridgeway, 14 Sept. 1839; Record of Assessments, Second Ward, 1820–39, MARC; John Cornwall Edwards, "A History of Nineteenth-Century Theatre Architecture in the United States" (Ph.D. diss., Northwestern Univ., 1963), 66.

42. On Brown, see Nevins, *Diary of Strong,* 1:162.

43. Society for the Reformation of Juvenile Delinquents, *Thirteenth Annual Report* (New York, 1838), 14–16; idem, *Sixteenth Annual Report* (New York, 1841), 23–25; Foster, *New York in Slices,* 101; Nevins, *Diary of Strong,* 2:410. For comments on the profitability of theaters from 1820 to 1850, see *Niles' Register,* 25 May 1822; *Advocate of Moral Reform,* 1 July 1849, 15 Dec. 1838; *Diary of Hone,* 273, 421–22.

44. *NPG,* 28 Dec. 1867; DAP, People v. Donahue, 14 Sept. 1843; People v. Cooper, 9 Sept. 1864. On private supper rooms, see DAP, People v. Ross, 7 March 1861; James D. McCabe, Jr., *Secrets of the Great City* (Philadelphia, 1868), 208; Buntline, *B'hoys,* 38. On dance halls, see Kernan, *Reminiscences,* 41–42 (Five Points); DAP, People v. Molineaux, 17 March 1825; Walt Whitman, "On Vice," in *The Uncollected Poetry and Prose of Walt Whitman,* ed. Emory Holloway (Garden City, N.Y., 1921), 1:6; Sanger, *History of Prostitution,* 524, 561–62.

45. Samuel B. Halliday, *Little Secret Sweeper; or, Life among the Poor* (New York, 1861), 182. On the number of crewmen in New York City, see Robert Albion, *The Rise of New York Port, 1815–1860* (New York, 1939), 398. The immigrant figure is in Edward K. Spann, *The New Metropolis: New York City, 1840–1857* (New York, 1981), 24. On hotel registrations, see Jefferson Williamson, *The American Hotel* (New York, 1930), 29–30.

46. Wilentz, *Chants Democratic,* 24–35, 50.

47. Jeanne Boydston, "To Earn Her Daily Bread: Housework and Antebellum Working-Class Subsistence," *RHR* 35 (1986): 19.

48. *Letters from John Pintard to His Daughter, 1816–1833,* Collections of the New-York Historical Society (New York, 1940), 1:170, 174.

49. McCabe, *Secrets,* 462–63; Junius Henri Browne, *The Great Metropolis: A Mirror of New York* (Hartford, 1869), 588–95; *Subterranean,* 29 July 1843, copy in DAP, Cases for 11 Aug. 1843. The men were twenty-two to twenty-five years in age.

50. Elizabeth Blackwell, *Counsel to Parents on the Moral Education of Their Children* (New York, 1881), 5. For a similar example of marriage brokers, see *New York Cupid* in Hanks to Hewitt, 2 Sept. 1887, MP 87-HAS-30. On courtship rituals and changes, see Rothman, *Hands and Hearts.*

51. On male reactions to the growing power of women in the family, see Mark C. Carnes, *Secret Ritual and Manhood in Victorian America* (New Haven, 1989); Daniel Scott Smith, "Family Limitation, Sexual Control, and Domestic Feminism in Victorian America," in *Clio's Consciousness Raised,* ed. Mary Hartman and Lois W. Banner (New York, 1974), 119–36; G. J. Barker-Benfield, "The Spermatic Economy: A Nineteenth-Century View of Sexuality," in *The American Family in Social-Historical Perspective,* ed. Michael Gordon (New York, 1978), 374–402; Peter T. Cominos, "Late Victorian Sexual Respectability and the Social System," *International Review of Social History* 8 (1963): 18–48, 216–50; Nancy F. Cott, "Passionlessness: An Interpretation of Victorian Sexual Ideology, 1790–1850," *Signs* 4 (1978): 219–36. Some historians have questioned the pervasiveness of the domestic ideal. See Carl Degler, *At Odds:*

Woman and the Family in America from the Revolution to the Present (New York, 1980), 30–50. Yet, in New York, the most vociferous critics of domesticity and middle-class conceptions of marriage like Victoria Woodhull, Tennessee Claflin, and Marx Edgeworth Lazarus received little support in white, middle-class households. See Taylor Stoehr, ed., *Free Love in America: A Documentary History* (New York, 1979). The best evidence suggests that by the midnineteenth century, the belief in and popularity of separate spheres bore some resemblance to middle-class reality. See Barbara Welter, "The Cult of True Womanhood, 1820–1860," *AQ* 18 (1966): 151–74; Ryan, *Cradle,* 18–59, 189–97; Kathryn Kish Sklar, *Catherine Beecher: A Study in Domesticity* (New Haven, 1973); Smith-Rosenberg, *Disorderly Conduct,* Nancy F. Cott, *The Bonds of Womanhood: "Woman's Sphere" in New England, 1780–1835* (New Haven, 1977); Suzanne Lebsock, *The Free Women of Petersburg: Status and Culture in a Southern Town, 1784–1860* (New York, 1984), 18–29. On the contradictions of this ideal for working-class New Yorkers, see Elizabeth Blackmar, *Manhattan For Rent, 1785–1850* (Ithaca, N.Y., 1989), 126–29.

52. Thompson, *Gay Girls,* 109 ("petticoat").
53. Nevins, *Diary of Strong,* 1:318.
54. Smith-Rosenberg, *Disorderly Conduct,* 90–108; David Crockett, *A Narrative of the Life of David Crockett of the State of Tennessee* (Nashville, 1834; reprint, 1973); James A. Shackford, *David Crockett: The Man and the Legend* (Chapel Hill, N.C., 1956). For other examples of sporting-male culture in nineteenth-century America, see David W. Rose, "Prostitution and the Sporting Life: Aspects of Working-Class Culture and Sexuality in Nineteenth-Century Wheeling," *Upper Ohio Valley Historical Review* 16 (1986): 7–31; John C. Schneider, "The Bachelor Subculture and Spatial Change in Mid-Nineteenth Century Detroit," *Detroit in Perspective* 3 (1978): 19–31. For more on the literature of sexual control, see Smith and Hindus, "Premarital Pregnancy," 537–70; James C. Mohr, *Abortion in America: The Origins and Evolution of National Policy, 1800–1900* (New York, 1978); John S. Haller and Robin M. Haller, *The Physician and Sexuality in Victorian America* (Urbana, Ill., 1974), 113–24; Carl Degler, "What Ought to Be and What Was: Women's Sexuality in the Nineteenth Century," *AHR* 79 (1974): 467–90; James Reed, *The Birth Control Movement and American Society: From Private Vice to Public Virtue* (Princeton, 1983): 3–63. For an excellent discussion of this literature, see Estelle B. Freedman, "Sexuality in Nineteenth-Century America: Behavior, Ideology, and Politics," *RAH* 10 (1982): 196–215.

Chapter 6 "Shoulder Hitters," Porno Kings, and Politicians

1. *The Complete Writings of Walt Whitman* (New York, 1902), 1:160.
2. Anonymous, *The Gentleman's Companion* (New York, 1870), 8.
3. Edward Van Every, *Sins of New York, as "Exposed" by the Police Gazette* (New York, 1930), 10–15, 74–79.
4. Allan Nevins and Milton Halsey Thomas, eds., *The Diary of George Templeton Strong* (New York, 1952), 2:211; Five Points House of Industry, *Monthly Record* (June 1858), 25; Citizens' Association of New York, *Sanitary Condition of the City: Report of the Council of Hygiene and Public Health* (New York, 1866), 67; *NPG,* 6 April, 8 June 1867; Thomas Butler Gunn, *The Physiology of New York Boarding Houses* (New York, 1857), 103; George Ellington, *The Women of New York; or, The Under-World of the Great City* (Burlington, Iowa, 1869), 206–12; Van Every, *Sins of New York,* 14. On the leading brothels, see Charles DeKock, *Guide to the Harems; or, Directory to the Ladies of Fashion in New York and Various Other Cities* (New York, 1855); Free Loveyer, *Directory to the Seraglios in New York, Philadelphia, Boston, and All the Principal Cities in the Union* (New York, 1859); *Gentleman's Companion.* Details on building size are in Record of Assessments, Eighth Ward, 1859, MARC. Winslow lived at 73 Mercer Street, Rowe at 21 Greene Street, and Pratt at 147 Mercer (or 597 Houston) Street. Pratt was

also listed at 29 Mercer Street in Record of Assessments, Eighth Ward, 1859. By the 1850s, the antebellum districts were declining as centers of commercial sex. The West Side had less than a quarter of the leading brothels in the city, and Corlears Hook was not even mentioned in guidebooks. Five Points housed under a fifth of the city's domiciles of prostitution by the Civil War. For data on this decline, see Timothy J. Gilfoyle, "City of Eros: New York City, Prostitution, and the Commercialization of Sex, 1790–1920" (Ph.D. diss., Columbia Univ., 1987), 51, 85.

5. Martin Clary, *Mid-Manhattan* (New York, 1929), 71 (Tweed); Elizabeth Kray, *A Walk through the SoHo Historic District with Walt Whitman* (New York, 1981), 1–3 (Whitman). Pfaff's Cafe was at 645 Broadway after 1856, Taylor's at 555 Broadway, the Bank Exchange at Howard and Broadway, and Platt's Saloon at 485 Broadway (under Wallack's). See *Tribune,* 10 March 1855; Kray, *Walk,* 9. For an excellent analysis of the social and political life of Broadway, see Elliot Gorn, " 'Good-Bye Boys, I Die a True American': Homicide, Nativism, and Working-Class Culture in Antebellum New York," *JAH* (74): 388–410. In 1859, over 450 establishments were listed between 444 and 680 Broadway. The most numerous were dry goods businesses (clothing, textiles, shoes, tailors, milliners, hatters)—114; visual arts (engravers, publishers, artists, photographers, lithographers)—58; furniture, sewing machines, and other hardware—52. There were also ten restaurants, nine billiard rooms, seven saloons, and seven hotels. Campbell's Minstrels played at Fellow's Opera House, Bryant's Minstrels at Mechanics Hall, and Wood's Minstrels at Marble Hall. See *Boyd's Pictorial Directory of Broadway* (New York, 1859), 50–59; Charles R. Rode, *The New York City Directory* (New York, 1842–55), 1st–13th publications; *Wilson's Business Directory* (New York, 1855–59). On theaters, see Mary C. Henderson, *The City and the Theater: New York Playhouses from Bowling Green to Time Square* (Clifton, N.J., 1973). On "monster" hotels, see Ivan Steen, "Palaces for Travelers: New York City's Hotels in the 1850's as Viewed by English Visitors," *New York History* 54 (1973): 24–51. Fellow's Opera House was formerly Mitchell's Olympic Theater and in 1860 became the New American Theater, one of the earliest concert saloons. See Edwin P. Kilroe, comp., "Skeleton Outline of the Activities of Michael Norton, 1839–1889," manuscript, 1 April 1938, NYHS, pp. 3–4, 179–83. On the absence of cafés and the prominence of hotel barrooms, see Edward Dicey, *Six Months in the Federal States* (London, 1863), 1:10–25. For related information, see Van Every, *Sins of New York,* 10–15, 74–79; J. F. Richmond, *The Institutions of New York* (New York, 1871), 116–17; William Perris, *Maps of the City of New York* (New York, 1859); George Bromley and E. Robinson, *Atlas of the Entire City of New York* (New York, 1879), plate 4.

6. James D. McCabe, Jr., *The Secrets of the Great City* (Philadelphia, 1868), 201–2; Ellington, *Women of New York,* 210; Junius Henri Browne, *The Great Metropolis: A Mirror of New York* (Hartford, 1869), 398 ("temptation"). Also see George G. Foster, *New York by Gas-Light, with Here and There a Streak of Sunshine* (New York, 1850), 40.

7. McCabe, *Secrets,* 208; DAP, People v. Ross, 7 March 1861; Ned Buntline, *The B'hoys of New York* (New York, 1850), 38; Foster, *New York by Gas-Light,* 37–40. For an example of a calling card, see the one for "The General," an establishment operated by Mrs. Caroline Rogers at 34 Howard Street in DAP, People v. Rogers, 27 March 1863. For a fictional account of private supper rooms with prostitutes, see Henry L. Williams, *Gay Life in New-York! or, Fast Men and Grass Widows* (New York, 1866), 53–55.

8. Quoted in Bayard Still, ed., *Mirror for Gotham* (New York, 1956), 199–200; Whitman, *New York Dissected,* 5–6. On sanitary inspection, see Citizens' Association, *Sanitary Condition,* 10, 26, 81, 138. Whitman reportedly had a sister-in-law who was a former streetwalker. See Harold Aspiz, *Walt Whitman and the Body Beautiful* (Urbana, Ill., 1980), 227.

9. Edward Crapsey, *The Nether Side of New York* (New York, 1872), 138–39. For streetwalkers in Madison Square and near the Fifth Avenue Hotel, see *Times,* 15 Nov. 1860.

10. Dicey, *Six Months,* 1:17; *NPG,* 6 April 1867; Citizens' Association, *Sanitary Condition,* 10, 26, 37, 67, 81, 138; Ellington, *Women of New York,* 206–12. Theaters and brothels were increasingly linked spatially after 1820. A breakdown of houses of prostitution within 2.5 blocks of a theater revealed the following:

Year	Number	Percentage of Total Houses
1820–29	30	11
1830–39	93	34
1840–49	87	42
1850–59	181	53
1870–79	102	24
1880–89	264	43
1900–09	463	41 (Manhattan only)
1910–19	617	28 (Manhattan only)

11. Citywide, 45 houses in 1855 were still operating in 1859. See Record of Assessments, Eighth and Fourteenth wards, 1855, 1859; DeKock, *Guide to the Harems;* Free Loveyer, *Seraglios; NPG,* 28 Dec. 1867. During the 1870s, West Twenty-seventh and West Twenty-sixth streets had 26 and 18 houses of prostitution, respectively. While Mercer Street had 7 houses, Wooster Street 27, and Greene Street 52, much of the prostitution had moved to the northern end of the streets past SoHo into Greenwich Village and above.

12. Kray, *Walk,* 6 (Whitman). A. T. Stewart, the department store founder, owned 18 Howard Street, on a block filled with brothels, but this specific address was never identified as such. Lorillard owned 28 and 30 Howard Street. See Record of Assessments, Eighth Ward, 1854, MARC; DeKock, *Guide to the Harems;* Free Loveyer, *Seraglios.* On Simers, see Moses Yale Beach, *Wealth and Biography of the Wealthy Citizens of New York City* (New York, 1845), 28; Pre-1917 Conveyance Liber 437, pp. 116–18, 8 May 1843; Record of Assessments, Eighth Ward, 1822–39. Simers's initial leases were at 103, 105, 107 Mercer Street. After 1826, no names are listed in the assessments for Simers's property. In 1843, Charles Hoyt transferred his "right, title, interest, estate, claim, and demand" on the houses and lots to Simers for $1.00. See Pre-1917 Conveyance Liber 437, p. 563, 26 Aug. 1843. Evidence that the property was used for prostitution is in DAP, Cases for 14 June 1826, 16 Aug. 1827. Simers also controlled property at 26 Walnut Street, 312 Water Street, 91 Cherry Street, and two unnumbered houses on Scammel Street. See Record of Assessments, Seventh Ward, 1832, 1835, 1837, 1839. Evidence that the Walnut and Water Street houses were used for prostitution is in DAP, Cases for 13 Aug. 1827, 17 Oct. 1828, 9 Aug. 1844, 21 Nov. 1846; *NPG,* 17 April 1847. The green-painted, Federal-style row house at 103 Mercer Street is one of the few remaining antebellum brothels still standing in SoHo, and probably the oldest parlor house structure remaining in New York City.

13. Eno owned 69, 71, 73, and 91 Mercer Street, which were some of the most expensive houses in the neighborhood, as well as 82 Greene Street and 142 Church Street. See Record of Assessments, Eighth Ward, 1854, MARC, DeKock, *Guide to the Harems;* Free Loveyer, *Sergalios.* Eno's wealth was valued at $150,000 at midcentury. By the 1880s, he was a millionaire. See Beach, *Wealthy Citizens,* 12; *NPG,* 31 May 1884. For more on Eno's real estate, see Record of Assessments, Eighth Ward, 1852–60; Pre-1917 Conveyance Records for Block 485; Amos R. Eno Balance Sheet, 1 May 1869, and Executors Sale, 1899, p. 3, both in Amos R. Eno Papers, Columbia Univ. Other Eno property in the heart of the sex district included 21, 25, 47, 67, 69, 95, 100, 102, and 109 Mercer Street; 26, 47, 49, 53, 55, and 80 Greene Street; 17, 20, 75, 101, 103, 112, and 114 Laurens Street. When Miss [Mary?] Walls and other tenants failed to pay rent at 49 Greene Street, Eno demanded payment from the surety. See Eno to John Boardman, 21 June 1861; Eno to Jacob Tatus, Aug. 1861; Eno to C. Valhert, 18 Dec. 1860 and May, 1861; Eno to Jahn and Feidler, May, 186?, all in Eno Papers. On Eno's direct involvement with his real estate, see the correspondence from 1858 to 1876 in the Eno Papers. For a rare demand that brothel owners be held liable and punished, see *Globe,* 27 Jan. 1849, in Daly Papers, Scrapbook 21, p. 67.

14. New York Secretary of State, Census of New York for 1855 (Albany, 1857), 330–407; idem, *Census of New York for 1865* (Albany, 1867), 420–71, 521; William W. Sanger, *The History of Prostitution: Its Extent, Causes, and Effects throughout the World* (New York, 1859), 600–606.

For a comparison with the total value of exports from New York City in 1860, see Robert G. Albion, *The Rise of New York Port, 1815–1860* (New York, 1939), appendix 9. To compare antebellum monetary values with late-twentieth-century ones, see Edward Pessen, *Riches, Class, and Power before the Civil War* (Lexington, Mass., 1973), 12–20. $1.00 in 1830 was equal to approximately $6.50 in 1970. By 1990, inflation had doubled the 1970 figure. Most nineteenth-century monetary values should be multiplied by a factor of thirteen for present-day comparisons.

15. On the number of brothels, see Citizens' Association, *Sanitary Condition,* 26, 37, 59, 67, 81, 96, 137. Addresses in Butt Ender, *Prostitution Exposed, or A Moral Reform Directory* (New York, 1839), DeKock, *Guide to the Harems,* and Free Loveyer, *Seraglios,* were compared with indictments in DAP, 1830–69, and PCP, 1830–59.

16. Taylor was usually accompanied by a police officer or another judge in his visits. See Robert Taylor Diary, NYPL, 14 Feb., 4, 17 April, 30 July, 1, 16, 29 Aug., 2, 16 Sept., 17, 18, 20, 21, 22, 23 Nov., 6, 17 Dec. 1846, 6 Jan. 1847; Matthew Hale Smith, *Sunshine and Shadow in New York* (New York, 1867), 371–72; Ellington, *Women of New York,* 198.

17. DAP, People v. Beach, 22 Nov. 1850. For an example of prostitutes in museums, see PCP, Box 7954, Bushnell v. Sylvester, 11 Feb. 1856. On Barnum's, see *New York Sporting Whip,* 11 Feb. 1843, in DAP, 22 March 1843; *Flash,* 24 July 1842, in DAP, People v. Wooldridge, 10 Aug. 1842; Harrison Gray Buchanan, *Asmodeus; or, Legends of New York* (New York, 1848), 55.

18. John D. Vose, *Seven Nights in Gotham* (New York, 1852), 43–48; *Whip,* 19 Feb. 1842; Ned Buntline, *The Mysteries and Miseries of New York* (New York, 1848), 3:126;

19. On Wood's raids, see *Tribune,* 20 Oct. 1856; Charles Lockwood, *Manhattan Moves Uptown* (New York, 1976), 121; Foster, *New York by Gas-Light,* 12–16, 89; idem, *New York Naked* (New York, 1850), 145. For an example of stripteases in brothels, see *Times,* 21 June 1859.

20. Buchanan, *Asmodeus,* 50–52; Franklin Walker and G. Ezra Dane, eds., *Mark Twain's Travels with Mr. Brown* (New York, 1940), 84–85. On the popularity of tableaus with the middle class, see Karen Halttunen, *Confidence Men and Painted Women: A Study of Middle-Class Culture in America, 1830–1870* (New Haven, 1982), 184–85.

21. Kilroe, "Michael Norton," 259, 270–72; Nevins, *Diary of Strong,* 4:183, 191. On Thompson and early burlesque, see Van Every, *Sins of America,* 65–88.

22. For concert halls in the 1850s, see DAP, People v. Finnigan, 28 Nov. 1859; People v. Muhler, 21 Nov. 1857; J. Frank ("Florry") Kernan, *Reminiscences of the Old Fire Laddies* (New York, 1885), 204; Henderson, *Theater,* 73–74; McCabe, *Secrets,* 308; *NPG,* 8 Dec. 1866.

23. *New York Sporting Whip,* 4 Feb. 1843 ("success"); 25 Feb. 1843 ("musical drinking shops"); *Whip,* 12 Feb. 1842 (Brown); Kilroe, "Michael Norton," 3–4 (New American Theater, 444 Broadway), 179–83 ("nudist"). The precise origin of the concert saloon is disputed. Several contemporaries alleged that the first one appeared in the old Chinese Assembly Rooms, 539–41 Broadway (corner of Spring Street), in the 1850s under the name of Melodeon. Parker R. Zellors, "The Cradle of Variety; The Concert Saloon," *Educational Theatre Journal* 20 (1968): 578–86, believes that the first concert saloon was founded in the late 1840s by William Valentine. The first use of the term "concert saloon" I found was in *Whip,* 29 Jan. 1842. Earlier influences, however, can be traced to the 1830s with Niblo's Garden and Vauxhall Garden. The former, established by William Niblo in 1829 as a "house and garden of entertainment," offered an alternative to the theater. By 1840, Niblo's was the leading summer theater in the city catering to New York's growing antebellum elite. In 1838, John Jacob Astor's Vauxhall Garden copied the concept and added a saloon to the premises. Only the short step of moving the stage production, singing, alcohol, and relaxing atmosphere indoors was required to create the concert saloon. During these years, London pubs added small stages to their interiors for madrigals, glees, operatic arias, instrumental solos, and comic songs. In 1849, Charles Morton opened Canterbury Arms in Lambeth, one of London's first concert saloons. See Museum of the City of London, "From Cyder Cellars to the Canterbury" (Exhibition, 1984); Gareth Stedman Jones, *Languages of Class* (Cambridge, Eng., 1983), 204–5; *NPG,* 8 Feb. 1879; Ronald Pearsall, *The Worm in the Bud: The World of Victorian Sexuality* (Harmondsworth, Eng., 1969),

85–88, 464. On the use of the term "concert hall," see Charles Gayler, *Out of the Streets: A Story of New York Life* (New York, 1869), 10.

24. Smith, *Sunshine and Shadow*, 669–70. On antebellum performances, see Lawrence W. Levine, "William Shakespeare and the American People: A Study in Cultural Transformation," *AHR* 89 (1984): 40–60. For complaints about the poor quality of the antebellum theater, see Walt Whitman, "Miserable State of the Stage," in *American Theater as Seen by Its Critics, 1752–1934*, ed. Montrose J. Moses and John Mason Brown (New York, 1934), 70–72. On concert saloon attendance, see Metropolitan Police, *Annual Report* (New York, 1866), 19–20.
25. Vose, *Seven Nights*, 119 (Leonard Street); Foster, *New York by Gas-Light*, 96–99 (Hastings); Ellington, *Women of New York*, 191. On Mott, see Nevins, *Diary of Strong*, 1:170; and Allan Nevins, ed., *The Diary of Philip Hone, 1828–1851* (New York, 1927), 575. On French balls, see *Times*, 2 Jan. 1876. The *New York Sporting Whip* had a regular column entitled "Balls" in 1842 and 1843.
26. DeKock, *Guide to the Harems*, 4; *Gentleman's Companion;* Butt Ender, *Prostitution Exposed*. On European guidebooks, see Lawrence Stone, *The Family, Sex, and Marriage in England, 1500–1800* (New York, 1977), 539; Pearsall, *Worm in the Bud*, 323.
27. Butt Ender, *Prostitution Exposed;* Ray Allen Billington, *The Protestant Crusade, 1800–1860* (New York, 1938), 98–117; Carl Wittke, *The Irish in America* (Baton Rouge, 1956), 118. For anti-evangelical satires and anti-Catholic novels that were even more pornographic, see David Reynolds, *Beneath the American Renaissance: The Subversive Imagination in the Age of Emerson and Melville* (New York, 1988), 64–65, 87. By midcentury, most large U.S. cities had guides to brothels. For an example, see A *Guide to the Stranger; or, Pocket Companion for the Fancy, Containing a List of Gay Houses and Ladies of Pleasure in the City of Brotherly Love and Sisterly Affection* (Philadelphia, 1849), cited in Marcia Carlisle, "Prostitutes and Their Reformers in Nineteenth Century Philadelphia" (Ph.D. diss., Rutgers Univ., 1982), 51. European documents dating to the Middle Ages sometimes referred to brothels as "abbeys." See Leah Lydia Otis, *Prostitution in Medieval Society: The History of an Urban Institution in Languedoc* (Chicago, 1985), 88.
28. Stone, *Family, Sex, and Marriage*, 537–40, 621–22, 674; Pearsall, *Worm in the Bud*, 93. For those who believe that clerical and reformer accounts exaggerated this phenomenon during the century, see the explicit description in DAP, People v. Bonfanti, 9 June 1824.
29. DAP, People v. Wooldridge, 22 March 1843; Nevins, *Diary of Strong*, 4:474 (Dix); *Weekly Rake*, 26 Nov. 1842; *Libertine*, 15 June 1842; *New York Sporting Whip*, 11 Feb. 1843; Peter C. Welsh, "Henry R. Robinson: Printmaker to the Whig Party," *NYH* 53 (1972): 25–53. A "Henry R. Robinson" had previously been charged with and acquitted of assault and battery. See DAP, People v. Robinson, 13 May 1836. Most of the publications were printed outside New York and distributed to booksellers throughout the city for a percentage. An 1842 municipal crackdown on all dealers in obscene books indicate that much of New York's pornography was highly commercialized and sold in the city's major business district between Wall and Fulton streets. For a list of eight prosecuted vendors and the publications, see DAP, People v. Ryan, People v. Robinson, 28 Sept. 1842. For later examples, see DAP, People v. Childs, People v. Matthew ?, People v. Carnes, all 21 June 1844; People v. Shaw, July 1844; People v. Wilson, 19 May 1854. For the 1850s, see Sanger, *History of Prostitution*, 522.
30. Anthony Comstock to Judge Gunning S. Redford, 21 Feb. 1872, in DAP, People v. Simpson, 5 Dec. 1871. For more examples of pornography, see DAP, People v. Carnes, 21 June 1844; People v. Shaw, July 1844; People v. Gazeley, 22 Sept. 1853; People v. Atchenson, 23 Feb. 1855; People v. Crown et al., 12 March 1855; People v. Brady, 12 Feb. 1858; People v. O'Connor, 15 June 1869; People v. Gomperts, 12, 29 July 1869; PCP, Box 7955, Rice v. Gillern, 22 March 1856.
31. *Tribune*, 21 March 1846, supplement; Charles Dickens, *American Notes* (New York, 1972), 135–36; Nevins, *Diary of Strong*, 4:430; idem, *Diary of Hone*, 275. For later criticism, see ibid., 518, 667–68. A few years later, however, the *Tribune* was quite willing to describe daily the sexual shenanigans of the actor Edwin Forrest during his divorce trial. See *Herald, Report of the Forrest Divorce Case* (New York, 1852).

32. *Life in New York,* undated copy in AAS ("frolic"); *Libertine,* 15 June 1842 ("colors"). The names of these publications changed slightly on occasion. The *Whip* was also the *New York Sporting Whip,* the *Flash* was the *True Flash,* and the *Rake* was the *Weekly Rake.* Most of these editors were tried for libel or obscenity. See DAP, People v. Wooldridge, 14 July 1842; People v. Scott and Vandewater, 14 July 1842; People v. Meighan, 14 July 1842, 8 Aug. 1842. All were convicted or pleaded guilty. On the *NPG* and other journals, see Reynolds, *American Renaissance,* 173–77.
33. *Rake,* 3 Sept. 1842 ("mirror"); *Whip,* 25 Dec. 1841 ("whip"); *Rake,* 3 Sept. 1842 ("image"); *Whip,* 25 Dec. 1841; *Whip,* 9 July 1842, copy in DAP, People v. Wooldridge, 14 July 1842; *New York Sporting Whip,* 4, 18, 25 Feb. 1843; 4 March 1843 ("Fornication"). For other examples of this, see the same, 28 Jan. 1843; *Whip,* 25 Dec. 1841, 1 Jan. 1842. See also *New York Sporting Whip,* 11 Feb. 1843, copy in People v. Wooldridge, 22 March 1843.
34. *Weekly Rake,* 30 July 1842, 24 Sept. 1842, 1 Oct. 1842; *Weekly Rake,* 22 Oct. 1842; July 1842 (Restelle). On venereal disease, see especially *Weekly Rake,* ? July 1842; *Rake,* 28 Jan. 1843; *New York Sporting Whip,* 5 March 1843.
35. James C. Mohr, *Abortion in America: The Origins and Evolution of National Policy, 1800–1900* (New York, 1978); *Sun,* 1, 5 Sept. 1840; George Thompson, *The Countess; or, Memoirs of Women of Leisure* (Boston, 1849), 37–41. For criticism of abortion and Restelle, see *Times,* 3 Nov. 1870, 26 Jan. 1871, 3 Sept. 1871; *Whip,* 19 Feb. 1843; *Flash,* 30 Oct. 1841. Restelle was also represented by David Graham, Jr., in 1847, but was convicted and served a year in prison on Blackwell's Island. The *Weekly Rake* and the *New York Sporting Whip* regularly ran ads for abortionists.
36. *Times,* 3 Nov. 1870, 30 Jan. 1873; DAP, People v. Evans, 7 March 1871. Ann Burns may have once been the proprietor of a house of prostitution at 32 Walnut Street in Corlears Hook. Mary Ann Burns was convicted of running such an establishment in 1842. See DAP, People v. Burns, 22 Feb. 1842. For an attack on newspapers advertising abortionists, see Nevins, *Diary of Strong,* 4:382. For an example of an abortion in a brothel, see Robert Taylor Diary, 14 Feb. 1846.
37. Nevins, *Diary of Strong,* 4:262. For more on the preventive society, see Timothy J. Gilfoyle, "The Moral Origins of Political Surveillance: The Preventive Society in New York City, 1867–1918," *AQ* (1986): 637–52.
38. *Whip,* 29 Jan. 1842; PCP, Box 7453, Atkinson v. Adams, 7 April 1839. In his examination of the District Attorney Indictment Papers before 1860, Michael Lynch found only twenty-two cases of sodomy. See Lynch, "Sodomy, Whitman, and Phrenology" (Paper delivered at New York Univ., 1 Feb. 1985). Historians still debate whether Whitman engaged in homosexuality. He never said so directly, but wrote frequently about male friends and acquaintances in his notebooks. See Paul Zweig, *Walt Whitman: The Making of the Poet* (New York, 1984), 141, 165, 187–89.
39. *Whip,* 29 Jan. 1842; 5 Feb. 1842 (Palmo); 12 Feb. 1842 ("unhallowed"); *Weekly Rake,* 1 Oct. 1842 ("enormities"), 30 July 1842. For other examples, see *Whip,* 26 Feb. 1842, 5 March 1842. For an example of a prosecution for homosexuality, see Jonathan Katz, *Gay American History* (New York, 1976), 45–51.
40. George Thompson, *City Crimes; or, Life in New York and Boston* (Boston, 1849), 138–40.
41. DAP, People v. Sewally, 16 June 1836. Sewally used the aliases Mary Jones and Eliza Smith. He was sentenced to three years in the state prison. See *Herald,* 17, 20 June 1836; *Sun,* 17 June 1836. An illustration of Sewally is in the Crime Folder, Prints Division, NYHS.
42. There is limited and fragmentary evidence that, in some brothels, young boys were available for homosexual clients. Several district attorney indictments accused madams of "harboring" young boys. In cases where the youths were there by force, the charge was usually described as "abduction." For harboring examples, see DAP, People v. Underwood, 12 Aug. 1812; People v. Hassan, 7 March 1816; People v. Pessinger, 12 July 1817. For abduction examples, see DAP, People v. James, 15 Sept. 1840; People v. Hermans, 3 May 1861; People v. Hammill, 16 Sept. 1861; People v. Monaise, 5 Aug. 1863; People v. Purpell, 14 May 1868; People v. Fisher, 11 Nov. 1874; PCP, Hines v. Blanchard, 19 Sept. 1836. If the language was carefully

and consistently employed, this difference could represent the existence of male homosexual prostitution, but such a conclusion can only be tentative. I am indebted to a discussion with Michael Lynch on this issue. For unelaborated references to "male prostitutes" in brothels, see *NPG*, 12 June 1847 (at 5 Manhattan Place), 2 March 1867 (at 23 Greene Street); DAP, People v. Wooldridge, 22 March 1843 (on the Bowery). The term "male prostitute" was ambiguous and sometimes synonymous with "sporting men" during the antebellum years. The word "homosexuality" was coined by Richard von Krafft-Ebing in 1869 and entered the English language only in the 1880s, through the work of Havelock Ellis. See Jeffrey Weeks, "Movements of Affirmation: Sexual Meanings and Homosexual Identities," in *Passion and Power: Sexuality in History,* ed. Kathy Peiss and Christina Simmons (Philadelphia, 1989), 70–71; Richard von Krafft-Ebing, *Psychopathia Sexualis, with Especial Reference to Antipathic Sexual Instinct,* trans. F. J. Rebman (Brooklyn, 1908).

43. George A. Chauncey, Jr., "Gay New York: Urban Culture and the Making of a Gay Male World, 1890–1940" (Ph.D. diss., Yale Univ., 1989), 20–58; on male and female prostitutes in the same areas and institutions, see 75–81; on the bachelor subculture tolerating fairies, see 87–88. Sporting men in New York mirrored eighteenth-century London in condemning effeminate homosexuality. Even "rakes" were less likely to have sex with other males after 1700. The adoption of the *Rake* as a titlehead for one sporting newpaper may have reflected similar attitudes a century later. See Randolph Trumbach, "The Birth of the Queen: Sodomy and the Emergence of Gender Equality in Modern Culture, 1660–1750," in *Hidden from History: Reclaiming the Gay and Lesbian Past,* ed. Martin Bauml Duberman et al. (New York, 1989), 129–40.
44. *Tribune,* 14 March 1844; *NPG,* 17 April 1847; Buntline, *Mysteries and Miseries,* 5:89.
45. CAS, *Seventh Annual Report* (New York, 1860), 6.
46. *Herald,* 12 Jan. 1849; *NPG,* 20 Jan. 1849; Buntline, *Mysteries and Miseries,* 5:90. On Boyd, see *McDowall's Journal,* Feb. 1835; James Ford, *Slums and Housing* (Cambridge, Mass., 1936), 95. After receiving a harsh sentence from Daly for his role in the Astor Place riot, Buntline reversed his position. See Buntline, *B'hoys,* 86–87; *Tribune, Globe, Ned Buntline's Own,* and *Fireman's Own* in Daly Papers, Scrapbook 21, pp. 66–71.
47. Whitman, "On Vice," 7.
48. Sanger, *History of Prostitution,* 19–20, 504–20, 629.
49. Citizens' Association, *Sanitary Condition,* 83, 106, 138; *Nation,* 21 Feb. 1867.
50. Crapsey, *Nether Side,* 145; *Nation,* 21 Feb. 1867. On the grand jury, see *Times,* 3 June 1876. On Folger and Park, see David J. Pivar, *Purity Crusade: Sexual Morality and Social Control, 1868–1900* (Westport, Conn., 1973), 51–62. The *National Police Gazette* recommended the registration and weekly inspection of prostitutes by the municipality, arguing that this would force public prostitutes to report houses of assignation in order to eliminate the competition. See *NPG,* 16 Feb. 1867.
51. Whitman, *Leaves of Grass,* in *Complete Writings,* 1:160.

Chapter 7 A "Gay" Literature

1. These quotations are from Asmodeus, *Sharps and Flats, or, The Perils of City Life* (Boston, 1850), 11–12, 49–52, 68.
2. George Thompson, *The Countess; or, Memoirs of Women of Leisure* (Boston, 1849), 37–39. On Restelle, see James C. Mohr, *Abortion in America: The Origins and Evolution of National Policy, 1800–1900* (New York, 1978), 48–53, 89–97, 125–28; Junius Henri Browne, *The Great Metropolis: A Mirror of New York* (Hartford, 1869), 582–87. Winslow and Hastings were described in *Whip,* 12, 19 March 1842; 23 April 1842 ("attention of all"). Jane (or Kate) Winslow was listed at 73 Mercer Street in Charles DeKock, *Guide to the Harems; or, Directory to the Ladies of Fashion in New York and Various Other Cities* (New York, 1855); the 1855 New York State Manuscript Census for New York City, Ward 8, Election District 1, no. 122. Hastings was listed at 50 Leonard Street in Record of Assessments, Fifth Ward, 1853 and 1854, MARC;

119 Mercer Street in DeKock, *Guide to the Harems;* Free Loveyer, *Directory to the Seraglios in New York, Philadelphia, Boston, and All the Principal Cities in the Union* (New York, 1859). Two Catharine Hastings were listed in the 1860 Federal Manuscript Census Schedules for New York City, Ward 7, Election District 3, no. 299, and Ward 6, Election District 2, no. 928. On Norman, see People v. Norman, 23 Nov. 1843, DAP. On Hastings attacking Buntline, see Peter G. Buckley, "The Case against Ned Buntline: The 'Words, Signs, and Gestures' of Popular Authorship," *Prospects* 13 (1988): 249–72.

3. On Foster, compare his *New York by Gas-Light, with Here and There a Streak of Sunshine* (New York, 1850), 32–36, with his *Celio: or, New York Above-Ground and Under-Ground* (New York, 1850), 35–39. On Buchanan, see *Asmodeus; or, Legends of New York* (New York, 1848), 31–35, 40, 92–94. Williams lived at 148 Leonard Street (1839), 22 Manhattan Place and 133 Reade Street (1842), and 72 Duane Street (1855). See People v. Ford, 28 Sept. 1842; People v. Mott, 20 Oct. 1842, both in DAP; DeKock, *Guide to the Harems;* 1855 New York State Manuscript Census for New York City, Ward 6, Election District 1, no. 125; 1860 Federal Manuscript Census Schedules for New York City, Ward 5, Election District 2, no. 676; *Whip,* 25 June 1842, 26 March 1842, 11 June 1842; *True Flash,* 4 Dec. 1841; *Weekly Rake,* 9 July 1842, 22 Oct. 1842; *Rake,* 1 Oct. 1842. Frances Okille was listed as the owner / occupant of 55 Leonard Street (valued at $12,000) in Record of Assessments, Fifth Ward, 1847–55, MARC. For documentation on Brown, see chapter 3. Annie Clark ran 43 Wooster Street from at least 1855 to 1859 and remained a leading madam after the Civil War at 68 West Houston Street in 1870 and 121 Elm Street in 1874. See DeKock, *Guide to the Harems;* Free Loveyer, *Seraglios;* Anonymous, *The Gentleman's Companion: New York City in 1870* (New York, 1870); People v. Clark, 19 Nov. 1874, DAP. On Livingston, see Vose, *Fresh Leaves from the Diary of a Broadway Dandy* (New York, 1852), 14; DeKock, *Guide to the Harems; Gentleman's Companion.*
4. Anonymous, *Revelations of Asmodeus; or, Mysteries of Upper Ten-Dom* (New York, 1849), 3; Thompson, *Countess,* 7–8; idem, *City Crimes; or, Life in New York and Boston* (Boston, 1849), 7–23; Buntline, *The Mysteries and Miseries of New York: A Story of Real Life* (New York, 1848), 5; Foster, *Celio,* 4. For another Foster claim of objectivity, see *New York by Gas-Light,* 5, 25.
5. David Reynolds, *Beneath the American Renaissance: The Subversive Imagination in the Age of Emerson and Melville* (New York, 1988), 55–58, 63–64, 351–52. For an insightful analysis of nineteenth-century popular culture and the commercialization of literature, see Michael Denning, *Mechanic Accents: Dime Novels and Working-Class Culture in America* (London, 1987). For similar themes on the prostitute in French literature, see Peter Brooks, *Reading for the Plot: Design and Intention in Narrative* (New York, 1984), 143–70.
6. Lambert A. Wilmer, *The Confessions of Emilia Harrington* (Baltimore, 1835), preface. On McDowall, see Carroll Smith-Rosenberg, "Beauty, the Beast, and the Militant Woman: A Case Study in Sex Roles and Social Stress in Jacksonian America," *AQ* 23 (1971): 562–84.
7. People v. Henry R. Robinson et al., 28 Sept. 1842, DAP. Robinson pleaded guilty to the charge. Also see Peter C. Welsh, "Henry R. Robinson: Printmaker to the Whig Party," *NYH* 53 (1972): 25–53. I am indebted to Georgia B. Barnhill of the American Antiquarian Society for information on Robinson.
8. Butt Ender, *Prostitution Exposed; or, A Moral Reform Directory* (New York, 1839); DeKock, *Guide to the Harems; Gentleman's Companion;* Anonymous, *The Gentleman's Directory* (New York, 1870).
9. Buntline, *Mysteries and Miseries;* idem, *Three Years After: A Sequel to the Mysteries and Miseries of New York* (New York, 1849); idem, *The B'hoys of New York: A Sequel to the Mysteries and Miseries of New York* (New York, 1850); idem, *The G'hals of New York: A Novel* (New York, 1850). For a recent examination of Buntline, see Buckley, "Case against Ned Buntline," 249–72.
10. *Three Years After,* 23 ("unwhipped villains"), 68 ("slaves"), 6 ("gayest moments"), 66–67 ("death"), 7 ("wretched").
11. Buntline, *G'hals,* 35, 96–105; idem, *Mysteries and Miseries,* 103; Thompson, *City Crimes,* 4–23; idem, *The Gay Girls of New York; or, Life on Broadway* (New York, 1854), 73; idem, *The Mysteries of Bond Street,* 35, quoted in Reynolds, *American Renaissance.*

12. Marie Louise Hankins, *Women of New York* (New York, 1861), 234–40; Buntline, *Mysteries and Miseries,* 4:103; 5:78–81 ("tired"); idem, *Three Years After,* 5–7; Eleanor Maria Ames, *Up Broadway, and Its Sequel: A Life Story by Eleanor Kirk* (New York, 1870); Thompson, *Gay Girls,* 11–12; John D. Vose, *Seven Nights in Gotham* (New York, 1852), 112. For other examples, see the characters of Anna in Foster, *New York by Gas-Light,* 29–33; Mary in Buntline, *G'hals of New York,* 146–48; the prostitutes in Buntline, *B'hoys of New York,* 64; Kate Brinley in Asmodeus, *Sharps and Flats,* 11–14, 70–75; Edith in Henry L. Williams, *Gay Life in New York! or, Fast Men and Grass Widows* (New York, 1866), 56–63. On the widespread popularity of this theme, see Adrienne Siegel, *The Image of the American City in Popular Fiction 1820–1870* (Port Washington, N.Y., 1981), 36–46. For a nonfiction critique of the double standard, see Browne, *Great Metropolis.*
13. Buntline, *Three Years After;* idem, *B'hoys of New York,* 186–87; Williams, *Gay Life in New-York,* 54–60.
14. *Celio,* 36. On Foster's importance, see Stuart M. Blumin, "Explaining the Metropolis: Perception, Depiction, and Analysis in Mid-Nineteenth-Century New York City," *JUH* 11 (1984): 9–38; Foster, *New York by Gas-Light,* ed. Stuart M. Blumin (Berkeley, Calif., 1990), introd. *Gas-Light* sold over 200,000 copies.
15. Foster, *Celio,* 35–36; idem, *New York Naked,* 154; *New York by Gas-Light,* 62. Also see Buchanan, *Asmodeus,* 25; Anonymous, *Revelations of Asmodeus,* 44; Williams, *Gay Life in New-York,* 61, 96. For similar images in another city, see George Lippard, *The Quaker City* (Philadelphia, 1845), 91. *The Quaker City* was the most popular American novel before Harriet Beecher Stowe's *Uncle Tom's Cabin.* See Reynolds, *American Renaissance,* 207.
16. Foster, *Celio,* 35–36.
17. Foster, *New York by Gas-Light,* 6–7; idem, *New York in Slices, by an Experienced Carver* (New York, 1849), 92, 96; Buntline, *Mysteries and Miseries,* 46–50; idem, *B'hoys,* 36; *Magdelena, the Outcast; or, The Millionaire's Daughter—A Story of Life in the Empire City* (New York, 1866). Also see the character of Kate Brinley in Asmodeus, *Sharps and Flats,* 11–14.
18. Osgood Bradbury, *Ellen Grant: or, Fashionable Life in New York* (New York, 185?); idem, *Ellen: The Pride of Broadway* (New York, 1865), 100; idem, *Female Depravity; or, The House of Death* (New York, 1857), 8–10, 20–22, 30–33, 36, 45. Eventually, Henderson and Hopkins reform, marry each other, and live happily ever after. Warnings about panel houses and the prostitutes were constantly mentioned in nonfiction accounts of New York. See Edward Crapsey, *The Nether Side of New York* (New York, 1872), 139–40; James D. McCabe, Jr., *The Secrets of the Great City* (Philadelphia, 1868), 107, 306–7; Matthew Hale Smith, *Sunshine and Shadow in New York* (Hartford, 1868), 306; George Ellington, *Women of New York; or, The Under-World of the Great City* (Burlington, Iowa, 1869), 203–4.
19. Joseph Holt Ingraham, *Frank Rivers; or, The Dangers of the Town* (New York, 1843); Anonymous, *Revelations of Asmodeus,* 10; Thompson, *Gay Girls,* 13. For nonfictional examples, see "the procuresses" Mary West and Louisa Acker in *New York Sporting Whip,* 4, 18 Feb. 1843.
20. Thompson, *Countess,* 13–16.
21. Ibid., 21.
22. Ibid., 8, 13, 37, 59–62.
23. Thompson, *Gay Girls,* 15–19.
24. Ibid., 72.
25. Ibid., 11.
26. Brooks, *Reading for the Plot,* 158–68.
27. Buntline, *Mysteries and Miseries,* 33–36; Foster, *Celio,* 15–16. Also see Thompson, *City Crimes,* 57–146; Reynolds, *American Renaissance;* Denning, *Mechanic Accents.*
28. Frank Greenwood, "Prostitution," *Life in New York* 1 (5 Oct. 1850); CAS, *Annual Reports* (New York, 1854–70); Five Points House of Industry, *Monthly Reports,* May 1858–April 1861; McCabe, *Secrets,* 286; Ellington, *Women of New York,* 172–73; Browne, *Great Metropolis,* 440, 536–41; William W. Sanger, *The History of Prostitution: Its Extent, Causes, and Effects throughout the World* (New York, 1859), 455–56.

29. McCabe, *Secrets,* 286–87, 296, 317; Ellington, *Women of New York,* 165–67, 190–92, 201–2, 235–37, 239–41.
30. Thompson, *Venus in Boston,* frontispiece; idem, *Gay Girls,* 10, 57; idem, *Countess,* frontispiece; Charles Lockwood, *Manhattan Moves Uptown* (Boston, 1976); Ellington, *Women of New York,* 184, 198, 244. For more on fashion and antebellum culture, see Karen Halttunen, *Confidence Men and Painted Women: A Study of Middle-Class Culture in America, 1830–1870* (New Haven, 1982), 33–123; James Thomas Flexner, *Nineteenth-Century American Painting* (New York, 1970).
31. Thompson, *Gay Girls,* 23; Anonymous, *Revelations of Asmodeus,* 38 ("gayer" and "gayeties"); Ellington, *Women of New York,* 241–42 ("gay world" and "gayety"); Williams, *Gay Life in New-York,* 8 ("vortex"); Anonymous, *Mysteries of New York* (Boston, 1845), 46–47 ("house of resort"); *Weekly Rake,* 12 Nov. 1842 ("gay seducers"); *New York Sporting Whip,* 11 Feb. 1843 ("gay sight"); *Whip,* 5 March 1842 ("gay nymphs"); 1 and 15 Jan. 1842 *("figurantes"); True Flash,* 4 Dec. 1841 ("gay sisters"); Sanger, *History of Prostitution.* For other uses of the term in connection with prostitution, "vice," or seduction, see James D. McCabe, Jr., *New York by Sunlight and Gaslight* (Philadelphia, 1882), 644; Charles Loring Brace, *The Dangerous Classes of New York, and Twenty Years' Work among Them* (New York, 1872), 118, 122; Asmodeus, *Sharps and Flats,* 67–68; Greenwood, "Prostitution." For Whitman's "Ode to a Common Prostitute," in *Leaves of Grass,* see *The Complete Writings of Walt Whitman* (New York, 1902), 1:161.

Chapter 8 "Bawdy Houses"

1. Timothy J. Gilfoyle, "The Moral Origins of Political Surveillance: The Preventive Society in New York City, 1867–1918," *AQ* 38 (1986): 637–52; Walter Kendrick, *The Secret Museum: Pornography in Modern Culture* (New York, 1987), 133–40; Paul S. Boyer, *Purity in Print: The Vice-Society Movement and Book Censorship in America* (New York, 1968), 1–35; Anthony Comstock, *Traps for the Young,* ed. Robert H. Bremner (Cambridge, Mass, 1967), introd.
2. DAP, People v. Richmond, 2 July 1878.
3. DAP, People v. DeForest, 2 July 1878. Also see Society for the Suppression of Vice Papers, Arrest Blotters, vol. 1, p. 120, Library of Congress.
4. Robert Taylor Diary, 14 Feb. 1846, 17 April 1846, 17, 18, 20, 21, 22, 23 Nov. 1846; 5, 6, 17 Dec. 1846; 6 Jan. 1847, NYPL; Allan Nevins and Milton Halsey Thomas, eds., *The Diary of George Templeton Strong* (New York, 1952), 1:114, 133, 170; 2:270; George Wilkes, *The Lives of Helen Jewett and Richard Robinson* (New York, 1849), 73, 124–26; *New York Sporting Whip,* 11 Feb. 1843, copy in People v. Wooldridge, 22 March 1843, DAP.
5. *Tribune,* 21 March 1846, supplement; Matthew Hale Smith, *Sunshine and Shadow in New York* (New York, 1867), 426.
6. Kym S. Rice, *Early American Taverns* (Chicago, 1983), 21, 31, 33–34, 103. Even the limited numbers of brothels functioned as liquor establishments during these years. When seven women were arrested for operating a string of illicit houses on James Street in 1811, their listed occupation was "innkeeper." See DAP, People v. Fitzpatrick, 11 Sept. 1812; People v. Rathbone et al., 15 Feb. 1811. City authorities before 1820 were lax in specifically identifying the type of prostitution in their records. Of 182 charges of prostitution from 1790 to 1809, only 42 were institutionally identifiable. From 1810 to 1819, 89 of 245 charges could be linked to a specific type of institution. For the former, 32 (76 percent) were inns, saloons, or taverns (27 along the East River dockfront); for the latter, 58 (65 percent) (48 along the East River dockfront). Since most of the prostitution was found in the East Dock area, a locale known for its grogshops and liquor stores, it is likely that this was a representative sampling.
7. *McDowall's Journal,* May, Oct. 1833; Butt Ender, *Prostitution Exposed; or, A Moral Reform Directory* (New York, 1839); Carroll Smith-Rosenberg, "Beauty, the Beast, and the Militant Woman," *AQ* 23 (1971): 562–84. The earliest use of the term "house of assignation" was in DAP, Cases for 3 July 1821.
8. Charles DeKock, *Guide to the Harems; or, Directory to the Ladies of Fashion in New York and*

Various Other Cities (New York, 1855); Free Loveyer, *Directory to the Seraglios in New York, Philadelphia, Boston, and All the Principal Cities in the Union* (New York, 1859). In Butt Ender, *Prostitution Exposed*, only six of the fifty-nine houses described in detail had over six resident prostitutes. On "public" and "private" brothels, see Ned Buntline, *The G'hals of New York* (New York, 1850), 201–2. For more on the emergence of elite brothels in the 1830s, see Patricia Cline Cohen, "Unregulated Youth: Masculinity and Murder in the 1830s City" (Paper delivered at the Annual Meeting of the Organization of American Historians, Louisville, 12 April 1991); and Cohen's forthcoming book on the Helen Jewett murder. On male wages, see Sean Wilentz, *Chants Democratic: New York and the Rise of the American Working Class, 1788–1850* (New York, 1984), 50–51, 117; Bruce Laurie, *Working People of Philadelphia, 1800–1850* (Philadelphia, 1980), 12.

9. On crowds of men outside brothels, see *Advocate of Moral Reform*, 15 Jan. 1837. For other examples of prostitutes accommodating clients in shorter than fifteen-minute intervals, see *McDowall's Journal*, 1 May 1833; Committee Report to the Humane Society, John Jay Papers, Reel 3; NYHS; *MCC*, 7:72–73 (18 March 1812); DAP, People v. Martin, 13 June 1825; Reports for 208–228 West 40th Street, Box 91, LWP: McCullough to Hewitt, 25 July 1888, MP 87-HAS-35; Cases of Delia Minsey and French Viola, Undated Reports on 144 West 32d Street; Undated Report on National Hotel, 3 Irving Place, all Box 91, LWP; Report of J. W. Brewster and Abel Whitehouse (on Flagelle's), 25 May 1905, Box 28, C14P. The first indictment to charge proprietors with operating a "bawdy house" was People v. Taff, 6 Feb. 1800, DAP.
10. Harrison Gray Buchanan, *Asmodeus: or, The Legends of New York* (New York, 1848), 35 (Pinteaux); DeKock, *Guide to the Harems;* Free Loveyer, *Seraglios; Whip*, 5 March 1842 ("ropes"); *Weekly Rake*, 9 July 1842 (Philadelphia). Also see *New York Sporting Whip*, 5 March 1843.
11. *Journal of Public Morals*, 7 March 1833; Walt Whitman, *New York Dissected*, ed. Emory Holloway and Ralph Adimari (New York, 1936), 94–96; Junius Henri Browne, *The Great Metropolis: A Mirror of Gotham* (Hartford, 1869), 548; Thomas Butler Gunn, *The Physiology of New York Boarding Houses* (New York, 1857), vii–x, 15–20, 65, 76–85, 96, 140, 152, 243. By the mid-1830s, there was a great rise in house rents in New York City. Any residence within two miles of Wall Street reportedly charged a minimum of $600 per year, and many went as high as $1,200. See *Niles' Register*, 11 Feb. 1837. At least fifty boardinghouses were in business in 1790 and triple that number by 1800. See Elizabeth Blackmar, "Re-walking the 'Walking City': Housing and Property Relations in New York City, 1780–1840," *RHR* 21 (1979): 140; idem, *Manhattan for Rent, 1785–1850* (Ithaca, N.Y., 1989), chap. 2–3; Mark Peel, "On the Margin: Lodgers and Boarders in Boston, 1860–1900," *JAH* 72 (1986): 813–34.
12. For an example, see DAP, People v. Swartz, 12 July 1850. On the difficulty of rent collection and the emergence of sublandlords and collecting agents, see Blackmar, *Manhattan for Rent*, chap. 7.
13. *Journal of Public Morals*, 7 March 1833.
14. The distribution of the various types of houses of prostitution was as follows (in percentages):

	1820–1829	*1830–1839*	*1840–1849*	*1850–1859*
Total Number	100	193	100	241
Brothels	69	64	43	57
Houses of Assignation	1	13	3	16
Saloons or Groceries	24	20	40	24
Panel Houses	0	0	14	1
Dance Halls	6	2	0	2

Brothels included boardinghouses, parlor houses, and tenements. For sources, see chapter 2, note 6. The proprietors of the houses of prostitution were compared and traced in *Wilson's Business Directory of New York City* (New York, 1855); New York State Census of 1855, Manuscript Schedules for New York County, Fifth Ward, First Election District, nos., 85, 87, 88, 108, 115, 175. For examples of brothels being listed as "boarding houses," see New York State Census of 1870, Manuscript Schedules for New York County, Eighth Ward, Second Election District, nos. 41, 43, 89; Third Election District, nos. 23, 28, 36, 37, 40, 41, 49, 50, 55. According to the 1855 census, at least four reputed houses of assignation accommodated prostitutes. Three of the houses had only one or two prostitutes, but Susan Palmer's had six. See New York State Census of 1855, manuscript schedules for New York County, Eighth Ward, First Election District, nos. 166, 194, 282, 297; Sixth Ward, First Election District, no. 101. For specific names and addresses, see DeKock, *Guide to the Harems,* and *The Gentleman's Companion: New York City in 1870* (New York, 1870). On the early development of row houses, see Gwendolyn Wright, *Building the Dream: A Social History of Housing in America* (New York, 1984), 24–40. The sources, in particular the District Attorney Indictment Papers, were sometimes unclear in describing the institutional form of prostitution. "Disorderly houses" that were not brothels had "whorring," "bawdy house," and "prostitution" crossed out or not mentioned in the indictment. These indictments usually involved saloons, gambling dens, or charges of fighting and quarreling. The percentage of unidentifiable institutions of prostitution was 60 percent in 1820–29, 29 percent in 1830–39, 52 percent in, 1840–49, and 27 percent in 1850–59. Most of the unidentified addresses were in Five Points and on the West Side, areas with much boardinghouse, parlor house, and tenement prostitution. In addition, some houses may have been termed "boarding houses" but provided no services, such as board, that would have distinguished them from a lodging or a tenement house. On the changing institutional structure of prostitution from 1870 to 1919, see note 2, chapter 11.

15. *McDowall's Journal,* 1 May 1833. For example, see PCP, Box 7447, Foot v. Marshal, 7 July 1835; Box 7954, Carpenter v. Simonson, 4 March 1856; Growlich v. Markle, 5 Aug. 1856; *NPG,* 18 July 1846.
16. On Valentine, see *Longworth's Directory* (New York, 1820–1827); Record of Assessments, Sixth Ward, 1826, 1827. Valentine was the owner / occupant at 85, 89, 91, 96, and 98 Cross Street. On Gillespie, see Record of Assessments, Sixth Ward, 1820–33; Pre-1917 Conveyance Liber 267, p. 201, 7 Dec. 1830. One year Gillespie lived at 150 Anthony Street, a property owned by James Ridgeway. In 1826, he leased John R. Livingston's house at 143 Anthony Street. In 1828, he was located at 130 Anthony Street. Finally, in 1833, Gillespie was listed in the assessment records at 130, 132, and 161 Anthony Street.
17. DAP, People v. Godeon, 11 April 1828, 13 Jan. 1829; People v. Jenkins et al., 16 April 1830; People v. Swartz, 12 July 1850, 21 May 1851; People v. Thompson, 25 Nov. 1840. Parker was known to control 247 and 308 Water Street before his murder in 1853. See *NPG,* 19 June 1847; DAP, 23 Sept. 1853.
18. The shoe shop was on West Tenth Street, near Sixth Avenue, the saloons at 41 Thompson Street and Bank Street, and the brothel at 18 Greene Street. See DAP, People v. Wellerdick, 23 March 1875.
19. *New York Sporting Whip,* 11 Feb. 1843, copy in DAP, People v. Wooldridge, 22 March 1843. For examples of residents complaining about prostitutes in their dwelling house, see PCP, Box 7447, Driscoll v. Shaw, 7 Aug. 1835; Box 7438, Lewis v. Donnelly, 26 Aug. 1824; Box 7439, Greaton v. Wilet, 6 July 1827; DAP, People v. Ross, 7 March 1861.
20. William W. Sanger, *The History of Prostitution: Its Extent, Causes, and Effects throughout the World* (New York, 1859), 553–54, DAP, People v. Williams, 13 April 1843; People v. Shannon, 19 April 1836; People v. Ridgeway, 14 Sept. 1839; People v. Brown, 25 May 1842; *McDowall's Journal,* May, 1834; *Times,* 7 Aug. 1855. Ridgeway's furniture was valued at $2,300. Jane Williams's weekly payments to him were about $42. Brown's furniture was insured by the Jefferson Insurance Company. Landlords charged $300 annually for basement rooms on Water Street. See Handwritten Report of E. G. Gerry, Statistics on Immorality and Crime in the Fourth Ward, Aug. 1853, CAS Records, CAS, New York City. On leased furniture, see *Whip,* 5 and 19 Feb. 1842, 16 April 1843.
21. On Miller, see *New York Sporting Whip,* 18 Feb. 1843. On Fairchild, see People v. Fairchild, 11 March 1861, DAP. For other examples, see DAP, People v. Timple, 8 April 1805; People

v. Ward, 13 Dec. 1817; People v. Blanchard, 15 Oct. 1829; People v. Sturges, 11 June 1821; People v. Bourne, 11 May 1829; People v. Barnes, 13 June 1845; People v. Weaver, 14 Sept. 1843; People v. Woods, 12 Aug. 1843; PCP, Box 7448, Bennet v. Pearce, 9 Nov. 1835. For examples after 1840, see DAP, People v. Weaver, 14 Sept. 1843; People v. Woods, 12 Aug. 1843; People v. Brown, 17 Dec. 1850. Philadelphia brothel keepers charged prostitutes three to four dollars plus half the "bed money." See Marcia Carlisle, "Prostitutes and Their Reformers in Nineteenth Century Philadelphia" (Ph.D. diss., Rutgers Univ., 1982), 104.

22. Citizens' Association of New York, *Sanitary Condition of the City: Report of the Council of Hygiene and Public Health* (New York, 1866), 37; DAP, People v. Strong, 9 Oct. 1843; People v. Bodell, 8 March 1847; People v. Malone, 26 Oct. 1850; PCP, Box 7437, Haviland v. Jones, 25 Aug. 1823; Box 7436, Speed v. Whitehead, 22 Nov. 1821. For other examples, see 108 Chapel Street, PCP, Box 7446, Popham v. Lincoln, 21 Dec. 1833.

23. See the cases cited in note 20 above. William Sanger found annual receipts over $26,000. See Sanger, *History of Prostitution,* 553–54. On workers' incomes, see Wilentz, *Chants Democratic,* 117; Laurie, *Working People,* 12.

24. New York State Census of 1855, Manuscript Schedules for New York County, Fifth Ward, First Election District, nos. 85, 87, 88, 92, 108; DAP, People v. Fairchild, 11 March 1861; James D. McCabe, Jr., *The Secrets of the Great City* (Philadelphia, 1868), 285–89; George Ellington, *The Women of New York; or, The Under-World of the Great City* (Burlington, Iowa, 1869), 198–206; *NPG,* 28 Dec. 1867. Adams and Brown were frequently mentioned in the *Whip,* and the *New York Sporting Whip* from 1841 to 1843. Dr. William Sanger concluded that a four-part hierarchy of brothels based primarily on cost, from rich to poor, existed. While some division was likely, it was not explicit in any sources I examined. See Sanger, *History of Prostitution,* 549–74, 600. On the number of women, see George J. Kneeland, *Commercialized Prostitution in New York City* (New York, 1917), 109. Most madams supervised five to twenty women and charged them one to three dollars for the weekly examination. In 1912, Kneeland found the following number of parlor houses: 20 charging clients fifty cents; 80, one dollar; 6, two dollars; 34, five to ten dollars; and 2, unknown. See his *Commercialized Prostitution,* 4.

25. DAP, People v. Thompson, 25 Nov. 1840; *NPG,* 28 Dec. 1867; Walt Whitman, "On Vice," in *The Uncollected Poetry and Prose of Walt Whitman,* ed. Emory Holloway (Garden City, N.Y., 1921), 1:6; PCP, Box 7438, Ross v. Baker, 12 July 1825; Samuel Prime, *Life in New York* (New York, 1847), 165. One Irish fraternal society thought the problem real enough to try to provide protection for female Irish immigrants arriving at Castle Garden, but it failed to raise sufficient funds for the task. See Hasia R. Diner, *Erin's Daughters in America: Irish Immigrant Women in the Nineteenth Century* (Baltimore, 1983), 122. For an example of fighting between rival houses of ill fame in Cherry and Water streets, see *Sun,* 3 Feb. 1834.

26. *NPG,* 17 July 1880 (window ads); *Whip,* 29 Jan. 1842 ("Cotillion"), 8, 15 Jan. 1842 *("figurantes"),* 12 Jan. 1842 ("dance houses"); Nevins, *Diary of Strong,* 1:170 (Mott). For another comment on the Mott ball, see Allan Nevins, ed., *The Diary of Philip Hone, 1828–1851* (New York, 1969), 575. For lists of balls and their patrons and participants, see *Whip,* Jan.–March 1842; *New York Sporting Whip,* 4, 18 Feb. 1843.

27. Kenneth Roberts and Anna M. Roberts, eds., *Moreau de St. Méry's American Journey, 1793–1798* (Garden City, N.Y., 1947), 313–14; Edward Crapsey, *The Nether Side of New York* (New York, 1872), 143; *McDowall's Journal,* May 1833; Smith, *Sunshine and Shadow,* 431; McCabe's *Secrets,* 300–301. Most houses of assignation charged one to two dollars per day or night; a good hotel would cost one to three dollars for the same. See Francis J. Grund, *The Americans in Their Moral, Social, and Political Relations* (Boston, 1837), 327.

28. *McDowall's Journal,* May 1833; Crapsey, *Nether Side,* 143; DAP, People v. Fowler, 11 Dec. 1848. The practice of "sitting in company" grew more prevalent after 1870. This is the only earlier reference I found. Most houses of assignation charged fifty cents per hour or one dollar per night. The number of couples is based on McDowall's figure of forty-eight assignation houses in 1833. On the "upper ten," see *Herald, Report of the Forrest Divorce Case* (New York, 1852), 88. On Jennison, see PCP, Box 7437, Collins v. Jennison, 21 June 1822; DAP, People v. Jennison, 10 Feb. 1823; People v. Johnson, 11 March 1828. Butt Ender, *Prostitution Exposed,*

lists "Mrs. Gennison" running a brothel with seven girls at 94 Cross Street in 1839. She was eighty years of age.

29. Peel, "On the Margins," 813–34. The dangers inherent in streetwalking, however, sometimes forced many to work in pairs or to substitute another dependency in the form of pimps. Undated Manuscript and Furnished Room House Reports for 321 East 12th Street, 40–42 1/2 St. Mark's Place, Boarding House Folders nos. 1–3; Typewritten Report, 1905, all in Box 91, LWP; Clippings, 3, 4 Jan. 1901, Box 32, C15P; Kneeland, *Commercialized Prostitution,* 43–45. After the Civil War, the term "assignation house" fell into disuse.
30. "Business Man" to Hewitt, 31 July 1888, MP 87-HAS-33. On the operation of furnished-room houses, see McElwain to Murray, 21 Sept. 1887, MP 87-HAS-29; Committee of Fourteen, *Annual Report* (New York, 1915), 10; Thomas Byrnes, *1886—Professional Criminals of America* (New York, 1886), 374–75. On mistaking furnished-room houses for brothels, see Jacobson to Mitchel, 22 Sept. 1910; Baker to Gaynor, 13 Oct. 1910; Hogan to Police Commissioner, 8 Oct. 1910, all in MP GWJ-17. For more on the close relationship of brothels and lodgings, see Rachel Amelia Bernstein, "Boarding-House Keepers and Brothel Keepers in New York City, 1880–1910" (Ph.D. diss., Rutgers Univ., 1984).
31. *Gentleman's Companion,* 10–11 ("badger"). For varied descriptions of panel houses, see DAP, People v. Fowler, 16 Nov. 1820; People v. Quin, 21 March 1840; People v. Concklin, 10 Aug. 1843; People v. Walsh, 11 Sept. 1843; People v. Foy, 20 June 1844; People v. Saunders, 17 Oct. 1845; People v. Roach, 3 June 1846; People v. Howard, 19 Feb. 1864; People v. Haggerty, 13 June 1865; PCP, Box 7437, Haviland v. Jones, 25 Aug. 1823; *NPG,* 16 May 1846, 19 June 1847; Crapsey, *Nether Side,* 139–40.
32. The quotation is in *Gentleman's Directory,* 11. On panel houses, see DAP, People v. Fowler, 16 Nov. 1820; People v. Pearsall, 11 Dec. 1840; People v. Sparks et al., 12 April 1849; People v. Hawley, 8 Dec. 1873. On Quin, see DAP, People v. Quin (two cases), 21 March 1840; William H. Bell Diary, NYHS, 6, 7 Feb., 13 May 1851; *Flash,* 10 July 1842, copy in DAP, 14 July 1842; McCabe, *Secrets,* 107. Unfortunately, neither Quin nor Stein is listed in any city directory for these years.
33. Wilson to Hewitt, 11 Oct. 1887, MP 87-HAS-29; Kealy to Walling (Mercer Street), 27 June 1879, MP 83-CE-26; Testimony of Lewis Oliver (St. Nicholas Hotel), June 1879, MP 83-CE-26. On the police, see *Times,* 30 Jan. 1876. Usually, panel house proprietors split the profits with local police officers. See *Lexow Committee,* 4:3615–23. Although some observers like Matthew Hale Smith charged that the "panel-thieving business [was] almost entirely in the hands of black women," numerous incidents demonstrate that robbery by prostitutes did not fit racist stereotypes. See Smith, *Sunshine and Shadow,* 306.
34. "A Landlord" to Hewitt, 3 Feb. 1888, MP 87-HAS-33. For other examples of panel houses, see Anonymous to Gardner, 6, 7 April 1974, McCullagh to Gardner, 3 April 1874; Walsh to Gardner, 6 April 1874, all in MP 80-HW-14; H.B. to Hewitt, 5 Dec. 1887, MP 87-HAS-28. On Lomax, see *Mazet Committee,* 2363–44, 2371–73. On bilking, see Various Reports on Disorderly Houses, Box 91, LWP. On prosecution, see *Mazet Committee,* 2461–79, 2504–17.
35. Smith, *Sunshine and Shadow,* 375–76; James D. McCabe, Jr., *New York by Sunlight and Gaslight* (Philadelphia, 1882), 476–78; DAP, People v. Howard, 19 Sept. 1878. On Woods, see *Gentleman's Companion,* 36; On the class divisions among prostitutes and brothels, see McCabe, *Secrets,* 208–9, 285–88; Crapsey, *Nether Side,* 138–39; Sanger, *History of Prostitution,* 549–66; Ellington, *Women of New York,* 173–87. For a comparison of the more businesslike and specialized organizational structure of Manhattan brothels, see Butt Ender, *Prostitution Exposed,* and *Gentleman's Directory.*
36. On Woods and the House of All Nations, see Hattie Ross Report, 1909, Folder 150, HLP; Anonymous to Hewitt ("House of All Nations"), 22 Aug. 1888, MP 87-HAS-35; Edward Van Every, *Sins of New York, as "Exposed" by the Police Gazette* (New York, 1930), 188 ("rounder"). On call boxes, see Clippings for 6 April 1901, Box 38, C15P. The Police Department licensed messengers working hotels, railroad stations, and ferries. See Chief Clerk to Reynolds, 16 May 1903, MP LS-5. First-class resorts employed as many as six servants, usually African-Americans, although this number seems to have diminished by the end of the century. Housekeepers

earned as much as twenty dollars per week. See New York State Census of 1855, Manuscript Schedules for New York County, Fifth Ward, First Election District, nos. 85, 87, 88, 108, 115, 175; *Lexow Committee,* 2: 1882–97; *Mazet Committee,* 182–90, 1549; "Virtue" to Hewitt, 25 Oct. 1888, MP 87-HAS-33; Cardwell and Reynolds to Hewitt, March 1888, MP 87-HAS-34; Williams to Murray, 13 Feb. 1888, MP 87-HAS-32; Anonymous to Grant, 4 Feb. 1889, MP 89-GHJ-39; Police Commissioner to Gaynor, 22 Jan. 1913, MP GWJ-71.

37. Newspaper Clippings, 18 Nov. 1900, C15P. For descriptions of parlor houses, see George Kneeland, "Commercialized Vice and the Liquor Traffic," *Social Hygiene* 2 (1916): 70; idem, *Commercialized Prostitution,* 3–23; *Times,* 9 June 1877; DeBarry to Hewitt, 23 Oct. 1888, MP 87-HAS-33; Statement of Louisa Kleuhenspies, 7 April 1887, MP 87-HAS-16; "Lady Resident" to Hewitt, 24 June 1888, MP 87-HAS-33; *Lexow Committee,* 2:1871; Undated Manuscript, pp. 6–7; Reports for 137–139, 151 West 26th Street; 56, 140 West 24th Street; 110 West 25th Street; 116, 118, 144 West 27th Street; 204 West 28th Street; 117, 118 West 29th Street; 108 West 31st Street; 123 West 32d Street; 208, 210, 212, 228 West 40th Street; and Undated Report, all in Box 91, LWP; Affidavits for 52 St. Mark's Place and 65 East Seventh Street, Box 15; Clippings, 3, 4 Jan. 1901, Box 32, all in C15P.
38. Committee of Fifteen, *The Social Evil* (New York, 1902), 183–85; Report of Sept. 1905; Undated Manuscript, Description of Cadets; Frances Kellor Manuscript, 17 Oct. 1905, Box 91, LWP.
39. Taxpayer to Hewitt ("modus operandi"), Sept. 1888, MP 87-HAS-32; Whitman, *New York Dissected,* 136–37; Cornelius Willemse, *Behind the Green Lights* (New York, 1931), 78; Report of Sept. 1905, Box 91, LWP. For the same in London, see Gareth Stedman Jones, *Outcast London: A Study in the Relationship between Classes in Victorian Society* (Harmondsworth, Eng., 1971), 62. Cabs continue to play an important role in directing men to prostitutes. See Richard Symanski, *The Immoral Landscape: Female Prostitution in Western Societies* (Toronto, 1981), 155–57.
40. *McDowall's Journal,* 1 May 1833; Committee Report to the Humane Society, John Jay Papers, Reel 3, NYHS; *MCC,* 7:72–73 (18 March 1812); DAP, People v. Martin, 13 June 1825; Reports for 208 to 228 West 40th Street, Box 91, LWP; McCullough to Hewitt, 25 July 1888, MP 87-HAS-35. On prices, see Affidavit for 64 to 66 Seventh Avenue, Box 18 C15P; Kneeland, *Commercialized Prostitution,* 4.
41. Kneeland, *Commercialized Prostitution,* 7, 13 ("stars"); Helen Campbell, *Darkness and Daylight, or, Lights and Shadows of New York Life* (Hartford, 1893), 210; Frances Kellor Manuscript, 17 Oct. 1907, p. 6, Box 91, LWP; DAP, People v. Rochelle, 17 April 1878. On "French" houses, see Affidavit for 100 West Third Street, Box 4; Affidavit for 30 and 32 Stanton Street, Box 10 ("unnatural practices"); Affidavit for 112 Third Avenue, Box 13; Affidavits for 83, 99, 100 West Third Street, Box 17, all in C15P; Charles W. Gardner, *The Doctor and the Devil: A Startling Exposé of Municipal Corruption* (New York, 1894), 56–57. Even the English blamed such activity on the French. See Ronald Pearsall, *The Worm in the Bud: The World of Victorian Sexuality* (Harmondsworth, Eng., 1969), 226, 331.
42. Gardner, *Doctor,* 56–57; DAP, People v. Henry ("segar"), 5 Feb. 1875; People v. Barnesciota ("lustful gaze"), 21 Sept. 1876. On oral sex and "indecent dances," see Undated Manuscript, pp. 6–7; Report of 121 West 49th Street, Sept. 1905, Box 91, LWP; Affidavit for 230 Thompson Street, Box 17, C15P; Kneeland, *Commercialized Prostitution,* 15; DAP, People v. Norton (Flaherty), 18 June 1874; People v. Hanson, 16 Oct. 1877; Neighbor to Hewitt, July 1888, MP 87-HAS-33.
43. See above, note 14.
44. Kneeland, *Commercialized Prostitution,* 96–98; Frances Kellor Manuscript, 17 Oct. 1907, p. 10, Box 91, LWP. Kneeland believed that prostitutes received only 20 percent of what they charged clients. Women who wanted to remain in brothel prostitution usually changed residences with a nearby brothel under control of the same madam.
45. William McAdoo, *Guarding a Great City* (New York, 1906), 92–93. On the impact of police raids later, see Murphy to Pfeiffer, 2 July 1911; Veiller to Mitchel, 18 April 1914, both in THC-Prostitution Folder, Box 168, CSS Papers. On complaints of increasing massage parlors, see "Friend of Justice" to Hewitt, 16 Oct. 1887; Campbell to Hewitt, 20 Nov. 1887, both in

MP 87-HAS-30. On ads, see clippings from *Morning Journal,* 27 Jan. 1889, MP 88-GHJ-39.

46. The "temples of love" quotation is in *Gentleman's Directory,* 15.
47. McAdoo, *Guarding a Great City,* 73; Raymond B. Fosdick, "Prostitution and the Police," *Social Hygiene* 2 (1916): 16. For similar conclusions, see Memo of 20 Nov. 1913, THC-Prostitution Folder, Box 168, CSS Papers; Jerome D. Greene, "The Bureau of Social Hygiene," *Social Hygiene* 3 (1917): 8–9; Committee of Fourteen, *Annual Report* (New York, 1912), 22; idem, *Annual Report* (New York, 1913), 27.

Chapter 9 SEXUAL POLITICS

1. *Diary of Cotton Mather,* 2:160, 229, 235, 283, 612, 767, quoted in Lawrence Stone, *The Family, Sex, and Marriage in England, 1500–1800* (New York, 1978), 526; Undated Report for the Society for the Suppression of Vice (approximately 1815); and Constitution for the New York Society for the Suppression of Vice ("happiness"), undated, Reel 3, both in John Jay Papers, NYHS.
2. Samuel Akesty (?) to Stephen Allen, 4 June 1827, Miscellaneous Papers no. 2, pp. 18–19, Stephen Allen Papers, NYHS; Raymond A. Mohl, *Poverty in New York, 1783–1825* (New York, 1971), 167–68, 195. By the 1850s, the Magdalen Society "was chiefly designed for such as were already lost to shame, or had worn themselves into dismissal even from the service of sin." See Five Points House of Industry, *Monthly Record* (July 1858), 67.
3. Carroll Smith-Rosenberg, *Religion and the Rise of the American City: The New York City Mission Movement, 1812–1870* (Ithaca, N.Y., 1971), chap. 4; idem, "Beauty, the Beast, and the Militant Woman in Jacksonian America," *AQ* 23 (1971): 562–84, reprinted in *Disorderly Conduct: Visions of Gender in Victorian America* (New York, 1985), 109–28; David J. Pivar, *Purity Crusade: Sexual Morality and Social Control, 1868–1900* (Westport, Conn., 1973), 25–27. The New-York Society of Public Morals was founded in 1833 for the eradication of all forms of vice—drinking, gambling, and prostitution. Explicitly promoting chastity, the society opposed a variety of theatrical exhibitions—circuses, the opera, puppet shows, juggling, dancing, cockfighting, and horse racing. See *Journal of Public Morals,* 7 March 1833. For examples in another city, see Roger Lane, *Policing the City: Boston, 1822–1885* (New York, 1977), 47.
4. CAS, *Second Annual Report* (New York, 1855), 9; Junius Henri Browne, *The Great Metropolis: A Mirror of New York* (New York, 1869), 522–27, 696; Hasia R. Diner, *Erin's Daughters in America: Irish Immigrant Women in the Nineteenth Century* (Baltimore, 1983), 134–38; Smith-Rosenberg, *Religion and the City,* chaps. 5, 7, 8. The Guardian Society home was at 32 East 30th Street. See Samuel B. Halliday, *The Little Street Sweeper; or, Life among the Poor* (New York, 1861), 238–40, 243, 300–318. In the next decade, organizations like the Children's Aid Society founded more industrial societies for young girls. On the expansion of female industrial schools to fight prostitution, see the following reports by the Children's Aid Society: *Third Annual Report* (New York, 1856), 19; *Tenth Annual Report* (New York, 1863), 10–14, 23–32, 42; *Thirteenth Annual Report* (New York, 1866), 32; *Fourteenth Annual Report* (New York, 1867), 4, 11; *Twenty-fourth Annual Report* (New York, 1876), 5. See also Edward K. Spann, *The New Metropolis: New York City, 1840–1857* (New York, 1981), 259; Amy Gilman Srebnick, "True Womanhood and Hard Times: Women and Early New York Industrialization, 1840–1860" (Ph.D. diss., SUNY, Stony Brook, 1979), 121–41.
5. DAP, Cases for 20 Sept., 26 Oct. 1850; People v. Gilroy et al., 23 Jan. 1852; People v. McCue, 22 April 1852. Five Points House of Industry, *Monthly Record* (July 1858), 69–70; ibid. (Aug. 1858), 76–78. The Five Points raid may have served as a model for other cities. See Lane, *Policing the City,* 65.
6. Allan Nevins and Milton Halsey Thomas, eds., *The Diary of George Templeton Strong* (New York, 1952), 1:217–18; *Herald,* 10 March 1855; *Tribune,* 14, 16, 21, 23, 28, 29, 30 March 1855; Spann, *New Metropolis,* 368–70.
7. Walt Whitman, *New York Dissected,* ed. Emory Holloway and Ralph Adimari (New York, 1936), 219; "On Vice," in *The Uncollected Poetry and Prose of Walt Whitman,* ed. Holloway

(Garden City, N.Y., 1921) 1:5–8. For similar expressions of discouragement by the Reverend John McDowall, see John M. Murtaugh and Sarah Harris, *Cast the First Stone* (New York, 1957), 208–9.

8. Five Points House of Industry, *Monthly Record* (Aug. 1858), 73–74. New York State, Secretary of State, *Census of 1855* (New York, 1857), xli. The Reverend Louis M. Pease of the House of Industry was an advocate of removing children from inner-city slums and placing them in rural institutions and farms, a policy implemented by the Children's Aid Society. See Five Points House of Industry, *Monthly Record* (Oct. 1858), 121–29. For more on female moral reform in the 1850s, see Lori D. Ginsberg, " 'Moral Suasion Is Moral Balderdash': Women, Politics, and Social Activism in the 1850s," *JAH* 73 (1986): 601–22.
9. Helen Campbell, *Darkness and Daylight; or, Lights and Shadows of New York Life* (Hartford, 1893), 219–21.
10. Pivar, *Purity Crusade*, 78–105; Roland Wagner, "Virtue against Vice: A Study of Moral Reformers and Prostitution in the Progressive Era" (Ph.D. diss., Univ. of Wisconsin, 1971), 25–38.
11. The most recent examinations of Comstock and Parkhurst are Timothy J. Gilfoyle, "The Moral Origins of Political Surveillance: The Preventive Society in New York City, 1867–1918," *AQ* 38 (1986): 637–52; John D'Emilio and Estelle B. Freedman, *Intimate Matters: A History of Sexuality in America* (New York, 1988), 159–67; Paul S. Boyer, *Purity in Print: The Vice-Society Movement and Book Censorship in America* (New York, 1968), 1–35; idem, *Urban Masses and Moral Order in America, 1820–1920* (Cambridge, Mass., 1978), 162–66, 171–72; Heywood Broun and Margaret Leech, *Anthony Comstock: Roundsman of the Lord* (New York, 1927); Anthony Comstock, *Traps for the Young*, ed. Robert H. Bremner (Cambridge, Mass., 1967), introd.
12. Nevins, *Diary of Strong*, 2:99; Wickham to Police Commissioners, 7 Oct. 1875, and Townsend to Wickham, 19 Aug. 1875, MP 81-WWH-25; *Lexow Committee*, 2825; Parkhurst to Police Commissioners, 16 Jan. 1894, MP 89-GTF-14. Similar charges by Mayor Edward Cooper are in MP 83-CE-29.
13. Edward Crapsey, *The Nether Side of New York* (New York, 1872), 13, 25–26; Nevins, *Diary of Strong*, 4:271.
14. Nevins, *Diary of Strong*, 2:99, 280, 282, 403.
15. On the ASPCA, see ASPCA, *Tenth Annual Report* (New York, 1876), 5–6, 37–49; *Scribner's Monthly* 17 (1879): 879. On the European origins of the humane society movement, see Roswell C. McCrea, *The Humane Movement* (New York, 1910), 5–12, 148; Charles D. Niven, *History of the Human Movement* (London, 1967). On the SPCC, see SPCC, *Fifth Annual Report* (New York, 1880), 7–8; John A. Kouwenhoven, *Adventures of America, 1857–1900: A Pictorial Record from Harper's Weekly* (New York, 1938), plate 144. On the national expansion of vice societies, see SSV, *Fifteenth Annual Report* (New York, 1889), 8–10. On English vice societies, see Ronald Pearsall, *The Worm in the Bud: The World of Victorian Sexuality* (Harmondsworth, Eng., 1971), 467–70. On the Philadelphia SPCC, see Marcia Carlisle, "Prostitutes and Their Reformers in Nineteenth Century Philadelphia" (Ph.D. diss., Rutgers Univ., 1982), 101–11. A fifth but minor organization, the Society for the Enforcement of Criminal Law, was founded in the late nineteenth century after Detective Joseph A. Britton broke with his mentor Anthony Comstock. It was primarily concerned with excise violations. See Letter of 4 July 1901, Box 42, C15P; Tully to Gaynor, 9 Dec. 1912, MP GWJ-88; Gunn to Grant, 28 July 1890, MP 88-GHJ-40.
16. *City Vigilant*, June, Dec. 1894; SPCC, *First Annual Report*, 25–27. Backgrounds on the SSV's incorporators can be found in Boyer, *Purity in Print*, 277. For information on the founders of the ASPCA, SPCC, and SPC, see Timothy J. Gilfoyle, "City of Eros: New York City, Prostitution, and the Commercialization of Sex, 1790–1920" (Ph.D. diss., Columbia Univ., 1987), appendix 2. Administrators for the CVL were listed in the monthly reports of the *City Vigilant* in 1894–95. For more on post–Civil War consensus, see Iver Bernstein, *The New York City Draft Riots: Their Significance for American Society and Politics in the Age of the Civil War* (New York, 1990), 195–257.
17. Gerry to Hewitt, 29 Sept. 1887, MP 87-HAS-37. Temperance and purity groups like the

Women's Christian Temperance Union, the Anti-Saloon League, the Prohibition party, the American Purity Alliance, and the Young Men's Christian Association sought change through the political process and legal system. Their activities assumed that new urban problems stemmed in part from inadequate laws. Therefore, these groups organized local option campaigns, worked for the election of supporters, and lobbied state legislatures for the passage of favorable laws. See Boyer, *Urban Masses,* chaps. 2–6, 9, 13; idem, *Purity in Print,* 1–35; Pivar, *Purity Crusade;* Joseph R. Gusfield, *Symbolic Crusade: Status Politics and the American Temperance Movement* (Urbana, Ill., 1963), 74–78; Carroll Smith-Rosenberg, "Beauty, the Beast, and the Militant Woman," 562–84; Ronald G. Walters, *American Reformers, 1815–60* (New York, 1978), chap. 1; SSV, *First Annual Report* (New York, 1875), 3; idem, *Fourth Annual Report* (New York, 1878), 10–11; idem, *Twentieth Annual Report* (New York, 1894), 5; idem, *Twenty-first Annual Report* (New York, 1895), 58. Howard Crosby blamed much of the vice on the rise of monopolies and "money power" and doubted that managerial changes would eliminate the problem. See Crosby, "The Dangerous Classes," *North American Review* 136 (1883): 346–52; *Commercial Advertiser,* 28 Dec. 1885. The ASPCA fought to eliminate dog and cock fights. See ASPCA, *Fourth Annual Report* (New York, 1870), 30–31, 16–17; idem, *Fifth Annual Report* (New York, 1871), 25–26. In contrast to the prominent role played by women in Great Britain in fighting legalized and other forms of vice, the lack of female involvement in preventive societies is striking. See Judith R. Walkowitz, *Prostitution and Victorian Society: Women, Class, and the State* (Cambridge, Eng., 1980).

18. Anthony Comstock, "The Suppression of Vice," *North American Review* 135 (1882): 485; Boyer, *Purity in Print,* 1–35. The SPC tried to get power to issue warrants, but failed. See SPC, *Report,* 16. For Comstock's early attacks on pornography, see DAP, People v. Beer, 17 April 1872; People v. Brooks, People v. McDermott, 14 March 1872; People v. Meeken, 26 April 1872; People v. Farrell, 30 April 1872; People v. Train, 19 Dec. 1872; People v. Nichols, 20 Dec. 1872; People v. Leslie, 28 Jan. 1873; People v. Shaw, 28 Oct. 1873; People v. Solomons and Bryant, 26 Jan. 1874. For selling condoms ("yarrels"), see DAP, People v. Sieckel, 6 June 1872. Most of these arrests occurred in the business district of the First Ward.

19. New York State, *Assembly Journal* (Albany, 1875), 1:71, 150, 677; idem, *Senate Journal* (Albany, 1875), 536; SPCC, *Constitution and By-Laws,* 7–9; idem, *Second Annual Report* (New York, 1877), 62; *Manual* (New York, 1888), 54–56; idem, *Third Annual Report* (New York, 1878), 69. On the influence of Europe in creating these laws, see Elbridge Gerry, "Cruelty to Children," *North American Review* 137 (1883): 71. The ASPCA was allowed to issue warrants and used it to protect horses from cruel and injurious labor. Sometimes, however, the ASPCA made arrests without issuing warrants. See ASPCA, *Seventh Annual Report* (New York, 1873), 5–7; idem, *Tenth Annual Report* (New York, 1876), 7. An informal source of preventive societies' power was found in the support of elected mayors. Throughout the 1870s and 1880s, for instance, Mayors William Wickham, Smith Ely, Jr., Edward Cooper, William R. Grace, and Abram S. Hewitt acted upon the recommendations of preventive societies in licensing concert halls, theaters, and other sites of urban amusements.

20. Most studies of vigilantism equate the phenomenon with violence. Here I use a broader definition of vigilantism, characterizing it as a form of violent or nonviolent extralegal police action resorted to when processes of law appear inadequate. Its goal is to suppress and eradicate a practice or behavior its organizers find intolerable or threatening to deeply held beliefs and values. For other studies of vigilantism, see Richard M. Brown, *Strain of Violence* (New York, 1975).

21. Parkhurst to Police Commissioners, 16 Jan. 1894, MP 89-GTF-14; SSV, *Twenty-first Annual Report,* 11. The Bergh quotation is from the Scrapbook 10, Box 108, Grace Papers. Examples of the perception of vice as subversive are in SSV, *Second Annual Report* (New York, 1876), 4; idem, *Third Annual Report* (New York, 1877), 7–9; *Times,* 21 April 1875; *NPG,* 8 Nov. 1879; Clippings for 1 Feb. 1901, Box 34, C15P. The CVL, Committee of Fifteen, and Potter were supporters of the preventive societies.

22. O. B. Frothingham, "The Suppression of Vice," *North American Review* 135 (1882): 49; *City Vigilant,* Feb. 1894, 20. On Comstock, see SSV, *Second Annual Report,* 4; idem, *Third Annual*

Report, 7–9. On Bergh, see ASPCA, *Tenth Annual Report*, 6. Comstock himself suffered from violent, physical attacks from opponents. See Comstock, *Frauds Exposed* (New York, 1880; reprint, Montclair, N.J., 1969), 418, 423; SSV, *First Annual Report*, 9; idem, *Second Annual Report*, 7.

23. *Times*, 20 Jan. 1880. On the futility of police raids as a means of eliminating vice, see *Lexow Committee*, 2:983–1009, 3:2861, 4:4207–15; *Mazet Committee*, 2372. On preventive societies demoralizing the police force, Box 34, 6 Feb. 1901 clipping, C15P.

24. Parkhurst to Devery, 12 Oct. 1893, MP 89-GTF-14; Committee of Fifteen Papers, Box 42, 3 Aug. 1901; Box 45, 10 Sept. 1901; Box 46, 11 Sept. 1901; Box 47, 4 Oct. 1901; SPC Papers, Box 13, Report of Cases, 17 May 1909. On the role of the Committee of Fifteen, see Jeremy P. Felt, "Vice Reform as a Political Technique: The Committee of Fifteen in New York, 1900–1901," *NYH* 54 (1973): 26–44.

25. *City Vigilant*, July 1894, 169 ("voluntarily undertook"); SSV, *First Annual Report*, 3; SPCC, *Fifth Annual Report*, 64–65; idem, *Ninth Annual Report* (New York, 1884), 22–23; SPC, *Report*, 17. The increasing activism of the SPCC is visible in its caseload. In 1876, it prosecuted 197 cases. The number rose to 1,035 (1,009 convictions) in 1882 and to 1,790 (1,729 convictions) in 1885. Large numbers of liquor violations were reported by the SPC, including over 200 by its second year. The number of convictions the ASPCA garnered increased from 66 in 1866 to 312 in 1871. See SPCC, *Second Annual Report*, 27; idem, *Eighth Annual Report;* idem, *Eleventh Annual Report* (New York, 1886), 53; SPC, *Third Report*, 29; ASPCA, *Second Annual Report* (New York, 1868), 40; *Fifth Annual Report*, 23.

26. James D. McCabe, Jr., *The Secrets of the Great City* (Philadelphia, 1868), 308–13. Gerry to Edson ("sinks of iniquity"), 23 Feb. 1883, MP 85-EF-10; SPCC, *Sixth Annual Report* ("western bravadoes"), 18–19, 40–41. Also see Gerry, "Cruelty to Children," 70–71; SSV, *Twenty-second Annual Report* (New York, 1896), 24; *Twenty-third Annual Report* (New York, 1897), 19–21; idem, *Fourth Annual Report* (New York, 1879), 16, 20, 24, 52; idem, *Ninth Annual Report*, 9, 25, 39, 59–61; idem, *Tenth Annual Report* (New York, 1885), 31–32, 65–66.

27. For descriptions of the surveillance activity by the SPCC in concert halls, see Gilfoyle, "Moral Origins," 637–52. Other studies that illustrate middle-class fears of an uncontrolled and oppositional working-class culture include Roy Rosenzweig, *Eight Hours for What We Will: Workers and Leisure in an Industrial City, 1870–1920* (Cambridge, Eng., 1983), 93–168, 204–28; Robert Sklar, *Movie-Made America: A Social History of American Movies* (New York, 1975), 3–47; Peter Burke, *Popular Culture in Early Modern Europe* (New York, 1978), 207–86.

28. Gerry to Grace, 28 July 1882, 2 Dec. 1882, MP 84-GWR-15; Gerry to Thomas C. T. Crain, 3 July 1882, MP 84-GWR-16; *Times*, 9 Dec. 1880; SPCC, *Fifth Annual Report*, 79.

29. SPCC, *Eleventh Annual Report*, 5–6, 8 ("a foreign theory"); SPCC, *Sixth Annual Report*, 6 ("to protect those"); *Eighth Annual Report* (New York, 1883), 55–57; Comstock, "Suppression of Vice," 488. Comstock's suspicion of working and poor people's ability to raise children can be found in *Frauds Exposed*, 146–47. For other examples of the SPCC's refusal to grant licenses, see W. L. Hagedorn to Hewitt, 10 Feb. 1887, and Jenkins to Hewitt, 18 Feb. 1887, MP 87-HAS-42; Gerry to Hewitt, 28 Jan. 1888, MP 87-HAS-18; Gerry to Grace, 10 June 1882, MP 84-GWR-15; Gerry to Charles McGeachy, Manager of Grand Infanta Troup, 24 Dec. 1880, MP 84-GWR-15; SPCC, *Fifth Annual Report*, 10; Gerry, "Cruelty to Children," 71–74. A good example of the Victorians' fear of the lewd and degrading effects of the theater is Rev. J. M. Buckley and John Gilbert, "The Moral Influence of the Drama," *North American Review* 136 (1883): 581–91. Evidence of middle-class support for child performers can be found, on the basis of addresses, in "Applications to Exhibit a Child," MP 90-SWL-49.

30. *Lexow Committee*, 1:80, 1083–84 ("at war"); 3:2965–67 (Goff quotation); William J. Gaynor, "Lawlessness of the Police in New York," *North American Review* 176 (1903) :19–20. For similar reservations, see Bird S. Coler, "Mistakes of Professional Reformers," *Independent* 53 (1901): 1406–7. On the SSV, see *Twenty-second Annual Report*, 12; idem, *Thirtieth Annual Report* (New York, 1904), 3–4. On the SPC, see Memo of Commissioner Frederick Grant, 21 July 1897, MP 90-SWL-45. Some of the SPC's undercover activity can be found in Box 13, SPC Papers.

31. Oversize no. 5, Obituary Clippings, March and April 1904; Box 106, Scrapbook 6, *Sun* Clipping, 22 May 1885; Box 63, Letterbook no. 10, W. R. Grace to John Grace, 13 May 1886, all in Grace Papers. The historian Kirby A. Miller places Grace "at the very peak of Irish-American society." See his *Emigrants and Exiles: Ireland and the Irish Exodus to North America* (New York, 1985), 496.
32. New York *Journal,* 7 July 1886, Box 109, Scrapbook 12, Grace Papers.
33. Box 105, Scrapbook 4, *Mail and Express* Clipping, 14 Jan. 1885; Box 107, Scrapbook 8, *Sunday Mercury* Clipping, 5 Nov. 1885, and Clippings for 15, 16 Nov. 1885; Box 108, Scrapbook 9, *Evening Post* Clipping, 17 Nov. 1885; Box 109, Scrapbooks 11 and 12; Box 112, Scrapbook 17, *Sun* Clipping, 1 Jan. 1887; Box 111, Scrapbook 16, clippings for 6 Oct. 1886, all in Grace Papers; *Lexow Committee,* 4:4374–82.
34. Brooklyn *Eagle,* 16 Nov. 1885. Grace was primarily concerned with economic and home rule issues. See Box 61, Letterbook no. 4, W. R. Grace to New York County Democracy, 26 Oct. 1881; Box 62, Letterbook 5, Speech to Chamber of Commerce, 2 May 1882; Box 107, Scrapbook 8, *Evening News* and *Evening Telegram* Clippings, 19 Oct. 1885, and Clippings for 20 Oct. 1885; Box 108, Scrapbook 9, *Times* Clipping, 10 Jan. 1886, all in Grace Papers.
35. Grace Papers, Box 107, Scrapbook 8, Clippings of 19 Sept., 8, 9, 13, 14 Oct. 1885. Some observers concluded that the Grant and Ward scandal eliminated Grace's chances for reelection. See Box 109, Scrapbook 12, *Tribune* Clipping, 5 July 1886, Grace Papers.
36. Box 108, Scrapbook 9, *Tribune* Clipping, 11 Dec. 1885; Scrapbook 10, *Times* Clipping, 17 Jan. 1886; Box 108, Scrapbook 9, *Times* clipping, 2 Dec. 1885; Grace to William Roberts, 12 Oct. 1886, Box 64, Letterbook 11, p. 125, all in Grace Papers. On Grace's mayoralty, see David C. Hammack, *Power and Society: Greater New York at the Turn of the Century* (New York, 1982), 133–35.
37. Well connected to the city's elite, Hewitt was a trustee at Cooper Union, Columbia, Barnard, the American Museum of Natural History, and the Metropolitan Museum of Art, president of the American Institute of Mining Engineers and the American Iron and Steel Association, and a member of the Small Charities Aid Association, Small Parks Association, City Club, and Citizens Union. See Allan Nevins, *Abram S. Hewitt: With Some Account of Peter Cooper* (New York, 1935); Hammack, *Power and Society,* 135–41.
38. New York City Police Department, *Report* (New York, 1887), 69–72; idem, *Report* (New York, 1888), 81–82. For similar complaints in the 1890s, see idem, *Report* (New York, 1897), 21. For numerous examples of Hewitt forwarding complaints to the police and their questionable denial of the charge, see the many letters to Hewitt in the following boxes: MP 87-HAS-12, 87-HAS-16, 87-HAS-18, 87-HAS-20, 87-HAS-26, 87-HAS-29, 87-HAS-34, 87-HAS-37, 87-HAS-42.
39. *New York v. Charlotte Ewer,* 30 Jan. 1894, MP 89-GTF-16. On the SPCC's support for child labor legislation, see SPCC, *Eleventh Annual Report,* 5–7; idem, *Manual* (New York, 1888), 83–85. On public baths, see Gerry to Hewitt, 8 June 1887, MP 87-HAS-16. The City Vigilance League formed a committee on baths in 1894. See Abbott to Strong, 22, 27 Jan. 1897, MP 90-SWL-35; *City Vigilant,* 1894, 240, 266. On establishing a city hospital for fighting certain diseases, see SPCC, *Eighth Annual Report,* 6. The ASPCA was a leader in fighting the importation of swill milk and contaminated food into the city. See ASPCA, *Second Annual Report* (New York, 1868), 6–8, 25–26; idem, *Fourth Annual Report,* 23–29; idem, *Fifth Annual Report,* 27.

Chapter 10 Sex Districts Revisited

1. Anonymous to Hewitt, 22 Sept. 1888, MP 87-HAS-33.
2. Edward Crapsey, *The Nether Side of New York* (New York, 1872), 142; *Times,* 3 June 1876; Committee of Fifteen, *The Social Evil* (New York, 1902), 69, 172; William McAdoo, *Guarding a Great City* (New York, 1906). For other views on the widespread presence of prostitution during the 1890s, see *Mazet Committee,* 5124–25.

3. To measure the physical movement of prostitution over time and space, I divided the city into neighborhoods consistent with their ward numbers and physical separation by major thoroughfares, as in chapter 2, note 6. In addition to the earlier antebellum neighborhoods and their specific boundaries, uptown New York was divided into the following communities: East Village—14th Street to Fifth Avenue to Clinton Place (Eighth Street) to Broadway to Houston Street to the East River; West Village—14th Street to Fifth Avenue to Clinton Place to Broadway to Houston Street to the Hudson River; Tenderloin—15th to 59th Street, west of Fifth Avenue; Lexington—15th to 59th Street, east of Fifth Avenue; West Side—60th to 110th Street, west of Central Park; East Side—60th to 110th Street, east of Central Park; Morningside Heights—111th Street to Morningside Drive to 122d Street to Hudson River; Manhattanville—123d Street to Convent Avenue to 133d Street to the Hudson River; Hamilton Heights—134th Street to St. Nicholas Terrace to Hamilton Terrace to 145th Street to Hudson River; West Harlem—111th Street to Morningside Avenue to St. Nicholas Avenue to 146th Street to the Hudson River to 155th Street to the East River to Fifth Avenue; East Harlem—111th Street to Fifth Avenue to East River; Washington Heights—north of 156th Street.

As in chapter 2, I included only places and individuals accused of the specific disorderly-conduct charge of prostitution. Other disorderly-conduct charges I disregarded, although many of the places probably accommodated prostitutes. Consequently, the following maps, tables, and figures for the decades after 1870 are a conservative measure and probably underestimate the levels of prostitution in New York. The sources for all tables and maps include DAP; MP; *The Gentleman's Companion: New York in 1870* (New York, 1870); CSS Papers; SPC Papers; LWP; C15P (the boxes in this collection have been reorganized and renumbered since I examined them); C14P; *Lexow Committee; Mazet Committee;* SPC, *Report* (New York, 1896); SPCC, *Annual Reports; Morning Journal.*

After plotting over 5,000 individual addresses with prostitution, I found the following neighborhood breakdown from 1870 to 1919. The figures below are percentages found in each neighborhood.

Neighborhood	*1870–1879*	*1880–1889*	*1890–1899*	*1900–1909*	*1910–1919*
Total Number	434	619	426	1,196 (Man). 1,251 (all)	2,196 (Man.) 2,423 (all)
Wall Street	6	.6	0	0	.1
East R. Docks	9	10	4	4	.7
(Old) West Side	1	.2	0	0	.1
Five Points	4	6	3	2	1
Lower E. Side	10	15	27	12	6
SoHo	20	7	2	5	.7
East Village	7	11	20	21	9
West Village	16	11	7	5	2
Tenderloin	23	28	35	42	32
Lexington	4	8	1	7	7
Above 59th and other	.2	3	1	4	50

After 1900, uptown neighborhoods like Morningside Heights (the new home of Columbia University after 1897), Manhattanville, Hamilton Heights (near the City College of New York), and Washington Heights reported significant amounts of commercial sex.

The sharp decline in recorded houses of prostitution from 1890 to 1899 reflects a problem of sources, which were less complete in this decade than before and after. Given that New York was considered a "wide open" city at that time, it is doubtful that prostitution decreased. Although prostitution after 1870 was more concentrated than during the antebellum years, the citywide ratio of addresses (of prostitution) to blocks (per neighborhood) never exceeded 3.33:1, and was usually below 3:1. For specific citywide and selected neighborhood ratios, see chapter 2, note 11. For an even more detailed breakdown of the physical concentration of prostitution by neighborhood during these years, see Timothy J. Gilfoyle, "City of Eros: New York City, Prostitution, and the Commercialization of Sex, 1790–1920" (Ph.D. diss., Columbia Univ., 1987), 355–56, 397–98.

Most of the literature on prostitution after 1850 describes it as segregated and organized around red-light districts. Ruth Rosen argues that New York prostitution was primarily in black and ethnic areas. See her *The Lost Sisterhood: Prostitution in America, 1900–1918* (Baltimore, 1982), 78–85. Ivan Light links American red-light districts with Chinatowns. See his "From Vice District to Tourist Attraction: The Moral Career of American Chinatowns, 1880–1940," *PHR* 43 (1974): 367–94. For similar arguments, see Neil Larry Shumsky, "Tacit Acceptance: Respected Americans and Segregated Prostitution, 1870–1910," *JSH* 19 (1986): 665–79; Shumsky and Larry M. Springer, "San Francisco's Zone of Prostitution, 1880–1934," *JHG* 7 (1981): 71–89; John C. Schneider, "Public Order in the Geography of the City: Crime, Violence, and the Police in Detroit, 1845–1875," *JUH* 4 (1978): 183–208; Marion S. Goldman, *Gold Diggers and Silver Miners: Prostitution and Social Life on the Comstock Lode* (Ann Arbor, 1981); Al Rose, *Storyville, New Orleans: Being an Authentic Illustrated Account of the Notorious Red-Light District* (University, Ala., 1974); Richard Symanski, *The Immoral Landscape: Female Prostitution in Western Societies* (Toronto, 1981).

4. Citizens' Association of New York, *Sanitary Condition of the City: Report of the Council of Hygiene and Public Health* (New York, 1866), 24–26; George Ellington, *The Women of New York; or, The Under-World of the Great City* (Burlington, Iowa, 1869), 232. For other reports see *Statesmen* Clipping, 25 May 1885, Scrapbook 6, Box 106, William R. Grace Papers, Columbia Univ.; Crapsey, *Nether Side,* 154. The median property values (land and building) of the houses of prostitution (or their addresses) after 1850 were as follows:

	1850	*1870*	*1880*
Mercer Street	$6,000	$18,000	$24,000
Greene Street	$5,200	$13,000	$13,500
Wooster Street	$5,000	$10,000	$10,000

See Record of Assessments, Eighth and Fifteenth wards, Years 1850, 1870, 1880, MARC.

5. Michael J. Doucet and John C. Weaver, "Material Culture and the North American House: The Era of the Common Man, 1870–1920," *JAH* 72 (1985): 561; Roy Lubove, *The Progressives and the Slums: Tenement House Reform in New York City, 1890–1917* (Pittsburgh, 1962), 257–60. Before 1870, there were few brothels north of 34th Street. See Citizens' Association, *Sanitary Condition,* 314, 330.
6. Thomas Byrnes, *1886—Professional Criminals of America,* ed. Arthur Schlesinger, Jr. (New York, 1886; reprint, New York, 1969); Herbert Asbury, *The Gangs of New York* (New York, 1928), 177; William T. Stead, *Satan's Invisible World Displayed; or, Despairing Democracy: A Study of Greater New York* (London, 1898), 99.
7. Astor built over 200 three- to five-story brownstones on West 44th, 45th, 46th, and 47th streets between Broadway and Ninth Avenue. See Charles Lockwood, *Manhattan Moves Uptown* (Boston, 1976), 250–52. On Clement Clarke Moore, see Elliot Willensky and Norval White, *The A.I.A. Guide to New York City* (New York, 1978), 104.
8. James D. McCabe, Jr., *New York by Sunlight and Gaslight* (Philadelphia, 1882), 574–75 ("handsomest"); Allan Nevins and Milton Halsey Thomas, eds., *The Diary of George Templeton Strong* (New York, 1952), 4:241.
9. John Tauranac, *Essential New York* (New York, 1979), 42–43, 49–50, 82–83. The named hotels were between 27th and 31st streets. See Perris and Brown, *Insurance Maps of the City of New York* (New York, 1877). On West 23d Street, see McCabe, *Gaslight,* 269–71. For other descriptions of the area, see Nevins, *Diary of Strong,* 4:253; Robert A. M. Stern, Gregory Gilmartin, and John Massengale, *New York 1900: Metropolitan Architecture and Urbanism, 1890–*

1915 (New York, 1984), 203. On the emergence of this area as an entertainment district, see M. Christine Boyer, *Manhattan Manners: Architecture and Style, 1850–1900* (New York, 1985), 44–84, 87–102.

10. McCabe called this New York's "Rialto" in the 1880s. See *Gaslight,* 153, 250–52; Cornelius W. Willemse, *Behind the Green Lights* (New York, 1931), 83–84; Mary C. Henderson, *The City and the Theater: New York Playhouses from Bowling Green to Times Square* (Clifton, N.J., 1973).

11. Edward Van Every, *Sins of New York, as "Exposed" by the Police Gazette* (New York, 1930), 188; George J. Kneeland, *Commercialized Prostitution in New York City* (New York, 1917), 4–5. After 1880, numerous Tenderloin brothels reached assessed values of over $15,000; by 1900, many had passed the $20,000 mark. I sampled the addresses cited for prostitution from 1870 to 1920 on those blocks with the largest number of brothels. The median values were as follows:

Year	*1870*	*1880*	*1890*	*1900*	*1910*
West 27th Street (6th–7th Aves.)	$6,500	$7,500	$7,000	$8,500	$22,500
West 29th Street (5th–6th Aves.)			16,000	24,000	52,800
West 29th Street (6th–7th Aves.)			6,000	5,000	19,500
West 40th Street (6th Ave.–Broadway)	8,000		21,000		46,000
West 40th Street (Broadway–8th Ave.)	6,000		5,500		12,500
West 43d Street (Broadway–8th Ave.)			15,000	18,000	31,000

See Record of Assessments, Wards 16, 20, 21, 22, for years 1870, 1880, 1890; Assessed Valuation of Real Estate in Manhattan, Blocks 802–805, 830, 831, 993, 1014, 1015, for years 1900, 1910, all in MARC. For locations of the theaters, see Gilfoyle, "City of Eros," appendix 1. A line of seven apartments behind Carnegie Hall called Oxford Union, on West 56th Street, was filled with prostitutes. See Box 109, CSS Papers. Behind the Waldorf-Astoria was a brothel at 27 West 33d Street. See Box 165, CSS Papers.

12. James D. McCabe, Jr., *The Secrets of the Great City* (Philadelphia, 1868), 293–94; Ellington, *Women of New York,* 244–59; "A Citizen" to Hewitt ("almost impossible"), 4 June 1887, MP 87-HAS-30; "Taxpayer" to Hewitt, 21 May 1888, MP 87-HAS-33; Van Every, *Sins of New York,* 194; Police Commissioner to Kline, 1 Oct. 1913, MP GWJ-76. On West 25th to West 27th streets, I compared *The Gentleman's Companion* with the following: New York State Census of 1870, Manuscript Schedules for New York County, County Clerk's Office, Hall of Records, nos. 8–14, 21, 67–69, 79–91, Ward 20, Election District 14; nos. 7, 8, 52, 53, 55–57, Ward 16, Election District 8; no. 212, Ward 16, Election District 7; Record of Assessment, Ward 20, MARC; Federal Census of 1870, Manuscript Schedules for New York County, NYPL, Reel 35, Ward 16, Election District 11, nos. 103, 105, 107; Reel 38, Ward 20, Election District 22, nos. 101, 103, 106, 107, 108, 109, 111, 112, 116, 119, 121, 123, 125, 127, 129, 130, 137, 138, 142, 146. The brothels were run by seven sisters from New England, one of whom was enticed into the business and who eventually recruited her six sisters. See John M. Murtaugh and Sarah Harris, *Cast the First Stone* (New York, 1957), 209–10. Also see Reilly to Murray, 16 April 1888, MP 87-HAS-32; "Anonymous" to Hewitt, May, 1888, MP 87-HAS-33; Willemse, *Green Lights,* 40–41; *NPG,* 12 April 1879.

13. A decade-by-decade breakdown of the houses of prostitution within 2.5 blocks of a concert saloon revealed the following:

Year	Number	Percentage of Total Houses
1870–79	214	49
1880–89	318	51
1900–09	351	29 (Manhattan only)
		28 (all boroughs)
1910–19	635	29 (Manhattan only)
(cabarets included)		26 (all boroughs)

On Sixth Avenue, see *NPG,* 29 Nov., 8 Oct. 1879; Van Every, *Sins of New York,* 186–88 ("saque"); "Pro Bono Publico" to Hewitt, 5 Oct. 1888, MP 87-HAS-34; Willemse, *Green Lights,* 66, 71; McCabe, *Gaslight,* 154, 253; Crapsey, *Nether Side,* 138–39. From 1865 into the 1880s, streetwalkers extended from West 14th to 35th Street on Sixth Avenue and from West 24th to 42d Street on Seventh Avenue. For other examples of streetwalkers on Sixth Avenue, see Johnson to Hewitt, May 1888; "Citizen" to Hewitt, 23 June 1888, both in MP 87-HAS-34; "A Citizen" to Hewitt, 25 May 1887, MP 87-HAS-28; Baker to Gaynor, 8 July 1910, MP GWJ-15; A. Kimbel to Hewitt, 7 July 1887, MP 87-HAS-29. On adjoining streets, see McDowell to Hewitt, 26 May 1887, MP 87-HAS-31; Brearton to Hewitt, 25 April 1887, MP 87-HAS-28. After 1890, streetwalkers were especially plentiful from 38th to 50th Street. See Kneeland, *Commercialized Prostitution,* 65–66 ("nightly"); Police Commissioners to Gaynor, 5 Dec. 1912, MP GWJ-57; New York City Police Department, *Annual Report for 1919* (New York, 1920), 37–38. On tenement districts in New York, see the maps in Kathy Peiss, *Cheap Amusements: Working Women and Leisure in Turn-of-the-Century New York* (Philadelphia, 1986), 94, 147; Robert DeForest and Lawrence Veiller, eds., *The Tenement House Problem* (New York, 1903), 1:194–95.

14. Charles W. Gardner, *The Devil and the Doctor: A Startling Exposé of Municipal Corruption* (New York, 1894), 59 (West 31st and 32d streets). On Soubrette Row, see *Mazet Committee,* 1551–55; Abstracts, 18 Jan. 1901, Box 1; Telegram, 18 Jan. 1901, Box 33, both in C15P. For houses 1–199 West 39th and 1–199 West 40th streets behind and across from the Metropolitan Opera House, see the numerous letters to Hewitt and Grant in MP 87-HAS-28, 87-HAS-32, 87-HAS-33, 87-HAS-39, 87-HAS-40; letters to Byrnes in MP 89-GTF-14; letters to Gaynor in MP GWJ-17, GWJ-35, GWJ-36, GWJ-37, GWJ-56; *Mazet Committee,* 2439; C15P, Boxes 20, 22, 23; Undated Reports, Box 91, LWP; SPC Papers, Box 13, Cases for 1911; CSS Papers, Boxes 165, 168. On French houses at 245, 247, 249 West 39th Street, see Investigator's Report (1905?), Box 91, LWP. Similar testimony is in Willemse, *Green Lights,* 68–69; McAdoo, *Guarding a Great City,* 91; Police Department, *Annual Report for 1919,* 37–38; *Mazet Committee,* 1551–55; Affidavits for 311 West 44th Street, March 1901, Box 24; Clippings for 30 Aug. 1901, Box 45, both in C15P. For more explicit street-by-street documentation on the pervasive brothels, see Gilfoyle, "City of Eros," appendix 5.
15. Praetori to Hewitt, 1887, MP 87-HAS-29; Citizen to Hewitt, 24 May 1887, MP 87-HAS-29 (in reference to West 24th Street); Clipping in *Evening World,* Sept. 1888, MP 87-HAS-33. For maps that show the functional integration of urban activities in the Tenderloin, see Perris and Brown, *Insurance Maps of the City of New York* (New York, 1871 and 1877). On the occupational diversity of West 26th and 27th streets, see Manuscript U.S. Census for 1870, Reel 38, Ward 20, Election District 22, pp. 2–5, 8–15.
16. *Times* ("Great White Way"), 21 July 1907; Affidavits for 340–342 West 59th Street, Box 24, C15P; Adam Clayton Powell, Sr., *Against the Tide: An Autobiography* (New York, 1938), 49, 55–56. The Denver Hotel was at 209 West 40th Street and the German Village at 147 West 40th Street. See Confidential Bulletin, 19 Dec. 1913, Box 3; Reports, 1913, Box 28, both in C14P; Police Commissioner to Woods, 11 Feb. 1914, MP MJP-17; Confidential Bulletin, 9 Sept. 1914, THC-Prostitution Folder, Box 168, CSS Papers. On streetwalkers, see Affidavits for 311 West 44th Street, March 1901, Box 24, C15P. On lines outside brothels, see Investigators Reports for 208, 210, 212, 228 West 40th Street, Box 91, LWP.

17. On "African Broadway" and black prostitution, see Jervis Anderson, *This Was Harlem: A Cultural Portrait, 1900–1950* (New York, 1982), 8–9; Willemse, *Green Lights,* 71. Also see Praetori to Hewitt, 29 Aug. 1887, MP 87-HAS-29. In 1914, J. L. Elliott of the Hudson Guild discovered black prostitutes in expensive, $40 per month apartments on West 28th Street. See Elliott to Headley, 25 June 1914, CSS Papers, Box 168, THC-Prostitution Folder.
18. Eden to Mitchel (black women soliciting), 14 Jan. 1914, MP MJP-17; Anonymous Letter attached to Acting Police Commissioner to Gaynor (West 37th Street), 22 July 1913, MP GWJ-74; "A Citizen" to Gaynor (West 40th Street), July 1913, MP GWJ-73; Powell, *Against the Tide,* 49. After 1910, A. B. Allen believed that West 29th Street was "practically the only block in the whole old 'Tenderloin' district where open soliciting" occurred. See letter of Allen attached to Police Commissioner to Kline, 11 Dec. 1913, MP GWJ-77; Police Commissioner to Gaynor, 26 Feb. 1912, MP GWJ-53.
19. On black and tans, see Willemse, *Green Light,* 42; *Times,* 12 April 1877. Similar reports are in Fahey to Police Commissioner, 25 Oct. 1910, MP GWJ-17; Report of 12 May 1913, Box 13, SPC Papers; Baker to Gaynor, 19 Oct. 1910, MP GWJ-17; Police Commissioner to Mitchel, 11 March 1914, MP MJP-18. On Johnson, see Gardner, *Doctor and the Devil,* 57.
20. Investigators Report on Wilkins's Café, 16 March 1910, Handwritten Report, Undated; Typed List of Houses, Arranged According to Streets, 1910; Report of Mrs. A. M. White, 2 April 1910; Report of William Pogue, 6 April 1911; Anonymous Report, 17 March 1910, all in Box 28, C14P. Edmunds's was at 147 West 28th Street, Wilkins's at 253 West 35th Street, Banks's at 206 West 37th Street, Herbert's at 331 West 37th Street, Diggs's at 336 West 37th Street, Welch's at 317 West 39th Street, Brown's at 323 West 41st Street, and Marshall's at 129 West 53d Street.
21. John W. Frick, *New York's First Theatrical Center: The Rialto at Union Square* (Ann Arbor, 1985), 1–9, 25–71, 89–90, 127–50; *Washington Square* (1880), in *The American Novels of Henry James,* ed. F. O. Matthiessen (New York, 1947), 171; Ralph Werther-Jennie June ("Earl Lind"), *The Female-Impersonators* (New York, 1922), 104–6; Willemse, *Green Lights,* 14 ("aristocracy"); Walt Whitman, "New York Dissected," in *New York Dissected,* ed. Emory Holloway and Ralph Adimari (New York, 1936), 18–19; Lockwood, *Manhattan,* 177–78, 290; Henderson, *Theater,* 113. Chickering Hall was at 135 Fifth Avenue, Huber's at 106–108 East 14th Street, and Luchow's at 110 East 14th Street. For another description of the wealthy residents on Fifth Avenue, see Edith Wharton, *The Age of Innocence* (New York, 1920, 1970), 1–101. For a description of Fifth Avenue as an attractive residential neighborhood, see Stern et al., *New York 1900,* 18, 307. For points of interest on Fifth Avenue, see McCabe, *Gaslight,* 165–77 *("par excellence");* Nevins, *Diary of Strong,* 4:347, 412, 417.
22. Citizens' Association, *Sanitary Condition,* 132 ("two cities"), 137–38 (brothels). On shanties, see CAS, *Seventeenth Annual Report* (New York, 1869), 34; Willemse, *Green Lights,* 150; Anonymous to Hewitt, 28 July 1887, MP 87-HAS-29; Affidavit for 179 West Houston Street, 6 March 1901, Box 5, C15P.
23. Anonymous to Hewitt ("fast women"), 28 May 1888, MP 87-HAS-32; Smith to Hewitt ("good time"), 16 Jan. 1888, MP 87-HAS-33; Anonymous to Hewitt ("bed houses"), 28 July 1887, MP 87-HAS-29; Anonymous to Hewitt ("thirteen girls"), 12 Dec. 1887, MP 87-HAS-28; Helen Campbell, *Darkness and Daylight, or Lights and Shadows of New York Life* (New York: 1893), 360. The median tax assessments of the East 13th Street brothels were similar to those on Allen Street: $7,000 in 1870, $8,500 in 1880, and $11,000 in 1890. See Record of Assessment, Wards 15, 17, Years 1870, 1880, 1890.
24. Frick, *Rialto,* 151–68; Frederick H. Whitin, "Obstacles to Vice Repression," *Social Hygiene* 2 (1916): 147. On homosexual streetwalkers, see Werther, *Female-Impersonators,* 106. On the frequent soliciting in front of St. George's Church on Stuyvesant Square, see Sommer to Committee of Fourteen, 2 Sept. 1909; Slade to Whitin, 16 Feb. 1910, both in Box 1, C14P. Slavin's Hotel and Saloon, 2 Union Square, was a "noted hang-out for fairies." See Committee of Fourteen to Woods, 1 June 1914, Box 28, C14P. On Union Square, see Anonymous to Hewitt, Aug. 1888, MP 87-HAS-35; Anonymous to Hewitt, 11 July 1888, MP 87-HAS-32;

Campbell, *Darkness and Daylight,* 203; Police Commissioner to Gaynor, 6 June 1911, MP GWR-34, and 12 July 1911, MP GWR-35; Kneeland, *Commercialized Prostitution,* 66; Davis to Whitin, 26 Feb. 1907, Box 1, C14P. Union Square had at least seventeen Raines Law hotels, eight furnished-room houses, and six saloons with prostitutes. See F. H. Burger to Gaynor, 8 Aug. 1910, MP GWJ-16.

25. Ellington, *Women of New York,* 168, 232 ("fashionable"). At 102, 103, 136, 138, 142, 149, and 156 East 22d Street were brothels during the 1860s and 1870s. See *Gentleman's Companion* (New York, 1870); Cases for 5 Feb. and 4 March 1875, DAP. On nearby hotels, see Perris and Brown, *Insurance Maps.* The 30th Street houses were between Madison and Fourth (later Park) avenues. See Lentilhan to Hewitt, 18 July 1887, MP 87-HAS-17. Grace lived at 31 East 31st Street. See Ivins to O'Neill, 3 Feb. 1881, Grace Papers, Box 61. Little prostitution existed in the area as late as 1866. See Citizens' Association, *Sanitary Condition,* 240–41. On Lexington Avenue, see *City Vigilant,* Jan. 1895; Anonymous to Hewitt, 11 May 1888; Lair to Hewitt, 25 July 1888, both in MP 87-HAS-33. East 23d Street between Lexington and Fourth avenues was also cited. See "23rd St. Resident" to Hewitt, 16 March 1888, MP 87-HAS-33. Arthur lived at 123 Lexington Avenue, off 28th Street.

26. Acting Police Commissioner to Gaynor, 18 July 1913, MP GWJ-74; Clapp to Headley, 30 June 1914, THC-Prostitution Folder, Box 168, CSS Papers. Also see *Lexow Committee,* 4:4092–100, 4277–85; Affidavits, Box 25, C15P.

27. Houghton to Hewitt, Aug. 1887, MP 87-HAS-29; "A Citizen" to Hewitt, 22 Sept. 1887, MP 87-HAS-28. Houghton lived on the south side of the park. On Bleecker Street, see McCabe, *Gaslight,* 275–76; Junius Henri Browne, *The Great Metropolis: A Mirror of Gotham* (Hartford, 1869), 372–80. Edward Cooper lived at 12 Washington Square North. See Grace Papers, Box 111, Scrapbook 16, *Evening Post* Clipping, 12 Oct. 1886. Wharton, Howells, and James lived at 1 Washington Square North. O'Neill, Dreiser, Reed, O. Henry, and Frank Norris lived at 61 Washington Square South. See Willensky and White, *A.I.A. Guide,* 66; Henderson, *Theater,* 185.

28. Snow to Hewitt, 13 June 1887, MP 87-HAS-28; Nimrod to Hewitt, May 1888, MP 87-HAS-32; Livellaru to Grace, 31 March 1885, MP 86-GWR-26; "A Near Neighbor" to Hewitt, 27 July 1888, MP 87-HAS-32; "A Friend" to Hewitt, 4 Sept. 1888, MP 87-HAS-32; Lockwood, *Manhattan,* 290. Edward Crapsey believed prostitution in this area occupied a middle ground between the expensive type in the Tenderloin and the poor resorts downtown. See his *Nether Side,* 138–39.

29. Citizen to Hewitt, June 1887, MP 87-HAS-28 ("from early"); Brogan to Murray, 9 July 1887, MP 87-HAS-28; Lederer to Grant, 8 Nov. 1889, MP 88-GHJ-39. For similar complaints, see Brogan to Murray, 29 March 1887; "Resident of the Ward" to Hewitt, 25 April 1887; "A Neighbor" to Hewitt, 26 Sept. 1887, all in MP 87-HAS-28; Connolly to Hewitt, 26 July 1887; "One Who Has to Pass Daily" to Hewitt, 13 Aug. 1887, both in MP 87-HAS-29; "Citizens" to Hewitt, 25 Aug. 1888, "Several Neighbors" to Hewitt, 13 May 1888, both in MP 87-HAS-32; Anonymous to Hewitt, 1 May 1888; "A Citizen" to Hewitt, 14 July 1888; Sinclare to Hewitt, 19 July 1888, all in MP 87-HAS-33; McCullough to Hewitt, 25 July 1888, MP 87-HAS-35; McHugh to Grant, June 1889, MP 88-GHJ-39; McCabe, *Gaslight,* 481; C15P, Box 5, Affidavit for 179 West Houston Street, 6 March 1901; Box 17, Affidavits for Bleecker and Wooster Street houses, 1901. For complaints of black prostitution, see Livellaru to Grace, 31 March 1885, MP 86-GWR-26; Anonymous to Hewitt, Nov. 1887, MP 87-HAS-27; Snow to Hewitt, 13 June 1887, MP 87-HAS-28.

30. Prive to Hewitt ("in the summer"), 24 April 1888, MP 87-HAS-33 (Prive lived at 162 Wooster Street); G.W.B. to Hewitt ("different women"), 19 Aug. 1887. MP 87-HAS-29; Anonymous to Hewitt ("harmless"), Dec. 1887, MP 87-HAS-33; New York Society for the Suppression of Vice, Arrest Blotters ("Busy Fleas"), Library of Congress, Book no. 2, 1875, pp. 119–21.

31. Coontown was the area bounded by Thompson, Sullivan, Broome, and Grand streets. See Crapsey, *Nether Side,* 155–59; Affidavit for 4 Sixth Avenue, Box 17, C15P; Lockwood, *Manhattan,* 290. The area was also called Arch Block, because of the open archway under the

houses connecting Thompson and Sullivan streets, midway between Broome and Grand streets. See also SPCC, *Fifth Annual Report* (New York, 1880), 62; *Eleventh Annual Report* (New York, 1886), 47–48; CAS, *Twenty-first Annual Report* (New York, 1873), 64.

32. "A Resident of the Fifteenth Ward" to Hewitt ("swarms"), Oct. 1887, MP 87-HAS-33; Taxpayer to Grant ("shameful manner"), 18 Jan. 1889, MP 88-GHJ-38; Affidavit for 230 Thompson Street ("unnatural acts"), 1901, Box 17, C15P. Also see Anonymous to Hewitt, Nov. 1887, MP 87-HAS-27; "Citizen" to Hewitt, 12 July 1887, MP 87-HAS-29; "Citizens" to Hewitt, 25 Aug. 1888, MP 87-HAS-32; Anonymous to Hewitt, May 1888, MP 87-HAS-34; *City Vigilant*, March 1894; Affidavits, Boxes 5, 17, C15P.
33. "Citizen from Hoboken" to Hewitt, 12 July 1888, MP 87-HAS-33; Brinkman to Hewitt, 17 Sept. 1887, MP 87-HAS-29; Springer to Hewitt, 18 July 1888, MP 87-HAS-33; C15P, Box 5, Affidavit for 179 West Houston Street, 6 March 1901; Willemse, *Green Lights*, 111, 115. See also Joe R. to Hewitt, 25 May 1887, and McDonnell to Murray, 3 June 1887, MP 87-HAS-28; Neighbor to Hewitt, 27 May 1888, MP 87-HAS-32; Mary Simkhovitch, *Neighborhood: My Story of Greenwich House* (New York, 1938), 112–13; New York City Police Department, *Annual Report for 1919* (New York, 1920), 35–36.
34. During this period, the neighborhood of the Lower East Side included everything south of 14th Street and east of the Bowery. The label East Village for the neighborhood between Houston and 14th streets is a recently adopted one.
35. Simkhovitch, *Neighborhood*, 64; Theodore Roosevelt Papers, Library of Congress, Reel 454, vol. 2, *Herald* Clipping, 28 Oct. 1895; F. H. McLean, "Bowery Amusements," in Univ. Settlement Society of New York, *Report* (New York, 1899), 14; *Times*, 28 March 1880; Campbell, *Darkness and Daylight*, 212, 422, 427–28; For similar descriptions of the Bowery, see Crapsey, *Nether Side*, 84–87; *NPG*, 6 Dec. 1879; Grace Papers, Box 106, Scrapbook 6, *Statesman* Clipping, 25 May 1885; Willemse, *Green Lights*, 11–12; Police Commissioner to Gaynor, 8 May 1911, MP GWJ-34; Burlingham and Persons to Woods, 1 Dec. 1914, Saloons Folder, Box 159, CSS Papers; Werther, *Female-Impersonators*, 203–5; Michael Batterberry and Ariane Batterberry, *On the Town in New York: From 1776 to the Present* (New York, 1973), 148–50. For an example of a nearby brothel on Chrystie Street, see "A Civilian" to Hewitt, 13 June 1887, MP 87-HAS-29.
36. Goetz to Gilroy, 20 June 1893, MP 89-GTF-14. Also see Veiller to Mitchel, 18 April 1914, THC-Prostitution Folder, CSS Papers, Box 168. Goetz was listed as the landlord at 186 Allen Street. See Record of Assessment, Ward 17, Years 1880, 1890. Allen Street houses of prostitution were less valuable than leading Tenderloin establishments, but were similar to those on East 13th Street near Union Square. The median assessment for Allen Street houses was $8,500 in 1880, $11,000 in 1890, $14,000 in 1900, and $30,000 in 1910.
37. "A Citizen" to Hewitt ("concubines"), 10 May 1887, MP 87-HAS-30; Davison to Hewitt ("indecent exposure"), 12 Sept. 1887, MP 87-HAS-29; "Citizen" to Hewitt ("useless to appeal"), 15 April 1888, MP 87-HAS-32; *Lexow Committee* ("tenements"), 2:1778–80. For similar complaints, see "Lovers of Law and Order" to Gilroy, 13 June 1893, MP 89-GTF-14; *Mazet Committee*, 1549; Raymond C. Spaulding, "The Saloons of the District," in Univ. Settlement Society of New York, *Report* (New York, 1899), 37.
38. Testimony of Sarah Holt, 18 Sept. 1887, MP 85-EF-10; SPCC, *Ninth Annual Report* (New York, 1884), 58; McCullagh to Murray, 11 April 1887, MP 87-HAS-29; Petition to Hewitt, 28 Aug. 1888, MP 87-HAS-33. Also see Workman of Brinkerhoof and Co. to Hewitt, 26 July 1887, MP 87-HAS-29; Henkel to Hewitt, 17 May 1888, MP 87-HAS-33; Affidavit for 15 Avenue B, Box 12; Affidavits, Box 6, both in C15P. Police arrested 961 women for streetwalking on Elizabeth Street from Feb. to Oct. 1888. See Meakim to Murray, 2 Oct. 1888, MP 87-HAS-33.
39. Affidavit for 84 East 10th Street, Box 15, C15P; *City Vigilant*, Feb. 1895; SPCC, *Ninth Annual Report*, 53–54.
40. Libby to Hewitt, 16 May 1888, MP 87-HAS-33; "A True Citizen" to Hewitt, 27 June 1887, MP 87-HAS-28; Goulden to Hewitt, 11 Jan. 1888, MP 87-HAS-33; "Citizen" to Hewitt, June 1888, MP 87-HAS-32. On Bleecker Street, see Keegan to Hewitt, 25 June 1887, MP 87-HAS-

28. For a listing of the numerous houses of prostitution on East Third and Fourth streets, see Box 16, Affidavits, 1901, C15P. For the Rivington Street area in the 1890s, see *Mazet Committee,* 2033–35. For complaints in this area, see Reports of H.K., 2 June, 10 July 1919, Box 34, C14P; Box 13, C15P; Report of Cases, 12, 26 April 1909, Box 13, SPC Papers; Memo of Headley to Veiller, 31 Dec. 1913, THC-Prostitution Folder, Box 168, CSS Papers; Kneeland, *Commercialized Prostitution,* 66. During the first half of 1910, police arrested ninety prostitutes on Stuyvesant Street, a thoroughfare known for its furnished-room houses with prostitutes. See Baker to Gaynor, 3 June 1910, MP GWJ-15. For a list of the numerous houses of prostitution in the East Village in 1913, see Police Commissioner to Kline, 29 Sept. 1913, MP GWJ-76.

41. On the concentration of prostitution below Canal Street, see above, note 3. For descriptions of the lower portion of Greenwich Street, see Trinity Church Men's Committee, *A Social Survey of the Washington Street District of New York City* (New York, 1914), 1; Citizens' Association, *Sanitary Condition,* 4; Berghold to Murray, 10 Dec. 1887, MP 87-HAS-37. On the Battery Tenderloin, see the illegibly signed letter to Hewitt, 14 Dec. 1887, MP 87-HAS-37; Harris to Hewitt, 15 June 1887, MP 87-HAS-29; Trinity Church Men's Committee, *Social Survey,* 49; Abstracts, 12 Jan. 1901, Box 1, C15P; Handwritten Investigator's Report, 7 June 1912, Box 28, C14P.

42. Campbell, *Darkness and Daylight,* 50–51; Anonymous to Hewitt ("shoved about"), 27 June 1888, MP 87-HAS-32. Collins to Grace ("exposed"), 5 March 1885, MP 86-GWR-26. On Gallus Mag, see Van Every, *Sins of New York,* 287–89. On Water Street, see the unmarked 1919 clipping attached to rear flap in Matthew Smith, *Sunshine and Shadow in New York* (Hartford, 1868), Columbia Univ.; New England Steamship Co. to Kline, 13 Nov. 1913, MP GWJ-77; CAS, *Twentieth Annual Report* (New York, 1872), 12; idem, *Twenty-second Annual Report* (New York, 1874), 61; *Times,* 9 April 1877; Tynan to Murray, 26 March 1884, MP 85-EF-10; Constituents to Hewitt, Oct. 1888, MP 87-HAS-32; Collins to Grant, 9 Oct. 1889, MP 88-GHJ-39; Carpenter to Williams, 15 Nov. 1889, MP 88-GHJ-40; *City Vigilant,* Feb. 1894; C15P, Box 3, Affidavits for Cherry Street; Police Commissioner to Gaynor, 12 June 1912, MP GWJ-54; Collins to Hewitt, 20 Dec. 1887, MP-HAS-31; Carpenter to Murray, 13 Feb. 1888; American Wax Match and Taper Co. to Hewitt, 29 Oct. 1887, MP 87-HAS-31. Water Street houses of prostitution consistently had some of the lowest median tax assessments in the city. They were $3,375 in 1840, $3,500 in 1850, $4,000 in 1860, $5,000 in 1870, and $4,500 in 1880. See Record of Assessment, Ward 4, Years 1840–80.

43. Statement of Thomas Miller, 25 May 1889, MP 88-GHJ-39; Affidavit for 143 Park Row, Box 3, C15P; Blatchly to Burlingham, 17 May 1912, Lodging Houses Folder, Box 15, C15P. Chatham Street's reputation grew so odious that property owners and businessmen in 1886 persuaded Mayor William Grace to change the name to Park Row. See *Sunday News* Clipping, 18 April 1886, Scrapbook 11, Box 109, Grace Papers.

44. Campbell, *Darkness and Daylight* 252, 558. For similar reports, see "Business Men and Property Owners" to Hewitt, 16 Oct. 1888, MP 87-HAS-33; Miller to Hewitt, 26 Oct. 1887, MP 87-HAS-30; *Lexow Committee,* 2:2245; C15P, Box 4, Affidavit for 12 Chatham Square; Police Commissioner to Gaynor, 20 June 1911, MP GWJ-34; 4 Feb. 1911, MP GWJ-33. On the beginnings of Chinatown after 1860, see Autobiography of George Appo, Box 32, SPC Papers; *Times,* 4, 22 March 1880; *City Vigilant,* March 1894.

45. McAdoo, *Guarding a Great City,* 170–71. Pell and Doyers streets (nicknamed Shinbone Alley) were notorious for their tenement brothels full of Irish, German, Italian, and American women servicing Chinese males. See "Businessmen and Property Owners" to Hewitt, 11 Sept. 1888, MP 87-HAS-33; George Washington Walling, *Recollections of a New York Police Chief* (New York, 1887), 419–28; Shumsky, "Tacit Acceptance," 666; Ivan Light, "From Vice District to Tourist Attraction: The Moral Career of American Chinatowns, 1880–1940," *PHR* 43 (1974): 370–71. The only Chinese females who could legally enter the United States after the Chinese Exclusion Act of 1882 were wives of merchants. For a description of "female slavery" in Chinatown, see *Times,* 30 April 1905.

46. Letter attached to Police Commissioner to Gaynor ("bare naked"), 11 April 1913, MP GWJ-

72. On prostitutes in the subway, see Gibbs to Mitchel, 24 Jan. 1914, MP MJP-17; Report of H.K., 12 Feb. 1919, Box 34, C14P. Policemen were also assigned to the 14th Street and Grand Central stations. Twenty-seven and 29 West 64th Street, across from the Century Opera House, and 206 and 222 West 67th Street, across from the Central Opera House, were houses of prostitution. See Boxes 109, 165, 168, CSS Papers. On Columbus Avenue and Broadway, see Kneeland, *Commercialized Prostitution,* 25, 46; Police Commissioner to Adamson, 10, 25, July 1912, MP GWJ-54. Louisa Brown rented 19 and 46 West 65th Street. See Clippings for 22 Aug. 1901, Box 44, C15P. For a complaint regarding black prostitutes, see "Citizen" to Gaynor, 3 May 1910, MP GWJ-15.

47. On Columbus Avenue, Central Park West, and Central Park, see Kneeland, *Commercialized Prostitution,* 66, 76; Illegibly signed letter ("Bachelor Quarters") to Headley, 25 June 1914, THC-Prostitution Folder, Box 168, CSS Papers. Little Coney Island was on West 110th Street, between Broadway and Central Park West. See Affidavits for 216 West 110th Street, 2839, 2832–34, and 2840 Broadway, 106, 108, 110, 112, West 109th Street, 101, 139 West 108th Street, Box 28; Clipping, 28 Jan. 1901, Box 33; Clipping, 18 Feb. 1901, Box 34; Clippings of 11 March 1901, Box 37, all in C15P; Illegibly signed letter to Headley, 25 June 1914; Memo of Headley to Veiller, 31 Dec. 1913, both in THC-Prostitution Folder, Box 168, CSS Papers; Whitin Report, 28 Jan. 1907; Charles A. Briggs Report, 26 June 1914, both in Box 28, C14P; Murtaugh and Harris, *Cast the First Stone,* 221. On Columbia's concern that vice was moving up Amsterdam Avenue, see the correspondence between Frederick Whitin and Frederic A. Goetz, Counsel of the Univ., July 1907, Box 1, C14P. The Metropolitan Elevated Railroad line opened in 1880 and went up Ninth (later Amsterdam) Avenue to 110th Street and curved over to Eighth Avenue and up to 116th Street. For a provocative discussion of land use and real estate politics in Morningside Heights during this period, see David Rosner, *A Once Charitable Institution: Hospitals and Health Care in Brooklyn and New York, 1885–1915* (Cambridge, Eng., 1982), 164–86.

48. Morgenstern to Peters, 17 June 1908, Box 1, C14P; Robinson to Hook 23 March 1911, Box 1, C14P; Report of Natalie and Albert Sonnischsen, 1912; Handwritten Report, 1913; Charles A. Briggs Report, 26 June 1914; Typed Report, 9 May 1914, all in Box 28, C14P. Chester's was located at 110th Street and Eighth Avenue; Pete's, at southwest corner of 112th Street and Eighth Avenue; Lynch's, at northwest corner of 114th Street and Eighth Avenue; Café St. Nick, at southwest corner of 125th Street and St. Nicholas Avenue; Tony's, at northwest corner of 125th Street and St. Nicholas Avenue; College Inn, at 319 West 125th Street; West End Casino, at 361 West 125th Street; and Alhambra Theater Café, at Seventh Avenue and 126th Street.

49. Jones to Headley, 26 June 1914, THC-Prostitution Folder, CSS Papers, Box 168; Robinson to Hook, 23 March 1911, Box 1, C14P. In this tabulation, I counted all blocks from 110th to 145th Street, east of Morningside and Edgecombe avenues. The small half blocks between Morningside Park and Eighth Avenue were counted as one each. Also see Committee of Fourteen, *Annual Report* (New York, 1916), 85–86. For some nineteenth-century examples of prostitution in Harlem, see S. H. Vial to Hewitt, 5 June 1887, MP 87-HAS-30; "Property Owners of E. 122nd Street" to Hooker, 15 June 1887, MP 87-HAS-29; "Resident" to Hewitt, 23 June 1887; Knowles to Hewitt, 22 April 1887, both in MP 87-HAS-28; *Mercury,* 12 June 1887. The Harlem House Hotel, at 116th Street and Third Avenue, was known for its prostitutes as early as 1890. See Confidential Bulletin, 26 Oct. 1914, THC-Prostitution Folder, Box 168, CSS Papers.

50. Prostitution also appeared along Second Avenue between 127th and 128th streets, as well as on Third Avenue from 99th to 102d Street. See Police Commissioner to Gaynor, 29 July 1912, MP GWJ-55, 14 Nov. 1910, MP GWJ-17, 19 April and 2 May 1911, MP GWJ-34; Anderson, *This Was Harlem,* 144; Gilbert Osofsky, *Harlem: The Making of a Ghetto,* 2d ed. (New York, 1971), 89, 117, 146. For other Harlem reports, see Inspector to Police Commissioner, 1 Aug. 1910, MP GWJ-15. Also see Ryan to First Deputy Commissioner, 22 July 1915, MP MJP-41; Acting Police Commissioner to Gaynor, 26 July 1913, MP GWJ-74. Residents complained about "the negroe guerilla bands that infest the section." See Fried to Kline, 13 Sept. 1913,

MP GWJ-77. On the rise of crime, see Police Commissioner to Gaynor, 20 Aug. 1913, MP GWJ-75. One police report estimated that thirty to forty disorderly houses were found from 133d to 135th Street. See Police Commissioner to Gaynor, 1 March 1912, MP GWJ-53. Since this was once a well-to-do neighborhood, the median tax assessments were comparatively high.

Year	*1900*	*1910*	*1920*
West 133d Street (5th to Lenox Avenue)	$14,500	$22,500	$45,000
West 134th Street (5th to Lenox Avenue)	14,500	20,500	14,500
West 134th Street (Lenox to Seventh Avenue)	16,000	26,000	20,000
West 135th Street (5th to Lenox Avenue)	4,500	48,000	39,000

See Assessed Valuation of Real Estate in Manhattan, Blocks 1730–33, 1917–19, Years 1900, 1910, 1920.

51. Report to Hook ("swell colored prostitutes"), 14 Aug. 1911; Handwritten Investigator's Reports, 29 May 1912, both in Box 28, C14P. Others with prostitution included Mrs. Walker's, at 19–21 West 135th Street; Roberts' Brothers, at 33 West 135th Street; Café Burney, at 56 West 135th Street; Connor's Rathskeller, at 69–71 West 135th Street; Young's Rathskeller, at 126 West 135th Street. See Whitin to Fred Moore, 15 Sept. 1911, Box 1, C14P. Ellington is quoted in Anderson, *This Was Harlem,* 170–74; Report of William Franklin, 1913, Box 18, C14P. The Lincoln was at 58 West 135th St. (1915), the Lafayette at 131st Street and Seventh Avenue (1912), and the Apollo on 125th Street near Eighth Avenue (1914). See Leroy Ostransky, *Jazz City: The Impact of Our Cities on the Development of Jazz* (New York, 1978), 200, 204–5.
52. Whitin to Jenkins, 22 March 1911; Whitin to Booraem, 23 May 1911, Box 1, C14P.
53. Gebhart to Committee of Fourteen, 24 July 1914, THC-Prostitution Folder, CSS Papers, Box 168. Roses ran brothels over a twenty-two-year period at 142 Chrystie Street, 173 Allen Street, 42 Stanton Street, 218 East Ninth Street and 176 Fulton Street, Brooklyn. See Anonymous to Committee of Fourteen, 19 Sept. 1911, C14P.
54. Inspector to Police Commissioner, 28 June 1910; Fosdick to Baker, 24 May 1910, MP GWJ-15; Police Commissioner to Adamson, 11, 21 Sept. 1911, MP GWJ-36; Police Commissioner to Gaynor, 5 Dec. 1911, MPM GWJ-37, 23 April 1913, MP GWJ-72, 27 June 1913, MP GWJ-73.
55. On Coney Island, see Mitchel to Gaynor, 1912, MP GWJ-87; Kent to McGuire, 11 July 1910, Box 1, C14P; Peiss, *Cheap Amusements,* 115–34. On Hamilton Avenue, see Typed List of Houses, Arranged According to Streets, 1910; Report of S. M. Auerbach, 27 July 1912, both in Box 28, C14P. For more on Brooklyn prostitution, see Committee of Fourteen, *Annual Report* (New York, 1913), 36–37; Police Commissioner to Gaynor, 1, 2 May, 21 June 1911, MP GWJ-34, 28 July 1911, MP GWJ-35; and 3, 10 Sept., 6 Nov., 2 Dec. 1912, MP GWJ-56; Woods to Mitchel, 17 April, MP MJP-18, and 9 July, 8 Aug. 1914, MP MJP-19; Whitin to Veiller, 9 Oct. 1914, THC-Prostitution Folder, CSS Papers, Box 168.
56. On the Bronx, see the letter attached to Police Commissioner to Gaynor, 16 May 1913, MP GWJ-73; Acting Police Commissioner to Gaynor, 26 July 1913, MP GWJ-74. On Queens, see Confidential Bulletin of Committee of Fourteen, 9 Sept. 1914, THC-Prostitution Folder, Box 168, CSS Papers.

Chapter 11 Concert Halls and French Balls

1. Elizabeth Blackwell, *Counsel to Parents on the Moral Education of their Children* (New York, 1881), 47; George J. Kneeland, *Commercialized Prostitution in New York City* (New York, 1913 and 1917), 65.
2. The percentage distribution of institutions of prostitution in New York from 1870 to 1919 was the following:

Institution Type	*1870–1879*	*1880–1889*	*1890–1899*	*1900–1909*	*1910–1919*
Number	288	426	218	1,152	2,165
Brothel	50	9	22	10	2
Furnished-Room House	23	26	20	11	5
Panel House	3	0	24	0	0
Massage Parlor	0	14	0	2	.5
Hotel	0	3	6	18	5
Saloon	18	22	9	12	6
Restaurant	.5	0	4	4	2
Cigar Store	0	8	2	3	.5
Tenement	4	4	4	34	77
Concert Saloon	.5	11	9	4	0
Theater	.5	0	0	0	0
Other	.5	3	0	2	1

For sources, see note 3, chapter 10; Timothy J. Gilfoyle, "City of Eros: New York City, Prostitution, and the Commercialization of Sex, 1790–1920" (Ph.D. diss., Columbia Univ., 1987), Appendixes 5 and 6. "Massage parlor" includes manicure parlors, "magnetic water treatment," beauty salons, hairdressers, vapor treatment, and baths; furnished-room houses include assignation and boardinghouses; saloons includes liquor stores, grocery stores, and oyster saloons; concert saloons include concert halls, dance halls; restaurants include cafés, soda water stores, and ice cream shops; and other includes dime museums, laundries, opium dens, poolrooms, candy stores, chiropodist offices, homosexual institutions, tailor shops, mechanics shops, cabarets, department stores, real estate offices, blacksmith shops, employment agencies, furniture stores, apartments, athletic clubs, harness shops, barbershops, banks, and private clubs. The sources did not always identify the type of prostitution, so these figures are only a rough estimate and must be used with caution. The percentages of unidentifiable institutions of prostitution were 34 percent in 1870–79, 31 percent in 1880–89, 49 percent in 1890–99, 8 percent in 1900–1909, and 11 percent in 1910–19. The total number of addresses for each decade are listed in note 3, chapter 10. On the Raines Law, see Claire Marie Renzetti, "Purity v. Politics: The Legislation of Morality in Progressive New York, 1890–1920" (Ph.D. diss., Univ. of Delaware, 1983).

3. Cornelius W. Willemse, *Behind the Green Lights* (New York, 1931), 69; Gunther Barth, *City People: The Rise of Modern City Culture in Nineteenth-Century America* (New York, 1980), 201; Parker R. Zellors, "The Cradle of Variety: The Concert Saloon," *Educational Theatre Journal* 20 (1968): 578–86; Helen Campbell, *Darkness and Daylight; or, Lights and Shadows of New York Life* (New York, 1893), 464–65. On the origins of the concert saloon, see chapter 7. On the rise of vaudeville, see Lewis A. Erenberg, *Steppin' Out: New York Nightlife and the Transformation of American Culture, 1890–1930* (Westport, Conn., 1981); Robert Snyder, *The Voice of the City: Vaudeville and Popular Culture in New York* (New York, 1989). For an overview of cultural life during these years, see William R. Taylor, "The Launching of a Commercial Culture: New York City, 1860–1930," in *Power, Culture and Place: Essays on New York City*, ed. John H. Mollenkopf (New York, 1988), 107–34. The number of concert saloons was hard to determine. Metropolitan Police, *Annual Report* (New York, 1866), 19–20, lists 223. Going

through registration materials in the Mayors' Papers, I only found 66 from 1870 to 1879 (38 with prostitution) and 93 from 1880 to 1889 (56 with prostitution). After the antiprostitution campaigns of Mayors Grace and Hewitt, the number dropped to 59 from 1890 to 1899 (22 with prostitution). See Gilfoyle, "City of Eros," appendix 7.

4. George Washington Walling, *Recollections of a New York Police Chief* (New York, 1887), 479 ("abandoned"); *Times,* 30 Jan., 1, 2, 5 Feb. 1876; *Evening Post,* 24 Sept. 1886, in Box 111, Scrapbook 15, Grace Papers; *Mazet Committee,* 2003; Keating to Grant, 1890, MP 88-GHJ-42; Allaire to Murray, 21 Nov. 1887, MP 87-HAS-37; Cassidy to Murray, 24 Jan., 5 Feb. 1889, MP 88-GHJ-41. For other descriptions, see James D. McCabe, Jr., *The Secrets of the Great City* (Philadelphia, 1868), 309–12; idem, *New York by Sunlight and Gaslight* (Philadelphia, 1882), 253–57, 489–90; *NPG,* 8 Dec. 1866, 15 Feb. 1879, 14 Feb. 1880; Gerry to Edson, 17 April 1884, Report on Tom Gould's, MP 85-EF-13; Report on Concert Saloons, 1893, MP 89-GTF-15; Berghold to Dilks, 11 Sept. 1880, 20 Oct. 1880, MP 83-CE-26; Warts to Murray, 22 July 1887; Williams to Murray, 29 April 1887, both in MP 87-HAS-37.

5. *World,* 5 Sept. 1886, Box 111, Scrapbook 15, Grace papers; Dilks to Walling, 5 May 1879, MP 83-CE-26; *World,* 23 March 1887, in MP 87-HAS-37; Meakim to Steer, 27 Nov. 1886; Hill to Grace, 1886, both in MP 86-GWR-26; Edward Crapsey, *The Nether Side of New York* (New York, 1872), 161–62; *The Gentleman's Companion* (New York, 1870), 13; Walling, *Recollections,* 484–85; *Lexow Committee,* 2:1827–50; Smith, *Sunshine and Shadow,* 435, and undated attached clippings, Columbia Univ.; McCabe, *Gaslight,* 612–15. For a possible assault-and-battery case against Hill, see People v. Hill and Finnegan, 27 June 1860, DAP. Hill's was located at 25 East Houston Street, on the corner of Crosby Street.

6. *NPG,* 22 Nov. 1879; Edward Van Every, *Sins of New York, as "Exposed" by the Police Gazette* (New York, 1930), 201–6.

7. Frederick H. Whitin, "Obstacles to Vice Repression," *Social Hygiene* 2 (1916): 147 ("Moulin Rouge"); Van Every, *Sins of New York,* 190. On the women, see Walling, *Recollections,* 480–82. For other descriptions, see *Mazet Committee,* 2004–5; Clippings of 25–29 July 1901, Box 42, C15P; *Evening Post,* 21 Nov. 1902; T. Allston Brown, *A History of the New York Stage from 1732–1901* (New York, 1903), 2:591. On McMahon, see Willemse, *Green Lights,* 70; *Times,* 10 Jan. 1886. On Haymarket raids, see *Times,* 8 June 1902, 13 Jan. 1903.

8. *NPG,* 8 June 1867 ("bevy"); Flood to Murray, 23 Dec. 1887, MP 87-HAS-29 (Palm Garden); Testimonies of John Bennett and William Waite, April, 1879, MP 83-CE-26 ("strip"); Gerry to Grace, 27 Jan. 1885, MP 86-GWR-26 (Liverpool). On sexual intercourse in concert saloons, see Undated Report on the Lyceum, 302 Bowery, Box 91, LWP; Albertson to McCullagh, 9 Nov. 1897, MP 90-SWL-45; Hogan to Strong, 18 Dec. 1896, MP 90-SWL-46; McLaughlin to Murray, 1892, MP 88-GHJ-42.

9. On American Mabille, 59 Bleecker Street, see *NPG,* 28 Aug. 1880; "Unfortunate Father" to Hewitt, 20 May 1887, MP 87-HAS-37; Walling, *Recollections,* 489. On Armory Hall, 158 Hester Street, see Voorhis to Hewitt, 31 March 1887, MP 87-HAS-37; Walling, *Recollections,* 489; Michael Batterberry and Ariane Batterberry, *On the Town in New York: From 1776 to the Present* (New York, 1973), 104, 157–58; Van Every, *Sins of New York,* 214–17; Police Report, 10 Jan. 1886, MP 86-GWR-26.

10. SSV, *Twenty-third Annual Report* (New York, 1897), 13. On the Columbia, see *NPG,* 27 Sept. 1879; DAP, People v. Schonberger, 26 March 1877; New York Society for the Suppression of Vice, Arrest Blotters, Library of Congress, vol. 2, pp. 83–84; Theatrical License Applications, Feb. and March 1879, MP 83-CE-26. On Tivoli, see SPCC, *Fourth Annual Report* (New York, 1879), 16, 20, 24. On Eighth Street, see Grace Papers, Box 105, Scrapbook 4, Clippings from Utica *Daily Observer,* 16 Jan. 1885, and *Dial,* 5 Feb. 1885.

11. When the Metropolitan was raided in 1875, the eighteen dancers were listed with aliases, a common practice for prostitutes. See DAP, People v. Campbell, Manning, et al., 10 Feb. 1875. The National was one Bowery theater with prostitutes. See SSV, *Twenty-fifth Annual Report* (New York, 1899), 16–17; "Honest" to Grant, Jan. 1889, MP 88-GHJ-39. Others claimed Bowery theaters had few prostitutes. See F. H. McLean, "Bowery Amusements," in Univ.

Settlement Society of New York, *Report* (New York, 1899), 16; William Young, ed., *Documents of American Theater History* (Chicago, 1973), 192–93. For a twentieth-century example of indecent performances, see the complaint against the Columbia Theater, at Broadway and 47th Street, in Police Commissioner to Gaynor, 24 Feb. 1911, MP GWJ-33.

12. Gerry to Grace, 4 Feb. 1882, MP 89-GTF-16. On the Windsor, see Testimony of George H. Young, Nov. 1883; Gerry to Edson, 5 Nov. 1883, MP-85-EF-10. On the New York, see Gerry to Edson, 5 Nov. 1883; Testimony of Augustine J. Wilson, 30 Nov. 1883; Wood to Edson, 30 Nov. 1883, all in MP 85-EF-10; Gerry to Edson, 24 Nov. 1884, MP 85-EF-13; Meakim to Murray, 27 April 1887, MP 87-HAS-37. On the New American, see Gerry to Edson, 5 Nov. 1883, MP 85-EF-10. Also see Murray to Walling, 19, 26 Sept. 1879, MP 83-CE-26; Gerry to Edson, 5 Nov. 1883; Campbell to Edson, 30 Nov. 1883, both in MP 85-EF-10; "A Citizen" to Hewitt, 3 Dec. 1887, MP 87-HAS-29; Brown to Hewitt, 6 June 1887, MP 87-HAS-37; Gerry to Crain, 1 Feb. 1889, MP 88-GHJ-49; Gerry to Grant, 22 Dec. 1892, MP 88-GHJ-92; Campbell, *Darkness and Daylight,* 464, 466; *NPG,* 3 Jan. 1880; Gerry to Hewitt, 21 Sept. 1887, MP 87-HAS-37; "Two Respectable Residents of the Sixth Ward" to Hewitt, 16 Sept. 1887, MP 87-HAS-37.
13. Testimony before Mayor Franklin Edson, 30 Nov. 1883, MP 85-EF-10. For other defenses of dime museums, see Kealy to Murray, 7 Dec. 1883; Alexander to Edson, Nov. 1883, both in MP 85-EF-10; Meakim to Murray, 5 Feb., 27 April 1887, MP 87-HAS-37; Acting Chief, Bureau of Licenses, to Epstein, 23 June 1903, MP LS-9. For most of the antebellum period, P. T. Barnum's American Museum was the foremost example in New York. See Mary C. Henderson, *The City and the Theater: New York Playhouses from Bowling Green to Times Square* (Clifton, N.J., 1973), 80.
14. Smith, *Sunshine and Shadow,* 217, 439; Crapsey, *Nether Side,* 163; Brogan to Murray, 23 April 1887, MP 87-HAS-30. See also Box 91, LWP, and letters in MP 87-HAS-37.
15. Allaire to Murray, 28 April 1887, MP 87-HAS-37 (Oriental); Ryan to Police Commissioner, 20 Aug. 1915, MP MJP-41 (Harlem Circle); Testimony for Armory Hall, 1889, MP 88-GHJ-41; "Law and Morality" to Hewitt, 17 Feb. 1888, MP 87-HAS-34 (Clarendon); Krumm to Hewitt, 7 Sept. 1887, MP 87-HAS-37 (Chrystie Street); Hutchinson to Hewitt, 8 April 1887, MP 87-HAS-16. Also see letters in MP 87-HAS-27 and 87-HAS-38; *Lexow Committee,* 1:1021.
16. Campbell, *Darkness and Daylight,* 471–72; Walling, *Recollections,* 485–86; William McAdoo, *Guarding a Great City* (New York, 1906), 100–101, 336.
17. Allan Nevins, ed., *The Diary of Philip Hone* (New York, 1927), 10–12, 54, 462–63; Notes on the Society for the Suppression of Vice, 1810, Reel 3, John Jay Papers, NYHS; Raymond A. Mohl, *Poverty in New York City, 1783–1825* (New York, 1971), 132. On balls in antebellum brothels, see most issues of the *Whip,* the *Sporting Whip,* and the *Rake,* 1841–43. For a fictional account of a fancy-dress ball, see Ann Sophia Stephens, *High Life in New York by Jonathan Slick* (New York, 1843), 49–54. For a general description of "fashionable balls and parties," see McCabe, *Gaslight,* 208–21. Laws prohibiting masked balls were passed to detect criminals, fight juvenile delinquency, and deter secret antirent organizations from meeting. These laws, however, were never enforced and were repealed in 1876. See *Times,* 2, 21 Jan. 1876. On the London Haymarket, see Mark Girouard, *Cities and People: A Social and Architectural History* (New Haven, 1986), 183.
18. *Tribune,* 10, 17 March 1855; *Times,* 16 Nov. 1871. Turner was a pugilist who fought the onetime heavyweight boxing champion and ward boss Thomas Hyer, an ally of John Morrissey, and was later implicated in the murder of his political rival Bill Poole. Wealthy merchants sponsored masked balls in their homes throughout the period. See Smith, *Sunshine and Shadow,* 36. On Tammany Hall and balls in the early twentieth century, see Hutchins Hapgood, *Types from City Streets* (New York, 1910), 62. For a visitor's observation, see William F. Cody, *Buffalo Bill's Own Story of His Life and Deeds* (New York, 1917), 246. I am indebted to Paul Hutton for this citation.
19. The above and similar quotes can be found in the *Times,* 26 Jan. 1871, 22 Jan. 1875, 19 Jan. 1886, 31 Jan. 1889, 8 Feb. 1893, 16 Jan. 1900; *NPG,* 1 Feb. 1879; Walling, *Recollections,* 491–92. Leading citizens were always invited to the French Ball. See Hewitt to Laxon, 15

Feb. 1888, Hewitt Letterbooks, NYHS. On the "respectable" nature of the patronage, see Ralph Werther–Jennie June ("Earl Lind"), *The Female-Impersonators* (New York, 1922), 182–85, 193; *Times,* 2 Jan. 1876, 18 Jan. 1874, 17 Jan. 1882, 29 Jan. 1890.

20. *Telegram* Clipping ("costumes"), 9 Jan. 1901, Box 32, C15P; Walling, *Recollections,* 492–96.
21. DAP, People v. Woodhull, Claflin, and Blood, 21 Jan. 1873, 4, 5 March 1874. Luther Challis was one of the accused men.
22. Comstock to Hewitt, 23 Feb. 1888, MP 87-HAS-18; Durand to Hewitt, 26 Feb. 1888, MP 87-HAS-18; *Lexow Committee,* 4:4577–81.
23. Detached Clipping, 1888, MP 87-HAS-18; *Telegram* Clipping, 9 Jan. 1901, Box 32, C15P. For similar stories, see *NPG,* 1 Feb. 1879; *Times,* 11 Feb. 1894.
24. *Lexow Committee* (Lemon), 3:3118–26; Walling, *Recollections,* 492, 494. On homosexual balls after 1890, see George A. Chauncey, Jr., "Gay New York: Urban Culture and the Making of a Gay Male World, 1890–1940" (Ph.D. diss., Yale Univ., 1989), 302–5.
25. Ibid.
26. On the Terrace Garden, see Whitin to Waldo, 23 Feb. 1912; Morrison to Israels, 1 Dec. 1912, Box 1, C14P. On the Harlem River Casino, see Natalie D. Sonnischsen Report, 26 Oct. 1912; T. W. Veness Report, 27 Oct. 1912, both in Box 28, C14P. On the New Amsterdam Opera House, 340 West 40th Street, see Report of D.O., 5 May 1919, Box 34, C14P.
27. SPC, *Third Report* (New York, 1879), 20–21; McCabe, *Gaslight,* 476–78; Lawrence to Hewitt, 23 July 1888, MP 87-HAS-33 (Bleecker Street); Blackwell, *Counsel to Parents,* 72–73, 50–51; Willemse, *Green Lights,* 68–69 (West 29th Street); *NPG,* 28 Aug. 1880 (Allen); SSV, *Twenty-seventh Annual Report* (New York, 1901), 10. For other examples, see Nicholas Francis Cooke, "The Honeymoon," in *Free Love in America: A Documentary History,* ed. Taylor Stoehr (New York, 1979), 194; William T. Stead, *Satan's Invisible World Displayed; or, Despairing Democracy: A Study of Greater New York* (London, 1898), 18–19; Margaret Marsh, "Suburban Men and Masculine Domesticity, 1870–1915," *AQ* 40 (1988): 168.
28. Anonymous to Comstock, June, 1887, MP 87-HAS-28; "A Poor but Respectable Lady" to Hewitt, 15 Feb. 1888, MP 87-HAS-32; Blackburn to Hewitt, 8 Sept. 1888, MP 87-HAS-33; Wagner to Gilroy, 24 July 1894, MP 89-GTF-14; Police Commissioner to Gaynor, 7 Aug. 1912, MP GWJ-55. For other examples, see Myer to Hewitt, July 1888, MP 87-HAS-33; L.P. to Hewitt, 25 Aug. 1887, MP 87-HAS-29; Lizzie O'Neil to Hewitt, 22 Feb. 1889, MP 87-HAS-35; Anonymous to Low, 2 Feb. 1903, MP LS-5; Police Commissioner to Gaynor, 28 June 1911, MP GWJ-34.
29. *Mazet Committee,* 941 (Van Wyck); Handwritten Report on Avenel Hotel, 8 July 1913, Box 28, C14P (Morgan); Campbell, *Darkness and Daylight,* 209. For a discussion of wealthy married men in New York regularly supporting mistresses after 1880, see Lois Banner, *American Beauty* (Chicago, 1983), 191. Van Wyck's testimony was somewhat confusing. Committee members questioned him on "male harlots" in New York, a subject on which he claimed ignorance. The mayor seems to have been referring to female prostitution and other typical forms of "vice," as seen in his statement "I know there are whores in every big city in the world." For an interpretation of this reference as male prostitution, see Jonathan Katz, *Gay American History* (New York, 1976), 68–69. For a fearful account of juvenile sexuality, including male homosexuality, see Pauline Goldmark, *West Side Studies: Boyhood and Lawlessness* (New York, 1914), 154–56. Observing the West 40th Street brothels from 8:20 to 11:00 P.M. on 28 Nov. 1911, agents for the SPC reported that at least 556 men entered the brothels. In earlier reports on nearby houses, investigators saw 18 men visit one in an hour and a half and another 19 men in twenty minutes. See Report for Nov. 1905, and Report on 140 West 24th Street, Box 91 LWP. For explicit examples of working-class males with prostitutes, see Police Commissioner to Gaynor, 13 Oct. 1911, MP GWJ-35; Description of 205 West 33d Street, Box 91, LWP.
30. Willemse, *Green Lights,* 69. A total of 196 men brought charges against prostitutes; 54 lived in the same ward as the prostitute, 72 in other parts of New York City, 25 in New Jersey and New York State, and 34 in other parts of the United States, and 15 were unknown. See *Mazet Committee,* 2461–79, 2504–17. Other arrest records add support to this trend. For example, eight men arrested in a Brooklyn hotel and house of assignation in East New York (2300 Fulton

Street) in 1910 were all residents of Manhattan (1) and Brooklyn (7). See Transcript to Police Commissioner, 4 March 1910, MP GWJ-14.

31. McCabe, *Gaslight,* 53 ("strangers"). On Italian immigration, see Samuel L. Baily, "The Adjustment of Italian Immigrants in Buenos Aires and New York, 1870–1914," *AHR* 88 (1983): 284–86. In 1900, Chinatown had a population of 6,321 men and only 183 women. See U.S. Bureau of the Census, *Twelfth Census of the United States: 1900* (Washington D.C., 1902), 2:138. This pattern was repeated nationwide. See Ivan Light, "The Ethnic Vice Industry, 1880–1940," *ASR* 42 (1977): 464–79. According to U.S. census figures, the male-to-female ratios were as follows:

	Total		*Native White*		*Foreign White*		*Black*	
	Male	*Female*	*Male*	*Female*	*Male*	*Female*	*Male*	*Female*
1880	100	104						
1890	100	103						
1900	100	102	100	103	100	99	100	103
1910	100	100	100	104	100	95	100	118
	100	95 (15–34 years)						
1920	100	101	100	104	100	95	100	110
	100	102 (18–44 years)						

New York's marriage rates conformed with national patterns, as the percentage of all unmarried American males over fifteen declined from 42 percent in 1890 to 35 percent in 1920. Percentages of married and unmarried males and females were as follows:

		Males		*Females*	
	Age	*Single*	*Married*	*Single*	*Married*
1910	15 or more	42%	54%	36%	53%
	15–24 yrs.	90%	10%	77%	23%
	25–44 yrs.	30%	68%	23%	71%
	45 or more	11%	77%	11%	54%
1920	15 or more	36%	59%	31%	57%

See U.S. Bureau of the Census, *Compendium of the Tenth Census* (Washington, D.C., 1882), 590; idem, *Compendium of the Eleventh Census: 1890* (Washington, D.C. 1894), 3:262–63; idem, *Abstract of the Twelfth Census, 1900* (Washington, D.C., 1904), 104; idem, *Twelfth Census of the United States: Population* (Washington, D.C., 1902), vol. 2, pt. 2, p. 138; idem, *Thirteenth Census of the United States: Abstract of the Census with Supplement of New York* (Washington, D.C., 1913), 602–4; idem, *Fourteenth Census of the United States: New York* (Washington, D.C., 1924), 36–40.

32. Kneeland, *Commercialized Prostitution,* 109–11. On the Mills Houses, see John Tauranac, *Essential New York* (New York, 1979), 79–81; James Ford, *Slums and Housing* (Cambridge, Mass., 1936), 346, 752–58.

33. Franklin H. Martin, ed., *Digest of the Proceedings of the Council of National Defense* (Washington, D.C., 1934), 150–51. On courtship problems, see Sondra R. Herman, "Loving Courtship or the Marriage Market? The Ideal and Its Critics, 1871–1911," *AQ* 25 (1973): 235–52. For more on the importance of "manhood" to late-nineteenth-century and early-twentieth-century males, see Nick Salvatore, *Eugene V. Debs: Citizen and Socialist* (Urbana, Ill., 1982), 46–47, 61–64, 171–72, 216–19, 228–30, 316–17; Leonard Ellis," Men among Men: An Exploration of All-Male Relationships in Victorian America" (Ph.D. diss., Columbia Univ., 1982); Mark C. Carnes, *Secret Ritual and Manhood in Victorian America* (New Haven, 1989).

34. Citizens' Association of New York, *Sanitary Condition of the City: Report of the Council of Hygiene and Public Health* (New York, 1866), 254; New York Association for Improving the

Conditions of the Poor, *Thirty-sixth Annual Report* (New York, 1879), 70 (I am indebted to Mary Beth Brown for this source); Affidavit for 136 Chrystie Street, Box 8, C15P; Clipping for 11 April 1901, Box 39; Clipping for 25 March 1901, Box 38; Minutes for 20 March 1901, all in C15P; Committee of Fifteen, *Social Evil,* 187.

35. Robert W. DeForest and Lawrence Veiller, eds., *The Tenement House Problem* (New York, 1903), 1:xv, 10, 19, 50–52; Kathy Peiss, "Charity Girls and City Pleasures: Historical Notes on Working-Class Sexuality, 1880–1920," in *Powers of Desire; The Politics of Sexuality,* eds. Ann Snitow, Christine Stansell, and Sharon Thompson (New York, 1983), 81. For another example, see Woods to Mitchel, 6 Oct. 1914, MP MJP-20.

36. DeForest, *Tenement House,* 1:386 (landlord); Veiller to Mitchel, 18 April 1914; Murphy to Pfeiffer, 2 July 1914, both in THC-Prostitution Folder, Box 168, CSS Papers. On tenement prostitution, see K.R. to Hewitt, 29 July 1887, MP 87-HAS-17; Clippings for 11 April 1901, Box 39, C15P; Headley to Burritt, 24 June 1914, File 60, Box 23, CSS papers; Kneeland, *Commercialized Prostitution,* 26–29, 117–18.

37. Kneeland, *Commercialized Prostitution,* 25; Committee of Fifteen Report, 1 Oct. 1901, Box 19, LWP; Memo (on high rate of prostitution), 20 Nov. 1913, THC-Prostitution Folder, Box 168, CSS Papers; Veiller to Murphy, 14 Feb. 1914, Box 168, CSS Papers; Headley to Burritt, 24 June 1914, File 60, Box 23, CSS Papers. Headley later thought that the problem was not as serious as first believed. See Headley to Burritt, 8 July 1914, File 60, Box 23, CSS papers.

38. Murphy to Pfeiffer, 2 July 1914, THC-Prostitution Folder, Box 168, CSS Papers. Also see Committee of Fourteen, *Annual Report* (New York, 1914), 31–32. On recidivism, see Committee of Fourteen, *Annual Report* (New York, 1915), 14; idem, *Annual Report* (New York, 1922), 35.

39. Kneeland, *Commercialized Prostitution,* 50–51.

40. Ibid., 45–50, 63–64; Handy to Hewitt ("cloak"), 22 June 1887, MP 87-HAS-16. Also see Neighbor to Grant, 26 Jan. 1889, MP 88-GHJ-39; Police Commissioner to Gaynor, 11 Jan. 1911, MP GWJ-33; Frank Moss, *The American Metropolis* (New York, 1897), 1:231, 339.

41. Anonymous to Gaynor ("for the purpose"), attached to Police Commissioner to Gaynor, 5 Aug. 1912, MP GWJ-55. One cigar store was the meeting place for eleven different social clubs. See Benjamin Reich, "A New Social Center: The Candy Store as a Social Influence," in Univ. Settlement Society of New York, *Report* (New York, 1899), 32–34. Rachel Goldcranz ran a house of prostitution in a Delancey Street cigar store without her children's discovering it. See SPCC, *Ninth Annual Report* (New York, 1884), 49–50. Because they were open on Sunday, some cigar stores sold liquor and other beverages illegally. "See "Hundreds of Saloon Keepers" to Hewitt, 9 June 1887, MP 87-HAS-16. There was only sporadic mention of prostitutes in cigar stores before 1880. The earliest I found was in the *Weekly Rake,* 22 Oct. 1842.

42. Freese to Grant ("nice girl"), 9 March 1889, MP 88-GHJ-39; J.T.R. to Hewitt (West 3d Street), 22 Aug. 1888, MP 87-HAS-32. For other examples, see Kneeland, *Commercialized Prostitution,* 62–65; Ballard to Hewitt, June 1887; "Tenant and Tenth Ward Democrat" to Hewitt, 22 April 1887; Testimony of Sophie Galle, 29 June 1887; Anderson to Hewitt, 11 Sept. 1887; Von Lossberg to Hewitt, 28 Aug. 1887; "A Tenant" to Hewitt, 28 May 1887; "One of Your Supporters" to Hewitt, 30 March 1887, all in MP 87-HAS-28; "Tenants of 85 Elizabeth Street" to Hewitt, 12 Aug. 1888, MP 87-HAS-32; Mayer to Hewitt, 25 June 1888; Citizen to Hewitt, 6 Oct. 1888; Seiffert to Hewitt, Jan. 1888, all in MP 87-HAS-33; Smith to Grant, 25 April 1889; Barrett to Grant, 27 Nov. 1889; Anonymous to Grant, 31 Jan. 1889; "Residents of 43 Eldridge Street" to Grant, 7 Dec. 1889, all in MP 88-GHJ-39.

43. When Goldstein was later arrested, she dropped the prostitution and ran a legitimate business. See Allaire to Murray, Nov. 1887, MP 87-HAS-28. For other quotes, see Anonymous to Hewitt (Second Avenue), 4 May 1887, MP 87-HAS-29; "One of a Good Many" to Hewitt (Delancey Street), 19 June 1888, MP 87-HAS-32; Anonymous Female to Hewitt (Hester Street), 7 Sept. 1888, MP 87-HAS-32; George Ellington, *The Women of New York; or, The Under-World of the Great City* (Burlington, Iowa, 1869), 171–72, 187–89. Even on Coney Island, the cigar store was a popular cover for the clandestine activities of prostitutes. See Acting Police Commissioner to Gaynor, 31 July 1913, MP GWJ-74. Institutions with exclusively male patrons were

not the only ones with prostitutes. Large department stores were sometimes accused of harboring prostitutes. See Minutes of 11 Oct. 1913, Box 13, SPC Papers. A Committee of Fourteen study in conjunction with the National Civic Federation, however, found no evidence of prostitution in an undercover investigation of Macy's. See Committee of Fourteen, *Department Store Investigation* (New York, 1915). On streetwalkers in Herald Square and near large department stores, see Baker to Gaynor, 1 Sept. 1910, MP GWJ-16.

44. Petition of Residents of East 30th Street to Hewitt, 15 Sept. 1887; Tomes to Hewitt, 14 Sept. 1887, both in MP 87-HAS-29. For examples of other cafés, see Confidential Bulletin, 18 Nov. 1914, THC-Prostitution Folder, Box 168, CSS Papers.

45. Undated Manuscript, pp. 3–5, and Soda Water Places Folder, Box 91, LWP. For an example of an Italian soda water place, see Police Commissioner to Gaynor, 4 May 1911, MP GWJ-34. Korn's was located at 232 East 14th Street, Litsky's at 228 East 14th Street, Steckles' at 98 Third Avenue, Ringschules' at 26 Second Avenue, Schwartsberg's at 45 Second Street, Kerner's at 244–246 East Ninth Street, Frisch's at 13 Second Street, and Elfenbein's at 123 Second Avenue. Also see Kneeland, *Commercialized Prostitution,* 30–33, 60–62; Report of H.K., 2 June 1919, Box 34, C14P.

46. Arrest Records of City Magistrates' Court, 6 Sept. 1904, MP MGB-10; Undated Reports, Box 91, LWP. Steckles provided bail for at least fourteen prostitutes in 1899 and thirty-two in 1902. See Police Memo, Fifteenth Precinct, 6 Oct. 1904, MP MGB-31. For an example of a downtown lunchroom with prostitutes (61 Ann Street), see "A Citizen" to Hewitt, 19 Nov. 1888, MP 87-HAS-34.

47. Williams to Byrnes, 29 Dec. 1893, MP 89-GTF-14. On saloon mortgages, see Kneeland, *Commercialized Prostitution,* 54–55. On other saloons, see Grant Holcomb, "John Sloan and 'McSorley's Wonderful Saloon,' " *American Art Journal* 15 (Spring 1983): 5–20; Batterberry, *On the Town,* 150–51.

48. On the Hertzes, see Saloonkeeper to Hewitt, April 1888, MP 87-HAS-33. On dealers, see Liquor Dealers Association, Second Assembly District to Hewitt, Sept. 1887, MP 87-HAS-29. Kneeland, "Commercialized Vice," 69–90, and Committee of Fifteen, *Social Evil,* 160, blamed saloons. On prostitutes boarding in saloons, see G.R. to Hewitt, 26 Aug. 1887, MP 87-HAS-29.

49. Davis to Edson (Chatham Street), 10 May 1884, MP 85-EF-10. Rook's saloon was at 37 East 13th Street. See Lawrence to Hewitt, 23 July 1888, MP 87-HAS-33; U.H. to Hewitt, Dec. 1887, MP 87-HAS-33; W.R. to Hewitt, 31 March 1887, MP 87-HAS-28; Martin to Grant, 5 Feb. 1889, MP 88-GHJ-40. For similar examples, see "Tenant" to Hewitt, 2 July 1888, MP 87-HAS-34; Schmidt to Hewitt, 30 Aug. 1888, MP 87-HAS-21; "A Sailor" to Hewitt, 30 Oct. 1888, MP 87-HAS-33; Muhn to Hewitt, 23 Aug. 1888, MP 87-HAS-35; DAP, People v. Noll, 24 March 1875. Most saloons charged men one dollar to use a room with a prostitute.

50. On couples, see Hutchinson to Hewitt, 2 May 1887, MP 87-HAS-28; "A Mother" to Hewitt, 2 July 1888, MP 87-HAS-35. On Geoghegan's, see *NPG,* 10 Jan., 10 July, 14 Aug. 1880. For more examples of the working-class patronage of saloons with prostitutes, see Allaire to Walling, 16 Jan. 1884, MP 85-EF-10; "Morality" to Hewitt, 8 April 1887, MP 87-HAS-29; Grant to Williams, 7 Jan. 1895, MP 90-SWL-44; Reardon to Gilroy, 7 Aug. 1894, MP 89-GTF-14.

51. Ashen to Grace, 17 Feb. 1881, MP 84-GWR-11 ("vilest"); McAdoo to Gaynor, 20 March 1913, MP GWJ-87; Committee of Fourteen, *Annual Report* (New York, 1912), 3; John D. Peters, "The Story of the Committee of Fourteen of New York," *Social Hygiene* 4 (1918): 363. Hiding their interest with dummy corporations and figurehead presidents (often the hotel bartenders), owners were difficult to trace. For descriptions of postbellum hotels, see McCabe, *Gaslight,* 142–53, 645–49; idem, *Secrets,* 44–45; Charles Lockwood, *Manhattan Moves Uptown* (Boston, 1976) 296; Henry S. Mower, *Reminiscences of a Hotel Man* (New York, 1912).

52. On Compton House, see "Truth" to Hewitt, 26 Sept. 1888, MP 87-HAS-35; "Citizen" to Hewitt, 27 Aug. 1887, MP 87-HAS-29; "An American" to Hewitt, 26 Oct. 1888, MP 87-HAS-34. On the Florence Hotel (Broadway and 26th Street), see "Citizen" to Hewitt, 24 Jan. 1888, MP 87-HAS-33. For another example, see "Citizen" to Grant, 16 Nov. 1889, MP 88-GHJ-40.

On King Edward Hotel, see Police Commissioner to Woods, 27 Feb. 1914, MP MJP-18; SPC, *Third Annual Report* (New York, 1879), 8–15.

53. Committee of Fifteen, *Social Evil,* 162–63 ("summer garden"); Affidavit for Maryland Kitchen, 254 West 34th Street, Box 23, C15P.

54. *Times* 22, 29 Aug. 1923; 17 Oct. 1926 (obituary). Luchow's was cited as a Raines Law hotel in 1910 because there were twenty-five rooms upstairs. See Burgher to Gaynor, 8 Aug. 1910, MP GWJ-16. Committee of Fourteen investigators, however, said that the rooms were never rented out and were occupied only by the male waiters. Prostitutes were only in the restaurant and saloon area. See Night Inspection Report by David Oppenheim, 5 Aug. 1918, Box 33, C14P. "Down Where the Wurzburger Flows" was a popular song about Luchow's. See Robert A. M. Stern et al., *New York 1900: Metropolitan Architecture and Urbanism* (New York 1983), 225; Batterberry, *On the Town,* 132–33.

55. Peters, "Committee of Fourteen," 363, 376; Kneeland, *Commercialized Prostitution,* 36; Reports in Raines Law I, II, III Folders, Box 91, LWP. The Regent was located at 28th Street and Sixth Avenue; Buchwald's, at 137 West 28th Street; the Bellwood, at 33d Street and Seventh Avenue; Nelson's, at 36th Street and Seventh Avenue; Roach's, at 38th Street and Seventh Avenue; McGirr's, at 38th Street and Sixth Avenue; Van Twiller, at the southeast corner of 25th Street and Lexington Avenue; Delevan, at 34th Street and Third Avenue; German Hotel, at 138–40 East 13th Street; St. Blaise, at 158 East 23d Street; Bergin Hotel, at northeast corner of 28th Street and Seventh Avenue; and Clinton Place Hotel, at 96 Sixth Avenue.

56. F. H. Whitin Report on 484 Third Avenue ("proposition pay"), 20 Feb. 1907, Box 28, C14P. On a good weekend, Flaggelle's made $400. See Report of J. W. Brewster and Abel Whitehouse, 2, 5 May 1905, Box 28, C14P. Since prosecution required clerks to know they were renting to prostitutes, proprietors placed the registration desk away from the hotel entrance. On "charity places," see Undated Reports on 245–49 West 39th Street; The National, 3 Irving Place; Metropolitan Hotel and Winter Garden, 278 Third Avenue; and Wundling's Hotel, 39 Third Avenue, all in Box 91, LWP; Kneeland, *Commercialized Prostitution,* 39–40. Prosecution of clerks was based on their accepting a female guest twice in the same night with different men. See Whitin, "Obstacles to Vice Repression," 156–57; Committee of Fourteen, *Annual Report* (New York, 1915), 18. By 1905, 1,150 of 1,407 certified hotels in Manhattan and the Bronx were "liquor law hotels." See Kneeland, *Commercialized Prostitution,* 34. When large numbers of brothels were raided and closed in 1907, many prostitutes simply set up new operations in hotels. See Kneeland, *Commercialized Prostitution,* 37–39.

57. Reports on Sans Souci, 100 Third Avenue, and National, 3 Irving Place, Box 91, LWP.

58. Committee of Fifteen, *Social Evil,* 160; Committee of Fourteen, *Annual Report* (New York, 1916), 34–35; Emma Goldman, *Living My Life* (Garden City, N.Y., 1934), 356. On hotels, see Theodore Roosevelt, *An Autobiography* (New York, 1914), 197; Committee of Fifteen, *Social Evil,* 166–68; Kneeland, *Commercialized Prostitution,* 34; Clippings for 25–27 Dec. 1900, C15P; Theodore Roosevelt Papers, Library of Congress, Reel 454, ser. 15, vol. 2; *Tribune,* 2 April 1896; Paul S. Boyer, *Urban Masses and Moral Order, 1820–1920* (Cambridge, Mass., 1978), 193, 210. The organization managed to get "underworld bills" introduced to remove police from the front of hotels if acquitted of vice charges and to grant defendants jury trials. None got out of committee. On the operation of hotels, see Undated Reports in Raines Law I, II, III Folders, Box 91, LWP; Report of Cases, 12 April 1909, Box 13, SPC Papers; Sanders to Board of Police Commissioners, 22 July 1897, MP 90–SWL–45; Police Commissioner to Woods, 11 Feb. 1914, MP MJP–17; George Kneeland, "Commercialized Vice and the Liquor Traffic," *Social Hygiene* 2 (1916): 73. On Union Square hotels, see Burgher to Gaynor, 8 Aug. 1910, MP GWJ–16. The combination of benefits and protection outweighed any loss of independence in making these hotels the most desirable places for prostitutes to work.

59. Holloran to Mitchel, 28 May 1915, MP MJP–41; Woods to Mitchel, 23 April 1914, MP MJP–20; Kneeland, "Commercialized Prostitution," 75. On reformers confusing Raines Law hotels with cabarets, see the reports on the German Village and other cabarets in Raines Law Hotel Reports, undated, Box 91, LWP. The best examination of cabarets is in Erenberg, *Steppin'*

Out. Erenberg argues that reformers like the Committee of Fourteen erroneously equated much of the activity in cabarets, including "shimmy dancing" and ragtime music, with prostitution. This was especially true in their annual reports. A careful reading of the unpublished investigators reports, however, shows that many of them made careful distinctions between prostitutes and other women. For typical examples, see Reports of Frederick Whitin, 1905–10, Box 28; Charles A. Briggs Reports, 7 April 1915, 24 March 1915, Box 28; Handwritten Reports, 29 May 1912, Box 28, all in C14P. For an excellent discussion of the business and organizational structure of cabarets and restaurants, see Lewis Erenberg, "Impresarios of Broadway Nightlife," in *Inventing Times Square: Commerce and Culture at the Crossroads of the World*, ed. William R. Taylor (New York, 1991), 158–69.

60. Investigator's Report, 12 Jan. 1919, Box 34 (Maxim's and Child's); Undated Typed Report, 1912, Box 28 (Pekin's); Charles A. Briggs Reports, 7 April 1915, 24 March 1915, Box 28 (Reisenweber's); Handwritten Reports, 29 May 1912, Box 28 (Green Turtle and Bustanoby's), all in C14P. Tucker was at Reisenweber's from 1916 to 1922. Cabarets were not licensed until 1912. See Erenberg, *Steppin' Out*, 65–66, 177–80. Policy changes by the liquor industry also encouraged concert saloons to give way to cabarets. In 1908, the Committee of Fourteen and the Central Association of the New York Liquor Dealers agreed to discontinue "disorderly practice" in saloons and prohibited pianos in rear rooms of saloons belonging to their organization, further separating live music from the saloon. See Confidential Bulletin, 12 June 1914, Box 168, CSS Papers; Committee of Fourteen, *Annual Report* (New York, 1912), 20–22; idem, *Annual Report* (New York, 1913), 33; Kneeland, "Commercialized Prostitution," 86–87.
61. Typed Report on College Inn, 9 May 1914, Box 28; Investigator's Report on Maxim's, 26 Feb. 1919, Box 34; Charles Briggs Report on Healy's, 15 April 1915, Box 28; T.T. Report on Pekin's, 10 Oct. 1914, Box 28, all in C14P. For other examples, see Investigators' Reports on Geneva Restaurant, Tokio, Alamo, and Banks's, 1914–19, Boxes 28 and 34, C14P.
62. Thomas Byrnes, *1886—Professional Criminals of America* (New York, 1886), xxi; Blackwell, *Counsel to Parents*, 51–52.

Chapter 12 Syndicates and Underworlds

1. *Lexow Committee*, 1:36; Memo of Howard to Police Commissioner, 12 April 1915, MP MJP-41.
2. William McAdoo, *Guarding a Great City* (New York, 1906), 80; Interview with Bingham, 1907, MP MGB-42; General Theodore A. Bingham, "The Organized Criminals of New York," *McClure's* 34 (1909): 62. On the power of captains, see Thomas Byrnes, *1886—Professional Criminals of America* (New York, 1886), xxi; McAdoo, *Guarding a Great City*, 222. On Erhardt, see Stenographers Report, Police Department Investigation, 1879, MP 83-CE-26. Roosevelt's comment is in New York City Police Department, *Annual Report* (New York, 1897), 13. In 1895, the state senator and Tammany Hall district leader George F. Roesch admitted that officials like himself wielded great influence in the obtaining of police appointments and promotions. See *Lexow Committee*, 2: 1261–301. For similar statements on the close ties of prostitution and the municipality, see Letterbook 1885–86, pp. 433–35, Box 79, William R. Grace Papers, Columbia Univ.; McAdoo, *Guarding a Great City*, 86; Matthew Hale Smith, *Sunshine and Shadow in New York* (Hartford, 1868), 176, 300; *Lexow Committee*, 1:34. Testimony before the Lexow committee could not be used against any of those testifying, which made this testimony unusually accurate and revealing. See *Lexow Committee*, 1:1011. For more on corruption problems, see Theodore Roosevelt, *An Autobiography* (New York, 1914), 176–96; Theodore Roosevelt Papers, Library of Congress, ser. 15, vol. 1, Clippings for June–Aug. 1895.
3. Cornelius W. Willemse, *Behind the Green Lights* (New York, 1931), 20; McAdoo, *Guarding a Great City*, 31–32. When he was police commissioner, Theodore Roosevelt ordered all police officers to resign from political clubs. See *Herald*, 17 May 1895, Reel 454, ser. 15, Theodore Roosevelt Papers. On police organization, see Wilbur Miller, *Cops and Bobbies: Police Authority in New York and London, 1830–1870* (Chicago, 1973), 29–34, 44, 94, 102–3; Eugene J. Watts,

"Police Response to Crime and Disorder in Twentieth-Century St. Louis," *JAH* 70 (1983): 341–56.

4. *Lexow Committee,* 1:460–64 ($20–$30). On the structure of the New York Democratic party and Tammany Hall, see Matthew P. Breen, *Thirty Years of New York Politics Up-to-Date* (New York, 1899), 38–39; McAdoo, *Guarding a Great City,* 88. For more on post–Civil War New York politics, see David C. Hammack, *Power and Society: Greater New York at the Turn of the Century* (New York, 1982), 3–30, 158–84.
5. New York State Senate, *Documents* (Albany, 1856), 142 ("the peace"), quoted in David R. Johnson, *Policing the Urban Underworld: The Impact of Crime on the Development of the American Police, 1800–1887* (Philadelphia, 1979), 178–79; Clipping, 17 Aug. 1901, Box 44, C15P; Anonymous to Hewitt ("bad female element"), 11 July 1888, MP 87-HAS-32; Praetori to Hewitt, 7 July 1887, MP 87-HAS-26; and 1887, MP 87-HAS-29. Praetori's parish was St. Francis of Assisi Roman Catholic Church, on West 31st Street. For a similar police statement a quarter century later, see Minutes of 15 Dec. 1913, Box 13, SPC Papers. Also see Adam Clayton Powell, Sr., *Against the Tide: An Autobiography* (New York, 1938), 55–56; Anonymous Police Document, 1896, and various letters of police captains to Conlin, 27 May 1896, all in MP 90-SWL-45.
6. "One Who Knows" to Hewitt, 30 May 1887, MP 87-HAS-16 ("woe"). On the Washington Square and Bleecker Street areas, see Anonymous to Hewitt, Dec. 1887, and 1 May 1888, both in MP 87-HAS-33. On Cherry Street, see Carpenter to Williams, 26 Jan. 1889; "Tenants" to Grant, 22 Jan. 1889, both in MP 88-GHJ-39. On the Tenderloin, see C.D. to Hewitt, 8 June 1887, MP 87-HAS-26; Prescott to Hewitt, 17 Nov. 1887, MP 87-HAS-17. On the Lower East Side, see Bannier to Hewitt, 26 June 1887. On new madams, see *Lexow Committee,* 4:4136–54, 4163–97. For more on the corrupt activities of Williams, see *NPG,* 22 June, 9 Nov. 1878; Moss to Hewitt, 1 June 1887, MP 87-HAS-16; Crosby, Smith, Praetori, Moss, and Hill to Hewitt, 1 Sept. 1887; Murray, Chatelan, and Crosby to Hewitt, 24 May 1887; Anonymous Madam to Hewitt, 1887, all in MP 87-HAS-26; Holmes to Murray, 1 June 1887, MP 87-HAS-28; *Lexow Committee,* 3:2917.
7. *Lexow Committee,* 1:954–64; 2:2752 (on Devery); 2:1536; 3:2752 (on Glennon); 1–2:1247–60 (on Schwartz); 1:1072–115; 4:4117–21 (on Parkhurst); *Mazet Committee,* 510–17, 2377–78; William T. Stead, *Satan's Invisible World Displayed: or, Despairing Democracy: A Study of Greater New York* (London, 1898), 126–28. For more on Glennon, see *Times,* 19 April 1901. When police received numerous complaints about a house, the captain usually raised "the ante." See *Lexow Committee,* 2:2286. For similar examples, see *Lexow Committee,* 1:1122–31; 2:1358; Affidavit for 8 James Street; 31 July, 1 Aug. 1901 Clippings, Box 3, C15P. It was not uncommon for city politicians to demand initiation fees for municipal positions. According to James McCabe, an appointment to the city attorney's office cost $10,000, and teachers had to pay $50 to $600 for an appointment. See McCabe, *The Secrets of the Great City* (Philadelphia, 1868), 66–67.
8. *Lexow Committee,* 4:4495–98.
9. On the coffee house, see *Lexow Committee,* 3:3105. On Chinatown, see Affidavits for 12 Chatham Square and 7 Mott Street, Box 4, C15P; Morgan to Edson, 23 Nov. 1883, MP 85-EF-10. On Thurow, see *Lexow Committee,* 1:1041–64; Stead, *Satan's Invisible World,* 131–33. On streetwalkers, see *Lexow Committee,* 1:35; 4:3615–23; Police Commissioner to Mayor, 20, 24, 27 Feb. 1911, MP GWJ-33; Police Commissioner to Gaynor, 5 June 1913, MP GWJ-73. For a streetwalker paying off policemen at Gramercy Park, see Minutes for 11 Dec. 1911, Box 13, SPC Papers.
10. Anonymous to Hewitt ("a well-known fact"), 28 July 1887, MP 87-HAS-29; *Lexow Committee,* 1–2:1247–60. In German-speaking neighborhoods, the wardman often knew the language. See Prescott to Hewitt, 17 Nov. 1887, MP 87-HAS-17; *Lexow Committee,* 2:1448. On Brogan, see "A Near Neighbor" to Hewitt, 27 July 1888, MP 87-HAS-32. On Hahn, see SPC, *Report* (New York, 1896), 49. Gannon was Mack's alleged lover. After Gannon was convicted for neglect of duty, they ran hotels and saloons at 29th Street and Sixth Avenue, 474 Sixth Avenue, 317 East 14th Street, and 431 Seventh Avenue, just south of 34th Street. See "A Victim" to Rocke-

feller, Undated, Box 28, C14P; Clippings for 29 Aug. 1910, Box 45; Clippings for 17 Sept. 1901, Box 46; Clippings for 3 Oct. 1901, Box 47; Clippings for 20 Sept., 14 Oct., 20 Nov. 1901, Box 49, all in C15P; Minutes of 11 Dec. 1911, Box 13, SPC Papers. On Miller, see "Business Men and Property Owners" to Hewitt, 16 Oct. 1888, MP 87-HAS-33. For another example of politicians frequenting specific brothels, see Maria to Hewitt, 8 June 1887, MP 87-HAS-28. Miller's house was at 335 West 20th Street. See Police Commissioner to Gaynor, 11 Jan. 1912, MP GWJ-52.

11. "A Near Neighbor" to Hewitt, 27 July 1888, MP 87-HAS-32; "Citizen" to Hewitt, 10 Aug. 1887, MP 87-HAS-29. The brothel was at 124 Prince Street and the station at 128 Prince Street. See "A True Democrat" to Hewitt, 21 Aug. 1887, MP 87-HAS-29. For a similar example on the Lower East Side, see *Lexow Committee,* 2:1669–79. In the antebellum period, the Fifth Ward Station House, at 16 Anthony Street, was surrounded by brothels. See D. T. Valentine, *Manual of the Corporation of the City of New York, 1845–1846* (New York, 1846), 60.

12. Keegan to Hewitt (Bleecker Street), 25 June 1887, MP 87-HAS-28; Wickham to Police Commissioners, 7 Oct. 1875, MP 81-WWH-25; H. Cole to Hewitt, 4 Oct. 1887, MP 87-HAS-28; "Morality" to Hewitt (Mr. Ryan), 8 April 1887, MP 87-HAS-29; "Morality" to Hewitt (sailor), 25 May 1887, MP 87-HAS-28; Anonymous to Hewitt (Fifth Avenue), 28 May 1888, MP 87-HAS-32; Mitchel to Gaynor, 1912, MP GWJ-87. For similar observations, see Anonymous to Hewitt, 12 Dec. 1887, MP 87-HAS-28; "Taxpayer" to Gaynor, 27 June 1910, MP GWJ-15; "Taxpayer" to Grant, 18 Jan. 1889, MP 88-GHJ-38.

13. *Times,* 14 July 1875. On police in front of brothels, see McAdoo, *Guarding a Great City,* 84–86. For similar examples, see Tresch to Grace, 25 Feb. 1881, MP 84-GWR-11; "Taxpayer" to Gaynor, 27 June 1910, MP GWJ-15. On Allaire and Williams, see Silberman to Hewitt, 27 June 1887, MP 87-HAS-28; Petition of "Business Men and Residents in 19th Precinct" to Hewitt, 27 May 1887, MP 87-HAS-26. Especially note the list of Bowery businessmen and shopkeepers denying the existence of prostitution in certain tenements and lodging houses in Williams to Murray, 23 Oct. 1888, MP 87-HAS-33.

14. *Lexow Committee,* 2:2287 ("turn up a dollar"); Parkhurst to Price, 16 Jan. 1894, MP 89-GTF-14. For examples of arresting innocent boardinghouse keepers, see the testimonies of Henrietta Hensing, Louisa Miller, and Caela Urchittel in *Lexow Committee,* 2:1448, 1558–65; 3:2943–54. One detective, a partner with a Brooklyn and Tenderloin madam, was promoted after completing a fake raid on a disorderly house over the head of a inspector whom he wanted removed. See "Citizen" to Gaynor, Oct. 1910, MP GWJ-17. Detective Cliff was promoted by the reformist police commissioner Theodore Bingham. Innocent working women returning home from their job were accosted and accused of prostitution by the police during the 1880s. On raids, see *Lexow Committee,* 3:2861; 4:4207–15 (Moss); *Mazet Committee,* 2372; 11 Aug. 1901 Clipping, Box 43, C15P; *City Vigilant,* Feb. 1894, p. 20; Undated Report for 235–239 West 39th Street, Box 91, LWP; Kneeland, "Commercialized Prostitution and the Use of Property," *Social Hygiene* 2 (1916); 566. For a similar account see "A Taxpayer" to Hewitt, 17 Oct. 1888, and Reilly to Murray, 26 Oct. 1888, both in MP 87-HAS-32. On payoffs, see *Lexow Committee,* 1:1069; 4:3624–38. Police officers sometimes worked through bondsmen to avoid corruption charges. See McAdoo, *Guarding a Great City,* 81–83. On the different levels of graft, see Undated Manuscript, p. 2, Box 91, LWP.

15. Bingham, "Organized Criminals," 65; The Joneses' brothels were at 21 and 32 Bayard Street. See *Lexow Committee,* 1:983–1009, 1011–21. On Bocks, see Mason to Hewitt, 16 Jan. 1888, MP 87-HAS-33. Hill was appointed marshal in 1881 and was an ally of William R. Grace. See *Herald,* 12 Dec. 1885. On the Owasco Club on Seventh Avenue, see Police Commissioner to Gaynor, 5 March 1913, MP GWJ-72. On the Flyder Association at Delancy and Eldridge streets, see Report for Oct. 1905, Box 91, LWP. On the Republican Hackett's Association at 144 Eighth Avenue, see Affidavits for 64–66 Seventh Avenue, Box 18, C15P. For other examples, Reports on 59 East Fourth Street and 2120 Third Avenue, Box 13, 26, 27, C15P. Voting in saloons and cigar stores was common. See William Mills Ivins, *Machine Politics and Money in Elections in New York City* (New York, 1887), 20–21.

16. Krammer also collected the weekly protection fees for the police. See Affidavits for 67 Cherry

Street and 8 James Street, Box 3, C15P. For an example of politicians frequenting specific brothels, see Maria to Hewitt, 8 June 1887, MP 87-HAS-28. Kelly's saloon was at 212 East 14th Street, and Hugo Langerfeld ran the Washington Hotel, 75 Third Avenue. See Undated Reports, Box 91, LWP. Other Tammany proprietors included Carroll, at 154 Fourth Avenue, and Gaffney, of the Stuyvesant Square Hotel, northeast corner of Ninth Street and Third Avenue. The retired police officer Owen Gallagher also ran a notorious Raines Law hotel with Louis Shapiro. The Hotel Irvington was at 119 East 14th Street. See Reports, 1913, Box 28, C14P. Another state senator reportedly ran a saloon and brothel at 13th Street and University Place. See SSV, *Twenty-seventh Annual Report* (New York, 1901), 22. The proprietor of the National Hotel, Mr. Allison, was a "political heeler" and associated with political clubs. See Undated Report on National Hotel, 3 Irving Place, Box 91, LWP.

17. Bingham, "Organized Criminals," 66 ("open markets"). The German Village was at 147 West 40th Street, opposite the Metropolitan Opera House. Hadden also controlled the Hotel Lafayette, at 562 Seventh Avenue, the Denver, at 207 West 40th Street, and the Atlan, at 159 West 34th Street. See Raines Law Hotel Reports, Undated, Box 91, LWP; Reports, 1913, Box 28, C14P; Committee of Fourteen Confidential Bulletins, 16 July, 9 Sept. 1914, Box 168, THC-Prostitution Folder, CSS Papers; Police Commissioner to Woods, 11 Feb. 1914, MP MJP-17; Committee of Fourteen, *Annual Report* (New York, 1914), 10–12; Fahey to Police Commissioner, 7 Oct. 1910, MP GWJ-17; Lewis Erenberg, *Steppin' Out: New York Nightlife and the Transformation of American Culture, 1890–1930* (Westport, Conn., 1981), 75. After coming to New York in 1886, Sam Paul ran gambling houses at Willett and Houston streets, 53 Attorney Street, 310 East Houston Street, 105 Second Avenue, and 98 Second Avenue. He was the ex-husband of the madam Frieda Shaw, who ran a brothel on West 29th Street off Broadway. They were married from 1904 to 1907. See Memo to Police Commissioner, 11 Sept. 1912, MP GWJ-87. Thurow also paid five dollars to a sergeant for each girl he released on bail. See *Lexow Committee,* 1:1041–64, 1115–22. On Fleck, see Abstracts for 19 April 1901, Box 1; Affidavits for 104–106 Bowery, Box 6; Clippings, 19 April 1901, Box 39, all in C15P; *Times,* 19 April, 3, 21, 29 May 1901.

18. Curry to Whitin, 19 March 1907, Box 1, C14P. For similar attacks, see Parkhurst's indictment of city government as a form of organized crime in SPC, *Report* (New York, 1896), 6–7.

19. Appell was proprietor of an Eighth Avenue concert saloon. His father was also a member of Tammany's committee on organization. See McCullagh to Byrnes, 15 Jan. 1895, McAvoy to Byrnes, 15 Feb., 3 May 1894; Appell to Gilroy, 27 Feb. 1894, all in MP 89-GTF-15. Gartner operated an establishment on Third Avenue. See Reilly to McDonough, 9 Feb. 1893, MP 89-GTF-15. Charles Krumm ran Kunstler Hall and was president of the German-American Independent Republican Association. See Krumm to Gilroy, 15 Feb. 1893, MP 89-GTF-15; Krumm to Burrows, 28 April 1897, MP 90-SWL-36. On Sullivan, see Complaints and Investigations, Police Department, Minutes of 1 Aug. 1908, MP MGB-120. On Hart, see Bingham, "Organized Criminals," 66. For a thoughtful and provocative interpretation of Sullivan, see Daniel Czitrom, "Underworlds and Underdogs: Big Tim Sullivan and Metropolitan Politics in New York, 1889–1913," *JAH* 78 (1991): 536–58.

20. *Times,* 10 Jan. 1886, in Grace Papers, Box 108, Scrapbook 9. For more on McMahon, See *Times,* 25 Jan. 1876. On Bennet, see Bennet to Hook, 24 Dec. 1910, Box 1, C14P. Eventually, Tammany's link with prostitution produced a split within the machine. In order to deflect charges of corruption by the Committee of Fifteen, Tammany appointed its own Committee of Five, headed by Lewis Nixon. When Nixon raided a downtown gambling den that had several Tammany men in attendance, including Maurice F. Holahan, president of the Board of Public Improvements, he angered several machine leaders, including Richard Croker and Nixon's "political godfather," Fire Commissioner John J. Scannell. See Clippings for 20 Feb. 1901, Box 35, and various clippings in Boxes 34–37, C15P.

21. On Oakey Hall, see *Times,* 16 Jan. 1875. On Street, see DAP, People v. Street, 23 Feb. 1875. The judge's name was Garvin. On Roesch, see *Lexow Committee,* 2:1261–301; Roesch to Gilroy, 5 Sept. 1893, MP 89-GTF-15. Roesch was an assemblyman in 1883–89, a state senator in 1890–93, and then a judge. On Engel and Hadden, see Bingham, "Organized Criminals,"

66. On Kernochan, see Third Deputy Commissioner to Mitchel, 23 Sept. 1915, MP MJP-41. The address was 234 West 14th Street. On Williams and Root, see *Lexow Committee,* 3:2925.

22. Wald to Holt, 16 Nov. 1910; Report of the Women's Prison Association, 14 Oct. 1910, both in Box 91, LWP; Whitin to Veiller ("fewer women"), 22 June 1911, Committee of Fourteen Folder, Box 109, CSS Papers; Judge Jonah J. Goldstein Interview, pp. 66, 341–43, Columbia Univ. Oral History Collection. Interestingly, during the 1930s, Goldstein was supported by Helen P. McCormick, counsel of the Brooklyn Women's Court Alliance and Samuel Markus, Counsel for the SPC. For a list of the array of reform and women's organization protesting the law, see Resolution of 19 Jan. 1911; Wald to Ivins, 6 Sept. 1910, both in Box 91, LWP. Similarly, in 1911, the San Francisco Board of Health required all prostitutes to be examined two times a week. See Neal Larry Shumsky and Larry M. Springer, "San Francisco's Zone of Prostitution, 1880–1934," *JHG* 7 (1981): 79.

23. The Committee of Fourteen referred to an "old syndicate" (before 1905) in its reports. See Typed List of Houses and Resorts of Prostitution, Arranged According to Street, 1910 and 1 Feb. 1912, Box 28, C14P. The first use of the term "organized crime" was applied to Tammany Hall in SPC, *Report* (New York, 1896), 6–7.

24. Orrin B. Booth, *The White Slave Traffic* (New York, 1899), 7–11; Kenneth Roberts and Anna M. Roberts, eds., *Moreau de St. Méry's American Journey, 1793–1798* (Garden City, N.Y., 1947), 302. On Farryall, see Christine Stansell, *City of Women: Sex and Class in New York, 1789–1860* (New York, 1986), 190. For other examples, see *NPG,* 31 Aug. 1867, 9 Nov. 1878. The best analysis of the "white slavery" phenomenon is Ruth Rosen, *The Lost Sisterhood: Prostitution in America, 1900–1918* (Baltimore, 1982), 38–50, 112–36.

25. Gerry to Crain (Wilson), 21 March 1889, MP 88-GHJ-49. On padrones, see McCabe, *Secrets,* 127; CAS, *Twenty-first Annual Report* (New York, 1873), 28–36; SPCC, *Fourth Annual Report* (New York, 1879), 39. On interurban networks, see Report on Mrs. Bush of Norfolk, Va., and the Tenderloin, in Box 28, C14P.

26. People v. Monaise, 5 Aug. 1863 (two cases), DAP. Monaise lived at 31 Church Street. For similar examples, see People v. Haskins, 23 Dec. 1874; People v. Fisher, 11 Nov. 1874, both in DAP.

27. Schuhmacher to Hewitt, June 1887, MP 87-HAS-29; "Opposite Neighbor" to Hewitt, Aug. 1888, MP 87-HAS-33; Bell Diary, 9, 17 July 1851. For unlicensed shops, see the entry for 29 May 1851.

28. SPC, *Third Report* (New York, 1879), 20. On intelligence recruiters, see *NPG,* 26 July 1884; *World* Clipping, July 1887, MP 87-HAS-17; *Woman's Municipal League Bulletin,* Jan. 1904; Undated Manuscript of Woman's Municipal League, both in Box 83; Undated Report on Wulfer's, Box 91, all in LWP.

29. Typed Information, Houses and Resorts of Prostitution, Arranged According to Streets, 1910 and 1 Feb. 1912, Box 28, C14P; Hattie Ross Report, 1909, Folder 150, HLP. George Kibbee Turner, "The Daughters of the Poor: A Plain Story of the Development of New York City as a Leading Center of the White Slave Trade of the World, under Tammany Hall," *McClure's* 34 (1909): 57. On the rise of gambling syndicates, see Johnson, *Policing the Urban Underworld,* 180. On organized crime in cities, see Mark Haller, "Urban Crime and Criminal Justice," *JAH* 57 (1970): 619–35; idem, "Organized Crime in Urban Society: Chicago in the Twentieth Century," *JSH* 5 (1972): 210–34. Schwartz's political headquarters was at 723 East Ninth Street. See Investigator's Report of Natalie D. Sonnischsen, June 1912, Box 28, C14P. On Lower East Side gangs, Jenna Weissman Joselit, *Our Gang: Jewish Crime and the New York Jewish Community, 1900–1940* (Bloomington, Ind., 1983), 23–53. On Paul Kelly (alias Paolo Vacarelli), see Humbert Nelli, *The Business of Crime: Italians and Syndicate Crime in the United States* (Chicago, 1976), 107, 109, 245.

30. Frank Moss, *The American Metropolis* (New York, 1897), 3:164–70. Incorporated with $50,000 in capital, the IBA had a burial plot in Washington Park Cemetery in Brooklyn. See Turner, "Daughters of the Poor," 47–52. On Hochstim, see Joseph E. Corrigan, "Magnates of Crime," *McClure's* 40 (1912): 5–8. On the IBA as the "Hochstim Club," see John M. Murtaugh and Sarah Harris, *Cast the First Stone* (New York, 1957), 216–17. For more on the syndicate and

Jewish prostitution, see Edward J. Bristow, *Prostitution and Prejudice: The Jewish Fight against White Slavery, 1870–1939* (Oxford, Eng., 1982), 160–80; Howard B. Woolston, *Prostitution in the United States prior to the Entrance of the United States into the World War* (New York, 1921), 86–90; Joselit, *Our Gang,* 49–52.

31. On Engel, see *Times,* 7 Jan. 1901; Herlihy Testimony, Box 1; Clippings, 4 Jan. 1901, Box 32; Clippings, 10 June 1901, Box 41, C15P; Raymond C. Spaulding, "The Saloons of the District," in Univ. Settlement Society of New York, *Report* (New York, 1901), 34–38; Stead, *Satan's Invisible World,* 88–93. On 123 Allen Street, see Pre-1917 Conveyance Records, Block 415, Lot 35, Liber 3, p. 7, 30 March 1891, Hall of Records. In 1896, Martin Engel gained full control of the property. See Liber 46, p. 396, 18 June 1896. On 102 Allen Street, see Block 414, Lot 37, Liber 144, p. 384, 3 Jan. 1906. For Engel's other transactions with the same property, see Liber 108, p. 110. 13 Feb. 1903; Liber 225, p. 219, 22 Oct. 1914.On 121 Allen Street, see Block 415, Lot 36, Liber 44, p. 102, 2 March 1896. For later transactions on the property, see Liber 50, pp. 6–10, 12 Nov. 1896; Liber 67, pp. 358–59, 4 Feb. 1899; Liber 78, p. 350, 14 May 1899; Liber 81, p. 203, 1 Aug. 1900. On George Washington Plunkitt, see William L. Riordan, *Plunkitt of Tammany Hall,* ed. Arthur Mann (New York, 1963). On Sullivan, see Czitrom, "Underworlds and Underdogs." On the Sans Souci and others, see Affidavits, Box 16, C15P; Raines Law Hotel Reports, Undated, Box 91, LWP. On Max Hochstim, see Affidavits for 102 Allen Street, Boxes 7, 10; Affidavit for 33 Madison Street, Box 3 all in C15P.

32. Clippings, 5, 6 Oct. 1901, Box 47, C15P; Turner, "Daughters of the Poor," 47; Corrigan, "Magnates of Crime," 8. A former member, Louis Weinraub of Brooklyn, gave state's evidence against Dr. Joseph Adler, a former president. See Frances Kellor Manuscript, 17 Oct. 1907, pp. 4–5, Box 91, LWP. On Spielberg as counsel for the IBA, see District Attorney Scrapbooks, New York County, 10 March 1913. On Smith, see *Mazet Committee,* 522, 2026; *Lexow Committee,* 3:2989, 3179–82; Moss, *American Metropolis,* 2:359. On Wissig, an ex-assemblyman, see "Mother" to Hewitt, 18 Sept. 1888, MP 87-HAS-34; Goetze to Gilroy, 20 June 1893, MP 89-GTF-14. Prior to entering politics, Wissig served a four-year prison term for burglary and later lost a bid for the state senate. He lived on Eldridge Street and ran a prostitute-filled saloon at Stanton and Allen streets. His son allegedly ran two Allen Street brothels. See *Lexow Committee,* 2:1536; 3:2752. The IBA met every other Thursday at 69 St. Mark's Place. For an exaggerated and highly moralistic account of Hochstim, see Moss, *American Metropolis,* 2:164–71, 227–41. On "enterprise" and "power" syndicates in the twentieth century, see Alan A. Block, *East Side–West Side: Organizing Crime in New York City, 1930–1950* (Cardiff, Eng., 1983).

33. The Sans Souci (later the Orpheum) was at 100 Third Avenue; the German Hotel, at 134–136 East 13th Street. See Typed Memo, 7 Sept. 1908, Box 1, C14P; Undated Report on Sans Souci, Box 91, LWP. Hochstim enjoyed five- and fourteen-year leases for rents ranging from $1,899 (1899–1904) to $3,750 (1915–20). See Pre-1917 Conveyance Records, Block 558, Lots 27 1/2, 30, Liber 60, p. 90, 23 Feb. 1899; Liber 130, p. 414, 27 Feb. 1905; Liber 170, p. 312, 16 May 1907. On the Princess Hotel, see Pre-1917 Conveyance Records, Block 804, Lot 34, Liber 11, p. 345, 19 April 1892; Liber 17, p. 344, 27 April 1893; Liber 29, p. 75, 25 May 1894; Liber 40, p. 100, 18 Sept. 1895; Liber 64, p. 355; 10 Oct. 1899; Liber 100, p. 7, 26 Jan. 1904. By 1914, Oestricher controlled several Tenderloin houses, including 217, 226, 228 West 28th Street and 330 West 52d Street. See "Tenement Houses and Owners Thereof," June 1914, THC-Prostitution Folder, Box 168, CSS Papers. On Mandelbaum and Lewine, see Pre-1917 Conveyance Records, Block 804, Lots 34, 35, Liber 142, p. 445, 9 Dec. 1908. Hochstim held a five-year lease at $16,000 per annum. On the lease transfer, see Block 804, Lots 34, 35, Liber 144, p. 419, 2 April 1909. In 1910, Mary Sipp sold 2025 Lexington Avenue to Beatrice Hirsch (53 Lenox Avenue) and Jennie Fromberg (238 West 106th Street) for $85,000. Shortly thereafter, Hirsch transferred the property to Annie Hochstim for a dollar, who in turn did the same with Gussie Deklade. See Pre-1917 Conveyance Records, Block 1772, Lots 52, 53, Liber 155, p. 334, 14 Oct. 1910; Liber 156, pp. 118–21, 22 Oct. 1910; Liber 154, pp. 363–65, 26 Oct. 1910; Liber 174, p. 60, 6 June 1913; Liber 173, p. 125, 6 June 1913. The Hotel

Lincoln was located at 1575 Broadway and 225 West 52nd Street, the Princess at 469 Sixth Avenue (northwest corner 28th Street), the Alt Heidelberg at 40–42 West 29th Street, the Crown at 36 West 29th Street, the Windsor (formerly called the Boulevard, Baltic, and Avenel) at 2025 Lexington Avenue (southeast corner, 124th Street).

34. Kellor Manuscript, pp. 2–3. By 1907, they worked with the Mutual Republican Club in the Thirteenth Ward of Philadelphia. See Bingham, "Organized Criminals," 66. For a list of the variety of ways pimps seduced or recruited young women, see Undated Manuscript, p. 8, Box 91, LWP. On Jewish-controlled prostitution, see Whitin to Mendes, 7 Jan. 1911, Box 1, C14P.

35. Ross Report, Box 150, HLP; U.S. Senate Immigrant Commission, *Importing Women for Immoral Purposes,* 61st Cong., 2d sess., Doc. 196 (Washington, D.C., 1909), 14–19; Typed Information, Houses and Resorts of Prostitution, Arranged According to Street, 1910 and 1 Feb. 1912, Box 28, C14P. According to the Committee, 53 houses were French-run or housed primarily French women, and 25 were Jewish, 25 black, 7 Italian, 2 Greek, 2 Chinese, 2 Swedish, and 1 Irish.

36. The French syndicate was headquartered at 124 West 29th Street and at the Franco-American Democratic Club at 117 West 28th Street. See Kellor Manuscript, quotations pp. 1, 6, 9; Statement of the Woman's Municipal League, 1909, Box 91, LWP; Clippings for 24 Oct. 1901, Box 47, C15P. Federal court convictions suggest that Italians were similarly engaged in trafficking women across the Atlantic. Some accused Irish groups like the "Sullivan men" and "McCarren men," named after their respective leaders, of promoting prostitution. See Bingham, "Organized Criminals," 62, and the list of federal convictions for white slavery in Anonymous, *Political Protection of the White Slave Trade* (n.p., 1910), 6–8, in Box 91, LWP. Chevallier's restaurant was at 133 West 45th Street. See Reports of J.S., 1, 5 Sept. 1915, 29, 31 Aug. 1919, Box 34, C14P. A third alleged syndicate was the "O.S. Club," but I have found no descriptive information on it. See Anonymous, *Political Protection,* 12.

37. For an example of the exaggerated influence of syndicates, see Ross Report, 1909, Folder 150, HLP. On Jerome, see *Times, Tribune, Sun,* all 22 Nov. 1902. On the Kehillah, see *Times,* 27 Jan. 1910. On the Rockefeller grand jury, see Presentment of Grand Jury of Court of General Sessions, 29 June 1910, Box 91, LWP; Claire Marie Renzetti, "Purity vs. Politics: The Legislation of Morality in Progressive New York, 1890–1920" (Ph.D. diss., Univ. of Delaware, 1983), 130–36. On the public misperception that the Rockefeller grand jury dismissed the existence of white slavery, see Rosen, *Lost Sisterhood,* 124–25.

38. Henry George, *Progress and Poverty* (New York, 1879), 340–41, 365; George Kneeland, "Commercialized Prostitution," 561; Committee of Fourteen, *Annual Report* (New York, 1916), 12; Newspaper Clippings (Gardiner), 2, 3 Dec. 1900, Box 31, C15P.

39. On police informing landlords, see *NPG,* 31 Dec. 1881. On landlords fearing "financial loss," see Committee of Fourteen, *Annual Report for 1912* (New York, 1913), 23. On landlords ignoring complaints, see Petition of 200 Families (on Roosevelt Street) to Hewitt, April 1887, MP 87-HAS-28; Anonymous (on Second Avenue) to Hewitt, 4 May 1887, MP 87-HAS-29; Smith to Hewitt, 15 Dec. 1888, MP 87-HAS-32; "Citizen" (on Allen Street) to Hewitt, 3, 6 Oct. 1888, MP 87-HAS-33; Konezny (on Monroe Street) to Grant, 12 June 1889; "Residents of 43 Eldridge Street" to Grant, 7 Dec. 1889, both in MP 88-GHJ-39; Anonymous (on West 66th Street) to Gaynor, 30 April 1911; Police Commissioner (on Columbus Avenue) to Gaynor, 28 June 1911, both in MP GWJ-34; Anonymous (on Third Avenue) to Gaynor, 5 Dec. 1911, MP GWJ-37; Police Commissioner (on St. Mark's Place) to Gaynor, 23 June 1913, MP GWJ-73; Acting Police Commissioner (on Second Avenue) to Gaynor, 26 July 1913, MP GWJ-74; Report on 307 West 11th Street, 5 Jan. 1914, Box 13, SPC Papers. On tenants' fear of eviction, see Anonymous (on Allen Street) to Hewitt, 20 June 1888, MP 87-HAS-32; Affidavit for 247 Stanton Street, Box 12, C15P.

40. On Hertz (39 Third Avenue), see Pre-1917 Conveyance Records, Block 465, Lot 5, Liber 177, p. 470, 1 April 1908. On Hearst, see Gaynor to Waldo, 3 Oct. 1912, MP GWJ-87. On Hearst's real estate, see Pre-1917 Conveyance Records, Block 1049, Lots 14–23, 44, 45; Liber 156, pp.

334, 417, 16 May 1913; Liber 157, pp. 111–15, 1 July 1913; Liber 158, p. 119, 9 July 1913; Liber 160, pp. 424–33, 21 April 1914. Hearst's development plans are outlined in Lindsay Chaney and Michael Cieply, *The Hearsts: Family and Empire—The Later Years* (New York, 1981), 265–68. On the Hearst-Gaynor rivalry, see W. A. Swanberg, *Citizen Hearst* (New York, 1961), 265–70; Roy Everett Littlefield III, *William Randolph Hearst: His Role in American Progressivism* (Lanham, Md., 1980), 263–69, 271. For another example of participation in prostitution by a city elite, see Joel Best, "Looking Evil in the Face: Being an Examination of Vice and Respectability in St. Paul as Seen in the City's Press, 1865–83," *Minnesota History* 50 (1987): 241–51.

41. On the Hertzes, see Pre-1917 Conveyance Records, Block 465, Lot 10, Liber 131, pp. 388–90, 15 Dec. 1904 (106 East Tenth Street); Block 465, Lot 11, Liber 164, p. 494, 20 March 1907 (108 East Tenth Street); Block 457, Lot 23, Liber 85, p. 308, 1 March 1901. Rosie Hertz leased 7 First Street to Phillip Hirsh for ten years and $3,000 annual rent. See Block 456, Lot 17, Liber 203, p. 146, 3 Dec. 1910. On Hertz's subleases, see Block 457, Lot 23, Liber 88, p. 53, 23 March 1901 (27 Second Street); Block 456, Lot 17, Liber 208, p. 12, 7 April 1911; Block 456, Lot 17, Liber 93, p. 422, 25 Feb. 1902. For more on the Hertzes and their bribery payments, see District Attorney Scrapbooks, New York County, 10, 15 March 1913; Closed Cases no. 93268, People v. Smith, 20 March 1913; no. 93267, People v. Meyer, 20 March 1913; no. 93200, People v. Heanly, 27 March 1913, all in New York Supreme Court in DAP. Falconer (alias Faulkner) controlled most of Second Street off the Bowery. See McCullagh to Murray, 25 May 1888, MP 87-HAS-33. On his leaseholds, see Record of Assessments, 17th Ward, 1890, 1895, in MARC; Pre-1917 Conveyance Records, Block 457, Liber 1079, p. 670, 17 Feb. 1869; Liber 1218, p. 544, 22 Aug. 1872; Liber 1306, p. 50, 12 Oct. 1874; Liber 1935, p. 41, 7 June 1886; Liber 2205, p. 169, 1 March 1889; Liber 46, p. 257, 11 June 1896.

42. Kneeland, "Commercialized Prostitution," 562; Natalie Sonnischsen Investigation of Sauter and Rollman, 1912, Box 28, C14P. Also see her investigation of property owned by Leon Sobel and the Louis Kean estate in the same box. Some sureties even provided bail for arrested madams. See DAP, People v. Wilson, 14 Feb. 1855. This is also the earliest example I found of a surety working with a brothel. For examples of agents renting to prostitutes, see DAP, People v. Roberts, 1862; People v. Flynn et al. (J. H. Rockwell, agent), 9 April 1874; Anonymous to Hewitt on C. D. Meyer of 14 First Street, 4 May 1887; "Citizen" to Hewitt on James A. Breen of 1242 Third Avenue, 2 May 1887; "A Sufferer" to Hewitt on A. Heyman of Broadway, 26 May 1887, all in MP 87-HAS-29; McAdoo, *Guarding a Great City*, 80.

43. On Sanders, see *Lexow Committee*, 2:1669–79. On Nelson, see *Mazet Committee*, 518, 1596–1600. From 1880 to 1899, Nelson's saloon, at 30th Street and Seventh Avenue, was only a block from Silver Dollar Smith's, at 31st Street and Seventh Avenue. See *Mazet Committee*, 522.

44. William W. Sanger, *The History of Prostitution* (New York, 1859), 554; Ross Report, Box 150, HLP ($50–$60 units); *NPG* ($52,000 brothel), 12 April 1879; Anonymous to Hewitt (Bleecker Street), 2 May 1888, MP 87-HAS-33; Investigators' Reports on Flagelle's, 1912, Box 28, C14P. On the close relationship between the various syndicates and real estate interests, see the numerous addresses in Hattie Ross Report, 1909, Box 150, HLP. The average commercial rent was less than $1,500 per year, or $125 per month. For a Tenderloin concert hall (Broadway Garden, on West 28th Street), see *Mazet Committee*, 501–17. For a twentieth-century brothel, see Kneeland, "Commercialized Prostitution," 563. These figures compare with those for other cities. For example, by the early twentieth century, San Francisco landlords recovered the initial cost of investment in less than a year. Some "cribs" earned $125,000 on an $8,000 investment. So lucrative was the business that banks, insurance companies, and real estate groups owned numerous bordellos. See Richard Symanski, *The Immoral Landscape: Female Prostitution in Western Societies* (Toronto, 1981), 158–61.

45. Apartments with only three or four prostitutes accumulated approximately $448 monthly, or almost $5,400 a year. The average numbers of prostitutes in each brothel type were fourteen and thirteen, respectively. See George J. Kneeland, *Commercialized Prostitution in New York*

City, (New York, 1917), 128–30; Kellor Manuscript, p. 9, Box 91, LWP. Chicago prostitution generated annual profits estimated to be $8.5 million. See Chicago Vice Commission, *The Social Evil in Chicago* (Chicago, 1911), 95.

46. For data on wage levels, see Olivier Zunz, *The Changing Face of Inequality: Urbanization, Industrial Development, and Immigrants in Detroit, 1880–1920* (Chicago, 1982), 227–28; Richard Sennett, *Families against the City: Middle Class Homes of Industrial Chicago, 1872–1890* (Cambridge, Mass., 1970), 84–87; Hammack, *Power and Society, 90–96.*
47. Hertz claimed that it was easy to make up the cost of the $500 initiation fee, the $100 per month protection fee, and even an $800 excise license. See Clippings for 5, 6 Oct. 1901 (Hertz), Box 47; Clippings, 29 Nov. 1901 (McGurk), Box 49, both in C15P; Fox to Hewitt (O'Donnell), 21 Dec. 1887, MP 87-HAS-28; District Attorney Scrapbooks, New York County, 10, 15 March 1913 ($250,000).
48. *NPG* (Talmage), 9 Nov. 1878; Anonymous to Hewitt (Brogan), Dec. 1887, MP 87-HAS-33; Turner, "Daughters of the Poor," 47; Committee of Fourteen, *Annual Report* (New York, 1922), 23, copy in Box 56, SPC Papers; Holde to Gaynor, 16 Feb. 1911, MP GWJ-33. The detective"s surname was Reynolds. See "A Resident of the Fifteenth Ward" to Hewitt, Oct. 1887, MP 87-HAS-33. For a complaint against Hermann, see Brogan to Murray, 28 Feb. 1890, MP 88-GHJ-40; *Lexow Committee*, 1:28.
49. On the similarity with Cincinnati's regulation system adopted in the 1890s, see Witte to Gaynor, 11 Sept. 1912, MP GWJ-87. On San Francisco's, see Shumsky and Springer, "San Francisco's Zone of Prostitution," 71–89. On New Orleans, see Al Rose, *Storyville, New Orleans* (University, Ala., 1974). On St. Louis, see James Wunsch, "The Social Evil Ordinance," *American Heritage* 333 (1982): 52–55. For national developments, see idem, "Prostitution and Public Policy: From Regulation to Suppression, 1858–1920" (Ph.D. diss., Univ. of Chicago, 1976). For de facto regulation in other American cities, see Best, "Looking Evil in the Face," 241–51; Ruth Rosen and Sue Davidson, eds., *The Maimie Papers* (Bloomington, Ind., 1977), xxv. On France, see Alain Corbin, *Women for Hire: Prostitution and Sexuality in France after 1850* (Cambridge, Mass., 1990). On Great Britain, see Judith R. Walkowitz, *Prostitution and Victorian Society: Women, Class and the State* (Cambridge, Eng., 1980).
50. On policemen being paid by industrial employers during strikes, see Minutes for 17 March 1919, Box 13, SPC Papers.

Chapter 13 White Slaves and Kept Women

1. Stephen Crane, *Maggie: A Girl of the Streets* (New York, 1960).
2. Crane to Hamlin Garland, March 1983, in R. W. Stallman and Lillian Gilkes, eds., *Stephen Crane: Letters* (New York, 1960), 14. For other interpretations, see Benedict F. Giamo, "On the Bowery: Symbolic Action in American Culture and Subculture" (Ph.D. diss., Emory Univ., 1987), 169–70, 209–12, 248–49, 261; Lawrence E.Hussman, Jr., "The Fate of the Fallen Woman in *Maggie* and *Sister Carrie*," in *The Image of the Prostitute in Modern Literature*, ed. Pierre L. Horn and Mary Beth Pringle (New York, 1984), 91–100. For a thoughtful account of the prostitute in literature during this time, see Laura Hapke, *Girls Who Went Wrong: Prostitutes in American Fiction, 1885–1917* (Bowling Green, Ohio, 1989). Unfortunately, I was able to obtain a copy of *Girls* only after this book was already in production.
3. James D. McCabe, Jr., *New York by Sunlight and Gaslight* (Philadelphia, 1882), 154, 476, 644; idem, *Secrets of the Great City* (Philadelphia, 1868), 109–10; Edward Crapsey, *The Nether Side of New York* (New York, 1872), 120, 142; Charles Loring Brace, *The Dangerous Classes of New York, and Twenty Years' Work among Them* (New York, 1872), 114–19. For examples of the seduction and suicide themes, see Crapsey, *Nether Side*, 144; SPCC, *Fourth Annual Report* (New York, 1879), 43–44; *Mazet Committee*, 2507–8; Undated Report on Wulfer's, Box 91, LWP; Orrin B. Booth, *The White Slave Traffic* (New York, 1899), 14–15, in Box 2, Charles L. Chute Papers, Columbia Univ.

4. Harriet Beecher Stowe, *We and Our Neighbors: or, The Records of an Unfashionable Street* (Boston, 1873), 263, 321–22; Elizabeth Stuart Phelps, *Hedged In* (Boston, 1870), 210.
5. T. W. Hanshew's, "Alone in New York: A Thrilling Portrayal of the Dangers and Pitfalls of the Metropolis," *New York Family Story Paper,* 16 April 1887, quoted in Joanne J. Meyerowitz, *Women Adrift: Independent Wage Earners in Chicago, 1880–1930* (Chicago, 1988), 58. On the monolithic view of prostitutes after 1850, see Mary P. Ryan, *Women in Public: Between Banners and Ballots, 1825–1880* (Baltimore, 1990), 72.
6. Caesar Lombroso and William Ferrero, *The Female Offender* (New York, 1897), 1–20, 98, 111 (quotation). For more on Lombroso, see Estelle Freedman, *Their Sisters' Keepers: Women's Prison Reform in America, 1830–1930* (Ann Arbor, 1981), 109–15.
7. George Kibbe Turner, "The Daughters of the Poor," *McClure's* 34 (1909): 45–61; William T. Stead, *Satan's Invisible World Displayed; or, Despairing Democracy: A Study of Greater New York* (London, 1898); Committee of Fifteen, *The Social Evil* (New York, 1902), 73; Booth, *White Slave Traffic,* 14–15; Jane Addams, *A New Consciousness and an Ancient Evil* (New York, 1912). The best examination of the white-slavery issue is Ruth Rosen, *The Lost Sisterhood: Prostitution in America, 1900–1918* (Baltimore, 1982), 38–50, 112–36. Also see Mark Thomas Connelly, *The Response to Prostitution in the Progressive Era* (Chapel Hill, N.C., 1980), 89–136; Egal Feldman, "Prostitution, the Alien Woman and the Progressive Imagination, 1910–15," *AQ* 19 (1967): 192–206; Edward J. Bristow, *Prostitution and Prejudice: The Jewish Fight against White Slavery, 1870–1939* (Oxford, Eng., 1982).
8. Leslie Fishbein, "From Sodom to Salvation: The Image of New York City in Films about Fallen Women, 1899–1934," *New York History* 70 (1989): 171–90.
9. George Kauffman, *The House of Bondage* (New York, 1910), 58, 69, 195, 238, 255, 365, 372, 382, 402, 465.
10. Ibid., 238.
11. David Graham Phillips, *Susan Lenox: Her Fall and Rise* (New York, 1917), 1:344.
12. Ibid., 2:243.
13. Freedman, *Their Sisters' Keepers,* 112–25.
14. Katharine Bement Davis, "A Study of Prostitutes Committed from New York City to the State Reformatory for Women at Bedford Hills," in George J. Kneeland, *Commercialized Prostitution in New York City* (New York, 1913); Mary Ruth Fernald et al., *Women Delinquents in New York State* (Montclair, N.J., 1969); William I. Thomas, *The Unadjusted Girl: With Cases and Standpoint for Behavioral Analysis* (Boston, 1923), 109, 116–20.
15. Howard B. Woolston, *Prostitution in the United States prior to the Entrance of the United States into the World War* (New York, 1921); Thomas, *Unadjusted Girl,* v, xii, 21–22, 119, 230–31. Thomas was also critical of the white-slavery argument, insisting that it was never "a quantatively important factor" in prostitution. See ibid., 150. On changing views of female sexuality after 1900, see Meyerowitz, *Women Adrift,* 110, 131–32.
16. Martin Green, *New York 1913: The Armory Show and the Paterson Strike Pageant* (New York, 1987), 131–35.
17. Marianne Doezema, *American Realism and the Industrial Age* (Cleveland, 1980), 57–59 (quotation); Green, *New York 1913,* 136–40. Sloan was a member of the Socialist party; Bellows and Henri were anarchists.
18. Edwin Mullins, *The Painted Witch: Female Body–Male Art: How Western Artists Have Viewed the Sexuality of Women* (London, 1985), 95–97; Theodore Reff, *Manet: Olympia* (New York, 1977), 114–18; Eunice Lipton, *Looking into Degas: Uneasy Images of Women and Modern Life* (Berkeley, 1986), 151–52, 163–64, 168–74, 179–81.
19. Mullins, *Painted Witch,* 215–22; Gotz Adriani, *Toulouse-Lautrec* (London, 1987). For a provocative account of female images by Western painters during these years, see Bram Dijkstra, *Idols of Perversity: Fantasies of Feminine Evil in Fin-de-Siècle Culture* (New York, 1986).
20. Charles Wisner Barrell, "The Real Drama of the Slums: John Sloan's Etchings," *Craftsman* 15 (1909): 562.
21. Bruce St. John, ed., *John Sloan's New York: From the Diaries, Notes, and Correspondence, 1906–1913* (New York, 1965), xx, 220–21.On Sloan's women as recognizable to contemporaries, see

Green, *New York 1913*, 175–78; Suzanne L. Kinser has argued that several other Sloan paintings also depicted prostitutes—notably, *3:00 a.m.* and *Sixth Avenue and Thirtieth Street* (1907). Her main evidence is the large feathered hats worn by the women. However, after 1890, both wealthy and theatrical women wore large hats. Furthermore, fashion standards increasingly broke down during these years as working- and middle-class women wore shorter skirts, makeup, and colorful hats. On the emergence of new dress standards, see Lois Banner, *American Beauty* (Chicago, 1983), 75–76, 189–94, and especially figs. 7, 25–29. Quite likely, many of the women Kinser categorizes as prostitutes were simply "bachelor girls." See her "Prostitutes in the Art of John Sloan," *Prospects* 9 (1984): 231–54.

22. David W. Scott and E. John Bullard, *John Sloan, 1871–1951: His Life and Paintings, His Graphics* (Washington, D.C., 1971), 87; Rebecca Zurier, *Art for the Masses: A Radical Magazine and Its Graphics, 1911–1917* (Philadelphia, 1988), 100.
23. Jane Myers and Linda Ayres, *George Bellows: The Artist and His Lithographs, 1916–1924* (Fort Worth, 1988), 18–22; Charlene Engel, "George W. Bellows' Illustrations for the *Masses* and Other Magazines and the Sources of His Lithographs of 1916–17" (Ph.D. diss., Univ. of Wisconsin, 1976), 112–15.
24. Zurier, *Art for the Masses*, fig. 14.
25. *Lexow Committee*, 2:1247–60 ("gentlemen"); *Mazet Committee*, 1996 (Hartig). For similar examples of twelve- to fourteen-year-olds in brothels, see SPCC, *Sixth Annual Report*, 48; idem, *Ninth Annual Report* (New York, 1884), 22–23, 64; idem, *Tenth Annual Report* (New York, 1885), 41; "A Father" to Hewitt, 6 Aug. 1887, MP 87-HAS-29; "Widowed Mother" to Hewitt, Sept. 1887, MP 87-HAS-28; Anonymous to Gaynor, 11 May 1910, MP GWJ-15; DAP, People v. Bleasby and Johnson, 4 Oct. 1876; People v. Hunt and Storey, 25 Sept. 1879; Affidavits for 554 1/2 Seventh Avenue and 116 West 27th Street, Box 21, C15P. On fifteen- to eighteen-year-olds, see DAP, People v. Battershall, 1 Sept. 1879; Watkins to Edson, 7 April 1884, MP 85-EF-10; Gilin to Hewitt, 25 Oct. 1888; and "Neighbor" to Hewitt, 15 July 1888; "Opposite Neighbor" to Hewitt, 19 July, Aug. 1888, all in MP 87-HAS-33; "A Father" to Hewitt, 21 Feb. 1888, MP 87-HAS-32; "An Old Citizen" to Hewitt, 25 July 1888, MP 87-HAS-35; SPCC, *Eighth Annual Report* (New York, 1883), 36; Anonymous to Grant, 13 Nov. 1889, MP 88-GHJ-39; Police Commissioner to Gaynor, 7 April 1911, MP GWJ-34, 15 Oct. 1912, MP GWJ-56, 6 Nov. 1912, MP GWJ-57, and 23 April 1913, MP GWJ-72. In numerous cases, the children of prostitutes lived with their mothers in brothels. For examples, see SPCC, *Fifth Annual Report* (New York, 1880), 50; "Neighbors" to Gilroy, 31 March 1894, MP 89-GTF-14; New York State Census Schedules for 1870, New York County, Ward 20, Election District 14, no. 79 (Mary Disbrow), no. 82 (Elizabeth Stanley), no. 83 (Ellen DeCamp); Ward 16, Election District 7, no. 14 (Ruckers); Ward 8, Election District 2, no. 39 (Conrads); Ward 8, Election District 3, no. 95 (Graf).
26. *NPG* ("peddlers of posies"), 1 March 1879. On flower selling, see SPCC, *Second Annual Report* (New York, 1877), 40–48; idem, *Third Annual Report* (New York, 1878), 39–40; idem, *Fourth Annual Report*, 52; idem, *Fifth Annual Report*, 83–84. On "the domestic lay," see Crapsey, *Nether Side*, 122–23. For an example of a child peddler being forced to have sex, see DAP, People v. Haskins, 9 March 1875.
27. *NPG*, 25 Feb. 1882.
28. Anonymous to Hewitt ("children talk"), April 1887, MP 87-HAS-28, (Sophia), 22 April 1888, MP 87-HAS-32. Henry's house was at 142 East 22d Street. See *Times*, 30 Jan. 1875. Mary Brooks was sentenced to a year in prison and a $250 fine for enticing young girls into her brothel. See SPCC, *Second Annual Report*, 32. For examples of consenting teenage sex, see "A Helpless Mother" to Hewitt, Feb. 1888, MP 87-HAS-34; SPCC, *Third Annual Report*, 29–30; "Mother" to Hewitt, 28 Jan. 1888,MP 87-HAS-33; Report of Natalie de Bogary, 16 May 1915, Strand Cafeteria Folder, Box 28, C14P. For a thirteen-year-old running off with her boyfriend, see Hendricks to Hewitt, 13 Feb. 1888, MP 87-HAS-32.
29. McCabe, *Secrets*, 294. Byrne worked in Rachel Howard's house at 148 East 32d Street. See SPCC, *Eighth Annual Report*, 43–44. I was unable to verify that seven sisters did indeed run

the West 25th Street brothels. Guidebooks and manuscript census schedules show that this street was filled with brothels, but none of the proprietors had the same surname. However, prostitutes and madams usually assumed aliases, so the tale remains plausible.

30. Statement of Louisa Kleuhenspies, 7 April 1887, MP 87-HAS-16 (Miller); SPCC, *Eighth Annual Report,* 27 (Langbein).

31. Case of Delia Minsey; Case of French Viola, Undated Report on 144 West 32d Street; Undated Report on 28 East 13th Street (Cooper and Siegel); Undated Report on Sharkey's (Lavatt); Undated Report on Sans Souci, 100 Third Avenue; Undated Report on National Hotel, 3 Irving Place, all in Box 91, LWP; Robert W. DeForest and Lawrence Veiller, eds., *The Tenement House Problem* (New York, 1903), 2:18, 20.

32. On female wages, see Elizabeth Ewen, *Immigrant Women in the Land of Dollars* (New York, 1985), 101, 246–47. In the years 1880–1930, the national female labor force grew from 2.6 million to 10.8 million. For New York, see U.S. Bureau of the Census, *Statistics on Women at Work* (Washington, D.C., 1907), 29. For national statistics, see idem, *Tenth Census of the United States, 1880: Population* (Washington, D.C., 1882), 1:712; idem, *Fifteenth Census, 1930: Population* (Washington, D.C., 1932), vol. 3, pt. 1, p. 12, cited in Meyerowitz, *Women Adrift,* xvii–xviii, 4, 145–46. Also see Alice Kessler-Harris, *Out to Work: A History of Wage-Earning Women in the United States* (New York, 1982), 102.

33. Williams to Hewitt (Minnie Brooks), 4 Nov. 1888, MP 87-HAS-33; "Truth" to Hewitt (hotels), 26 Sept. 1888, MP 87-HAS-35. Hill's establishment was at 129th Street and Third Avenue. See Dalton to Hewitt, 4 April 1888, MP 87-HAS-33. Lester's house was at 50 East 13th Street. See "Citizen" to Hewitt, 12 Jan. 1888; "Business Man" to Hewitt, 31 July 1888, MP 87-HAS-33; DAP, People v. Lester, 9 Nov. 1876. For other examples of houses of assignation, see "Resident of Allen Street" to Hewitt (Weindorf's, 102 Allen Street), 26 Oct. 1887, MP 87-HAS-29; anonymous to Edson (Keckmeyer's, 414 Fourth Avenue), Sept. 1883, MP 85-EF-10; SPCC, *Sixth Annual Report,* 68; idem, *Eleventh Annual Report* (New York, 1886), 37–38; DAP, People v. Kaltenhausers, 13 Nov. 1876; People v. Haskins, 23 Dec. 1874; Anonymous to Hewitt, Nov. 1888, MP 87-HAS-33. For examples of ten- to fifteen-year-old prostitutes in saloons, see SPCC, *Fourth Annual Report,* 31; idem, *Sixth Annual Report,* 20; "An Anxious Mother" to Hewitt, 4 Oct. 1887, MP 87-HAS-28; "Citizen and Taxpayer" to Hewitt, 11 Sept. 1887, MP 87-HAS-29; Police Commissioner to Gaynor, 7 Nov. 1912, MP GWJ-57. For hotels, see Affidavit for 109 West 37th Street, Box 20, C15P. On dime museums, see Testimonies of Wilson and Young, Nov. 1883; Gerry to Edson, 5 Nov. 1883, both in MP 85-EF-10; Anonymous to Hewitt, 1 May 1888, MP 87-HAS-33. Gerry listed twenty-seven girls aged ten to fifteen he claimed were prostitutes and had been "ruined" in the New American Museum. On child prostitution in England during this period, see Deborah Gorham, " 'The Maiden Tribute of Modern Babylon' Reexamined: Child Prostitution and the Idea of Childhood in Late-Victorian England," *Victorian Studies* 21 (1978): 353–79.

34. Booth, *White Slave Traffic,* 14–15. On Bushein, see SPCC, *Eighth Annual Report,* 28, 47.

35. Emma Goldman, *Living My Life* (New York, 1934), 91–93.

36. Kathy Peiss, "Charity Girls and City Pleasures: Historical Notes on Working-Class Sexuality," in *Powers of Desire: The Politics of Sexuality,* ed. Ann Snitow et al. (New York, 1983), 75–84; idem, *Cheap Amusements: Working Women and Leisure in Turn-of-the-Century New York* (Philadelphia, 1986); Meyerowitz, *Women Adrift,* 104–7, 112–19. For an example of the confusion of some observers, see the description of the dance hall at the City and Suburban Homes model tenement at 541 East 78th Street, in Acting Police Commissioner to Gaynor, 5 July 1913, MP GWJ-74.

37. Handwritten reports of Charles Briggs on Sennett's Café, 440 Westchester Avenue; Gilligan's, 364 East 149th Street; and Lennett's, in 1914; Typed Report on Schramm's Music Hall, 544 Westchester Avenue, 9 Aug. 1914, Box 28, C14P. On prostitutes coming from other cities, see *Mazet Committee,* 2368.

38. Memoranda on Riverside Casino ("out for the money"), 110th Street, off Broadway, 17 June 1908, Box 1, C14P; Handwritten Report on Klyberg and Freeney's, 25 May 1912, Box 28,

C14P; Undated Report by J. B. Beers on on Raines Law Hotels (in Harlem), Box 91, LWP. For other examples, see Affidavit for 93 First Street, Box 16, C15P; Acting Police Commissioner to Gaynor, 18 Aug. 1913, MP GWJ-75.

39. These cases are in DAP, People v. Baker, 27 April 1876; People v. Mass, 17 Nov. 1875; People v. Barber, 13 Sept. 1878; Handwritten Report, 6 July 1913, Box 28, C14P; Stenographer's Minutes, City Magistrate's Court (Emma Dale), 13 Dec. 1911,MP GWJ-52. Dale lived at 214 West 108th Street. Testimony of Sheidhauer, 3 May 1888, MP 87-HAS-32. When he was released, Sheidhauer's wife deserted him. For another example, see DAP, People v. Kraus, 25 April 1870.

40. Elizabeth Blackwell, *Counsel to Parents on the Moral Education of Their Children* (New York, 1881), 65–66. The cases are in Mayer to Hewitt, 25 June 1888, MP 87-HAS-33; "Neighbor" to Hewitt, 15 July 1888; Ryan to Murray, 23 July 1888, both in MP 87-HAS-33; DAP, People v. Dannenberg, 26 March 1878. For more details on Marks, see Gerry to Hedges, 25 May 1895; Marks to Strong, 21 May 1895, both in MP 90-SWL-49. Marks also appears in *Lexow Committee,* 1:1061–69; 3:2750–51. On DelPaul, see SPCC, *Eighth Annual Report,* 29. For similar examples, see Reports for 17 March 1919, Box 13, SPC Papers. Twentieth-century studies show that the overwhelming majority of prostitutes *chose* the occupation and had little interest in rehabilitation. See Richard Symanski, *The Immoral Landscape: Female Prostitution in Western Society* (Toronto, 1981), 227.

41. Committee of Fifteen, *Social Evil,* 80–81; *NPG,* 18 Jan. 1879 (60,000); U.S. Senate Immigrant Commission, *Importing Women for Immoral Purposes,* 61st Cong. 2d sess., Doc. 196 (Washington, D.C., 1909), 7–10; Undated Report on 28 East 13th Street (Cooper and Siegel); Undated Report on Sharkey's (Lavatt), both in Box 91, LWP. On women living alone, see U.S. Bureau of the Census, *Statistics on Women at Work,* 29; Kessler-Harris, *Out to Work,* 102; Meyerowitz, *Women Adrift.* The Davis survey is in Kneeland, *Commercialized Prostitution,* 195, 235. Family problems, especially orphanage, were the most cited (46 percent), with "personal" problems, "bad company," and a desire for pleasure and money equaling 43 percent.

42. Kneeland, *Commercialized Prostitution,* 103, 257. Of the 540 who gave occupations, the breakdown was as follows: 117 department store clerks, 28 small-store clerks, 27 servants, 79 houseworkers, 9 chambermaids, 72 actresses, 72 factory operatives, 25 office workers, 31 stenographers, 8 teachers, 9 telephone operators, 13 milliners, 18 waitresses, 4 nurses, 4 booksellers, 4 artists, 2 models, 1 translator, 17 dressmakers, and 101 unknown.

43. Miner to Wald, 8 April 1913, Box 91, LWP. On the poor working conditions of most hotel servants, see Porter to Hewitt, 17 May 1888, MP 87-HAS-20. One 1910 study found that nearly 78 percent of all female criminals were domestic servants. Another study found that despite making up only 18 percent of the female wage-earning population, servants composed 60 percent of all female prisoners. See Kessler-Harris, *Out to Work,* 103. Nationally, between 1870 and 1900, the supply of domestic servants only rose 50 percent, while demand doubled. At the same time, the percentage of working women who were domestic servants declined from 48 percent in 1870 to 24 percent by 1900, indicating the shift to factory work. See I. M. Rubinow and Daniel Durant, "The Depth and Breadth of the Servant Problem," *McClure's* 34 (1910): 576–85.

44. Undated Manuscript, p. 3, Box 91, LWP.

45. On the fifty-cent houses, see Booth, *White Slave Traffic,* supplement. On Williams and the French prostitute, see Typed Information, Houses and Resorts of Prostitution, Arranged According to Street, 1910, Report for 138 West 32d Street. On Delancey Street, see Testimony of Mrs. Weiner, 1901, Affidavit for 30 Stanton Street, Box 10, C15P. On concert saloon prostitutes, see Undated Report on Sans Souci, 100 Third Avenue. At the National Hotel, one woman brought in six different men in little more than one hour. See Undated Report on National Hotel, 3 Irving Place, both in Box 91, LWP.

46. People v. Fishers, 10 May 1876, DAP; Undated Report on 151 West 26th Street ("good trade"); Undated Report on Coleman, both in Box 91, LWP; Brogan to Murray, 26 July 1888, MP 87-HAS-33.For similar accounts, see Welsing to Murray, 8 Oct. 1887, MP 87-HAS-28; Police Commissioner to Kline, 24 Nov. 1913, MP GWJ-77; idem to Gaynor, 29 Aug. 1911, MP GWJ-

35; Symanski, *Immoral Landscape,* 184. Further evidence that prostitutes moved often among brothels was found by comparing West 25th, 26th, and 27th streets in U.S. Census Manuscript Schedules for 1870, New York County, Ward 16, Election District 11; Ward 20, Election District 22; and New York State Census Schedules for 1870, New York County, Ward 20, Election District 14. In most cases, the madams' names matched and the boarders' names differed. On temporary and occasional prostitution nationwide, see Woolston, *Prostitution in the United States,* 38–50. For another example of the transiency of prostitutes, see the testimony of Augusta Thurow in *Lexow Committee,* 1:1061–69.

47. Whiten to Rosenstein, 14 Oct. 1913, Box 2, C14P; Committee of Fourteen, *Annual Report* (New York, 1922) in Box 56, SPC Papers. Ledyne worked in Mrs. Brown's brothel at 223 Greene Street for five years. See *Lexow Committee,* 4:3624–38.

48. Feldman, "Prostitution," 192–206. For those arrested in 1908 and 1909, they numbered 2,093. Among immigrants, 154 (7 percent) were French, 225 (11 percent) were Jewish, and 31 (1 percent) were Italian. See U.S. Senate Immigrant Commission, *Importing Women for Immoral Purposes,* 11–14. This was the sole study indicating that immigrants streetwalked while the native-born worked in brothels.

49. Of 1,106 prostitutes, 762 (69 percent) were American-born and originated from the following states: 347 from New York (31 percent), 95 from Pennsylvania (9 percent), 63 from New Jersey (6 percent), 35 from Ohio (3 percent), and 26 from Connecticut (2 percent). The 344 foreign-born (31 percent) came from the following countries: 107 from Russia (10 percent), 72 from Germany (7 percent), 35 from Austro-Hungary (3 percent), and 32 from England and Scotland (3 percent). See Kneeland, *Commercialized Prostitution,* 101, 174–75. I sampled the months of Oct. and Dec. 1914–17, Women's Court File Cards (arrests), Boxes 66–68, C14P. The breakdown by birthplace and race appears in the following table (numbers in percentage):

Birthplace	*1914*	*1915*	*1916*	*1917*
Unrecorded	20	53	55	61
U.S.A.	52	21	20	18
Russia	6	6	3	2
Italy	2	2	2	0
Germany/Austria	7	7	8	8
Ireland	3	5	6	2
Other Europe	9	5	5	8
Latin America	1	1	1	2
African-American	35	22	20	26
Total Number	271	190	86	120

50. Compiled from Undated Raines Law Hotel Reports and Undated Boarding House and Parlor House Reports, Box 91, LWP.

51. Kneeland, *Commercialized Prostitution,* 190–91. The best description of the social backgrounds of prostitutes nationwide from 1900 to 1918 is in Rosen, *Lost Sisterhood,* 137–68.

52. Kneeland, *Commercialized Prostitution,* 107; J.A.S. Report on "Street Conditions," 1918, Box 33, C14P. On the decline of child beggars after 1890, see Helen Campbell, *Darkness and Daylight; or, Lights and Shadows of New York Life* (Hartford, 1893), 170–73. The Committee of Fourteen study was based on 91 women sentenced in the Jefferson Market Night Court, Box 91, LWP. They gave their ages as follows: ten were 16–19 years; nine, 20–21 years; twenty-three, 22–23 years; thirty, 24–25 years; fourteen, 26–27 years; and five, 28–29 years. Compiled from women sentenced in the Jefferson Market Night Court, Box 91, LWP. In sampling for age, I took the month of Dec. 1919, in Women's Court File Cards, Box 66–68, C14P. Ages were not recorded until 1919. The breakdown was this: none were under 15 years; nine, 16–19 years; twenty-seven, 20–22 years; twenty-eight, 23–25 years; and eighty-one, 26 or older.

53. A Mr. Paresis operated numerous Tenderloin brothels over a two-decade period; his last known house was at 204 West 28th Street. See Undated Report, Box 91, LWP. Kate Woods first appeared in U.S. Census Manuscript Schedules for 1860, New York County, Ward 17, Election District 10, no. 159; Ward 12, Election District 3, no. 1081. Also see Anonymous, *The Gentleman's Companion: New York in 1870* (New York, 1870); New York State Census Schedules for 1870, New York County, Ward 16, Election District 8, no. 53; U.S. Census Manuscript Schedules for 1870, New York County, Ward 16, Election District 11, no. 45; Record of Assessment, 1870, Ward 16, Entry for 105 West 25th Street. In 1909, Woods was working at 122 West 41st Street. See Hattie Ross Report, 1909, HLP. Kitty Mack was at 40 West Fourth Street in 1874 and 343 West 58th Street and 241 West 52d Street in 1913. See DAP, People v. Mack, 9 April 1874; Police Commissioner to Kline, 24 Nov. 1913, MP GWJ-77. Annie Grey was at 114, 206, and 214 West 46th Street in 1910. See Typed Information, Houses and Resorts of Prostitution, Arranged According to Street, 1910, Box 28, C14P. On Virginia Dallafind, 165 Hester Street, see Police Commissioner to Gaynor, 16 Aug. 1911, MP GWJ-35. On Elizabeth Hartel, see SPC, *Report* (New York, 1896), 46. On Lucy A. Rogers, 131 West 15th Street, see Affidavit, Box 20, C15P; Committee of Fourteen, *Annual Report for 1915–16* (New York, 1917), 50–51.

54. Sources are inconsistent on the age and place of birth of Fisher. She was listed at 105 West 27th Street in U.S. Census Manuscript Schedules for 1870, New York County, Ward 20, Election District 22, no. 105; New York State Census Schedules for 1870, New York County, Ward 20, Election District 14, no. 81. Also see DAP, People v. Fisher, 10 May 1876; Undated Reports on 109, 144 West 27th Street, Box 91, LWP. The houses were 106, 112, 116 West 31st Street. See Holmes to Murray, 1 June 1887, MP 87-HAS-28. On Wiener, see Cassidy to Murray, 11 Oct. 1888, MP 87-HAS-33; Herlihy and Wiener Testimony, 11 Feb. 1901, Box 1, C15P. On De Camp, see U.S. Census Manuscript Schedules for 1870, New York County, Ward 20, Election District 22, no. 109; New York State Census Schedule for 1870, New York County, Ward 20, Election District 14, no. 83; *NPG,* 8 Nov., 6 Dec. 1879. On Roses, see Anonymous to Committee of Fourteen, 19 Sept. 1911, Box 1, C14P. Roses was at Kaiser Hoff, 142 Christie Street, 173 Allen Street, 42 Stanton Street, and 218 East 9th Street. For another example, see DAP, People v. Pearl, 9 March 1877.

55. DeForrest, born in 1835, was a German Jew and controlled brothels at 224 Greene Street and 48 West Fourth Street. See New York Society for the Suppression of Vice, Arrest Blotters for 1875, pp. 119–21, Library of Congress; DAP, People v. DeForrest, 9 April 1874. Brown's houses were 120, 122 West 31st Street. See Bogart to Hewitt, 30 July 1888, MP 87-HAS-33. Livingston ran 210, 214 West 40th Street and 150 West 45th Street. Grey operated 114, 206, 214 West 46th Street, the last for thirty years. See Typed Information, Houses and Resorts of Prostitution, Arranged According to Street, 1910 and 1 Feb. 1912, Box 28, C14P. Shaw's houses were at 103, 123 West 28th Street. See *Lexow Committee,* 2:1882–97, 1922–25. For more on multiple houses, see Hattie Ross Report, 1909, Folder, 150, HLP.

56. The Hermanns' houses were at 111, 133, 136, 137, 139, 141 West Third Street. They bought no. 138 from Mr. Friend in 1891 for $13,000. Rent in no. 139 was $75 per month; in no. 136, $110 per month (later rented as a private home for only $40). Hermann claimed that the police paid her $1,700 to abandon her houses, although she later opened one in the Tenderloin at 112 West 32d Street before being forced out by the police. See *Lexow Committee,* 4:4117–21, 4136–54, 4163–97, 4207–15. For a similar story, see the testimony of Augusta Thurow, 1:1072–1115. On rent figures, see Ewen, *Immigrant Women,* 116–21.

57. Typed List of Houses and Resorts of Prostitution, Arranged According to Street, 1910 and 1 Feb. 1912, Box 28, C14P; Joseph E. Corrigan, "Magnates of Crime," *McClure's* 40 (1912): 5. The Hertzes lived and worked at 103 East Fourth Street in 1888 (Tenant to Hewitt, 2 July 1888, MP 87-HAS-34); 13 East First Street in 1892–94 (*Lexow Committee,* 2:1763–70); 7, 9, 13, 15, 17 East First Street (Affidavits, Box 1, C15P), 12 Stanton Street (Box 10, C15P), all in 1901; Booth, *White Slave Traffic,* 16. They later lived on Keap Street in Brooklyn.

58. Committee of Fourteen, *Annual Report* (New York, 1913), 23; Idem, *Annual Report* (New York, 1914), 10–12. On Hertz's wealth, see District Attorney Scrapbooks, New York County, 10

March 1913. On police officers receiving graft from her, see Closed Cases no. 92368, People v. Smith, 20 March 1913; no. 93267, People v. Meyer, 20 March 1913; no. 93200, People v. Heanly, 27 March 1913, all in New York Supreme Court, DAP. On Hertz's conviction (13 Feb. 1913) and one-year sentence, see Whiten to Glynn, 19 Nov. 1913; Potter to Hooke, 20 Nov. 1913, both in Box 3, C14P; *Times*, 27, 30 April 1913; 18 Jan. 1914.

59. Anonymous Madam to Hewitt ("pure necessity"), 1887, MP 87-HAS-26. On Smith, see *Times*, 5 Oct. 1887. On Sanford and Schwartz, see *Lexow Committee*, 1:983–1009; 1–2:1247–60. A German immigrant married to the expressman Morris Cohen, Schwartz rented the upper floors of their East Houston Street domicile in 1893 from the first-floor leaseholder for $40 and paid the standard $500 initiation and $50 per month fees to the local wardman for the "permit" to do business. She raised the money from a Park Row jeweler and offered the police a mortgage on the house and furniture.

60. Anonymous Madam to Hewitt, 1887, MP 87-HAS-26. One madam admitted she managed to save $3,000 over the years, but given her cash flow, it was a paltry sum. For every $150 she made, she managed to keep only $20 to $30, or 13 to 20 percent. See affidavit for 8 James Street, Box 3, C15P.

61. *Lexow Committee*, 2:1358; Tynan to Cooper (Harris), 23 May 1880, MP 83-CE-26.

62. Sources are often incomplete and fail to provide names of proprietors at specific addresses. Nevertheless, a limited breakdown by gender of the known proprietors from 1870 to 1919 shows the following:

	Below Canal St.	*Lower East Side*	*Greenwich Village*	*Tender-loin*	*Lexington & East Side*	*West Side & above 110th St.*	*Total (%)*
				1870–1879			
Males	49	20	22	12	1		104 (24%)
Females	84	26	93	86	14		303 (70%)
Couples	10	6	5	3	3		27 (6%)
				1880–1889			
Males	17	36	48	33	14	3	151 (36%)
Females	7	46	63	93	34	1	244 (58%)
Couples	1	10	11	1	2	1	26 (6%)
				1890–1899			
Males		24	31	21	1		77 (39%)
Females		72	23	21	1		117 (59%)
Couples		2	3				5 (3%)
				1900–1909			
Males	33	24	92	170	44	20	383 (71%)
Females	4	15	24	88	11	3	145 (27%)
Couples	1	1	7	2			11 (2%)
				1910–1919			
Males	7	8	19	56	17	57	164 (50%)
Females	1	7	33	69	13	36	159 (49%)
Couples			6	5	2	1	14 (1%)

For sources, see chapter 10, note 3.

63. Committee of Fourteen, *Annual Report for 1915–16*, 50–51.

Chapter 14 UNDERMINING THE UNDERWORLD

1. Charles W. Gardner, *The Doctor and the Devil: A Startling Exposé of Municipal Corruption* (New York, 1894), 24, 26, 46, 47, 50, 57, 73; William T. Stead, *Satan's Invisible World Displayed; or, Despairing Democracy: A Study of Greater New York* (London, 1898), 48–55.
2. Robert F. Walsh, *Dr. Parkhurst's Crusade; or, New York after Dark* (New York, 1892), 16, 31, 37. On its first use, the term "organized crime" was applied to Tammany Hall when Parkhurst was head of the SPC. See SPC, *Report* (New York, 1896), 6–7.
3. SPC, *Report,* 47–48, 83; Gardner, *Doctor,* 25. Gladden is quoted in Paul S. Boyer, *Urban Masses and Moral Order in America, 1820–1920* (Cambridge, Mass., 1978), 171. Peck compared each with the abolitionist William Lloyd Garrison and the prison reformer John Howard of Great Britain. See SSV, *Twentieth Annual Report* (New York, 1894), 28.
4. Abstracts, 23 Sept. 1901, Box 1, C15P; Charles P. Parkhurst, *My Forty Years in New York* (New York, 1923), 171–74, 178–79, 181, 187; *City Vigilant,* Jan., Dec. 1894; *Herald,* 21 Sept. 1895.
5. *City Vigilant,* Jan., May 1895.
6. *Lexow Committee,* 5 vols.; David C. Hammack, *Power and Society: Greater New York at the Turn of the Century* (New York, 1982), 147–50; Jeremy P. Felt, "Vice Reform as a Political Technique: The Committee of Fifteen in New York, 1900–1901," *New York History* 54 (1973): 39; Roy Lubove, "The Progressive and the Prostitute," *Historian* 24 (1962): 317–24. From 1885–1886, Moss successfully closed down most of the brothels on West 27th Street that operated under the protection of the notorious Captain Alexander Williams, by employing private detectives, procuring evidence, attracting media attention, and getting police from other precincts to conduct raids. See *Herald,* 20 Dec. 1885, and *Evening Post,* 24 Dec. 1885, in Scrapbook 9, Box 108, Grace Papers; *Star* Clipping, 13 June 1887, MP 87-HAS-17; *Lexow Committee,* 3:2827–33.
7. *Mazet Committee,* 5 vols; Clippings of 17, 19, 24 Nov., 2, 3 Dec. 1900, Box 31, C15P.
8. Claire Marie Renzetti, "Purity vs. Politics: The Legislation of Morality in Progressive New York, 1890–1920" (Ph.D. diss., Univ. of Delaware, 1983), 101–6; David J. Pivar, *Purity Crusade: Sexual Morality and Social Control, 1868–1900* (Westport, Conn., 1973), 215; Mark Thomas Connelly, *The Response to Prostitution in the Progressive Era* (Chapel Hill, N.C., 1980), 12. The coalition of women's groups recommended a system of "public industries" for women to earn a living wage, and the elimination of fines that only discriminated against women. Women involved also included the wives of Frank Damrosch, Richard W. Gilder, Charles Russell Lowell, Charles Parkhurst, and Henry Villard and Miss Julia Phelps. See Clippings for 11, 15 March 1901, Box 37; Clippings for 1, 2 Feb. 1901, Box 34, C15P.
9. Clippings for 28, 29 Nov. 1901, Box 31; 17 Aug. 1901, Box 44; 1, 3, 4 Oct. 1901, Box 47, all in C15P; Felt, "Committee of Fifteen," 26–31. Members included Felix Adler, founder of the Ethical Culture Society; William Baldwin, president of the Long Island Railroad; Joel B. Erhardt, president of the Lawyers Surety Co.; Austen Fox, lawyer; John S. Kennedy, director of the National Bank of Commerce; William O'Brian, president of the Workingmen's State Federation; Alexander Orr, president of the Rapid Transit Co.; George Peabody of Spencer, Trask, and Co.; George Putnam, publisher; John Rhodes, president of Greenwich Savings Bank; Jacob Schiff, partner at Kuhn, Loeb and Co.; Edwin Seligman, professor of political economics at Columbia University; Andrew Smith, Central Federated Union; Charles S. Smith, professor of Romance languages at Columbia University; Charles Stewart Smith, banker and former Chamber of Commerce president. See Renzetti, "Purity vs. Politics," 108–9; Roland R. Wagner, "Virtue against Vice: A Study of Moral Reformers and Prostitution in the Progressive Era" (Ph.D. diss., Univ. of Wisconsin, 1971), 76–110.
10. Felt, "Committee of Fifteen," 38–50. Jerome sat on the Court of Special Sessions.
11. Veiller to Murphy, 14 Feb. 1914, and Veiller to Mitchell, 18 April 1914, both in Box 168, THC-Prostitution Folder, CSS Papers; Clippings for 6 March 1901, Box 36; Clippings for 25 March 1901, Box 38; Clippings for 11 April 1901, Minutes for 20 March 1901, Box 39, all in C15P; Robert W. DeForest and Lawrence Veiller, eds., *The Tenement House Problem* (New

York, 1903), 2:17–19 (Adler). On Adler, see Roy Lubove, *The Progressives and the Slums: Tenement House Reform in New York City, 1890–1917* (Pittsburgh, 1962), 33, 105, 119, 188–90, 214. On the limits of earlier reform efforts to regulate landlords, see Elizabeth Blackmar, *Manhattan for Rent, 1785–1850* (Ithaca, N.Y., 1989), 263–67.

12. Morgenstern to Peters, 17 June 1908, Box 1, C14P. The original Committee of Fourteen included the Reverend Lee W. Beattie, settlement house worker and minister at Madison Square Presbyterian Church (Parkhurst's church); William S. Bennett, Republican congressman and counsel to the Anti-Saloon League; Francis M. Burdick, Columbia Univ. professor; the Reverend William Daly of the Paulist Fathers; Rabbi Bernard Drackman of Zichron Ephraim Congregation; Edward J. McGuire, lawyer and member of St. Vincent de Paul Society; Rabbi Pereira Mendes, of Shearith Israel and president of the New York Board of Jewish Ministers; the Reverend John Peters, Morningside and Riverside Heights Association and canon at St. John the Divine; George Putnam, publisher and Committee of Fifteen member; Thomas H. Reed, Anti-Saloon League; the Reverend Howard H. Russell, Anti-Saloon League; Isaac Seligman, banker (and brother of Edwin Seligman); Mary Simkhovitch, settlement house worker; Lawrence Veiller, Tenement House Commission; and Frederick Whitin. Later members included Ruth Standish Baldwin, New York Probation and Protective Association; Frances Kellor, College Settlements Association; William McAdoo, former congressman and police commissioner; William J. Schieffelen, drug merchant; and Henry L. Stimson, Republican congressman and later secretary of war. See letters in Box 91, C14P; Committee of Fourteen, *Annual Report for 1918* (New York, 1919), 68–72; Wagner, "Virtue against Vice," 113–49.
13. Committee of Fourteen, *Annual Report* (New York, 1916), 18, 28; Felt, "Committee of Fifteen," 42. On the moral surveillance of preventive societies and their offspring quietly evolving into political surveillance, see Timothy J. Gilfoyle, "The Moral Origins of Political Surveillance: The Preventive Society in New York City, 1867–1918," *AQ* 38 (1986): 648–49.
14. Whitin to Peters, 17 Nov. 1906, and Whitin to Rosenstern, 14 Oct. 1913, Box 1, C14P; Raymond B. Fosdick, "Prostitution and the Police," *Social Hygiene* 2 (1916): 11, 18.
15. Whitin to Rosenstern, 14 Oct. 1913, Box 1, C14P.
16. On the success of the Committee of Fourteen, see George J. Kneeland, *Commercialized Prostitution in New York City* (New York, 1917), 164. The Prentice Law of 1906 cut the number of hotels with bars from 1,304 in 1905–06 to 650 in late 1906. See Peters to Reed, 6 June 1906, Box 1, C14P; John D. Peters, "The Story of the Committee of Fourteen of New York," *Social Hygiene* 4 (1918): 376; Kneeland, *Commercialized Prostitution,* 35. In 1912, 400 of the 425 ten-room hotels were for men only. On the Buildings Bureau, see Hopper to Peters, 28 July 1905; Peters to Delany, Oct. 1905, both in Box 1, C14P.
17. Whitin to Hinman, 11 Jan. 1911, Box 1, C14P. The first Night Court was at the Jefferson Market Court, which was also the first court in the city to employ the fingerprint system. On its conception and failure to remedy the plight of New York's prostitutes, see John M. Murtaugh and Sarah Harris, *Cast the First Stone* (New York, 1957), 221–23, 230, 244.
18. United Surety Company to Peters, 25 Aug. 1909; Committee of Fourteen to American Fidelity Co., 30 Aug. 1909; and other correspondence with breweries and surety companies, 1905–11, Box 1, C14P. Periodically, brewers complained about unlicensed bars in New York City. For an example, see H. B. Wheatcroft, Secretary of the Association of the United Lager-Beer Brewers of New York City to Edson, 17 March 1882, MP 85-EF-8. After 1896, all liquor licenses required an excise bond but gave no discretionary power to excise officials over the surety companies that issued the bond. The injunction and abatement law allowed the municipality, if the owner was convicted, to restrict all use of the property up to one year. See Committee of Fourteen, *Annual Report* (New York, 1912), 8–9, 27; idem, *Annual Report* (New York, 1913), 24–25; idem, *Annual Report* (New York, 1914), 17, 23–24; idem, *Annual Report* (New York, 1916), 13–16. On efforts to attack landlords, see Report of Cases, 17 May 1909, Box 13, SPC Papers; Confidential Bulletin, 26 April 1917; Court Opinion in *Tenement House Department v. Lucy A. McDevitt,* 25 May 1915, both in Box 165, Committee of Fourteen Folder, CSS Papers; Memo, Howard to Police Commissioner, 12 April 1915, MP MJP-41. From 1911 to 1915, twenty-one states and the District of Columbia passed abatement laws.

See Richard Symanski, *The Immoral Landscape: Female Prostitution in Western Society*. (Toronto, 1981), 194–96.

19. On settlement house reformers, see Frances A. Kellor, "The Protection of Immigrant Women," *Atlantic Monthly* 101 (Feb. 1908): 246–55; Lillian Wald, *The House on Henry Street* (New York, 1915), 293–94; Allen F. Davis, *Spearheads for Reform: The Social Settlements and the Progressive Movement, 1890–1914* (New York, 1967), 94. On Rose Livingston, see Folders 152 and 159, HLP. On the influential role of Rockefeller, see Allen to Peters, 4 Jan. 1909, Box 1, C14P; Peters, "Committee of Fourteen," 360–61, 365, 386; Frederick H. Whitin, "Obstacles to Vice Repression," *Social Hygiene* 2 (1916): 146–50; Jerome D. Greene, "The Bureau of Social Hygiene," *Social Hygiene* 3 (1917): 3. On the committee's cooperation with the Committee of One Hundred, see Moskowitz to Whitin, 11 Aug. 1909; Mitchell to Whitin, 12 Nov. 1909, both in Box 1, C14P. For a general overview, see Lubove, "Progressive and the Prostitute," 308–30.
20. For a comprehensive list of these organizations, see Kneeland, *Commercialized Prostitution*, 263–81.
21. In 1908, the Anti-Saloon League began its state-by-state drive for prohibition. See Robert Wiebe, *The Search for Order, 1877–1920* (New York, 1967), 290.
22. Fosdick, "Prostitution and the Police," 16; Unsigned Memo ("closing the town"), 20 Nov. 1913, THC-Prostitution Folder, Box 168, CSS Papers; Committee of Fourteen, *Annual Report* (New York, 1913), 27; idem, *Annual Report* (New York, 1912), 22; idem, *Annual Report* (New York, 1914), 9; idem, *Annual Report for 1915–16* (New York, 1917), 50 ("Bowery"). For examples of men forced to solicit prostitutes on the street, see Minutes for 8 Feb. 1918, Box 13, SPC Papers; Numerous Reports in Hotel Investigations Folder, 1918–21, Box 34, C14P. The first example of a "call girl" I found was at 48 East 29th Street in 1901. See Affidavit for 203 West 48th Street, 4 March 1901, C15P. For a later example, see Minutes of 31 March 1913, Box 13, SPC Papers.
23. Committee of Fourteen, *Annual Report for 1929* (New York, 1930), 35. On the decline of the brothel, see chapter 8. Havelock Ellis believed that the brothel was declining throughout the world by the early twentieth century. See Ellis, *Studies in the Psychology of Sex* (New York, 1906), 4:302–3.
24. Committee of Fourteen, *Annual Report* (New York, 1922), 10; idem, *Annual Report* (New York, 1925), 7–8; idem, *Annual Report* (New York, 1926), 23; idem, *Annual Report for 1928* (New York, 1929), 10, 18–19. The committee still considered "commercialized prostitution" a serious social problem, especially regarding venereal disease. On New York in the 1920s, see William E. Leuchtenburg, *The Perils of Prosperity, 1914–32* (Chicago, 1958), chap. 12.
25. Committee of Fourteen, *Annual Report for 1929*, 35; "The Nation's Infamy," *Literary Digest*, 14 May 1927; "Trade Routes of White Slavers," *Survey* 59 (15 Jan. 1928): 486–88; Willoughby C. Waterman, *Prostitution and Its Repression in New York City, 1900–1931* (New York, 1932), 46–48. On Luciano, see Alan A. Block, *East Side–West Side: Organizing Crime in New York City, 1930–1950* (Cardiff, Eng., 1980).
26. Mary M. Simkhovitch, *Neighborhood: My Story of Greenwich House* (New York, 1938), 66–67; Confidential Report of Paige to LaGuardia, 19 Aug. 1936, Box 755, Mayor's Commission on Conditions in Harlem, Fiorello LaGuardia Papers, MARC. I am indebted to Cheryl Greenberg for this source. For similar conclusions on the visible decline of prostitution, see Greene, "Bureau of Social Hygiene," 8–9; Peters, "Committee of Fourteen," 367–68; Magnes to Gaynor, 25 May 1913, Box GWJ-76, MP; Minutes of 6 May 1912, Box 13, SPC Papers; Joseph L. McGoldrick, "The New Tammany," *American Mercury* 15 (1928):9. On the decline of the Tenderloin, the Rialto, and the Broadway streetwalker, see Jerome Myers, *Artist in Manhattan* (New York, 1940), 50–53.
27. Report of H.K., 22 March 1919; Report of D.O., 27, 30 Dec. 1919; and Other Reports for 1918 and 1919 in Box 34, C14P; New York City Police Department, *Annual Report for 1919* (New York, 1919), 37–38; Major Bascom Johnson, "Next Steps," *Social Hygiene* 4 (1918): 10–11; "Report on Barney's," 22 Dec. 1927, Box 36, C14P (Bloomingdale's). On theater ushers, see H. Kahen Report on Olympic Theater, East 14th Street, 18 March 1919; H. Kahen Report on B. F. Kahn's Union Square Theater, 56 East 14th Street, 23 June 1919, both in Box 33

C14P. On restaurant waiters, see Reports on Child's Restaurant, Columbus Circle, 12, 19 Jan. 1919, Box 35, C14P; Frederick Whitin, "Sexual Perversion Cases in New York City Courts, 1916–1921," Bulletin no. 1480, 12 Nov. 1921, Box 88, C14P. For examples of former brothels and hotels convicted of disorderly-house charges converting themselves to furnished-room houses in the 1920s, see George A. Chauncey, Jr., "Gay New York: Urban Culture and the Making of a Gay Male World, 1890–1940" (Ph.D. diss., Yale Univ., 1989), 174. The decline of prostitution may have been an international phenomenon. For example, Paris reported a decrease in brothels from 220 in 1892 to 40 in 1912, and similar declines in aggregate numbers. See Whiten to Bierhoff, 21 Jan. 1913, Box 2, C14P.

28. On redevelopment in the Tenderloin, see Martin Clary, *Mid-Manhattan* (New York, 1929), 75–80; Emanuel Tobier, "Manhattan's Business District in the Industrial Age," in *Power, Culture and Place: Essays on New York City,* ed. John H. Mollenkopf (New York, 1988), 85–86; Carl Condit, *The Port of New York: A History of the Rail and Terminal Systems from the Beginning to Penn Station* (Chicago, 1980), 152–53; Elliot Willensky and Norval White, *The A.I.A. Guide to New York City,* 2d ed. (New York, 1978), 127, 270. On the privacy of the apartment, see James Ford, *Slums and Housing* (Cambridge, Mass., 1936), 430–31.

29. Allan M. Brandt, *No Magic Bullet: A Social History of Venereal Disease in the United States since 1880* (New York, 1985), chap. 2. Prior to 1915, prostitution was illegal only in streets or tenements. The 1915 revision of the criminal code widened the definition of "vagrant" to include a "person who offers to commit prostitution." See Committee of Fourteen, *Annual Report for 1920* (New York, 1921), 26.

30. U.S. Bureau of the Census, *Historical Statistics of the United States, Colonial Times to 1970* (Washington, D.C., 1975); Ira Rosenwaike, *Population History of New York City* (Syracuse, 1972), 91–99.

31. Before 1915, prostitutes who did not solicit in streets or tenements were not guilty of any offense in New York. See Committee of Fourteen, *Annual Report for 1920,* 26. Also see PCP, Box 7456, People v. Ella ?, 1841; Committee of Fourteen, *Annual Report* (New York, 1915), 3; *McDowall's Journal,* June 1833; Symanski, *Immoral Landscape,* 83, 88; Review of Iowa Injunction and Abatement Law, 1909, Box 138, Samuel Lindsey McCune Papers, Columbia Univ. For the difficulty of prosecution in colonial New York, see Douglas Greenberg, *Crime and Law Enforcement in the Colony of New York, 1691–1776* (Ithaca, N.Y., 1976), 96–98. For examples of other cities, see Roger Lane, *Policing the City: Boston, 1822–1885* (New York, 1977), 168.

32. Daniel Czitrom, "Underworlds and Underdogs: Big Tim Sullivan and Metropolitan Politics in New York, 1889–1913," *JAH* 78 (1991): 536–58. On police replacing prostitution with gambling, see District Attorney Scrapbooks, New York County, 10 March 1913, MARC. On the Committee of Fourteen's effort to reform saloons and surety companies, see the correspondence from 1905 to 1911 in Box 1, C14P.

33. On booking, see Block, *East Side–West Side,* 141–48.

34. Judge Jonah J. Goldstein Interview, pp. 66, 341–43, Columbia Univ. Oral History Collection; Typed Report on the Problem of Prostitution in New York and a Plan for Meeting It, Women's City Club and League of Woman Voters, 1935, Box 56, SPC Papers. The report also recommended stronger enforcement of laws against the exploiters of prostitutes, free clinics to treat venereal disease, sex education in schools, and replacement of punitive treatments with social treatments for offenders. The Committee of Fifteen was one of the first reform groups to recommend that prostitution no longer be treated as a crime. See *The Social Evil* (New York, 1902), 176. On the changing image of young single women in cities after 1920, see Joanne J. Meyerowitz, *Women Adrift: Independent Wage Earners in Chicago, 1880–1930* (Chicago, 1988), 123–26.

35. Brandt, *No Magic Bullet,* chaps. 2 and 4.

36. Alice Kessler-Harris, *Out to Work: A History of Wage-Earning Women in the United States* (New York, 1982), 224, 228; James Reed, *The Birth Control Movement and American Society* (Princeton, 1983), 59. On increasing female wages after 1920, see Meyerowitz, *Women Adrift,* 29–36.

37. Kathy Peiss, *Cheap Amusements: Working Women and Leisure in Turn-of-the-Century New York* (Philadelphia, 1986), 95–114; Lewis A. Erenberg, *Steppin' Out: New York Nightlife and the Transformation of American Culture, 1890–1930* (Westport, Conn., 1981).
38. Paula Fass, *The Damned and the Beautiful: American Youth in the 1920s* (New York, 1977), 55, 63, 72–75, 93. This highly detailed and researched account of American youth and sexuality during the 1920s never discusses the role of prostitution. On the companionate wife during the 1920s, see Sheila Rothman, *Woman's Proper Place: A History of Changing Ideals and Practices, 1870 to the Present* (New York, 1978). On the rise of masculine domesticity, see Margaret Marsh, "Suburban Men and Masculine Domesticity, 1870–1915," *AQ* 40 (1988): 165–86; idem, "From Separation to Togetherness: The Social Construction of Domestic Space in American Suburbs, 1840–1915," *JAH* 76 (1989): 506–27.
39. Fass, *Damned and the Beautiful*, 392–93; Paul C. Glick, *American Families* (New York, 1957), 45.
40. Alfred Kinsey et al., *Sexual Behavior in the Human Male* (Philadelphia, 1948), 411.
41. Prince Morrow, *Social Diseases and Marriage* (New York, 1904), 342; David M. Kennedy, *Birth Control in America: The Career of Margaret Sanger* (New Haven, 1970), chap. 2.
42. For different parts of this synthesis, see Fass, *Damned and the Beautiful*, 3–167, 260–90, 365–76; Brandt, *No Magic Bullet*, 123–33; Kennedy, *Birth Control in America*, 89–98; Kathy Peiss and Christina Simmons, eds., *Passion and Power: Sexuality in History* (Philadelphia, 1989), 9–10. On the criminalization of abortion, see James C. Mohr, *Abortion in America: The Origins and Evolution of National Policy, 1800–1900* (New York, 1978). John Boswell argues that the first half of the twentieth century was the most homophobic era in American history. See Boswell, *Christianity, Social Tolerance, and Homosexuality: Gay People in Western Europe from the Beginning of the Christian Era to the Fourteenth Century* (Chicago, 1980), 23. My interpretation of sexuality after World War I departs slightly from that of John D'Emilio and Estelle B. Freedman, *Intimate Matters: A History of Sexuality in America* (New York, 1988), 173, 233–34, 239–74, which sees the 1920s as a period of significant change in sexual mores. Although certain types of previously untolerated behavior and discussion were more acceptable, these changes affected only a minority of Americans and were confined to the middle classes and to marital, heterosexual activity. A more dramatic transformation occurred after 1960.
43. On the "sacralizing" of the child, see Viviana A. Zelizer, *Pricing the Priceless Child: The Changing Social Value of Children* (New York, 1985), 11–13.
44. On Fox, see Lary May *Screening Out the Past: The Birth of Mass Culture and the Motion Picture Industry* (New York, 1980), 152–53.
45. On Victorians as sexually repressed, see Steven Marcus, *The Other Victorians: A Study of Sexuality and Pornography in Mid-Nineteenth-Century England* (New York, 1964); Peter T. Cominos, "Late Victorian Sexual Respectability and the Social System," *IRSH* 8 (1963): 18–48, 216–50. Recent works arguing that Victorians were more liberated include Carl Degler, "What Ought to Be and What Was: Women's Sexuality in the Nineteenth Century," *AHR* 79 (1974): 1468–91; idem, *At Odds: Women and the Family in America from the Revolution to the Present* (New York, 1980); Peter Gay, *The Bourgeois Experience from Victoria to Freud*, vol. 1, *The Education of the Senses* (New York, 1984), and vol. 2, *The Tender Passion* (New York, 1986). On some faults with these approaches, see Carol Zisowitz Stearns and Peter N. Stearns, "Victorian Sexuality: Can Historians Do It Better," *JSH* 18 (1985): 625–34.

BIBLIOGRAPHY

Collections and Manuscripts

New York City Municipal Archives and Records Center

Records of Assessment, 1800–97 (by wards), 1898–1920 (by blocks).
District Attorney Indictment Papers, Court of General Sessions, 1790–1879.
District Attorney, Closed Cases, New York County, 1900–15.
District Attorney Scrapbooks, New York County, 1900–15.
New York City Mayors' Papers, 1840–1920.
Police Court Papers, 1820–60.

New York City Hall of Records

State of New York. Census for 1855, New York City Schedules, County Clerk's Office.
State of New York. Census for 1870, New York City Schedules, County Clerk's Office.
New York City Land Title Registrations. Pre-1917 Conveyance Records, Office of the City Register.
Record of Wills and Index Record.

New York Public Library

Committee of Fifteen Papers, 1900–02 (the boxes in this collection have been rearranged and renumbered since I examined them).
Committee of Fourteen Papers, 1905–32.
Charles P. Daly Papers.
Hotel Publishing and Advertising Co. *Map of the City of New York.* New York, 1886.
New York City, Court of General Sessions, 1866–78. Recorder John K. Hackett Records.
Robert Taylor Diary, 1846–47.
Ullitz, Hugo. *Atlas of the Borough of Manhattan.* 4 vols. New York, 1906, updated to 1916.
U.S. Census for New York City. Manuscript Schedules, 1860 and 1870 (microfilm).

New-York Historical Society

Stephen Allen Papers.
William H. Bell (policeman) Diary, 1850–51.
New York City Census and Jury Book, 1816 (microfilm).
Abram Hewitt Mayoral Letterpress Copybooks, 1887–88.
John Jay Papers—Papers of the Society for Suppression of Vice and Humane Society.

Edwin P. Kilroe, comp. "Skeleton Outline of the Activities of Michael Norton, 1839–1889" Typewritten manuscript, 1 April 1938.
Robert R. Livingston Papers.

Columbia University, New York City

Dr. Alexander Anderson Diary, 1793–97.
[Anonymous]. *Plan of the City of New York Showing Wards, Senate, and Congressional Districts.* New York, 1870.
Bromley, George W., and Walter S. Bromley. *Atlas of the City of New York.* 5 vols. Philadelphia, 1899.
Burr, D. H. *Map of the City of New York.* New York, 1837.
Charles L. Chute Papers, 1899–1913.
Committee of Fourteen Papers in Community Service Society Papers.
Duer Family Papers.
Dripps, M. *New York City, County, and Vicinity.* New York, 1866.
Amos Eno Papers, 1857–80.
Jonah J. Goldstein Interview. Oral History Collection.
William R. Grace Papers.
Hayward, G. *Map of the City of New York.* New York, 1850.
Hooker, W. *Plan of the City of New York.* New York, 1817.
Hooker, William. *Map of the City of New York.* New York, 1831.
Seth Low Papers.
Samuel Lindsey McCune Papers.
New York Society for the Prevention of Crime Papers.
Lillian Wald Papers.

New York State Library, Albany, New York

House of Refuge Papers.

Schlesinger Library, Harvard University

Harriet Laidlaw Papers.

Library of Congress, Washington, D.C.

Blackwell Family Papers.
Desobry, P. *The Fireman's Guide: A Map of the City of New York Showing the Fire Districts, Fire Limits, Hydrants, Public Cisterns, Stations of Engines, Hooks and Ladders, Hose Carts, etc.* New York, 1834.
Harrison, John F. *Map of City of New York Extending Northward to Fiftieth Street.* New York: M. Dripps, 1851.
New York Society for the Suppression of Vice. Arrest Blotters.
Perris, William. *Maps of the City of New York Surveyed under Directions of Fire Insurance Companies.* New York, 1859.
Perris and Browne. *Insurance Maps of the City of New York.* New York: Perris & Browne, 1867, 1870, 1871, 1874, 1875, 1877, 1880, 1884.
Theodore Roosevelt Papers.

Printed Primary Sources

American Society for the Prevention of Cruelty to Animals. *Annual Report.* New York, 1867–1900.
Ames, Eleanor Maria. *Up Broadway, and Its Sequel: A Life Story by Eleanor Kirk* New York, 1870.
Anonymous. *The Gentleman's Companion: New York City in 1870.* New York, 1870[?].
Anonymous. *Helen Leeson: A Peep at New York Society.* Philadelphia, 1855.
Anonymous. *Mysteries of New York.* Boston, 1845.

Anonymous. *Revelations of Asmodeus; or, Mysteries of Upper Ten-Dom*. New York, 1849.
Anonymous. *The Three Widows; or, The Various Aspects of Life in Gotham. By a Member of the New York Bar*. New York, 1849.
Anonymous. *The Truly Remarkable Life of the Beautiful Helen Jewett*. New York, 1880.
Baer, Warren. *Champagne Charlie; or, The Sports of New York*. New York, 1868.
Bangs, Edward, ed. *Journal of Lt. Isaac Bangs, 1776*. Cambridge, Mass., 1890.
Beach, Moses Yale. *Wealth and Biography of the Wealthy Citizens of New York City*, New York, 1845.
Belden, E. Porter. *New York: Past, Present, and Future*. New York, 1849.
Bingham, General Theodore A. "The Organized Criminals of New York." *McClure's* 34 (1909): 62–68.
Blackwell, Elizabeth. *Counsel to Parents on the Moral Education of Their Children*. New York, 1881.
———. *Rescue Work in Relation to Prostitution and Disease*. New York, 1882.
Brace, Charles Loring. *The Dangerous Classes of New York, and Twenty Years' Among Them*. New York, 1872.
Bradbury, Osgood. *The Belle of the Bowery*. Boston, 1846.
———. *Ellen Grant: or, Fashionable Life in New York*. New York, 185?.
———. *Ellen: The Pride of Broadway*. New York, 1865.
———. *Female Depravity; or, The House of Death*. New York, 1857.
Breen, Matthew P. *Thirty Years of New York Politics Up-to-Date*. New York, 1899.
Bristed, Charles Astor. *The Upper Ten Thousand: Sketches of American Society*. New York, 1852.
Browne, Junius Henri. *The Great Metropolis: A Mirror of New York*. Hartford, 1869.
Buchanan, Harrison Gray. *Asmodeus; or, Legends of New York*. New York, 1848.
Buckingham, J[ames] S[ilk]. *America: Historical, Statistic, and Descriptive*. London, 1841.
Buckley, Rev. J. M., et al. "The Moral Influence of the Drama." *North American Review* 136 (1883): 581–606.
Buntline, Ned [Edward Zane Carroll Judson]. *The B'hoys of New York: A Sequel to the Mysteries and Miseries of New York*. New York, 1850.
———. *The G'hals of New York: A Novel*. New York, 1850.
———. *Magdalena, the Outcast: or, The Millionaire's Daughter—A Story of Life in the Empire City*. New York, 1866.
———. *The Mysteries and Miseries of New York*. New York, 1848.
———. *Three Years After: A Sequel to the Mysteries and Miseries of New York*. New York, 1849.
Byrnes, Thomas. *1886—Professional Criminals of America*. New York, 1886. Reprint. New York: Chelsea House, 1969.
Campbell, Helen. *Darkness and Daylight; or, Lights and Shadows of New York Life*. Hartford, 1893.
Census Office, Department of the Interior. *Report on the Social Statistics of Cities*. Vol. 18. Washington, D.C., 1856.
Children's Aid Society. *Annual Reports*. New York, 1854–79.
Citizens' Association of New York. *Sanitary Condition of the City: Report of the Council of Hygiene and Public Health*. New York, 1866.
Cody, William F. *Buffalo Bill's Own Story of His Life and Deeds*. New York, 1917.
Committee of Fifteen. *The Social Evil*. New York, 1902.
Committee of Fourteen. *Annual Reports*. New York, 1912–16.
———. *Department Store Investigation*. New York, 1915.
Comstock, Anthony. *Frauds Exposed*. New York, 1880. Reprint. Montclair, N.J.: Patterson Smith, 1969.
———. "The Suppression of Vice." *North American Review* 135 (1882): 484–89.
———. *Traps for the Young*. Edited by Robert H. Bremner. Cambridge: Belknap Press, Harvard Univ. Press, 1967.
Cooke, Nicholas Francis [A Physician]. *Satan in Society*. Cincinnati, 1876.
Corrigan, Joseph E. "Magnates of Crime." *McClure's* 40 (1912): 1–11.
Crane, Stephen. *Maggie: A Girl of the Streets*. 1893. Reprint. New York: Fawcett, 1960.

Crapsey, Edward. *The Nether Side of New York*. New York, 1872.
Crosby, Rev. Howard. "The Dangerous Classes." *North American Review* 136 (1883): 345–52.
Deems, Rev. Charles F. "Street Begging." *North American Review* 136 (1883): 389–95.
DeForest, Robert W., and Lawrence Veiller, eds. *The Tenement House Problem*. 2 vols. New York, 1903.
DeKock, Charles [Old Man of 25]. *Guide to the Harems; or, Directory to the Ladies of Fashion in New York and Various Other Cities*. New York, 1855. (in possession of Prof. Leo Herskowitz, Queens College, New York).
Dicey, Edward. *Six Months in the Federal States*. 2 vols. London, 1863.
Duer, William A. *Reminiscences of an Old New Yorker*. New York, 1867.
Ellington, George. *The Women of New York; or, The Under-World of the Great City*. Burlington, Iowa, 1869.
Ellis, Havelock. *Studies in the Psychology of Sex*. 4 vols. New York: Harper, 1906 and 1936.
Ender, Butt. *Prostitution Exposed; or, A Moral Reform Directory*. New York, 1839. (in possession of Prof. Leo Hershkowitz, Queens College, New York).
Five Points House of Industry. *Monthly Reports*. May 1858–April 1861; April 1876–April 1898.
Fosdick, Raymond B. "Prostitution and the Police." *Social Hygiene* 2 (1916): 11–19.
Foster, George G. *Celio: or, New York Above-Ground and Under-Ground*. New York. 1850.
———. *Fifteen Minutes around New York*. New York, 1853.
———. *New York by Gas-Light, with Here and There a Streak of Sunshine*. New York, 1850.
———. *New York in Slices, by an Experienced Carver*. New York, 1849.
———. *New York Naked*. New York, 1850.
Free Loveyer. *Directory to the Seraglios in New York, Philadelphia, Boston, and All the Principal Cities in the Union*. New York, 1859.
Frothingham, O. B. "The Suppression of Vice." *North American Review* 135 (1882): 489–95.
Gans, Howard S. "In the Matter of the Lawlessness of the Police—A Reply to Mr. Justice Gaynor." *North American Review* 176 (1903): 287–96.
Gardner, Charles W. *The Doctor and the Devil: A Startling Exposé of Municipal Corruption*. New York, 1894.
Gayler, Charles. *Out of the Streets: A Story of New York Life*. New York, 1869.
Gaynor, William J. "A Government of Laws, Not of Men." *North American Review* 176 (1903): 282–86.
———. "Lawlessness of the Police in New York." *North American Review* 176 (1903): 10–26.
Gerry, Elbridge T. "Cruelty to Children." *North American Review* 137 (1883): 68–75.
Goldman, Emma. *The Traffic in Women and Other Essays on Feminism*. Edited by Alix Kates Shulman. Albion, Calif.: Times Change Press, 1970.
Goldmark, Pauline. *West Side Studies: Boyhood and Lawlessness*. New York, 1914.
Green, Jonathan H. *The Secret Band of Brothers, of the American Outlaws*. Philadelphia, 1847.
———. *Twelve Days in the Tombs*. New York, 1850.
Greene, Jerome D. "The Bureau of Social Hygiene." *Social Hygiene* 3 (1917): 1–9.
Grund, Francis J. *The Americans in Their Moral, Social, and Political Relations*. Boston, 1837.
Gunn, Thomas Butler. *The Physiology of New York Boarding Houses*. New York, 1857.
Halliday, Samuel B. *The Little Street Sweeper; or, Life among the Poor*. New York, 1861.
Hankins, Marie Louise. *Women of New York*. New York, 1861.
Hapgood, Hutchins. *Types from City Streets*. New York, 1910.
Hardie, James. *The Description of New York*. New York, 1827.
Herald. Report of the Forrest Divorce Case. New York, 1852.
Hoffman, John T. *Annual Message*. Albany, N.Y., 1871.
Ingraham, Joseph Holt. *Frank Rivers; or, The Dangers of the Town*. New York, 1843.
Ivins, William Mills. *Machine Politics and Money in Elections in New York City*. New York, 1887.
Johnson, Major Bascom. "Next Steps." *Social Hygiene* 4 (1918): 9–23.
Kauffman, George K. *The House of Bondage*. New York, 1910.
Kernan, J. Frank ("Florry"). *Reminiscences of the Old Fire Laddies*. New York, 1885.

Kneeland, George J. *Commercialized Prostitution in New York City*. New York, 1917.
———. "Commercialized Prostitution and the Use of Property." *Social Hygiene* 2 (1916): 561–72.
———. "Commercialized Vice and the Liquor Traffic." *Social Hygiene* 2 (1916): 69–90.
Lippard, George. *The Empire City; or, New York by Day and Night*. New York, 1850.
———. *Margaret Dunbar; or, Leaves from New York Life*. New York, 1853.
———. *The Midnight Queen; or, Leaves from New York Life*. New York, 1853.
———. *New York: Its Upper Ten and Lower Million*. Cincinnati, 1853.
———. *The Quaker City*. Philadelphia, 1845.
Lombroso, Caesar, and William Ferrero. *The Female Offender*. New York, 1897.
McAdoo, William. *Guarding a Great City*. New York, 1906.
McCabe, James D., Jr. *New York by Sunlight and Gaslight*. Philadelphia, 1882.
———. *The Secrets of the Great City*. Philadelphia, 1868.
Mackaye, Steele. "Safety in Theaters." *North American Review* 135 (1882): 461–70.
McLean, F. H. "Bowery Amusements." In Univ. Settlement Society of New York. *Report* (1899): 14–19.
Minutes of the Common Council of the City of New York. New York, 1917.
Mitchell, Donald G. *Reveries of a Bachelor; or, A Book of the Heart*. New York, 1850.
Mitchell, John I. "Political Bosses." *North American Review* 135 (1882): 363–73.
Morrow, Prince. *Social Diseases and Marriage*. New York. 1904.
Moses, Montrose J., and John Mason Brown, eds. *American Theater as Seen by Its Critics, 1752–1934*. New York: Norton, 1934.
Moss, Frank. *The American Metropolis*. 3 vols. New York, 1897.
Mower, Henry S. *Reminiscences of a Hotel Man*. New York, 1912.
Myers, Jerome. *Artist in Manhattan*. New York, 1940.
Nevins, Allan, ed. *The Diary of Philip Hone, 1828–1851*. New York: Dodd, Mead, 1927.
Nevins, Allan, and Milton Halsey Thomas, eds. *The Diary of George Templeton Strong*. 4 vols. New York: Macmillan, 1952.
New York City, Board of Aldermen. *Semi-Annual Report of the Chief of Police*. Document 50. New York, 1853.
New York City, Board of Commissioners of the Metropolitan Police. *Annual Report*. New York, 1866–72.
New York City, Police Commissioner. *Annual Report*. New York, 1906–10.
New York City, Superintendent of Metropolitan Police. *Report*. New York, 1860.
New York City, General and Deputy Superintendent of Metropolitan Police. *Quarterly Report*. New York, 1858.
New York City, Police Department. *Report*. New York, 1885–89, 1891–96, 1898, 1901–04, 1911–12, 1914–17, 1919.
New York Society for the Prevention of Crime. *Report*. New York, 1878, 1879, 1896.
New York Society for the Prevention of Cruelty to Children. *Annual Report*. New York, 1875–90.
———. *Gerry's Manual*. New York, 1888, 1902, 1913.
New York Society for the Suppression of Vice. *Annual Report*. New York, 1875–1907.
New York State, Secretary of State, *Census for 1855*. Albany, 1857.
New York State, Secretary of State, *Census for 1865*. Albany, 1867.
New York State Assembly. *Report of the Metropolitan Police*. Albany, 1858.
New York State Assembly. *Special Committee Appointed to Investigate Public Officers and Departments of the City of New York*. 5 vols. Albany, 1900. (Mazet Committee).
New York State Senate. *Investigation of the Police Department of New York*. 5 vols. Albany, 1895. (Lexow Committee).
New York State, Governor. *Annual Report of Board of Commissioners of Metropolitan Police*. Albany, 1864, 1865.
Parkhurst, Charles P. *My Forty Years in New York*. New York, 1923.

———. *Our Fight with Tammany*. New York, 1895.

Peters, John D. "The Story of the Committee of Fourteen of New York." *Social Hygiene* 4 (1918): 347–88.

Phelps, Elizabeth Stuart. *Hedged In*. Boston, 1870.

Phillips, David Graham. *Susan Lenox: Her Fall and Rise*. New York, 1917.

Powell, Adam Clayton, Sr. *Against the Tide: An Autobiography*. New York, 1938.

Prime, Samuel. *Life in New York*. New York, 1847.

Raeder, Ole M. *America in the Forties*. Translated and edited by Gunnar J. Malmin. Minneapolis, 1929.

Rees, James. *Mysteries of City Life*. Philadelphia, 1849.

Reich, Benjamin. "A New Social Center: The Candy Store as a Social Influence." In Univ. Settlement Society of New York. *Report* (1899): 32–34.

Reynolds, David S., ed. *George Lippard: Prophet of Protest*. New York: Peter Lang, 1986.

Richmond, Rev. J. F. *The Institutions of New York*. New York, 1871.

Roberts, Kenneth, and Anna M. Roberts, eds. *Moreau de St. Méry's American Journey, 1793–98*. Garden City, N.Y., 1947.

Roosevelt, Theodore. *An Autobiography*. New York, 1914.

Ross, Joel H. *What I Saw in New York*. Auburn, N.Y., 1851.

Rubinow, I. M., and Daniel Durant. "The Depth and Breadth of the Servant Problem." *McClure's* 34 (1910): 576–85.

St. John, Bruce, ed. *John Sloan's New York: From the Diaries, Notes, and Correspondence, 1906–1913*. New York, 1965.

St. John de Crèvecoeur, Michel Guillaume. "Letters." *Magazine of American History* 2 (1878): 748–51.

Sanger, William W. *The History of Prostitution: Its Extent, Causes, and Effects throughout the World*. New York, 1859.

Simkhovitch, Mary M. *Neighborhood: My Story of Greenwich House*. New York, 1938.

Slick, Jonathan. *Snares of New York; or, Tricks and Traps of the Great Metropolis*. New York, 1879.

Sloan, John. *Gist of Art*. New York, 1939.

Smith, Matthew Hale. *Sunshine and Shadow in New York*. Hartford, 1868.

Spaulding, Raymond C. "The Saloons of the District." In Univ. Settlement Society of New York. *Report* (1899), 34–38.

Stead, William T. *Satan's Invisible World Displayed; or, Despairing Democracy: A Study of Greater New York*. London, 1898.

Stephens, Ann Sophia. *High Life in New York*. New York, 1843.

Stokes, I. N. Phelps. *The Iconography of Manhattan Island, 1498–1910*. 5 vols. New York, 1912.

Stowe, Harriet Beecher. *We and Our Neighbors: or, The Records of an Unfashionable Street*. Boston, 1873.

Syrett, Harold C., ed. *The Gentleman and the Tiger: The Autobiography of George B. McClellan, Jr.* Philadelphia, 1956.

Thomas, William I. *The Unadjusted Girl: With Cases and Standpoint for Behavioral Analysis*. Boston, 1923.

Thompson, George. *The Brazen Star: or, The Adventures of a New-York M.P.*, New York, 1853.

———. *City Crimes; or, Life in New York and Boston*. Boston, 1849.

———. *The Countess; or, Memoirs of Women of Leisure*. Boston, 1849.

———. *The Gay Girls of New-York; or, Life on Broadway*. New York, 1854.

Turner, George Kibbee. "The Daughters of the Poor: A Plain Story of the Development of New York City as a Leading Center of the White Slave Trade of the World, under Tammany Hall." *McClure's* 34 (1909): 45–61.

U.S. Senate Immigration Commission. *Importing Women for Immoral Purposes*. 61st Cong., 2d sess. Doc. 196. Washington, D.C., 1909.

Vose, John D. *Fresh Leaves from the Diary of a Broadway Dandy*. New York, 1852.

———. *Seven Nights in Gotham*. New York, 1852.

Walling, George Washington. *Recollections of a New York Police Chief.* New York, 1887.
Walsh, Robert F. *Dr. Parkhurst's Crusade; or, New York after Dark.* New York, 1892.
Welsh, James H. *The Root of the Municipal Evils.* New York, 1875.
Werther, Ralph–Jennie June. *The Female-Impersonators.* New York: Medico-Legal Journal, 1922.
Whitin, Frederick H. "Obstacles to Vice Repression." *Social Hygiene* 2 (1916): 145–63.
Whitman, Walt. *New York Dissected.* Edited by Emory Holloway and Ralph Adimari. New York, 1936.
———. "On Vice." In *The Uncollected Poetry and Prose of Walt Whitman,* edited by Emory Holloway. Vol. 1. Garden City, N.Y., 1921. Pp. 5–8.
Wilkes, George. *The Lives of Helen Jewett and Richard Robinson.* New York, 1849.
Willemse, Cornelius W. *Behind the Green Lights.* New York, 1931.
Williams, Henry L. *Gay Life in New-York! or, Fast Men and Grass Widows.* New York, 1866.
Wilmer, Lambert A. *The Confessions of Emilia Harrington.* Baltimore, 1835.
Winchell, Alexander. "Communism in the United States." *North American Review* 136 (1883): 454–66.
Woolston, Howard B. *Prostitution in the United States prior to the Entrance of the United States into the World War.* New York, 1921.
Young, William C., ed. *Documents of American Theater History.* 2 vols. Chicago, 1973.

Newspapers and Journals

Advocate of Moral Reform and Family Guardian
City Vigilant
Flash
Herald
Journal of Public Morals
Libertine
McDowall's Journal
Niles' Register
New York Sporting Whip
Sun
Tenderloin
Times
Tribune
Weekly Rake
Whip

City Directories

Boyd's Pictorial Directory of Broadway. New York, 1859.
Longworth, Thomas. *American Almanac, New York Register, and City Directory.* New York, 1820.
Mercein, William A. *City Directory, New York Register, and Almanac.* New York, 1820.
Rode, Charles R. *The New York City Directory,* 1st–13th Publications. New York, 1842–55.
Wilson's Business Directory. New York, 1855–59.

Secondary Sources

Adams, Grace, and Edward Hutter. "Sex in Old New York." *American Mercury* 52 (1941): 550–57.
Adriani, Gotz. *Toulouse-Lautrec.* London: Thames and Hudson, 1987.
Albion, Robert G. *The Rise of New York Port, 1815–1860.* New York: Scribners, 1939.
Appleby, Joyce. "Defining the Public Realm." *Reviews in American History* 12 (1984): 198–202.
Asbury, Herbert. *The Gangs of New York: An Informal History of the Underworld.* New York: Knopf, 1927.
Aspiz, Harold. *Walt Whitman and the Body Beautiful.* Urbana: Univ. of Illinois Press, 1980.

Barnett, Harold C. "The Political Economy of Rape and Prostitution." *Review of Radical Political Economics*. 8 (1976): 59–68.

Batterberry, Michael, and Ariane Baterberry. *On the Town in New York: From 1776 to the Present*. New York: Scribners, 1973.

Baym, Nina. *Woman's Fiction: A Guide to Novels by and about Women in America, 1820–1870*. Ithaca: Cornell Univ. Press, 1978.

Beall, Otho T., Jr., "*Aristotle's Master Piece* in America: A Landmark in the Folklore of Medicine." *William and Mary Quarterly*, 3d ser., 20 (1962): 207–22.

Bernstein, Iver. *The New York City Draft Riots: Their Significance for American Society and Politics in the Age of the Civil War*. New York: Oxford Univ. Press, 1990.

Bernstein, Rachel Amelia. "Boarding-House Keepers and Brothel Keepers in New York City, 1880–1910." Ph.D. diss., Rutgers Univ., 1984.

Best, Joel. "Careers in Brothel Prostitution: St. Paul, 1865–1883." *Journal of Interdisciplinary History* 7 (1982): 597–619.

Blackburn, George M., and Serman L. Ricards. "The Prostitutes and Gamblers of Virginia City, Nevada: 1870." *Pacific Historical Review* 48 (1979): 239–58.

Blackmar, Elizabeth. *Manhattan for Rent, 1785–1850*. Ithaca: Cornell Univ. Press, 1989.

———. "Re-walking the 'Walking City': Housing and Property Relations in New York City, 1780–1840." *Radical History Review* 21 (1979): 131–48.

Bloch, Avital. "The Remolding of American Sexual Attitudes: The Bureau of Social Hygiene, 1911–1934." Master's thesis, Columbia Univ., 1980.

Boyer, Paul S. *Purity in Print: The Vice-Society Movement and Book Censorship in America*. New York: Scribners, 1968.

———. *Urban Masses and Moral Order in America, 1820–1920*. Cambridge: Harvard Univ. Press, 1978.

Boyle, Thomas. *Black Swine in the Sewers of Hampstead*. New York: Viking, 1989.

Bridges, Amy. *A City in the Republic: Antebellum New York and the Origins of Machine Politics*. Cambridge: Cambridge Univ. Press, 1984.

Bristow, Edward J. *Prostitution and Prejudice: The Jewish Fight against White Slavery, 1870–1939*. Oxford: Clarendon, 1982.

Brooks, Peter. *Reading for the Plot: Design and Intention in Narrative*. New York: Knopf, 1984.

Broun, Heywood, and Margaret Leech. *Anthony Comstock: Roundsman of the Lord*. New York: Literary Guild of America, 1927.

Brown, Michael. "Times Square." *Preservation* 1 (Jan. 1982): 1–23.

Brown, Richard Maxwell. *Strain of Violence: Historical Studies of American Violence and Vigilantism*. New York: Oxford Univ. Press, 1975.

Brown, T. Allston. *A History of the New York Stage from 1732 to 1901*. 3 vols. New York: Dodd, Mead, 1903.

Buckley, Peter G. "The Case against Ned Buntline: The 'Words, Signs and Gestures' of Popular Authorship." *Prospects: An Annual of American Culture Studies* 13 (1988): 249–72.

———. "Culture, Class and Place in Antebellum New York." In *Power, Culture and Place: Essays on New York City*, edited by John H. Mollenkopf. New York: Russell Sage, 1988.

———. "To the Opera House: Culture and Society in New York City, 1820–1860." Ph.D. diss., SUNY, Stony Brook, 1984.

Bullough, Vern L. "Problems and Methods for Research in Prostitution and the Behavioral Sciences." *Journal of the History of the Behavioral Sciences* 1 (1965): 244–51.

Bullough, Vern, and Bonnie Bullough. *Prostitution: An Illustrated Social History*. New York: Crown, 1978.

Burnham, John C. "American Historians and the Subject of Sex." *Societas: A Review of Social History* 2 (1974): 307–16.

———. "The Progressive Era Revolution in American Attitudes toward Sex." *Journal of American History* 59 (1973): 885–907.

Butler, Anne M. *Daughters of Joy, Sisters of Misery: Prostitutes in the American West, 1865–90*. Urbana: Univ. of Illinois Press, 1985.

Carlisle, Marcia. "Prostitutes and Their Reformers in Nineteenth Century Philadelphia." Ph.D. diss., Rutgers Univ., 1982.

Carnes, Mark C. *Secret Ritual and Manhood in Victorian America*. New Haven: Yale Univ. Press, 1989.

Chauncey, George A., Jr. "Gay New York: Urban Culture and the Making of a Gay Male World, 1890–1940." Ph.D. diss., Yale Univ., 1989.

Clark, Norman H. *Deliver Us from Evil: An Interpretation of American Prohibition*. New York: Norton, 1976.

Cohen, David Steven. *The Ramapo Mountain People*. New Brunswick: Rutgers Univ. Press, 1974.

Cohen, Patricia Cline. "The Helen Jewett Murder: Violence, Gender, and Sexual Licentiousness in Antebellum America." *National Women's Studies Association Journal* 2 (1990): 374–89.

Cominos, Peter T. "Late Victorian Sexual Respectability and the Social System." *International Review of Social History* 8 (1963): 18–48, 216–50.

Connelly, Mark Thomas. *The Response to Prostitution in the Progressive Era*. Chapel Hill: Univ. of North Carolina Press, 1980.

Conzens, Michael P., and Kathleen Neils Conzens. "Geographical Structure in Nineteenth Century Urban Retailing: Milwaukee, 1836–1890." *Journal of Historical Geography* 5 (1979): 45–66.

Cook, Adrian. *The Armies of the Streets: The New York City Draft Riots of 1863*. Lexington: Univ. Press of Kentucky, 1974.

Corbin, Alain. *Women for Hire: Prostitution and Sexuality in France after 1850*. Cambridge: Harvard Univ. Press, 1990.

Cordasco, Francesco, and Thomas Monroe Pitkin. *The White Slave Trade and the Immigrants: A Chapter in American Social History*. Detroit: Blaine-Ethridge Books, 1981.

Cott, Nancy F. *The Bonds of Womanhood: "Women's Sphere" in New England, 1780–1835*. New Haven: Yale Univ. Press, 1977.

———. *The Grounding of Modern Feminism*. New Haven: Yale Univ. Press, 1987.

———. "Passionlessness: An Interpretation of Victorian Sexual Ideology, 1790–1850." *Signs* 4 (1978): 219–36.

Czitrom, Daniel. "Underworlds and Underdogs: Big Tim Sullivan and Metropolitan Politics in New York, 1889–1913." *Journal of American History* 78 (1991): 536–58.

Denning, Michael. *Mechanic Accents: Dime Novels and Working-Class Culture in America*. London: Verso, 1987.

Dijkstra, Bram. *Idols of Perversity: Fantasies of Feminine Evil in Fin-de-Siècle Culture*. New York: Oxford Univ. Press, 1986.

Ditzion, Sidney. *Marriage, Morals, and Sex in America: A History of Ideas*. New York: Norton, 1969.

Doezema, Marianne. *American Realism and the Industrial Age*. Cleveland: Cleveland Museum of Art, 1980.

DuBois, Ellen Carol, and Linda Gordon. "Seeking Ecstasy on the Battlefield: Danger and Pleasure in Nineteenth-Century Feminist Sexual Thought." *Feminist Studies* 9 (1983): 7–25.

Dudden, Faye E. *Serving Women: Household Service in Nineteenth-Century America*. Middletown, Conn.: Wesleyan Univ. Press, 1983.

Dunn, Waldoff. *The Life of Donald G. Mitchell*. New York: Scribners, 1922.

Durkheim, Emil, *The Rules of Sociological Method*. Translated by Sarah A. Solovay and John H. Mueller. New York: Free Press, 1966.

Engel, Charlene S. "George W. Bellows' Illustration for the *Masses* and Other Magazines and the Sources of His Lithographs of 1916–17." Ph.D. diss., Univ. of Wisconsin, 1976.

Erenberg, Lewis A. *Steppin' Out: New York Nightlife and the Transformation of American Culture, 1890–1930*. Westport, Conn.: Greenwood, 1981.

———. "Impresarios of Broadway Nightlife." In *Inventing Times Square: Commerce and Culture at the Crossroads of the World*, edited by William R. Taylor. New York: Russell Sage, 1991.

Erikson, Kai. *Wayward Puritans: A Study in the Sociology of Deviance*. New York: Wiley, 1966.

Evans, Richard J. "Prostitution, State and Society in Imperial Germany." *Past and Present,* no. 70 (1976): 106–29.

Fass, Paula. *The Damned and the Beautiful: American Youth in the 1920s.* New York: Oxford Univ. Press, 1977.

Feldberg, Michael. *The Turbulent Era: Riot and Disorder in Jacksonian America.* New York: Oxford Univ. Press, 1980.

Feldman, Egal. "Prostitution, the Alien Woman and the Progressive Imagination, 1910–15." *American Quarterly* 19 (1967): 192–206.

Felt, Jeremy P. "Vice Reform as a Political Technique: The Committee of Fifteen in New York, 1900–1901." *New York History* 54 (1973): 24–51.

Finnegan, Frances. *Poverty and Prostitution: A Study of Victorian Prostitutes in York.* Cambridge: Cambridge Univ. Press, 1979.

Fishbein, Leslie. "From Sodom to Salvation: The Image of New York City in Films about Fallen Women, 1899–1934." *New York History* 70 (1989): 171–90.

Ford, James. *Slums and Housing.* Cambridge: Harvard Univ. Press, 1936.

Freedman, Estelle B. "Sexuality in Nineteenth-Century America: Behavior, Ideology, and Politics." *Reviews in American History* 10 (1982): 196–215.

———. *Their Sisters' Keepers: Women's Prison Reform in America, 1830–1930.* Ann Arbor: Univ. of Michigan Press, 1981.

Freedman, Estelle B., and John D'Emilio. *Intimate Matters: A History of Sexuality in America.* New York: Harper and Row, 1988.

Gay, Peter. *The Bourgeois Experience, Victoria to Freud.* 2 vols. New York: Oxford Univ. Press, 1984–86.

Giamo, Benedict F. "On the Bowery: Symbolic Action in American Culture and Subculture." Ph.D. diss., Emory Univ., 1987.

Gilfoyle, Timothy J. "The Moral Origins of Political Surveillance: The Preventive Society in New York City, 1867–1918." *American Quarterly* 38 (1986): 637–52.

———. "Policing of Sexuality." In *Inventing Times Square: Commerce and Culture at the Crossroads of the World,* edited by William R. Taylor. New York: Russell Sage, 1991.

———. "Strumpets and Misogynists: Brothel 'Riots' and the Transformation of Prostitution in Antebellum New York City." *New York History* 68 (1987): 144–65.

———. "Urban Geography of Commercial Sex: Prostitution in New York City, 1790–1860." *Journal of Urban History* 13 (1987): 371–93.

Gilje, Paul A. *The Road to Mobocracy: Popular Disorder in New York City, 1763–1834.* Chapel Hill: Univ. of North Carolina Press, 1987.

Girouard, Mark. *Cities and People: A Social and Architectural History.* New Haven: Yale Univ. Press, 1986.

Goldman, Marion S. *Gold Diggers and Silver Miners: Prostitution and Social Life on the Comstock Lode.* Ann Arbor: Univ. of Michigan Press, 1981.

Goode, William J. "The Historical Importance of Love." In *Explorations in Social Theory.* New York: Oxford Univ. Press, 1973.

Gorham, Deborah. " 'The Maiden Tribute of Modern Babylon' Reexamined: Child Prostitution and the Idea of Childhood in Late-Victorian England." *Victorian Studies* 21 (1978): 353–79.

Gorn, Elliot J. " 'Good-Bye Boys, I Die a True American': Homicide, Nativism, and Working-Class Culture in Antebellum New York City." *Journal of American History* 74 (1987): 388–410.

———. *The Manly Art: Bare-Knuckle Prize Fighting in America.* Ithaca: Cornell Univ. Press, 1986.

Grant, James Wilson. *The Memorial History of the City of New York.* 4 vols. New York, 1893.

Green, Martin. *New York 1913: The Armory Show and the Paterson Strike Pageant.* New York: Scribners, 1987.

Greenberg, Douglas. *Crime and Law Enforcement in the Colony of New York, 1691–1776.* Ithaca: Cornell Univ. Press, 1976.

Grimsted, David. *Melodrama Unveiled: American Theater and Culture, 1800–1850.* Chicago: Univ. of Chicago Press, 1968.

Groneman, Carol. "Working-Class Immigrant Women in Mid-Nineteenth Century New York: The Irish Woman's Experience." *Journal of Urban History* 4 (1978): 257–71.

Gusfield, Joseph R. *Symbolic Crusade: Status Politics and the American Temperance Movement.* Urbana: Univ. of Illinois Press, 1963.

Haller, John S., and Robin M. Haller. *The Physician and Sexuality in Victorian America.* Urbana: Univ. of Illinois Press, 1974.

Halttunen, Karen. *Confidence Men and Painted Women: A Study of Middle-Class Culture in America, 1830–1870.* New Haven: Yale Univ. Press, 1982.

Hammack, David C. *Power and Society: Greater New York at the Turn of the Century.* New York: Russell Sage, 1982.

Hapke, Laura. *Girls Who Went Wrong: Prostitutes in American Fiction, 1885–1917.* Bowling Green, Ohio: Bowling Green Univ. Press, 1989.

Headley, Joel Tyler. *The Great Riots of New York, 1712–1873.* Edited by Thomas Rose and James Rodgers. New York: Arno, 1970.

Henderson, Mary C. *The City and the Theater: New York Playhouses from Bowling Green to Times Square.* Clifton, N.J.: James T. White, 1973.

Henriques, Fernando. *Prostitution and Society: A Survey—Primitive, Classical, and Oriental.* New York: Citadel Press, 1962.

———. *Prostitution in Europe and the Americas.* New York: Citadel Press, 1963.

Herman, Sondra R. "Loving Courtship or the Marriage Market? The Ideal and Its Critics, 1871–1911." *American Quarterly* 25 (1973): 235–52.

Hills, Patricia. "John Sloan's Images of Working-Class Women: A Case Study of the Roles and Interrelationships of Politics, Personality, and Patrons in the Development of Sloan's Art, 1905–16." *Prospects: The Annual of American Culture Studies* 5 (1980): 157–96.

Hirata, Lucie Cheng. "Free, Indentured, and Enslaved: Chinese Prostitutes in Nineteenth-Century America." *Signs* 5 (1979): 3–29.

Holcomb, Grant. "John Sloan and 'McSorely's Wonderful Saloon.' " *American Art Journal* 15 (Spring 1983): 5–20.

Horlick, Allan Stanley. *Country Boys and Merchant Princes: The Social Control of Young Men in New York.* Lewisburg, Penn.: Bucknell Univ. Press, 1975.

Horn, Pierre L., and Mary Beth Pringle, eds. *The Image of the Prostitute in Modern Literature.* New York: Unger, 1984.

Ichioka, Yuji. "Ameyuki-san: Japanese Prostitutes in Nineteenth-Century America." *Amerasia Journal* 4 (1977): 1–17.

Jeanniere, Abel. *The Anthropology of Sex.* Translated by Julie Kernan. New York: Harper and Row, 1967.

Johnson, Claudia D. "That Guilty Third Tier: Prostitution in Nineteenth-Century American Theaters." In *Victorian America,* edited by Daniel Walker Howe. Philadelphia: Univ. of Pennsylvania Press, 1976.

Johnson, David R. *Policing the Urban Underworld: The Impact of Crime on the Development of the American Police, 1800–87.* Philadelphia: Temple Univ. Press, 1979.

Joselit, Jenna Weisman. *Our Gang: Jewish Crime and the New York Jewish Community, 1900–1940.* Bloomington: Indiana Univ. Press, 1983.

Kessler-Harris, Alice. *Out to Work: A History of Wage-Earning Women in the United States.* New York: Oxford Univ. Press, 1982.

Kinser, Suzanne L. "Prostitution in the Art of John Sloan." *Prospects: The Annual of American Culture Studies* 9 (1984): 231–54.

Kinsey, Alfred C., Wardell C. Pomery, and Clyde E. Martin, *Sexual Behavior in the Human Male.* Philadelphia: Saunders, 1948.

Lampard, Eric E. "The Social Impact of the Industrial Revolution." In *Technology in Western Civilization,* edited by Melvin Kranzberg and Carroll W. Pursell, Jr. Vol. 1. New York: Oxford Univ. Press, 1967.

Lane, Roger. *Policing the City: Boston, 1822–1885.* New York: Atheneum, 1977.

———. *Roots of Violence in Black Philadelphia, 1860–1900.* Boston: Harvard Univ. Press, 1986.

Lebsock, Suzanne. *The Free Women of Petersburg: Status and Culture in a Southern Town, 1784–1860*. New York: Norton, 1984.

Light, Ivan. "The Ethnic Vice Industry, 1880–1940." *American Sociological Review* 42 (1977): 464–79.

———. "From Vice District to Tourist Attraction: The Moral Career of American Chinatowns, 1880–1940." *Pacific Historical Review* 43 (1974): 367–94.

Lipton, Eunice. *Looking into Degas: Uneasy Images of Women and Modern Life*. Berkeley: Univ. of California Press, 1986.

Lockwood, Charles. *Manhattan Moves Uptown*. Boston: Houghton Mifflin, 1976.

Lubove, Roy. "The Progressive and the Prostitute." *Historian* 24 (1962): 308–30.

McCrea, Roswell C. *The Humane Movement*. New York: Columbia Univ. Press, 1910.

McGovern, James R. " 'Sporting Life on the Line': Prostitution in Progressive Era Pensacola." *Florida Historical Quarterly* 54 (1975): 131–41.

Marcus, Steven. *The Other Victorians: A Study of Sexuality and Pornography in Mid-Nineteenth-Century England*. New York: Norton, 1964.

Marks, Lara. "Jewish Women and Jewish Prostitution in the East End London." *Jewish Quarterly* 34 (1987): 6–10.

Marsh, Margaret. "From Separation to Togetherness: The Social Construction of Domestic Space in American Suburbs, 1840–1915." *Journal of American History* 76 (1989): 506–27.

———. "Suburban Men and Masculine Domesticity, 1870–1915." *American Quarterly* 40 (1988): 165–86.

May, Lary. *Screening Out the Past: The Birth of Mass Culture and the Motion Picture Industry*. New York: Oxford Univ. Press, 1980.

Metropolitan Museum of Art. *Memorial Exhibition of the Work of George Bellows*. New York, 1925.

Meyerowitz, Joanne J. *Women Adrift: Independent Wage Earners in Chicago, 1880–1930*. Chicago: Univ. of Chicago Press, 1988.

Micknish, Janet Eileen. "Legal Control of Socio-Sexual Relationships: Creation of the Mann White Slave Traffic Act of 1910." Ph.D. diss., Southern Illinois Univ., 1980.

Miller, Wilber R. *Cops and Bobbies: Police Authority in New York and London, 1830–1870*. Chicago: Univ. of Chicago Press, 1973.

Mohl, Raymond A. *Poverty in New York, 1783–1825*. New York: Oxford Univ. Press, 1971.

Mollenkopf, John Hull, ed. *Power, Culture and Place: Essays on New York City*. New York: Russell Sage, 1988.

Monaghan, Frank, and Marvin Lowenthal. *This Was New York: The Nation's Capital in 1789*. Garden City, N.Y.: Doubleday, 1943.

Morris, Lloyd. *Incredible New York: High Life and Low Life of the Last 100 Years*. New York: Random House, 1951.

Murtaugh, John M., and Sarah Harris. *Cast the First Stone*. New York: McGraw-Hill, 1957.

Mullins, Edwin. *The Painted Witch: Female Body–Male Art: How Western Artists Have Viewed the Sexuality of Women*. London: Secker and Warburg, 1985.

Myers, Jane, and Linda Ayres. *George Bellows: The Artist and His Lithographs, 1916–1924*. Fort Worth: Amon Carter Museum, 1988.

Nadel, Stanley. *Little Germany: Ethnicity, Religion and Class in New York City, 1845–80*. Urbana: Univ. of Illinois Press, 1990.

Nissenbaum, Stephen. *Sex, Diet, and Debility in Jacksonian America: Sylvester Graham and Health Reform*. Westport, Conn.: Greenwood, 1980.

Ostransky, Leroy. *Jazz City: The Impact of Our Cities on the Development of Jazz*. Englewood Cliffs, N.J.: Prentice-Hall, 1978.

Otis, Leah Lydia. *Prostitution in Medieval Society: The History of an Urban Institution in Languedoc*. Chicago: Univ. of Chicago Press, 1985.

Peiss, Kathy. "Charity Girls and City Pleasures: Historical Notes on Working-Class Sexuality, 1880–1920." *Powers of Desire: The Politics of Sexuality,* edited by Ann Snitow, Christine Stansell, and Sharon Thompson. New York: Monthly Review Press, 1983.

———. *Cheap Amusements: Working Women and Leisure in Turn-of-the-Century New York.* Philadelphia: Temple Univ. Press, 1986.

Peiss, Kathy, and Christina Simmons, eds. *Passion and Power: Sexuality in History.* Philadelphia: Temple Univ. Press, 1989.

Peel, Mark. "On the Margins: Lodgers and Boarders in Boston, 1860–1900." *Journal of American History* 72 (1986): 813–34.

Perry, Mary Elizabeth. " 'Lost Women' in Early Modern Seville: The Politics of Prostitution." *Feminist Studies* 4 (1978): 195–211.

Pivar, David J. "Cleansing the Nation: The War on Prostitution, 1917–21." *Prologue* 12 (1980): 29–40.

———. *Purity Crusade: Sexual Morality and Social Control, 1868–1900.* Westport, Conn.: Greenwood, 1973.

Reed, James. *The Birth Control Movement and American Society.* Princeton: Princeton Univ. Press, 1983.

Reff, Theodore. *Manet: Olympia.* New York: Viking, 1977.

Renzetti, Claire Marie. "Purity vs. Politics: The Legislation of Morality in Progressive New York, 1890–1920." Ph.D. diss., Univ. of Delaware, 1983.

Reynolds, David. *Beneath the American Renaissance: The Subversive Imagination in the Age of Emerson and Melville.* New York: Knopf, 1988.

Rice, Kym S. *Early American Taverns.* Chicago: Regnery Gateway, 1983.

Richards, Leonard L. *"Gentlemen of Property and Standing": Antiabolition Mobs in Jacksonian America.* New York: Oxford Univ. Press, 1970.

Richardson, James F. *The New York Police: Colonial Times to 1901.* New York: Oxford Univ. Press, 1970.

Richardson, Joanna. *The Courtesans: The Demi-monde in Nineteenth Century France.* Cleveland: World, 1967.

Riegel, Robert E. "Changing American Attitudes towards Prostitution, 1800–1920." *Journal of the History of Ideas* 29 (1968): 439–52.

Rose, Al. *Storyville, New Orleans: Being an Authentic, Illustrated Account of the Notorious Red-Light District.* University: Univ. of Alabama Press, 1974.

Rosen, Ruth. *The Lost Sisterhood: Prostitution in America, 1900–1918.* Baltimore: Johns Hopkins Univ. Press, 1982.

Rosen, Ruth, and Sue Davidson, eds. *The Maimie Papers.* Bloomington: Indiana Univ. Press, Feminist Press, 1977.

Rossiaud, Jacques. "Prostitution, Youth, and Society in the Towns of Southeastern France in the Fifteenth Century." In *Deviants and the Abandoned in French Society: Selections from the "Annales,"* edited by Robert Forster and Orest Ranum. Baltimore: Johns Hopkins Univ. Press, 1978.

Rothman, Ellen K. *Hands and Hearts: A History of Courtship in America.* New York: Basic Books, 1984.

Rothman, Sheila. *Woman's Proper Place: A History of Changing Ideals and Practices, 1870 to the Present.* New York: Basic Books, 1978.

Rubin, Gayle. "The Traffic in Women: Notes on the 'Political Economy' of Sex." In *Towards an Anthropology of Women,* edited by Rayna R. Reiter New York: Monthly Review Press, 1975.

Salvatore, Nick. *Eugene V. Debs: Citizen and Socialist.* Urbana: Univ. of Illinois Press, 1982.

Schneider, John C. "Public Order and the Geography of the City: Crime, Violence, and the Police in Detroit, 1845–1875." *Journal of Urban History* 4 (1978): 183–208.

Scobey, David Moisseiff. "Empire City: Politics, Culture, and Urbanism in Gilded-Age New York." Ph.D. diss., Yale Univ., 1989.

Scott, David. *John Sloan.* New York: Watson-Guptill, 1975.

Scott, David, and E. John Bullard. *John Sloan, 1871–1951: His Life and Paintings, His Graphics* Washington: National Gallery of Art, 1976.

Sears, Hal. *The Sex Radicals.* Lawrence: Univ. of Kansas Press, 1977.

Shumsky, Neil Larry. "Tacit Acceptance: Respectable Americans and Segregated Prostitution, 1870–1910." *Journal of Social History* 19 (1986): 665–79.

Shumsky, Neil Larry, and Larry M. Springer. "San Francisco's Zone of Prostitution, 1880–1934." *Journal of Historical Geography* 7 (1981): 71–89.

Siegel, Adrienne. "Brothels, Bets, and Bars: Popular Literature as a Guidebook to the Urban Underground, 1840–70." *North Dakota Quarterly* 44 (1976): 6–22.

———. *The Image of the American City in Popular Literature 1820–1870*. Port Washington: Kennikat Press, 1981.

Silver, Nathan. *Lost New York*. New York: Schocken, 1967.

Smith, Daniel Scott. "Family Limitation, Sexual Control, and Domestic Feminism in Victorian America." In *Clio's Consciousness Raised: New Perspectives on the History of Women*, edited by Mary Hartman and Lois W. Banner. New York: Harper and Row, 1974.

Smith, Daniel Scott, and Michael S. Hindus, "Premarital Pregnancy in America, 1607–1971: An Overview and Interpretation." *Journal of Interdisciplinary History* 5 (1975): 537–70.

Smith-Rosenberg, Carroll. "Beauty, the Beast, and the Militant Woman: A Case Study in Sex Roles and Social Stress in Jacksonian America." *American Quarterly* 23 (1971): 562–84.

———. *Disorderly Conduct: Visions of Gender in Victorian America*. New York: Knopf, 1985.

———. *Religion and the Rise of the American City: The New York City Mission Movement, 1812–1870*. Ithaca: Cornell Univ. Press. 1971.

Spann, Edward K. *The New Metropolis: New York City, 1840–1857*. New York: Columbia Univ. Press, 1981.

Srebnick, Amy Gilman. "True Womanhood and Hard Times: Women and Early New York City Industrialization, 1840–1860." Ph.D. diss., SUNY, Stony Brook, 1979.

Stansell, Christine. *City of Women: Sex and Class in New York, 1789–1860*. New York: Knopf, 1986.

———. "The Origins of the Sweatshop: Women and Early Industrialization in New York City." In *Working-Class America: Essays on Labor, Community, and American Society*, edited by Michael H. Frisch and Daniel J. Walkowitz. Urbana: Univ. of Illinois Press, 1983.

———. "Women, Children, and the Uses of the Streets: Class and Gender Conflict in New York City, 1850–1860." *Feminist Studies* 8 (1982): 309–35.

———. "Women of the Laboring Poor in New York City, 1820–1860." Ph.D. diss., Yale Univ., 1979.

Stearns, Carol Zisowitz, and Peter N. Stearns. "Victorian Sexuality: Can Historians Do It Better?" *Journal of Social History* 18 (1985): 625–34.

Steen, Ivan. "Palaces for Travelers: New York City's Hotels in the 1850's as Viewed by English Visitors," *New York History* 54 (1973): 24–51.

Stern, Robert A. M., Gregory Gilmartin, and John Massengale. *New York 1900: Metropolitan Architecture and Urbanism, 1890–1915*. New York: Rizzoli, 1983.

Stevens, John D. *Sensationalism and the New York Press*. New York: Columbia Univ. Press, 1991.

Stoehr, Taylor, ed. *Free Love in America: A Documentary History*. New York: AMS Press, 1979.

Symanski, Richard. *The Immoral Landscape: Female Prostitution in Western Societies*. Toronto: Butterworths, 1981.

Thomas, Keith, "The Double Standard." *Journal of the History of Ideas* 20 (1959): 195–216.

Tomes, Nancy. " 'A Torrent of Abuse': Crimes of Violence between Working-Class Men and Women in London, 1840–1875." *Journal of Social History* 11 (1978): 328–45.

Trumbull, Charles Gallaudet. *Anthony Comstock, Fighter*. New York: Fleming H. Revell, 1913.

Walkowitz, Judith R. *Prostitution and Victorian Society: Women, Class, and the State*. Cambridge: Cambridge Univ. Press, 1980.

Walters, Ronald G. "Sexual Matters and Historical Problems: A Framework for Analysis." *Societas* 6 (Summer 1976): 157–75.

Waterman, Willoughby Cyrus. *Prostitution and Its Repression in New York City, 1900–1931*. New York: Columbia Univ. Press, 1932.

Weinbaum, Paul O. *Mobs and Demagogues: The New York Response to Collective Violence in the Early Nineteenth Century*. Ann Arbor: Univ. of Michigan Press, 1979.

ACKNOWLEDGMENTS

IN THE COURSE of this project, I incurred numerous debts. Daniel Barron, George Chauncey, Jr., Philip Costello, Dennis Cremin, Gregory DeBenedictis, Nan Fairhurst, Gaines Foster, Julia Foulkes, Henry Graff, David Johnson, Barbara Klaw, Felicia McNeil, Burl Noggle, Eric Reisenauer, Charles Royster, Sara Rude, Mary Ryan, Ken Scherzer, Christiana Schoenbacher, James Shenton, John Tone, and Martha Wagner read the entire manuscript and offered invaluable criticism and support. Portions were read by Iver Bernstein, Henry Binford, Avital Bloch, Allan Block, Mary Elizabeth Brown, Joan Jacobs Brumberg, Mark Carnes, Deborah Dugan, Lewis Erenberg, Peter Goheen, Mark Kaminsky, Peter Levy, Eric Lott, the late Michael Lynch, Servando Ortoll, George Pozzetta, David Sloane, and Judith Stanley.

Several people, in addition to their comments, offered much more help than I deserved. Elizabeth Blackmar and Tara Fitzpatrick gave me so many handwritten and constructive criticisms that it took me several years to address them. Sigmund Diamond, in both lectures and private conferences, taught me how to carefully apply social science theory to history. Patricia Cline Cohen prevented me from committing several egregious errors of fact and interpretation regarding the Jewett-Robinson affair, as well as generously sharing her work and ideas with me. Eric Foner encouraged me to take chances and use my imagination in interpreting the most difficult sources. During his term as a Gannett Center fellow at Columbia University, John Stevens not only shared his research but also provided me with many lunches, for which I am most grateful. Daniel Czitrom and Rosalind Rosenberg offered much appreciated words of advice, encouragement, and commentary at critical stages. Because she laboriously read three or four different versions of the manuscript, Myra Sletson is probably the happiest to see its completion. And in numerous conversations, Doron Ben-Atar forced me to question my own moralistic assumptions and acted as my sounding board for frustrations about this manuscript and life.

Other individuals at Columbia University provided advice and assistance during my years as a college student, Ph.D. candidate, and faculty member—in particular, Henry Coleman, the late Arnold Collery, Roger Lehecka, Hollis Lynch, Leora Neter, the late James Parker, the late Robert Randall, Rosalind Rosenberg, Michael Rosenthal, Jack Salzman, and Barbara Tischler. I am especially grateful for a Harry J. Carman Fellowship from the college and a Herbert Lehman Fellowship from the state of New York. Sadly, New York no longer funds the Lehman program, without which this book would never have been written. I also profited from comments and support offered at various conferences and institutions where I presented different portions of the manuscript: in particular, the Harry Van Arsdale, Jr., School for Labor Studies, State University of New York (especially by Priscilla Murolo and Steve Tischler); the Institute for Research on Women and Gender at Columbia University; the South Street Seaport Museum; the Transformation of Philadelphia Project at the University of Pennsylvania; the annual meetings of the American Studies Association, the Society of American Planning History, the Organization of American Historians, the Midwest Journalism and Mass Communications Historians, the New York State History Conference; and the history departments at the California State University, Hayward; the University of California, San Diego; the University of Florida; the George Washington University; the Louisiana State University; Loyola University of Chicago; the University of New Mexico; and San Jose State University.

The patience and assistance of librarians and archivists at Columbia University, the Library of Congress, the New-York Historical Society, the New York State Archives, and the New York Public Library enabled me to locate and examine the resources necessary for this study. Georgia Barnhill, Joyce A. Tracey, Dennis Laurie, and Jack Simpson at the American Antiquarian Society, Worcester, Massachusetts, provided invaluable assistance on short notice. Leo Hershkowitz graciously allowed me to interrupt his own work to examine pertinent manuscripts in his personal collections. Patti Schor, Shirley Smith, and Mark Tatara of the Center of Instructional Design at Loyola University of Chicago patiently endured my picayune demands concerning maps and illustrations. My colleagues in the Department of History and the Halas Center at Loyola provided an intellectually stimulating and warm environment that allowed me to complete this book. Special thanks are in order to Idilio Gracia-Pena, Kenneth Cobb, Evelyn Gonzalez, and Leonora Gidlund of the New York City Municipal Archives and Records Center. During the four years of research on this book, they made me feel welcome and appreciated despite my requesting over one thousand boxes from the basements of the Hall of Records and the Tweed Courthouse.

Although some did not always realize it, numerous friends and associates enabled me to persevere in this project with their words of encouragement and humor. I am thankful to Michael Ackerman, Adele Alexander, John Alexander, Paula Alexander, Robert and Ellen Andrew, Jo Ben-Atar, Marianna Bernunzo, the Reverend Robert Bierley, S. J., Patricia Brennan, Robert and Laurie Bucholz, Anthony Cardoza, Jimmy Carson, Sheldon Cohen, James Connolly, Jr., Maureen Connolly and her family, Judy Cook, Mary Curtin, Bob Cvornyek, Steve Deyle, Michael Fraser, Vivian Fried, Marc Friedberg, Joseph and Gloria Gagliano, Kathy Garrahan, Geoffrey Giles, Mary Gilfoyle, Paul Gilfoyle and his family, Steve Hart, Harrison Henry, Susan Hirsch, Clifton Hood, Gemma Kallaugher, Ilwon Kang, Ted Karamanski, Michael Kessler, David King, Harriet Kram, Diane Krejsa, David and Roberta Kishbaugh, Margaret Kishbaugh and her family, Joseph Lynch, Catherine Mardikes, Larry and Joan McCaffrey, Michael and Jennifer McCarthy, Eileen McMahon, Chris McNickle, Patricia Mooney-Melvin, Gerard and Benardine Norton and their family, Charles O'Byrne, Daniel Parker, Kathryn Parlan, Charisse Parrot, Linda Pattee Gilfoyle, Harold Platt, Lee Podair, Ann Scott, Steve Shapiro, Joel Siegel, Diane Slaine, Scott Smith, Martin Suto, the Reverend Luke Travers, O.S.B., Sylvia Toyos, Michael Valmas, Ellen Waugh, David Wazer, Ray Weissman, Eric Wertzer, Richard Wolff, Carol Woodward, Joseph Wright, and Cedric Yap.

Hilary Hinzmann at W.W. Norton patiently endured my overdue drafts and intelligently prodded me to keep working even when I thought I was done. His faith and persistence have resulted, I hope, in a better book. My greatest professional debt belongs to Kenneth T. Jackson. Beginning with his class in American urban history, when I was a Columbia College sophomore, to his biting but honest criticism of this manuscript, he nurtured and encouraged me in innumerable ways. From discussions on gentrification to shooting hoops in the gym, he has been my mentor, critic, surrogate parent and personal confidant. His infectious enthusiasm for the city, his scholarship, and his modesty changed the way I look at the world and will be my models in my career. He, his wife, Barbara, and son, Kevan, allowed me to share in their greatest triumphs and tragedies, and for that I am forever grateful.

For the past several years, family members have quietly wondered why I chose this topic of study. My parents, after sending their children to parochial school for a dozen years, no doubt wondered at some moments what went wrong. Putting confusion aside, they offered unquestioning moral, financial, and emotional support during good times and bad. Mary Rose Alexander, whom I met when this project was nearly complete, demonstrated equal faith and confidence with much less reason for doing so. Most of the good things in my life today are the result of her unwavering presence and innumerable sacrifices. Her ultimate endorsement is one I will never forget. Together with my brother Jerry and my aunt Margaret Norton, these kind people have given me their devoted love and loyalty, personal strength, and sympathy for the underdog. And that is a debt I can never repay.

INDEX